COPING WITH CRISIS: THE RESILIENCE AND VULNERABILITY OF PRE-INDUSTRIAL SETTLEMENTS

Rural Worlds: Economic, Social and Cultural Histories of Agricultures and Rural Societies

Series Editor: Richard W. Hoyle, University of Reading, UK

We like to forget that agriculture is one of the core human activities. In historic societies most people lived in the countryside: a high, if falling proportion of the population were engaged in the production and processing of foodstuffs. The possession of land was a key form of wealth: it brought not only income from tenants but prestige, access to a rural lifestyle and often political power. Nor could government ever be disinterested in the countryside, whether to maintain urban food supply, as a source of taxation, or to maintain social peace. Increasingly it managed every aspect of the countryside. Agriculture itself and the social relations within the countryside were in constant flux as farmers reacted to new or changing opportunities, and landlords sought to maintain or increase their incomes. Moreover, urban attitudes to the landscape and its inhabitants were constantly shifting.

These questions of competition and change, production, power and perception are the primary themes of the series. It looks at change and competition in the countryside: social relations within it and between urban and rural societies. The series offers a forum for the publication of the best work on all of these issues, straddling the economic, social and cultural, concentrating on the rural history of Britain and Ireland, Europe and its colonial empires, and North America over the past millennium.

www.ashgate.com/ruralworlds

Coping with Crisis: The Resilience and Vulnerability of Pre-Industrial Settlements

DANIEL R. CURTIS
Utrecht University, Netherlands

Routledge
Taylor & Francis Group
LONDON AND NEW YORK

First published in paperback 2024

First published 2014 by Ashgate Publishing

Published 2016 by Routledge
4 Park Square, Milton Park, Abingdon, Oxon OX14 4RN

and by Routledge
605 Third Avenue, New York, NY 10158

Routledge is an imprint of the Taylor & Francis Group, an informa business

Publisher's Note
The publisher has gone to great lengths to ensure the quality of this reprint but points out that some imperfections in the original copies may be apparent.

British Library Cataloguing in Publication Data
A catalogue record for this book is available from the British Library

The Library of Congress has cataloged the printed edition as follows:
Curtis, Daniel R.
Coping with crisis : the resilience and vulnerability of pre-industrial settlements / by Daniel R. Curtis.
pages cm. -- (Rural worlds : economic, social and cultural histories of agricultures and rural societies)
Includes bibliographical references and index.
ISBN 978-1-4724-2004-6 (hardcover)
1. Crisis management--Europe--History. 2. Organizational resilience--Europe--History. 3. Disasters--Social aspects--Europe--History. 4. Communities--Europe--History. 5. Europe--Rural conditions--History. I. Title.
HD49.C873 2014
307.72094'0902--dc23

2013051054

ISBN: 978-1-4724-2004-6 (hbk)
ISBN: 978-1-03-292048-1 (pbk)
ISBN: 978-1-315-57423-3 (ebk)

DOI: 10.4324/9781315574233

In memory of Ken

Lo! Where the heath, with withering brake grown o'er,
Lends the light turf that warms the neighbouring poor;
From thence a length of burning sand appears,
Where the thin harvest waves its wither'd ears;
Rank weeds, that every art and care defy,
Reign o'er the land and rob the blighted rye;
There thistles stretch their prickly arms afar,
And to the ragged infant threaten war;
There poppies nodding, mock the hope of toil,
There the blue bugloss paints the sterile soil ... .

George Crabbe

Contents

List of Figures — *ix*
List of Tables — *xi*
Preface — *xiii*
Abbreviations and Contractions — *xvii*
Measurements — *xxi*

1 Defining Settlement 'Resilience' and 'Vulnerability' and Introducing the Historiography — 1

2 The Theoretical Framework — 23

3 Parasite or Stimulant? The Divergent Impact of the City of Florence upon its Surrounding Rural Hinterlands, 1300–1580 — 63

4 Settlement Decline before the Black Death? Dealing with Pressure on Resources in Two Regions of Medieval Cambridgeshire, 1200–1340 — 105

5 Village Communities and Commercialisation: The Rise of Large Tenant Farmers and its Impact on Settlements in the Dutch River Area, 1300–1600 — 147

6 A North Sea Coastal Area Under Pressure of Land Consolidation. Transition from a Farmers' Republic to an Unequal Polder Society in the Oldambt of Groningen, 1700–1900 — 181

7 Exploring Long-Term Inequality and Agro-Towns in the Kingdom of Naples, 1600–1900: A Comparative Study in Apulia — 223

8 Conclusion — 265

Bibliography — *273*
Index — *379*

List of Figures

1.1	Western Europe and the location of the case studies	20
3.1	Major medieval cities and towns of central Italy	68
3.2	Florentine territories (*contado* and *distretto*), 1574	69
3.3	What types of society were the Florentine *contado* and the Casentino Valley, 1300–1580?	101
3.4	Predicted strategies for resource management in the Florentine *contado* and Casentino Valley, 1300–1580	102
3.5	Predicted levels of settlement resilience or vulnerability in the Florentine *contado* and Casentino Valley, 1300–1580	102
4.1	The three 'provinces' of England according to Brian Roberts and Stuart Wrathmel	111
4.2	Layout of the Bourn Valley parishes with distribution of moats	113
4.3	Layout of the East Chilford parishes with distribution of moats	114
4.4	Manorial fragmentation in Barton in the late thirteenth century	132
4.5	What types of society were the Bourn Valley and East Chilford, 1200–1340?	142
4.6	Predicted strategies for resource management in the Bourn Valley and East Chilford, 1200–1340	143
4.7	Predicted levels of settlement resilience or vulnerability in the Bourn Valley and East Chilford, 1200–1340	143
5.1	Location of the Betuwe in the Northern Low Countries, c.1600	151
5.2	The Central Dutch River Area with the Betuwe located	152
5.3	Contrasting medieval reclamation patterns in the Betuwe	154
5.4	Distribution of Mariënweerd *uithoven* (1350) and locations of large tenant farms (1550) in the Betuwe	170
5.5	Size of tenant farms leased from Mariënweerd, 1456/1550 (divided by tenants)	171
5.6	Size of tenant farms leased from Mariënweerd, 1456/1550 (divided by area)	172
5.7	What type of society was the Betuwe, 1300–1600?	178
5.8	Predicted strategies for resource management in the Betuwe, 1300–1600	179
5.9	Predicted levels of settlement resilience or vulnerability in the Betuwe, 1300–1600	179

6.1 Location of the Oldambt in the Northern Low Countries, c.1700 183
6.2 Farm sizes in the Oldambt, 1630–1832 (divided by total landholders) 204
6.3 Farm sizes in the Oldambt, 1630–1832 (divided by total area) 204
6.4 Isolated farms on the Kroonpolder and Stadspolder, 1832 206
6.5 Farmhouses on the main street and labourer houses on the side-road, 1832 (Nieuw Beerta) 207
6.6 Development of the polders in the Dollard, c.1550–1923 212
6.7 What type of society was the Oldambt, 1700–1900? 218
6.8 Predicted strategies for resource management in the Oldambt, 1700–1900 219
6.9 Predicted levels of settlement resilience or vulnerability in the Oldambt, 1700–1900 219
6.10 What type of society was the Oldambt, 1500–1700? 221
6.11 Predicted strategies for resource management in the Oldambt, 1500–1700 221
6.12 Predicted levels of settlement resilience or vulnerability in the Oldambt, 1500–1700 222

7.1 Rough locations of main agro-town areas of Southern Italy 224
7.2 Map of Apulia and locations of towns 231
7.3 Ascoli Satriano in 1703 235
7.4 Population trends in comparison: Ascoli Satriano and Locorotondo, 1595–2010 237
7.5 Distribution of dispersed *trulli* in Locorotondo, end of the twentieth century 239
7.6 What type of society was Ascoli Satriano and Locorotondo, 1600–1900? 260
7.7 Predicted strategies for resource management in Ascoli Satriano and Locorotondo, 1600–1900 261
7.8 Predicted levels of settlement resilience or vulnerability in Ascoli Satriano and Locorotondo, 1600–1900 261

8.1 What types of societies were the case studies? 265
8.2 Predicted strategies for resource management in the case studies 265
8.3 Predicted levels of settlement resilience or vulnerability in the case studies 266
8.4 Number of 'matches' between predicted and actual strategies for resource management 266
8.5 Number of 'matches' between predicted and actual levels of settlement resilience or vulnerability in the case studies 267
8.6 Societies on the 'boundary' 268

List of Tables

2.1 The breakdown of Tyrannoland (1200–1550) into quantifiable configurations 38
2.2 The four basic types of pre-industrial society 38

3.1 Concentrated settlements in the Casentino Valley, 1427 75
3.2 Population trends in the Casentino, 1427–1552 76
3.3 Wealthiest 10 heads of household in the Casentino Valley, 1427 86
3.4 The breakdown of the Florentine *contado* (1300–1580) into quantifiable configurations 100
3.5 The breakdown of the Casentino Valley (1300–1580) into quantifiable configurations 101

4.1 Distribution and status of medieval moats in East Chilford and the Bourn Valley 112
4.2 Estimated numbers of households in the Bourn Valley and East Chilford, 1086–1327 119
4.3 Social distribution of land in the Bourn Valley and East Chilford, 1279 133
4.4 Landholding sizes in the Bourn Valley and East Chilford, 1279 138
4.5 The breakdown of the Bourn Valley (1200–1340) into quantifiable configurations 142
4.6 The breakdown of East Chilford (1200–1340) into quantifiable configurations 142

5.1 Population trends for regions in Betuwe and surrounding area, 1369–1630/50 159
5.2 Social distribution of landownership in the Western Betuwe, 1300–1600 (%) 173
5.3 The breakdown of the Betuwe (1300–1600) into quantifiable configurations 178

6.1 Population figures for the Oldambt, 1795–1899 190
6.2 Occupational distribution of the Oldambt population by parish, 1807 (%) 198
6.3 Occupational distribution of the Oldambt population by parish, 1813 (%) 199
6.4 Oldambt agricultural sector, 1862 (%) 201
6.5 Social distribution of landownership in the Oldambt, 1721 (%) 207

6.6 The breakdown of the Oldambt (1700–1900) into quantifiable configurations 218
6.7 The breakdown of the Oldambt (1500–1700) into quantifiable configurations 220

7.1 Access to land in Locorotondo (1749) and Ascoli Satriano (1753) (%) 248
7.2 Social distribution of land in Locorotondo (1749) and Ascoli Satriano (1753) 248
7.3 Gini indexes for villages in the Cosentino area of Calabria, mid-eighteenth century 250
7.4 Gini indexes for various places in the Mediterranean, twentieth century 253
7.5 The breakdown of Ascoli Satriano (1600–1900) into quantifiable configurations 260
7.6 The breakdown of Locorotondo (1600–1900) into quantifiable configurations 260

Preface

> We never think entirely alone: we think in company, in a vast collaboration; we work with the workers of the past and of the present. [Across] the whole intellectual world, each one finds in those about him the initiation, help, verification, [and] encouragement that he needs.
>
> Antoine Sertillanges, La vie intellectuelle, 1920.

I have always been interested in the places where people live. I often find myself asking: how did these people end up living here? Is it by choice or necessity? How do they spend their time and how do they make a living? Travelling can take you to some of the most picturesque or exciting spots in the world, but I have always had a fascination for the mundane and the ordinary. Indeed, my favourite place in Italy is not Florence as one of the 'cultural centres' of the Renaissance, the villas and vineyards of the rolling Tuscan hills, the antiquities of Rome, the Alpine mountains, or the tranquil lakes of Como or Garda, but is actually encapsulated in a small, rather drab and ordinary town in Apulia which goes by the name of Ascoli Satriano. Between the nineteenth century and the Second World War, this town was home to the mass ranks of agricultural labourers working for wages on large latifundist estates. Since the mid twentieth century, the story of the town has been one of perpetual decline and stagnation: the population has halved in size, former residents have emigrated north in search of work, and much that remains is the elderly or the underemployed youth. Ecological and environmental degradation has reduced local agricultural yields to such low levels that there is a concomitant reliance on state subsidies. Yet as an outsider and a visitor to this town well off the tourist trail some years ago, it provided a special sense of atmosphere and soul not to be replicated in any of the towns of greater 'grandeur' in Italy. This book is written with that exact aesthetic in mind – placing great value in the 'ordinary people' and the places they reside.

Of course this is an academic book, and thus has academic influences too, which may be clear to those historians who encounter this work by chance. In particular, I have from my earliest days as an undergraduate been inspired by the Annales School with their belief in approaching historical developments over the *longue durée* and their passion for the story of the ordinary – the peasant, the farmer, the worker, the soil. However, my explicit focus on power and property as the basic foundation point for divergent historical developments in the pre-industrial period has some roots in the Neo-Marxist School – in particular, my greatest intellectual influence being that of Prof. Robert Brenner. These frameworks are not altogether fashionable anymore, however, and it is with that realisation that in more recent years I have become influenced by other ideas such the New Economic Geography associated with Paul Krugman and the Douglass North-inspired New Institutional Economics. The most fascinating work and inspiration for this book, however, is almost certainly the twin publications of *Guns, Germs, and Steel* and *Collapse* by Prof. Jared Diamond. There is not one academic in the world who could have written those books, and while many may not agree with his argumentation or material, it is undeniable that his influence on academia and on the wider public has been immense. It is through him that I have learnt it is better to write something which is open to criticism than write something conservatively and left to gather dust on bookshelves.

Of course, a preface necessitates many offerings of gratitude to those who have helped along the way – and there have been many. I am most indebted to my PhD supervisor at Utrecht University, Prof. Bas van Bavel, whom I have come to appreciate not just as a brilliant scholar, but a kind and generous person with a sharp sense of humour. It was my great fortune to stumble across his path. Other individuals have made vital contributions. Prof. Maarten Prak has always shown great confidence in my work at Utrecht and I thank him for providing me with some funding to finish this book. Through his warmth and genuine concern for other people, to my mind Maarten is the 'model scholar' to which many of us should aspire. Further I thank in no particular order members of Bas van Bavel's own research group, Dr Auke Rijpma, Dr Jessica Dijkman, and Dr Jaco Zuijderduijn for comments on past papers. The same goes for Prof. Tine De Moor and Prof. Oscar Gelderblom. I am grateful also to Prof. Jan Luiten van Zanden, another incredibly impressive scholar at Utrecht, for charitably providing me with paid work during tricky periods. The Social and Economic History Department at Utrecht University is an outstanding institutional setting for anyone considering research there – in my opinion currently the best in the world in this discipline. Elsewhere I thank Dr Otto Knottnerus for imparting his considerable wisdom on the Oldambt region of Groningen to me and for driving me precariously around snow-covered polders in the depths of winter. I am particularly grateful to Dr Michele Campopiano also, who has not only co-authored papers with me, but took the time to improve my Italian. I have received helpful advice on individual chapters from some of the most revered scholars working on pre-industrial societies and economies such as Prof. Chris Dyer and Prof. Chris Wickham. I must also thank Dr Susan Oosthuizen, who laid the foundations of my research some years ago as a supportive supervisor of an MPhil thesis at the University of Cambridge. The comments from both Richard Hoyle as series editor and the anonymous peer reviewer went right to the 'core' issues, and helped shape the book in its final stages.

Naturally there are many friends that have helped me over the years; too numerous to list individually, though a large amount of my gratitude goes to my partner Qijun. When writing a book like this, it is inevitable that some periods are arduous and lonely, but being with Qijun has made the later phases of this task a much more enjoyable and fulfilling process. Finally, I am especially indebted to my parents and grandparents, for without their support over the years, this book never would have come to fruition.

D.R.C. Rotterdam, 2014

Abbreviations and Contractions

Some of the works cited in the bibliography and footnotes appear many times. In the interests of space, frequently appearing journal articles, printed primary sources, and names of archives are shortened or abbreviated.

Archives

ASA – Archivio di Stato di Arezzo
ASB – Archivio di Stato di Bari
ASC – Archivio di Stato di Cosenza
ASF – Archivio di Stato di Firenze (Florence)
ASN – Archivio di Stato di Napoli (Naples)
ASP – Archivio di Stato di Pisa
ASEM – Archivio Storico dell'Eremo e Monastero di Camaldoli
BCP – Biblioteca Comunale di Poppi
BNF – Biblioteca Nazionale Centrale di Firenze (Florence)
BL – British Library (London)
CCRO – Cambridgeshire County Record Office (Shire Hall, Cambridge)
CUL – Cambridge University Library
ERO – Essex Record Office (Chelmsford)
GELA – Gelders Archief (Arnhem)
GA – Groninger Archieven (Groningen)
KCA – King's College Archives (Cambridge)
MCA – Merton College Archives (Cambridge)
NADH – Nationaal Archief Den Haag (The Hague)
PCA – Pembroke College Archives (Cambridge)
RAR – Regionaal Archief Rivierenland (Tiel)
SCC – St. Catherine's College Archives (Cambridge)
SWB – Streekarchivariaat West-Betuwe (Geldermalsen)
TNA – The National Archives (Kew) [formerly PRO – Public Record Office]

Primary Sources Abbreviated

Inquisitions Post Mortem – IPM
Oorkondenboek van het Sticht Utrecht – OSU
Regesto di Camaldoli – RC
Rotuli hundredorum – RH
Victoria County History – VCH

Journals Abbreviated

Agricultural History Review – AgHR
American Historical Review – AHR
Annales: Economies, Sociétés, Civilisations – Annales: ESC
Archeologia Medievale – AM
Archivio Storico Italiano – ASI
Bijdragen en Mededelingen Verenigingen Gelre – BMGelre
BMGN: Low Countries Historical Review – BMGN
Bulletin van de Koninklijke Nederlandse Oudheidkundige Bond – Bulletin KNOB
Comparative Studies in Society and History – CSSH
Continuity and Change – C&C
Economic History Review – EcHR
English Historical Review – EHR
Explorations in Economic History – ExEH
Historisch Kring West Betuwe – HKWB
International Review of Social History – IRSH
Journal of Economic History – JEH
Journal of Family History – JFH
Journal of Historical Geography – JHG
Journal of Interdisciplinary History – JIH
Journal of Medieval History – JMH
Landscape History – LH
Past and Present – P&P
Proceedings of the Cambridge Antiquarian Society – PCAS
Revue Belge de Philologie et d'Histoire – RBPH
Studi Storici – SS
Tijdschrift voor Sociale en Economische Geschiedenis – TSEG

Individual Words Contracted

Agricultural – Agr.
American – Amer.
Archives – Arch.
Association – Assoc.
Editor – Ed. (editors – Eds)
Environmental – Env.
European – Europ.
Geographical – Geog.
Historical – Hist.
Institute – Inst.
International – Int.
Journal – J.
Medieval – Med.
Philosophical – Phil.
Political – Pol.
Proceedings – Proc.
Quarterly – Quart.
Review – Rev.
Series – Ser.
Society – Soc.
Studies – Stud.
Transactions – Trans.
Unpublished – Unpub.

Measurements

Wherever possible, the modern metric system of measuring has been used to aid the comparative process. Thus weight is measured in kilograms and grams, area is measured in hectares, distance in metres and kilometres, and litres for volume.

1 hectare (10,000 square metres) = 2.47 acres

However, it is difficult to give reliable conversions for differing monetary systems due to the frequently changing values. Debasement meant that 240 *denari* did not always equate to 1 pound of silver.

1 pound = 20 shillings = 240 *denari* [1/3 of a pound = 1 mark]

Chapter 1
Defining Settlement 'Resilience' and 'Vulnerability' and Introducing the Historiography

> Civilizations are fragile, impermanent things. This fact inevitably captures our attention, and however we might wish otherwise, prompts disturbing questions.
>
> Joseph Tainter[1]

Outline of the problem

This book tries to provide an answer to one main question. Why in the pre-industrial period were some settlements resilient and stable over the long term while other settlements were vulnerable to crisis? Indeed, what made certain human habitations more prone to decline or even total collapse, than others? All pre-industrial societies had to face environmental challenges at some point, many of which had origins that were exogenous to the societies themselves, such as bubonic plague, earthquakes, and (some) floods. Similarly, pre-industrial societies could face economic or agricultural challenges as direct or indirect victims of developments caused by actors from 'outside' such as harsh state taxation, warfare, or expropriation of property. In addition to these 'exogenous' problems, pre-industrial societies also faced problems of their 'own making': challenges which were, at least in part, the outcome of endogenous processes such as (some) harvest failures and subsistence crises, social revolts, population pressure on finite resources, fires, and soil erosion. How then can we explain why some societies were able to overcome or negate these problems, while other societies proved susceptible to failure, as settlements contracted, stagnated, were abandoned, or even disappeared entirely?

Historiography

This book is not the first work to explicitly focus on concepts such as stability or crisis in settlements in the pre-industrial period, although it is one of the first works to explicitly deal with the terms 'resilience' and 'vulnerability', which have

1 Tainter, *The Collapse of Complex Societies.*

recently been made fashionable in the contemporary social sciences but have not truly been embedded into historical disciplines as yet. This section looks at the build-up to our state of knowledge of the resilience and vulnerability of pre-industrial societies, which provides the background for the definition of what is meant by these terms used in this book.

Malthusian Ideology and the Population-Resources Framework

The population-resources framework was at one time employed to explain why societies and settlements failed in the pre-industrial period, often founded upon an underlying theory of 'Malthusian Crisis'. Although Malthus-inspired explanations have for a long time become unfashionable in academic circles (indeed history shows that 'natural Malthusian limits' were rarely reached),[2] the paradigm has had some high-profile resurrection – in particular Gregory Clark's *A Farewell to Alms*.[3] In these explanations, societies failed to combat the destabilising effects of demographic pressure on an (often) finite pool of resources, which put the future sustainability of settlements in danger. It is the story of people outstripping resources, straining the natural environment, and leading to an inevitable breaking point. Even modern-day societal collapses have been explained with recourse to this framework, such as the terrible genocide in Rwanda in 1994.[4] On a global level, some scholars believe that modern humanity has 'overshot' its carrying capacity for certain resources,[5] and much emphasis in modern sustainable development strategies has been on a demographic transition to lower fertility regimes.[6]

There have been some famous advocates of the population-resources framework in social and economic history of the pre-industrial period: Sir Michael Postan, Georges Duby, Bernard Slicher van Bath, and Wilhelm Abel, to name but a few. In their interpretation, the collapse of settlements across Europe around the time of the Black Death simply capped off what was already a long-term trend towards stagnation and decline anyway.[7] According to the theory, relentless population growth in Europe from roughly the eleventh century reached a critical point around the end of the thirteenth century. The retraction in settlement during the 1300s was only inevitable given high pressure on existing resources. In effect, population in these pre-industrial societies operated

[2] A point asserted in Van Bavel and Thoen, 'Rural history and the environment', 22.

[3] Clark, *A farewell to alms*, esp. 1–18. Clark's basic principles are also endorsed in a (poorly written) paragraph in the recent McCloskey, *Bourgeois dignity*, 272–3.

[4] André and Platteau, 'Land relations under unbearable stress'.

[5] Rees, 'Carrying capacity'.

[6] Brander, 'Viewpoint: sustainability: Malthus revisited?'.

[7] Classic works being Postan, 'Some agrarian evidence'; Slicher van Bath, *De agrarische geschiedenis van West-Europa*; Duby, *L'économie rurale*; Abel, *Agrarkrisen*.

under a natural 'Malthusian ceiling' which could not be passed.[8] Apparently, their argument was strengthened by the fact that so many societies had expanded cultivation into so-called 'marginal' lands, peripheral area unsuited to arable or intensive farming. The numerous late-medieval deserted villages were the telling evidence of this vulnerability.[9] Woodland began to re-encroach upon formerly tilled areas in some parts from the late 1200s onwards.[10] Over time, such a view has been disputed,[11] and empirical research has since shown that settlements in the 'marginal' areas did not decline any more than settlements in the 'old-settled' areas,[12] and the 'supply' constraints were not necessarily as acute as Postan initially suggested.[13] Furthermore, the timing of settlement abandonment in medieval Western Europe has been questioned; in certain parts it likely occurred during the fifteenth century, rather than in the period up to the Black Death.[14] Over-population and environmental degradation theories have also been used for explaining crises in habitation in pre-industrial China,[15] though once again they have been more recently refuted.[16]

Even if the Malthusian notion of the inevitability of population outstripping resources is not taken up, scholars have still explained the vulnerability of settlements through demographic pressures on limited resources. Indeed, recent literature puts more emphasis on the human capacity to protect or degrade their environment, a scholarship more directly influenced by our now greater awareness of climate change and the growing importance and crystallisation of disciplines such as 'environmental history' within academia.[17] Rapid decline of habitation, whether in the pre-industrial or post-industrial age, has been framed in a general story of humans' destruction of their natural environment.

---

8 Also used to explain long-term population trends in the early modern period; Le Roy Ladurie, *Les paysans de Languedoc*; 'L'histoire immobile'.

9 Dyer and Jones (eds), *Deserted villages revisited*; Beresford, *Lost villages*; Abel, *Die Wüstungen*; Beresford and Hurst, *Deserted medieval villages*; Hilton, 'Villages désertés'; Le Roy Ladurie and Pesez, 'Les villages désertés en France'; Romano and Corbin (eds), *Villages désertés*; Gissel et al., *Desertion and land colonization*; Antonson, 'The extent of farm desertion'; Coulet, 'Encore les villages disparus'; Humm, *Villages et hameaux disparus.*

10 Jager, 'Die Ausdehnung der Wälder', 305.

11 Particularly by those emphasizing the capacity for technological innovation in the Middle Ages; Kitsikopoulos, 'Technological change'. For an overview of critical reaction to population-focused explanations see Bailey and Hatcher, *Modelling the Middle Ages*.

12 Dyer, 'Retreat from marginal land'; 'Villages in crisis', 29; 'Deserted medieval villages', 33; Bailey, 'Concept of the margin', 1–17.

13 Dunsford and Harris, 'Colonization', 35; Bailey, *A marginal economy?*, 85–97.

14 Austermann, 'Archäologische Forschungen zu den mittelalterlichen Siedlungen'.

15 Chao, *Man and land*; Huang, *The peasant family*.

16 Lavelly and Bin Wong, 'Revising the Malthusian narrative'.

17 McNeill, 'Observations'.

Frequently, settlement decline is associated with the chopping-down of too many trees or the over-exploitation or ruination of the soil. These sorts of population-resources frameworks have captured the general public's imagination and have been used to explain the mysterious disappearance of the Ancient Mayan civilisation of Central America or even the end of the Roman Empire.[18] Indeed, the fascination with these famous societal collapses can explain the international best-seller status of author Jared Diamond, who has even written a book with the title *Collapse: How Societies Choose to Fail or Succeed*, as if to emphasise the role of human decision-making in the process and disassociate himself from purely environmentally deterministic literature. A basic point put forward in this work is that societies and settlements were most vulnerable when they failed to halt degradation of natural resources caused by commerce or population growth.[19]

Domination, Expulsion, and Violence

Imbalance in power and its application (often from 'outside') is another avenue through which the resilience or vulnerability of settlement has been considered. Some societies were vulnerable to decline because of the high chances of violent expropriation. This could come in the form of the forcible expulsion of people from an area; for example, the *Moriscos* (former Muslim population) were expelled from the Kingdoms of Aragon and Valencia in 1610 by King Phillip II, which led to irreversible contraction of former settlements.[20] Elsewhere powerful landowners went in search of royal edicts so they could throw out the inhabitants of swamps and woodlands in order to make way for new land reclamation projects.[21] Inhabitants of the Rio Grande region of New Mexico were pushed out of their large pueblo villages during the period of sixteenth- and seventeenth century Spanish colonisation.[22] In some cases, it has been said that agriculturalists that had lost the means of production and had become proletarian workers on large farms frequently found that their susceptibility to eviction from their homes by landlords rose.[23] The same connection between expropriation of land by dominant powers and the vulnerability of settlement is just as applicable in the modern context: one example is the 'land reform' scheme in Zimbabwe instigated by Robert Mugabe, which by the year 2000 had manifested itself in the violent invasion and seizure of white farmers' lands.[24]

18 Culbert, 'Collapse of Classic Maya'; Chew, *World ecological degradation*, 93.

19 Diamond, *Collapse*, 6–7, 35, 487, 490, 516.

20 Salas, 'La evolución demográfica aragonesa'.

21 Morera, 'Environmental change', 86.

22 Kulisheck, 'Pueblo population movements'.

23 Crais, *White supremacy and black resistance*, 218–9.

24 Shaw, 'They stole our land', 75–89.

Neo-Marxist scholars, in particular, have tended to emphasise the capacity of elites such as lords or wealthy landowners to use extra-economic powers and jurisdictions to evict subordinate tenants from their homes as and when they wanted, especially in the interests of land enclosure.[25] This has been labelled a 'depopulation hypothesis'.[26] Indeed, villagers were sometimes moved to make way for monastic granges.[27] Debt and pressure from landlords sometimes forced peasants to give up their property.[28] However, this view has been slightly nuanced by empirical research from England, where it has been suggested that although this could have happened in theory, rarely did it occur in practice.[29] In a small abandoned hamlet near Bordeaux in the fourteenth century, lords had to wait for the rights of any possible heirs to be extinguished before claiming and reassigning the land and property.[30] Rather than evicting tenants, a more common problem for lords in Western Europe (particularly in the wake of the Black Death) was actually forcing subordinates to stay and pay rents.[31] A similar reappraisal of the power of seigneurial lords to evict tenants has also been applied to areas of pre-industrial Eastern Europe.[32] Furthermore, this kind of argumentation tends to end up reducing communities capable of active thought and decision-making to mere passive victims.

Nonetheless, even if dominant powers did not always follow through with expropriation of land and housing of their subordinates in the pre-industrial period, certainly they could speed up settlement decline. In one paper it was explicitly suggested that 'a link between the number of landowners and vulnerability to contraction was apparent', emphasising the power of dominant large landowners to alter settlement structures with changes in land use such as imparking or enclosure.[33] This kind of story is even enshrined in contemporary literature, such as the poems of Oliver Goldsmith witnessing the destruction of an old village in 1770:

---

[25] Brenner, 'Agrarian class structure'; Tawney, *The agrarian problem*, xiii, 264, 283.

[26] Dyer, 'Villages in crisis', 30.

[27] Rösener, 'Economie cistercienne', 131; Fossier, 'Economie cistercienne', 64.

[28] Ulsig, *Danske adelsgodser*, 46–53.

[29] Overton, *Agricultural revolution*, 180; Dyer, 'Occupation of the land', 81; Hilton, *The English peasantry*, 191–3; Platt, *Monastic grange*, 76–93. Especially given the high costs associated with the eviction process as described in Guinnane and Miller, 'Bonds without bondsmen', 113.

[30] Boutruche, *La crise d'une société*, 524–7.

[31] Britnell, 'Feudal reaction'; Harris, 'Wastes'.

[32] Blum, *The end of the social order*, 103. Many studies emphasising the stability of tenant holdings in the face of seigneurial pressure; for example see Wetherell, Plakans and Wellman, 'Social networks'; Zeitlhofer, 'Besitztransfer in frühneuzeitlichen ländlichen Gesellschaften'; Hagen, *Ordinary Prussians*.

[33] Neave, 'Rural settlement contraction', 130.

> But times are altered: trade's unfeeling train
> Usurp the land, dispossess the swain;
> Along the lawn, where scattered hamlets rose,
> Unwieldy wealth and cumbrous pomp repose ...
> ... Those healthful sports that graced the peaceful scene,
> Lived in each look, and brightened all the green;
> These, far departing, seek a kinder shore,
> And rural mirth and manners are no more.[34]

Literature on the 'open' and 'closed' parishes of England in the eighteenth and nineteenth centuries emphasises how powerful landlords limited and stopped the lower orders living in the same parish, in order to reduce the poor rate.[35] Cottages were destroyed and labourers driven into towns, resulting in them having to walk many kilometres to work.[36] Elsewhere, capricious state taxation has been cited as one key reason for the breakdown and disintegration of rural communities, for example, in some parts of sixteenth-century mainland Greece.[37] In some cases, as with the Highland Clearances in Scotland, people were forcibly displaced by aristocratic landowners such as the Duke of Sutherland under the pretext of agricultural and 'social improvement'.[38]

Often the capacity for dominant groups to use violence and warfare has been cited as a reason for the vulnerable status of settlements. It should come as no surprise that numerous pre-industrial (and post-industrial)[39] settlements were either abandoned or destroyed as a result of warfare, while even in the twenty-first century, millions of people in underdeveloped countries are displaced from their homes. At the time of writing, an estimated 9 million Syrians have fled their homes since the outbreak of civil war in March 2011, seeking refuge in Jordan, Turkey, Lebanon and Iraq, or internally displaced.[40] The Eighty Years' War led to the entire destruction of fishing villages in the Low Countries,[41] while in Germany, famine, sickness, and the abandonment of farms were just some of the consequences of the Thirty Years' War – even if the 'devastating' extent of these

---

34 Goldsmith, *The deserted village*, 11–12.

35 Holderness, 'Open and close parishes'. Although a wider range of reasons than simply the poor law have been discussed in Banks, 'Nineteenth century scandal', 54.

36 Snell, 'Settlement, poor law and the rural historian'; Sheppard, 'East Yorkshire's agricultural labour force'.

37 Parry, 'The Ottoman Empire'; Wagstaff, 'War and settlement desertion', 305; Antoniadis-Bibicou, 'Villages désertés en Grèce'.

38 Tindley, 'The Iron Duke'.

39 A classic example being almost total settlement desertion caused through Arab-Israeli conflict; Harris, 'War and settlement change'.

40 See Migration Policy Centre, 'Syrian refugees'.

41 Tys and Pieters, 'Understanding a medieval fishing settlement'.

consequences has had a long history of debate.[42] Military destruction inflicted further miseries on the lives of 'ordinary' rural folk, who already were struggling to maintain subsistence.[43] The presence of soldiers did not just mean killings but it also brought exactions and plundering, the destruction of fields and dikes, and the outbreak of contagious diseases.[44] Warfare also disrupted trade networks leading to shortages in produce.[45] Farming systems were disrupted: the second Arab invasions (*Hilali*) in parts of Berber Morocco in the eleventh and twelfth centuries led to the entire collapse of the pastoral economy.[46]

Some areas of the countryside were so vulnerable that people avoided building there altogether. In parts of the Mediterranean, such as Sicily, the threat of brigandage and fears over public order were so severe that it has been suggested that nobody dared live anywhere but the towns.[47] To live isolated in the countryside was to expose oneself to all kinds of danger. Governments did not always ensure safety for their populations, and sometimes actively contributed to settlement vulnerability in pursuit of their own interests. In the first half of the twentieth century, governmental officers of the Afenmai district of Nigeria caused hill-dwelling communities to abandon their lands by burning their homes.[48] Even in the very recent history of China, the damming of the Yangtze River (made possible through funding from a number of loans from international commercial banks and corporate bonds) has led to the forcible relocation of settlements and the flooding of villages and land – a process that the rural communities had no power to prevent.[49]

Environmental Determinism

Although environmental determinism is becoming less frequently invoked on its own as an explanatory framework, it is still used (particularly in studies on a global scale) to explain why some habitations around the world are more vulnerable to crisis or collapse than others.[50] Certainly it cannot be denied that

---

42 Abel, *Agricultural fluctuations*, 155–6; Hagen, 'Seventeenth-century crisis', 327–8; Theibault, *German villages in crisis*.

43 Thoen, 'Warfare and the countryside'; Adriaenssen and 't Hart, 'Farming communities at risk'; Adriaenssen, *Staatsvormend geweld*.

44 Hahn, 'Kriegserfahrungen von Kindern und Jugendlichen', 6; Albini, *Guerra, fame, peste*.

45 Munro, 'Changing fortunes of fairs'.

46 Lawless, 'Lost Berber villages', 118.

47 Blok, *Mafia of a Sicilian village*; Weber, *The city*, 82.

48 Bradbury, *The Benin Kingdom*, 113; Gleave, 'Hill settlements', 45.

49 Jing, 'Rural resettlement'; 'Villages dammed'; Heming, Waley and Rees, 'Reservoir resettlement'; Stone, 'Three Gorges dam'.

50 Weiss and Bradley, 'What drives societal collapse?'.

there are certain parts of the globe more favourable to human settlement than others. The emergence of the world's first settled farming systems in the 'Fertile Crescent' of the Middle East from about 9000 BCE has been put down to high levels of fertility in the soils which support sown agriculture.[51] According to some scholars, settlement and agriculture in Western Europe before 1300 benefited from more stable and predictable climatic conditions than those seen in the late Middle Ages.[52] This changed with the so-called 'Little Ice Age': a global cooling in temperatures following the 'warm period' of the high Middle Ages.[53] Indeed, in general it has been suggested that Northern Europe bore the brunt of the terrible and unpredictable weather conditions much more than the South – particularly in Scandinavia.[54] Exceptionally cold mountain regions such as Iceland became more susceptible to avalanches.[55] However, very recent research is now suggesting that the Mediterranean parts of Europe were equally hit by adverse climatic conditions and the differences only lay in the precise timing of events such as severe rainfall – making habitation equally vulnerable to the elements.[56] Even today climate change informs general views on societal vulnerability, sometimes in very simplistic terms with an almost paranoid narrative of migration from the 'Global South' to the 'safer' shores of developed countries.[57] Such simple causal links are disputed and contested by scholars, however.[58] Indeed, top disasters studies scholar Greg Bankoff has urged us away from an uncritical Western discourse of a Global South conceived of as disease ridden, inhospitable places – poverty stricken and disaster prone in equal measure.[59]

---

51 Diamond, *Guns, germs, and steel*, 79–90; Bellwood, *The first farmers*, 44–66.

52 Bailey, 'Per impetum maris'; Utterstrom, 'Climate fluctuations'; Parry, *Climatic change*, 85.

53 The Little Ice Age is often attributed to the sixteenth century, although some have argued for a long-term cooling starting from the early fourteenth century; see Pfister, Schwarz-Zanetti and Wegmann, 'Winter severity', 103.

54 Campbell, 'Nature as historical protagonist', 310; Briffa et al., 'Influence of volcanic eruptions', 450; Kalela-Brundin, *Climate information from tree rings*, 15–16, 199–203; Leijonhufvud, *Grain tithes*, 255–8.

55 Le Roy Ladurie, 'Climat et récoltes'.

56 See the recent superb Alfani, *Calamities and the economy*. Also Camuffo and Enzi, 'Reconstructing the climate'; Mariani, 'Clima ed agricoltura'; Pavese and Gregori, 'Analysis of six centuries'. Recently there has been some debate as to whether the 'Little Ice Age' occurred at all; Kelly and Ó Gráda, 'Waning of the Little Ice Age'; White, 'The real Little Ice Age'; Büntgen and Hellmann, 'The Little Ice Age in scientific perspective'.

57 For a debate on this issue see Homer-Dixon, 'On the threshold'; Oels, 'From "securitization" of climate change'; Barnett and Adger, 'Climate change, human security'.

58 Dun and Gemenne, 'Defining environmental migration'.

59 Bankoff, 'Rendering the world unsafe'.

While pre-industrial Western and Eastern Europe had its environmental problems in the form of storms,[60] and even experienced disastrous earthquakes in the South,[61] scholars nonetheless inevitably acknowledge that environmental dangers were (generally) more severe in Asia, Africa, or America if taken on a global comparative level. Hurricanes were a constant threat in tropical climates, and it is well-known that the plantation economies of the Caribbean suffered when strong winds tore the flimsy wooden shacks to pieces.[62] Many settlements faced the potential threat of volcanoes, earthquakes, and tsunamis, as they were located close to converging tectonic plates, and many societies had to deal with fluctuating and extreme temperatures, causing blizzards, hailstorms, droughts, and heat-waves. Hot and dry areas of the world had to deal with the possibility of bushfires, which could (and still do) spread rapidly through wooded areas. Unpredictable weather conditions led to some of the deadliest flooding of the Yellow, Yangtze, and Huai Rivers in China in the nineteenth and twentieth centuries.[63]

Settlement vulnerability has also been considered in connection with the spread of disease. Marshland societies faced the threat of malaria, especially in warmer climates, and people were fearful of venturing into these areas.[64] More significant in the literature, however, has been the work on European colonists exposing contacted peoples to new germs – and therefore disease epidemics. According to some authors, most significantly in the work of Alfred Crosby, the arrival of Columbus in the New World brought about one of the greatest population disasters in history.[65] In that sense, the vulnerability of societies has been reduced to the chances of biology – something that has not gone without criticism.[66] Such environmental vulnerability was not 'one-way' either: it has been noted that European colonists also came to the Americas inadequately prepared, physically and psychologically, to cope with the new environment they had to face.[67] Early colonists at Jamestown, Virginia, were beset with

60 De Kraker, 'Reconstruction of storm frequency'; 'Storminess'; Kiss, 'Floods and weather'.

61 Boschi et al., *Catalogo dei forti terremoti.*

62 Mulcahy, *Hurricanes and society.*

63 Pietz, *Engineering the state*, 61–70; Kueh, *Agricultural instability*, 182.

64 Snowden, 'Fields of death'; Bruce-Chwatt and De Zulueta, *Rise and fall of malaria*; Roy Meterns and Terry, 'Dying in paradise'; Dobson, 'Marsh fever'.

65 Crosby, *Ecological imperialism*, 195–216; 'Infectious disease', 123; *The Columbian exchange*, 38; 'Virgin soil epidemics'; Thornton, *American Indian holocaust*; McNeill, *Plagues and peoples*, 177; Guerra, 'El efecto demográfico de las epidemias'.

66 See the critique of the literature in Alchon, *A pest in the land.*

67 Kupperman, 'The puzzle of the American climate', 1277.

psychological problems leading to loss of appetite and malnutrition as a result of the alien and uncomfortable new surroundings.[68]

Urban Expropriation and Flight to the City

In Western Europe, the rise of cities and towns and the formalisation of territorial jurisdictions over their hinterlands from the late Middle Ages onwards in particular have been associated with a destabilising and detrimental effect on settlements in the countryside – often fuelling rural-urban migration.[69] This is often set within a 'flight to the city' narrative, where urban centres attract an influx of the poor.[70] Difficult conditions for rural people caused by expropriation of their land by wealthy or powerful urban interest groups were often exacerbated by 'pull' opportunities offered by the cities themselves.[71] Indeed, in an influential theory posited by Tony Wrigley for England, he showed the interconnectivity of the 'push' and 'pull' factors by emphasising links between land accumulation and industrial development. According to Wrigley, agricultural progress and the consolidation of large farms in England led to increased demand for manufactured products and services, which set in motion flight to the city undertaken by proletarians in search of non-agricultural work.[72]

Land consolidation caused by investment and encroachment of urban interest groups in late-medieval and early-modern Europe often preceded a mass exodus of rural people to the city.[73] Features associated with this downward demographic trend include high unemployment and a paucity of opportunity for work, proletarianisation, settlement collapse, and a general trend of movement (permanent or temporary) towards the city in search of work. Indeed, it was a central tenet of a famous thesis by Charles Tilly that pre-industrial agricultural labourers were more migratory and more likely to be involved in rural-urban movement than landholding peasants who were 'relatively immobile'.[74] Other scholars, such as Jerome Blum, also noted the connection between the incidence of permanent or temporary migration from countryside to city, mainly by the

[68] Kupperman, 'Apathy and death'.

[69] Curtis, 'Florence and its hinterlands'. Also Epstein, 'Cities, regions'; 'Town and country'.

[70] Glaeser, *Triumph of the city*, 70.

[71] Cipolla, *Before the Industrial Revolution*, 92; Lucassen and Willems, 'Why people want to live in the city'.

[72] Wrigley, 'Men on the land'; 'Urban growth'. A view influenced by Jones, 'Agricultural origins of industry'.

[73] On the general process see Curtis, 'Impact of land accumulation'.

[74] Tilly, 'Migration in modern European history', 53. Also Flinn, *European demographic system*, 23; Grigg, *Dynamics of agricultural change*, 110–13.

impoverished and the landless in search of work.[75] By the nineteenth century, the poor were looking even further afield – attempting to find their fortune through dangerous transatlantic migration to Argentina or North America.[76] It also laid the seeds for political unrest as proletarian workers (both agricultural and urban) formed conscious identities as a social group, and began to revolt against the political mainstream.[77]

Urban expropriation of rural property-holders in the late-medieval Florentine *contado* in Tuscany, Italy, coupled with harsh fiscal oppression and the imposition of the onerous demands of *mezzadria* (sharecropping), led to mass migration from the countryside into Florence.[78] As a result, village settlements collapsed, farm plots were abandoned, and the rural poor eventually swelled the impoverished suburbs of Florence, often to the south and the east. A similar trend can be seen in many of the city-states of Northern Italy in the transition from the late Middle Ages to the early modern period as urban expropriation of peasant lands became a general phenomenon.[79] Newly proletarianised rural people had little option but to migrate to various cities and towns in search of food and work.[80] Of course, widespread rural-urban migration put more pressure on those that remained in the countryside, as peasant assistance in the maintenance of things like complex hydraulic works completely unravelled.[81] The consequence was increased susceptibility to flooding, in turn causing a vicious circle of outward migration.[82] In fact, it has been shown that in tougher economic periods, the swarm of rural people upon the cities in search of employment and food was so great that many urban governments chose to close their gates to keep out beggars and vagrants.[83] Peasants taking refuge in the cities were removed and sent back to work in the countryside.[84]

The association of land consolidation with downward demographic trends in the countryside has also been a feature of literature much later in the pre-industrial period.[85] In the late sixteenth and seventeenth centuries, the Beaujolais area of France was converted to wine-cultivation through urban finance; three quarters of the land passed into non-residents' hands leading to a mass exodus

75 Blum, *The end of the social order*, 111.
76 Wokeck, *Trade in strangers*.
77 Dunbabin, 'Revolt of the field'; Lane, 'Agricultural labourers and rural violence'.
78 See Chapter 3 of this book. Also Curtis, 'Florence and its hinterlands'.
79 An overview of urban land accumulation in Cherubini, 'La proprietà fondiaria'.
80 Curtis and Campopiano, 'Medieval land reclamation', 30.
81 Curtis and Campopiano, 'Medieval land reclamation', 30.
82 Guidoboni, 'Human factors'; Alfani, 'Population and environment', 581.
83 Gutton, *La société et les pauvres*, 104–6.
84 Ronchini (ed.), *Statuta communis Parmae*, 72–3.
85 On the general process see Lucassen and Lucassen, 'The world we lost'.

of rural dwellers.[86] Other areas of France such as the Beauce and the countryside close to Toulouse also experienced a shift from rural to urban landownership, but on a less pronounced scale.[87] This set the backdrop to the kinds of migration described in Paul-André Rosenthal's classic, *Les sentiers invisibles*.[88] Similar high levels of rural-urban migration after proletarianisation have been plotted for parts of Wallonia,[89] and in the Ruhr Valley of Germany.[90] In Andalusia, dismantlement and expropriation of vast expanses of the commons worsened the economic condition of the poor to such an extent that many emigrated in droves to nearby towns.[91] The concept of 'flight from the land' was invoked by famous scholars focusing on nineteenth-century Prussia and Germany, including Max Weber.[92]

The vulnerability of rural settlements in many areas has arguably increased into the twentieth and twenty-first centuries with the dissemination of highly dominant urban culture, the development of technological solutions, and the fact that so many rural people are now divorced from the agricultural productive processes.[93] Isolated mountain regions have been highlighted as particularly vulnerable in this regard.[94] Furthermore, expropriation has continued into the modern period: after the Iranian Revolution, for example, continued and exacerbated inequalities in land distribution led many rural peasants to swell the cities instead, so much so that whole villages in some regions were abandoned.[95] A major concern of governments in both 'developed' and 'underdeveloped' nations is the skewed distribution of people towards main centres, while the peripheries suffer from depopulation, the so-called 'brain drain' (flight of young educated people), and a remaining elderly population to support.[96] In rural Africa, many villages have an over-representation of women, children, and the elderly.[97] Similar distorted demographic profiles have been noted in Russian villages.[98] Not only this, but mass rural-urban migration is also seen by scholars as

86 Gruter, *La naissance d'un grand vignoble*, 83–91.

87 Jacquart, *La crise rurale*, 724–5; Béaur, *La marché foncier à la veille de la Révolution*, 186–204; Frêche, *Toulouse*, 164–8, 191–2; Goubert, *Beauvais et le Beauvaisis*.

88 Rosenthal, *Les sentiers invisibles*.

89 Oris, 'Cultures de l'espace'.

90 Hochstadt, *Mobility and modernity*; Jackson, *Migration and urbanisation*.

91 Gilmore, 'Class consciousness', 154.

92 A historiography provided in Grant, *Migration and inequality*, 34.

93 In general see Bunce, *Rural settlement in an urban world*. For a specific recent study see Collantes, 'Decline of agrarian societies'.

94 Collantes and Pinilla, 'Extreme depopulation'.

95 Parsa, *Social origins of the Iranian Revolution*, 265.

96 Huang, Orazem and Wohlgemuth, 'Rural population growth', 615.

97 Yacoob and Kelly, 'Secondary cities in West Africa', 5.

98 Pallot, 'Rural depopulation', 655.

increasing the vulnerability of cities and towns, as the ranks of the poor become confined to huge slums with poor infrastructure – Sao Paolo and Mumbai as two of the classic examples.[99]

Disaster Studies: 'Natural' Events as Social Processes

Much of the existing scholarship mentioned above on the resilience or vulnerability of settlements focuses on exogenous conditions, or at least 'bad things' which can happen to human habitations. Essentially settlements that were vulnerable to crisis had to contend with an assortment of difficult environmental, political, or economic conditions, whether that was war, climate change, flooding, oppressive taxation or expropriation. It has also been recognised that societies could add to these challenges by creating problems of their own making: things like soil subsidence or erosion, deforestation, general lawlessness, or simply population pressure on limited resources.

One way in which the resilience or vulnerability of human habitation has been approached in more recent times, however, is through an increasingly fashionable discipline of 'disaster studies'. Instead there is now a growing literature based on solid empirical ground which sees disasters, for example, not as mere natural events but as social processes which test the organisational capabilities of societies to limit destabilisation and move onto a stage of recovery.[100] Such crises are now seen as 'nature-induced' rather than 'natural'.[101] Thus according to this discipline the distinction between 'exogenous' and 'endogenous' crises has faded somewhat. Even 'exogenous' crisis is now seen as 'social' with its effects dictated and directed by the arrangement of societies themselves. The establishment of this kind of theory actually owes much to the early work of Nobel Prize-winning development economist Amartya Sen who famously used the Bengal famine of 1943 to argue that mass starvation was not the result of a basic lack of food but more the result of distorted systems of access to food.[102] A good example of the idea of 'natural events' as 'social processes' in the historical literature can be found in practice on the island of St. Vincent in the Caribbean: two different sets of coastal plantations experienced the same terrible shock of the eruption of Mount Soufrière in 1812, yet while one group of cultivators doubled their

99 Kruger, 'Taking advantage of rural assets'; Jacobi, 'Environmental problems in Sao Paolo'; Pelling, *Vulnerability of cities*, 59.

100 For explicit reference to this kind of approach see Tierney, 'From the margins to the mainstream?'; Blaikie et al. (eds), *At risk*; Pelling, *Vulnerability of cities*.

101 Pfister, 'Learning from nature-induced disasters', 18.

102 Sen, *Poverty and famines*; Sen and Drèze, *Hunger and public action*. For other famines; Tilly, 'Food entitlement'; Walter, 'Social economy of dearth', 81–2; Sen's interpretation of the Great Bengal Famine of 1943–4 has been somewhat adapted, however, in the recent O'Grada, 'The ripple that drowns?'.

output after this event, another group recovered only three-quarters of their pre-disaster output, five years after the eruption.[103] Essentially different societies came up with different coping strategies in the face of crises: seventeenth-century accounts from Cambridge show that in response to outbreaks of plague, the afflicted were isolated from the healthy in a 'pest house' while local joiners were paid 'for making barrows to carry corpses'.[104] In the same period in Amersfoort, infected houses were cordoned off and evacuated in response to this epidemic.[105]

Another famous early proponent of the idea that it is societies rather than exogenous conditions that hold the key to societal resilience or vulnerability was Joseph Tainter. He suggested that while invasions, crop failures, or disease may be the direct causes of the collapse of human habitation, the roots of vulnerability are actually inherent in the structure of societies themselves.[106] In his theory on social complexity, Tainter argues that as societies become more complex, they need higher levels of 'energy' input to maintain their increasing levels of complexity. So, for example, governmental costs could grow to the point that they undermined a state's ability to react to problems.[107] Resilience or vulnerability is then dependent on society to solve its problems, to develop its own coping strategies. Troubled times pushed some pre-industrial societies into creating systems of mutual support and cohesion.[108] However, there were times when mutual support broke down: an extreme example is the devastating famines connected to the agricultural and economic policies of Mao Zedong and the 'Great Leap Forward' in China between 1958 and 1962 where in some of the most heavily pressurised areas, survival simply came down to an ability to outwit and pilfer from the State and from equally impoverished neighbours.[109] This same sort of framework has been used to explain the decline of habitation on Easter Island. According to Tainter's interpretation, the inhabitants erected large statues (*moai*) as a form of religious reverence to their ancestors. It was believed that this display of reverence would in turn be rewarded with future prosperity – thus stimulating an intensification of statue-production. Since the isolated geographical position meant the islanders could not rely on trade and the market, statue-production disturbed an already-delicate ecosystem, leading to resource-exhaustion through deforestation and increased competition for scarce resources used in reverent display.[110] Accordingly, Tainter is explicitly

103 Smith, 'Volcanic hazard in a slave society'.

104 CCRO, PB X/18.

105 UA, Stichting Armen de Poth te Amersfoort, 1342–1999, 0100, no. 582.

106 Tainter, *Collapse of complex societies*.

107 Phillips, 'Growth and decline of states'.

108 Clark, 'Social welfare and mutual aid', 405–6; Cuny, *Disasters and development*, 86.

109 Thaxton, *Catastrophe and contention*; Dikötter, *Mao's Great Famine*.

110 In line with work emphasizing environmental mismanagement rather than the disturbing effects of European contact; Bahn and Flenley, *Easter Island*; Van Tilburg,

critical of what he judges to be 'simplistic' explanations for vulnerability based on capitalistic over-exploitation of resources.[111]

The limitations of Tainter's work, however, lie in the lack of empirical testing of very grand ideas. In fact, Tainter himself went so far as to say of his work that 'factual matters will be discussed, but they are never of major importance'![112] Indeed, a limitation on much of the 'collapse' literature is that it remains focused on the level of 'grand civilisations', in periods where documentary evidence is sparse or non-existent, and it becomes difficult to verify or test empirically the bold frameworks.[113] Many scholars are unsure as to whether they agree with Tainter's thesis because (a) they remained unconvinced by the basic wealth of historical evidence and (b) there is little framework set up to actively test his assertions.[114] Probably this is why his thesis has attracted far less public attention than the work of Jared Diamond.

More recently, a few scholars have begun to point to the positive role of social and economic equality in allowing societies to better deal with potentially disastrous shocks and calamities – in contexts which are more testable. One consistent claim in the disaster studies literature of the past 10 or even 20 years has been that the poorer segments of society are more vulnerable than the privileged and wealthy, especially in the face of harsh environmental shocks.[115] It was, after all, Karl Marx who once quipped that the Great Irish Famine 'killed poor devils only'.[116] Disasters are said to be more severe in poor countries,[117] and exacerbated particularly in conditions of corrupt political regimes.[118] Not so long ago this kind of idea was proposed and pushed forward by Ted Steinberg, who argued in a somewhat polemical book that natural disasters in American history (a) hit impoverished people harder than wealthier segments of society and (b) could have had their destructive effects reduced if society had been rearranged in a less polarised manner.[119] The failure to maintain the levees around New Orleans before Hurricane Katrina has been linked to distortions within the US political system: powerful interest groups had no political incentive to make

Easter Island; Stevenson and Haoa, 'Diminishing agricultural productivity'; Orliac, 'Wooded vegetation'.

111 Tainter, 'Archaeology of overshoot'.

112 Tainter, *Collapse of complex societies*, 43.

113 Examples include Homer-Dixon, *Upside of down*; Schwartz and Nichols (eds), *After collapse*; Yoffee and Cowgill (eds), *Collapse of ancient states*.

114 See the sceptical reviews in Trigger, 'Review', 374–5; Jones, 'Review', 634; Blanton, 'Review', 421–3. For a truly negative review see Bowerstock, 'Review', 119–21.

115 Blaikie et al. (eds.), *At risk*, 46–61; Wijkman and Timberlake, *Natural disasters*.

116 Marx, *Capital*, 704.

117 Kahn, 'The death toll'; Strömberg, 'Natural disasters'.

118 Escaleras, M. et al., 'Public sector corruption'.

119 Steinberg, *Acts of God*. Also noted in Fothergill and Peek, 'Poverty and disasters'.

adequate investments in a city with a large proportion of African American residents (roughly 60% of the population in 2010), and a large proportion of poor households.[120] Elsewhere in the aftermath of the earthquake in Haiti in 2011, many of the poor peasants did not even have the legal documents needed to prove ownership of their ruined lands, many of which dated all the way back to the division of the French colonial plantations in the early 1800s.[121]

A further literature has put forward the argument that risks from turbulent environmental events have tended to be greater for the poor, the elderly, racial and ethnic minorities, the less educated or illiterate, and the politically disenfranchised.[122] To cite some illustrative examples, the 1948 flood at Vanport in the United States led to social housing being torn down to make space for industrial development. The significant African American population either had to crowd into (basically segregated) neighbourhoods or be excluded from the area altogether.[123] African Americans were similarly victimised after the events of Hurricane Katrina: they were characterised as 'rampaging thugs' and even turned away at gunpoint from refuges.[124] Further back in time, it was Chinatown which bore the brunt of looting after the 1906 San Francisco Earthquake and it was Chinatown residents who were victimised after being forcibly moved into new settlements.[125] It was ethnic Koreans who were victims of rape, looting and civil violence after the 1923 Great Kanto earthquake in Tokyo.[126] Similar arguments have been made along gender lines.[127] Elsewhere, other scholars have suggested that disaster response in underdeveloped countries such as the regrouping of people into villages in Rwanda after the 1994 genocide failed because of a lack of cultural attention to distinctive arrangement of societies at the local level.[128]

One issue with this literature, however, is that it is not often grounded in historical research – at least not far back in time. The hypotheses are more frequently about contemporary or modern societies, and thus the long-term responses and consequences of disasters are not easy to discern. Indeed, the tsunami of Fukushima and Hurricane Katrina caused terrible short-term damage, misery and disruption, for example – yet long-term social and economic consequences will

---

120 Shughart, 'Katrinanomics'.

121 Lundahl, *The political economy of disaster*.

122 Bankoff, Frerks and Hilhorst (eds), *Mapping vulnerability*; Bankoff, 'Constructing vulnerability'; Dorsey, 'Globalizing justice'; Bullard, *Dumping in Dixie*; Hartman and Squires (eds), *No such thing as a natural disaster*; Dash, Peacock and Morrow, 'And the poor get poorer'; Rodríguez and Barnshaw, 'Social construction of disasters', 220.

123 Pearson, '"A menace to the neighbourhood"', 177; Skovgaard, 'Oregon voices'.

124 Cooper and Block, *Disaster: Hurricane Katrina*.

125 Bolton, *Recovery for whom?*.

126 Ryang, 'Great Kanto earthquake'.

127 Fothergill, 'Gender, risk, and disaster'.

128 Van Leeuwen, 'Rwanda's Imidugudu programme'.

not be discernible for some time.[129] Strong statements by disaster studies scholars such as 'poorer or more inequitable societies are more vulnerable' are interesting and provocative, and yet they remain for the most part as untested statements and intuitive or logical descriptions. There has been little explicit attempt to set up systematic comparative research projects to test these hypotheses, and one thing is for sure, this test certainly has not been performed on historical societies to the same extent.[130] Yet it is clear that past 'pre-industrial' societies can be used almost as a 'laboratory' for testing hypotheses with societal relevance to the present, and this is useful because the consequences over the long term can be discerned – unlike with present-day calamities.[131] Furthermore, some scholars have shown that contemporary disasters actually have very deep roots in historical developments: for example, the terrible earthquake in Peru in 1970 has been linked back to Spanish colonial practices some 500 years previous.[132]

Thus some opportunities still remain for further research. In particular, while the hypotheses offered by much of the new disaster studies literature sound intuitively correct, the approach remains on a descriptive level and not an analytical one. A systematic comparative framework dealing with coping strategies of societies against exogenous crises has barely been attempted. If scholars have used a historical perspective, mostly this is conducted as a one-off experiment on an individual case.[133] For example, recent research has asserted a view that the city of Lisbon and the surrounding rural hinterlands responded favourably to the earthquake of 1755.[134] Although in the short-term the effects were serious with high numbers of casualties and loss of capital goods, it has been argued that some of the long-term structural and institutional recovery was positive leading to economic reform – thus supporting a controversial idea that disasters and hazards can be a 'force for good' as seen in the commercial developments after the Great Fire of Hamburg in 1842 or urban transformation after the 1944 earthquake in Argentina.[135] Yet the problem is that research such as this is not placed in a comparative perspective and so we have nothing to really judge this recovery against:[136] was the Lisbon case really so special in comparison with the societal response to other strong earthquakes such as in Carinthia in

---

129 Ganapati, Cheng and Ganapati, 'Resilient rural communities', 100.

130 Schenk, 'Historical disaster research'.

131 Lübken, 'Chasing a ghost?', 6; Bankoff, 'Time is of the essence'.

132 Oliver-Smith, 'Peru's five-hundred-year earthquake'.

133 A criticism made in the excellent Bankoff, *Cultures of disaster*; Lübken and Mauch, 'Uncertain environments'.

134 Pereira, 'Opportunity of a disaster'; Aguirre, 'Better disaster statistics'.

135 Schubert, 'Great Fire of Hamburg'; Healey, *Ruins of New Argentina*, 296–8.

136 Only one explicitly comparative approach has been found; Romá, 'El terremoto de Lisboa'. Another has compared twentieth-century earthquakes in Southern Italy; Parrinello, 'Post-disaster migrations'.

1348,[137] eastern Sicily in 1693,[138] Calabria in 1783,[139] San Francisco in 1906,[140] or Messina in 1908,[141] where other coping strategies have been identified? Furthermore, of those few works that have approached societal interaction with crises and traumatic events from a historical angle, there has been a more frequent tendency to focus on mentality and cultural responses.[142] In that sense, a systematic comparative approach to the resilience or vulnerability of pre-industrial habitations against exogenous crises focusing predominantly on economic and social institutions has still to be written.

Introducing the Approach Taken in this Book

This book has been stimulated by the questions and hypotheses put forward by the recent 'disaster studies' literature – in particular, placing the arrangement of societies at the forefront of the theoretical framework. Essentially it is suggested that the resilience or vulnerability of habitation has less to do with exogenous crises themselves, and more with endogenous societal responses which dictate (a) the extent of destruction caused by crises and the capacity for society to protect itself, and (b) the capacity to create a sufficient recovery over the medium and long term. However, new ground is broken in this book by offering an approach which is (a) explicitly historical, (b) empirically testable, and (c) systematically comparative.

In the theoretical framework outlined in the next chapter, it is suggested that the way societies were organised in the pre-industrial period impacted significantly on the strategies those societies devised for exploiting their resources and the types of institutions those societies were able to lay down, which in turn dictated the extent to which some settlements were stable and resilient over the long term (perhaps in the face of serious crises) while other settlements were vulnerable to failure and even collapse. A system is first devised for identifying particular 'types of pre-industrial societies' based around levels of equality/inequality and dynamism/persistence in property and power distribution. These distributions in power and property were essentially the 'social context' behind the emergence of different kinds of modes of economic exploitation and institutions for managing resources. Some of these resource-management

[137] Rohr, 'Man and natural disaster'; Borst, 'Das Erdbeben von 1348'.

[138] Condorelli, *Un tirrimoti ranni*.

[139] Tobriner, 'La casa baraccata.

[140] Strupp, 'Dealing with disaster'.

[141] Parrinello, 'Post-disaster migrations'.

[142] For example see Jakubowski-Tiessen, 'Gotteszorn und Meereswüten'; Gestrich, 'Religion in der Hungerkrise'; Kempe, 'Noah's flood'; Lange, 'Bilder eines Deichbruchs'; Forquet, 'Das Erdbeben in Basel'; Oberholzner, 'An act of God'.

strategies and institutions ended up being 'favourable' for the resilience of settlements, while other strategies and institutions became 'unfavourable' – leading to settlement vulnerability.

Defining 'Resilience' and 'Vulnerability' of Pre-Industrial Settlements

First of all though, before moving onto the theoretical framework, there needs to be from the outset a clear idea of what is meant by a 'resilient settlement' in the face of such crises, and how is this distinguished from a 'vulnerable settlement'? In effect, how is the term 'crisis' measured in this study? Overall there are three main markers or indicators employed in this book for measuring the extent to which a pre-industrial settlement was resilient or vulnerable against exogenous crises: (i) population decline or stagnation (epitomised by number of deaths caused by an exogenous event or its connected problems, or number of people outwardly migrating to new areas), (ii) loss or degradation of agricultural land, and (iii) destruction of housing and capital goods. Thus, a 'highly resilient settlement' would be one that (despite experiencing, for example, flooding) experienced low numbers of casualties or at least recovered its population quickly and was able to retain its population even during hard times, put in measures to lessen or limit ruination of agricultural land, and either did not experience great destruction to housing and capital goods, or at least was able to reconstruct very quickly. In contrast, a 'highly vulnerable settlement' would be one that upon experiencing similar severe problems (such as flooding), experienced high numbers of casualties which perhaps never even recovered over the long term or led to widespread outward migration from the region in search of better opportunities, experienced terrible ruination of the local environment including ruination and loss of agricultural land, and suffered great losses to capital goods and housing – often never rebuilt to the same standard.

Book Layout

The rest of this book proceeds as follows. In Chapter 2, the general theoretical framework for explaining resilience or vulnerability of pre-industrial settlements is laid out and explained in greater detail. In chapters 3–7, this theoretical framework is then tested empirically. Each chapter represents a case study of a region in Western Europe sometime between the Middle Ages and the nineteenth century. These case studies have been confined to different parts of the Low Countries, England, and Italy, with the exact locations and time periods of all the case studies plotted on the map below. One reason for the selection of these cases is that they allow us to further probe into the relationship between the intrinsic arrangement of society and resilience or vulnerability in the face of challenging conditions. Indeed, all kinds of different societal constellations are covered through these case studies with a variety of socio-political contexts and economic characteristics. This selection includes peasant-dominated societies such as the medieval Casentino Valley in the Apennines of Central Italy or Locorotondo in Central Apulia with strong peasant associations, places which knew strong formalised manorialism and lordship such as the Betuwe in the Central Dutch River Area (before becoming agrarian-capitalist in the early modern period), and places which experienced a transition from free peasant farming to agrarian capitalism on coastal polders such as the Oldambt of north-east Groningen. It also includes rural regions which were tied very closely in a political and jurisdictional sense to cities and urban governments, such as the late-medieval Florentine *contado* and Florence or Ascoli Satriano (in Northern Apulia) and the Neapolitan State based in Naples, but also includes rural regions (close to cities such as Cambridge) which had much looser political connections to urban centres. A wide range of societal characteristics is presented from this limited number of case studies.

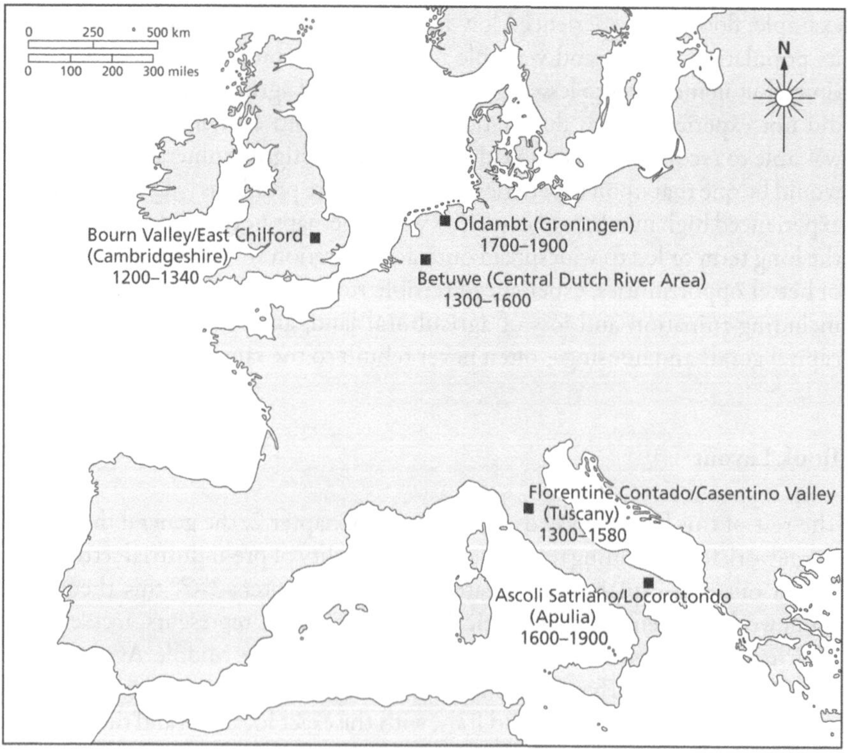

Figure 1.1 Western Europe and the location of the case studies

For each case study, archival manuscript, cartographic, archaeological, and printed primary and secondary source material is used to reconstruct the 'type of society', the strategies for resource management, and the settlement development between the particular dates chosen. At the end of each chapter, it is shown where each case study fits into the general theoretical framework presented in Chapter 2. Chapter 8 is the final one in the book and brings together all of the data from the five case studies and lays it out side by side to test against the overall theoretical framework. Do the findings fit the hypothesised outcomes? It is here we learn whether it is fair to say that settlement resilience or vulnerability stems from endogenous societal organisation itself, rather than mere exposure to differing exogenous conditions or 'bad things', and if that is so, what type of pre-industrial society was more likely to stave off crises than others.

Chapter 2

The Theoretical Framework

In this chapter, a new theoretical framework is constructed which may be used to explain how some settlements were resilient and other settlements were vulnerable to decline or crisis in the pre-industrial period. It has three main facets. First, a basic principle is that the very base or foundation of pre-industrial society is made up of alignments in property and power. That is to say, all social and economic developments in the pre-industrial period can be linked back to the distribution and changeability of property and power. Thus, a system is offered for distinguishing and differentiating between a number of basic 'types of pre-industrial society' based on the configuration of property distribution at the user level, the social distribution of property at the owner level, and the balance of power between social interest groups. Second, it is argued that these distinctive 'types of society' each led to very particular strategies for managing and exploiting their resources, in the face of a number of pressures such as commercialisation and ecological degradation – some favourable and others unfavourable. Third and finally, these strategies and institutions for managing resources ultimately determined the path in which settlements would develop. In that sense, the distribution and capacity for change in configurations of power and property strongly impacted on the way resources were handled and exploited through institutions, which in turn dictated to what extent some human habitations were resilient over the long term against all kinds of crisis while other settlements were highly susceptible to failure and collapse when faced with the same kinds of problem.

Power and Property as the Foundation Behind Different 'Types of Society'

The point of departure for the theoretical framework in this book is that the essential characteristics of each pre-industrial society were forged through the arrangement of both property at the user level, social distribution of property at the owner level, and the balance of power between social interest groups. The concepts of property and power are the foundations for understanding pre-industrial development. Each of these configurations in a particular pre-industrial society could be assessed as either 'egalitarian' or 'polarised' (i.e. measured in terms of equality), and at the same time 'dynamic' or 'persistent' (i.e. measured in terms of capacity for change). So, for example, in one particular pre-industrial society, the distribution of property could be assessed as 'egalitarian-persistent', while in another pre-industrial society 100 km away, the distribution of property could be assessed as 'polarised-dynamic'. The very first question then is what is meant by these terms? How do we begin to assess property, social distribution of property, and balance of power within a society as 'egalitarian' or 'polarised', and 'dynamic' or 'persistent'?

Property

Egalitarian property configurations were characteristic of pre-industrial societies which divided land up equally. Even though between the Middle Ages and the nineteenth century it would be rare to find any society in the world that had totally equal distributions of land, naturally some societies were more equal than others. One problem to overcome was deciding how to distribute property to the next of kin. That is to say the equitable distribution of property sometimes had its origins in egalitarian inheritance practices. Many pre-industrial societies practiced partible inheritance, whereby land and assets were evenly distributed between heirs regardless of age or sex. However, one of the (perhaps unwanted) side effects of this practice (especially when combined with population pressure and finite resources) was the proliferation of miniscule holdings that supported nobody.[1]

In contrast, polarised property configurations were characteristic of pre-industrial societies with a large proportion of land consolidated in the hands of just a few dominant individuals or institutions. Just like in many countries today, the distribution of property in the pre-industrial world was frequently highly polarised.[2] It has been said that this inequality often went hand in hand with (capitalistic) economic expansion, and only slackened off in a stage of maturity.[3] In Western Europe, however, it has been shown that increased inequality in the distribution of property and resources occurred gradually from the late Middle Ages through to the eighteenth century (with regional divergences in timing and magnitude) in conditions of both economic growth, stability, and stagnation.[4] When property distribution became polarised, it often meant large sections of pre-industrial societies had lost access to the means of production and had to resort to working on other people's lands. Polarised property distribution may

1 Segalen, *Fifteen generations of Bretons*, 83–4; Meriwether, *Kin who count*, chp. 4; Berkner, 'The stem family'; Brennan, James and Morill, 'Inheritance, demographic structure, and marriage'; Goss, 'Handing down the farm'.

2 For a global overview of twentieth-century disparities in property distribution see Frankema, *Has Latin America always been unequal?*, 213–8.

3 Van Zanden, 'Tracing the beginning".

4 See the trends towards increased early-modern inequality discussed in recent literature; Alfani, 'Wealth inequalities'; Van Bavel, 'Rural development'; 'Medieval origins of capitalism'; Santiago Caballero, 'Income inequality'; Reis et al., 'How unequal were the Latins?'; McCants, 'Inequality among the poor'; Hanus, 'Real inequality'.

have been exacerbated or crystallised in place by unequal inheritance practices. Impartible inheritance often ensured that large estates descended through the same family for generations,[5] and powerful lords often supported single-heir inheritance to maintain economically viable units for rent.[6] In some cases, women were expressly forbidden or discouraged from inheriting land in a patrilineal system, in order to maintain a generational hold over an estate.[7] Other women, particularly from elite families with large patrimonies to preserve, were prevented from marrying in order to prevent the breakup of estates,[8] or at least were urged to marry 'horizontally' to distant relatives instead.[9]

Dynamic property configurations were basically those where change could occur. People could accumulate and consolidate landed estates, and even work their way up the social and economic ladder from sometimes meagre beginnings. Thus, it refers to those pre-industrial societies where social mobility was high (and land was frequently a status symbol). An essential facet of a dynamic property configuration was a fluid land market, where land could be transferred between parties unhindered. It has been argued that integral to this development was the establishment of clear, inalienable property rights, perhaps rooted in the formalisation of 'Roman Law'.[10] In theory, clear property rights reduced the number of potential 'stakeholders' in a piece of land, in the process reducing the barriers for transfer, and this could be made more secure by, for example, increasing registration of transactions in public courts from the late Middle Ages onwards.[11] Some have even suggested that these conditions paved the way for the emergence of agrarian capitalism in Europe.[12] Clear property rights also sometimes proved to be fertile conditions for the establishment of a fluid lease market in land, and leased land tended to transfer hands even more frequently than by sale.[13] Dynamic property configurations were also sometimes helped by flexible inheritance practices. Indeed, no society was a completely helpless prisoner of inheritance custom as Malthusian perspectives have often dictated.[14] Societies often used tactical or even delayed marriages,[15] non-receiving heirs

---

5 Karl O'Brien, 'Final considerations', 255.

6 De Haan, *In the shadow of the tree*, 157.

7 Cohn, *Women in the streets*, 8–15; Wheaton, 'Family and kinship', 625–7.

8 Visceglia, *Il bisogno di eternità*.

9 Visceglia, 'Linee per uno studio unitario', 445.

10 Van Bavel, *Manors and markets*, 168.

11 Van Bavel, 'Organisation and rise of land and lease markets'; 'The land market in the North Sea area', 130–1; Feller, 'Quelques problèmes liés à l'étude'; Wickham, 'Land sales'.

12 Brenner, 'Agrarian roots of European capitalism'; 'Agrarian class structure'.

13 Van Bavel, 'Emergence and growth of short-term leasing'; 'Land, lease and agriculture'.

14 Innes, *State and society*, 81; Razi, 'Family, land and the village community', 366–7.

15 Mundy, 'Family, inheritance, and Islam'; Brown, *In the shadow of Florence*, 40–41.

were put through institutions such as religious orders,[16] and inheritance rights were even surrendered through side-payments.[17] The same family could at times adopt combinations of partible and impartible inheritance.[18] These flexible inheritance practices often required a less familial and generational attachment to particular farms and pieces of land.[19]

Persistent property configurations characterised those pre-industrial societies where the distribution of property was very difficult to shift. It could easily have applied as much to egalitarian societies with little economic stratification or social hierarchy as to polarised societies with all the land in the hands of the powerful or wealthy. Property could not be easily transferred between parties. It has been argued that a key facet in this may have been the absence of clear, inalienable property rights. Indeed in parts of medieval Europe or Japan, it may even be incorrect to speak of 'landownership'; ownership was not over 'land' per se but over a complicated bundle of rights and obligations associated with the land.[20] Land could have a number of different stakeholders or jurisdictions, preventing easy transfer,[21] and sometimes preventing further reclamation or investment in drainage.[22] For example in Northwest Germany, a clear division can be made between the coastal marshes where land transactions were common due to few feudal ties, and the stagnant land market in the manorialised districts.[23] Even as late as the eighteenth century, full and exclusive rights to property were not the rule in most parts of the pre-industrial world.[24] In some cases, land often was only transferred with prior permission of lords. Medieval lords in England were fearful of the transfer of free land to customary tenants in case the land status changed over time and they lost their associated labour obligations.[25] Other blocks to land transfer were the much-despised tallages and recognitions, which made land transfer a costly process, especially where the manorial system

16 Molho, *Marriage alliance*, 344–5.

17 Powers, 'Islamic inheritance system'.

18 Livingstone, *Out of love*.

19 Dansma and Kok, 'Ingedroogde harten?'; Whittle, 'Individualism and the family-land bond'; Sabean, *Property, production and family*, 18.

20 Van Bavel and Hoyle, 'Social relations, property and power', 12; Saito, 'Land, labour and market forces in Tokugawa Japan', 170.

21 Congost and Santos, 'Working out the frame', 15–23; Ostrom, 'Design principles', 27–9.

22 Hoyle, 'Disafforestation', 377 ; Gritt, 'Making good land', 2.

23 Brakensiek, 'Farms and land'; Achilles, *Vermögensverhältnisse Braunschweigischer Bauernhöfe*.

24 Béaur, *La terre et les hommes*, 24.

25 Brooke and Postan (eds), *Carte nativorum*, xxix; Schofield, *Peasant and community*, 65–9.

was strong.[26] Similarly, in eighteenth- and nineteenth-century Russia, serfs were able to purchase land, but only in their 'lord's name' and with risk of arbitrary confiscation.[27] In the rural hinterlands of Evora in Southern Inland Portugal, central government political discourse meant that the free transfer of property for 'private gain' was stigmatised as going against the 'common good'.[28] There were also occasions where societies had families with strong (perhaps even emotional) attachments to their land, and in that regard were not willing to part with it easily.[29] However as a counter point to that, it has been shown that even 'familial' land markets sometimes could offer high turnover rates of land.[30]

Social Distribution of Property

Social distribution of property is different from property distribution, and it was an important distinction in the pre-industrial period. Land was not always worked or used by the interest groups that 'owned' it. Egalitarian social distribution of property refers to those societies where a high proportion of non-elite residents had a grip on the land. That is to say this was characteristic of societies where the people who performed the hard labour on the land (i.e. peasants), also owned the land. Even some developing countries today such as China are characterised by rural villages with resilient peasantries – in the face of pressures such as urban capital, a globalising economy, and state transformation.[31] This contrasts with a polarised social distribution of property where a high proportion of the land lay in the hands of interest groups 'outside' of the rural society in question. Essentially these were societies dominated by absentee interest groups. From the late Middle Ages onwards in Western Europe, this kind of absentee involvement became more pronounced as towns and the countryside became more closely politically and economically connected.[32] Urban institutions and wealthy merchants, office-holders, regents, and speculators began investing in land in the countryside, either by the reclamation of new areas, the expropriation of the existing rural producers, or even capitalising on the declining position of rural elites such as aristocratic lords and ecclesiastical institutions.[33]

Dynamic social distribution of property was where the proportions of landownership changed between interest groups over time. In some areas of

---

26 Genicot, *L'économie rurale Namuroise*, iii, 78–9; Thoen, *Landbouwekonomie*, 411.

27 Dennison, 'Contract enforcement', 15.

28 Serrão and Santos, 'Land policies', 7.

29 De Haan, *In the shadow of the tree.*

30 French and Hoyle, 'English individualism refuted', 617–8.

31 Bramall and Jones, 'Fate of Chinese peasantry', 270.

32 Curtis, Van Onacker and De Keyzer, 'Parasite or stimulant?', 1.

33 Curtis, 'Impact of land accumulation'; Curtis and Campopiano, 'Medieval land reclamation'.

Western Europe, the late Middle Ages brought about such dynamic change: for example, feudal lords and ecclesiastical institutions (in the context of a late-medieval economic crisis) began to lose their grip on property and jurisdictions, and instead urban interest groups swooped in to fill this vacuum.[34] In other cases new social interest groups gained more dominant positions at the expense of aristocrats. In parts of England, prosperous free tenant farmers from roughly the late thirteenth century onwards began to consolidate to such an extent that sometimes it was hard to distinguish between a free tenant with plentiful land and a small manorial lord with very weak jurisdictions.[35] New developments in factor markets such as the proliferation of different types of leases frequently allowed new powerful groups of large tenant farmers to emerge in the countryside: relatively wealthy rural people who may have ultimately descended from peasant families.[36] By the eighteenth and nineteenth centuries all across Western Europe, former feudal and especially common lands were being privatised and put up for sale by auction.[37] As a result, 'old' elite social groups such as the barons and rural aristocrats lost out while 'new' emerging forces such as grain speculators and the urban bourgeoisie profited. In that sense, these kinds of structural changes in the social distribution of property did not transfer more property from elites to non-elites, but rather between 'new forms' of elites.[38]

This situation contrasted with social distribution of property which was much more stable and persistent. In some cases, whatever demographic or economic changes that occurred, landownership stayed in the same hands over many centuries.[39] Thus, for example, in a 'Brennerian' explanation of pre-industrial historical development, the French peasantry's ability to retain their grip over property over the long term posed an institutional block to the development of agrarian capitalism, and in turn, may have delayed the coming of the Industrial Revolution in France. At the same time, the capacity of manorial lords in England to retain their grip over land (despite demographic and economic changes), allowed them to exploit their property indirectly leading to the emergence of large lease farms and agrarian capitalism, which in turn may have been the ripe contextual conditions for the early Industrial Revolution in England.[40]

---

34 Epstein, 'Cities, regions'; 'Town and country'.

35 Curtis, 'A comparative study', 40.

36 Van Cruyningen, 'Profits and risks'; Chittolini, 'Alle origini delle "grandi aziende"'; Occhipinti, 'L'economia agraria in territorio milanese'; Baars, 'Oorspronkelijke verkaveling'.

37 Congost and Miguel Lana (eds), *Cerrados, debates abiertos*; Deméelas and Vivier (eds), *Les propriétés collectives*.

38 Mooers, *Making of Bourgeois Europe*, 70–71.

39 Van Bavel, 'Land, lease, and agriculture'.

40 Brenner, 'Agrarian class-structure'; 'The agrarian roots'.

Power

Egalitarian configurations of power characterised those pre-industrial societies that knew great freedoms: extra-economic exactions were low or absent, jurisdictional control and coercion was minimal, and potential elite interest groups lacked the tools to perpetuate their power. Many societies that experienced more egalitarian distributions of power were founded in Western Europe from the high Middle Ages onwards, where land reclamation created conditions of personal, legal, and economic freedom for colonists. In a hugely influential article published more than 50 years ago in the *American Historical Review*, Bryce Lyon introduced us to his connection between 'medieval real estate developments and freedom' by noting that 'for well over a hundred years historians specialising in agrarian institutions of the Middle Ages have suggested that the vast land reclamation characterising the eleventh and twelfth centuries in Western Europe contributed to the emancipation of the common man'.[41] The egalitarian configuration of power often had its origins in the favourable distribution of concessions and freedoms granted to colonists.

For example, in the Low Countries, territorial lords such as the Bishop of Utrecht or the Count of Flanders managed to usurp complete regalian rights over vast expanses of wasteland after the collapse of the Carolingian Empire in the tenth century.[42] Rather than reclaiming these wastelands to economically exploit them directly, territorial lords looked to colonise these new lands in order to broaden their territorial hold, thereby expanding their tax base. The consequences of this were highly significant for future development within parts of the coastal Low Countries. Territorial lords such as the Bishop of Utrecht lured colonists to the scarcely inhabited Holland marshes by offering concessions such as personal freedoms from serfdom and full peasant property rights to the land.[43] The rural people that reclaimed the Holland peat-lands between the tenth and fourteenth centuries barely knew of the manor or seigneurial dues.[44] In fact, many of the colonists in the Holland peat-lands actually originated from heavily manorialised societies and were looking to escape the constrictions of serfdom, further inland (for example in the Central Dutch River Area).[45] Each colonist received a standardised strip of land of their own but also enjoyed favourable jurisdictions over the wasteland which allowed them to continue to

---

41 Lyon, 'Medieval real estate developments', 47.

42 Van Cruyningen, 'State, property rights and sustainability', 184.

43 Van der Linden, *De cope*, 160–82; 'Het platteland in het Noordwesten'.

44 De Vries and Van der Woude, *First modern economy*, 159–65. Although recent archaeological evidence has revealed the wider presence of ninth- and tenth-century manorial *hoven* than previously acknowledged; Dijkstra, *Rondom de mondelingen van Rijn en Maas*, 261.

45 Van Bavel, *Manors and markets*, 86–7.

reclaim as much of the marshes as they wanted until they met up with a natural boundary or were stopped by someone else's property.[46] Village communities in the Frisian and German coastal marshes such as in Schleswig-Holstein also had similar freedoms to reclaim land, though here permission often was sought from territorial lords.[47] As a result of the reclamation of the marshes, these societies knew great personal freedoms and secure rights to their lands with few onerous obligations.

Whereas reclamation through the manorial or feudal context often necessitated and promoted unfreedom, public territorial authorities did not require this same personal control over labour and surplus. Village communities in these freer societies often had direct control over poor relief, judicial affairs, water management, as well as collecting taxes, organising military duties, and maintaining internal order. Jurors could be elected as representatives of the community in local courts, and villages in the freer societies of the medieval coastal areas of the Low Countries frequently developed their own by-laws.[48] Societies with more equitable distributions of power and shallower social hierarchies sometimes revolted if encroachments were made into their perceived rights for self-government and independence.[49] Quite often they were helped by their particular reclamation contexts; territorial lords as public authorities often supported the position of colonists in direct antagonism to the powers of seigneurial lords.[50] The high level of organisation needed to manage complicated environments such as marshes or fragile heaths crystallised communal village identities.[51]

Colonists were also enticed into new settlements carved out of the forest in the twelfth and thirteenth centuries with the promise of reductions in manorial dues.[52] In parts of Southern France in the eleventh and twelfth centuries, new areas of settlement known as '*sauvetés*' were established by monasteries and priories who offered protection and place of refuge in exchange for bringing new land into cultivation,[53] although lords also offered similar conditions in their so-called '*castelnaux*'.[54] In a similar period in the Odenwald region of Southern Germany, the monastery of Lorsh stimulated the emergence of new linear forms

---

46 De Vries, *Dutch rural economy*, 56.

47 Allemeyer, *'Kein Land ohne Deich ... !'*, 139.

48 Hoppenbrouwers, "Op. zoek naar de 'kerels'", 230–1; Ehbrecht, 'Gemeinschaft, Land und Bund'.

49 Schmidt, 'Hochmittelalterliche Bauernaufstände'; Van Bavel, 'Rural revolts'.

50 Steurs, 'La région'.

51 Spufford, *Contrasting communities*, 122; De Keyzer, 'The common denominator'.

52 Berger and Delaborde (eds), *Recueil des actes de Philippe Auguste*, i, no. 51.

53 Higounet, 'Hospitaliers'.

54 Simon, 'Les castra du Néracais'.

of habitation by offering privileges to colonists.[55] At Paderborn in Westphalia in Northern Germany, skilled builders were enticed into the area on the promise of receiving excellent wages and secure property rights, in order to carry out Bishop Meinwerk's building projects.[56] Similar concessions and freedoms (although not nearly to the same extent) guided the well-known German colonisation movement into the Slavic territories of Eastern Europe.[57] Tenants with harsh obligations as serfs in the Rhineland looked to escape by seeking free tenures east of the Elbe.[58] For example, privileges from the Prince Bishop of Passau such as freedom of movement, free marital rights, and free property transactions, enticed settlers into difficult forested areas in Bavaria in the 1300s, stimulating the distinctive linear villages known as *Waldhufendorfen*.[59]

In contrast, polarised power configurations were those where dominant groups used whatever tools available to maintain a hold over the rest of society. Many medieval communities were exposed to harsh exactions and onerous jurisdictions, only weakening in England, parts of France and Germany, and Scandinavia, after the Black Death.[60] In the harshest manorialised areas of Europe such as central England or Burgundy, as well as owing fealty to the lord, tenants had to perform a number of customary works (*corvées*) on manorial demesnes and had to pay customary death duties such as the heriot, ask permission for marriage between servile women (*merchet*), and migration was sometimes restricted.[61] Dominant lords laid out plots for their subordinate tenants in 'landscapes of lordship'.[62] The physical remnants of seigneurial dominance in Europe were reflected in the tradition of castle building and particularly associated with Norman territorial advances in the eleventh and twelfth centuries.[63] In Eastern Europe it has even been argued that coercion and consolidation of power over

---

55 Nitz, *Die ländliche Siedlungsformen*, 83–112; 'The Church as Colonist'.

56 Irsigler, 'Divites und Pauperes'.

57 Bartlett, *Making of Europe*.

58 Richter, 'Kulturlandschaft und Wirtschaft', 129; Ribbe, 'Die Anfänge von Berlin/Cölln', 7.

59 Veit, *Passau*, 287–8, 442–3; Nitz, 'Planmäßige Siedlungsformen', 61.

60 For the weakening of manorial structures and lordly jurisdictions in Europe after the Black Death see Dyer, *An age of transition?*; 'The ineffectiveness of lordship'; Bois, *Crise du féodalisme*; Hilton, 'A crisis of feudalism?'; Genicot, 'Crisis'. Although even after the Black Death new forms of repression emerged in the attempt to control the movement and actions of wage labourers; Beier, 'A new serfdom', 56.

61 Searle, 'Seigneurial control of women's marriage'; Faith, 'Seigneurial control of women's marriage'; Postan and Titow, 'Heriots and prices'.

62 Faith, *The English peasantry*, 224–44; Verhulst, *Carolingian economy*.

63 Martin, 'Note sur l'habitat fortifié médiéval'; Loud, 'Continuity and change in Norman Italy'.

subordinates increased after the Middle Ages (known as the 'Second Serfdom'),[64] while other scholars have noted late growth of *corvée* labour in Byzantium.[65] Coercion intensified, furthermore, in Catalonia in the late-medieval transition.[66] These geographical disparities in power configurations after the Black Death have been framed in a story of a 'Great Divergence' across regions of Europe – the beginnings of divergent development between North and South, West and East.[67]

Polarised power configurations did not end with manorial or feudal contexts, however. In the late Middle Ages, the practice of serfdom was on the wane in Europe, but in many places newly repressed rural societies emerged out of land colonisation conducted through the framework of an exploitative relationship between cities and the countryside. As urban agglomerations grew in size, number and stature, the numbers of 'non-productive' or dependent citizens also grew.[68] Cities realised they had to (a) create more direct and explicit legal relationships with their hinterlands, and (b) economically exploit these hinterlands more intensively. In that sense, urban institutions, governments and burghers became the new 'feudal lords' of the late Middle Ages and early modern period in Europe.[69] Urban governments tried to settle people in uninhabited areas to reclaim unproductive wastelands in order to produce enough food to support their swelling non-agricultural populations. In many regions of pre-industrial Europe, urban authorities tightened their jurisdictions over their close countryside, levying taxes in kind and coin, and forcing rural communities into a more subordinate position.[70] In some cases, as with late-medieval Castile, urban dominance over the countryside grew to such levels that the monarchy tried to keep their power in check.[71]

Polarised power configurations were also a feature of geographical areas colonised by strong centralised states looking to implement and enforce sophisticated systems of taxation. These were to be found, in particular, all across the early-medieval Middle East where water was brought to former arid

---

64 Brenner, 'Economic backwardness', 44; Kochanowicz, 'Polish economy'; Zytkowicz, 'Trends of Agrarian economy in Poland, Bohemia and Hungary'; Kriedte, *Peasants, landlords and merchant capitalists*, 69. However the extent of a 'Second Serfdom' is now being revised in Cerman, 'Social structure'; Hagen, 'Village life'; Peters (ed.), *Gutsherrschaftsgesellschaften im europäischen Vergleich*; Aymard, 'L'Europe moderne'.

65 Laiou, 'The agrarian economy'.

66 Freedman, *Origins of peasant servitude*, 174–7.

67 Pamuk, 'The Black Death'.

68 Curtis, 'Florence and its hinterlands'; Curtis and Campopiano, 'Medieval land reclamation'.

69 Epstein, 'Cities, regions and the late medieval crisis'; 'Town and country'.

70 Jones, *Italian city-state*.

71 Del Val Valdivieso, 'Urban growth'; Rucquoi, 'Pouvoir royal'.

soils in delicate ecological balances. Indeed in Iraq, agricultural expansion and extension of cultivation was encouraged by powerful centralised states, which used reclamation as a framework for legitimising new arrangements of taxation.[72] In the late Sasanian period (fifth–sixth centuries), the state used expansion through irrigation works to crystallise and expand its taxation reach.[73] Water was taken from rivers such as the Tigris and the Euphrates using networks of canals, and brought to dry wastelands, fuelling an expansion of settlement.[74] Irrigated agriculture collapsed with the end of the Sasanian Empire, though the emergence of a second centralised state after the Arab Conquest re-stimulated a similar system of land reclamation and taxation.[75] The Umayyad Abbasid caliphs, anxious to extend their financial bases by increasing direct control of royal estates, completed some reclamation projects.[76] Other lands were colonised through land grants, whereby cultivators were given tax cuts for reviving land out of tillage. This crystallised the system of large estates, as only the wealthy had the resources to undertake such difficult work.[77] Through these reclamation works, a system of nepotism and patronage was created with large tracts of wasteland going to a small group of favoured aristocratic elites – often to the ruin of smallholders.

Dynamic power configurations applied to those pre-industrial societies where the balance of power was very changeable and there was constant competition for dominance. Power and dominance (particularly in the Middle Ages) was often exerted through custom and contract, though demographic and economic pressures often made this subject to change: lords had to deal with inflation and in turn devaluation of rents, often causing seigneurial interests to wane and offering opportunities for new social groups.[78] Dynamic distributions of power then were often characteristic of societies where dominant interest groups were reliant on control over labour rights rather than land. In many places power was divided between a number of interest groups such as territorial lords, urban institutions, local seigneurial lords, urban burghers, and rural communities. For example, in the Campine region of Brabant in the Southern Low Countries, a special triangular set of social relations developed between local lords, territorial lords, and urban governments. In this area, the classical manorial system was

---

72 Campopiano, 'Land tax 'alā l-misāha and muqānama'; 'State, land tax and agriculture'.

73 McAdams, 'Intensified large-scale irrigation'.

74 Archaeological evidence discussed in McAdams, *Land behind Baghdad*; McAdams and Nissen, *The Uruk countryside*. Written evidence on the Persian Kings' investment in water infrastructures; Rahimi-Laridjani, *Die Entwicklung der Bewässerungslandwirtschaft*, 457; Morony, 'Landholding in seventh-century Iraq', 155–7.

75 Campopiano, 'State, land tax and agriculture'.

76 Lapidus, 'Arab settlement'.

77 Ashtor, *Social and economic history of the Near East*, 46; Morony, 'Landholding'.

78 North and Thomas, *Rise of the Western World*, 59–61.

never firmly introduced and feudal ties were entirely weak. This lack of feudal stranglehold was caused by local lords' rivalry with the main territorial lord, the Duke of Brabant, who, after claiming *bona vacantia* over certain territories, attracted immigrants to his settlements by offering liberties and secure property rights to privileged towns and villages through charters.[79] Consequently, the local lords had to grant the same privileges to their communities, in order to maintain their *seigneurie*.[80] By the late Middle Ages, this conflict between territorial and local lords had changed into an alignment of interests, in order to negate the growing power of cities: feudal lords became new allies of the Duke.[81]

Often cities had rival competitors for jurisdiction and control over the countryside from rural aristocrats, and sometimes even had competition from other cities or towns as part of an urban network or hierarchy.[82] In the '*behetría*' system of medieval Castile, intra-noble conflict was rife and disputes between lay and ecclesiastical lords often opened up room for peasants to secure some level of freedom.[83] Societies with dynamic power balances also had a number of actors who were prepared to resist and revolt against perceived injustices committed by elite powers. Some communities used peaceful techniques and adopted the political language of their superiors to achieve political objectives,[84] while other revolts were more short-term expressions of temporary disaffection,[85] often linked to harsh taxation,[86] or perceived local injustices.[87] Dynamic power distributions could also be seen at the wider governmental or 'state level'. One of the key characteristics identified by Charles Tilly for pre-industrial Western Europe was the incidence of repeat conflict across regions and the rapid rise and decline of small states very close to one another;[88] this is especially clear when contrasted with the persistence of large centralised states such as those which developed in pre-industrial China.[89]

---

79 De Wachter, 'Opname van de Kempen'; Steurs, 'La région entre Dommel et Peel'.

80 Steurs, 'Seigneuries et franchises'.

81 Van Uytven, 'Vorst, adel en steden'.

82 Waley, *Italian city-republics*, 84–5; Stabel, *Dwarfs among giants*.

83 Alfonso Antón, 'Conflict in the behetrías', 294.

84 Some revolts had overarching long term political objectives as noted in Van Bavel, 'Rural revolts'; 't Hart, 'Een boerenopstand'; Harvey, *Jack Cade's rebellion*; Hobsbawm and Rude, *Captain Swing*; Neveux, *Les révoltes paysannes*; Poulsen, 'Schleswigsche Bauern'; Katajala, 'Against tithes and taxes'.

85 Debated in Hilton, *Bondsmen made free*, 214–32.

86 Nicolas, *La rébellion française*.

87 Lorenzen-Schmidt, 'Gutsherrschaft über reiche Bauern'; Hauptmeyer, 'Bäuerlicher Widerstand'.

88 Tilly, *Coercion, capital*.

89 Bin Wong, *China transformed*.

Persistent power configurations on the other hand could not be shifted easily. It was either the case of one dominant group having very little competition from other rival forces or that there was a complete power vacuum with no one to fill it. One of the facets of the stability in the inequitable power distribution in Southern Italy well into the eighteenth century was that even though 'feudalism' was in terminal decline, barons and former feudal lords were still able to retain their power over the long term by consolidating landed estates through tactical marriage strategies and using violence and imperfections in the labour market to put down any destabilising groups from below.[90] Scottish magnates consolidated power over vast territories and controlled rural labour for centuries without outside interference from central government.[91] The durability of such inequitable distribution in power relations could often be attributed to the high costs of developing new structures and legitimising new ideologies from scratch.[92] Pre-existing established infrastructures were therefore maintained regardless of perceived inefficiencies and injustices.[93] In any case institutions do not work inevitably to the highest level of efficiency or 'rationality' but frequently are adapted (or remain persistent) to serve the needs of dominant interest groups with high levels of bargaining power.[94] Essentially it was not always easy to enact political change – a point demonstrated by the persistence of long-standing autocratic dictatorships in, for example, Myanmar and the Gambia, even today.[95] In a similar way, new ideals of liberal democracy have not been internalised by Turkmenistan or Azerbaijan, despite the collapse of the Soviet Union.[96]

Quantifying and Measuring Property and Power

Thus to reiterate, at the very foundation of pre-industrial society, there were many kinds of configurations in distribution of property at the user level, social distribution of property ownership, and balances of power between interest groups, which could be assessed as either 'egalitarian' or 'polarised', and at the same time 'dynamic' or 'persistent'. To aid the comparative process used in this book, each of these configurations could be given a quantifiable figure as far as conceivably possible, which is a method adapted from renowned sociologist

90 Astarita, *Continuity of feudal power*; Dal Lago, *Agrarian elites*.
91 Smout, *Scottish people*, 31–9.
92 Tilly, *Durable inequality*.
93 Mayhew, 'Ascription', 313.
94 Ensminger, *Making a market*; Haller, *Understanding institutions*, 22.
95 Haber and Menaldo, 'Do natural resources fuel authoritarianism?'
96 Dilli, 'Persistent global gaps', 4.

Charles Ragin, who devised a way of bridging the gap between qualitative and quantitative research.[97]

Property distribution at the user level, social distribution of property ownership, and power balances between interest groups all can be given a score, or more precisely two scores. If property at the user level was assessed as 'egalitarian', it received a score of 1, while if it was 'polarised', it received a score of 0. Property was deemed to be 'egalitarian' (i.e. a score of 1) if the Gini index of land distribution was lower than 0.65.[98] If property distribution received a figure of 0.75 or more on the Gini index, however, it was deemed 'polarised' (i.e. a score of 0). If the Gini index was between 0.65 and 0.74, then the assessment was neither 'egalitarian' nor 'polarised' and received an 'intermediate' score of 0.5. How were these cut-off points devised? First of all, recent literature on inequality in the distribution of wealth and property across Western Europe has suggested that Gini indexes of around 0.7 were very common in small towns and rural areas in the pre-industrial period.[99] Second, although 0.65 or lower may not seem very 'egalitarian', in a relative sense it is. Indeed, across pre-industrial Europe it is very difficult to find many regions with a Gini index (for property, not income) of less than 0.5. Additionally, if property was assessed as 'dynamic', it received a second score of 1, while if it was 'persistent', it received a second score of 0. Property was 'dynamic' if there was either a change in the Gini index over time (at least by a figure of 0.1), however, if the Gini index remained very stable with barely any change over time, property would be regarded as 'persistent'. If the Gini index changed by just a figure of around 0.05 over time, then property at the user level would be deemed neither 'dynamic' nor 'persistent' but 'intermediate' and received a score of 0.5. If there was no data to assess the change in Gini indexes over time, the score would also be 0.5: however, if there was qualitative evidence from manuscripts for a land or lease market where significant amounts of property was clearly changing hands frequently, then property at the user level would be deemed 'dynamic'.

If social distribution of property (at the owner level) was assessed as 'egalitarian', it received a score of 1, while if it was 'polarised', it received a score

---

97 Ragin, *The comparative method.*

98 Also known as the 'Gini coefficient'. The Gini index is a measure of statistical dispersion developed in 1912 by Corrado Gini in a paper '*Variabilità e mutabilità*'. A value of '0' is equivalent to total equality, where all stakeholders have exactly the same amount of resources. A value of '1' is equivalent to total inequality, where only one stakeholder has all the resources. All Gini indexes are calculated with the aid of concentration statistics software found at <www.wessa.net>. As with many quantitative techniques for measuring inequality, there are some inbuilt limitations to the Gini index, such as its tendency to give a lower figure for smaller samples of data. Fortunately when measuring distributions of property in restricted rural areas, large differences in the numbers of landholders is generally not massive.

99 Van Zanden, 'Kuznets Curve', 645–7; Alfani, 'Wealth inequalities', appendix.

of 0. An 'egalitarian' social distribution of property was that where the rural inhabitants had high levels of ownership over the land: that is to say at least 55 per cent of the land in the hands of non-noble farmers or peasants. 'Polarised' social distributions of property typically had higher levels of 'absentee' landownership, and in these cases non-noble rural farmers or peasants owned less than 45 per cent of the total land. If rural peasants or farmers owned between 45 and 54 per cent of the land, then the social distribution of landownership received an intermediate figure of 0.5. 'Dynamic' social distributions of property were those where there was a change of at least 20 per cent in the distribution between 'absentee' social groups such as urban institutions, burghers, and nobles, and 'in-living' social groups such as peasants or farmers. The social distribution of property was regarded as 'persistent' when there was less than a 10 per cent change in the distribution between 'absentee' and 'in-living' social groups. If the shift in the social distribution of landownership was between 10 and 19 per cent, it was deemed neither 'dynamic' nor 'persistent' and received a score of 0.5.

If power was assessed as 'egalitarian', it received a score of 1, while if it was 'polarised', it received a score of 0. The assessment of power is more complicated in the sense that it is a blurrier concept that does not readily allow for quantification. This is a more qualitative assessment based on the distribution of jurisdictions, votes, rights, privileges and access across all the major social groups. 'Egalitarian' distributions of power were those societies where jurisdictions, votes, rights, privileges, and access to institutions were distributed evenly amongst social groups; 'polarised' distributions of power were those where the same concepts were consolidated in the hands of one dominant social group. Power was assessed as 'dynamic' if these same jurisdictions, votes, rights, privileges, and access to institutions changed between social groups over time (perhaps after conflict between interest groups), while 'persistent' power meant that the social distribution of these concepts remained stable and changed little over time.

Historical research is never that simple, however. There are undoubtedly going to be many cases where there is no data available to make a judgement. In those cases, the configuration in question was given a score of 0.5. Thus, in sum, property at the user level, social distribution of property, and alignments on power all received two scores: either a 1, 0, or 0.5, depending on how 'egalitarian' or 'polarised' they were, and either a 1, 0, or 0.5, depending on how 'dynamic' or 'persistent' they were.

Identifying the 'Types of Pre-Industrial Societies'

The way distinctive 'types of societies' are distinguished from each other is by simply calculating two average scores (one for the 'egalitarian'/'polarised' opposition, and one for the 'dynamic'/'persistent' opposition) of user-level property, social distribution of property, and balance of power taken together. This can be better shown in a simple table for the fictional pre-industrial society of '*Tyrannoland*' in the period 1200–1550. An average of the two scores is taken.

Table 2.1 The breakdown of Tyrannoland (1200–1550) into quantifiable configurations

	Egalitarian-Polarised	Dynamic-Persistent
Property	0	0.5
Social distribution of property	0	0.5
Power	0	0
Total scores	**0**	**0.33**

Tyrannoland was judged to have been 0 on the egalitarian or polarised scale, and 0.33 on the dynamic or persistent scale. What do these scores mean? If a society received a total score of 0 to 0.49 in the first column, it could be considered 'polarised'. If in the same column however, it received a total score of 0.51 to 1, it could be considered 'egalitarian'. Likewise, if a society received a total score of 0 to 0.49 in the second column, it could be considered 'persistent', while a total score of 0.51 to 1 rendered it 'dynamic'. Thus, for example, the pre-industrial society of *Tyrannoland* between 1200 and 1550 could be considered 'polarised-persistent'. The four basic types of society based on this idea are shown in the table below.

Table 2.2 The four basic types of pre-industrial society

Egalitarian/polarised score	Dynamic/continuous score	Type of society
0.51–1	0–0.49	Egalitarian-persistent
0–0.49	0.51–1	Polarised-dynamic
0.51–1	0.51–1	Egalitarian-dynamic
0–0.49	0–0.49	Polarised-persistent

Occasionally one of the columns will end up exactly half-way between 'egalitarian' and 'polarised', or 'dynamic' and 'persistent'. If this happens, the column is assessed as 'intermediate'. The consequences of this occurrence are discussed in more detail in Chapter 8.

Linking 'Types of Pre-Industrial Societies' and Strategies for Exploiting Resources

Managing Resources in Egalitarian-Persistent Societies: Protectionist Strategies

Pre-industrial societies classified as egalitarian-persistent were interested in maintaining the status quo. To do this, they used a number of *protectionist strategies* to share or avoid risks, lessen the potentially disturbing and unpredictable effects of the market, and create a favourable balance between population and resources. Rather than adapting to demographic, environmental, and economic changes, these societies built strategies to shield themselves from potentially destabilising effects of commercial and population pressure on resources, and furthermore, made sure these destabilising risks were well divided amongst inhabitants.[100] Protectionist forms of risk-management were only taken up in those societies with highly egalitarian social distributions of risk: that is to say, in those societies with highly egalitarian and stable distributions of power and property. *As a result, these societies produced settlements that did not change very much, but at the same time were very resilient and effective at seeing off periods of crisis.*

How did egalitarian-persistent societies go about implementing these protectionist strategies, and what did they consist of? One of the ways was the implementation of an open-field system which spread across Western Europe from the early Middle Ages and into parts of Eastern Europe by the late Middle Ages and early modern period.[101] The open-field system helped settlements withstand 'Malthusian crises' caused by population increases on finite levels of resources. Indeed, the proliferation of this field system through many parts of Western Europe in the Middle Ages is a good example, since it may have gone hand in hand with exceptional population growth between the tenth and thirteenth centuries,[102] although admittedly the open fields did emerge in some areas earlier than the ninth century.[103] In theory, as population levels increased, the need for rural inhabitants to divide their resources up in a more equitable manner became more acute. The open fields allowed for a more egalitarian division of land as every household's landholding was divided up into small morsels and scattered across the fields,[104] while the community

100 The social division of risk noted in Bankoff, 'Dangers to going it alone'.

101 For an overview and chronology see Renes, 'Grainlands'.

102 A sceptical view on the link between open-field proliferation and demographic pressure is found in Lewis, Mitchell-Fox and Dyer, *Village, hamlet and field*, 213–6.

103 Oosthuizen, 'New light'.

104 Hoffmann, 'Medieval origins of the common fields'. Holdings could be divided with strict equality; for example see Hilton, *Economic development of some Leicestershire*

often lived in a concentrated village at the heart of these fields.[105] The same risk-limitation concerns still inform the persistence of fragmented land distributions in parts of Asia and Africa today.[106] Not only did scattering make transport and labour costs more equal, but it was also an exercise in risk-management, as no single person could monopolise the best soils; if one field harvest failed, this was not disastrous.[107] Furthermore, it has now been suggested that agricultural productivity of these scattered fields was actually not inevitably lower than fields farmed in consolidated enclosures.[108] The open fields were often an exercise in sustainable ecological management. As one particular 'sub-type' of the open fields, the 'common fields'[109] was a system whereby one of the fields (usually one out of three but could be more variation)[110] could spend time fallow, thus not exhausting the nutrients in the soil.[111] In places where grazing area was limited, the common fields had significant benefits in providing access for village livestock to stubbles and fallow, which could most easily be arranged if all strips in a field were sown at the same time with a crop taking the same length of time to ripen for harvest.[112] The importance of access to the commons for small peasants should not be underestimated: Jane Humphries once suggested that even access for as little as two cows for a commoner in eighteenth-century England could be the equivalent economic value as 6 months of wages for a fully-employed male agricultural labourer.[113]

In turn, this system fostered further collective action as local people had the opportunity to band together into small groups to manage plough-teams

---

estates, 153–5; Roden, 'Field systems of the Chiltern Hills', 349; Brown, 'Arable land as commons', 445–8.

105 Although the link between open-field formation and settlement concentration is still debated; Oosthuizen, 'Medieval field systems and settlement nucleation'.

106 Heston and Kumar, 'Persistence of land fragmentation'; Simmons, 'Land fragmentation in developing countries'; Sengupta, 'Fragmented landholding'; Nguyen, Cheng and Findlay, 'Land fragmentation and farm productivity'; Najafi and Bakhshoodeh, 'Effects of land fragmentation'; Jabarin and Epplin, 'Impact of land fragmentation'; Blarel et al., 'Economics of farm fragmentation'; Anantha Ram et al., 'Subdivision and fragmentation'.

107 Dahlman, *Open field system*, 111–4; Fox, 'Ecological dimensions'; McCloskey, 'English open fields'; 'The prudent peasant'; Bailey, 'Beyond the Midland field system', 160.

108 Allen, *Enclosure and the yeoman*; Clark, 'Commons sense'.

109 On the definition of the 'common fields'; Thirsk, 'The common fields', 3. In some cases the open fields and the common fields have been unclearly associated as one and the same thing; for example in the earlier work of Clark, 'Commons sense', 73.

110 Of course this is an idealized description of a system which could offer considerable variation. On this variation across Western Europe; Hildebrandt, 'Systems of agriculture', 287–8.

111 Pretty, 'Sustainable agriculture'; Campbell, 'Ecology versus economics'.

112 Oosthuizen, 'Anglo-Saxon Kingdom of Mercia', 156.

113 Humphries, 'Enclosures, common rights and women', 23-31.

and oxen were sometimes collectively acquired (often expensive for any one person anyway).[114] As Tine De Moor has iterated, these forms of collectively-pooled resources could offer substantial economies of scale.[115] Smallholding peasants in particular could take advantage of the lowering of transaction costs connected with maintaining flocks of herds of animals, and many had interests in the collective investments that could be made into drainage facilities and boundary markers and fences.[116] Indeed, 'exclusion costs' such as the fencing off of open spaces sometimes were very high, and so did not always compensate for any apparent advantages of privatisation.[117] This kind of arrangement was even more crucial in areas marked by poor access to credit and capital facilities, and it is well-known now that rural credit did not permeate through to the medieval countryside of Western Europe in equal measure.[118] The benefits of collectively farming the open fields were also in societal regulation and maintenance of 'sociable behaviour': the harvests were able to be supervised by the community (against potential thieves) and grazing on the stubbles could be maintained and enforced in an orderly fashion.[119] This social control characteristic for small communities was sometimes cheaper than top-down monitoring and enforcement mechanisms.[120] Thus the common fields, like other types of collective system for managing resources, also frequently acted as an 'information-enhancing' institution – dispersing 'resource knowledge' across a wider segment of the population.[121] In the common-field system, each participant had a number of obligations to meet, for example, only grazing animals on the fields at certain times of the year, and good practice was often enforced by the common members themselves.[122] Nonetheless, there were occasions when members of the community failed to fulfil the obligations, did not adhere to the rules, or caused disturbances for others.[123] Therefore, in some places good practice was enforced by more formal councils.[124] In sum, the open fields (and even more so with the common fields as a sub-type) were one way

114 Rösener, *Bauern im Mittelalter*, 151.

115 De Moor, 'Silent Revolution'.

116 Tan, 'The bull is half the herd', 472.

117 Iriarte-Goñi and Miguel Lana, 'The 'Concurrence' and 'Hierarchization' of Rights to Property', 131.

118 Schofield and Lambrecht (eds), *Credit and the rural economy*; Briggs, *Credit and village society*.

119 Vardi, 'Construing the harvest', 1424–7; Ault, *Open-field farming*, 27–40.

120 Laborda Pemán and De Moor, 'A tale of two commons', 13.

121 Casari, 'Emergence of endogenous legal institutions', 220.

122 De Moor, 'Avoiding tragedies'.

123 Tawney, *The agrarian problem*, 161–2.

124 For example the *Dorfgenossenschaft* in Germany; Rösener, *Peasants in the Middle Ages*, 46. Also the *bystämman* in Sweden; Moberg, *History of the Swedish people*, i, 40.

in which the inhabitants of settlements within egalitarian-persistent societies managed their resources carefully and with one eye on risk-avoidance and risk-management, in the process also compensating for their lack of individual access to capital and credit, thereby increasing the resilience of the habitation against crises and misfortune.

Another protectionist strategy was to impose a system of regulated common rights over the pastures, wastelands, marshes and woodlands.[125] Many scholars have shown how the formalisation of common rights from the high Middle Ages onwards were used to prevent over-exploitation of the local resources, thereby sustaining rural communities. In the 1960s, a highly influential paper entitled 'The tragedy of the commons' suggested common pooling of resources were inevitably bound to fail, for when population increased to a certain level, members of the system would begin 'free-riding', thus bringing down the community with them.[126] In a way this paper was a product of its time, when Malthusian-style explanations for how pre-industrial societies and economies developed were at their strongest. The problem with this view was it was not grounded in historical research and merely operated at the theoretical or hypothetical level, and thus this paper has now been resoundingly dismissed by historians and social scientists, in particular with the ground-breaking scholarship of Elinor Ostrom.[127] The institutional management of resources through the commons had high significance for many regions of Europe in the pre-industrial period, where communal property forms sometimes lingered on until the nineteenth century.[128] All across the pre-industrial world, there is evidence of communities actively defending and preserving their perceived rights to marshes and woodlands, in the face of would-be colonists.[129] This was also the case for local rights to use water.[130] In parts of Asia and Africa, commons still play an integral role in the sustenance of many rural societies today, while

---

125 The risk-avoidance qualities of the commons asserted in the framework of De Moor, 'Silent Revolution', 227. Also see Curtis, 'Tine De Moor's 'Silent Revolution''.

126 Hardin, 'Tragedy of the commons'.

127 Ostrom, *Governing the commons*; Ostrom, Walker and Gardner, 'Covenants with and without a sword'; Dahlman, 'The tragedy of the commons that wasn't'.

128 For a chronology see De Moor, Shaw-Taylor and Warde (eds), *Management of common land*.

129 Dyer, 'Conflict in the landscape'; Birrell, 'Common rights in the medieval forest'; Manaresi (ed.), *I placiti del 'Regnum Italiae'*, i, no. 36; Andreolli and Montanari, *L'azienda curtense*, 194–6; Menant, 'Les chartes de franchises'; Bland, Brown and Tawney (eds), *English economic history*, 88–9.

130 Heimpel, 'Die Federschnur'; Blickle, 'Wem gehörte der Wald?; Devailly, *Le Berry*, 361.

many contemporary fisheries are collectively self-governed.[131] The commons helped balance population and resources (and in the face of commercial pressures) by putting restrictions on grazing, limiting the cutting-down of trees for private gain,[132] and the management of water supplies and sources. Formal institutions such as courts developed in order to examine infringements made on the commons.[133] Corporate control of the commons sometimes involved close supervision.[134] Sanctioning and punishment of 'bad practice' was an effective tool to deter individual expropriation of collective resources,[135] and formalised collective action (as opposed to informal or oral tradition) had the advantage also of being more effective enforcement to external outsiders.[136] As a result of this protectionist strategy, egalitarian-persistent societies were shielded from commercial and population pressures on resources, which if unchecked could have brought ruin to the settlements.

Another protectionist strategy was de-specialisation, whereby households would engage in a range of economic activities in order to stave off crisis. In egalitarian-persistent societies, the extraction of large amounts of surplus to support a steady flow of rents and taxes was not needed. Rather than 'putting all the eggs in one basket', rural producers wanted to know that if the grain harvest failed (which it did frequently), they could rely on fishing and hunting rights or products from the forest. Woodlands and wastelands provided fuel, pasture, and building materials for communities, often distributed and accessed through collective institutions or the commons.[137] Chestnuts were a popular subsistence food, particularly in the mountainous Apennines of Central Italy.[138] Animals were hunted in the forest (although hunting in the forest did in some cases become the reserve of the elite),[139] and marshes were good environments for hunting and fishing.[140] In fact, wetland environments and streams provided

---

131 For contemporary commons see Agrawal and Chhatre, 'Explaining success on the commons'; Agrawal and Ostrom, 'Collective action'; Ribot, 'Theorizing access'. For fisheries see Acheson, 'Maine lobster industry'; McCay and Jentoft, 'From the bottom up'.

132 Sommé, 'Règlements, délits et organisation des ventes dans la forêt de Nieppe'.

133 Schütte, 'Markenrecht und Markengerichtsbarkeit'; Hayhoe, 'Litigation and the policing of communal farming', 52.

134 For an illustrative case in Japan; McKean, 'Japanese experience with scarcity'.

135 Tukker, 'Sanctionering en controle'.

136 Casari, 'Emergence of endogenous legal institutions', 201.

137 Van Zanden, 'Paradox of the Marks', 131.

138 Andreolli, 'Formule di pertinenza e paesaggio'; Cherubini, 'La 'civiltà' del castagno'; Coltelli, 'La civiltà del castagno'.

139 Especially for furs; Delort, *Le commerce des fourrures*, i, 108–17.

140 Montanari, *L'alimentazione contadina*, 34–5, 48–9, 268–70; Rippon, *Transformation of coastal wetlands*.

a diverse range of fish for communities and religious institutions.[141] Societies which based their economies around these kinds of concerns had less interest in land reclamation, and in fact, it has been revealed in an important article in the *American Historical Review* that the more intensive use of the land supported by dikes and mills ended up disturbing the good functioning of the ecosystems that these societies depended upon.[142] Recent literature has suggested that the risk-management ethos of the commons may have combined well with those small peasant societies pursuing highly diversified economic portfolios, such as that identified for the medieval and early-modern mountain regions of the Western Adriatic ,[143] and some have even argued that restricted specialisation of production was one condition (among others) that led to the optimal operation of the commons.[144] In some cases, risk-averse societies created mixes of grains for cultivation, which produced lower yields but a greater chance that all of the sown seeds would succeed.[145] In contrast to what Donald McCloskey and John Nash argued,[146] medieval peasants also stored grain (it did not need to be *either* open fields *or* grain storage – both tactics were not mutually exclusive)[147] and furthermore given the institutional restrictions and poorly functioning commodity markets in some areas,[148] was not a 'lost investment' but had almost an opportunity cost of zero.[149] As a result of the protective and risk-avoidance strategies used, settlements were not entirely wiped out by disastrous events such as failed harvests or cattle pestilences, and limited problems of environmental degradation.

Managing Resources in Polarised-Dynamic Societies: Short-Termist Strategies

Pre-industrial societies classified as polarised-dynamic were dominated by powerful interest groups, who were interested in using the plethora of techniques available to increase their particular grip on power or wealth. To do this, they used a number of *short-termist strategies* to extract what they could out of the available resources, but at the same time making the rest of society

---

141 Hoffmann, 'Economic development and aquatic ecosystems', 636; 'Fishing for sport', 886–7; Trexler, 'Measures against water pollution'.

142 Hoffmann, 'Economic development and aquatic ecosystems'.

143 Panjek, 'Not demesne but money'.

144 Miguel Lana, 'From equilibrium to equity', 165.

145 Pretty, 'Sustainable agriculture'.

146 McCloskey and Nash, 'Corn at interest'.

147 An 'either-or' kind of debate continued in Fenoaltea, 'Risk, transaction costs'; 'Transaction costs, Whig history'.

148 Hoppenbrouwers and Van Zanden, 'Restyling the transition from feudalism to capitalism', 22–6.

149 Komlos and Landes, 'Anachronistic economics', 37–8.

highly exposed to potential disasters such as famine and flooding. *As a result, these societies produced settlements that could rise up and change very rapidly as a result of short-term economic gains (for limited groups), but at the same time could quickly contract or collapse as a result of precarious exposure to unpredictable and unfavourable events.*

One of the short-termist strategies that polarised-dynamic societies undertook was large-scale capital-intensive land reclamation for commercial profit, which took off in Europe during the early modern period (as opposed to the earlier more labour-intensive reclamations of the eleventh to thirteenth centuries).[150] This was the process by which rich investors and institutions brought 'unused', 'waste', or simply 'unproductive' land into more intensive use. In the pre-industrial era, this could come in the form of the assarting of woodlands, the clearing of bushes, the development of irrigation systems, or the drainage of wetlands, in order to create new land. However, although the large-scale reclamation of new lands such as the conversion of marshlands to fertile polders allowed for the rapid emergence of new settlements (so-called polder villages), created more jobs for agricultural workers,[151] and made profits for already-wealthy investors, it also brought with it a lot of problems. It is well-known that land reclamation could produce serious negative environmental effects, often leading to the degradation of ecosystems.[152] Many delicate ecosystems were disturbed by private reclamation of precariously balanced collective property regimes.[153] Often these problems were externalised with knock-on effects for other societies. It has been shown in Southern France that the planned drainage of the marshes around Arles by rich investors from Amsterdam could have had disastrous effects on the nearby town of Tarascon. The loss of the Arles marshes in the seventeenth century could have led to the disappearance of an important safety valve, easing water pressure in Tarascon. In protest the citizens of Tarascon mobilised themselves through riots and violence.[154]

In China, reclamation of lowland marshes along parts of the Yangtze River by already-large landowners during different phases of the Ming and Qing periods was propped up by the state, looking to indirectly benefit from agricultural intensification with commercialisation and urbanisation in the core areas of the Yangtze. The tax concessions and favourable conditions for these acquisitive landlords led to increasingly polarised frontier societies, which in turn created environmental problems. In previous centuries, water management functioned by apportioning levies on households according to the amount of land they

150 For the chronological differences see Richards, *The unending frontier*.

151 Van Bavel, 'Markets for land', 527.

152 Curtis and Campopiano, 'Medieval land reclamation', 33.

153 Pichard, 'L'espace absorbé par l'économique?'.

154 Morera, 'Environmental change', 92–3.

had benefitting from the system.[155] However, after land reclamation and consolidation, the state often failed to make absentee landowners responsible for their dike repairs (in fact conceding control over water to local elites by the nineteenth century)[156] – to the detriment of local ecosystems and vulnerable settlements.[157] In the Dongting Lake area of the Central Yangtze region, large landowners refused to do away with problem dikes (which were creating high water pressures), simply because they did not want to lose their investments in new lands (made more valuable in the context of the Qing demographic and commercial boom).[158] The severe floods of the nineteenth and twentieth centuries in this region have been blamed on the deteriorating water management systems linked to the reclamation process.[159] Polarisation also led to outward migration of a large population from new polder areas, thus making it difficult to gain the tax base necessary to maintain the water management structures,[160] a feature also noted in the collapse of water management and flooding in Egypt close to the Nile after the Black Death.[161] Pressure on the system was also exacerbated by reclamations in the highlands by newly proletarianised and impoverished migrants referred to as 'shack people', causing erosion and landslides.[162]

Similar problems existed in the British Punjab of the late eighteenth century, where the British government aimed to consolidate power there by offering land grants to elite caste members (encouraging land reclamation) and thus keeping powerful interest groups onside.[163] However this unregulated reclamation process, while further entrenching social and economic polarisation in the rural Punjab by enriching an already elite group of landowners,[164] created negative knock-on effects in nearby areas dominated by poorer peasants – including heightened water pressures and flooding.[165] This kind of reclamation also

---

155 Li, 'Beneficiary pays'.

156 Bin Wong, 'China before capitalism', 9. Paralleling the move towards a more laissez-faire attitude towards its community-based granaries; Will and Bin Wong, *Nourish the people.*

157 Elvin, 'Water control', 96; Perdue, 'Official goals', 762.

158 Perdue, 'Official goals', 748; Liu, 'Dike construction'; Ho, *Studies on the population of China*, 227–30.

159 Morita, 清代水利史研究, 森田明[著 (A study of water management in the Qing dynasty), 50–80; Elvin and Ninghu, 'Engineering the sea', 86. On the general environmental problems caused by reclamation in China see Elvin, 'Three thousand years of unsustainable growth'; 'Environmental legacy of Imperial China'; Edmonds, *Patterns of China's lost harmony*, chp. 2.

160 Perdue, 'Official goals', 754.

161 Borsch, 'Environment and population'.

162 Osborne, 'Local politics'; Averill, 'Shed people'; Vermeer, 'Mountain frontier'.

163 Ali, 'Punjab canal colonies', 133–45, 171–4.

164 Alavi, 'Politics of dependence'; Ahmad, *Class and power in a Punjabi village.*

165 Ali, 'Malign growth?', 124.

stimulated settlement into areas never inhabited before (because they were prone to flooding) bringing more poor people into vulnerable situations.[166] Social manipulation through colonisation often ended in violent protest from marginalised groups.[167]

Furthermore, newly colonised polarised-dynamic societies often embarked on economic exploitation that was wholly unsuited to the water management systems put in place. In colonial Guanajuato, the reclamation of new cultivated land and the move away from a previously well-balanced extensive grazing economy proved to be a dangerous move that threatened the economic well-being of the region. Agriculturalists began to plant grains in order to sell at high prices to European silver miners; however, wheat required consistent irrigation, which made poor farmers far more susceptible to harvest failure through unpredictable climatic events including flooding and drought.[168] Elsewhere the conversion of swamps to rice fields in colonial Georgia simplified the hydrography of the coastal plains, making them more prone to unpredictable flooding.[169]

The extractive nature of polarised-dynamic societies also meant dominant interest groups either did not care about the potential degradation of the woodlands and soils, or simply had no need or requirement to take responsibility for their actions (often as external actors).[170] It is no coincidence that the most extreme frontier societies produced by European colonisation of the Americas led to destabilising ecological processes culminating in some of the most severe environmental problems in the world.[171] While the initial environmental effects of the English, Dutch and French settlement may have been modest,[172] the cultivation of sugar cane changed all that, and within a few decades in the seventeenth century, whole islands were losing their tree cover – certainly in

166 Weil, 'The rivers come', 14. On general failures of colonial policy towards irrigation, famine, and habitation in British India see Ahuja, 'State formation'. On the general phenomenon of poorer people living in inherently more hazardous sites see Boustan et al., 'Moving to higher ground'; Kim, 'How much more exposed are the poor to natural disasters?'.

167 Grove, *Ecology, climate, and empire*, 208–11; Sunseri, 'Reinterpreting a colonial rebellion'; Howard, 'Ecological marginalization'.

168 Endfield and O'Hara, 'Degradation, drought, and dissent'.

169 Stewart, *What nature suffers to groe*.

170 Myers and Tucker, 'Deforestation in Central America'.

171 Richardson, *The Caribbean in the wider world*, 31; Grove, *Green Imperialism*; Arnold, *The problem of nature*; Beinart and Hughes, *Environment and empire*. A thesis challenged by Max Edelson, 'Clearing swamps, harvesting forests'; Donahue, *The great meadow*, xv; Breen, *Tobacco culture*. They have instead argued for the adaptability of plantation agriculture to environmental change.

172 Innes, 'The pre-sugar era'.

Barbados and the Leeward Islands.[173] French colonists on St. Croix performed slash and burn activities over the entire area of the island.[174] Cuba went the same way (although later in the nineteenth century) where large tracts of forest were swept away under new sugar-orientated production.[175] A clear result of woodland clearance was the ruination and erosion of the soils.[176] In Martinique, this meant the soil could not retain moisture, leaving settlements entirely vulnerable to droughts.[177] Aside from the demands of cultivation, these sorts of frontier societies inevitably needed resources necessary for the sustenance of society such as fuel. Much was imported (e.g. coal from England), though many trees were still cut as timber for buildings.[178] Indeed, instead of concentrating on resource management in line with reclamation activity, interest groups looked to more intensive labour exploitation (through slaves) to recompense for declining fertility.[179] The ecological changes stimulated by reclamation in the Caribbean had profound consequences for the peasant subsistence societies which developed after the emancipation of the slaves, who found themselves working tiny plots (in marginal areas) and faced with entirely eroded and degraded soils, making survival much more difficult.[180] The same sight of hillsides washed away by erosion after reclamation was seen in large parts of Portuguese Brazil.[181] In some cases such as the westward expansion of the North American frontier into California, the pursuit of one highly valuable resource put the inhabitants at high risk.[182] Once the gold was mined to extinction, settlements that once supported life were soon abandoned, becoming so-called 'ghost towns'.[183]

Short-termist strategies also reduced the likelihood of protective and sustainable institutions being laid down, such as water management structures. If they did appear, they were frequently mal-configured. Water management responsibilities often fell away in polarised pre-industrial societies, particularly in places characterised by high levels of absentee landownership. This argument has been supported by empirical research on the polder reclamations in coastal

173 Watts, *The West Indies*, 219; Bridenbaugh and Bridenbaugh, *No peace beyond the line*, 268.

174 Dirks, *The black saturnalia*, 16.

175 Moreno Fraginals, *The sugarmill*, 76–7.

176 Harris, *Plants, animals, and man*.

177 Kimber, *Martinique revisited*, 180–1.

178 Sheridan, *Sugar and slavery*, 115.

179 Richardson, *Caribbean migrants*, 56–7.

180 Richardson, 'Slavery to freedom'.

181 Dean, *With broadax and firebrand*; Augusto Padua, 'European colonialism and tropical forest destruction'.

182 Dasmann, 'Environmental changes before and after the Gold Rush'.

183 Lachman, 'Golden promises, abandoned dreams'; Nadeau, *Ghost towns*.

regions of the Low Countries; particularly by Tim Soens.[184] As Soens carefully shows, the water management system began functioning less effectively in the transition from the late Middle Ages to the early modern period when property was consolidated in the hands of rich urban burghers and institutions and worked by a group of large tenant farmers.[185] Absentee owners had less interest in investing income derived from the rents back into effective water management (when costs exceeded yields), thereby leaving some reclaimed polders highly susceptible to environmental collapse.[186] Tenant farmers had all the incentives to reap as much as they could through over-exploitation to the detriment of long-term environmental sustainability: economic rationalisation dictated investment, not ecological sensitivity.[187] As Soens himself notes, 'an unequal distribution of flood risk was often the result of unequal or deteriorating land rights mediated by an unequal or deteriorating access to the decision making process in flood risk management'.[188] Repeat flooding after the storms in fifteenth- and sixteenth-century coastal Zeeland and Flanders could be testament to sub-optimal water management,[189] although the 'free-rider' problem was arguably even more severe on the North German coastline.[190]

Managing Resources in Egalitarian-Dynamic Societies: Flexible Strategies

Pre-industrial societies classified as egalitarian-dynamic had the *flexibility* and freedom to respond to demographic, environmental, or commercial changes in a 'pro-active' way. While egalitarian-persistent societies used strategies to limit exposure to potentially disturbing forces such as the market or to negate the effects of population pressure on finite resources, egalitarian-dynamic societies could flexibly move exploitation strategies to account for changes – and even benefit from the emergence of markets. *As a result, these societies produced settlements which drew their resilience in the face of crises from the adaptive strategies devised for economic exploitation of resources. It was a case of adaptation to survive.*

184 Soens, *De spade in de dijk?*; 'Polders zonder poldermodel?; 'Explaining deficiencies of water management'; 'Floods and money'. Related to this is the recent revision of the so-called Dutch 'poldermodel' in Van Tielhof, 'Op. zoek naar het poldermodel'; Van Dam, 'Water en land'.

185 Soens, 'Origins of leasehold'; Thoen, 'Social agrosystems'.

186 Soens, *De spade in de dijk?*, 73–105; 'Floods and money', 348–50.

187 One reason cited for adopting sharecropping contracts instead in Hoffman, 'Economic theory of sharecropping'.

188 Soens, 'Social distribution of land', 147.

189 See Buisman and Van Engelen, *Duizen jaar weer, wind en water*; De Kraker, 'Flood events'; 'Reconstruction of storm frequency'; Gottschalk (ed.), *Stormvloeden en rivieroverstrommingen*; Van Tielhof, 'Texel'.

190 Norden, *Eine Bevölkerung in der Krise*, 225–6.

There were a number of flexible strategies for managing resources that egalitarian-dynamic societies employed, often inter-related. The first was a widening of economic portfolios (on a regional level), but in contrast to egalitarian-persistent societies, a specialisation of production at the household or individual producer level. The second was a movement towards rural proto-industrialisation – taking a step away from traditional agriculture. Essentially economic activities could be adapted to changing economic conditions such as rising or falling wages and prices, or environmental degradation, or the emergence of new markets. For example, in late-medieval and early modern Holland, where exposure of the top-layer of soil and subsidence of the peat made arable farming difficult for the peasant farmers,[191] the local population transformed the economy into one dominated by proto-industry to such an extent that by the onset of the sixteenth century, 50 per cent of the rural population was working 'outside agriculture'.[192] This can be connected to a series of weak urban guilds (relative to many urban guilds seen in other parts of Western Europe), which were unable or unwilling to prevent rural production of items like cloth and beer, and furthermore, were not able to put any restrictions on the mobility and actions of workers.[193] These kinds of adaptive strategies for managing resources were often exacerbated in those places which faced land hunger or the soil was very poor for cultivation.[194]

Specialisation and investment in the late Middle Ages was further enhanced by the well-functioning and unrestricted markets for capital and credit, which was available to a wide section of the population, both urban and rural.[195] As noted for Württemburg in Germany, borrowing was not always a sign of distress but a positive strategy to serve productive purposes.[196] In the early modern period, risks in rural Holland also began to be negated by investment in capital markets.[197] Even poor households resorted to this.[198] In contrast to the egalitarian-persistent societies which tried to protect themselves from the market, egalitarian-dynamic societies exploited the market in order to stand a better chance of survival. Indeed, this is entirely the hypothesis laid out by

---

191 De Boer, *Graaf en grafiek*, 222; Van Dam, 'Sinking peat bogs'.

192 Van Zanden, 'A third road to capitalism?'; 'Taking the measure', 135–9; Van Bavel, 'Early proto-industrialization'. An overview of the literature on the late-medieval transition of the Holland economy can be found in Gubbels, 'Boeren, bezit en bodemproblemen'.

193 Van Bavel, 'Rural wage labour ', 65–6; Epstein, *Freedom and growth*, 115–42.

194 Marfany, 'Is it still helpful to talk about proto-industrialization?', 948; Terrier, *Les deux âges de la proto-industrie*, 78–99; Panjek, 'Not demesne but money', 305–7.

195 Zuijderduijn, *Medieval capital markets*, 242–6; 'Accessing a medieval capital market'; Zuijderduijn, Van Zanden and De Moor, 'Small is beautiful'; 'Microcredit'.

196 Ogilvie, Küpker and Maegraith, 'Household debt', 136.

197 Zuijderduijn and De Moor, 'Spending, saving, or investing?'.

198 Zuijderduijn and De Moor, 'Preferences of the poor'.

Erik Thoen for the labour-intensive cultivation of tiny plots of cash crops in inland Flanders which were sold in urban markets, an effective way of dealing with the high levels of land fragmentation due to population pressure in the region.[199] Rural producers actively used the market as a survival strategy – not exactly 'coerced' as Robert Brenner would have it,[200] but also nothing like the 'Industrious Revolution' hypothesis suggested by Jan de Vries who emphasised aspirational consumption in the countryside.[201]

Egalitarian-dynamic societies used the market in a flexible manner. Through the egalitarian distributions of power and property, egalitarian marketing frameworks for commodities logically emerged which were not dominated by powerful interest groups. Political actors had limited ability to structure market and polity towards their exclusive benefits.[202] Institutional barriers and exclusive privileges were almost non-existent in egalitarian configurations.[203] In these egalitarian market configurations, there were no restrictions on certain people having to use certain trading venues. 'Outsiders' had freedom and accessibility to this kind of marketing structure, and few people were explicitly excluded from the exchange process.[204] Institutions were set up to ensure good contract enforcement between producers and traders, often through courts.[205] Frequently creditors and debtors, landlords and tenants, masters and servants, and farmers and peasants, set up personal relationships of reciprocity to prevent either party from taking advantage of the other.[206] Furthermore, there was usually a plethora of marketing opportunities. In Holland, inhabitants could choose from a number of rural and urban marketing venues for their produce and furthermore, this vast network of marketing opportunities often amounted to informal trading sites.[207] In Europe, many new settlements actually sprung up in the high and late Middle Ages as small market centres and trading posts.[208] By flexibly using the market with high levels of participation and inclusion, settlements in egalitarian-dynamic societies were resilient against potentially disruptive events

199 Thoen, 'Commercial survival economy'.

200 Brenner, 'Agrarian roots'.

201 De Vries, 'The Industrial Revolution and the Industrious Revolution'; 'Peasant demand patterns'.

202 Greif, *Institutions*, 401.

203 Gelderblom, 'Decline of fairs and merchant guilds'.

204 Dijkman, *Shaping medieval markets*, 89–96.

205 Greif, 'Institutions and impersonal exchange'.

206 Ronsijn, 'Mediated and unmediated market dependence'; Hoffman, *Growth in a traditional society*; Lambrecht, 'Reciprocal exchange'.

207 Dijkman, *Shaping medieval markets*, esp. chp. 3.

208 Britnell, 'Proliferation of markets in England'; Lalik, 'Märkte des 12. Jahrhunderts in Polen', 364; Toubert, 'Les statuts communaux', 499; Jones and Kupper, 'Villes, bourgs et franchises', i, 145.

such as the deterioration of the natural environment. In that sense, it was not the market per se which acted as a protective-shield for rural societies, but the precise socio-political context in which the market functioned.

Managing Resources in Polarised-Persistent Societies: Restrictive-Coercive Strategies

Societies classified as polarised-persistent were dominated by interest groups, which were interested in maintaining the status quo. Interest groups used *restrictive or coercive strategies* to strengthen their grip on power and wealth, often through extra-economic extraction. By way of these restrictions, the rest of society was limited in its ability to implement adaptive strategies, and this lack of flexibility left large sections of the population further exposed than necessary to potential disasters such as harvest failure and flooding. However, on the other hand, coercion could at times be used by powerful interest groups to force subordinates into doing things which improved the sustainability of the society, such as maintaining water defence features. *As a result, these societies produced settlements which were narrowly more resilient in the face of crises than settlements in polarised-dynamic societies, but still much more exposed than settlements in egalitarian-dynamic and egalitarian-persistent societies – essentially 'vulnerable' rather than 'highly vulnerable'.*

For example, just as in 'egalitarian-persistent' societies, the open-field system could also become a feature of 'polarised-persistent' societies. Powerful interest groups such as manorial lords were often influential in laying out the open fields (the manorial demesne was often divided into small plots and mixed in with tenant plots), and was organised in negotiation with village communities.[209] Often the strips were regularly distributed in the fields, highly suggestive of ordered planning from above.[210] Furthermore, in societies dominated by seigneurial authorities, frequently there were concessions made by lords for their subjects to make use of their wastelands and to allow access to woodland resources at certain times of the year.[211] Indeed, both common fields and common rights to pastures and woodlands existed in these more inequitable societies, just as they did in the 'egalitarian-persistent' societies. However, in these cases the multifarious benefits of the commons did not descend upon each inhabitant of a rural community in equal measure – the social distribution of these benefits was far more restricted and exclusive. Indeed, as now established by the likes of Ostrom on a theoretical level and confirmed by De Moor and Leigh Shaw-

209 Nash, 'Customary measure'.

210 Gardiner, 'Planned medieval land division'; Meibeyer, 'Der Rundling'; Harvey, 'Regular field and tenurial arrangements'.

211 Menant, 'Les chartes de franchises', 239–40; Fumagalli, *Terra e società*, 62–3; Bruhl and Violante (eds), *Honorantie Civitatis Papiae*, 20; Venditelli, 'Diritti ed impianti di pesca', 407.

Taylor on a more empirical historical level, the commons were rarely 'open access' or a complete 'free for all' as conceived of by Hardin, and not some form of 'primitive communism'.[212] Just as private property forms work to the exclusion of others, so too did collective property forms. As well summarized by Maïka De Keyzer in a recent paper, 'When a wide variety of interest communities were able to create a balanced distribution of power, inclusive access rights could be maintained. Imbalanced distributions of power, where one particular group was able to monopolise the village and/or the government of the institution...led to restrictive access regimes'.[213] In some contexts it is clear that the many identified benefits of the commons could reach down the social hierarchy and help even the very poorest of society to eke out a miserly living,[214] yet in other contexts the commons, as a malleable institution, could just as easily be shaped to the interests of more powerful groups and elites – in the process possibly detrimental to the poorest within society and the very 'vehicle' through which inequality manifested itself.[215] In many cases the commons even supported both outcomes simultaneously: giving the very poor a small package of rights as a contribution to meagre subsistence (as in the right to hunt and take wood), yet at the same time entrenching a dominant position of those with access to 'better' rights (especially with regard to grazing).[216] In effect, the mere presence of institutions such as the commons did not inevitably give the poorest and most vulnerable segments of society enhanced security of livelihood – it depended on the precise socio-political context in which they operated.

Nonetheless there are some examples in 'polarised-persistent' societies of measures being taken to improve the resilience of habitation. For example, powerful seigneurial lords in many areas of Western Europe stimulated the concentration of inhabitants into fortified villages (*incastellamento*), often on hill-tops, for the purpose of collecting a labour force large enough to colonise

212 De Moor, 'Participating is more important than winning'; Shaw-Taylor, 'Labourers, cows, common rights'.

213 De Keyzer, 'The impact of different distributions of power', 521.

214 For example the more 'open access' regimes of the Campine area of Brabant or across vast areas of Scandinavia; De Keyzer, 'The common denominator'; Sundberg, 'Nordic common lands'.

215 Examples of very restricted access rights to common pool resources are everywhere across pre-industrial Europe, particularly in the early modern period; for example see De Keyzer, 'The impact of different distributions of power'; De Moor, 'Avoiding tragedies', esp. 17; Marcos Martín, 'Before the Liberal *desamortizaciones*', 118; Royo, 'Manifestations of difference', 94; McKean, 'Success on the commons', 262; Curtis, 'Is there an agro-town model for Southern Italy?'.

216 A duality noted in Iriate-Goñi, 'Common lands in Spain'.

new areas, or simply as a way of crystallising and securing territorial power.[217] As a result, settlements became more defensible, encouraging investment in defensive structures such as walls and castle towers. In Japan, domain lords (*daimyo*) even tried to exact financial contributions from their subjects in order to rebuild structures, especially after bouts of warfare.[218] A key concern was raising sufficient revenues to perform obligatory public works that benefited agriculture.[219] In that sense, polarised-persistent societies dominated by elites, who exploited their resources through coercive strategies, could have interest groups which benefited from helping sustain their village communities. After all, the power of manorial lords and lay aristocrats was built on the back of subordinate peasants as extra-economic power and not necessarily financial muscle.[220]

Polarised-persistent societies also had interest groups which invested in structures necessary for the resilience and protection of settlements, such as water management institutions. Elite aristocratic landlords were able to confirm impositions on colonists, forcing them to dig and maintain canals.[221] Colonists were fined and lost usufruct rights if land was not tilled.[222] Near Mantova, the monastery of S. Benedetto in Polirone forced rural communities to clear land near the Po River and repair the dikes.[223] In a land grant from the same monastery, every inhabitant of Villabona had to build and maintain dikes to protect their fields.[224] Lords were able to use reclamation projects to move and settle whole communities in new areas, thereby strengthening their territorial presence.[225] Lords also took advantage of ancient communal and collective duties for water management by reasserting them as seigneurial obligations – effectively imposing their will on collective organisation.[226] After the conquest of Lleida in the twelfth century, the Counts of Barcelona and Urgell made sure they maintained and improved the irrigation structure for the surrounding

---

217 Feller, *Les abruzzes médiévales*, chp 6; Toubert, *Dalla terra ai castelli*; Settia, *Castelli e villaggi*; Andrews, 'Castelli e incastellamento'; Bourin, *Villages médiévaux en Bas-Languedoc*; Bazzana, Guichard and Poisson, *Habitats fortifiés*; Martin Viso, 'Riflessioni sull'incastellamento'; Kreutz, *Before the Normans*, 134–5.

218 Hauser, 'Osaka Castle'.

219 Berry, 'Public peace'.

220 Raftis, *Tenure*, 21.

221 Dugsdale, *History of imbanking*, 69–71; Galloway, 'Storm flooding', 178.

222 Panero, *Terre in concessione*, 84–94; Fumagalli, 'L'evoluzione dell'economia agraria', 1032–3.

223 Castagnetti, *Le comunità rurali dalla soggezione signorile*, 7.

224 Torelli (ed.), *Regesto mantovano*, i, 365–6.

225 Bacchi, 'Conquista del territorio', 144–9.

226 Provero, 'Le corvées nelle campagne', 375–7.

villages.[227] Lords also invested in other elements of necessary infrastructure such as bridges.[228]

Similarly, urban governments tried to enforce labour works on rural communities in the interests of water management. In the second half of the eleventh century, the urban administration of Pavia asked nearby communities to work the locks of the Ticino River.[229] Rural communities became compelled in the thirteenth and fourteenth centuries to colonise wastelands, as attested to by numerous city statutes.[230] The statutes of Reggio Emilia ordered the assarting of trees near the village of Rivalta.[231] Cities invested in canals to expand irrigation of the fields.[232] Cities also struck up agreements with large rural landowners, such as a pact between Bologna and a consortium of lords who agreed to work on a canal that brought water from the Reno River to the city.[233] Elsewhere the statutes of Parma in the thirteenth century indicated that any rural communities benefitting from the canal which ran across the lands of Sant'Ilario, Taneto, and Prato Ottesola, had to maintain the structure.[234] The statutes of Ferrara around the same time clearly show that officials of the city had to discuss with the inhabitants of local communities any matters regarding the improvement of water management, and furthermore, it is indicated that rural communities were supposed to provide a labour force to work the embankments of the rivers.[235] Coercion could lead to the construction of an infrastructure which helped with the resilience of settlements against environmental problems such as flooding – however, it must also be noted that this infrastructure was still to some extent precarious. For example, in England it has been shown that when manorial lords took a step back from direct management of their demesnes, the rationale for investing in the physical structures needed to stave off environmental problems also disappeared.[236]

The coercive nature of 'polarised-persistent' societies also inadvertently stimulated the emergence of some important structures from the bottom-up. In medieval Western Europe, the formalisation of seigneurial territories and jurisdictions at the local level led to the crystallisation of the rural commune, either as an outgrowth of seigneurial structures or established in direct opposition

227 Bolòs, 'Changes and survival', 328.
228 Harrison, 'Bridges'.
229 Grillo, 'Comuni urbani e poteri locali', 45–6.
230 Fumagalli, 'Il paesaggio si trasforma', 104–5; Fantoni, *L'acqua a Milano*, 39.
231 Campanini (ed.), *I rubricari degli statuti comunali*, 31–58; Cerlini (ed.), *Consuetudini e statuti reggiani*, 23.
232 Boucheron, 'Water and power'; Menant, *Campagnes lombardes*, 197–200.
233 Balestracci, 'La politica delle acque urbane', 442.
234 *Monumenta Historica ad provincias parmensem*, 382.
235 Zupko and Laures, *Straws in the wind*, 69.
236 Galloway and Potts, 'Marine flooding'.

as a counterweight to the powers of the banal *signorie*.[237] As a result, settlements began to crystallise themselves into more stable concentrations, which can be explained 'less in the power of the *signoria* itself, than in the growing sense of coherence and local identity of the inhabitants of the territories focused on the seigniorial centre'.[238] Territorial crystallisation, often informed by coercive structures from above, led to settlement concentration, which compelled and enabled villagers to work more closely together, particularly in coordinating agricultural activities and regulating access to ever scarcer resources.[239] This 'communal' function of villages, however, was still often maintained under the direction of strong lordships.[240] Furthermore, it has recently been suggested that the vertical hierarchy of serfdom, which deployed communal social capital to enforce manorial interests in exchange for benefits enjoyed by the 'communal oligarchy', often simply benefited the village elites and the manorial lords to the detriment and increased vulnerability of the poorer common folk.[241] In that sense these institutional responses were shaped and dictated by a very select group within society.[242]

Indeed, 'polarised-persistent' societies were also based around coercive strategies for managing resources with restrictions which could stop rural people from making necessary adaptations to ensure survival in the face of crises. First of all, many (though certainly not all) manorialised societies supported demesne agriculture, which often (though not always) required subordinate tenants to provide the labour (to varying degrees) to exploit these fields for the lord or ecclesiastical institution – taking time out of their own fields and leading to the exhaustion of peasant production.[243] Even where the demesne system was not employed or the lord did not own much land, they still upheld a number of customary rights and jurisdictions (banalities), all of which ate into the surplus of the tenants (to varying degrees),[244] and ranged from basic recognition fees (to express fidelity to the lord), death and marriage duties, and transaction fees for the transfer of land. Lords were generally more successful at raising these than customary rents.[245] Peasants could make recourse to the market and even increase output to stave off tough times,[246] but this was not always enough to

---

237 Van Bavel, *Manors and markets*, 93.

238 Wickham, *Mountains and the city*, 339.

239 Van Bavel, *Manors and markets*, 93.

240 Steurs, *Naissance d'une région*.

241 T. Dennison and S. Ogilvie, 'Serfdom and social capital'.

242 Ogilvie, 'Whatever is, is right?'.

243 Brenner, 'Agrarian class structure', 33, 45

244 Post, 'Manorial amercements'.

245 Dyer, 'Changes', 306.

246 Biddick, 'Missing links'; Campbell, 'Economic rent'.

sustain rising total factor productivity.[247] Landlord incentives for innovation in agriculture were initially diminished by their ability to just extend demesne farms or exploit forced labour,[248] although more recent literature has suggested that lordly capital investment was often higher than previously accepted[249] – particularly after the Black Death.[250] Inflation and demographic decline often weakened the value of extra-economic power over subordinates (who asserted their own customary rights and opposed attempted rent increases)[251] – this is the basic premise behind John Hatcher's highly revisionist view that it was often the villeins and not the free tenants who had the most advantageous position by the late Middle Ages in England.[252] However, lords continued to seek new ways to make up for this loss of income: after the Black Death, English lords would spend much energy converting customary tenures to competitive ones, though with mixed success.[253] In Bohemia, nobles were quite effective in employing new restrictions on peasant mobility,[254] and the imposition of coercive labour laws have been noted for late-medieval Norway (with support from the King),[255] in Denmark after the Black Death,[256] in Bavaria and Tyrol,[257] and in parts of Portugal.[258] Fixed cash payments were replaced in some areas by payment in usable agricultural produce as protection against inflation.[259]

Another of the restrictive strategies employed in 'polarised-persistent' societies was limitations on economic activities. Manorial lords punished members of rural communities for production without license.[260] Local communities in need of wood for fuel and housing were prevented from going into forests with seigneurial restrictions and were actively punished for doing so.[261] Often this simply led to unregulated poaching and pilfering instead.[262] The

---

247 Britnell, 'Specialization'; Epstein, *Freedom and growth*, 49–52.

248 Dribe, Olsson and Svensson, 'If the landlord so wanted ...', 747; Postan and Hatcher, 'Population and class relations', 65–6.

249 Campbell, *English seigniorial agriculture*.

250 Stephenson, 'Risk and capital formation', 208–9.

251 Campbell, 'Agrarian problem', 8; Razi, 'Struggles', 105–7.

252 Hatcher, 'English serfdom'. Later supported by Kanzaka, 'Villein rents', 608–14.

253 Overton, *Agricultural revolution*, 151–8; Spufford, *Contrasting communities*.

254 Agnew, *The Czechs*, 58.

255 Sogner, 'Legal status', 178.

256 Orrman, 'Conditions', 581–3, 600–602.

257 Abreu, 'Beggars'; Baquero Moreno, *Marginalidade e conflitos*, 27.

258 Mitterauer, 'Die Wirtschaftspolitik', 20–2.

259 Clark, *State and status*, 151.

260 Schofield, 'Social economy of the medieval village', 42.

261 Birrell, 'Peasant deer poachers'.

262 Lalanne, 'Le domaine des Prémontrés de Belval', 305; Zadora-Rio, 'Parcs à gibier', 134.

same restrictions were often imposed in the colonial context by authorities such as the Dutch East India Company in Java or Taiwan, preventing those who could not afford the license to hunt in the woodlands.[263] In Northern Italy, Flanders, and Germany, rural economic portfolios were often limited by urban guild restrictions.[264] Urban and central governments after the Black Death also frequently tried to manipulate and impose fixed wage levels on many of these economic activities.[265] As Venice began to expand its *terraferma* in the fifteenth century, it made sure it rigorously regulated all economic activities within its rural hinterlands.[266] Some of the strongest blocks to economic activities in the countryside were imposed in the Po Valley, where legal proceedings were started up against entrepreneurs from small communities in the late-medieval *contado* of Mantua who were making cheap woollen cloth.[267] Manufacturing did not appear in the Mantua countryside at all until the eighteenth century.[268] The rural *contado* of Bologna was also rigorously controlled and production of valuable goods such as silk was almost entirely concentrated within the city itself.[269] Rural people who defied the guilds were resented: shoemakers operating outside Milan were regarded as parasites by the shoemaking guilds.[270]

Indirect modes of exploitation could also be considered restrictive-coercive, such as sharecropping, which continued well into the twentieth century in places as diverse as Italy, Mexico, Brazil, and India. Under this system, the producer theoretically received all of the credit, capital and equipment needed to run their enterprise from a wealthier landlord, but this relationship between tenant and landlords often descended into one of dependency and subordination.[271] Many scholars have pointed to the connection between poverty and sharecropping, although development economists tend to present it more positively.[272] This sort of (quasi) indirect mode of exploitation occurred

263 Boomgaard, 'Oriental nature', 273; Koo, 'Deer hunting'.

264 Malanima, *La decadenza*, 154; Van Zanden and Prak, 'State formation', 212.

265 Kelter, 'Das deutsche Wirtschaftsleben'; Scholliers, 'Vrije en onvrije arbeiders'; Boyer, '1245–1380', 254–5.

266 Ciriacono, 'Venise et ses villes', 288–9.

267 Belfanti, 'Town and country', 311.

268 Belfanti, 'Dalla città alla campagna'.

269 Poni, 'Per la storia del distretto industriale serico', 98–9.

270 Merlo, *Le corporazioni*, 44; Belfanti, *Mestieri e forestieri*, 103–10.

271 Emigh, 'Loans and livestock'.

272 For traditional dismissive views of sharecropping see Hoffman, *Growth in a traditional society*; O'Brien, 'Path dependency'. Some have questioned whether sharecropping was more a symptom of poverty rather than a cause; Yun, 'Economic cycles', 134. More favourable views of sharecropping are usually associated with development economists; Finkler, 'From sharecroppers to entrepreneurs'; Boadu, 'Efficiency of share contracts'; Bell, 'Alternative theories of sharecropping'.

when there were real malfunctions in the labour, credit, and capital markets (not enough access to either).[273] These kinds of factor markets also included highly restricted legislation on labour movement and actions, and inefficient and poorly accessible credit markets (particularly for rural producers) with high interest rates.[274] Elsewhere in parts of the Mediterranean such as Southern Italy and Andalusia, labour-intensive and capital-extensive monoculture grain estates worked through a system of *latifundia* were crystallised in place (in different chronological phases) because dominant large landowners (former feudal lords, barons, and grain speculators) had no interest in modifying the system, were more concerned with urban life, and were afraid of investing finance into agricultural systems where soils were poor, droughts were frequent, and returns unpredictable or consistently low.[275]

The market was also another way of exploiting resources in polarised-persistent societies: markets for commodities were set up entirely dominated by powerful interest groups. Towns created market monopolies or coerced the flow of commodities into one particular trading centre.[276] Rural producers were forced to sell their goods at designated markets rather than search for the best price in other trading venues, and would suffer punishments if found disobeying the legislation.[277] In the late Middle Ages, the formalisation of urban jurisdiction over wider rural hinterlands led to the emergence of highly regulated and monopolised networks of markets. Frequently rural producers who were told where and what to cultivate were also told they had to sell their output in specialised city markets.[278] Cities took exclusive and prioritised access to the food supply of their hinterlands enforcing monopolies up to the sixteenth century (and sometimes beyond).[279] Price controls, bans on exporting, and forced sales during times of scarcity occurred in many rural areas in Northern Italy, for example.[280] Inevitably, this led at times to unpredictable market regulation and frequently high transaction costs.[281] Some towns were given charters of liberties to recognise the fact they were compulsory trading venues for rural producers.[282] The *bastide* towns which emerged in parts of Southern France during the

---

273 Curtis, 'Florence and its hinterlands'.

274 Van Bavel, 'Markets for land'; Cohn, 'After the Black Death'.

275 Mack Smith, *Latifundia in modern Sicilian history*; Aymard, 'Mesures et interprétations de la croissance'. Although we have been warned not to project continuity too far back in time in the classic Epstein, *An island for itself*, 163.

276 On this process more generally see Epstein, 'Cities, regions'; 'Town and country'.

277 Ronchini (ed.), *Statuta communis Parmae*, 44–6, 60–61, 178–80.

278 Stabel, *De kleine stad*, 226–7; Bianchi and Granuzzo (eds), *Statuti di Verona*, 546–7.

279 Stabel, *Dwarfs among giants*, 163–4; Ciriacono, 'L'economia regionale veneta', 45.

280 Zanetti, *Problemi alimentari*, 40–50; Farolfi, *Strutture agrarie e crisi cittadina*, 35–6.

281 Tocci, *Le terre traverse*, 280–89.

282 Rutte, *Stedenpolitiek*, 125–7.

thirteenth and fourteenth centuries were founded by large landowners and lords interested first and foremost in securing taxes on all trade performed at the market.[283] Manorial lords also tried to reserve particular privileges for accessing markets – such as the medieval burgesses and the seigneurial concessions to instigate trade through burgage tenure.[284] Heavy tolls and taxes imposed on the transportation of produce also deterred producers from using distant markets or new ones emerging,[285] which was further exacerbated if there were few safe places to store perishable items such as grain.[286] Certain dominant groups received privileged rights over facilities for the storage of grain.[287] Where commodity markets were restricted, difficult to find and enter, or unsafe, the barriers to trade pushed producers towards a more subsistence-orientated exploitation.[288]

In sum, coercive-restrictive strategies used for managing and exploiting resources in 'polarised-persistent' pre-industrial societies limited the capacity for populations to adapt to new conditions and inhibited their flexibility; in turn this left the settlements more exposed to unexpected crises with many living a precarious existence and the only option left was to migrate – frequently to the city.

Summary of Hypothesis and Measurement of Resilience and Vulnerability of Settlements

The basic premise of the theoretical framework employed in this book is that pre-industrial society can be divided into four basic types based on an assessment of how egalitarian or polarised (i.e. a test of equality), and dynamic or persistent (i.e. a test of change) its key configurations of property and power were. These particular 'types of societies' ended up exploiting resources in different ways with vastly different types of institutions.

'Egalitarian-persistent' societies exploited their resources using protectionist strategies with one eye on risk avoidance and risk management. As a result, they produced very resilient settlements over the long term, particularly in the face of exogenous crises such as harvest failures and pestilence, though possibly did not change much. According to the measurements of resilience and vulnerability outlined in Chapter 1, these societies exhibited none of the three negative

283 Higounet, *Les villeneuves de Piémont*, esp. 130–9; *Nouvelle approche sur les bastides*, esp. 32–5.

284 Britnell, 'Proliferation of markets in England'; Galloway, 'Town and country', 117–8; Goddard, 'Small boroughs'.

285 Weststrate, 'Organisation of trade and transport'.

286 Small, 'Grain for the Countess', 60–1.

287 Kaplan, *Provisioning Paris*, 66–79.

288 Hoppenbrouwers and Van Zanden, 'Restyling the transition', 22–6.

indicators for settlement vulnerability – population trends (epitomised in either deaths or outward migration), loss and degradation of agricultural land, and destruction of housing and capital goods.

'Polarised-dynamic' societies exploited their resources using short-termist strategies with the intention of interest groups extracting in a commercial sense as much as they possibly could from finite resources, but in the process exposing the wider population to more risk. Sustainable infrastructures and institutions often failed to develop. As a result, they produced settlements which possibly could rise up very quickly through short-term economic gain, but also were susceptible to rapid decline – maybe even total collapse. These societies could exhibit all of the three negative indicators for settlement vulnerability.

'Egalitarian-dynamic' societies exploited their resources flexibly by responding to change – often taking production in new directions in direct response to the opportunities presented by the market. As a result, they produced adaptable settlements which could grow organically and furthermore got their resilience from the inherent adaptability of society. These societies perhaps only exhibited one of the three negative indicators for settlement vulnerability after experiencing forms of exogenous crisis.

Finally, 'polarised-persistent' societies tended to exploit their resources using coercion and restriction. As a result, they produced entirely dependent settlements which could benefit from infrastructures necessary for long-term resilience (laid down through coercion), but at the same time faced inbuilt restrictions on their decision-making processes, which could lead to a failure to adapt to new conditions, and therefore exposure to settlement decline or even collapse. These settlements, therefore, were moderately vulnerable to exogenous crises, and could exhibit as many as two out of the three negative indicators for settlement vulnerability.

Chapter 3

Parasite or Stimulant? The Divergent Impact of the City of Florence upon its Surrounding Rural Hinterlands, 1300–1580

From the high Middle Ages onwards in Western Europe, cities or towns and the countryside became more closely connected, both politically and economically. Indeed, some of the most influential economic historians of the past have put at the core the role of urban–rural relations in fostering the processes by which capitalism emerged in Europe.[1] It was after all, Adam Smith, who exclaimed that 'the great commerce of every civilised society is that carried on between the inhabitants of the town and those of the country'.[2] Many scholars have put forward a view that the level of urbanisation in pre-industrial Europe was highly dependent on the organisation and level of productivity in agriculture in the countryside.[3] Cities reaped the rewards of surplus produce taken from the countryside, but at the same time it has been said that rural regions enjoyed the fruits of integration with urban markets, as urban growth stimulated development of commercialised agriculture.[4]

Thus, the growth of London through the high Middle Ages stimulated agricultural production in the rural hinterlands, leading to the emergence of highly commercialised arable and pastoral farms in East Anglia.[5] London's brewing industry, furthermore, stimulated cultivation of new types of grain.[6] Elsewhere in England, the growing demand for produce from the Cambridge colleges from the 1400s onwards encouraged surrounding rural regions to specialise in different agricultural and economic activities – the South-Eastern Uplands supplying charcoal and wood for fuel and the Fens providing pastoral goods.[7] The same incentives for commercialised pastoral farming have been

---

1 Marx, *Capital*, i, 4; Weber, *Economy and society*, ii, 1323; Wallerstein, *The modern world-system*.

2 Smith, *Wealth of nations*, 168.

3 Hoffman, *Growth in a traditional society*, 170–85; Wrigley, 'Parasite or stimulus'; Grantham, 'Divisions of labour'.

4 Grantham, 'Espaces privilégiés'; Masschaele, *Peasants, merchants and markets*.

5 Campbell et al., *A medieval capital*; Keene, 'Medieval London', 103–4.

6 Galloway, 'London's grain supply'.

7 Lee, 'Feeding the colleges'.

traced in the countryside around the German town of Thüringen in the early modern period.[8] In Northern France, considerable urban demand from Paris for agricultural produce encouraged farmers in the Paris Basin to put financial investment into increasingly modernised farms.[9] For arable regions, urban-produced manure (from Paris, for example) allowed for greater fertility of soils and improved productivity.[10] Some areas such as the Central Dutch River Area began to orientate their agricultural enterprises towards specialised horse breeding – a lucrative business.[11] Even in poorly urbanised areas such as Apulia in Southern Italy in the eleventh and twelfth centuries, the establishment of small urban centres was enough to stimulate economic activity in the rural hinterlands.[12] Furthermore, rural areas poorly endowed with fertile soils were still able to benefit from urbanisation by establishing new forms of proto-industry or diversifying – for example, brick production in the late-medieval Holland peat-lands or the establishment of viticulture on sharecropping farms in Catalonia.[13] New trends in urban consumption and patterns of demand also created other opportunities for rural producers to cater to.[14]

This urban–rural relationship was not always mutually beneficial, however. While some rural regions enjoyed the fruits of integration with urban markets as urban growth stimulated the development of commercialised agriculture, other rural regions were exploited through oppressive jurisdictions linked to urban territorial expansion.[15] The proximity of an expanding town did not guarantee prosperity for the surrounding countryside as noted for the late-medieval development of Colchester.[16] Urbanisation sometimes did not even result in increased specialisation in production in the countryside: wealthy urban elites invested in farms simply for their own non-market access to basic foodstuffs.[17] Swiss and Italian towns, in particular, stunted rural economies with heavy taxation.[18] Some of the strongest urban exploitation and domination over the countryside was evident in the city-states of Northern Italy in the late Middle Ages and early modern period.[19] Urban investment in landownership in the

---

8 Held, *Zwischen Marktplatz und Anger*, 108–10.

9 L. Vardi, *Land and the loom*.

10 Moriceau, *Les fermiers de l'Ile-de-France*, 660–61.

11 Van Bavel, 'Land, lease and agriculture', 36.

12 Oldfield, 'Rural settlement and economic development', 342–3.

13 Van Bavel and Van Zanden, 'The jump-start of the Holland economy', 505; Marfany, 'Is it still helpful to talk about proto-industrialisation?'.

14 Blondé and Van Damme, 'Retail growth'.

15 Epstein, 'Cities, regions'; Scott, *Freiburg and the Breisgau*, 31–46.

16 Britnell, *Growth and decline in Colchester*, 141–58.

17 Soens, Van Onacker and Dombrecht, 'Metropolis and hinterland?', 82.

18 Scott, *The city-state in Europe*, 173.

19 Chittolini, 'Cities, city-states'.

countryside led to dispossession of rural producers and high levels of economic polarisation.[20] The last vestiges of the commons were encroached upon and parcelled out,[21] and furthermore, urban investment in land reclamation became an effective framework for the legitimisation of urban legislation over the countryside.[22] Urban governments supported colonisation of new territories through jurisdictions that subsumed rural communities into their governmental structure.

Rather than fall onto one side of a debate as to whether cities and towns were 'good' or 'bad' for economic development, it is simply accepted in this chapter that pre-industrial urbanisation had differing effects on the development of rural economy and society, with the impact highly dependent on context. Indeed, rural societies were not necessarily passive victims of urban whims, but could oppose urban interests to the point of antagonism.[23] Over the course of time, rural societies could loosen the exploitative hold that urban interest groups held over them, a process traced for the late-medieval *contado* of Perugia.[24] Furthermore, rural societies did not always have to direct trade towards big cities (regardless of their span of influence); evidence points to a diversity of marketing opportunities appearing from the Middle Ages onwards in the countryside.[25]

Thus, the central question addressed in this chapter instead is *why* were some pre-industrial rural societies vulnerable to urban dominance, while other rural societies were more resilient – even positively benefiting from their connection to urban environments? What were the causal mechanisms behind these divergent responses? Why did some rural societies benefit from increasing urban influence while others were reduced to poverty and decay? That question is explored in this chapter by comparing the fortunes of two rural regions of Tuscany between the fourteenth and sixteenth centuries, and how they were affected in different ways by the growth of the city of Florence. A contrast is drawn between the Florentine *contado*, an area of plains and hills encircling Florence, which suffered settlement contraction and abandonment in the late Middle Ages, and a mountainous region (in the *distretto*) more distant from Florence known as the Casentino Valley, which simultaneously experienced the

---

20 Epstein, 'The peasantries of Italy', 89; Rossini, *Le campagne Bresciane*, 33, 124, 195; Gullino, 'Quando il mercante costruì la villa'.

21 Panjek, 'Beni comunali'; Comino, 'Sfruttamento e ridistribuzione di risorse collettive'; Rao, 'Risorse collettive'.

22 Campopiano, 'Land clearance'.

23 Kälin, *Die Urner Magistraten-Familien*, 14; Körner, 'Trotz, Hochmuot und Rebellion'; Bierbrauer, 'Die Ausbildung bäuerlicher Landschaften', 100.

24 Blanshei, 'Population, wealth, and patronage'.

25 Britnell, 'Proliferation of markets in England'; Lalik, 'Märkte des 12. Jahrhunderts in Polen', 364; Jones and J-L. Kupper, Villes, bourgs et franchises', i, 145; Dijkman, *Shaping medieval markets*, chp. 3.

crystallisation of settlement into concentrated villages around flourishing local markets, encouraging barter and specialisation.[26]

This chapter is organised as follows. In the first section, the basic growth and development of the city of Florence between the high and late Middle Ages is plotted and the increased sphere of urban influence crystallised in the Florentine territorial government is described. In the second section, the divergent effects of outside urban influence on settlement development are illustrated. For the *contado*, the settlement situation is described for the period before 1300, followed by an account of the contraction in habitation in the late Middle Ages. This is contrasted with an area of the *distretto* known as the Casentino Valley, where it is shown that settlement after 1300 became clustered into concentrated settlements around blossoming market centres. In order to highlight the different levels of rural resilience or vulnerability to urban encroachment, the three measurements outlined in Chapter 1 are used – population trends, degradation and ruination of agricultural land, and destruction or devaluation of housing and capital goods. In the third section, it is shown that the different levels of societal resilience or vulnerability exhibited in the two areas was linked to different ways each society arranged its economic portfolios and modes of resource exploitation. In section four, the deep-lying reasons for this divergent development are considered: why did settlements in the *contado* decay in the late Middle Ages under urban pressure, while a blossoming set of villages appeared in the Casentino? It is suggested in this section that the extent to which a city was a parasite or a stimulant to pre-industrial rural societies depended on the configuration of rural societies themselves. The favourable set of institutions for exploiting resources in the Casentino Valley was linked to (a) a more egalitarian and stable distribution of property and (b) a balanced equilibrium of social interest groups able to form a counter force to urban domination. In the final fifth section, these findings are placed into the wider theoretical framework described in Chapter 2.

Florence: Urbanisation and the Growth of the City-State

Even after the political, economic and demographic disruption caused by the decline of the Western Roman Empire, Italy remained 'a land of cities', with a distinctive urbanised character in the early Middle Ages.[27] Nonetheless, it was not until the tenth century that the urban population of Northern and Central Italy

---

[26] The link between medieval settlement concentration and specialisation of production has been made in Higounet, 'Congregare populationem'.

[27] Wickham, *Early medieval Italy*, 4–5.

really expanded, possibly doubling between 1000 and 1300.[28] By 1300, around one-fifth of the population of Northern and Central Italy lived in cities, three times the level of urbanisation seen in other parts of Western Europe.[29] Tuscany conformed to this general trend of urbanisation between 1000 and 1300, and, furthermore, was one of the most densely populated regions of Europe before the Black Death, supporting 60 people per km^2 around 1300.[30] In the twelfth century, however, Florence was still arguably the least important of all the major Tuscan cities which included Lucca, Pisa, Arezzo, Prato and Siena. It was only in the thirteenth century that it grew in size and significance, increasing from 10,000 to 110,000 inhabitants between 1175 and 1300.[31] By 1300, Florence had risen to almost 'metropolitan' status by medieval standards and was the home to companies (such as the Peruzzi) with world trading interests and leading banking agencies.[32] Just before the Black Death, over half of the population of the Florentine territory lived in Florence.[33]

As Florence grew during the thirteenth century, so did its need for supplies of food and produce. Evidence from the fourteenth century suggests that Florence was consuming annually 4,000 oxen, 60,000 sheep, 20,000 goats, 30,000 pigs, and 25 million quarts of wine, as well as 1,300 bushels of grain daily.[34] As a result, the city became more reliant on its trading network with Southern Italy, which provided large quantities of grain and pottery.[35] Other products such as spices, (some) textiles, paper, and stone were imported from Asia.[36] The problem with this reliance on imports was acutely felt when prices were high, however.[37] Furthermore, food shortages were common, forcing the Florentine government to fall back on its international networks for the supplies it needed.[38] One solution was to be more self-sufficient in the production of food, something which could be achieved by a more intensive exploitation of the surrounding countryside in Tuscany.[39] By 1300, the Florentine administration

---

28 Malanima, 'Urbanisation', 99–102.

29 Van Bavel, 'Markets for land', 505.

30 Epstein, *Freedom and growth*, 71.

31 Petralia, 'Lo sviluppo dell'economia toscana medievale', 119–20.

32 Luzzati, 'Firenze e le origini della banca moderna', 433–4; De la Roncière, *Un changeur florentin*; Hunt, *Medieval super-companies.*

33 Ginatempo and Sandri, *L'Italia delle città.*

34 Lopez, 'Trade of medieval Europe: the South', 369; Pinto, *Il libro del Biadaiolo*, 77; De la Roncière, 'Le vignoble florentin', 126.

35 Abulafia, 'Southern Italy and the Florentine economy'; Britnell, 'Towns of England and Northern Italy', 29.

36 Balard, 'Le commerce du blé'.

37 Goldthwaite, 'I prezzi del grano'.

38 Pinto, 'Commercio del grano'.

39 De la Roncière, 'Alimentation et ravitaillement', 185.

began to extend its influence and authority over the countryside, over wider areas, imposing jurisdictions, reclaiming marsh and woodlands, levying new taxes, and even subduing 'rival' Tuscan towns.[40] As is explained in the next section, however, Florence did not affect the entire Tuscan countryside in the same way. In some places Florentine influence caused rural decay and ruin, while other areas withstood the exploitative tendencies of the city and even indirectly benefited from the growth of Florence.

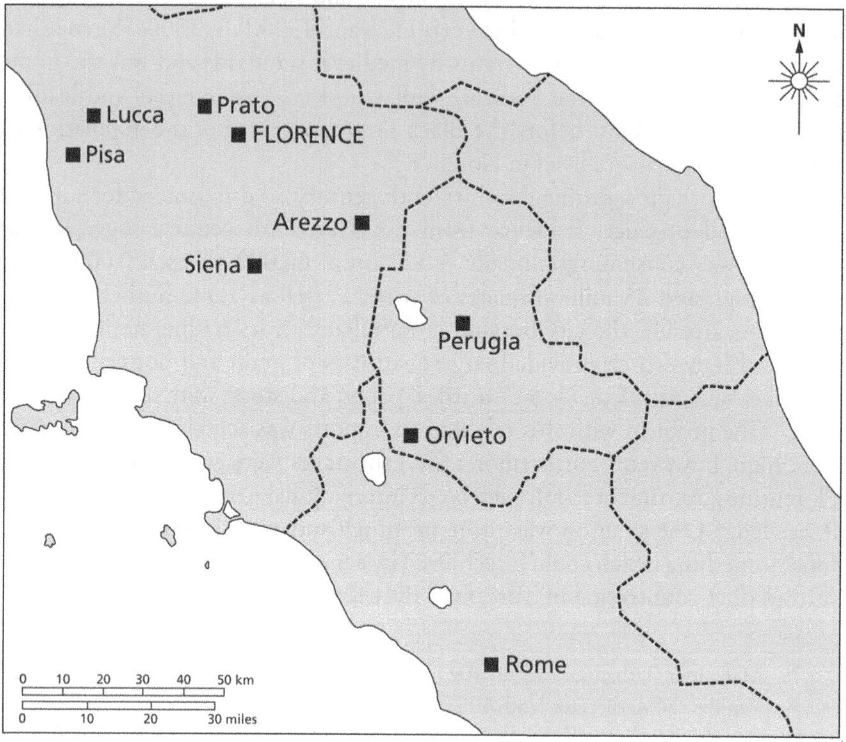

Figure 3.1 Major medieval cities and towns of central Italy

Settlement Resilience and Vulnerability in the Late-Medieval Tuscan Countryside

Although the Florentine territory by 1427 extended over around 11,000 km^2, only around 4,900 km^2 of this was considered *contado*. Indeed, the *contado*

---

[40] Epstein, 'Cities, regions', 19–20, 36–42.

represented only the plains and hills closely encircling the city of Florence, running from Empoli and Prato in the west to the Arno and Sieve rivers in the east.[41] The *contado* was distinct from the *distretto*: it consisted of the rural areas which had formerly been under feudal jurisdiction before coming under the control of the Florentine commune, while the more distant *distretto* was brought under control much later.[42] Some parts of Tuscany never fell into Florentine dominion, such as the Republic of Lucca, while the State of Siena was not conquered outright until 1555.[43]

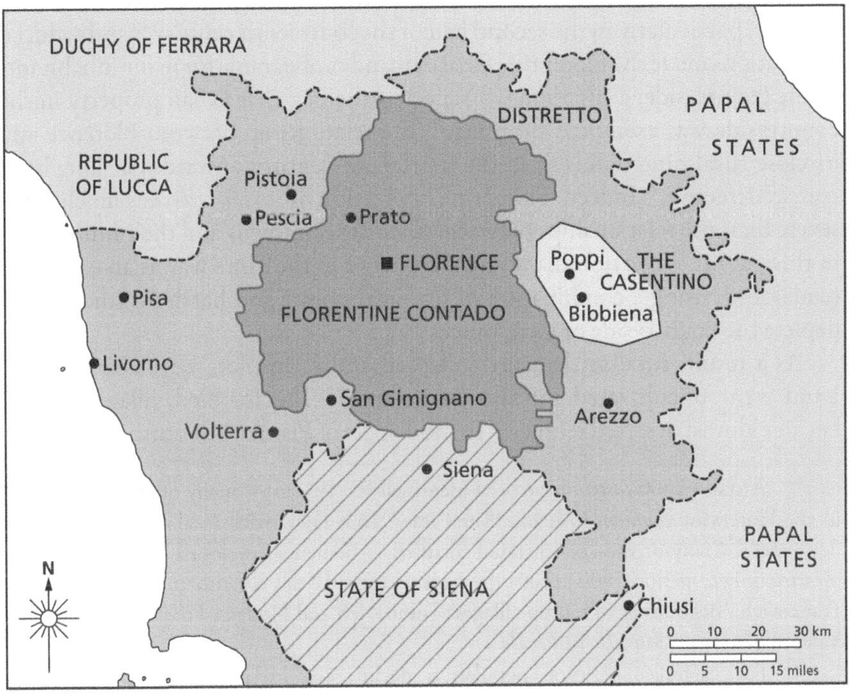

Figure 3.2 Florentine territories (*contado* and *distretto*), 1574

In the Florentine *contado*, the evidence for decay and ruin from the beginning of the fourteenth century onwards is in the contracting settlements and long demographic downturn. Before 1300, the landscape of the *contado*

41 Najemy, *A history of Florence*, 97.
42 Brucker, *Renaissance Florence*, 5; De la Roncière, *Prix et salaires*, ix–x.
43 Maria Pult Quaglia, 'Early modern Tuscany', 130–1.

was a patchwork of *castelli* or *castri* (fortified villages perhaps with a castle), open or loosely clustered settlements known as *casali*, small hamlets, and some isolated aristocratic structures focused on *curtes* or ecclesiastical granges.[44] In accordance with the general trend in Western Europe, many of these population centres grew in size between the eleventh and thirteenth centuries, thus the countryside by 1300 was teeming with rural folk. However after 1300, the rural population began to suffer a major reduction through a series of severe plagues, poor harvests and harsh Florentine fiscal oppression, so much so that by the time of the Florentine *catasto* in 1427, the population may have been a third of what it was at the end of thirteenth century.[45] The combination of heightened tax pressure, particularly in the second half of the fourteenth century,[46] and reduced populations made the Florentine fiscal demands unbearable for many inhabitants of the countryside, a situation worsened by the fact that urban property in the countryside was exempted from tax.[47] The relationship between Florence and its close rural hinterlands from the fourteenth century onwards has long been seen as defective.[48] Indeed, Florentine oppression of its *contado* was much more severe than the relationships between other Tuscan towns and their hinterlands in this period.[49] The dominant city-state acted in the same way as an extractive feudal lord, using a combination of financial power and harsh jurisdictions to deplete the countryside of its resources.[50]

As a result, rural settlements collapsed and farm plots were abandoned.[51] Land went uncultivated for lack of tenants.[52] The fortified villages (*castri*) became almost deserted refuges.[53] In the district of Pistoia, just north of Florence,

---

[44] Around 2400 *castelli* have been identified for Tuscany – many of which were sited in the Florentine *contado*; Osheim, 'Rural Italy', 163; Francovich et al., 'Verso un atlante dei castelli'. Many of the concentrated fortified settlements developed before the typical *incastellamento* period (900–1100), perhaps as early as the seventh or eighth centuries; Francovich, 'Beginnings of hilltop villages'; Francovich and Hodges, *Villa to village*, 61–74; Valenti, *L'insediamento altomedievale*.

[45] For examples of rural population decline see Herlihy, 'Population, plague'; *Medieval and Renaissance Pistoia*, 64–6; Fiumi, 'La popolazione del territorio volterrano-sangimignanese'; 'La demografia fiorentina'.

[46] Including the despised *gabelles*; De la Roncière, 'Indirect taxes', 185–9.

[47] Molho, *Florentine public finances*, 23–36.

[48] See negative views offered in Becker, *Florence in transition*, ii, 181–8; Molho, *Florentine public finances*, 24.

[49] Caferro, 'City and countryside in Siena'; Meek, *Lucca*, 112.

[50] Epstein, 'Cities, regions'; 'Town and country'.

[51] Herlihy, 'Santa Maria Impruneta'; Conti, *La formazione della struttura agraria*, iii, 78; Kotel'nikova, 'Tendenze progressive', 124–7; Klapisch-Zuber and Day, 'Villages désertés en Italie', 442–3, 437–8; Klapisch-Zuber, 'Villaggi abbandonati'.

[52] Jones, 'Florentine families', 196; ASF, Catasto, no. 307, f. 438r.

[53] Jones, *Italian city-state*, 166.

inhabitants fell from 37,598 in 1244 to just 8,969 in 1404.[54] Rural people fled to the city in search of work, hoping to be absorbed into urban building industries.[55] Indeed, the rural poor eventually swelled the impoverished suburbs of Florence, often to the south and the east.[56] Florence was no respite for the impoverished country-folk, however, as increased migration into the city caused real wages to sink and pauperism and crime to rise, deepening the antagonism between rich and poor.[57] As early as the thirteenth century, Florentine hospitals and charitable foundations swelled with the impoverished and destitute.[58] Even wealthier members of rural society began to migrate to the city, unimpressed with the heightened tax demands upon them as a result of depopulation.[59]

The impression of the *contado* during the late Middle Ages seems to be one of widespread impoverishment.[60] The *catasto* of 1427 in particular, tells a general story of rural misery, instability and insecurity in the countryside close to Florence, with many on the verge of famine and supported only by charity.[61] Only 4 per cent of Tuscan movable wealth was in the hands of *contado* inhabitants, rural people had no liquid assets, and the constant demand for rents and taxes drained the countryside of coins.[62] Loans to rural tenants by urban landlords increasingly went unpaid.[63] The population of the *contado* declined all the way up to the mid-fifteenth century and only recovered much later, during the first half of the sixteenth century.[64]

Such evidence for settlement vulnerability was not seen everywhere in the Tuscan countryside, however. The more distant rural areas of Tuscany which came much later under Florentine jurisdiction were known as the '*distretto*', and were often (though not always) mountainous. This applied to the area known as the Casentino Valley, 30 km east of Florence, where some of its communes, such as Poppi, were only brought under Florentine administration as late as

---

54 Herlihy, 'Population, plague'.

55 Guarducci and Ottanelli, *I servitori domestici*, 19–30; Nenci, 'Ricerche sull'immigrazione dal contado'.

56 Faini, 'Da Bagno a Ripoli a Firenze'.

57 De la Roncière, 'Pauvres et pauvreté'; 'Condition des salariés'; Caduff, 'Publici latrones', 505, 515.

58 Trexler, 'Foundlings of Florence', 260; Pullan, 'Support and redeem', 177; Henderson, *Piety and charity*.

59 Herlihy, 'Santa Maria Impruneta', 266–9; Plesner, *L'émigration de la campagne*.

60 Herlihy and Klapisch-Zuber, *Les toscans*, 241–60, 272–9.

61 Brucker, 'Florentine voices'; 'Bureaucracy and social welfare'; Mazzi, 'Ai margini del lavoro'.

62 Van Bavel, 'Markets for land', 519.

63 Mazzi and Raveggi, *Gli uomini e le cose*, 290–300.

64 Herlihy and Klapisch-Zuber, *Tuscans and their families*, 73.

1440.[65] The evidence for the argument that parts of the *distretto* responded more favourably to the rise of the city of Florence is that some areas did not suffer the same settlement contraction, land abandonment, and general dilapidation as described for the *contado* in the late Middle Ages. Pestilence did reach these mountain communities and Florentine taxation in the *distretto* was an even higher rate than in the *contado*.[66] Yet Samuel Cohn has shown that mountain people of northern and eastern Tuscany did not migrate in droves to Florence, in contrast to an earlier picture of impoverishment that Giovanni Cherubini painted.[67] If people of the *distretto* were forced to move on, they simply chose another mountain village, sometimes even crossing the passes into Romagna.[68] In fact, in the Casentino Valley from around 1300 onwards there blossomed a wide network of concentrated villages, which were often compacted around small coherent market centres, catering for local, regional and urban demand.

Prior to the fourteenth century, settlement was dispersed across the landscape in the Casentino. An excellent source for the reconstruction of the valley between the eleventh and thirteenth centuries is the book of charters belonging to the great landowning monastery of Camaldoli (founded in 1005).[69] In this *Regesto di Camaldoli*, over 55 per cent of the houses mentioned during the eleventh century were positioned outside of the castle walls and identifiable by the name given to the field in which they were located.[70] Some of the field-names closer to the Arno were lost later in the eleventh and twelfth centuries due to flooding of the river banks.[71]

Most of the charter references mention *castelli* (fortified villages) or *casali* (often open villages) by name, which gives each settlement a clear territorial definition. However a large number of houses are mentioned as being located in specific fields (*avocabula*) pertaining to that settlement. For example, it was noted at Ornina in 1030 that 'there are ... two houses, and three enclosed lands and vines, and four pieces of land that are positioned in the territory of the people of S. Leozheri situated at Plano in the casale Ornina ... one of these houses and enclosures are in the fields that are known as Runco'.[72] A concept of

65 Benadusi, *A provincial elite*, 22.

66 For plague in the *distretto* see Cherubini, 'La carestia del 1346–47'. For higher taxation in the mountains compared to the plains see Cohn, 'Inventing Braudel's mountains', 404.

67 For the positive view of Tuscan mountain society see Cohn, *Creating the Florentine State*, 55–112; 'Highlands and lowlands'; 'Insurrezioni contadine'. For mountain poverty see Cherubini, 'Il montanaro della novellistica'.

68 Cohn, 'Demography', 187.

69 On the foundation by Romualdo di Ravenna see Tabacco, 'La data di fondazione'; Kurze, 'Campus Malduli'; Vedovato, *Camaldoli e la sua congregazione*, 16–21.

70 My data from Schiaparelli, Baldesseroni and Lasinio (eds), *Regesto di Camaldoli*.

71 RC, i, 15, 19, 50–1, 112, 145, 160, 228, 387, 416, ii, 763, 805, 862, 937.

72 RC, i, no. 108. My translation of the Latin.

a 'village' or settlement is offered (the *casale* Ornina), but the evidence suggests that the houses were built on specific fields, in this case at Runco. Runco was likely a new cultivated and settled area of Ornina as the word originates from the Latin word '*runcare*', referring to deforestation and reclamation.[73]

If the *casale* Ornina was at all a concentrated settlement in the eleventh century, there would have been no need to label houses in specific fields or locations. Houses would just be listed as present within the confines of the village, perhaps with the most topographic information afforded being next to whom their house was positioned. Between 1027 and 1041 houses at Ornina were mentioned in 11 separate charters, each in a different place.[74] Three of these dwellings were clearly positioned within their own enclosure. The *casale* of Ornina did not appear to have had a physical centre at all, being just a scattered number of dwellings in different fields known as Antreriora, Arconiano, Lavaclo, Petra Rondinaia, Posticcio, Pratella, Sigalare, Faito, Runco, Arconiano and Plano. Ornina was at the extreme end of the dispersed spectrum. The settlement of Contra also had a dispersed pattern. Between 1013 and 1099 houses were mentioned nine times, seven of which were located in separate fields.[75] Freggina also had housing mentioned nine times between 1019 and 1047, two-thirds with specific field-locations,[76] while Gello had twelve houses listed from 1019 to 1099, of which ten were scattered.[77] Ventrina also was a clearly dispersed settlement, for all but one of its eleven houses mentioned between 1009 and 1078 were recorded in specific fields.[78] Very little sign of concentrated settlement can be taken from the documents for the eleventh-century Casentino, perhaps only at Monte in the Partina area. One of the toponyms at Monte known as 'Musileo' became an independent *casale* in the 1080s. Corezzo and Contra too were listed as '*avocabula*' at various points in the eleventh century, though eventually in the twelfth century established themselves as independent *casali*.[79] The change from *avocabulum* to *casale* status is not outright proof of increased concentration of settlement: indeed it may be that these sites had simply more houses attributed to them but continued to be distributed in a dispersed pattern.

Castle building was a common process in the valley during the eleventh and early twelfth centuries, but this did not stimulate settlement concentration. Although the big ecclesiastical institutions did not involve themselves in this process, castles were built by territorial lords such as the Bishop of Arezzo and smaller local lords. The castle-building process in the Casentino can be divided

---

73 Saggioro, 'Insediamenti', 90; Montanari and Baruzzi, 'Silva runcare', 101.

74 RC, i, nos 88, 108, 131, 196.

75 RC, i, nos 31, 35, 94, 118, 125, 126, 152, 184, 457, 621.

76 RC, i, nos 49, 52, 149, 232, 235, 237, 240.

77 RC, i, nos 46, 546, 583, 593, 612, 606, 609, 612, 616.

78 RC, i, nos 16, 27, 183, 204, 461, 402.

79 RC, i, nos 60, 90 and 82, 118.

into two key phases. Phase one was the earliest castles built by the Bishop of Arezzo, big feudal families such as the Guidi or donations by emperors such as Henry II.[80] These castles were largely built before 1050: Sarna (980), Marciano (1008), Nibbiano (1011), Castel Focognano (1028), Strumi (1029) and Montecchio (1049). Furthermore there were some castles first mentioned after 1050, although they were likely built much earlier than that date. These include Vezzano (1052), Castel Castagnaio (1063), Fronzola and Gello (1065), Bibbiena (1114), Chiusi (1119), Poppi (1191)[81] and Romena (1164). Phase two was a later group of castles which were built after 1050 through the affirmation of a local elite, often as fees from the Bishop of Arezzo. These include Gressa (1078), Soci (1079), Ragginopoli (1081), Partina and Lierna (1095), Papiano (1091), Moggiona (1107), Teggiano and Lorenzano (1111) and Serra and Riosecco (1114).[82]

The *castelli* in the Casentino emerged as an expression of social status and political control by 'capitaneal' families (originally vassals of a bishop) looking to distinguish themselves as aristocrats from mere freemen. Indeed, there was no wall between the social strata – freemen could aspire to aristocratic status through their actions. Yet the problem was that local power was still linked to landholding. Due to fragmented landownership networks, these founders of *castelli* actually tended to have only partial control over them. Thus the castle in the Casentino may have been a political symbol, and it was more often than not an isolated aristocratic residence, but significantly they were rarely population centres and their demographic effect was negligible. As Chris Wickham concludes '[*castelli*] were simply small additions to a continuing network of dispersed settlement' and '*incastellamento* as a population movement had so far little effect on the zone'.[83] The Casentino had numerous lords who did not try to force people into their *castelli*. The castles had a function as a political symbol and an expression of social status, but were not major economic centres shown elsewhere.[84]

In the late Middle Ages, however, this settlement structure changed. In contrast to a largely dispersed settlement pattern between the eleventh and thirteenth centuries, by 1427 around two-thirds of the houses were located in concentrated villages in the Casentino Valley (see Table 3.1). Through the fifteenth and sixteenth centuries this proportion likely increased to levels closer

80 Molducci, 'L'incastellamento dei conti Guidi'; Bargiacchi, 'I castelli dei conti Guidi'.

81 Bargiacchi, 'I conti Guidi e l'incastellamento'.

82 Cortese, 'L'incastellamento nel territorio di Arezzo'.

83 Wickham, *Mountains and the city*, 269–306, q. 300.

84 Settia, *Castelli e villaggi*, 258–68; Fiumi, *Storia economica e sociale di San Gimignano*, 28–111.

to 75 per cent.[85] In the 1427 *catasto* houses were often recorded as clustered around central *corte* or *piazze*, and often explicitly located inside the castle walls. It appears the fourteen and fifteenth centuries were particularly important for coherent village formation in the Casentino Valley, despite the fact that these mountain communities had to deal with bouts of pestilence and plague and increasing urban taxation and encroachment from Florence. For example the settlement of Marciano was recorded in a Florentine inspection of Aretine *castelli* in 1385 as having castle walls but only 12 'malcontent' residents.[86] By 1427 it had 35 households which could mean as many as 160 inhabitants. Although this may partially have been down to some level of population increase, more likely it was caused by the restructuring of scattered settlement, as families began to orientate themselves into larger concentrated villages. Possibly the breakdown of other settlements such as Contra, which became a dispersed assortment of *poderi* leased by the monastery of Camaldoli, prompted peasant-cultivators to converge on the villages.

Table 3.1 Concentrated settlements in the Casentino Valley, 1427

No. of houses	1546
No. of huts	308
Concentrated in a *castello* (%)	27
Houses in a concentrated village (%)	63
Dispersed or isolated houses (%)	37

Source: ASF, Catasto, nos. 179–81, 246, 250, 330.

Through the fifteenth and at least the first half of the sixteenth century these clusters of habitation likely became more concentrated and more populous, an argument supported by comparing the population figures from the 1427 *catasto* with a state census from 1552. Although some of the settlements cannot be compared (for example, Poppi has population figures for 1552, but did not appear in the *catasto*, while settlements such as Montecchio were recorded in 1427 but received no population figures for 1552), the table below shows a general trend towards the increased size of the villages of the Casentino.

85 For example 44 out of 60 houses in Moggiona in 1574 were inside castle walls; ASF, Corporazioni religiose soppresse dal Governo Francese, no. 39.

86 Pasqui (ed.), *Arezzo*, iii, no. 859. The poor state of Marciano may have been down to a series of exceptionally unfortunate harvests; see ASF, Diplomatico, Olivetani d'Arezzo, 8 August 1346.

Table 3.2 Population trends in the Casentino, 1427–1552

Settlements	Population, 1427	Population, 1552	Index of change (100 = same)
Pezza	50	39	78
Pratovecchio and Stia	693	865	125
Raggiolo	329	546	167
Banzena	63	187	297
Bibbiena	941	1472	156
Campi	131	301	230
Gello	203	161	79
Giona	36	46	128
Gressa	104	393	378
Marciano	158	161	102
Serravalle	63	264	419
Soci	256	94	37
Partina	122	300	246
Coffia	50	173	346
Ortignano	675	654	97
Romena	153	88	58
Strapetegnoli	54	124	230
Cetica (S. Agnoli)	599	872	146
Cetica (S. Pancrazio)	455	759	167
Garliano	261	538	206
Vado and Castello S. Niccolo	589	236	40
Total	**5985**	**8273**	**138**

Sources: ASF, Catasto, nos. 179–81, 246, 250, 330; BNF, Magliabechi, ii, 120.

Out of the villages for which comparable data is available, the population levels in 1552 appear to have been bolstered by more than a third of what they were in 1427. This contrasts with the slow recovery of settlement in the *contado*, where population only began to increase slowly again in the sixteenth century and did not reach its pre-Black Death level again until the mid-eighteenth century.[87] Not every settlement increased in size in the Casentino but, if anything, that supports the hypothesis for a general process of increased concentration in habitation throughout the late Middle Ages. Indeed those settlements in 1427 that were still scattered, or small hamlets in 1427 such as Pezza or Gello, became even smaller by the mid-sixteenth century, perhaps revealing a trend of movement away from these sites and into the concentrated market centres

[87] Najemy, *History of Florence*, 97.

such as Marciano, Pratovecchio or Bibbiena. Settlement in the Casentino only started to decline at the end of the sixteenth century in the context of a declining pastoral trade and the reappearance of severe pestilence.[88]

Late-medieval concentration of settlement in the Casentino Valley was linked to the close grouping of inhabitants around small market centres and points of production, which was stimulated by increased marketing of diverse products to satisfy increased urban and regional demand. Some of the settlements grew into flourishing small towns such as Poppi, which had grocery shops, bakeries, butchers, druggists, barbers, tailors, and cobblers.[89] In 1427 the Casentino already had an assortment of bakers, barbers, belt-makers, spice-sellers, blacksmiths, innkeepers, leather harness makers, doctors, notaries, millers, merchants, saddlers, shoemakers, soldiers, tailors, weavers, and weapons makers.[90] Fifteen per cent of those heads of household listed in the *catasto* were tradesmen, although the proportion could have been higher with job plurality; for example, Bartolo Rampino of 'unknown status' lived in Stia and had a shop there, while Antonio Cecco, 'peasant cultivator', had a smith's workshop in Marciano.[91] Houses and shops came to be increasingly huddled around the market centres, and by the late Middle Ages markets or fairs were in existence at Soci, Poppi, Pratovecchio, Stia, Strada, Porciano, Romena, Castel San Niccolò, and Bibbiena.[92]

In sum, a real divergence in the settlement resilience or vulnerability seems to have been established in the Tuscan countryside, especially in light of increased Florentine interference and encroachment in the late Middle Ages.

---

88 BNF, EB, 15, no. 2; ASF, Carte Strozziane, i, no. 24. For pestilence in the early seventeenth century see BCP, 'Relazione della peste in Poppi nel 1630 e memorie della più distinte famiglie della stessa città scritta da Bernardo di Giuliano Lapini nel XVII secolo', no. 160. The only signs of economic decline in the Casentino are at the end of the sixteenth century; for example see the temporary outward migration to the Maremma in search of work in ASF, Pratica segreta, no. 174, fo. 1, no. 178, fos 5–6.

89 ASF, Decima granducale, no. 6852, fos 1–21v.

90 From my database of ASF, Catasto, nos 179–81, 246, 250, 330.

91 ASF, Catasto, no. 179, fos 417, 471.

92 For early evidence of markets see RC, i, nos 559–60, 705, ii, no. 1063. Later markets and fairs see ASF, Reale Arcispedale di Santa Maria Nuova, no. 474, fos 27r, 105r, no. 475, fos 86v, 78v–79r. Market centres with a distinctive triangular design have been dated to the fourteenth century such as Pratovecchio and Stia in Cherubini and Francovich, 'Forme e vicende degli insediamenti', 875.

Linking Settlement Resilience and Vulnerability with Resource Exploitation

The growth of Florence into a dominant city-state by 1300 had a great impact on the Tuscan countryside but as suggested above, the effects were by no means homogeneous. Why did the *contado* suffer from settlement contraction, abandonment, and outward migration towards the city, while other areas of Tuscany (such as the Casentino Valley) were able to withstand Florentine exploitative tendencies, and furthermore, even benefited from heightened urban demand for rural produce? In line with the general theoretical framework posited in Chapter 2, it is argued that this may have been connected to the particular strategies for resource management that either society employed. The settlement divergence seen in the late-medieval Tuscan countryside was connected to (a) different arrangements in the essential modes of exploitation and (b) different configurations of their economic portfolios.

Modes of Exploitation

It is often put forward by medievalists specializing in the late Middle Ages that the Black Death was a turning point in the fortunes of ordinary rural peasants vis-à-vis their traditional elite oppressors, seigneurial or feudal lords. The late Middle Ages did not bring any kind of increased political or economic freedom for rural inhabitants of the *contado*, however. In fact, the growth of Florence during the thirteenth century, and the consolidation of its territorial power in the centuries thereafter, led to quite the opposite – a retraction in the basic economic freedoms of rural producers. As described above, the city-state of Florence acted similarly to an extractive feudal lord, using its financial and jurisdictional power to deplete the countryside of resources.[93]

The restrictions on the rural population to choose their own economic path was linked to the malfunctioning factor markets (in labour, credit, and capital), which encouraged urban landlords to install onerous sharecropping regimes in the countryside. Serfdom had disappeared from the *contado* by the thirteenth century so urban landlords could not invoke extra-economic coercion,[94] and the fourteenth-century population decline caused by plague and fiscal oppression prevented the emergence of large tenant farms of the sort seen in Lombardy due to restricted availability of wage labour.[95] Consequently, urban landlords rearranged their lands into compact farms (*poderi*) and forced households to

93 Epstein, 'Town and country', 466–9.

94 Jones, 'From manor to mezzadria', 211–4. See the thirteenth-century Florentine legislation against serfdom in one village community in ASF, Provvisioni Registri, no. 4, fo. 78.

95 On the situation in Lombardy see Chittolini, 'Alle origini delle 'grandi aziende''.

work on them in sharecropping contracts (*mezzadria*).[96] Occasionally, *poderi* were leased on fixed terms to rural 'middlemen', who then re-leased the farms on sharecropping contracts to peasant families.[97] *Poderi* and sharecropping was not just a phenomenon in the Florentine *contado* but appeared in the hinterlands of towns and cities across Marche, Umbria and Emilia.[98] These farms included all the buildings needed to run the enterprise: huts, barns, furnaces, stables, dovecotes, wells, and cellars.[99] *Poderi* were not always entirely new constructions however; many were simply adapted pre-existing *curtes*, demesnes, or even *castelli*.[100]

The lack of labour made sharecropping the obvious solution for urban landlords who wanted a supply of food in order to be more self-sufficient, did not want to be involved in the direct demands of farming, and did not want to be too concerned with supervision.[101] The rural inhabitants of the *contado*, lacking both capital and access to credit, had to accept their fate as sharecroppers. Indeed, credit markets in the *contado* were local and isolated, forcing peasants to contract debts with their landlords, increasing their susceptibility to expropriation.[102] Wealthy urban citizen, Bongianni Gianfigliazzi, had 22 identifiable *poderi* in the *contado*, and this was by no means exceptional.[103] The Medici family by the sixteenth century had consolidated enormous stretches of land in the close rural hinterlands.[104] Florentine administration backed up acquisition with oppressive legislation, freezing wages, setting high food prices and blocking labour movement.[105] It was even the duty of some of the tenant families to physically carry the portion of produce destined for the urban landlords to Florence.[106] The tenant households working the sharecropping farms faced a number of imposed

---

96 A massive literature of which the best is probably Klapisch-Zuber, 'Mezzadria e insediamenti rurali'.

97 Emigh, 'Mystery'.

98 Epstein, 'Peasantries of Italy', 91.

99 Stopani, *Medievali 'Case da Lavoratore'*, 19; Biasutti, *Casa rurale nella Toscana*, 14.

100 Comba, 'La dispersione dell'habitat'; 'Le origini medievali', 386; Jones, 'From manor to mezzadria', 228.

101 See the debate between two well-known scholars in Epstein, 'Tuscans and their farms'; 'Moral hazard'; Galassi, 'Tuscans and their farms'.

102 On the lack of credit see Hopcroft and Emigh, 'Divergent paths', 15–6; Botticini, 'A tale of benevolent governments', 170; Zuijderduijn, *Medieval capital markets*, 242–6. On the link between lack of credit and sharecropping see Ackerberg and Botticini, 'Choice of agrarian contracts', 242. On personal bonds and risks of expropriation see Emigh, 'Loans and livestock', 714.

103 Piffanelli, 'Sustanze e beni nel contado fiorentino', 14.

104 Nanni, 'Lorenzo agricolture'; Maria Pult Quaglia, 'Aspetti della proprietà fiorentina'.

105 Van Bavel, 'Markets for land', 524; Cohn, 'After the Black Death'.

106 Jones, 'Florentine families', 195.

restrictions – tenants were even gaoled for speaking disrespectfully to their landlords.[107] Evictions were frequent and tenant turnover was high.[108] What characterised the modes of exploitation in the *contado* was the complete lack of flexibility and choice.

The situation was quite different in the Casentino Valley and much of the northern and eastern mountain regions of the *distretto* at large. Sharecropping was not unknown in the *distretto*, particularly in the fifteenth century, although it was not the dominant mode of exploitation as in the *contado*. Large ecclesiastical institutions such as the monastery of Camaldoli did create a series of *poderi*, essentially subdivided former granges and *curtes*, although these were usually leased out on fixed terms (usually three years) and rents were fixed pre-agreed amounts rather than percentages of surplus.[109] In 1427 the monastery of Camaldoli was a strong community of around 300 monks and lay brothers, and so it made sense to adapt the rents from the *poderi* to whatever the monastery needed the most.[110] In the fifteenth and sixteenth centuries, tenants paid in combinations of cash, piles of wood, grain, legumes, eggs, bread, chickens, beans, oil, pork, and even a few days' labour on the monastery's demesnes.[111] In complete contrast to the declining rents shown by David Herlihy on the *poderi* of Impruneta in the *contado* (where landlords lowered the amounts to attract tenants), the rents on the Casentinese *poderi* increased between the middle of the fourteenth and the end of the fifteenth century, indicative of a buoyant economy and population. For example, the Castaldo Benedenti for the '*Podere Cutrino*' at Monte paid Camaldoli a rent of 110 *staia* of grains and 25 *staia* from his vineyards and orchards in 1349 but in 1481 the rent was 188 *staia* of grains, 300 pounds of pork, 2 chickens, a pair of capons, 200 eggs and a cell of wood – a significant increase even when accounting for inflation.[112] The number of *poderi* also increased substantially; Camaldoli had just six documented in 1328 but over 30 by the onset of the sixteenth century. Using this system, the monastery of Camaldoli went from strength to strength in the late Middle Ages, curious given the general decline in monasteries in Central Italy at this time.[113] Camaldoli sold off land during hard times but this was more a policy of efficient economic organisation rather than true bouts of crisis: giving up distant peripheral lands at Borsemulo in 1319, where profits were insufficient

---

107 McArdle, *Altopascio*, 167.

108 Caiati, 'The peasant household', 124–5.

109 ASF, Camaldoli, nos 117–8, 136, 183, 589, 935; ASF, Corporazioni religiose soppresse dal Governo Francese, no. 39, fo. 7r.

110 ASF, Camaldoli, no. 191, fo. 255v.

111 Jones, 'A Tuscan monastic lordship'.

112 ASF Camaldoli, no. 117, fo. 123; no. 136, fo. 4.

113 On monastic decline see Cipolla, 'Une crise ignorée'; Herlihy, 'Church property', 98. Debated in Chittolini, 'Un problema aperto'; Stumpo, 'Problema di ricerca'.

to make it worthwhile.[114] More frequently, the monastery leased out distant lands, for example in Romagna.[115] Camaldoli thrived while its Benedictine neighbour towards Arezzo, S. Fiora, was reduced to a handful of monks in the late thirteenth century, caught in a culture of debt and owing money to Aretine banks and citizens of Florence.[116]

What was most striking about modes of exploitation in the Casentino Valley in contrast to the *contado* was the great variety and flexibility in the tenurial structures. The mountain regions of Tuscany have generally been painted as rather 'backward' and conservative places; little 'feudal enclaves' where manors and serfdom lingered on well into sixteenth century under the influence of ecclesiastical institutions or lay aristocratic families such as the Guidi or Ubertini.[117] Such a picture is only half true. Demesne agriculture did continue in some places all the way into the sixteenth century such as at the mountain village of Moggiona where customary labour works were performed.[118] However, these demesnes did not resemble anything like the classic bi-partite estates seen in Northern Europe during the high Middle Ages.[119] Most of the demesnes in the Tuscan *distretto* were small, customary labour was not particularly onerous, and *corvées* were more symbolic than having any economic significance.[120] Actually between the fourteenth and sixteenth centuries in the eastern mountains of Tuscany, there were a great variety in tenurial forms, some fixed ancient rents based more on custom and fidelity, alongside newer tenancies more linked to the market value of the land and paid in cash or kind.[121] Indicative of this flexibility in modes of exploitation was the constant and rapid switching between direct and indirect agricultural management. For example, one *podere* in the mountain village of Monte was worked by a former *castaldo* (lay brother) as a tenant in 1328, in 1332 it returned back to the monks of the hermitage at Camaldoli, and then in 1334 it once again was worked by the same tenant, the former *castaldo* Benuccio.[122]

---

114 Mittarelli and Costadoni (eds), *Annales Camaldulenses*, ix, no. 271.

115 ASF Camaldoli, no. 590, fos 53, 56v, 137v, 138v.

116 Grossi, *Le abbazie benedettine*, 114–25; Penco, *Storia del monachesimo*, 430. Also ASA, S. Fiora, no. 704; Pasqui (ed.), *Arezzo* , ii, no. 481.

117 For example see Baldari and Farina, 'Il Casentino'.

118 ASF, Camaldoli, no. 183, fo. 13.

119 Cherubini, 'Aspetti della proprietà fondiaria', 5; Jones, *Italian city-state*, 72–4.

120 For extent of demesne between 1000 and 1250 see RC, i, nos 50, 106, 153, 170, 266, 376, 503, 535, ii, no. 713, iii, no. 1231; Pasqui (ed.) *Arezzo* , i, no. 169; Manaresi (ed.), *I placiti del 'regnum Italiae'*, i, 373. For the light obligations see an inventory in RC, ii, nos 724, 750. For symbolism of labour works see Jones, 'An Italian estate', 30.

121 Increasingly in kind from the 1200s onwards in Tuscany; Kotel'nikova, 'Rendita in natura'.

122 ASF, Camaldoli, no. 117, fos 123–43.

In mountain areas such as the Casentino Valley, the diverse tenurial structure meant local people could be tenant farmers or (less frequently) sharecroppers on *poderi*, they could cultivate their own lands, exploit the common woodlands and pastures, or work as wage labourers or as customary tenants on demesnes. Increasingly in the *contado*, the options were sharecropping, migration, or hunger.

Economic Portfolios

The increased economic integration of late-medieval Florence and its *contado* only served to limit and restrict the pool of economic activities that could be performed in this close rural hinterland. Paolo Malanima suggested the limited number of economic activities (for example a lack of proto-industries) in the *contado* was explained by the fact that *mezzadria* and proto-industry were incompatible.[123] Judith Brown refined this argument slightly by suggesting instead that it was the precise combination of mixed cropping on labour intensive activities such as viticulture that simply left no time for industrial side-projects.[124] As Brown also remarked however, the lack of economic diversity probably was sown before the dissemination of *mezzadria*, in the general demographic crisis of the fourteenth century. Urban investors and landlords saw no reason to set up rural industries in the *contado* because of the absence of a ready labour pool, made worse by the fact that landlords simply adapted the sizes of their farms to whatever household structure and availability of labour was present.[125] There was simply no incentive for rural craft occupations and industries to develop in the *contado*, which had a circular effect in stimulating further demographic and settlement contraction. Those rural inhabitants who did not fit into a sharecropping family or were unsuccessful sharecroppers had little choice but to migrate to the city.

In some of the mountain regions outside of the *contado*, the situation was completely different. Even before 1300, inhabitants and institutions of the Casentino Valley followed quite diverse economic portfolios, based mainly around a subsistence economy.[126] Peasants practised a mixed pattern of cultivation and small-scale silvo-pastoral farming, some cheese and wine was produced, and mountain dwellers were particularly reliant on the consumption of chestnuts, which were high in protein.[127] The growth of Florence during the thirteenth century and its increased contact with the *distretto* during the

123 Malanima, *La decadenza*, 66, 88.

124 Brown, "Economic decline' of Tuscany', 110–11.

125 Van Bavel, 'Markets for land', 523.

126 Wickham, *Mountains and the city*.

127 The chestnut was a key food resource across most of the Apennines. Cherubini, 'La 'civiltà' del castagno'; Andreolli, 'Formule di pertinenza e paesaggio'; Zagnoni, 'La

fourteenth and fifteenth centuries only served to widen the range of economic activities performed in the region – though individual households themselves became more specialised in their production.[128] Certainly from 1300 onwards (and perhaps beginning sometime in the 1200s), a wide range of products and goods were being sold in concentrated villages crystallising around local market centres, catering for the rise in Florentine demand (particularly since Florence could not get certain products from its *contado*, given the limitations discussed above).

Pastoral farming, in particular, became more commercially orientated in the late Middle Ages.[129] The suggestion this may have begun as early as the thirteenth century is indicated by the existence of some extremely large flocks: in 1239 in the eastern mountains, the Gualdrada family inherited 4,600 sheep, cattle, and goats, after the assets of the aristocratic Guidi family had been subdivided.[130] Through the fourteenth and fifteenth centuries, the Casentino Valley became so renowned for larger-scale pasturing that people from outside the area began to periodically graze their animals there too. In 1419, one Florentine put 600 sheep on Camaldoli's pastures, in that year narrowly more than the monastery itself.[131] These rights of grazing came at a great cost, since Camaldoli charged high cash rents for such privileges. In the same valley, over half of the inhabitants had access to animals, and a third had sheep, cattle or both.[132] For every five plots of arable recorded in the *catasto*, there were four plots of either pasture or woodland: an extremely high ratio of cultivated to grazing land.[133] In some places there were even more pasture and woodland plots than arable, for example double in the higher areas of Raggiolo and Ortignano, and that is without even considering any land held in common.[134] Furthermore institutions such as Camaldoli began to organise pasture into coherent blocks such as the 12-hectare unit at Campo

coltivazione del castagno'. Small wooden huts appeared in the forest for storage of chestnuts; Balducci, 'La dimora silvo-pastorale appenninica', 305–6.

128 A number of different mountain activities are described in Cherubini, 'Risorse, paesaggio et utilizzazione agricola'; 'Paesaggio agrario, insediamenti'; 'La società dell'Appennino', 130–31; *Una comunità dell'Appennino*; 'La società dell'Appennino settentrionale (sec. 13–15)'.

129 In contrast to the view that pastoral farming was a 'traditional subsistence economy' in the eastern mountains argued in Herlihy and Klapisch-Zuber, *Tuscans*, 121.

130 Davidsohn, *Storia di Firenze*, i, 1157.

131 Jones, 'A Tuscan monastic lordship', 180.

132 Database compiled from ASF, Catasto, nos 179–81, 246, 250, 330.

133 ASF, Catasto, no. 179, fos 257r–315r, no. 180, fos 331r–350v, 410v–416v, 371r–405r, 223r–248v, 627–688, no. 250, fos 449r–481r, 338v–365r, no. 246, fos 331r–354v.

134 ASF, Catasto, no. 180, fos 627–688, no. 179, fos 161–252.

Drezzale at Serravalle or the 10-hectare unit they created at Siepi by 1576.[135] Demand for pasture was so high that Camaldoli leased out all of its meadows at Asqua in 1515 to local farmers.[136]

The commercialised pastoral economy of the late-medieval Casentino was supported by the emergence of long-distance transhumance – the seasonal and organised movement of animals from one grazing location to another. The lay *signorie* and large institutions saw they could profit from this development, enticing inhabitants into the system by offering transit rights and better regulation of grazing.[137] In 1419 it was noted that animals from the Casentino arrived en masse to the winter pastures by the coast of the Maremma, and a permanent economic link between the two regions was thereby crystallised in the fifteenth century.[138]

The new pastoral economy supported a flourishing local production of woollen cloth in the area.[139] Tuscan towns had for a long time marketed country-made cloth, though this was something that the Florentine administration actually came to resent for they wanted to preserve this activity as a solely urban preoccupation.[140] During the late fifteenth and early sixteenth centuries, concerted attempts were made to control production of Casentinese cloth and its marketing.[141] A vital piece of evidence for this notion was the concern of the urban guild of Prato in 1541 about the increasing volume of woollen cloth introduced into the city and made in the Casentino.[142] The Prato guild eventually forbade the introduction of Casentinese cloth except through fairs, despite the fact Casentinese merchants had always sold products in that town and at Impruneta.[143] Nonetheless we have evidence of a large sale to a merchant from Bologna in the thirteenth century and by 1400 Florentine citizens were doing the same, despite increasing restrictions put on Casentinese cloth by the city.[144] There were many instances of evasion of the restrictions imposed on Casentinese cloth.[145] By the beginning of the sixteenth century shops with looms and dying

135 ASF, Camaldoli, no. 183, fo. 114v; ASF, Corporazioni religiose soppresse dal Governo Francese, no. 39, fo. 9.

136 ASF, Camaldoli, no. 123, fo. 173.

137 Cherubini, 'La società dell'Appennino settentrionale', 133.

138 Imberciadori (ed.), 'Il primo statuto della dogana', 123–4.

139 Della Bordella, *L'arte della lana*, 59–131.

140 Kotel'nikova, 'La produzione dei panni di lana'; Cherubini, 'Risorse, paesaggio', 103.

141 Malanima, *La decadenza*, 154.

142 ASF, Pratica segreta, no. 157, fos 58v–64v.

143 ASF, Arte della Lana, no. 15, fos 54v–55r, 79r–81r.

144 ASA, Fondo di Murello, no. 1269, fo. 7; Melis, *Aspetti della vita economica medievali*, i, 536–7.

145 Benadusi, *A provincial elite*, 88.

equipment were appearing right along the banks of the Arno River.[146] It was only at the end of the sixteenth century that cloth production declined in the Casentino, as was a general trend for Tuscany.[147]

The growth of the pastoral economy stimulated by the demand from cities such as Florence encouraged the emergence of local rural elites converging around the small market villages. From mediocre origins in the fifteenth century, a band of wool manufacturers, artisans, shopkeepers, notaries and petty landowners became a local ruling elite in Poppi by the mid-sixteenth century.[148] These families used the burgeoning commercial production of wool to establish strangleholds over local administrative positions and politics, and when the wool trade declined at the end of the sixteenth century, these local elites instead resorted to land concentration and accumulation.[149] Families from lowly backgrounds achieved success very quickly, establishing their enterprises in the heart of villages and marketing their produce in the same centres. Indeed through the *catasto* we can plot the emergence of a local well-to-do, owning multiple houses, and differentiated from the rest by the high quantities of cattle and sheep they possessed. By 1590, one Valerio Cascesi had accumulated 16 wool shops in the Casentino.[150]

The commercialisation of the Casentino and the marketing of produce was not limited to the pastoral economy however. Six of the ten wealthiest inhabitants of the Casentino in 1427 were 'other sorts' of tradesmen – not necessarily aristocrats.

One of the most important activities in the late-medieval Casentino Valley was not only the production of iron as a raw material using the many mills and foundries powered by the fast-flowing Arno River, but also the manufacture of finished products out of the material.[151] Two fifteenth century account books belonging to two ironworkers, Deo di Buono da Tracorte and his son Giovanni da Stia, provide a fantastic insight into this commercialised activity, and the relationship between iron production and manufacture of weapons, tools and

---

146 BNF, Magliabechi, no. 359, *Descrizione delle cose più essenziali e relevanti del Casentino con diversi ragguagli delle famiglia e persone, scritto l'anno 1666 da Giuseppe di Scipione Mannucci*, 112.

147 Nonetheless both Stia and Poppi were still two of the most important cloth-producing locations in Tuscany as late as 1660, despite the decline; ASF, Misc. Medicea, no. 459.

148 Benadusi, 'Rethinking the state'; *A provincial elite*.

149 Benadusi, 'Ceti dirigenti locali'.

150 ASF, Decima granducale, no. 6852, fo. 200r.

151 In contrast to Pistoia and Pescia where iron had to be imported from Elba; Herlihy, *Medieval and Renaissance Pistoia*, 173–5; Brown, *In the shadow of Florence*, 107.

Table 3.3 Wealthiest 10 heads of household in the Casentino Valley, 1427

Head of household	Taxable fortune (florins)	Location	Occupation
Cristofano Battista	861	Bibbiena	Spice seller
Giovanni Antonio	622	Bibbiena	Unknown
Landino Francesco	550	Bibbiena	Spice seller
Giovanni Antonio	526	Stia & Pratovecchio	Belt-maker
Andrea Meo	505	S. Martino a Vado	Peddler (Merchant)
Piero Antonio	476	S. Martino a Vado	Smith
Franceschi Matteo	447	S. Niccolo a Vado	Smith
Stefano Giovannino	441	Stia & Pratovecchio	Peasant cultivator
Venturicci Niccolo	425	Bibbiena	Peasant cultivator
Nanni Niccolo	394	S. Maria in Castello	Peasant cultivator

Source: ASF, Catasto, nos 179–81, 246, 250, 330.

machinery.[152] The premises of the two men were clearly situated in the heart of villages and served a commercial purpose. Giovanni built himself a tavern near to a shop which had just been constructed in Porciano and he had a shop in the centre of Stia.[153] We are told that goods were sold at local fairs in Vado and other unspecified places, and at a local market in Pratovecchio.[154] A great variety of products were made from iron according to the books, in particular axes and saws used by local woodcutters. Some of the products were made using old iron bought from inhabitants in the valley, which was reworked into new objects. Interestingly the ironworkers did not rely on middlemen to provide them with the iron, for they were close enough to the foundries themselves to ensure consistent supplies.[155] Between January 13 1469 and June 9 1471, the duo received 1,118 pounds of iron from Biagio di Piero di Lorenzo di Stia. The fifteenth century was the peak of iron production in the valley and numerous sources record forges serving this purpose. Three iron forges located close to the river near Raggiolo were in the hands of the aristocratic Ubertini family in the

152 ASF, Reale Arcispedale di Santa Maria Nuova, nos 474–5. Attention brought to the source by De Angelis, 'Intorno all'attività di Deo di Buono'.

153 For the shop see ASF, Reale Arcispedale di Santa Maria Nuova, no. 474, fos 19r, 24r, 34r, 53r, 62r, 71r, 75r, 98r, 102r. For the tavern see *Idem*, no. 474, fos 79r, 87r, 94v, 113r, 124v, 143r.

154 For Vado see ASF, Reale Arcispedale di Santa Maria Nuova, no. 474, fo. 105r. For unspecified markets see *Idem*, no. 474, fo. 27r, no. 475, fo. 86v. For Pratovecchio see *Idem*, no. 475, fos 78v–79r.

155 The positions of the foundries is given in Barlucchi, 'La lavorazione del ferro'.

fourteenth century.[156] The significance of iron was highlighted in the books of Arezzo merchant, Lazzaro Bracci, who talked of the 'great iron of the Casentino' and how he had bought ample quantities from markets in Bibbiena.[157] Thus we see the close relationship between two commercialised enterprises in the valley: raw iron production and manufactured production of iron objects serving the needs of the local population but also sold in the market centres to meet regional and urban demand.

The number of mills in the Casentino increased in the fourteenth and fifteenth centuries, a sure sign of increasing commercialisation of production, and although many were associated with iron foundries, mills were needed for crushing grain and presses were needed for grapes and olives.[158] Seigneurial monopoly of the rights over mills was a trait common in much of Western Europe from the tenth century onwards, and the Casentino was no different in that regard. A pool of evidence shows various mills belonging to high-status seigneurial families. Commonly mills were rented to local inhabitants who then acted as millers for the communities close by. For example, Niccolo di Iacopo da Muglio rented a mill in Partina from the Guidi family for a period of two years in 1350, which allowed him the monopoly of milling activities not just for Partina but perhaps also Lierna and Ragginopoli.[159] The miller took a cut of the profits but provided 18 *staia* of grain to the Count every month, which amounted to 1 *staia* of grain (said to be approximately the total grain produced from 0.2 hectares of land) from every inhabitant of the three settlements mentioned per year.[160] Other mills were leased out by the Guidi in the fourteenth century in the Casentino, while Camaldoli did the same for its mills in Soci and Partina.[161]

Another significant commercial venture was the timber trade, as the Arno River allowed for the transportation of this produce. Lumber cut by saw mills in the area was put on rafts and floated down the river to buyers.[162] The monastery of Camaldoli was also prominent in the timber trade and offered a concession on 3,000 pieces of wood to Florentine Guiduccio Tolosini for 2,000 florins in 1317

[156] Bicchierai, *Il castello di Raggiolo*, 65–71.

[157] Melis, 'Momenti dell'economia del Casentino', 195–6. On the trading activities of Lazzaro Bracci in this area see Melis, 'Lazzaro Bracci'.

[158] A basic distribution for the Casentino is given in Muendel, 'The 'French mill'', 218. However there are more; Marignani, 'I mulini ad acqua della zona casentinese'.

[159] However in general, mills in the valley were tiny and numerous and difficult to monopolise for whole communities; Pappacio, 'I mulini e i porti'; 'Mulini, pescaie e porti'.

[160] Cherubini, 'La 'bannalità' del mulino', 225. Rent payment in grain by millers was apparently common in Tuscany; see Pampaloni (ed.), *Firenze al tempo di Dante*, nos 177–9.

[161] ASF, Notarile Antecosimiano, nos 92–4; ASF, Camaldoli, no. 125, fo. 55r, no. 136, fo. 1v.

[162] ASF, Reale Arcispedale di Santa Maria Nuova, no. 475, fos 81r–82v.

(normally they were 2,500 florins).[163] They also demanded some of their rents to be paid in wood on their *poderi* at Monte, Lonnano, Bucena and Contra.[164] Some wood was used locally by tradesmen however, who crafted tools out of beech and used it to heat their homes during long, hard winters.[165] The trade in wood from the forest also stimulated other local industries such as charcoal burning, an important resource for blacksmiths.[166] Raggiolo had a long history of close control over its communal woodland resources.[167] In the statutes for nearby Bibbiena, strong regulations were put on hunting activities in the nearby woodlands, and in particular the amount of game that could be made available for sale at urban markets.[168]

Casentinese wine was also highly prized and found a willing urban market. Of all the goods recorded in the assets of households in the *catasto*, barrels of wine were the most valuable, and the large number stored by some families indicates these were intended for sale.[169] Vineyards were very common in the valley and were generally the highest valued of all lands in the *catasto*. Unlike the fragmented pieces of arable and pasture, these were more often coherent units kept *in clausura* and formed part of an isolated *podere*, or alternatively were attached to the houses and walls of the concentrated *castelli*. Camaldoli also saw the commercial sense in producing good wine and kept vineyards in demesne well into the sixteenth century, such as the 'Vigna dei Romiti' at Pratovecchio.[170] Another commercial pursuit was the sale of bees and the production of honey. Hives were everywhere in the Apennines and the Casentino was no exception.[171] More affluent local families owned furnaces and produced mortar and roof tiles.[172] The monks of Camaldoli developed and distributed a number of different medicines and remedies from their pharmacy at the monastery.[173] Arezzo was a key market for leather from the thirteenth century onwards but leather was also bought by important Florentines such as the Datini Company. In a letter written to Giuliano di Tommaso of Poppi, they described a payment of 115 florins for

---

163 Cacciamani, *L'antica foresta di Camaldoli*, 56.

164 ASF, Camaldoli, no. 589, fo. 13.

165 Ciampelli, *Badia Prataglia*, 49–50; Zagnoni, 'Comunità e beni comuni', 18.

166 Seghi, *Alla macchia*.

167 Bicchierai, 'La lunga durata dei beni comuni'.

168 ASF, Statuti delle comunità autonome e soggette, Bibbiena (1373-1553), Rubrics XX, no. 79. With thanks to Cristina Arrigoni Martelli for making this source known to me.

169 Niccolo Nanni stored 70 barrels at his farm at S. Maria in Castello in ASF, Catasto, no. 179, fo. 67.

170 Jones, 'A Tuscan monastic lordship', 179.

171 ASA, Fondo di Murello, no. 1269, fo. 27r.

172 ASF, Decima granducale, no. 6852, fos 48r, 72r, 200r.

173 Cacciamani, 'L'antica farmacia di Camaldoli'.

the leather of revered 'hairy' buffaloes.[174] The leather trade also stimulated a host of local shoemaking businesses listed in the *catasto* and a register from a shoemaker from Poppi confirms his locally sourced leather.

The production of chestnuts, important from the twelfth century onwards, continued to have significance, and while this activity leaned more towards peasant self-sufficiency rather than market production, evidence suggests the activity became at least partially commercialised. Collecting chestnuts was a risky and difficult task which involved climbing trees. Many richer proprietors of the chestnut trees gave this work to day labourers and in the Casentino an owner paid men (often in kind) to collect and clean chestnuts ready for sale.[175] Another commercial activity in the Casentino was the 'growth industry' of wet-nursing and foster care of children from foundling homes in Florence. Other scholars have used the archives of urban charitable institutions to show the development of this micro-economy in the mountain regions to the east of Florence.[176] Castello San Niccolo in the Casentino was mentioned by 24 separate wet-nurses in documents of the *Ospedale degli Innocenti* in Florence, suggesting that institution had set up a network of contacts for this village.[177] Popular song lyrics frequently alluded to an association between the Casentino and wet-nursing.[178]

A final commercial activity undertaken in the Casentino in the late Middle Ages was trout fishing in the Arno River – trout was a food with a willing elite market in many parts of medieval Western Europe.[179] We know the frequency and scale of this activity thanks to Florentine legislation, concerned not only about losing food upstream but also poisoning of the river.[180] In 1450 the city threatened people of the Casentino with substantial fines if caught poisoning the river with lime and nut shells.[181] 'Priests, clerks or other religious lay brothers' were revealed as guilty parties, showing it was not the act of desperate peasants but organised efforts of large institutions like Camaldoli, who sold the fish at market. By the seventeenth century, fishing in the river by Stia and Poppi had been outlawed completely.[182] Florence grew increasingly restless as they failed to profit from diverse commercial ventures undertaken in the Casentino in the late Middle Ages.

---

174 Melis, 'Momenti', 196–7.

175 Cherubini, 'La civiltà', 274.

176 Klapisch-Zuber, 'Blood parents'; Takahashi, 'I bambini'; Trexler, 'Foundlings of Florence'.

177 Gavitt, *Charity and children*, 227.

178 Singleton (ed.), *Canti carnascialeschi*, nos 29, 94.

179 Hoffman, 'Economic development and aquatic ecosystems', 649–50.

180 Trexler, 'Measures against water pollution', 462–7.

181 ASF, Provvisioni Registri, nos 175–6.

182 Pignoni, *Bando, e prohibizione di non poter pescare*. Found in the BNF.

Property and Power

Thus far it has been suggested that the divergent settlement responses in the Tuscan countryside to increased (outside) urban encroachment and influence was linked to the different ways in which the two different societies in the *contado* and the *distretto* exploited their resources. In the *contado* the economic portfolios were entirely restricted and inflexible, and the modes of exploitation only benefited a select dominant elite group to the detriment of wider society. In the *distretto* in contrast, the economic portfolios were much broader and flexible, and the modes of exploitation allowed surplus to descend much further down the social hierarchy, benefiting a wider section of inhabitants. The question of course remains – why? In this section it is suggested in line with the general theoretical framework posited in Chapter 2 that the configurations of property and power were at the core and foundation of all social and economic development. In fact it is hypothesised that those societies (such as in the *distretto*) best equipped to fend off potential urban exploitation were made up of favourable configurations of property and power which were essentially egalitarian and flexible. Those societies vulnerable to urban exploitation (such as the *contado*) were made up of more inequitable and persistent configurations of property and power. The extent to which Florence was able to be a parasite or a stimulant to pre-industrial rural societies depended on (a) the distribution (and social distribution) of property in the countryside, and (b) the equilibrium of social interest groups in the countryside able to form a counter force (or not) to urban domination. Essentially, the deep arrangement of property and power in pre-industrial societies facilitated or limited the extent to which favourable or unfavourable strategies (and institutions) for resource exploitation could develop.

Contado

One of the main features of the Florentine *contado* in the late Middle Ages was its high level of economic polarisation, particularly with regard to the social distribution of landownership. From the fourteenth century onwards, wealthy Florentine burghers purchased large portions of land in the *contado*. This accumulation process was not a Tuscan phenomenon but occurred within many city-states all across late-medieval Northern and Central Italy.[183] Landownership in the countryside was one way urbanites could diversify their commercial

[183] Cherubini, 'La proprietà fondiaria'.

portfolio,[184] become more self-sufficient in food production,[185] and even assert a certain social prestige, as evidenced by the construction of residential villas in the second half of the fifteenth century.[186] Thus social distribution of land in the late-medieval *contado* became increasingly inequitable. By the time of the *catasto* in 1427, only 18 per cent of the land in the *contado* was owned by rural inhabitants, declining to 14 per cent by the end of the fifteenth century.[187] Taxable wealth (land, animals, surplus) in the *contado* was distributed highly unequally with a Gini index of 0.8.[188] The *catasto* is a good source for calculating Gini indexes because it seems to have included many households who did not own or have access to any taxable wealth, thus the poorest were included (even if they themselves did not pay tax). In some parishes such as Montecalvi, none of the rural households owned any land whatsoever.[189] In the town and territory of San Gimignano in 1332, over four-fifths of the inhabitants were described as poor or property-less.[190] Furthermore, over 60 per cent of the landowners there were townspeople.[191] Even ecclesiastical institutions accumulated land in the *contado* to the detriment of local peasants, as seen in many bitter disputes between the monastery of Settimo and inhabitants of S. Martino la Palma.[192] Impoverishment was intensified by continual urban expropriation which reduced common land to almost nothing through the course of the fourteenth century.[193]

The rural inhabitants of the *contado* were neither well-placed to counter urban acquisition of property in the countryside or the imposition of onerous jurisdictions or sharecropping regimes. In particular, rural inhabitants in the *contado* had very weak security on property rights, and urban courts tended to side with urban landowners and speculators.[194] The lack of liquid wealth in

---

184 Emigh, *The undevelopment of capitalism*, 128; Goldthwaite, *The building of Renaissance Florence*, 49–50.

185 Pinto, 'Coltura e produzione dei cereali', 283; Kotel'nikova, 'Artigiani-affittuari nelle città'.

186 Lillie, *Florentine villas*, 23–38; Gobbi Sica, *The Florentine villa*, 326. Scholars have suggested the noble lifestyle exhibited by the nouveaux riche in late-medieval Tuscany damaged commerce; Pinto, 'Honour and profit', 85.

187 Conti, *La formazione della struttura agraria moderna*, ii, 97–102, 395–411.

188 Taken from calculations using a database from Herlihy and Klapisch-Zuber (eds), *Census and property survey of Florentine domains*.

189 Van Bavel, 'Markets for land', 513.

190 Balestracci, 'Lavoro e povertà', 567.

191 Fiumi, *San Gimignano*, 140.

192 De la Roncière, 'A monastic clientele?', 62.

193 De la Roncière, 'Rentabilité, bien commun, écologie'.

194 Van Bavel, 'Markets for land', 507–8; 'Organisation and rise of land and lease markets', 29.

the countryside prevented villagers from calling upon legal aid to support their claims.[195] With no assets to fall back on, rural landowners were highly vulnerable to urban creditors, who looked to seize property from heavily indebted peasants.[196] Examples of extortion for sums not repaid can be found in the fifteenth-century documents.[197] Of those documented rural crimes which involved an urban party, 61 per cent were Florentine citizens prosecuting peasants who had violated their property rights in the mid-fourteenth century, increasing to 89 per cent by the mid-fifteenth century; in contrast, peasants prosecuting urban citizens went from 27 per cent of cases in 1344, but had disappeared entirely from record some 100 years later.[198] We have to take into account also the fact that rural landowners had to pay much higher rates of tax than urbanites with land in the countryside – heightening their vulnerability.[199]

Such insecurity in rural property structure in the Florentine *contado* was connected to the distorted alignment of power and political interests in the region. As early as the first decades of the twelfth century, a doctrine had already emerged suggesting that Florence had a legitimate claim to the countryside in its immediate environs.[200] Many of the closest rural communes were brought to heel by the city very quickly, such as Fiesole in 1125 and the *castrum* of Montebuoni in Impruneta in 1135.[201] Between the eleventh and thirteenth centuries, important rural nobles relocated from the *contado* to Florence (for example, the Medici moved to the city from the Mugello in the late twelfth century), but always retained patronage rights over the churches and monasteries, and connections in rural *borghi* of origin.[202] Ultimately, this meant that by the beginning of the fourteenth century, there was no alignment of local power structures in the *contado* able to stand up to Florentine jurisdictional, fiscal and landed encroachment. There were no rural interests standing in direct opposition to urban interests, simply because there was no sharp distinction made between rural and urban. The rural *signori* or *nobili* of the *contado* were, at the same time, urban citizens or burghers.[203] While in parts of medieval Flanders, for example, strong oppositions grew up between powerful interest groups such as the urban guilds, territorial lords, and seigneurial lords (cultivating a real rural–urban opposition), the interest groups of Florence and the *contado* were one and the

195 Osheim, 'Countrymen and the law'.

196 Emigh, 'Forms of property rights or class capacities?', 40 ; Polica, 'An attempted 'reconversion' of wealth'.

197 For example ASF, Provvisioni Registri, no. 109, fos 61–2.

198 Cohn, 'Criminality and the state'.

199 Cohn, *Creating the Florentine State*, 71–81.

200 Santini (ed.), *Documenti dell'Antica Costituzione del Comune di Firenze*, nos 1–2.

201 Davidsohn, *Forschungen zur älteren Geschichte von Florenz*, i, 358, 392–6, 416.

202 Brucker, *Florence, the Golden Age*, 28; Bertelli, *Il potere oligarchico*, 47–8.

203 A similar point made for Luccan countryside; Wickham, *Community and clientele*.

same.[204] As the ratio of rural to urban magnates declined through the 1300s, it became increasingly impossible to tell whether a baronial family was of 'rural' or 'urban' origin, and even the notion of 'gentility' came to be seen as an urban concept, linked to city residence and citizenship.[205] This bond between city and countryside was reinforced by a network of landed and patrimonial relationships and the very fact that, despite the rise of Florence as an international commercial hub, Florentine economic fortunes were still undoubtedly tied up in agrarian interests.[206] The lack of strong oppositional rural interest groups and the lack of autonomy for rural inhabitants to pursue their own economic interests facilitated the late-medieval Florentine encroachment into the rural *contado*.[207] There was not even feudal resistance from ecclesiastical powers, since Florentine bishops had already sown the seeds of their expansion of rural estates in the eleventh century – eventually developing them by the thirteenth century into territorial lordships which became the very rural communes that facilitated Florence's control of its *contado*.[208]

Distretto: The Casentino Valley

The rise of Florence did not create the same deep polarising effects in the *distretto* as in the *contado*. While Florentine jurisdiction increasingly extended out into the distant mountains by the fifteenth century, urban landownership did not follow suit. Samuel Cohn, working on a large number of notarial charters to trace the workings of the Florentine land market, found almost no mention of urban landownership in the Apennines to the east and north.[209] In fact much of the land in the *distretto* remained in the hands of rural inhabitants throughout the late Middle Ages.[210] In the Casentino over half of the households recorded in 1427 were local cultivators who owned their own land (scattered plots), and over three-quarters of the population lived in their own houses (i.e. not rented).[211] Approximately 35 per cent of the land was in the hands of ecclesiastical institutions, the monastery of Camaldoli being one of the largest landowners in

---

204 Blockmans, 'Stadt, Region und Staat'; Nicholas, 'Town and countryside'.

205 Jones, *Italian city-state*, 280, 300–301. Linked to this was the cult of chivalry and courtly life as described in Larner, 'Chivalric culture in the age of Dante', 120.

206 Jones, *Economia e società nell'Italia medievale*, 44, 345; Hoshino, 'Per la storia dell'arte della lana', 49.

207 Aymard, 'From feudalism to capitalism', 191.

208 Dameron, *Episcopal power*, 45, 69, 195; Conti, 'Le proprietà fondiarie del vescovado di Firenze'.

209 Cohn, *Creating the Florentine state*, 22–4.

210 Epstein, 'Peasantries of Italy', 89.

211 ASF, Catasto, nos 179–81, 246, 250, 330.

the region.[212] Forty-five per cent of the land belonged to either local tradesmen or peasant farmers, 15 per cent belonged to rural nobles, while only a very tiny remainder was in the hands of urbanites (and these were mainly Aretine, not Florentine). Accordingly the distribution of taxable wealth in 1427 was highly equitable: a Gini index of 0.58 (in comparison to 0.8 in the *contado*). The peasant-owner property structure of the Tuscan mountains remained stable well into the early modern period. For example, in the mountain village of Moggiona in 1576, less than 1 hectare out of a total 323 belonged to a Florentine owner.[213] The Gini index for distribution of land in the same village and year was 0.55 (and 0.46 when removing ecclesiastical institutions; 0.42 when removing ecclesiastical institutions and 'outsiders'). High peasant property-ownership was not solely characteristic of the Casentino Valley either, for in other parts of the *distretto* smallholders held as much as 85 per cent of the land.[214]

It is difficult to discern whether the lack of Florentine accumulation of land in the *distretto* was down to a lack of incentive or a general inability. However, there were more barriers to land polarisation in the mountains than exhibited in the *contado*. A basic issue may have just been distance: land acquired in the mountainous *distretto* was simply too far to be able to administer easily. An argument purely on distance is dubious however, when one considers that the area around Pisa became dominated by Florentine landowners looking to exploit the fertile plains for grain production and to control trade through the coastal ports.[215] Pisa was further away from Florence than, for example, the Casentino. Furthermore, it has been shown that transportation costs between the Casentino and Florence were not prohibitively high, for account books suggest the costs of bringing 100 pounds of wool from Poppi to Florence was just 4 per cent of the cost of the wool.[216] In that case the lack of incentive for urban land acquisition in the *distretto* may have had something to do with the poor fertility of the soils. The climate and soils supported a wide range of crops in the eastern mountains, although not high yields in anything.[217] Furthermore the heavy clays and steep slopes were unsuited for medieval cultivation techniques. Probably more

212 ASF, Catasto, no. 191, fo. 235v.

213 ASF, Corporazioni religiose soppresse dal Governo Francese, no. 39, fo. 172.

214 Cherubini et al., 'La proprietà fondiaria in alcune zone del territorio senese'. Also high peasant landholding recorded at Val di Cecina and the Valdarno in ASF, Catasto, nos 116–7, 886.

215 Epstein, 'Market structures', 94; Chittolini and Fasano Guarini, 'Citta soggette e contadi nel dominio fiorentino'; Mallett, 'Pisa and Florence', 432. Pisan country folk strongly opposed Florentine encroachment; Luzzati, 'I contadini e la guerra di Pisa'.

216 Brown, ''Economic decline' of Tuscany', 110.

217 Modern statistics suggest very low crop yields but it is always dangerous to equate modern soils with medieval ones; Barbieri, *Memoria illustrativa della carta della utilizzazione del suolo*, 24.

important, however, was that the amount of cultivable land in the northern and eastern mountains of Tuscany was much smaller than in the plains and hills closer to Florence. The valleys and slopes were often densely covered in ancient forests, and if any prospective Florentine burgher had hopes of constructing a series of sharecropping farms this far out, there was a good chance they would first have to chop a lot of trees down. In other areas of northern Italy such as the Po Valley, cities and towns offered favourable concessions to new colonists to drain marshes and cut down trees for arable and vineyards, but given the significant demographic downturn in the Florentine *contado*, it is difficult to see where Florentine landlords could have mobilised manpower for this task.

Furthermore, it was not just the physical task of cutting down trees which dissuaded potential Florentine investors and landowners: many of the forests in the *distretto* were protected by highly valued common rights. Such was the reliance on woodland that hardly any attempt was made to cut down trees for arable or settlement. In the Casentino Valley in 1279, even the Prior of Camaldoli was forbidden to cut wood to repair houses of the hermitage without first consulting the wider monastic community.[218] These sorts of restrictions were still well in use some 300 years later, as a series of charters between 1563 and 1575 strictly forbade the monks of Camaldoli to cut down trees in the forest without first consulting the local communities and the monastery.[219] The increasing use of charters in the late Middle Ages to regulate pastoral resources in a more formalised manner has been noted for other mountain regions of Italy.[220]

Grazing rights in the mountains also were rigorously guarded, as seen for the mountain community of Raggiolo in the sixteenth century, where a cap of 2,000 was put on the number of animals that could pasture in the forests of the commune.[221] One area of the forest was marked out as 'banned' and a charge was levelled on any unwanted animals found there, while an area known as the '*pastura di Prata*' in 1545 was reserved only for animals belonging to Raggiolo villagers.[222] The forested slopes around Pratovecchio became a contested space, serving as a meeting place for the people of Raggiolo, Carda, Calletta, Cetica and Garliano to discuss their grazing arrangements and the boundaries involved.[223] In a mountain area further north of the Casentino, on the Tuscany-Romagna border, the aristocratic Alberti family had to resolve a point of contention between two communities (Baragazza and Castiglione) over the territorial boundaries of the

218 Mittarelli and Costadoni (eds), *Annales Camaldulenses*, vi, no. 242.

219 ACC, Atti Capitolari, no. 156, fos 3r, 5r, 14v, 18r–19r, 21r, 25v, 36r, 43r, 45r–50r, 54r–60r, 68r–69r, 76r, 84r–87r, 95r.

220 Casari, 'Emergence of endogenous legal institutions'.

221 For management of commons at Raggiolo see ASF, Notarile Antecosimiano, nos 9495–7.

222 ASF, Statuti delle comunità autonome e soggette, no. 696, fos 49r–50v, 18v, 34v.

223 Bicchierai, *Una comunità rurale toscana*, 86–7.

commons.[224] The importance and stability of common resources in areas of the *distretto* may have provided further difficulties for Florentine land acquisition – acting as an important rural 'layer' or 'barrier' to urban encroachment. Villages and institutions clung on tightly to their highly guarded communal rights over pastures and forests, preventing both sales to private parties and assarting of new land.

The lack of urban expropriation, the preservation of peasant-farmer property structures, and the effective long-term maintenance of collective management of resources was linked to the balanced equilibrium of social interest groups participating in the region. Indeed, although Florence slowly extended its jurisdiction further into the *distretto* during the fourteenth and fifteenth centuries, it was a process not without its problems, and furthermore, Florence probably did not exert the sort of dominant authority it would have liked (particularly when taken in comparison with the *contado*). Valley communities such as the Valdinievole to the west of Florence enjoyed extended periods of independence from urban territorial subjection,[225] while the Alpi Fiorentine to the northeast experienced almost permanent fiscal and corporate exemptions.[226] It was exceedingly difficult to penetrate the assorted layers of power and jurisdictions in the distant mountains, where there existed a peculiar balance of seigneurial, territorial, ecclesiastical, communal, and village interests. Illustrative of the tension between rural *signori* in the *distretto* and the commune of Florence is the wealth of material describing assaults on Florentine merchants passing through the Alpi degli Ubaldini.[227] The aristocratic families of the Guidi and Ubertini had land, jurisdictions and castles all over the mountains of Romagna and the Casentino (even though it was slightly checked by partible inheritance creating warring factions).[228] The Florentine administration strategically founded new towns and villages close to the Apennines to the north and east of the city, in order to compete in an area dominated by rebellious nobles.[229]

Some of the mountain communities were very strong, often aligning themselves with seigneurial interests in order to stave off rising Florentine

224 Abatantuono and Righetti, *I conti Alberti*, 232–3.

225 Calamari, 'La lega dei comuni di Valdinievole'.

226 Guasti (ed.), *I capitoli del comune di Firenze*, i, 89–90.

227 Villani, *Cronica*, i, 48–9, 203, 287–90, iii, 308–9, iv, 279–80, 289–90; Sterpos, 'Evoluzione delle comunicazioni transappenniniche', 13; Sacchetti, *Il libro del rime*, 225. Also Larner, 'Crossing the Romagnol Appennines'; Cherubini, 'Appunti sul brigantaggio'.

228 Sestan, 'I conti Guidi'; Casini, 'Minor rural aristocracy'; Rinaldi, 'Le origini dei Guidi'.

229 Osheim, 'Rural Italy',166; Francovich, Boldrini and Di Luca, 'Archeologia delle terre nuove'; Fabbri, *Statuti e riforme del comune di Terranuova*, intro.

interference.[230] The *signori* in turn recognised the benefits of keeping rural communities 'on-side', granting mountain villagers their own control over the operation and regulation of the forests.[231] In the mountains in the direction of Arezzo, villagers under the jurisdiction of the Ubertini suggested they enjoyed living 'in peace under the dominion of their true *signore*'.[232] Rural communities and seigneurial lords often teamed up in order to maintain control of settlements and territories. For example, in an episode of peasant insurrection in 1391 in Raggiolo, inhabitants of the village petitioned the troops of the aristocratic lords of Pietramala to assist them in regaining control of the village.[233] Life as feudal subjects to these lords was by no means perfect, but it was a lot better than the harsh rates of taxation they would have to pay to the Florentine administration. As it happened, the villagers regained their castle at Raggiolo, and although Florentine troops later exacted retribution by burning some of the village to the ground, the Florentine administration also realised the need for concession and compromise in these mountain areas – including a 5-year tax exemption for the villagers affected by the conflict.[234]

Lay aristocrats and villagers put up strong resistance to save their jurisdictions. Some villages were conceded to the Florentine administration in the mid-fourteenth century, such as Pratovecchio in 1343, Castel San Niccolo in 1348, or Bibbiena in 1359, but others took much longer to bring to heel.[235] The Palagio branch of the Guidi family in Stia only fell to Florentine administration in 1402, and Count Francesco Guido only lost the town of Poppi as late as 1440 because he made the error of aligning his interests with that of Filippo Maria Visconti, the Duke of Milan.[236] Furthermore, even where Florence did take control of settlements and territories in the mountains, there was always some tricky negotiation to consider. The aristocratic Ubertini family managed to save their jurisdictions over the villages of Chitignano, Rosina, and Taena in the late fourteenth century, by making tactical concessions elsewhere.[237] The balance of seigneurial and communal interests in parts of the *distretto* proved to be awkward obstacles for the Florentine state to overcome.

---

230 Pirillo, 'Il popolamento tra signorie territoriali'; Bicchierai, 'La signoria dei conti Guidi', 115.

231 Zagnoni, 'Comunità e beni comuni nella montagna'.

232 ASA, Diplomatico, pergamene e carte varie, no. 91. Also for the peasant *fideles* of the Ubertini and Guidi see Cohn, 'Demography', 200.

233 Indeed, the people of Raggiolo and the Guidi lords had a long history of cooperative treaties drawn up; De la Roncière, 'Fidélités, patronages, clientèles dans le contado florentin', 37.

234 Cohn, *Creating the Florentine state*, 125.

235 Pasqui (ed.), *Arezzo* , iii, no. 832.

236 Beni, *Guida del Casentino*, 250–51; Bicchierai, *Una comunità rurale toscana*, 13.

237 Cherubini, 'La signoria degli Ubertini'.

Conclusion

The demographic rise of Florence in the thirteenth century, and the crystallisation and expansion of its territorial domain in the fourteenth and fifteenth centuries had a great impact on the surrounding Tuscan countryside. These effects were not homogeneous, however: the extent to which they were 'positive' or 'negative' was dictated by the intrinsic arrangement of the rural societies themselves. In the *contado*, the lack of rural interest groups to stand up to dominant urban elites facilitated urban encroachment into the countryside. This contributed to a distorted property structure, whereby urban expropriation of country-dwellers' land was made easier by urban courts siding with urban landowners and speculators. The skewed property structure eventually lent itself to imperfections in other societal constellations: the disappearance of welfare systems such as the commons, the imposition of *mezzadria* to counter defective balances in factor markets (land, labour, capital), and the restricted economic portfolios which followed. All of these resource management strategies and institutional configurations which emerged in the *contado* heightened the vulnerability of rural society – epitomised in the mass exodus to the city in search of work, the contraction and abandonment of agricultural lands, and the vacated *castelli* and *casali* which were left behind.

In contrast, the balanced equilibrium of various social interest groups in the Casentino Valley of the more distant *distretto* acted as a shield against urban predations, and prevented easy urban encroachment and expropriation of rural dwellers' property. This was made more secure by the effective and durable functioning of the collective property systems – particularly in the forests. As a result this more balanced and equitable power and property structure gave inhabitants the incentive and freedom to install beneficial and adaptive institutions leading to heightened resilience. These included the high tenurial flexibility and modes of exploitation exhibited, but also the diverse economic portfolio, where surplus descended the social hierarchy. The resilience of the late-medieval Casentino in contrast to the *contado* can be identified in its crystallisation of the coherent village structure, lack of outward migration, quick recovery and stabilisation after the demographic nadir, a protection of the existing agricultural lands, and limited signs of farm abandonment and destruction.

Fitting the Findings into the Theoretical Framework

In this final section, the information taken from the comparative case study in late-medieval Tuscany is placed into the theoretical framework outlined in Chapter 2.

Property, Social Distribution of Property, and Power

In the Florentine *contado*, property was distributed unequally. In 1427, it exhibited a Gini index of 0.8 for taxable wealth; this is more than the 'polarised' mark of 0.75 set out in Chapter 2. Unfortunately, this Gini index was only possible for 1427, and thus it is difficult to make comparisons about the changeability of this figure over the long term. However, the general evidence for land transactions, transfer, and expropriation is overwhelming in the literature, and with that in mind is considered 'dynamic'. In contrast, the Casentino Valley in the Florentine *distretto* exhibited a more egalitarian distribution of property. A Gini index of 0.58 was calculated for taxable wealth from the 1427 Catasto; this is lower than the 0.65 mark set out in Chapter 2. Although not directly comparable, a Gini index of 0.55 for land distribution in a mountain village in the Casentino in 1576 suggests that this configuration was quite stable over the long term. Certainly there was no sign of consolidation or mass accumulation of land either by urbanites or within the stratifications of peasants themselves. However, indirect evidence from the literature does show a level of land transfer (both sale and donations), and it is unclear how important this was in a relative or a quantitative sense. With that in mind, an 'intermediate' figure of 0.5 is given for the 'dynamic-persistent' opposition.

The social distribution of landownership in the Florentine *contado* was clearly highly polarised. Only 18 per cent of the land in 1427 was in the hands of rural inhabitants, declining by the end of the fifteenth century to around 14 per cent. Furthermore, only 9 per cent of the land in 1427 was in the hands of local farmers or peasants, while urbanites held 60 per cent of the land. The change in social distribution of land is hard to discern with precise quantitative data over the long term – that is, from the fourteenth century into the early modern period. However, it is clear that a structural change happened in the social distribution of land in the late Middle Ages – quite different from what was apparent before 1300. The evidence for urban Florentine encroachment and consolidation is abundant, and for that reason, the social distribution of landownership can be assessed as 'dynamic'. The social distribution of property was quite different in the Casentino Valley. Almost no land in 1427 was in the hands of wealthy Florentines with the only urban landownership being less than 1 per cent and being of Aretine origin instead. Small peasant landownership was high at around 45 per cent of the total area, but the actual amount of land belonging to 'local' inhabitants or institutions was higher given the presence of local aristocrats and the great landowning monastery of Camaldoli. The figure of 45 per cent puts the Casentino Valley at an 'intermediate' status in terms of social distribution of landownership, and received a score of 0.5. The social distribution of land is harder to assess in terms of changeability, though evidence from select villages such as Moggiona at the end of the sixteenth century suggests the essential distribution of landownership did not undergo any significant changes (certainly nowhere near a 20 per cent shift) – and is therefore assessed as 'persistent'.

Power, as mentioned in Chapter 2, is assessed more qualitatively. In the *contado* it is clear there was an imbalance in the distribution of jurisdictions, rights, privileges, and access to institutions, and furthermore, there were no real strong rural interest groups able to counter the dominant urban ones – thus they were 'polarised'. Probably, however, this situation must also be classified as 'persistent', because the roots of this distorted alignment in political and power interests in the region were sown much earlier in the high Middle Ages when many of the rural communes were brought to heel very quickly by the feudal authority of the city. In contrast, power was distributed in a much more egalitarian manner in the Casentino Valley (as in many of the mountain regions to the north and east of Florence), where rights, privileges, and jurisdictions were shared and negotiated by a large number of different social groups. This situation was also quite changeable: in the eleventh to thirteenth centuries, jurisdictional battles were taking place between territorial lords such as the Bishop of Arezzo and the local seigneurial lords such as the Guidi. Monasteries also were engaged in conflict with the Bishop of Arezzo, while some institutions such as Prataglia were subsumed by more successful ones such as Camaldoli. In the late Middle Ages seigneurial lords such as the Guidi began to lose their grip on power, as concessions were made towards village communities in the hope of forging alignments against Florentine encroachment. Such a shifting balance is indicative of a 'dynamic' power balance in the region.

Table 3.4 The breakdown of the Florentine *contado* (1300–1580) into quantifiable configurations

	Egalitarian-Polarised	Dynamic-Persistent
Property	0	1
Social distribution of property	0	1
Power	0	0
Total scores	**0**	**0.67**

Type of society: polarised-dynamic.

Table 3.5 The breakdown of the Casentino Valley (1300–1580) into quantifiable configurations

	Egalitarian-Polarised	Dynamic-Persistent
Property	1	0.5
Social distribution of property	0.5	0
Power	1	1
Total scores	**0.83**	**0.5**

Type of society: egalitarian-intermediate.

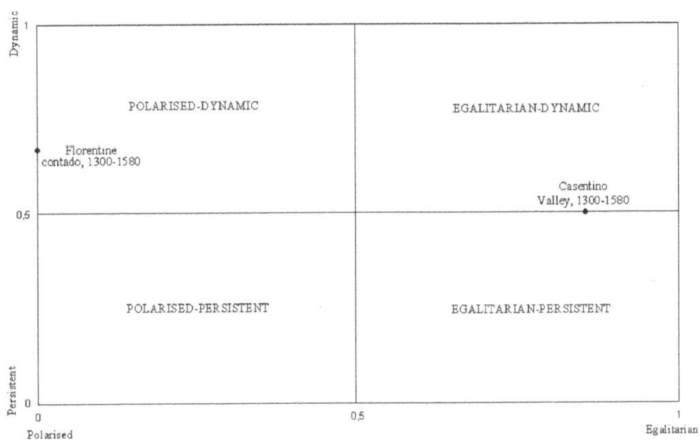

Figure 3.3 What types of society were the Florentine *contado* and the Casentino Valley, 1300–1580?

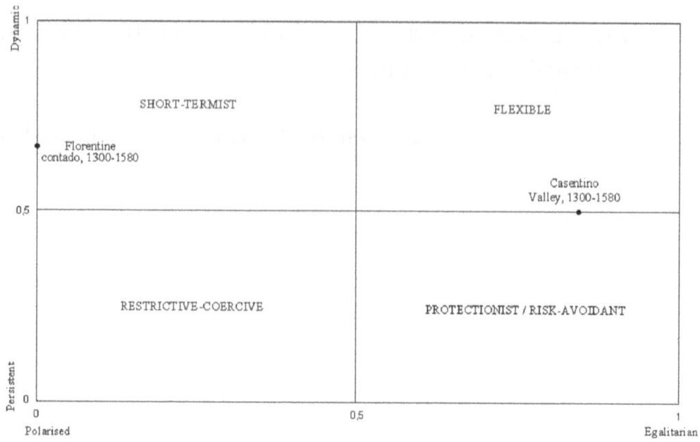

Figure 3.4 Predicted strategies for resource management in the Florentine *contado* and Casentino Valley, 1300–1580

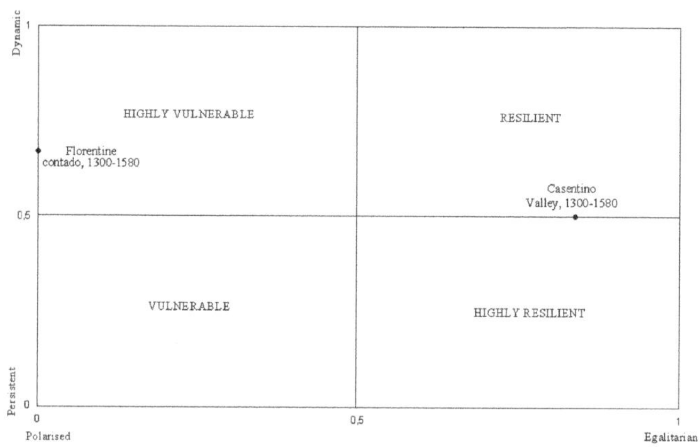

Figure 3.5 Predicted levels of settlement resilience or vulnerability in the Florentine *contado* and Casentino Valley, 1300–1580

Assessing the Theoretical Model

The society of the Florentine *contado* in the late Middle Ages has been assessed as 'polarised-dynamic'. According to the principles of the theoretical framework, this would mean that these arrangements of property (at the user level), social distribution of property, and power, led logically to 'short-termist' strategies for resource exploitation, and in turn 'highly vulnerable' settlements.

The 'highly vulnerable' status of settlements in the Florentine *contado* suggested by the principles of the theoretical framework is confirmed by what actually can be discerned from the empirical evidence. Indeed, in order to achieve 'highly vulnerable' status, a society needed to exhibit clearly all three of the indicators or markers for settlement vulnerability defined in Chapter 1. When faced with encroachment from outside by the city, the *contado* displayed a slow demographic recovery after the cumulative effects of plague, pestilence, and flooding, exhibited a strong trend of outward rural to urban migration stimulated by harsh taxation, showed retraction and abandonment of cultivated areas, and former physical structures such as *castelli* were left abandoned. The only problem with the 'predictions' of the theoretical framework in this case may be found in the classification of the strategies for resource management as 'short-termist'. Given the extractive modes of exploitation which emerged, such as the imposition of sharecropping, guild protectionism, and harsh taxation, this would be better classified as 'restrictive-coercive'. This shows that although we can create theoretical models which cater as much as possible for nuances and historical context, nothing ever fits perfectly into an ideal sociological model. Nonetheless, the basic principle that the society of the Florentine *contado* in the late Middle Ages was vulnerable holds firm.

The society of the Casentino Valley in the late Middle Ages has been assessed as 'polarised-intermediate'. An intermediate status was given to this society because it was not possible to clearly determine on the axis of change whether this was a society of dynamism or persistence: it exhibited aspects of both. According to the principles of the theoretical framework, this would mean that these arrangements of property (at the user level), social distribution of property, and power, led logically to a combination of 'flexible' and 'protectionist / risk avoidant' strategies for resource exploitation, and in turn either 'resilient' or 'highly resilient' settlements.

The 'resilient' or 'highly resilient' status of settlements in the Casentino Valley suggested by the principles of the theoretical framework is confirmed by what actually can be discerned from the empirical evidence. Indeed, in order to achieve 'highly resilient' or 'resilient' status, a society needed to exhibit either none or just one of the indicators or markers for settlement vulnerability defined in Chapter 1. Indeed, populations recovered and stabilised quite quickly after the demographic nadir seen at the end of the fourteenth and the beginning of the fifteenth century, and in a period often characterised as a breakdown in settlement structures in Central Italy (after 1300), this was exactly the time when coherent concentrated villages came to be formed. There was no sign of land going out of use, and non-agricultural land was protected by common rights. Similarly there was little evidence of widespread destruction of infrastructures or abandonment of housing – only some limited signs of small hamlets being vacated with inhabitants moving into newly formed settlements. The strategies for resource management as the link between 'type of society' and 'settlement resilience/vulnerability' is also confirmed by what happened in practice. As one may note, the Casentino Valley had an intermediate status between 'dynamism' and 'persistence', thereby occupying a position between 'protectionism' and 'flexibility'. In line with this, there is evidence for some classic 'protective / risk avoidant' strategies such as the commons to protect the valuable forest economy and the diversification of economic activities, yet at the same time there were also 'flexible' strategies such as the widening of the economic portfolio (at the regional level, but specialisation at the household level) and adaptability of tenurial structures and modes of exploitation in order to actively benefit from the opening up of new urban markets.

Chapter 4

Settlement Decline before the Black Death? Dealing with Pressure on Resources in Two Regions of Medieval Cambridgeshire, 1200–1340

At the time of the Domesday Book in 1086 there may have been 2 or 2.5 million people in England,[1] but by (roughly) 1300 the population may have been anything from 4.4 to 7 million, depending on whose interpretation you take.[2] After this increase in population through the eleventh to thirteenth centuries however, came a late-medieval decline. It is common knowledge that a decline definitely happened of course, but less consensus is on the timing of this demographic (and some say economic) crisis. One older Malthusian interpretation associated most closely with Sir Michael Postan noted that the surge in population in England between the eleventh and the thirteenth centuries put an enormous strain on what was essentially a finite amount of resources (for example, land).[3] As a result of the need to bring more land into cultivation, arable farming was increasingly extended to the 'marginal areas', areas with poor, infertile soils which were not suited to this kind of agriculture.[4] Early-medieval England was a far more thickly forested place than in the high and late Middle Ages.[5] Accordingly, the over-exploitation of natural resources by the late thirteenth century eventually led to the reversal of the upward demographic trend, and set in motion a process

---

1 A figure of 2 million in Moore, "Quot homines?". A figure up to 2.25 million in Bartlett, *England under the Norman and Angevin Kings*, 290–6. Recent revision has suggested around 2.5 million; Hinton, 'Demography: from Domesday and beyond', 31.

2 A figure of 4.38 million based on available arable in Campbell, *English seigniorial agriculture*, 388, 402. Higher levels of peasant productivity led to a revised figure of 5.46 million in Stone, 'Consumption of field crops', 19–21. Other estimates have been higher; figures of 6 million and 7 million provided respectively in Bartlett, *England under the Norman and Angevin Kings*, 290–97; Hallam, *Rural England*, 244–7. A (very) rough range from 4.5 to 6.5 million suggested in Hatcher, *Plague, population*, 71.

3 In particular see Postan, 'Some agrarian evidence'.

4 Postan and Hatcher, 'Population and class relations', 75–6. The difficult environment of the 'margins' even appears in very recent explanatory frameworks; for example see the late-medieval settlement decline described for parts of County Durham in Jones, 'Contrasting patterns of village and hamlet desertion', 19.

5 Wickham, 'European forests'.

of contraction in settlement and cultivation a long time before the Black Death hit England.

This kind of 'early-stagnationist' framework was supported by scholars working in other areas of Western Europe (to various extents) such as Georges Duby, Wilhelm Abel, and Bernard Slicher van Bath.[6] It was also a thesis well-defended and extended in England by some of Postan's best-known supporters.[7] These ideas eventually came to be criticised, however, by those who rejected the notion of a Malthusian ceiling on population levels, and aimed to show how the arrangement of society and economy itself could have prevented early contraction of population. Robert Brenner emphasised instead Neo-Marxist principles of extra-economic coercion,[8] Esther Boserup (and more recently Harry Kitsikopoulos) argued for medieval societies' capacity to implement technological change and increase agricultural productivity,[9] and Richard Britnell and James Masschaele emphasised the effects of commercialisation and peasants' capacity to use the market to negate crises.[10] Postan was criticised on a more explicitly empirical level by Chris Dyer and Mark Bailey, who showed that the so-called 'marginal areas' were not necessarily abandoned any quicker than the 'old-settled areas'.[11]

However, even if one does not necessarily subscribe to Postan's explanatory framework of the 'margins', there is evidence to show that population and settlement did begin to contract before the Black Death in some places – particularly by those scholars working on their own micro-regions.[12] A number of settlements were deserted or abandoned before the Black Death.[13] Indeed, the notion of early contraction in settlement is not illogical given that Western Europe suffered a spate of plagues and subsistence crises in the early fourteenth century – in particular, the Great Famine of 1315 to 1322.[14] Indeed recent evidence has suggested that the physiological stress caused by the early fourteenth century famines, together with the lack of dairy caused by Great Bovine Pestilence of 1319 to 1320, may have caused a chronic shortage of vital

---

6 Although it must be noted that Postan never formally associated himself with this group of scholars; Verhulst, 'Medieval socio-economic historiography', 91.

7 Titow, *English rural society*, 64–96; Miller, 'The English economy', 39.

8 Brenner, 'Agrarian class structure'.

9 Boserup, *Conditions of agricultural growth*; Kitsikopoulos, 'Technological change'.

10 Britnell, *Commercialisation*; Masschaele, *Peasants, merchants and markets.* A good outline of the debates can be found in Bailey and Hatcher, *Modelling the Middle Ages*.

11 Bailey, 'Concept of the margin'; Dyer, 'Retreat from marginal land'.

12 Slota, 'The land market', 146; Britton, *The community of the vill*, 132–43; Dewindt, *Land and people in Holywell-cum-Needingworth*, 166–70.

13 Dyer, 'Deserted medieval villages'.

14 Kershaw, 'The Great Famine'. For a Western European context see Jordan, *The Great Famine*.

proteins for generations after, in turn making people more susceptible to further environmental crises.[15] Considerable environmental evidence has pointed to the onset of climatic instability in the early fourteenth century,[16] and there is much evidence for the worsening of peasant welfare and the increasing susceptibility of rural societies to subsistence crises.[17] That being so, Lawrence Poos showed for Essex that population began to decline around the time of these famines and on into the post-plague era, while Judith Bennett noted a similar chronology.[18] In Suffolk, Richard Smith suggested a general population stagnation up to the time of the famines starting in 1315 and then marked decline up to 1348.[19] John Hatcher emphasised the high mortality rates in England in the period 1300–1348, a view supported very recently by an essay arguing for a very particular 'medieval demographic system' in contrast to a post-plague one.[20] Additionally, it seems that from the onset of the fourteenth century, the founding of new towns ceased almost entirely.[21]

In contrast, however, some scholars such as Bruce Campbell have shown some evidence antithetical to this early-stagnation hypothesis. While acknowledging the basic fact that the early fourteenth century was a time of severe crisis, he has emphasised the capacity of English agriculture to at least withstand Malthusian pressures.[22] In that respect, ultimate population decline was still more attributable to the devastating effects of the Black Death, as Campbell notes: 'it was the massive and fortuitous loss of life in the Black Death of 1348–49 that took the demographic tension out of the equation'.[23] Barbara Harvey had much earlier taken this view with a more explicit and stronger attack on the Postan thesis.[24] Other scholars have also argued for a 'later' population decline.[25] Under this interpretation, settlement and cultivation did not contract in England until much later in the fourteenth century, perhaps supported by the fact that the highest proportion of settlement desertions in England can be identified to the

15 DeWitte and Slavin, 'Between famine and death'.

16 Campbell, 'Nature as historical protagonist'.

17 Bailey, 'Peasant welfare'; Schofield, 'Dearth'; Kitsikopoulos, 'Standards of living'.

18 Poos, 'Rural population of Essex'; Bennett, *Women in the medieval English countryside*, 228–9.

19 Smith, 'Families and their land', 54.

20 Hatcher, *Plague, population, and the English economy*, 65–6; Benedictow, 'New perspectives'.

21 Hilton, 'Small town society'; 'Medieval market towns'.

22 Campbell, 'Population pressure'; 'Arable productivity'.

23 Campbell 'Agrarian problem', 64.

24 Harvey, 'The population trend in England between 1300 and 1348'.

25 Razi, *Life, marriage, and death*, 27–32; Hallam, 'Population movements in England', 511; Russell, 'The pre-plague population of England', 21; Lomas, *North-East England*, 160.

period 1370–1520, after the ravages of the Black Death.[26] For some scholars, the plague could be considered entirely exogenous and independent of the social and demographic framework.[27]

It is not the intention in this chapter to support either an 'early-stagnationist' or a 'Black Death-focused' interpretation. Instead it will just be accepted that in England, some regions experienced early contraction of settlements perhaps from as early as the end of the thirteenth century onwards, while other regions held out much longer and only suffered contraction through the Black Death in the mid-fourteenth century.[28] The question addressed in this chapter is that given difficult or challenging conditions towards the end of the thirteenth and early fourteenth centuries, such as population pressure on resources and frequent plagues and pestilences, why did some societies withstand these pressures much better than others which proved more vulnerable? What accounts for this difference in timing? This question is approached through a comparative perspective by looking at two rural societies in medieval Cambridgeshire from the rough period of 1200 to 1340. While one area (East Chilford) in south-east Cambridgeshire showed signs of settlement vulnerability well before the Black Death, another area (the Bourn Valley) just 15km to the west did not suffer such a strong contraction (which happened later), possibly hinting to a greater role played by the plague. Put simply, why did East Chilford suffer from settlement vulnerability from the end of the thirteenth century onwards (under population-resources pressures and frequent pestilences and plagues) while the Bourn Valley was resilient for longer – only succumbing eventually to the serious problems of the Black Death?

The rest of the chapter proceeds as follows. In the first section, the Cambridgeshire case study will be introduced by way of describing the development of settlement in the two regions prior to 1200, emphasising the different settlement and occupation contexts in both. In the second section, the indicators for late-medieval settlement vulnerability or resilience are assessed for the two regions. It shall be shown that in East Chilford, the difficult pressures had already led to settlement contraction by the rough period of the late thirteenth or early fourteenth centuries. However, in contrast, the Bourn Valley, although showing some signs of pressure, did not suffer the same extent of decline and did not suffer real demographic crisis until later in the fourteenth century – possibly through the Black Death. In that sense the different markers or indicators for resilience or vulnerability (described in Chapter 1) are elaborated upon. In the third section, it is shown that the differing extent of resilience or vulnerability in the face of difficult economic

26 Dyer, *Making a living in the Middle Ages*, 350.

27 Herlihy, *Black Death*, 38.

28 A regional diversity in timing suggested in Smith, 'Demographic developments'.

and environmental pressures on resources was dictated by the divergent strategies and institutions for resource exploitation that each society adopted. In the fourth section, the deep-lying reasons for this divergent development are considered: why did settlements in East Chilford decay earlier than in the Bourn Valley under resource pressure? It is suggested in this section that this was connected to the configuration of the rural societies themselves. The favourable or more protective sets of institutions or methods for exploiting resources in the Bourn Valley were linked to (a) a more egalitarian distribution and social distribution of property, and (b) a more egalitarian distribution of power between social groups. In the fifth section some conclusions are made and in the final sixth section, these findings are placed into the wider theoretical framework described in Chapter 2.

Settlement Context of the Bourn Valley and East Chilford Prior to 1300

The rural settlement pattern of Central England seen today stands in stark contrast to the settlement pattern of the South-East or North-West. The Midland Belt of England is characterised by concentrated settlements (often large villages),[29] while East Anglia in the South-East, for example, has a dispersed pattern of small hamlets and isolated farmsteads. The differences between the Central and South-Eastern regions of England have long been acknowledged by scholars, contrasting landscapes characterised as 'champion' against 'woodland', 'planned' against 'ancient', or simply the 'central province' against the 'south-eastern province'.[30] It is likely that the divergence in settlement patterns between these two areas of England developed at least at some stage in the Middle Ages.[31] It is a logical suggestion to make given that most scholars accept that habitation in Central England became increasingly clustered within concentrated settlements in a process sometime between 700 and 1200, even if the exact timing and intensity of settlement concentration varied within the

[29] However, the number of small hamlets identified in the 'Midland Belt' of England has grown; Fox, 'The Wolds'; Dyer, 'Villages and non-villages'; Taylor, 'Dispersed settlement in nucleated areas'; Jones and Lewis, 'The Midlands', 190–91.

[30] Roberts and Wrathmell, *Region and place*, 1–10; *An atlas of rural settlement*, 2, 5, 15. Roberts and Wrathmell's 'provinces' idea was based on a long historiography which had already identified different landscape boundaries in England; Gray, *English field systems*; Beresford and Hurst, *Deserted medieval villages*, 66; Roberts, *Rural settlements in Britain*, 16; Rackham, *History of the countryside*, 4–5.

[31] As suggested in Roberts and Wrathmell, *Region and place*, 134–46.

province.[32] The same process of settlement concentration did not happen in South-East England.

Cambridgeshire is a county which is divided down the middle by the proposed settlement boundary (based on nineteenth-century cadastral mapping) between Central and South-Eastern England. In the west it is a landscape of wide open views and concentrated villages, while in the east it is characterised by little woods, hedgerows and narrow twisting lanes, and small hamlets and isolated farmsteads.[33] Thus, in accordance with expectations, the Bourn Valley (West Cambridgeshire) contains a number of concentrated villages, while East Chilford (South-East Cambridgeshire) contains small hamlets and scattered farms.

Given a general consensus that habitation in Central England became more concentrated at various stages between 700 and 1200, it is entirely logical to suggest that the settlement divergence between the Bourn Valley and East Chilford occurred sometime within this period of the Middle Ages. It is not the intention of this chapter to be any more explicit on the dates than that, to avoid being dragged into a polemical debate amongst British historians and archaeologists on the 'origins of nucleated settlement' in England.[34] All that will be said is that by 1200, the concentration of settlement in the Bourn Valley had been more or less completed. Evidence supports this assertion – the best of which is arguably the distribution of moated dwellings in the two areas, particularly given that it is widely accepted that they proliferated in a rough phase running from the early thirteenth to early fourteenth century in England.[35] In the Bourn Valley, 75 per cent of moats were situated at the heart of concentrated settlements, suggesting that people by the thirteenth century were already choosing to live in villages. This point is strengthened by the fact that most of these moats were not manorial residences of lords but owned by wealthy peasant tenants. This social group probably wanted to ostentatiously flaunt their economic fortunes to their neighbours as visible expressions of

32 Hamerow, *Early medieval settlements*, 120–4; 'Settlement mobility and the 'Middle Saxon shift'; Taylor, *Village and farmstead*, 130–31; Williamson, *Shaping medieval landscapes*, 14.

33 The contrast in the landscapes noted in Taylor, *Cambridgeshire landscape*. A landscape difference highlighted visually in Martin and Satchell, "'Wheare most inclosures be".

34 See the historiographical essay in Astill, 'The long and the short'.

35 Wilson, *Moated sites*, 28; Le Patourel, *Moated sites of Yorkshire*, 16–9; 'Documentary evidence', 27; Roberts, 'Historical geography of moated homesteads'; 'Moated sites in Midland England'; 'Moats and mottes'; 'Moated sites'; Le Patourel and Roberts, 'The significance of moated sites', 46–7, 51; Emery, 'Moated settlements in England', 384; Oosthuizen, 'Medieval greens'. By the end of the fourteenth century moated sites were transformed into ornamental gardens instead; Taylor, 'Medieval ornamental landscapes'.

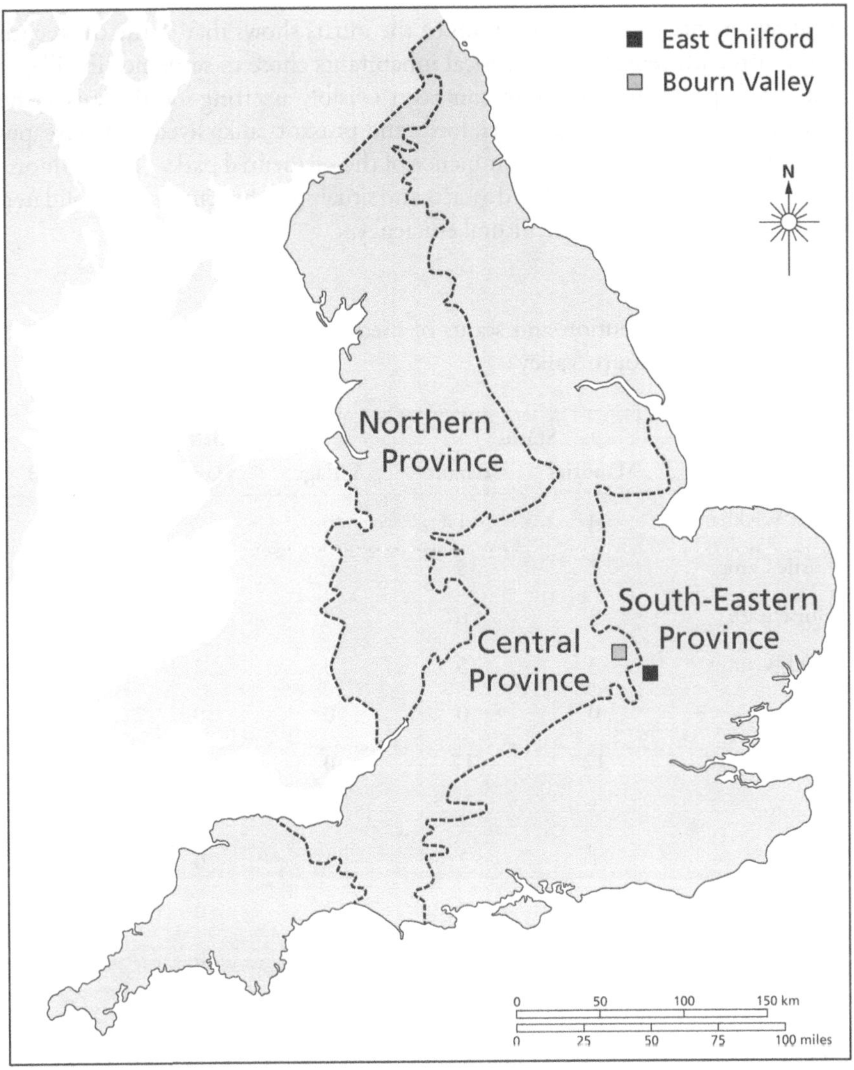

Figure 4.1 The three 'provinces' of England according to Brian Roberts and Stuart Wrathmel

social status (moats were predominantly status symbols),[36] perhaps inspired by the 'landscapes of lordship' created by seigneurial lords with their manor house overlooking subordinate tenant plots. In East Chilford, moats were scattered widely across the parishes, some belonging to manors and some belonging to

36 Taylor, 'Medieval moats in Cambridgeshire'.

wealthy tenants. The lonely position of the moats shows that in the thirteenth and fourteenth centuries, many local inhabitants chose to settle not in villages but in a dispersed formation. In contrast to visibly asserting social status at the heart of concentrated settlements, lords and peasants alike lived in 'landscapes of exclusion' inspired by the prominence of the seigneurial park.[37] Furthermore, these moats were often woodland assarts and situated at the centre of consolidated land units for increased agricultural efficiency.

Table 4.1 Distribution and status of medieval moats in East Chilford and the Bourn Valley

	Status		**Position**		
	Manorial	**Tenant**	**Village**	**Hamlet**	**Isolated**
West Wickham	4	1	0	2	3
Castle Camps	2	5	0	1	6
Horseheath	3	6	0	1	8
Shudy Camps	3	5	0	2	6
Bartlow	0	0	0	0	0
East Chilford	**12**	**17**	**0**	**6**	**23**
Kingston	2	1	1	0	2
Barton	1	2	2	0	1
Toft	0	0	0	0	0
Harlton	1	1	2	0	0
Eversden	1	3	4	0	0
Bourn Valley	**5**	7	**9**	**0**	**3**

Source: Cambridgeshire Historic Environment Record, Shire Hall, Cambridge.

[37] As noted elsewhere in an important article by Dyer, 'Conflict in the landscape', 27. Castle Camps parish in East Chilford was dominated by the seigneurial park belonging to the Earl of Oxford and all moats respected its boundaries; Taylor, 'Cambridgeshire earthworks surveys'.

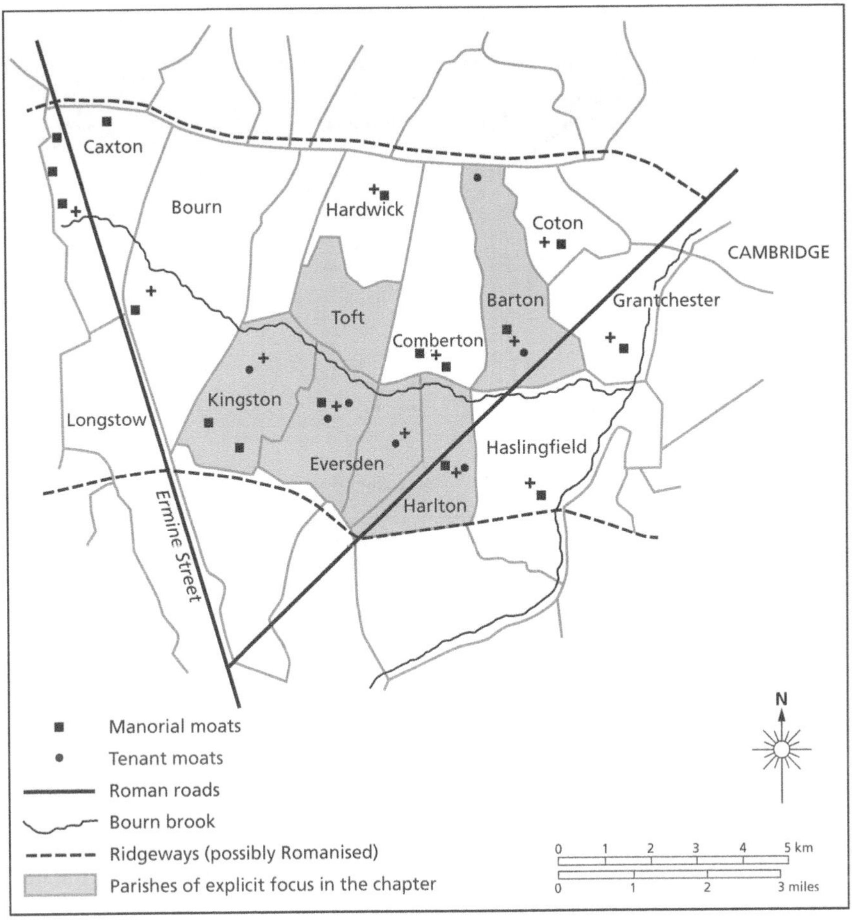

Figure 4.2 Layout of the Bourn Valley parishes with distribution of moats
Source: Cambridgeshire Historic Environment Record, Shire Hall, Cambridge.

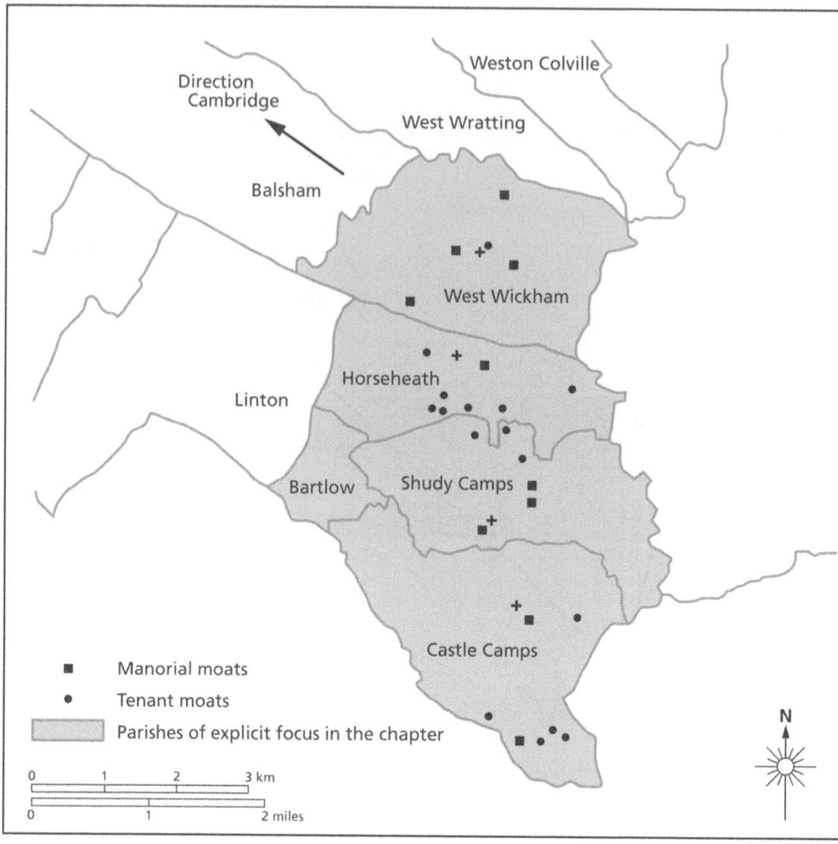

Figure 4.3 Layout of the East Chilford parishes with distribution of moats
Source: Cambridgeshire Historic Environment Record, Shire Hall, Cambridge.

Some work on settlement development prior to 1200 in the Bourn Valley has already been conducted by Susan Oosthuizen. However, while her evidence for the long-term development of field systems and boundaries is highly convincing,[38] the paucity of good available evidence for settlement development means that her conclusions on patterns of early-medieval habitation are logical but less certain, something which Oosthuizen acknowledges in her book herself.[39] In short, Oosthuizen argues for a two-stage development of concentrated settlement in the Bourn Valley, the first being the informal clustering of habitation around

38 Oosthuizen, 'New light'; 'Roots of the common fields'; 'Prehistoric fields'; 'Two- and three-field systems'.

39 Oosthuizen, *Landscapes decoded*, 59–64, 145–8.

points of common pasture and meadow contiguous with the working of a 'proto-common field system' based on very ancient readapted boundaries.[40] The second stage of concentration apparently occurred from the eleventh century onwards, as settlement shifted due to the formalisation of a more orthodox system of open fields.[41]

Archaeological evidence supports the view taken from the moated sites that settlement in East Chilford was dispersed by 1200, and probably here we can be more confident in our assertions in saying that settlement in this region had always been dispersed.[42] Scattered pottery distributed widely across the landscape suggests this, with a number of artefacts from the Iron Age.[43] The same wide distribution also goes for Roman pottery and coins, not to mention the isolated remains of Roman villas and one of the finest burial sites in Britain.[44] Anglo-Saxon pottery is also scattered widely,[45] there are some Anglo-Saxon burial sites,[46] plus there is also the good fortune of having the precise location of an isolated Anglo-Saxon manor set within the thick woodlands at Yen Hall in the parish of West Wickham. We know its location through the continued existence of a moat (first recorded in 1315 and likely a thirteenth-century construction) and its date because of its appearance in a charter from 974 as the manor of Eanheale, which amounted to three hides granted by King Edgar to his thegn Elfhelm Polga.[47] The only movement towards concentrated habitation in East Chilford before the thirteenth century was in the form of very small hamlets.

---

40 Oosthuizen, 'Medieval settlement relocation'; 'Saxon commons'; 'Medieval settlement plans'; 'Ancient greens'.

41 A two-phase process as noted elsewhere in Brown and Foard, 'The Saxon landscape', 74; Foard, 'Systematic fieldwalking', 370; Taylor, 'Nucleated settlement'. Informal early-medieval clustering around points of pasture argued for in Davison, 'The evolution of settlement', 18–9; Warner, *Greens, commons and clayland colonization*, 32.

42 In nearby Essex it has been shown that the pattern of dispersed settlement and irregular enclosures existed in the Roman period or possibly earlier; Williamson, 'The Roman countryside'; Rodwell, 'Relict landscapes in Essex'; Rackham, 'Medieval landscape of Essex'.

43 Parsons, 'A Romano-British site in Horseheath'; Haverhill and District Archaeological Group, 'Yen Hall', 10; Charge, 'Castle Camps'; Powell (ed.), *VCH of Essex. Roman Essex*, iii, 42–3. Also some Palaeolithic and Mesolithic finds have turned up; Salzman (ed.), *VCH*, i, 253; Wymer (ed.), *Mesolithic sites*, 135.

44 Eckhardt et al., 'The Bartlow Hills'; Eckhardt, 'Roman barrows'; Powell (ed.), *VCH Essex*, iii, 39–45; Brocklebank, 'The Bartlow Hills'; Astin, Eckhardt and Hay, 'Resitivity imaging survey'; Fox, *Archaeology of the Cambridge region*, 185, 226, 231.

45 Browne et al., 'Archaeological notes'; Charge, 'Cropmark survey reports', 141, 147.

46 Boddington, 'Models of burial, settlement and worship'; Lethbridge, 'A cemetery at Shudy Camps'; Meaney, *Early Anglo-Saxon burial sites*, 69.

47 Birch (ed.), *Cartularium Saxonicum*, iii, 628–31. For background see Taylor, 'Medieval moats in Cambridgeshire', 244; *Cambridgeshire landscape*, 51, 72, 90; Salzman (ed.), *VCH*, ii, 43; Reaney, *Place-names*, 113; Wright (ed.), *VCH*, vi, 118.

As the Norman castle belonging to Aubrey de Vere (the Earl of Oxford) was constructed in the late eleventh or twelfth century, the Earl would have needed a close pool of labour to build the castle and dig the moat.[48] The small cluster of habitation was temporary, however, and probably uprooted when the castle fell into disrepair or when the Earl's seigneurial park became extended.[49] Thus, the tenants probably were shifted into the small informal clusters which appeared around greens at Camps Green and Olmstead.[50]

In sum, it is highly likely that a settlement divergence had appeared in Cambridgeshire by the thirteenth century: the Bourn Valley was characterised by large concentrated villages while East Chilford contained small loosely clustered hamlets and dispersed farmsteads. This is the spatial context upon which the following discussion into the development of late-medieval settlement resilience or vulnerability can take place.

Settlement Resilience and Vulnerability in the Bourn Valley and East Chilford, Late Thirteenth and Early Fourteenth Centuries

The indicators of settlement resilience or vulnerability in the two regions of Cambridgeshire around the late thirteenth and early fourteenth centuries are as stipulated in Chapter 1 and are threefold: population movements, ruination or loss of agricultural land, and loss of capital goods and housing. However, before going deeper into this, an appreciation of the methodological challenges needs to be outlined with particular reference to the limitations of the sources. Demographic information can be taken from a number of manuscript sources for medieval England – four well-known ones were available for our two areas of Cambridgeshire including the Domesday Book of 1086, the Hundred Rolls of 1279/80, the Lay Subsidy of 1327, and the Poll Taxes of 1377–81. The Domesday Book was England's first truly impressive survey of landholding across the whole of the country carried out by William I. The Hundred Rolls were similarly a central government inquiry into landholding, although only rolls for parts of Eastern, Midland, and South-East England survive. It is likely that the whole of England was intended to be surveyed but the enormity of the administrative task meant that it was aborted mid-process.[51] Fortunately the

48 Taylor, 'Cambridgeshire earthworks surveys', 38–41.

49 Way, *The impact of imparkment*, 64, 229. Entry into and activities in the seigneurial park were punished; for example see *Calendar of Patent Rolls, 1281–1292*, ii, 97; *Calendar of Patent Rolls, 1313–1317*, iii, 63.

50 Some habitation remained at Olmstead until the sixteenth century, after which it almost entirely disappeared; Wright (ed.), *VCH*, vi, 36–7; ERO, D/D Q 1, no. 1.

51 Raban (ed.), *A second Domesday?*.

largest body of complete Hundred Roll returns comes from Cambridgeshire.[52] The Lay Subsidy was a tax of a fifteenth, not on land but on moveable goods such as livestock and corn, while the Poll Taxes in contrast were assessed at a flat rate of 4 denarii per capita.

The Domesday Book, the Hundred Rolls, and the Lay Subsidy were seemingly all assessed at the 'head of household' level and so can be compared directly without population multipliers, but more caution is needed for comparing these to the Poll Tax of 1377 which was a tax on the whole of the adult population over the age of 14.[53] Problems specific to each of the sources also emerge, however. To begin with the Domesday Book, we cannot be sure in this landholding assessment how systematically settlements were recorded.[54] For example, the book lists the number of tenants at 'Camps' (Shudy and Castle Camps – two parishes in East Chilford). Yet did this assessment also include Nosterfield, Olmstead, Camps Green, and Northo' too, which all were or became secondary settlements within the parish? We cannot be sure how rigorous was the assessment of secondary settlements which lay in proximity to the main vills.

Most of the key problems, however, regard the use of the Hundred Rolls. For other parts of England such as Warwickshire, attempts have been made to discern population trends by comparing data taken from the Domesday Book and the Hundred Rolls without properly accounting for limitations of the Hundred Rolls.[55] The problem with simply counting the number of tenants in each parish in 1279 is that not every landholder recorded in a parish lived in that parish.[56] Indeed, for the purposes of the Cambridgeshire cases, it was actually very common for landholders in the East Chilford parishes to hold land across numerous parish boundaries. In that case, the figure taken from simply a count of the tenants may be too high – thus over-emphasising a population increase between the eleventh and thirteenth centuries and by the same token over-emphasising late-medieval demographic decline when compared to the fourteenth-century data. Instead of counting tenants, there is the possibility of counting 'messuages' in the Hundred Rolls. Yet this too causes some consternation. For a start, there are some real doubts about the meaning of the term 'messuage'. Were all houses referred to as 'messuages', or were there other forms of habitation not considered 'messuages'? Basically we are unsure whether messuages recorded in the rolls really represented the entirety of housing, and we are unsure how rigorous the compilers of the source were in recording habitations.

---

52 Approximately 60 per cent of the pages of the Record Commission edition are devoted to the Cambridgeshire and Huntingdonshire circuit.

53 A minefield of methodological problems leading to inflated population totals; McKintosh, *Autonomy and community*, 126–30.

54 Muir, *Yorkshire countryside*, 114.

55 Harley, 'Population trends'.

56 A point put forward in John, 'Population change'.

Further problems exist when comparing the Hundred Rolls with the Lay Subsidy. Indeed, the numbers of heads of households recorded in the Lay Subsidy of 1327 were likely far too low – a problem exacerbated when one considers that figures taken from the Hundred Rolls could easily be too high, creating a false perception of steep demographic decline. The number of fiscal paupers not taxed in the Lay Subsidy is unknown but given the economic difficulties associated with the late thirteenth and early fourteenth centuries, it was probably high.[57] Edward Britton suggested in fact that it was only the upper echelons of the peasantry who paid this tax, but his argument was based on a flawed categorisation system which crudely equated local office-holding with wealth.[58] Other scholars have suggested that not all the tenants were in a position to pay the tax,[59] and that is not to mention those who evaded taxation successfully, which may have been anything from 5 to 25 per cent of the population.[60] In effect, these sources are too problematic to be used for formulating total population figures in an exact absolute sense,[61] but that does not mean they cannot be used to create a general insight into relative sizes of settlements in a comparative sense.[62]

Given these source limitations, how does this inform the methodology employed in this chapter? To negate the problem in the Hundred Rolls of landholders appearing many times in different parishes, a new method has been used. First, all messuages are counted because these are clearly dwellings of some description and represented a household. To this figure were added some landholders without messuages, however, more care was made to not include landholders which appear in a number of parishes. In fact, of those landholders who appeared in multiple parishes, they were only recorded as resident in the parish where they had the most significant landholding. Although this methodology is by no means perfect, it is as cautious and considered as one is likely to get.[63] Of course, the careful examination of repeat names in the

57 Dyer, 'Were late medieval English villages 'self-contained'?', 17.

58 Britton, *Community of the vill*, 70–6.

59 Dyer, *Lords and peasants*, 106; Harvey, 'Population trend', 28. Though a much higher proportion of tenants paying the subsidy has been suggested in Franklin, 'Gloucestershire's medieval taxpayers', 22–5.

60 Smith, 'Demographic developments', 48. High levels of evasion of the lay subsidies has been argued in Hadwin, 'Medieval lay subsidies', 207; Rigby, 'Urban society'.

61 Asserted very negatively in Willard, *Parliamentary taxes*, 181; Salzman, 'Early taxation', 40–43.

62 As performed in Harley, 'Settlement geography of early medieval Warwickshire'.

63 The difficulty and problems with matching names in English medieval documents has been discussed in a long methodological debate connected with court rolls; Razi, 'Toronto School's reconstitution of medieval peasant society', 143–4; Bennett, 'Spouses, siblings and surnames'; Poos and Smith, 'Legal windows'; Razi, 'The use of manorial court rolls'; Poos and Smith, 'Shades still on the window'; Razi, 'Demographic transparency of manorial court

Hundred Rolls is possible in this comparative study because the areas of focus are small. Finally, in order to account for those who evaded the Lay Subsidy in 1327, 15 per cent has been added to the figure (between the 5 to 25 per cent estimates suggested by other scholars).

Table 4.2 Estimated numbers of households in the Bourn Valley and East Chilford, 1086–1327

	1086	1279	1327	Multiplier 1086–1279	Multiplier 1279–1327
Castle Camps	27	83	48	3.07	0.58
Shudy Camps	22	85	32	3.86	0.38
Horseheath	29	66	30	2.28	0.46
Bartlow	n/a	32	15	n/a	0.47
West Wickham	33	50	58	1.52	1.16
East Chilford	**111**	**316**	**183**	**2.84**	**0.58**
Barton	31	85	52	2.74	0.61
Harlton	20	57	49	2.85	0.86
Kingston	21	67	64	3.19	0.96
Eversden	26	46	62	1.77	1.35
Toft	23	50	34	2.17	0.68
Bourn Valley	**121**	**305**	**261**	**2.52**	**0.86**

Sources: Otway-Ruthven, 'Cambridgeshire Domesday'; Caley and Illingworth (eds), *RH*, ii, 420–30, 510–20, 562–4, 568–9; Evelyn-White (ed.), *Cambridgeshire Lay Subsidy 1327*.

It is clear that the Bourn Valley and East Chilford both experienced significant population growth between the eleventh and thirteenth centuries. The ratios of 2.84 and 2.52 are in line with what was expected, given that the literature on high-medieval population growth has suggested roughly a doubling or tripling of people in England. In addition, it has been said that Cambridgeshire had one of the most densely settled landscapes of the twelfth and thirteenth centuries.[64] However, population in East Chilford took a far earlier contraction than that of the Bourn Valley. Both regions showed demographic decline between 1279 and 1327, but East Chilford's was far more pronounced. In fact, the decline of

rolls'. The late thirteenth century was in particular a period of instability in surnames which could represent occupation, nickname, or kinship group; Harvey, *A medieval Oxfordshire village*, 126–7.

64 Miller and Hatcher, *Medieval England: rural society and economic change*, 144.

East Chilford in this period was at a higher rate than that seen between 1327 and 1377 (a period including the Black Death), where it is calculated that the downward demographic multiplier was 0.63.[65] In contrast in the Bourn Valley, the multiplier of 0.86 shows a less severe decline between 1279 and 1327, and instead population was halved (multiplier of 0.5) in the period including the Black Death. However, as noted above, we must only accept these trends very cautiously given the limitations of the sources.

Fortunately, further indicators can be used to show the difference in settlement vulnerability between the Bourn Valley and East Chilford around the late thirteenth and early fourteenth centuries – in particular, evidence for contracting cultivation. It was said for Camps Manor in Castle Camps parish that the grain yield there had declined by two-thirds between 1291 and 1340, while in the same period in Bartlow, Shudy Camps, and Horseheath, a combined 81 hectares had gone out of cultivation.[66] In fact, Chilford Hundred contained vills with some of the highest proportions of land going uncultivated in the first half of the fourteenth century in Cambridgeshire, while the Bourn Valley in contrast was one of the regions with least evidence for land going out of cultivation in the same period.[67]

The different levels of vulnerability can also be shown by the archaeological and place-name evidence used for the desertion of medieval settlements. Only one medieval deserted settlement can be discerned for the Bourn Valley: that of Pincote, which apparently was located in Kingston Wood of Kingston Parish in the eleventh and twelfth centuries, but disappeared thereafter.[68] Another desertion of a hamlet known as Whitwell (an independent vill in 1086) occurred, but this did not happen until the sixteenth century.[69] In contrast, the landscape of East Chilford was far more unstable and has evidence for far more deserted and shifted settlements from the Middle Ages.[70] A settlement known as Barsey was mentioned together with Shudy Camps in 1272, and yet all that remains now is an isolated moated site at 'Barsey Farm'.[71] As mentioned already, a significant settlement also had grown up around the Castle of the Earl of Oxford at Castle Camps in the eleventh century, though by some point in

---

[65] Figures from 1377 calculated from Fenwick (ed.), *Poll taxes of 1377, 1379 and 1381*, iii, 71–2.

[66] TNA, C135/28/17, no. 8; C135/222, no. 15; Vanderzee (ed.), *Nonarum Inquisitiones*, 213–15.

[67] Baker, 'Evidence in the "Nonarum Inquisitiones"', 525–6.

[68] Reaney, *Place-names*, 163.

[69] Beresford, *Lost villages*, 344; Taylor, *Cambridgeshire landscape*, 139.

[70] Oosthuizen, 'Deserted medieval settlements'.

[71] Reaney, *Place-names*, 106.

the late Middle Ages this was already deserted.[72] A settlement called Northo' (or Northey) near Shudy Camps was mentioned in 1200 and was the site of a number of free tenants still in 1279, but by the late Middle Ages had disappeared completely.[73] Another settlement near Shudy Camps known as Nosterfield was mentioned in the Domesday Book, but all that is left now is the remains of some empty moated sites.[74] Settlement at Olmstead Green was recorded in 1235, yet by 1279 this was reduced to a just a handful of free tenants, and once again the only remains today is a single farm with some moats.[75] Already mentioned was the settled site at Yen Hall, north of West Wickham, which was the location of a late Anglo-Saxon manor and was later moated.[76] This manor (Enhale) still had a number of free, customary, and cottar tenants in 1279, and yet quickly came to be abandoned as a settled site. Further late-medieval deserted sites were to be found close to the small medieval market town of Linton such as 'Catley', which was mentioned in 1279 but represented only by a singular farmhouse by the late-medieval period.[77] The settlement structure in East Chilford was much more unstable than in the Bourn Valley from the end of the thirteenth century onwards.

That is not to create a false impression that the Bourn Valley was in any way a 'great' place to live in the period before the Black Death. The 1320s and the 1330s in particular was a difficult period and rural inhabitants suffered immensely. Indeed, nearby Dry Drayton (only a handful of kilometres away) has been described as utterly impoverished during the 1320s and 1330s, and it is difficult to see how the Bourn Valley would have been any different.[78] Other West Cambridgeshire regions have received similar negative evaluations.[79] The expansion of the cultivated arable through open fields in the thirteenth century, likely exacerbated any environmental problems which occurred in the fourteenth century. The culture of land hunger moved cultivation into the most unsuitable areas of the parishes – the high exposed boulder clays or the heavy water-logged gault clays of the valley bottom. It is inevitable drainage problems

---

[72] Taylor, 'Cambridgeshire earthworks surveys'; *Cambridgeshire landscape*, 121; Beresford and Hurst, *Deserted medieval villages*, 184.

[73] Reaney, *Place-names*, 105; Wright (ed.), *VCH*, vi, 49.

[74] Reaney, *Place-names*, 105–6; Beresford, *Lost villages*, 345.

[75] Oosthuizen, 'Deserted medieval settlements'.

[76] Birch (ed.), *Cartularium Saxonicum*, iii, 628–31; Taylor, 'Medieval moats', 244; *Cambridgeshire landscape*, 51, 72, 90; Salzman (ed.), *VCH*, ii (London 1948) 43; Reaney, *Place-names*, 113; Wright (ed.), *VCH*, vi, 118.

[77] Reaney, *Place-names*, 110.

[78] Ravensdale, 'Population changes', 207.

[79] Bowden, 'Agricultural prices', 614–5; Farmer, 'Prices and wages, 1350–1500', 444, 448; Lee, 'Tracing regional and local changes in population and wealth', 34, 40; Maddicott, 'The English peasantry', 302, 316.

would have occurred as a result. In fact, Lord Constantine Mortimer actually requested a papal induct to allow him to conduct Mass at his own chapel next to his isolated manor at Kingston Wood on the grounds that travelling the distance to the village was too precarious with regard to the flooding and deep mud.[80] In Grantchester (one of the closest villages to Cambridge), the manor of Burwash was still valued at a decent 16 marks in 1311, but after terrible waterlogging of the meadows and ruination of the farm house, it only drew rents of 3 pounds by 1355.[81] The difficulties experienced in the Bourn Valley later in the fourteenth century are also shown by the cases of indebted landholders losing their land to local creditors. For example, John Wyot was a prolific local source of credit to villagers in the Bourn Valley as seen from the court rolls of nearby Oakington.[82] Chris Briggs has suggested that Wyot from his base in Dry Drayton and Comberton capitalised on the failure of many of his debtors to pay their debts (such as William Fraunce in 1316), thereby acquiring a wide span of land in the Bourn Valley.[83] Elsewhere there is evidence that a number of men from the village of Barton owed money to Cambridge Jews, and were in danger of forfeiting their property.[84] In that sense, both the Bourn Valley and East Chilford experienced difficulties during the late thirteenth and early fourteenth centuries caused by pressure on resources, climatic changes, environmental degradation, and outbreaks of repeat plague and subsistence crises. It was just that East Chilford was at a higher level of vulnerability than the Bourn Valley, where the Bourn inhabitants were able to alleviate their problems to a greater extent.

Linking Settlement Resilience and Vulnerability with Resource Exploitation

Why did East Chilford experience a more pronounced settlement decline than the Bourn Valley starting before the Black Death? It is argued in this section that this was likely linked to the essential structural changes in the modes of exploitation experienced in East Chilford (and surrounding area) from the late thirteenth century onwards. A level of instability occurred in this region as a result of (a) a transition towards a more pastoral economy, and (b) a transition towards large lease farming by prosperous free peasant tenants. This economy could not support the large numbers of inhabitants created by high-medieval population growth and led ultimately to a reversal of demographic fortunes. Where grain production required large seasonal workforces, pastoral farming

[80] Bliss (ed.), *Calendar of papal registers*, ii, 161.

[81] TNA, C134/22/10; C135/131/8, no. 19.

[82] CUL, QC, 3 and 4 (Oakington court rolls).

[83] Briggs, 'Creditors and debtors', 137–9.

[84] KCA, BAR, nos 11, 76. Attention brought to this source by Briggs, 'Seigniorial control of villagers' litigation'.

only needed a small band of specialised stock keepers through the year such as the four shepherds in the Hundred Rolls at West Wickham (where one is actually accused of stealing sheep).[85] The Bourn Valley dealt much better with the potential problems caused by population growth. Instead the Bourn Valley exhibited much greater structural stability in its modes of exploitation characterised by (a) the long maintenance of arable cultivation supported through the open-field system, and (b) the maintenance of demesne farming and the restricted opportunities for large lease farmers to consolidate land. This economy was far better at achieving a balance between inhabitants and work opportunities, despite the stress caused by high-medieval population growth and early fourteenth-century plagues and failed harvests. The result was a more resilient set of settlements, which only were truly decimated after the Black Death.

The increased prominence of a pastoral economy and the emergence of lease farms from the late thirteenth century onwards were in many ways interlinked processes. By the time of the Hundred Rolls in 1279, arable fields extended for over 80 per cent of the Bourn Valley parishes, while in East Chilford it was 60 per cent, although this figure was much lower given that the Hundred Rolls did not systematically record the large amounts of wooded areas in the region and certainly not the commons. The same does not apply for the Bourn Valley because almost all of the woodland had already been chopped down by the end of the thirteenth century.[86] The importance of sheep in East Chilford is shown by the sale of large quantities of wool (as well as timber) at the nearby small town of Linton, which had received a grant for a weekly market and fair from 1240.[87] In 1347, a number of the East Chilford parishes had to provide wool to King Edward III, in what was termed a 'forced loan' of 20,000 sacks (although there was little chance of repayment) in order to finance continuing war with France.[88] It was calculated that each sack was to be 165 kg, thus Shudy Camps contributed around 2 sacks, Horseheath around 3.5 sacks, and Bartlow 1 sack.[89] What is interesting is not the total amount but the composition of the contributions to this loan in East Chilford. In Horseheath just 37 per cent of the wool came from manorial flocks, while in Shudy Camps it was just 29 per cent. A significant proportion was made up of wool taken from prosperous free tenants, which

[85] Watkins, 'Cattle grazing', 12; Caley and Illingworth (eds), *RH*, ii, 429–30, 568–9; PRO, *Assizes held at Cambridge*, 11.

[86] Oosthuizen, 'Field-names'.

[87] *Calendar of Charter Rolls, 1226–1257*, i, 294. Also see Clapham, 'Linton'. For timber in Linton see PCA, Barham, AA, nos. 2–3. Also for another De Furneaux market and fair see *Calendar of Charter Rolls, 1257–1300*, ii, 262.

[88] Lloyd, *English wool trade*, 200–2; Harriss, *King, parliament and public finance*, 450–55.

[89] TNA, E179/242/8, fos 6–7; *Calendar of Close Rolls, 1341–1343*, vi, 122.

reveals how sheep farming had been well and truly taken up in the area by this emerging social group.

Pastoral land became highly valued in the late thirteenth century. Sampson of Frankenhoe rendered 3s 8d per annum for just less than half a hectare of pasture in the Hundred Rolls, which was 13 times the average money rent for the same amount of arable in the area (3.25d).[90] The commons were present in parts of East Chilford such as the 24 hectares in the eastern corner of the parish of West Wickham (known as 'The Shrubs') which linked up with 40 hectares of common grazing to the north around the green at Weston Colville.[91] However, an increasing trend was towards securing private access to grazing – particularly by lords and wealthy tenants of East Chilford preserving their own fold-courses. The fold-courses could either be the right to graze sheep over other tenants' arable lands during fallow periods (in the irregular open fields in the very far west of the parishes) or in specifically created enclosures (probably more common in East Chilford) – generally typical for East Anglian agricultural systems.[92] One example is William le Harper, a wealthy local tenant who lived at Horseheath. He paid a subsidy at Shudy Camps of 3s in 1327 and managed to consolidate 35 hectares across four parishes, later coming to hold the 43-hectare estate that belonged to John de Mimiac in the Hundred Rolls.[93] Even though he already had two houses according to the rolls, by securing the quit-rents to Robert de Plessy's holding (as of 1280) centred on the moats at Cardinal's Farm, he acquired extra pasture for his animals by recovering a fold-course for his sheep which belonged to the Bernham fee that the land was originally devised from.[94] The maintenance of sheep-folds was important in East Chilford and Waltham Abbey rigorously guarded theirs at the beginning of the fourteenth century for their rectory.[95]

The emergence of a mixed economy of arable and sheep farming in the region went hand in hand with a simultaneous process of manorial demesne fragmentation and the proliferation of indirect exploitation through leasehold. As early as the second half of the thirteenth century, direct demesne agriculture by manorial lords was on the wane in East Chilford. Demesnes began to be sold or leased out piecemeal to tenants. In the fourteenth century this process intensified as larger units or even whole demesnes were offered to successful tenants and low-level gentry through sale or leasehold, as economic conditions worsened

90 Caley and Illingworth (eds) *RH*, ii, 427.

91 Caley and Illingworth (eds), *RH*, ii, 569; CUL, QC, 52, no. 101; Add. MS. 6081, fos 2v, 24v; Wright (ed.), *VCH*, vi, 185–7.

92 See Bailey, 'Sand into gold'.

93 Caley and Illingworth (eds) *RH*, ii, 428; *Calendar of Patent Rolls, 1307–1313*, i, 159; *IPM AD 1336–1347*, viii, 242–3; *IPM AD 1377–1384*, xv, 106–7; TNA, C137/34/2; C139/37/4; C143/75/12.

94 BL, Add. MS. 5823, fos 244, 257.

95 BL, Cott. MS. Tib. C., no. 9, fo. 131.

for large landowning manorial lords.[96] This contributed to the consolidation of new agricultural units in the thirteenth and fourteenth centuries, often with the isolated moated farmhouses at the centre.

Lord Emery Peche exploited his manor in West Wickham through leasehold from the late 1200s onwards. It comprised of 144 hectares of arable in 1280 and yet was supported by only one customary tenant to work the demesne. It sold its last villein to a man from St. Albans (80 km away in Hertfordshire) with no land or connections in the parish in 1304.[97] That the lord in 1327, John Bernham, was assessed at a paltry 12d in the Lay Subsidy suggests that considerable economic misfortune occurred in the early fourteenth century, or direct operations within the manor were completely downsized.[98] By the end of the fourteenth century the whole demesne was at lease.[99] The manors of Enhale, Streetly and Le Hayes at West Wickham all reduced their demesnes and focused less on direct management by the late thirteenth century. The ancient manor of Enhale had 130 hectares of arable in 1280, yet by 1320, 99 hectares of this was alienated between 13 tenants.[100] By 1338 only 73 hectares remained in demesne.[101] La Hayes Manor had 144 hectares demesne in 1280 but was entirely leased out by 1366.[102] The lord of the manor, Stephen de la Hayes, also had his estate in Horseheath subinfeudated (subinfeudation after the Norman Conquest in England was the process by which a social superior granted away land to 'followers' or vassals, lay or ecclesiastical[103]) by the time of the Hundred Rolls and divided up between Geoffrey of Horseheath, Nicholas son of Adam Mersey and Waltham Abbey in Essex.[104] Streetly Manor in West Wickham retained some customary labour services into the fourteenth century although the Hundred Rolls showed that the land held by its customary tenants was minimal (5 hectares) and by the end of the fourteenth century this manor was leased out in its entirety too.[105] The same trend of disintegrating demesnes

---

96 The same chronology seen elsewhere in England, beginning with piecemeal leasing and later whole demesnes en-bloc; Dyer, *An age of transition?*, 195; Lomas, 'Priory of Durham and its demesnes', 341, 345; Miller and Hatcher, *Medieval England: rural society*, 236; Britnell, *Winchester pipe rolls*, 32; Du Boulay, 'Who were farming the English demesnes?'; Mate, 'Farming out of manors'; Searle, *Lordship and community*, 257–66; Harvey, 'Leasing of the abbot of Westminster's demesnes'.

97 BL, Add. MS. no. 5823, fos 58v, 102v.

98 Evelyn-White (ed.), *Cambridgeshire lay subsidy 1327*, 26.

99 BL, Add. MS. no. 5823, fo. 102v.

100 TNA, CP40/236, nos 52d, 301d.

101 TNA, C135/54/9.

102 BL, Add. MS. no. 5823, fos 57v, 232v.

103 Thomas, 'Subinfeudation', 397; Harvey, 'The knight', 5–9.

104 Caley and Illingworth (eds) *RH*, ii, 421.

105 TNA, C133/94/5, no. 3; BL, Add. MS. no. 5823, fo. 107v.

can be observed in Castle Camps. The large demesne of Camps Manor held by the Earl of Oxford showed earlier signs of fragmentation. An Inquisition Post Mortem of 1262–63 revealed that the arable amounted to 300 hectares, yet that had shrunk to 243 in 1331 and to 219 hectares in 1371.[106] The value of the manor declined from 100 marks in 1315 to 15 pounds in 1371.[107] Although the Camps Manor demesne was still partly directly farmed in 1371, by 1432 it was totally leased out to William Peyt.[108] The Prior of Ely had a manor at the small hamlet of Northo' in the thirteenth century (and probably twelfth century), but by the time of the Hundred Rolls this had already been divided up between 16 free tenants.[109] It may have represented a sort of collective tenancy seen elsewhere in England over former manorial demesnes.[110]

Thus, late-medieval retraction in settlement and cultivation in East Chilford between 1279 and 1327 occurred simultaneously with great changes in the modes of economic exploitation in the region. New lease farms emerged out of the ashes of the manorial system with its occupants moving instead towards more mixed farming with an emphasis on pastoral activity. Manorial lords were not able to extract labour through extra-economic means for their demesnes and the only option for the large free tenant farmers to obtain labour was by hiring wage workers. The prohibitive costs of this inevitably played a role in the general conversion to a more pastoral economy, where less labour was needed. The combination of intense demographic growth up to the late thirteenth century with the reduction in employment opportunity likely led under pressure to the early reversal of demographic fortunes in East Chilford, a process intensified by the lack of evidence for any significant proto-industries or by-employments to emerge in the region, as well as the loss of an important 'safety valve' through increased encroachment and expropriation of the peasants' common pastures, to the extent that free tenants in some cases resisted and sued Lord William de Colville for depriving them of access to the heaths.[111]

This early rupture in the modes of exploitation in East Chilford never occurred in the Bourn Valley, which was actually a model of stability in its economic and agricultural exploitation in the late Middle Ages. A great deal of evidence points to the stability of arable farming in the Bourn Valley during the late Middle Ages – which happened to go hand in hand with the resilience of direct demesne management. In 1280, almost 80 per cent of the total parish areas were arable fields. It seems that arable fields really extended

[106] Kosminsky, *Studies*, 97; TNA, C135/28/17, no. 8; C135/222, no.15.

[107] TNA, C143/118/4; C135/222, no.15.

[108] BL, Add. MS. no. 5861, fo. 91v.

[109] Caley and Illingworth (eds), *RH*, ii, 428.

[110] See Hoyt, 'Farm of the manor'; Hallam (ed.), *Agrarian history*, ii, 674.

[111] *Curia Regis rolls*, vii, 286.

across the Bourn Valley during the twelfth century,[112] likely stimulated by high demographic pressure on existing resources, and were managed through communal cropping shifts.[113] Thirty examples of ridge and furrow survive in the Bourn Valley parishes and their wide distribution even in some of the more dubious areas for arable cultivation such as the upper ridges and poorly drained valley bottoms reveal how it had extended into the marginal parts of each parish. By the thirteenth century, grazing was becoming increasingly reduced to the stubbles close to the Bourn Brook, demonstrated by the reduction in meadows from 64 hectares in 1086 to 16 hectares in 1280.[114] Although it is conceded that ridge and furrow can also often be evidence for post-medieval land-use, the location of the ridge and furrow on these marginal areas suggests they were of medieval origin since once arable cultivation retracted after the mid-fourteenth century, these lands reverted back to scrub land and were never touched by the plough again.[115] Access to woodlands also became increasingly restricted, and those that remained were in the hands of seigneurial lords or converted into deer parks.[116] Apart from access to the lush meadows close to the Bourn Brook, access to pasture was limited and thus necessitated significant arable cultivation of fodder crops.[117]

The focus on arable farming continued through the fourteenth century, even after the Black Death. William Castelacre, who held most of the land in Eversden in 1397, had most of his wealth tied up in grain: 300 quarters of wheat, 140 quarters of barley and 360 quarters of dredge.[118] His flock of 120 sheep was worth 90s in total but his store of grain was valued at 4,220s. Some of this grain would have been used for household use throughout the year, though much was produced for sale, perhaps in nearby Cambridge or even one of the weekly village markets such as the one founded in Kingston in 1306.[119] Indeed, evidence from neighbouring parishes has shown villeins in the thirteenth and fourteenth

---

112 See the evidence of twelfth-century assarts made into demesnes at Harlton in Longeville (ed.), *Newington Longeville charters*, 75–6.

113 Postgate, 'Open fields of Cambridgeshire'; 'Field systems of East Anglia', 294–5, 297. Although it has been noted that common control of the fallow did not seem to be enforced stringently here; Bailey, 'Beyond the Midland field system', 163.

114 Otway-Ruthven, 'Cambridgeshire Domesday'; Caley and Illingworth (eds), *RH*, ii, 420–30, 510–20, 562–4, 568–9.

115 See the situation in Kingston in 1340 in Vanderzee (ed.), *Nonarum Inquisitiones*, 208.

116 Baldwin St. George had a deer park in Kingston in 1269; *Calendar of Patent Rolls, 1266–1272*, vi, 388. Lord Constantine Mortimer claimed 40 hectares of woodland for himself in 1355; TNA, C135/137/3.

117 Sapoznik, 'Peasant agriculture'.

118 *Calendar of Inquisitions Miscellaneous, Chancery*, vi, 97–8.

119 *Calendar of Charter Rolls, 1300–1326*, iii, 72.

centuries carrying their lords' grain to Cambridge market as a service.[120] The close proximity to Cambridge kept the costs of transportation of grain low for the manorial producers.[121] Some agricultural produce may even have found its way into markets outside of Cambridgeshire given the generally decent quality of the waterways in the eastern countries.[122] Grain was shipped down to London as part of a trade route which included the ports of East Anglia.[123] The actual process of milling the grain, however, was undertaken locally, as reference can be found for at least one manorial mill in each of the Bourn Valley parishes.[124] Overall, it is difficult to find much reference to pastoral farming in the late Middle Ages: the classic early-modern sheep enclosures did not disrupt the common fields very much in this part of Cambridgeshire.[125] In Harlton no mention of sheep farming is made until a reference to a fold-course in 1561.[126]

Continuity in arable farming in the Bourn Valley was connected to the stability of direct demesne management by the manorial lords. Manorial lords here were unrelenting in their direct exploitation of their lands, which even continued long after the disastrous effects of the Black Death. Such a system lingered on into the fifteenth century in some cases, in line with what has been found across other parts of lowland England.[127] In Eversden, Robert Hoo managed the largest demesne farm in the parish by retaining heavy labour services in the late thirteenth century sufficient for the cultivation of the demesne, and by the end of the fourteenth century Eversden Manor was still being farmed directly.[128] A rental from 1382 and a court roll from 1385 reveal that even at

---

120 Miller, *Abbey and Bishopric of Ely*, 84–5.

121 It has been calculated that the price of carriage of grain amounted to about seven per cent of the purchase price in 1339 for a trip from St. Ives to Cambridge – the Bourn Valley was much closer; Masschaele, *Peasants, merchants, and markets*, 210.

122 Langdon, 'Inland water transport'.

123 Owen (ed.), *Making of King's Lynn*, 49–50.

124 SCC, 6/175, nos 15–6; Salter (ed.), *Cartulary of the Hospital of St. John the Baptist*, i, no. 46; Salzman (ed.), *VCH*, i, 345, 421; TNA, CP25(1)/26/44, no. 20; CP25(1)/26/49, no. 17; CUL, QC, 59, no. 36; *RH*, ii, 514; BL, MS Lansdowne Manuscripts, no. 375, fo. 134; MC, Muniments, nos 5394–6.

125 Cunningham (ed.), *Common rights*, 175.

126 TNA, E150/106/2.

127 In many areas of lowland England demesne agriculture continued till c.1400 though in not many places did it continue far into the fifteenth century; Campbell, *English seigniorial agriculture*, 28–9. See the 'Indian Summer' of demesne farming in Stone, *Decision-making*, 80–120. Examples of demesne agriculture continuing after the Black Death in England are numerous; Holmes, *Estates of the higher nobility*, 114–5; Mate, 'Agrarian economy', 341, 344–9; Dyer, *Lords and peasants*, 121–49; Bailey, *A marginal economy?*, 232–4, Hilton, *Economic development of some Leicestershire estates*.

128 Caley and Illingworth (eds), *RH*, ii, 510–1; *Calendar of Inquisitions Miscellaneous, Chancery*, vi, 97–8.

these late dates, tenants still owed some labour services.[129] We also know about the lingering demesne management here from a number of presentments made by leading villages through the courts against the mismanagement of the demesnes by bailiffs between 1385 and 1398, supporting the view that by end of the fourteenth century it had become very difficult to find qualified demesne managers.[130] Elsewhere in Harlton, the lord of the largest manor in the parish enlarged and consolidated the demesne rather than leasing pieces out in the fourteenth century. The Hundred Rolls show the manor was fragmented in 1280, as lower gentry or local free tenants held moderate estates of Lady Isabel Paunton. By the early fourteenth century however, the Harlton Manor was extending its demesne and growing at the expense of other holdings in the parish. Ludes Manor passed into the same ownership as Harlton Manor by 1388 and two other manors joined in the fifteenth century.[131] The same manor could still be identified in 1524 as one large demesne farm with a wealthy aristocratic owner.[132] The two largest manors in Kingston in 1280, Kingston Wood and Kingston St George, also were directly farmed through the fourteenth century. In 1280 both manors had at least some villeins to provide customary labour services, but interestingly also had three influential 'free' tenants who owed a few days ploughing in addition to their money rent.[133] Between 1280 and 1355 the Kingston Wood demesne increased by 12 hectares, owing largely to the consolidation of demesne pasture and meadow.[134] As late as the sixteenth century the Kingston Wood demesnes were kept in hand by an aristocratic family, the Chamberlains, enlarged and consolidated further by uniting their lands with Kingston St George Manor and Depdens Manor, an estate that originated from land consolidation by free tenant Geoffrey of Soham in the thirteenth century.[135] Demesnes of the two principle manors at Toft were kept in hand during the fourteenth and fifteenth centuries and showed marginal increases in area; one of these, Leventhorpe's Manor, went from 24 hectares in 1280 to 32 hectares in 1355.[136]

The stability of arable cultivation and direct demesne management through the 'pressure period' of the late thirteenth and early fourteenth century allowed

---

129 CUL, QC, 15, no. 67; QC, 11, 10th Jan 1985.

130 Briggs, 'Monitoring demesne managers', 190–94; Stone, *Decision-making*, 216–23.

131 Illingworth (ed.), *Placitorum in domo capitulari Westmonasteriensi asservatorum abbreviatio*, 217–9.

132 TNA, E179/81/130, fo. 4.

133 Caley and Illingworth (eds) *RH*, ii, 514.

134 TNA, C135/137/3.

135 TNA, C142/63/33; E150/74/4; C142/170/12; CP25(2)/93/835; BL, Add. Ch. 44797.

136 Caley and Illingworth (eds) *RH*, ii, 519–20; *IPM AD 1352–1361*, x, 393; Salzman (ed.), *VCH*, ii, 71.

for a continuity in employment opportunity in the Bourn Valley. This stability also helped crystallise in place the open-field system (which remained in place all the way into the nineteenth century up to parliamentary enclosure), which gave the local inhabitants some protection against demographic, ecological and economic stress (the theoretical benefits of which are outlined in Chapter 2). Within the framework of the open-field strip system, the less economically prosperous members of Bourn Valley society were able to deal with pressures on resources by fragmentation of holdings. Geoffrey Kyne of Toft is a classic example of this process, holding just over 3 hectares in seven miniscule plots from seven different landlords in 1279.[137] Although not an endlessly sustainable strategy, fragmentation of small holdings in conditions of pressure on resources was also facilitated by what seems to have been a flexible system of land transfer between smallholders. At Barton between 1200 and 1329, 123 charters show tiny selions (strips of open-field arable) being passed between private individuals – often small tenants.[138] It has been suggested in the literature that high-intensity sales of very small plots was often a peasant strategy of reducing risk and staving off starvation in tough periods.[139]

Evidence also shows villagers 'trading down' towards poorer quality grains such as barley and rye during the early fourteen century, and both lords and peasants began intermixing wheat with other grains in order to guard against total failure of one crop.[140] Dredge (a mixture of oats and spring barley) made up almost two-thirds of recorded tithe from nearby Oakington in 1321,[141] used not commercially for brewing as stated by Bruce Campbell for Norfolk but for peasant animal fodder.[142] Dredge was one of the most stable-yielding and flexibly used crops, and furthermore, it negated to some extent the problems caused by bringing higher proportions of land into cultivation, being a less soil-exhaustive crop than maslin or wheat.[143] However, it is clear that open-field agriculture, fragmentation, land transfer, and the stability in demesne arable farming was not always an inevitable strategy for success in the face of resource pressures.

137 Caley and Illingworth (eds) *RH*, ii, 518–20.

138 KCA, BAR/4, nos 6–11, 13–40, 42–103, 105–16, 122–32, 134–6, 138. Work with these charters has been done in Briggs, 'Credit and the freehold land market'.

139 Campbell, 'Population pressure'; Bekar and Reed, 'Open fields, risk, and land divisibility'; Davies and Kissock, 'The feet of fines'.

140 Elrington (ed.), *VCH*, v, 167–8. On 'trading down' during crisis or pressure periods see Appleby, 'Grain prices and subsistence crises'. The inter-mixing of peasant grains as a protectionist strategy has been noted in Stone, 'Consumption of field crops', 19; Raftis, 'East Midlands', 339.

141 CUL, Q, 3, no. 2.

142 Campbell, *English seigniorial agriculture*, 244, 266–7. Asserted in Sapoznik, 'Productivity of peasant agriculture', 18.

143 Pretty, 'Sustainable agriculture' 5; Sapoznik, 'Productivity of peasant agriculture', 21.

Plenty of evidence exists for the desertion of villages in classic open-field areas of Central England prior to the Black Death.[144] As is noted in the next section, it was the particular property and power context in which demesne agriculture was embedded in the Bourn Valley which allowed it to function effectively.

Power and Property

The differing levels of resilience or vulnerability of settlements in the Bourn Valley and East Chilford in Cambridgeshire before the Black Death was connected to the different modes of exploitation of resources each society undertook – a divergence taking place from roughly the late thirteenth century onwards. One society experienced great structural economic changes while the other was built on small adaptions within an already entrenched system. The question of course remains, why the divergence in economic systems? It is argued in this section that much was built upon the differing underlying configurations of property, social distribution of property, and power – all very much interrelated.

One of the key differences between the two regions was the social distribution of property. If one only looks at the surface, tenurial structures at first glance do appear quite similar in the late Middle Ages. The value of the Hundred Rolls lies in the information provided on smaller lay landlords who rarely left archives of their own.[145] Thus it is possible to see that in both areas there existed a high complexity of manorial structure and complicated networks of tenurial relationships.[146] Manors were small and numerous, conforming to Kosminsky's notion of the 'sub-manor' which according to him, 'properly speaking cannot be called manors at all'.[147] In fact there was very little demarcation between free tenants who held considerable lands from several different lords and with sub-tenants of their own, and manorial lords whose manors sometimes included lands held from other landlords on temporary lease or permanent tenure.[148] The *Nomina Villarum* of 1316 showed five manorial lords in Barton in the Bourn Valley, and four manorial lords in West Wickham in East Chilford, to illustrate this point.[149]

---

144 Dyer, 'Deserted medieval villages'.

145 Kosminsky, *Studies*, 97; Campbell, 'Agrarian problem', 25; Raban (ed.), *A second Domesday?*, 6; Barg, 'Social structure of manorial freeholders', 109.

146 Similar to nearby Norfolk; Campbell, 'Complexity of manorial structure'. Recognised explicitly for Cambridgeshire in Kosminsky, 'Services and money rents', 30.

147 Kosminsky, 'Hundred Rolls', 23.

148 The difficulties of defining manors is a theme addressed in Postan, 'The manor in the Hundred Rolls'; Bailey (ed.), *The English manor*, 1–17.

149 PRO, 'Nomina Villarum: Comitatus Cantebrigie', 152–7.

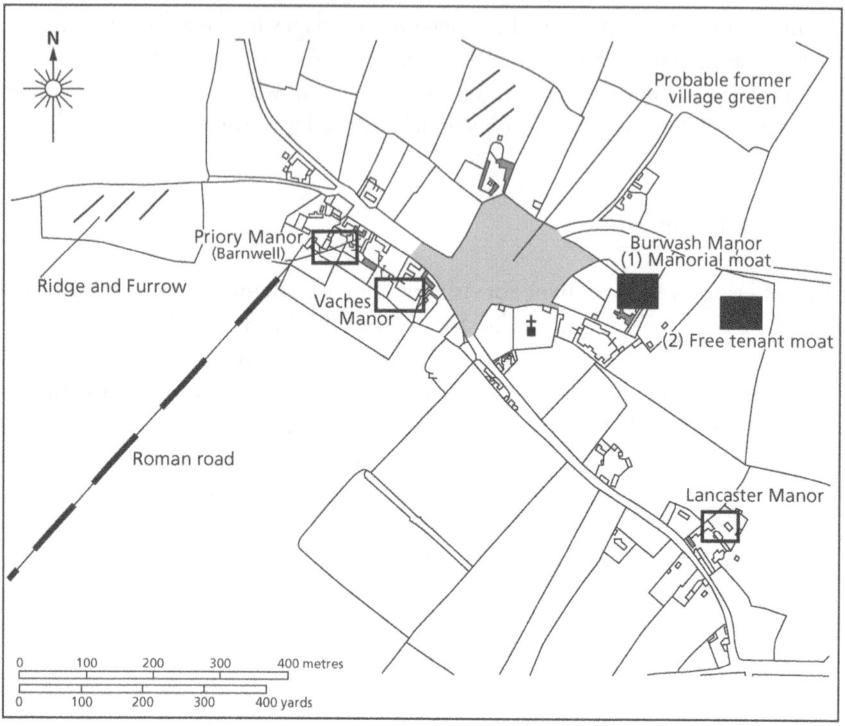

Figure 4.4 Manorial fragmentation in Barton in the late thirteenth century
Notes: Additions made with the help of Oosthuizen, 'New light on the origins of open field farming?'. Adapted version of 1841 tithe map: CCRO, P 10/27/1.

In both the Bourn Valley and East Chilford, tenants held lands from numerous lords. For example, William Jake of Eversden in 1280 held 22 hectares from 11 different landlords of various rents, including a tiny 8-hectare 'demesne' which was held as a quarter of a knight's fee and had been subinfeudated through five different hierarchies of men.[150] From very meagre origins he had constructed himself a moat on one side of the High Street, and on the other side had carefully laid out plots of land for his own tenants – aping the style of the greater seigneurial lords. He had worked his way up as one of the local '*coqs de village*', for he was included as one of the recurrent witnesses to land transactions in 1275.[151] A similar situation can be discerned from East Chilford; William le Harper held 34 hectares from 13 different landlords scattered across

[150] Caley and Illingworth (eds) *RH*, ii, 511–2.
[151] CCRO, 588/T124.

four different parishes in 1280, and later took control of the 32-hectare manor formerly belonging to Robert de Plessy.

On closer inspection, however, there were some important differences with regard to social distribution of property in the two regions. The differences lay in the composition of the demesnes and large farms. Although in both areas manors were numerous, complex, and (relatively) small, the average size of manorial demesnes was much smaller in the Bourn Valley. In East Chilford demesnes averaged 83 hectares each, while in the Bourn Valley they were just 49 hectares on average in 1279. Just a handful of kilometres north of the Bourn Valley, recent research has similarly highlighted the small areas for demesnes in the parish of Oakington.[152] This is a curious finding, because the Bourn Valley lies in the 'Midland Belt' of Central England identified by Roberts and Wrathmell, and has long been seen as distinctive from South-East England due to its larger manors, more often coterminous with the territory of the parish. In fact, in East Chilford manorial demesne occupied around 40 per cent of the total land in the five parishes studied – almost double the proportion of demesne recorded for the Bourn Valley in 1279. The total demesne recorded for all the regions covered in the Hundred Rolls accounted for between a quarter and a third of total land, thus East Chilford was well above this average and the Bourn Valley below.[153]

Table 4.3 Social distribution of land in the Bourn Valley and East Chilford, 1279

	Bourn Valley		**East Chilford**	
	Hectares	**%**	**Hectares**	**%**
Free tenants	1125	47	1017	37
Customary tenants or villeins	466	19	359	13
Manorial demesne	538	22	1090	40
Ecclesiastical demesne or glebe	287	12	286	10
Total	2416	100	2752	100

Source: Caley and Illingworth (eds), *RH*, ii, 420–30, 510–20, 562–4, 568–9.

As well as the smaller demesnes, more land in the Bourn Valley was held by labour rents than in East Chilford: 22 per cent of total cultivated land compared with 11 per cent in 1279. Even though the Bourn Valley had high levels of personal freedom amongst its inhabitants (relative to other areas in Central

152 Sapoznik, 'Productivity of peasant agriculture', 6.

153 Calculation offered in Campbell, 'Land, labour, livestock', 149.

England),[154] many very wealthy free tenants were still required to perform labour services on the demesnes. It has long been noted that the distinctions between customary and free tenants in late-medieval England were not always clear-cut.[155] For example, three influential free tenants to Lord William Mortimer provided a week's worth of ploughing in addition to their cash rent.[156] Some of the Kingston tenants were actually required to do labour works on another manor in Foxton, which is understandable given William and his successor Constantine Mortimer were lords of manors elsewhere in Cambridgeshire and Norfolk.[157] Harvest was a time of particularly oppressive (highly despised) labour obligations in the form of boon works such as those demanded by the Priory of Barnwell over its tenants at Barton.[158] Labour works were demanded at the nearby Crowland Abbey manor in Oakington until at least the end of the fourteenth century,[159] while it has been shown elsewhere in and around Cambridge that labour demands as some form of rent continued unabated.[160] The only problem for the owners and managers of the demesne farms may have been the low labour productivity indicative of a reliance on customary works.[161] At the same time, the smaller size of the demesnes in the Bourn Valley meant it did not require as much labour to meet the demands of cultivating them. Thus, it was the higher amount of labour rents, the smaller total area of demesnes, and the ability to get free tenants to do customary works that made direct demesne management much more viable over the long term in the Bourn Valley. As asserted in Campbell and Bartley's recent '*Atlas*', demesnes were of greater relative significance in areas with small manors,[162] and small estates of the gentry were known to have derived as much as 40 per cent of their income from the demesne in the fourteenth century.[163] Any shortfalls were made up through wage labour, as recorded for demesnes at nearby Little Gransden and on the farms of well-to-do peasants at nearby Cottenham.[164] However, it has been noted at nearby Oakington that customary

154 Possibly linked back to its status even in the eleventh century as a place dominated by moderate 'sokemen' rather than powerful lords; Oosthuizen, 'Sokemen and freemen'.

155 Hilton, 'Freedom and villeinage'.

156 Caley and Illingworth (eds) *RH*, ii, 514.

157 Moor, *Knights of Edward I*, iii, 206–7; Blake, 'Norfolk manorial lords', 241, 270, 286.

158 Clark and Maitland (eds), *Liber Memorandum Ecclesie de Bernewelle*, 302–4.

159 CUL, QC, 6, nos 5–6; QC, 8, no. 4; Page, *Estates of Crowland Abbey*, 126–8.

160 Maitland, 'History of a Cambridgeshire manor', 422; Bailey, 'Prior and Convent of Ely', 18.

161 Stone, 'Productivity of hired and customary labour', 651–5.

162 Campbell and Bartley, *England on the eve*.

163 Coss, *Origins of the English gentry*, 83–4.

164 BL, Cott. MS. Claud C., no. 9, fos 149–52; Page, 'Customary poor-law', 128.

services remained remarkably stable long after the Black Death, while little increase was made in the wages of hired labourers.[165]

In contrast, East Chilford had very small proportions of land rented out to tenants with the expectation of receiving extra-economic labour works in return – certainly not enough to support any kind of large grain demesne farms. Here there was 13 hectares of demesne for every tenant owning labour services, while in the Bourn Valley it was only 3.5 hectares of demesne.[166] Three-quarters of all tenant land in East Chilford had their rents commuted to either produce or cash by 1279, and it only increased during the course of the fourteenth century. Thus the only way the shortfall in labour could have been addressed in East Chilford was to employ significant numbers of wage labourers.[167] It is on this point that we can understand why East Chilford made such a conversion to demesne fragmentation, tenant farming through leases, and ultimately a move towards a mixed pastoral economy. Manorial lords had lost their extra-economic means of coercion and the large sizes of the demesnes had created an imbalance in the ratio of land to labour. It was inevitable such structural changes to the economy would then occur given the prohibitive costs (linked to market rather than custom) associated with employing mass ranks of wage labourers.

Demesne fragmentation provided the contextual opportunity for large tenant farms to emerge in East Chilford, but of course it required the incentive and desire of a group of local peasants to take up such opportunities through consolidation and accumulation. Indeed, the manorial demesnes that were sold, leased or alienated in the thirteenth and fourteenth centuries came into the hands of the lower gentry or free tenants with improving economic fortunes. Economic stratification and polarisation became much higher in East Chilford in comparison with the Bourn Valley. Already by 1327, wealthy tenants were being assessed at higher subsidies for moveable assets than manorial lords,[168] and these well-to-do free tenants were beginning to dominate positions within the Cambridgeshire juries.[169] They consolidated land into large units around their isolated farmhouses and their moats visibly expressed their heightened social and economic status. The social composition of these prosperous free tenants and their attempts to accumulate land can be reconstructed in some cases by the Feet of Fines, which despite some limitations (including differing levels of detail

165 Sapoznik, 'Peasant agriculture at Oakington', 170–200.

166 Caley and Illingworth (eds) *RH*, ii, 420–30, 510–20, 562–4, 568–9.

167 A point asserted more generally for the early 1300s in Campbell and Bartley, *England on the eve*, 268.

168 Evelyn-White (ed.), *Cambridgeshire lay subsidy 1327*, 25–7. Although it is difficult to know what 'taxable wealth' meant to subsidy assessors; Biddick, 'Missing links', 281.

169 Scales, 'Cambridgeshire Ragman Rolls', 560. Also Asaji, 'The Baron's War'.

and preciseness), does throw some light on these developments over the long term of the late Middle Ages.[170]

A perfect example is the Sewale family of West Wickham, who can be traced in the twelfth and thirteenth centuries as local tenants.[171] By the time of the Hundred Rolls John Sewale had compiled 12 hectares which he held of Emery Peche, lord of Bernhams Manor.[172] He continued to purchase land which ended up in the hands of his heir, John, who by 1315 held over 41 hectares.[173] The high status of his farmhouse is indicated by the fact that in 1322 he granted his sister Margery a solar attached to his hall with a granary, bakery and stables.[174] The farmhouse was positioned in the small hamlet of West Wickham and was moated.[175] The later occupant Thomas Sewale was recorded as occupying Bernhams Manor in 1361, which suggests (given the thirteenth-century links with Emery Peche) that the farmhouse and consolidated lands of the Sewales were created by acquiring land from the demesne of Bernhams Manor.[176] Their moated farmhouse was either the former manor house associated with Bernhams or newly constructed on the sub-division of previous demesne land.

William Berardshay is another good example. In 1280 he held 32 hectares in West Wickham, which were subinfeudated from an estate of the Earl of Oxford.[177] Such layers of patronage were the foundations behind the whole feudal system.[178] William consolidated land around his moated residence in Shudy Camps on the site now known as 'Barsey's Farm'. Over 20 hectares had been acquired there by 1280, all held from different owners for large cash rents.[179] William continued to build his landholding around his isolated farmhouse in Shudy Camps and in 1296 purchased 36 hectares from Robert de Say, an aristocratic landowner who held a vast estate in the locality.[180] From very humble origins based on the acquisitive tendencies of a local tenant, the farm and landholding grew in the fourteenth and fifteenth centuries to comprise a manor known as 'Berardsheys'.[181]

---

170 On their potential; Yates, 'The market in freehold land'.

171 BL, Add. MS. no. 5823, fos 58r, 229r, 231v–232v; Illingworth (ed.), *Placitorum*, 148.

172 CUL, QC, 52, no. 9; Caley and Illingworth (eds.) *RH*, ii, 569.

173 BL, Add. MS. no. 5823, fos 94, 102–3, 229–31v; CUL, QC, 52/22; TNA, CP25(1)/27/57, no. 7.

174 BL, Add. MS, no. 5823, fo. 230v.

175 Charge, 'Crop mark survey', 141, 148.

176 *IPM AD 1352–1361*, x, 530. Thomas Sewale also had lands further north in West Wratting; Wright (ed.), *VCH*, vi, 193–4.

177 Caley and Illingworth (eds.) *RH*, ii, 569.

178 The classic work being Maitland and Pollock (eds), *History of English law*.

179 Caley and Illingworth (eds) *RH*, ii, 428–9.

180 TNA, CP25(1)/26/43, no. 31; BL, Add. MS. no. 5823, fo. 252.

181 TNA, CP25(2)/51/270, no. 2.

Elsewhere William le Harper held 34 hectares across four parishes in 1280 and from numerous different owners, though it is likely that he resided in Shudy Camps given that he was assessed there for 3s in the 1327 Lay Subsidy.[182] The *VCH* suggests that by the early 1300s he had bought the fee of 43 hectares which in 1280 had belonged to John de Mimiac, held from the Earl of Oxford.[183] William le Harper built up his landholding in the Nosterfield area of Shudy Camps in the late thirteenth and early fourteenth centuries and his residence was one of many moats in the area. William also acquired land in Horseheath around two moats located at Cardinal's Farm, which was formerly a fee held by Robert de Plessy in 1280.[184] When he died in 1347 he passed on an estate of 53 hectares to Richard, son of Henry of Wykes, showing how he had built up great landholdings from meagre beginnings.[185]

The same capacity and desire to accumulate land holdings and more polarised internal distinctions between different strata of tenants or peasants did not occur in the Bourn Valley. Of course there were free tenants in the Bourn Valley – in fact nearly half the land in the five parishes studies was classified as 'free'. It is also clear that some prosperous free tenants did live in the Bourn Valley, as noted by Oosthuizen in identifying the owners of moated sites at the heart of the villages.[186] However, East Chilford had twice as many landholders with 40 hectares to their name than in Bourn Valley. Landed estates of freemen in the Bourn Valley were moderate at best. Whereas tenants in East Chilford accumulated consolidated blocks of demesne, and added to this through assarting of woodland,[187] any aspiring free tenant in the Bourn Valley not only had to deal with the fact that demesne was less likely to be offered by manorial lords for lease, but also that their opportunities for consolidation were highly limited given the spatial fragmentation of parcels connected to the open-field system. In nearby Oakington, manuscript sources similarly show very little sign of consolidation of landed estates by peasants, even after the Black Death.[188] The typical holding there still remained around 4.5 hectares with only a few exceptions.[189] The Gini-index for land distribution in 1279 is indicative of this divergence between the two areas: land was distributed fairly equally in the Bourn Valley with a figure of 0.59, while in East Chilford the distribution was more inequitable with a figure

182 Caley and Illingworth (eds.) *RH*, ii, 420–9, 569; Evelyn-White (ed.), *Cambridgeshire lay subsidy 1327*, 26.

183 Wright (ed.), *VCH*, vi, 52.

184 BL, Add. MS, no. 5823, fo. 250.

185 TNA, CP25(1)/28/67, no. 21; E179/242/8, fo. 5.

186 Oosthuizen, 'Medieval greens'.

187 Curtis, 'A comparative study', 70–85.

188 CUL, QC, 3, no. 4, fos 15–7; QC, 4, no. 12, fos 8–9. Not much change seen from the situation in 1279 in Oakington; Caley and Illingworth (eds), *RH*, ii, 448–50.

189 Sapoznik, 'Productivity of peasant agriculture', 6.

of 0.7. This disparity probably only widened during the fourteenth century with the continued consolidation of lease land in East Chilford.

The other side of the coin, of course, was that as a small group of successful tenants appeared in East Chilford, a substantial group of less fortunate peasants were squeezed out – often to the point of destitution. Fifty-three per cent of the tenants in East Chilford in 1279 had two hectares or less of land, compared to forty-three per cent in the Bourn Valley. Partible inheritance practices only pushed fragmentation of smallholdings further, as noted in other parts of East Anglia.[190] The proportion of small 'peasant farms' in the Bourn Valley (as opposed to tiny cottar holdings or larger consolidated holdings) of 3 to 10 hectares was much higher: nearly half of all the tenants compared to 38 per cent of tenants in East Chilford in 1279. These tiny freeholders in East Chilford, in line with what has been noted elsewhere, paid higher unit values of rent than any other rural social group – indicative of their high vulnerability.[191] Prosperous free tenants with large holdings also sublet parts of their acquired estates, but at full competitive market rents,[192] thereby intensifying economic polarisation in the region. Nowhere is this better demonstrated than in the case of John le Squier at Shudy Camps who sublet just 2.5 hectares to seven sub-tenants.

Table 4.4 Landholding sizes in the Bourn Valley and East Chilford, 1279

Sizes of holdings (hectares)	**Proportion of tenants (%)**	
	Bourn Valley	**East Chilford**
Under 3	43.9	53.2
3–6	30.6	23.6
7–10	18	14.4
11–20	5.2	4.9
21–40	1.6	2.4
Over 40	0.8	1.5

Source: Caley and Illingworth (eds) *RH*, ii, 420–30, 510–20, 562–4, 568–9.

190 Razi, 'Myth of the immutable English family', 15–8.

191 In line with what has been noted in Campbell, 'Agrarian problem', 22; Kanzaka, 'Villein rents', 510–11.

192 An exploitative internal stratification similar to what has been noted in Smith, 'Kin and neighbors'; Fox, 'Exploitation'.

Conclusion

Although the Bourn Valley was hit hard (like many villages across Western Europe) by the Black Death, its settlement structure proved to be quite resilient in the period before the Plague. In contrast, East Chilford showed signs of vulnerability (particularly in consideration of demographic pressure on resources and poor harvests and repeat plagues at the beginning of the fourteenth century) much earlier – perhaps already beginning in the late thirteenth century. East Chilford between 1279 and 1327 had higher levels of population decline than the Bourn Valley, higher levels of abandonment and ruination of agricultural land, and more abandoned settlements – many likely deserted before the Black Death.

The reasons for the different intensity and chronology of settlement decline between the two Cambridgeshire regions can be linked to the different modes of exploitation. Essentially the stability in the demesne farming system, the continuation of the open-field system and arable cultivation, and small tactics like fragmentation of land, flexible transfer of small plots, and the mixing of grains, allowed the Bourn Valley to retain its 'poorer' section of its population more readily. In East Chilford, the emergence of large tenant farms, the lack of substantial proto-industries or by-employments, encroachment into the commons, and the switch to pastoral farming, restricted employment opportunities and pushed more inhabitants to the margins of subsistence, and East Chilford settlements began to contract already in the late thirteenth century. Indeed East Chilford fell into one of those areas of medieval England identified by Greg Clark, where under- or unemployment was rife.[193] The root causes for these two divergent economic paths can be found in the deep-lying divergences in property and power exhibited in the two regions. The stability of the economy in the Bourn Valley can be put down to the structural difficulties limiting land consolidation and the emergence of tenant farming, and the more balanced match-up between labour needs and labour supply. The rupture in the economy in East Chilford was made possible by the divergent social distribution of land, including a higher proportion in the hands of larger manors and where tenants found it much easier to consolidate and accumulate land – often to the detriment of their less fortunate neighbours. East Chilford inhabitants became exposed to the vicissitudes of the market much earlier than the Bourn Valley inhabitants who protected themselves through custom. In that sense this chapter supports the view taken by Bruce Campbell that much of the early fourteenth-century crisis was compounded not by lordly extraction from subordinates, but by tenant on tenant extortion.[194]

---

193 Clark, 'Labour productivity', 232.

194 Campbell, 'Agrarian problem'.

Fitting the Findings into the Theoretical Framework

In this final section, the information taken from the comparative case study in late-medieval Cambridgeshire is placed into the theoretical framework outlined in Chapter 2.

Property, Social Distribution of Property, and Power

In East Chilford, property was distributed quite unequally. A Gini-index of 0.7 has been calculated for property distribution there, which is precisely on the boundary mark for inequality already justified in Chapter 2. Unfortunately, this Gini-index was only possible for 1279, and thus it is difficult to make comparisons about the changeability of this figure over the long term. However, the general evidence for land transactions and land transfers is overwhelming, particularly when plotting the fortunes of individual free tenant farmers who are seen from a variety of sources accumulating land and leased land over the period in question. Indeed, inequality only likely became more exaggerated through the fourteenth century through this process. With that in mind, East Chilford received a 'dynamic' status for property. In contrast, the Bourn Valley exhibited a more egalitarian distribution of property. A Gini-index of 0.59 was calculated from the Hundred Rolls, under the 0.6 mark set out in Chapter 2. Again the Gini-index figure was only possible for one year, thus it is hard to assess the capacity for change in property distribution. Charters do reveal that land changed hands frequently, even down to the lowest members of the social hierarchy, however it is difficult to assess this clearly in a quantitative or a relative sense. There was much less sign of land consolidation and accumulation in the Bourn Valley during the fourteenth century, and most of the charters detail very tiny plots of land exchanged between peasants or donated to ecclesiastical institutions. With that in mind, an intermediate figure of 0.5 is given for the 'dynamic-persistent' opposition.

The social distribution of landownership in the Bourn Valley was highly equitable. Almost two-thirds of the total land was in the hands of local peasants or more prosperous farmers, while aristocratic landownership was quite restricted at just 22 per cent and urban landownership was nothing – indicative of the lack of penetration of Cambridge capital into the countryside. Again the change in social distribution of land is hard to discern with precise quantitative data over the long term, however the stability of manorial demesne farming (even after the Black Death) and the lack of evidence for consolidation and accumulation by an acquisitive strata of peasantry suggests the situation was persistent between the thirteenth and fourteenth centuries. The situation in East Chilford was slightly different. Rural peasants and farmers had a significant stake in the social distribution of property in the region, with half of the land in the hands of this (broad) social group in 1279. However, aristocratic or noble landownership was also significant in this region, and twice as much land was manorial demesne in East Chilford as in the Bourn Valley. As a result the social distribution of property was given an 'intermediate' status here. The social distribution of land is harder to assess in terms of changeability, though a key process identified in this chapter has been the rise of a group of lower gentry or prosperous peasants from the late thirteenth century onwards, consolidating parts of fragmented demesne by sale or lease. In that sense, a shift in emphasis from manorial lords to rural farmers is indicative of a level of dynamism in the property structure.

In some ways, the Bourn Valley was quite 'free' when compared to other regions of Central England. Manors were small and numerous, much land was in the hands of free tenants, and extra-economic coercion was not at the level seen elsewhere in high and late-medieval England. Yet at the same time, demesne agriculture was maintained past the Black Death, and this was aided by the lingering presence of some coercive duties – including some which were actually put on quite prosperous free tenants. Later in the fourteenth century, some tenants raided and plundered a manor house at Eversden (leading to the death of Justice of the Peace, Sir Edmund Walsingham), connected with discontent stimulated in the Peasants' Revolt.[195] Given this complex situation, power distribution in the Bourn Valley was assessed as 'intermediate'. The lingering presence of customary duties until late in the fourteenth century is also indicative of its 'persistent' status. Despite being more polarised in its distribution of land than the Bourn Valley, East Chilford was freer. Three-quarters of all tenants in East Chilford had their rents commuted to either produce or cash by 1279, and it only increased during the course of the fourteenth century – customary obligations were very minor. Many former customary tenants of the Earl of Oxford had bought their freedom and were recorded as 'molmen'. Of course the late thirteenth to the early fourteenth century was also a period of dynamism: it represented a shift in power from the old manorial lords struggling to maintain their demesnes to a new strata of prosperous free tenants.

---

195 Palmer and Saunders (eds), *Documents relating to Cambridgeshire villages*, 27–8.

Table 4.5 The breakdown of the Bourn Valley (1200–1340) into quantifiable configurations

	Egalitarian-Polarised	Dynamic-Persistent
Property	1	0
Social distribution of property	1	0
Power	0.5	0
Total scores	**0.83**	**0**

Type of society: egalitarian-persistent.

Table 4.6 The breakdown of East Chilford (1200–1340) into quantifiable configurations

	Egalitarian-Polarised	Dynamic-Persistent
Property	0	1
Social distribution of property	0.5	1
Power	1	1
Total scores	**0.5**	**1**

Type of society: intermediate-dynamic.

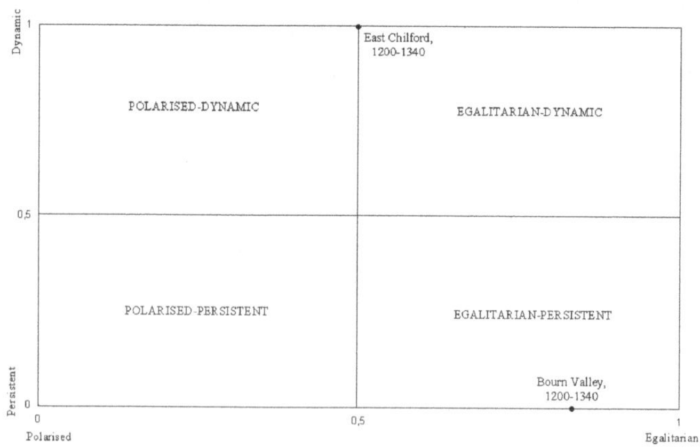

Figure 4.5 What types of society were the Bourn Valley and East Chilford, 1200–1340?

Figure 4.6 Predicted strategies for resource management in the Bourn Valley and East Chilford, 1200–1340

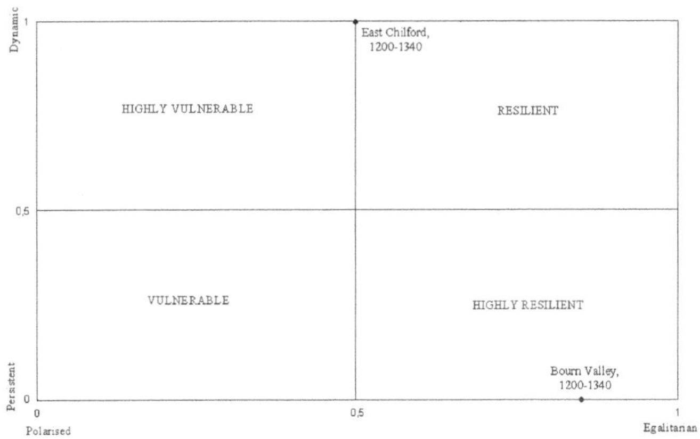

Figure 4.7 Predicted levels of settlement resilience or vulnerability in the Bourn Valley and East Chilford, 1200–1340

Assessing the Theoretical Model

The society of the Bourn Valley from 1200 to 1340 has been assessed as 'egalitarian-persistent'. According to the principles of the theoretical framework, this would mean that these arrangements of property (at the user level), social distribution of property, and power, led logically to 'protectionist' or 'risk-avoidant' strategies for resource exploitation, and in turn 'highly resilient' settlements.

The 'highly resilient' status of settlements in the Bourn Valley suggested by the principles of the theoretical framework is confirmed by the evidence, to an extent. In order to achieve a 'highly resilient' status, a society needed to exhibit none of the indicators or markers for settlement vulnerability defined in Chapter 1. In the face of demographic pressure on resources and the difficult agricultural crises occurring repeatedly in the early fourteenth century, there seems to be no sign of a structural collapse in rural society in the Bourn Valley. No villages were abandoned or deserted during this period and land continued to be cultivated up to the furthest corners of each parish – not retracting until after the Black Death. As seen between 1279 and 1327, population levels also seemed to be highly resilient with a much more moderate stagnation (after the high-medieval population boom) than that seen in East Chilford and elsewhere in England. Of course there was a level of population decline – however moderate – and thus this may question whether the Bourn Valley can truly be labelled 'highly' resilient from 1200 to 1340. It was resilient, for sure, but the emphasis on 'highly' (given the strict application of our indicators for settlement vulnerability) is disputable. The connections of the model between power and property constellations, to resource management strategies, to settlement resilience or vulnerability are confirmed by the evidence, nonetheless. The 'egalitarian-persistent' arrangement of property, social distribution of property, and power did in fact lead to a number of protectionist strategies: the long stability of the open-field system worked through a system of common rights, land fragmentation, and small plot transfer in times of need, for example.

The society of East Chilford between 1200 and 1340 has been assessed as 'intermediate-dynamic'. The intermediate axis for equality is because this society sat in the middle ground on the spectrum. According to the principles of the theoretical framework, this would mean that these arrangements of property (at the user level), social distribution of property, and power led logically to a combination of 'short-termist' and 'flexible' strategies for resource exploitation, and in turn to settlements with some vulnerability – but not exhibiting all the signs of vulnerability as would be the case for a society with entirely 'short-termist' strategies. In fact this combination of 'short-termist' and 'flexible' strategies led to 'vulnerable' status normally equated with 'restrictive-coercive' strategies.

The 'vulnerable' status of settlements in East Chilford suggested by the principles of the theoretical framework is confirmed by what actually can be discerned from the empirical evidence. Indeed, in order to achieve 'vulnerable' status, a society needed to exhibit two of the indicators or markers for settlement vulnerability defined in Chapter 1. Certainly land went out of production and returned to wasteland in the early fourteenth century. It is also clear that demographic retraction had started early in East Chilford – well before the Black Death. With regard to the destruction or depreciation of capital goods and housing, this is more difficult to say without clearer evidence. Certainly settlements were unstable and hamlets were being abandoned at various stages in the late Middle Ages, though at present we cannot say whether this is simply shifting to another site close by. The strategies for resource management as the link between 'type of society' and 'settlement resilience/vulnerability' is also confirmed by what happened in practice. Indeed, some 'short-termist' strategies such as the emergence of large tenant farming, the conversion to more specialised pastoral economy, and the expropriation of the commons occurred, heightening the exposure of rural society to vulnerability, yet these were at least partially off-set by the widespread and unhindered access to local markets from those low down on the social hierarchy.

Chapter 5

Village Communities and Commercialisation: The Rise of Large Tenant Farmers and its Impact on Settlements in the Dutch River Area, 1300–1600

The proliferation of concentrated settlements in Western Europe during various phases between the eighth and thirteenth centuries has been explained with recourse to many different theoretical frameworks[1] – be it through the application of power and *incastellamento*, local autonomy and territorial crystallisation from the bottom up, or the reorganisation of agricultural field systems.[2] Another framework through which rural settlement concentration has been explained is increased commercialisation of the medieval economy, especially from the high Middle Ages onwards. Under this kind of interpretation, rural regions enjoyed the fruits of increased integration of urban markets with commercialised agriculture: the growth of towns and their markets stimulated production in the countryside.[3] Many new high- and late-medieval settlements appeared through the reorganisation of trading patterns with more specialised modes of exchange. In Sicily, for example, some were based around the formation of permanent markets, while others were more transient and temporary and based around rural fairs.[4] The transitory nature of some of these new settlements was especially visible in parts of the south of France, where many rural centres went into a cycle of decline and re-emergence.[5] Coastal villages were formed around specialisation in non-agricultural activities such as fishing,[6] while in some mountain areas, high- and late-medieval concentrations of settlement occurred with the crystallisation of people around small local markets and points of

1 A broad chronology applied in Hamerow, *Early medieval settlements*, 120–4.

2 On these frameworks see Curtis, 'Emergence of concentrated settlements'.

3 Clark, *European Cities*, 44–5 ; Grantham, 'Espaces privilégiés'; Masschaele, *Peasants, merchants and markets*.

4 Epstein, *An island for itself*, chp. 4.

5 Higounet, *Paysages et villages neufs*, 417–38; Germain, 'Les migrations'; Higounet-Nadal, *Perpignan*.

6 Tys and Pieters, 'Understand a medieval fishing settlement'; Fox, *Evolution of the fishing village*.

production, as a result of increases in urban demand for mountain produce such as meat, wool, and wood.[7]

Thus urban demand had a knock-on effect in the countryside, as many new small concentrated settlements sprang up all across Western Europe from the high Middle Ages as rural market centres and trading posts.[8] At the very least, village centres of exchange provided for all the needs of the peasant population, and substantial tenants could be a major source of demand for produce themselves.[9] However, many of these marketing opportunities and institutions were hijacked by powerful sectional and group interests.[10] Lords often granted explicit privileges to certain settlements in the hope of stimulating market centres, and profiting in turn from trade.[11] Some of the larger villagers expanded into small towns as a result of their status as compulsory trading venues for their hinterlands.[12] In the south of France, lords created *bastides* with the prime intention of securing a reservoir of taxes on all trade performed at the market.[13] They served the function of regulating and stabilising traffic in food and textile produce.[14] Many were built with clear grid or circular plans ('*circulades*') based around a market centre.[15] Similarly in Lombardy, the weak position of territorial lords such as the Sforza in the mid-fifteenth century led them to grant jurisdictional independence and autonomy for a number of new rural communities (provoking urban hostility) who crystallised their settlements around markets.[16] Thus in effect, people began to congregate themselves around central squares or greens in a growing culture of barter and trade,[17] and some of these central trading areas can be recognised even today with very distinctive shapes.[18]

However, one of the consequences of commercialisation in late-medieval Western Europe was also economic stratification and polarisation. Of course

---

7 Curtis, 'Florence and its hinterlands'. Also Chapter 3 of this book.

8 Britnell, 'Proliferation of markets'; Lalik, 'Märkte des 12. Jahrhunderts', 364; Jones and Kupper, 'Villes, bourgs et franchises', i, 145; De la Roncière, *Florence*, iii, 951–1013; Toubert, 'Les statuts communaux', 499.

9 Duby, *Early growth*, 162–80; Dyer, *Standards of living*, chp. 6.

10 Epstein, 'Regional fairs', 462. Also see Dyer, 'Consumer'.

11 Goddard, 'Small boroughs'; Taylor, 'Medieval Market Grants'.

12 Rutte, *Stedenpolitiek*, 125–7.

13 See the classics; Higounet, *Les Villeneuves*, 130–9; *Nouvelle approche sur les bastides*, 32–5.

14 Higounet, 'Les origines'.

15 Pawloski, 'Villes et villages circulaire'.

16 Chittolini, 'I capitoli'; 'Governo ducale'; 'Legislazione statutaria'.

17 Higounet, 'Congregare populationem'.

18 As in parts of Tuscany; Cherubini and Francovich, 'Forme e vicende degli insediamenti', 875.

even before the late Middle Ages, social and economic hierarchies had existed in many parts of Western Europe. The most obvious example is the distinction made between lords, often aristocratic and wielding jurisdictional powers, and the peasants or tenants; essentially the 'common folk'. It would be wrong, however, to simply draw an opposition between an elite lordship and a homogeneous mass of rural agriculturalists. Even within one village, there could be numerous social, tenurial, and legal statuses among the peasantry.[19] Although nearly all tenants had to owe some sort of fealty to either a local or territorial lord, some owed more customary dues and had to perform more onerous obligations to their lord than others. In some parts of Western Europe, there was a distinction made between 'serfs' (the unfree) and 'freemen', while certain tenants were able to effectively 'buy' their freedom by commuting customary works into money rents.

Through commercialisation and market integration in late-medieval Europe, these essential stratifications simply became more pronounced within rural societies.[20] Outside the very basic distinctions between lord and peasant, aristocrat and commoner, serf and freeman, new stratifications grew between '*les coqs du village*' and other poorer, less successful inhabitants.[21] Peasants began to produce more surpluses for markets and began to accumulate and consolidate their own landed estates. Social and economic mobility was higher in the late Middle Ages and groups of very wealthy and locally significant, well-to-do rural tenants or farmers were able to emerge from previously very meagre origins as peasants. Consequently, new avenues for disputes between villagers arose, as communities often descended into internal conflict.[22] Successful tenants could pass onto others the exactions and extortions practised by those at the top of the social hierarchy such as lords.[23]

In this chapter, it is considered how this level of increased internal stratification in the late Middle Ages at the local level affected the resilience or vulnerability of settlements. In contrast to the positive interpretation of market integration and village proliferation depicted above, it is clear that economic polarisation could also pose challenges for rural habitations. While a minority became rich through investment and accumulation in land and real estate, less fortunate members of rural society often lost their land, became pauperised, and often ended up as proletarians working as wage labourers on their more

---

19 Menant and Jessenne (eds), *Les élites rurales*; Aparisi and Royo (eds), *Beyond lords and peasants*.

20 Van Bavel, 'Medieval origins of capitalism', 72–7.

21 Duby, *L'économie rurale*, ii, 524, 591; Hilton, *The English peasantry*, 40–1.

22 Bourin, 'Peasant elites and village communities'; Hilton, 'Les communautés villageoises' ; Hanawalt, *Crime and conflict*.

23 Campbell, 'Agrarian problem', 59; Rigby, *English society*, 48–9. Also in the urban context; Keene, 'Property market', 218.

successful neighbour's lands.[24] What happened to these people and how stable were their lives as a result? What happened when common property forms disappeared or when many rural inhabitants became excluded from major 'community' decisions?[25] The connection between commercialisation of the late-medieval economy in Western Europe and the resilience or vulnerability of rural settlement is explored.

These questions are approached in this chapter by zooming in on the commercialisation of a rural region in the Northern Low Countries: the Betuwe in the western part of the Central Dutch River Area from roughly 1300 to 1600. As plotted skilfully in a number of publications by Bas van Bavel, this region was one of the earliest societies to experience commercialisation in the Low Countries. It was also an 'old-settled' region of the Low Countries, which had already established some concentrated village settlements from the Merovingian period. How did late-medieval commercialisation come to affect these settlements in the Betuwe? In the first section, the context of village formation is elaborated upon for the period before the fourteenth century. In the second section, the development of settlement in the period 1300 to 1600 is traced with a particular focus on increased vulnerability in habitation into the early modern period. This vulnerability is measured by the three indicators described in Chapter 1. In the third section, it is argued that this increased vulnerability of settlement in the region was linked to specific changes in the modes of economic exploitation and strategies for resource management resulting from increased market integration and commercialisation. In particular, focus is put on the early decline of the manorial system before 1300, the development of a market in short-term leases, the emergence of large tenant farmers, and a move towards very specialised forms of capital-intensive, labour-extensive pastoral farming. In the fourth section, it is shown that this situation had deep roots in a particular configuration of property and power. Emphasis is put on the long-term persistence of polarised property distribution between social groups and poorly contested balances of power (despite an early decline of the manorial system). This is all summarised in the conclusion in the fifth section, and in the sixth section these findings are placed in the wider theoretical framework described in Chapter 2.

24 Shaw-Taylor, 'Rise of agrarian capitalism'; Glennie, 'In search of agrarian capitalism'.

25 Hoppenbrouwers, "Op. zoek naar de kerels", 232–7; Soens, 'Polders zonder poldermodel?'.

The Formation and Crystallisation of Villages in the Betuwe

The Betuwe is located in the northern part of the Low Countries in a central inland area known as the Central Dutch River Area: a general territory which follows the Waal River (a main distributary branch of the Rhine).

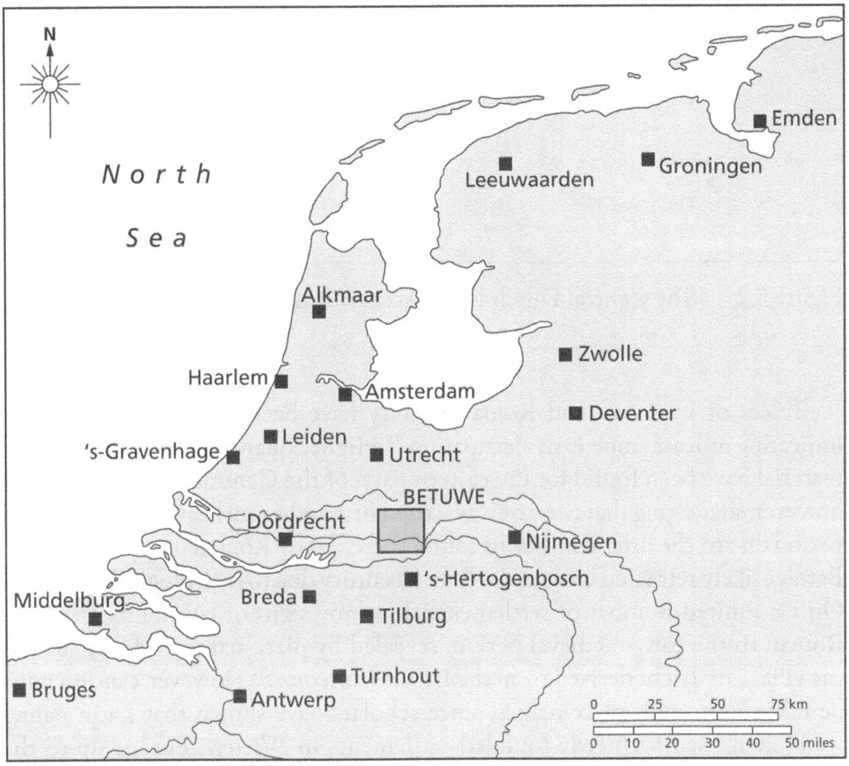

Figure 5.1 Location of the Betuwe in the Northern Low Countries, c.1600

The Betuwe is the most westerly region of the Central Dutch River Area (perhaps more specifically can be called the 'Western Betuwe') and is administratively distinct from other areas further east such as the Neder-Betuwe and the Over-Betuwe. The Betuwe is also bordered to the west by the Vijfheerenlanden (literally 'land with five lords') which has an environment more characteristic of the Holland peat marshes, and to the south by the Bommelerwaard. The Betuwe is made up of four smaller administrative districts known as Land van Buren, Tielerwaard, the Ambt van Beesd and Rhenoy, and Land van Culemborg.

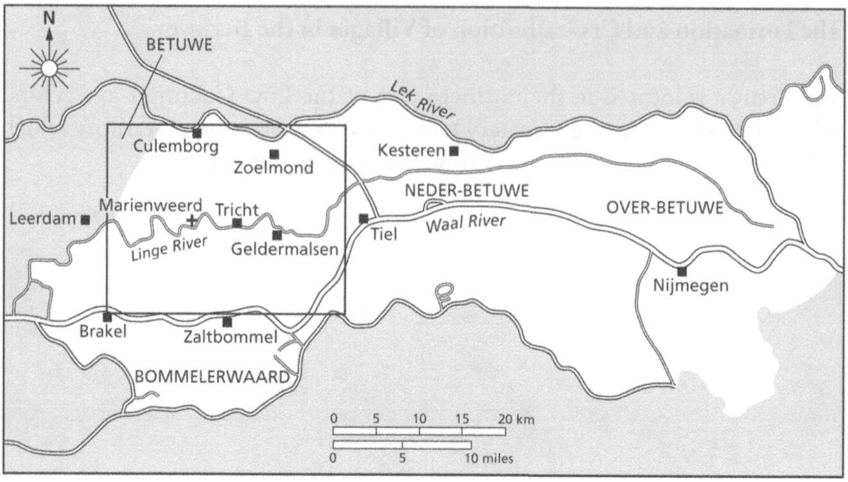

Figure 5.2 The Central Dutch River Area with the Betuwe located

Traces of Iron Age and Roman pottery have been found in the Betuwe, indicating at least some early occupation.[26] Higher quantities of archaeological material have been found for the eastern parts of the Central Dutch River Area however, suggesting that the east was settled first and more heavily in the Roman period due to the drier conditions found there.[27] Any Roman occupation in the Betuwe likely retracted around the fourth century due to hydrological problems. Only a limited number of settlements show any signs of continuity from the Roman to the early-medieval period, revealed by place-name evidence such as the village of Tricht derived from the Latin '*Trajectum*'.[28] However, caution must be taken even with place-names, since scholars have shown that Latin names were often used for newly founded settlements in Western Europe up to the seventh century.[29]

Today most of the significant villages in the Betuwe are found straddling the Linge River which bisects the region down the middle. Many of these

---

26 Taconis and Verhelst, 'Archeologische verkenningen'.

27 Modderman, 'Het oudheidkundig onderzoek van de oude woongronden'; Willems, 'Romans and Batavians'; Folkerts, 'Op. zoek naar Romeinen en Batavieren'. Archaeological finds in the river area have increased through excavation prior to the construction of a road known as the '*Betuweroute*' connecting Rotterdam and Zevenaar; Goudswaard, 'Archeologie en Betuweroute'.

28 Henderikx, *De beneden-delta van Rijn en Maas*, 43; Blok, 'De eigen inbreng van de plaatsnaamkunde', 236–7. A limited continuity in settlement argued in Van Es, 'Volksverhuizing en continuiteit'.

29 Roblin, *Le terroir de Paris*, 89–91.

settlements originated in the late Merovingian period, indicative of a Frankish re-occupation between the sixth and eighth centuries after a probable population nadir following the collapse of the Western Roman Empire.[30] For example, Buurmalsen is one such village with Merovingian origins, characterised by a more rounded structure with houses clustered around a central green (in Dutch a '*brink*').[31] However, most of the settlements along the Linge appeared later in the Carolingian period, and instead can be identified by a more linear, stretched physical form, yet often still combining this curiously with a central green.[32] The Carolingian settlements can also be identified by the way they incorporated the suffix *-heem* into their names, something developed in the late Frankish period.[33] Many of the river-edge villages expanded with demographic growth in the eighth and ninth centuries, fuelled by the crystallisation of the manorial system and the desire to reap rewards of colonisation and agricultural expansion.[34] The small town of Culemborg started out as a small agricultural settlement with block-parcels dating back to these centuries.[35] Population growth likely waned slightly at the end of the ninth century with political unrest (including Viking attacks) but started up once again from the late tenth century.[36]

The reason why people lived in settlements close to the Linge River was because this was the highest land and therefore less affected by flooding and drainage problems.[37] The higher lands were dry enough to support arable agriculture, thus around the villages developed arable open-field complexes made up of an irregular distribution of scattered block-parcels.[38] Remnants of these complexes can still be discerned from the landscape today.[39] It was not until the eleventh century that much of the lower-lying basins away from the Linge River began to be reclaimed – these were areas poorly suited to supporting cultivation or settlement. During the eleventh and twelfth centuries nonetheless, some limited

30 Bult and Hallewas, 'Archaeological evidence for the early-medieval settlement around the Meuse'.

31 Harten and Schuyf, 'Possible planned medieval villages'.

32 The difference between the two types of concentrated settlement are discussed in Den Uyl, 'Dorpen in het rivierengebied'; Renes and Van de Ven, 'Siedlung und Landschaft'; Harten, 'Dorpen in het rivierengebied'.

33 Blok, *De Franken*, 125–30.

34 For arguments of this type elsewhere in North-West Europe see Despy, 'Villes et campagnes'; Devroey, 'Mansi absi'.

35 Renes, 'Culemborg-Redichem'; 'Culemborg en omgeving'.

36 Henderikx, *De beneden-delta van Rijn en Maas.*

37 Renes, *Op. zoek naar de geschiedenis van het landschap*, 70–71.

38 Blok, 'De enken'; Harten, 'Oude nederzettingsvormen', 73–5; Edelman, 'Oudheidkundige resultaten van de bodemkartering', 321–2; Edelman, and Edelman-Vlam, *Over de perceelsnamen*, 11–15.

39 Weijschedé et al., *Gaafheid van bodem*, 33.

attempts were made to settle away from the main villages. The marshy lower-lying lands began to be colonised through 'cope-style' reclamations, bringing more land into use, and being more reminiscent of the colonisation projects seen in the 'Great Reclamation' of Holland between the ninth and thirteenth centuries with long, narrow, standardised strip divisions.[40] Evidence for these late reclamations is the surviving field-patterns which were in stark contrast to the block-parcels of the older-cultivated complexes: for example, the old cultivated Mariënweerdse Veld belonging to the abbey of Mariënweerd contrasted with the strip-formation of Vretstrooy close to the small hamlet of Paveien.

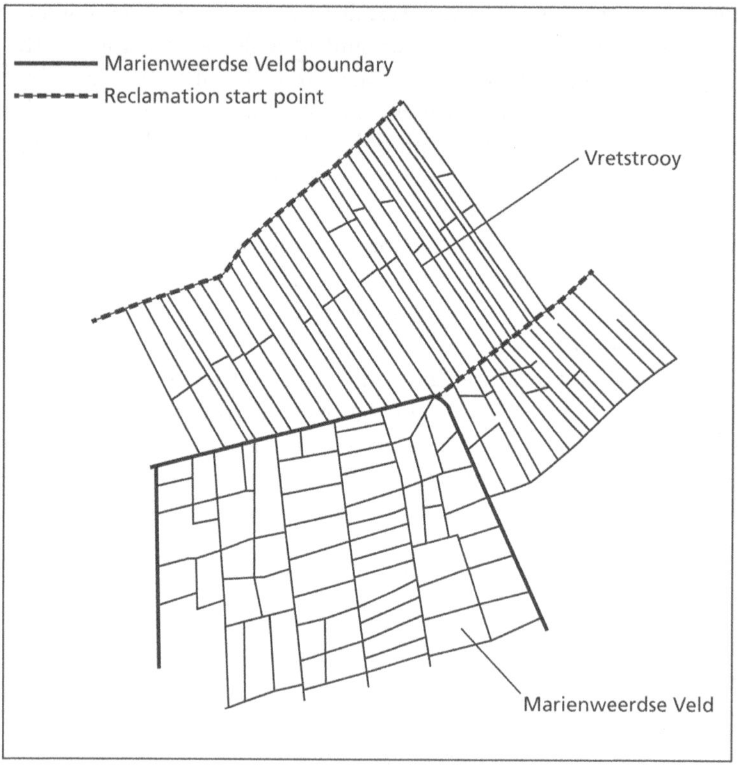

Figure 5.3 Contrasting medieval reclamation patterns in the Betuwe

[40] Van Bavel, 'Mariënweerd'.

Settlement was attempted in such an isolated position as Paveien as early as 1100 because a parish church appeared there, and later the abbey of Mariënweerd took tithes from 20 farms in 'De Geer te Paveien'.[41] However, despite these early attempts at colonisation of the marshy basins, settlement this far from the main villages was neither extensive nor long-lasting. The church of Paveien disappeared not so long after its foundation, sometime between 1166 and 1210.[42] The pace and style of land reclamation in this part of the Betuwe had a role to play in the abandonment of the lower-lying areas (alongside the obvious environmental precariousness), since the lowering of the soil level caused by oxidation of the exposed peat left isolated settlements susceptible to flooding.[43] The soils were further ruined by the almost complete disappearance of trees as colonisation was extended.[44]

It is still not entirely certain who performed the initial reclamations of the lower-lying, poorly drained marshes. Much of the reclamation work began before the foundation of the Mariënweerd (1129), so the role of this Norbertine abbey can be discounted[45] (scholars have tended to emphasise the role of Norbertine expansion in land reclamation).[46] Probably much of the basins were reclaimed in the eleventh and twelfth centuries by aristocratic families such as the Van Cuijks, although some of the very earliest reclamation may even have been undertaken by the Bishop of Utrecht.[47] This assertion is supported by the fact that aristocratic families from an early date owned a great deal of feudal and allodial (free) land in the Betuwe during the Middle Ages; not just the Van Cuijks but also the families of Arkel, Culemborg, and Spijk. Much of their land was located on the older-cultivated areas (as scattered plots) and they had multiple houses in the river villages (for example, Lord Willem van Tuil had 15 hearths in Deil, while the Lord of Enspijk had seven in that village in 1630).[48] However, they also owned lands in the lower-lying basins, for example, the 68

---

41 Renaud, 'Het kerkhof van Paveien'; Beltjes, 'Het kerkhof van Paveie'; Muller and Bouman (eds), *OSU*, i, no. 327. On reclamation in this area see Van Doorninck and Van Veen (eds), *Acten betreffende Gelre en Zutphen*, 29–31.

42 Beltjes and Blommers, 'Eer Culemborg was ...', 106.

43 Pouw, 'Onontgonnen geschiedenis', 19.

44 Mulder, 'Het veranderende landschap', 71–3.

45 Van Bavel, 'Stichtingsplaats, ontginning en goederenverwerving', 46.

46 Andreae Fockema, *Studien over Waterschapsgeschiedenis*; Saint-Denis, 'Les débuts du temporel de Saint-Martin de Laon'; Mostert, 'De goederen van de abdij Berne'; Niermeyer, 'Het klooster Berne'.

47 For the early influence of the Bishop of Utrecht in the Betuwe see Sloet, Van Veen and Martens van Sevenhoven (eds), *Register op. de leenaktenboeken*, 427; Graswinckel (ed.), *Het oud-archief der gemeente Arnhem*, nos 150, 332, 379.

48 GELA, Archief van de Familie van Randwijck, 6090, no. 1324.

hectares of feudal property belonging to the Van Cuijks in the isolated '*Geeren*' area of Buurmalsen.[49]

Despite the periodic and ill-fated attempts at settlement away from the main villages close to the Linge River, it was clear that any permanent habitation in the lower-lying areas would only be achieved if the drainage situation was much improved. This only happened from the late thirteenth century onwards when a more coherent system of dikes was laid down. The Diefdijk was constructed in 1284 to protect the neighbouring Vijfheerenlanden from water flowing down across the Betuwe from the Neder-Betuwe in the east, and was consistently raised in the fourteenth century.[50] At the other end of the Betuwe, the Linge was dammed by Tiel in 1306.[51] Yet even after these innovations, water-related problems remained and small hamlets and farmsteads such as Paveijen, Parijs, Rietveld, Voorkoop and Lanxmeer were abandoned. The dikes may have helped with the drainage of the marshes but they also contributed to the build-up of water-pressure, which if chroniclers from the fifteenth century can be believed, often culminated in severe floods.[52] Constant repairs had to be made to the dikes.[53] Indeed, the abbey of Mariënweerd suffered badly from floods and lost most of their winter supplies in grain when the Linge dike broke in 1432 and 1433.[54] Furthermore, parts of the lower-lying lands were temporarily submerged under water during the winter, even as late as the seventeenth century, as noted in fiscal records from 1650.[55]

Thus, although attempts were made to improve conditions ready for settlement in the lower-lying areas, people in the Betuwe continued mainly to reside within the key river-edge villages all the way into the fifteenth century. Furthermore some of these villages increased in size up to the fourteenth century: for example, archaeological fieldwork has shown new houses continuing to be built before the 1320s in Zandwijk, near Tiel.[56] These villages were crystallised in place also by fortified physical structures. In the Carolingian period this came in the form of basic fortifications from local elites,[57] later to be replaced by fortified manor houses and castles of aristocratic families and manorial lords of the high

49 Kort (ed.), 'Reportorium op. de Cuykse lenen', no. 6.

50 Renes, 'Historisch Culemborg', 2.

51 Stein, 'Rivierverleggingen'.

52 Kuys (ed.), *Tielse kroniek*, 164–7.

53 Van Heiningen, *Dijken en dijkdoorbraken*.

54 Gottschalk (ed.), *Stormvloeden en rivieroverstromingen*, ii, 261–91; GELA, Abdij Mariënweerd te Beesd 2, 1170, no. 112.

55 GELA, Staten van het Kwartier van Nijmegen en hun Gedeputeerden, 0003, no. 368.

56 Verhelst et al., *De nederzetting Zandwijk*, 61.

57 The kinds of structures discussed in Heidinga, 'From Kootwijk to Rhenen'; Van Es, 'Friezen, Franken en Vikingen'; Janssen, 'Tussen woning en versterking'.

Middle Ages,[58] and finally in the form of moated sites of the lesser nobility – built to show off power, status, and pretention.[59] Many high-status residences were moated in the river-edge villages of the Betuwe: for example, the village of Deil had at least seven traceable through archaeological evidence.[60] Likely this was linked to the high number of knights residing there in the late Middle Ages,[61] and one castle, 'Bulckestein', is clearly identifiable with the aristocratic Van Tuyll family.[62] Indeed, while moats in Coastal Flanders or parts of England have been associated with prosperous free tenants and peasant farmers,[63] the moats in this part of the Northern Low Countries seem to have been more restricted to the nobility, regardless of how low down on the aristocratic hierarchy the moat owner fell.[64] Many of the high-status sites were also positioned on raised mounds known as *terpen* – partly for water defence, partly for status reasons.[65] Just to the south of the Betuwe in the Bommelerwaard, whole villages such as Brakel were raised.[66]

Settlement Vulnerability in the Late-Medieval and Early-Modern Betuwe

It is clear that a pattern of firmly established concentrated villages had emerged along the Linge River in the Betuwe – crystallised in a number of phases of the medieval period. In the transition between the late Middle Ages and the early modern period, however, some changes began to be made to the settlement structure. As a result of improvements made to drainage in the Betuwe during the thirteenth and fourteenth centuries, more successful attempts at habitation in the lower-lying areas were made, and from roughly the late fifteenth century (but more intensely in the sixteenth century) new isolated farms began to appear away from the main villages. Indeed, while there were barely any settlements away

58 The kinds of structures discussed in Janssen, 'Castles of the Bishop of Utrecht'; 'Archaeology of the medieval castle'.

59 The kinds of structures discussed in Schuyf, 'Beyond the castle'.

60 Schuyf, 'Beyond the castle'; Van der Aa, *Aardrijkskundig woordenboek der Nederlanden*, iii, 204.

61 GELA, Archief van de Familie van der Capellen, 0467, no. 278.

62 Van Goelst Meijer, 'Het verdwenen kasteel', 5.

63 Verhaeghe, 'Moated sites in Flanders'; Tys, 'Medieval moated sites in Coastal Flanders'; Roberts, 'Historical geography of moated homesteads'; Emery, 'Moated settlements in England', 384.

64 In Holland; Hoek, 'Moated sites in the County of Holland'; Bult, 'Moated sites in their economical and social context'. In the Central Dutch River Area; Van Doesburg, 'Medieval castles', 76.

65 Bosschaert and Driessen, 'Terpen'.

66 Berendsen, *Landschappelijk Nederland*, 113.

from the main villages in 1300, by 1600 there were well over 100 farmhouses dispersed in the fields.

However, this change in the settlement structure seemed to occur simultaneously with the first real contraction and stagnation in the main villages themselves. Although no absolute population figures exist for the Betuwe prior to the Black Death, in line with simultaneous developments elsewhere in Western Europe, it is likely that the Western Betuwe experienced demographic growth between the eleventh and thirteenth centuries and reached a population plateau towards the beginning of the fourteenth century, perhaps ending with the 'Great Death' mentioned by chroniclers of the period in reference to the plagues of 1316.[67] From this point onwards in the 1300s, population levels declined, exacerbated by the impact of the Black Death – however, figures from the Tielerwaard (an administrative district within the Betuwe) suggest that between 1382 and 1470 population recovered by around 17 per cent. This recovery is curious given the mid-fifteenth century was a time of well-documented plagues in the Dutch river area.[68] Nonetheless between 1470 and 1630/50 (the period when new isolated farms began to be built), population once again tumbled to a lower level than in 1369. This demographic decline in the transition from the late Middle Ages to the early modern period was mirrored in the nearby Bommelerwaard. Population did not decline significantly in the Tielerwaard; around 14 per cent between 1470 and 1630/50, and was not that different in 1630/50 from what it was in 1369. However, since the figures from 1369 represented a real population nadir (given the mid-century Black Death), the fact that population was even nearly the same in 1630/50 reveals strong stagnation at a low-level over the long term. The Betuwe did not recover at all well from the fourteenth-century crises. Similar patterns of long-term decline were seen in the Neder-Betuwe to the east. In total around 18,000 people lived in the Betuwe, Neder-Betuwe, and Bommelerwaard combined in the late fourteenth century, but even though this population figure was at a real nadir after the Black Death, some 250 years later in the early seventeenth century it was still basically the same level – real long-term stagnation and no recovery. The Over-Betuwe contained at least 7,300 people in 1470, but by the mid-seventeenth century had lost about 10 per cent of its population. These trends are supported by data on declining numbers of births and the increasing age of marriage in the region. According to van Bavel, the low nuptiality in the region was demonstrated most clearly in the rural households who had little or no land (a sizeable group by the sixteenth century), and had

[67] With particular reference to the Central Dutch River Area see Meister (ed.), 'Niederdeutsche Chroniken', 51. Also nearby Xanthen along the Rhine; Weiler (ed.), *Urkundenbuch des Stiftes Xanten*, i, no. 462.

[68] Blockmans, 'Social and economic effect of the plague'.

on average between one and a half to two children less than families with land.[69] There was no point having children if a household did not have land for them to work on – a basic premise of the small nuclear households seen in eighteenth- and nineteenth-century century Apulia in Southern Italy.[70]

Table 5.1 Population trends for regions in Betuwe and surrounding area, 1369–1630/50

	Tielerwaard	Bommelerwaard	Neder-Betuwe	Over-Betuwe
1369	5,835	5,800	6,200	—
1382/94	5,429	6,900	6,600	—
1470	6,385	—	6,400	7,300
1630/50	5,485	6,200	6,400	6,700

Sources: Van Schaïk, *Belasting, bevolking en bezit*, 273–7; Brusse, *Overleven door ondernemen*, 28–32; Van Bavel, 'People and land'.

In that sense, after forming and crystallising across the *longue durée* of the early and high medieval period, the 'old' village centres began to experience prolonged contraction from the crisis period of the fourteenth century all the way through to the seventeenth century – despite the emergence of new farmhouses in isolated parts. Although very few of the main villages showed any signs of complete disappearance, some settlements did experience strong collapses such as Zoelen and Kerk-Avezaath – already breaking down in the late 1200s with some farms abandoned by the early fourteenth century.[71] More archaeological evidence on settlement contraction from the late Middle Ages onwards would be extremely valuable, but unfortunately archaeologists still put more precedence on Roman and early-medieval structures than those from the late-medieval period.[72] The contraction of the villages in the early modern period was further compounded by the miseries inflicted by incessant warfare. The village of Buren was attacked on several occasions in the fifteenth century, and suffered further ruination of its church and castle by occupying Spanish

69 Van Bavel, 'People and land', 24.

70 Da Molin, 'Family forms'.

71 Oudhof, 'Sporen en structuren'; Botman and Kenemans, 'Sporen en structuren'; Van Renswoude, *Archeologische onderzoek*; Van Doesburg and Schut, *Die hofstat tot Zoelen*.

72 Van Doesburg, Hesselink and Smit, 'Het Rivierengebied', 7. Also the late-medieval wooden building foundations do not survive as well as those from the early-medieval period in general.

troops in 1575. Buurmalsen and Tricht were also badly afflicted,[73] while the aristocratic residents of the Huis van Zoelen decided that it was preferable to burn their house themselves and flee before the troops arrived.[74]

Linking Settlement Vulnerability with Resource Exploitation

What caused this long contraction in settlement between the fourteenth and seventeenth centuries in the Betuwe? Why did the village communities respond so poorly to the repeat crises of the fourteenth century, and why did this stagnation also occur simultaneously with the emergence of new isolated settlement forms? In this chapter it is shown that this process was connected to essential changes in the ways resources were exploited from the late Middle Ages onwards. In particular, focus is put on (a) the decline of direct demesne management and the emergence of capital-intensive, labour-extensive, pastoral tenant farms, (b) the inability to create any significant proto-industries, and (c) the expropriation of the commons as a rural safety net.

In the high Middle Ages, the Central Dutch River Area was highly manorialised. In fact, the strong manorial system before 1300 helped crystallise the series of concentrated settlements straddling the Linge River.[75] A classic association has tended to have been made between scattered distribution of arable plots such as in an open-field system, manorialisation, and concentrated village settlement.[76] It was originally thought that the 'classic' bipartite manor of large demesne and associated serf tenements was completely absent in the Northern Low Countries, though recent work has done much to dispel that notion, and they were certainly present in the Central Dutch River Area.[77] More specifically, manors with bipartite demesnes were present in the Betuwe (with variations in their form and organisation), although they also existed together with manors with demesnes of '*type dispersé*' – small clustered demesnes with scattered tenant properties.[78] Demesnes were exploited with unfree labour taken from the local settlements straddling the Linge River and then increasingly in the high Middle Ages supplemented by wage labour. In order to make this

[73] Dekker, 'Buurmalsen'.

[74] Van Ingen, 'Enige wetenswaardigheden', 8.

[75] As alluded to in Dekker, *Het Kromme Rijngebied*, 31–8; Van Es, Van Doesburg and Van Koningsbruggen, *Van Dorestad naar Wijk bij Duurstede*, 34–43.

[76] For the historiography see Curtis, 'Emergence of concentrated settlements'.

[77] For the original view see Verhulst and De Bock-Doehaerd, 'Social-economische leven tot circa 1000'. Studies revising this position include Buitelaar, *Stichtse ministerialiteit*; Braams, *Weyden en zeyden*; Dekker, *Het Kromme Rijngebied*.

[78] Palmboom, *Het kapittel van Sint Jan te Utrecht*. The diversity in 'types' of manor and demesne near the Rhine are discussed in Verhulst, 'La diversité du régime domanial'.

system work, the serfs were given land to support themselves, which tended to be scattered plots in the open fields (on the highest lands) close to the villages.

In this early heavily manorialised society, rural tenants did not 'own' land per se but merely had access to a package of rights, benefits, and obligations associated with it. Often there were multiple stakeholders in one piece of land, thus adding an extra obstacle to its potential transfer between parties. Land transfer tended to be only conducted with the prior permission of the seigneurial lord, particularly with the holdings of unfree tenants such as serfs. Until the thirteenth century it was actually forbidden to sell an estate in fiefdom in many parts of Western Europe – at least in theory, though not always the case in practice.[79] The payment of a fee to the lord on the transfer of the land was another institutional obstruction and occasionally lords blocked transfers altogether.[80] It is significant then that seigneurial jurisdictions began to wane in the Betuwe during the late thirteenth century in line with a general collapse in the manorial system. For example, the large landowning abbey of Mariënweerd had trouble controlling 70 men on one of their manors at Zoelmond in 1259, who refused to accept their serf status and deserted.[81] By 1300 manorialism had almost completely vanished and bipartite manors worked by dependent serfs had disappeared.[82] Only very small remnants of customary duties remained in the Tielerwaard.[83] Thus despite being a region of strong manorialism, this system also was dismantled very quickly and came to an abrupt end. What this decline allowed, however, was the early emergence of clear inalienable private property rights in the Betuwe informed by the slow infiltration of Roman Law.

First of all, the loss of extra-economic means of coercion meant that aristocratic lords and ecclesiastical institutions no longer had the propensity to exploit their estates directly. Through the fourteenth century, large landowners instead decided to exploit their land indirectly by leasing it out to local peasant tenants. We know a lot about this process thanks to the survival of a number of 'leasebooks' belonging to the large landowning abbey of Mariënweerd.[84] Mariënweerd sub-divided substantial portions of their estates into randomly scattered parcels of about 2.5 hectares each and a patchwork of randomly distributed lease plots emerged in the Betuwe, each worked by a host of different local tenants – many of whom a couple of generations previous may have had serf status.[85] In 1442 (the date of the first available leasebook), there were around 200 different tenants using Mariënweerd land. The unrestricted nature

79 Genicot, *L'économie rurale Namuroise*, i, 125–59.

80 Opsommer, *'Omme dat leengoed es thoochste dinc van der weerelt'*, 422–7.

81 Van Bavel, *Mariënweerd*, 227–8.

82 Van Bavel, *Manors and markets*, 86; Kuys, 'Dagelijkse heerlijkheden', 3.

83 To the Duke of Gelre, for example; Meihuizen (ed.), *De rekening*, 89.

84 For the potential and limitations of this source see Van Bavel, 'Pachtboek'.

85 Van Bavel, 'Land, lease and agriculture', 29.

of the lease market and the fact that it was short-term (land went up for lease at public auction every 6 to 10 years)[86] allowed for a flexible spatial rearrangement of scattered agricultural plots. Quite simply, the farmer who paid the highest price at public auction for the piece of land secured the tenancy. In the course of the fifteenth century, tenant farmers became more selective about which parcels they wanted to lease and with clever organisation and patient management over the long term they could refocus their plots into consolidated farm units. This is essentially the origins of the 100 (and more) isolated farmhouses which emerged in the Betuwe away from the older established concentrated villages.[87]

These new tenant farms in the Betuwe were commercialised and orientated towards buoyant urban markets (especially in Holland) and they followed very capital-intensive but labour-extensive modes of exploitation.[88] Indeed in a general sense, the Duchy of Guelders became more economically and politically connected to the west, loosening its traditional links with principalities in the German Lower Rhine area such as Cleves and Cologne.[89] Very small amounts of surplus were lost in taxation (with the exception of river tolls exacted by territorial lords),[90] which meant more could be invested in the farms. Surplus was used to improve the hydraulics with drainage mills – highly significant in a sodden environment. The enclosure of land into consolidated farm units also reduced transportation and storage costs for products and materials and less time was wasted travelling between plots. Large-scale producers such as the abbey of Mariënweerd acquired a number of strategically placed '*stadshoven*' to store produce in the towns of Culemborg, Zaltbommel, Grave and Cologne.[91] The commercial orientation of these farms went hand-in-hand with a widespread transition from arable to pastoral farming. Even those that did continue with arable cultivation did so with an emphasis on fodder crops and oats for the feeding of animals.[92] Accounts and tithe registrations show that in 1364, only a third of the agricultural land in the Land van Culemborg (an administrative district in the Betuwe) was used as arable, and by 1450 this had declined to just

---

86 For public auctions in river area see Kuys, *De ambtman in het kwartier van Nijmegen*, 164–9. For public auctions in the Land van Culemborg see Cerutti (ed.), *Hoofdstukken uit de Nederlandse rechtsgeschiedenis*, 192. For public auctions in the general Rhineland area see Nève, 'De overdracht van onroerend goed'; Kastner, *Das Schoffenbuch der Stadt Zülpich*, 12–4.

87 Van Bavel, 'Land, lease and agriculture', 31.

88 Ibid., 35–9.

89 Alberts, 'Gelderland'.

90 Weststrate, *In het kielzog van moderne markten*, 106–7; Westermann (ed.), *De rekeningen van de landsheerlijke riviertollen*, 49–88. Other rights of the Duke of Guelders listed in Van Schaïk, 'Taxation, public finances', 263.

91 GELA, AMtB 2, 1170, no. 106.

92 Hoppenbrouwers, 'Agricultural production and technology'.

under a fifth of the total land.[93] Similarly in the Ambt of Beesd and Rhenoy (another administrative district), 48 per cent of the land was arable in 1364 but this declined to just over a third by 1400.[94] Conversion from arable to pastoral farming during the fourteenth and fifteenth centuries was most pronounced in the lower-lying areas away from the Linge River, where heavy soils and poor drainage hampered ploughing. Many sixteenth-century tenant farmers opted to move further towards extensive agriculture, indeed high prices were being paid for meat and dairy produce in the 1500s. The Betuwe became a prominent area for horse-breeding and ox-fattening in the fifteenth and sixteenth centuries, while farmers with sufficient capital invested in orchards necessary for market-orientated fruit production.[95] Farmers took advantage of local markets for horses, cattle, and oxen, which developed in the nearby towns and villages of Beusichem, Culemborg, Nijmegen, Tiel, and Zaltbommel from the second half of the fifteenth century onwards.[96] Another form of extensive agriculture which developed in the late Middle Ages was the exploitation of duck decoys (to trap ducks),[97] which could only be constructed by tenant farmers with sufficient capital.[98]

In short, the result of these realignments in the rural economy meant rural producers who possibly had lost out to more competitive neighbours in the lease market for land also struggled to find work as wage labourers on the new farms. Work was available in the 'Mariënweerdse Veld' which was retained partly as demesne by the abbey of Mariënweerd as late as the sixteenth century for their own provisioning, but this provided employment for just 25 fixed contract workers, 25 temporary workers for the harvest, and 20 single-day workers for times outside the harvest.[99] The lack of work was exacerbated by tenant farmers

---

93 Although some caution must be taken with using tithes to measure agricultural productivity and land under cultivation; see Dejongh and Thoen, 'Arable productivity in Flanders', 33; Dodds, 'Estimating arable output', 254–7.

94 Van Bavel, 'Valuation of arable productivity', 305–6.

95 Van Bavel, 'Land, lease and agriculture', 35–6.

96 On markets in the Betuwe see Benders, 'Item instituimus ibidem singulis annis nundinas', 649–51, 664–5; Den Hoed, 'Beschouwingen rond de Culemborgse stadsrechtbrief', 349–50. On the development of horse fairs from the late fourteenth century onwards in the Betuwe see Dijkman, *Shaping medieval markets*, 60–61. On horse markets in the Betuwe see Van Bavel, *Mariënweerd*, 450–51; Van den Hombergh, 'Brugman en de broodnijd'.

97 Van Bavel, 'Eendenkooien'; Van Tielhof, 'Eendenkooien'.

98 GELA, Waardenburg, no. 584; Nassause Domeinen, no. 148, fo. 231r; ORA Deil, no. 1089, fo. 141v. Many of these decoys were found in low-lying marshes with some belonging to hereditary leasers of the Convent of Mary Magdalene at Wijk bij Duurstede; RAR, Archief Dijkstoel Beesd, 1552–1838, Verpondingen over Beesd 1690, no. 26.

99 Van Bavel, *Mariënweerd*, 436–42.

securing labour from migrant workers who originated from as far as 150 km away in parts of Overijssel (Eastern Netherlands) and who were liable to accept much lower wages.

The lack of employment opportunity in agriculture was compounded by the lack of employment opportunity outside of farming. No significant proto-industries developed in the Betuwe to take on those without agricultural work – just three per cent of the total workforce had proto-industrial employment.[100] This contrasted with the nearby countryside of Holland, where rural producers compensated for the worsening of agricultural conditions such as soil subsidence by occupying themselves in non-agricultural activities.[101] In South and Central Holland, around 45 per cent of rural inhabitants were classified as 'non-agricultural' at the beginning of the sixteenth century.[102] The inhabitants of the Betuwe, however, did not have these options: roughly 80 per cent of households in the mid-sixteenth century were in agricultural work.[103] As well as an absence of proto-industries, there was very limited intensive production of industrial crops such as flax or hops, in contrast to what was produced on tiny peasant plots in inland Flanders.[104] The only hops cultivated were by the abbey of Mariënweerd, which were sold at urban markets in Holland and Nijmegen.[105] Possibly the only significant work away from labouring on the farms was the wage labour needed for maintaining the dikes, which is unsurprising given the wet environment and the frequent breakages.[106]

Another reason for the contraction of the settlements in the late-medieval to early modern transition in the Betuwe may have been connected to the absence or loss of welfare systems that the rural poor could fall back on. Common land never played a dominant role in the economy of the Central Dutch River Area during the Middle Ages (especially in comparison to the east such as Drenthe or Overijssel) but it was not completely absent either.[107] At the beginning of the fourteenth century, there was around two per cent of land under common ownership in the Betuwe, since a large proportion had already been parcelled out into private ownership before documents started making explicit references

100 Van Bavel, 'Proto-industrie tussen de Gelderse rivieren?'.

101 On soil subsidence see De Boer, *Graaf en grafiek*, 222; Van Dam, 'Sinking peat bogs'. On non-agricultural opportunities in late-medieval Holland see Van Zanden, 'A third road to capitalism?'; Van Bavel, 'Early proto-industrialization'.

102 Van Zanden, 'Taking the measure', 135–9.

103 Van Bavel, 'Rural wage labour', 45.

104 Van Bavel, 'Landbouw, bosbouw en visserij'. On intensive peasant cultivation in inland Flanders see Thoen, 'Commercial survival economy'.

105 De Jonge, 'De hopteelt', 78.

106 Van Bavel, *Mariënweerd*, 377–9, 385, 428–9.

107 The area of the Low Countries where common land was important is shown in Hoppenbrouwers, 'Use and management of commons'.

to it.[108] There were two types of common land in the Betuwe.[109] The first was land totally unsuitable for arable cultivation in the lowest of the low-lying marshes away from the Linge River, often used for grazing. The second was the common grazing opportunities on the arable complexes close to the villages, particularly seen in the Land van Buren. In the villages of Buren, Beusichem, and Erichem, there was a combined 85 hectares of common land in total, most of which was divided between three arable fields, and this lasted well into the seventeenth century when it was finally usurped by high-status landowners such as the Count of Buren.[110]

The commons in parts of the Betuwe initially may have helped formalise the crystallisation of concentrated villages during the early and high Middle Ages. Peasants resided around the edges of centrally placed greens which had communal functions and in fact, a precondition of entry into the system was ownership of one of the houses tied to old inheritance rights.[111] The early disappearance of this system in much of the river area, or at least the continual encroachment onto the commons during the fourteenth to sixteenth centuries, likely exacerbated the shrinkage of the villages in the transition into the early modern period. Local peasants did begin to protest to magistrates at their increased exclusion from the common property regime, however, large landowners and tenant farmers of the Betuwe had absolutely no interest in sustaining such a peasant economy, thereby speeding its ultimate decline.[112] This was facilitated to some extent by the fact that the peasants only had limited use-rights on the commons, but actual ownership remained safely in the hands of local lords.[113] In sum, the previous safety net of the commons was completely disintegrated.

It is in this economic context that we can understand the long stagnation of village settlements after the crisis period of the fourteenth century. The combination of underemployment caused by capital-intensive pastoral farming, poorly developed proto-industries, and the absence of good welfare systems to fall back on (which were in any case exclusive and restrictive) made it very difficult for the most unfortunate of rural inhabitants to survive in the Betuwe. As noted earlier, widespread divorcement of rural producers from the land also gave households no incentives to produce more children – thereby slowly reducing nuptiality. The lack of opportunity in the Betuwe was compounded by

---

108 Reference to very small pieces of common land are still found in the Betuwe, however, even as late as the seventeenth century; for example GELA, Familie Pieck, 0480, no. 46.

109 Van Bavel, *Transitie en continuïteit*, 274–8.

110 Koch and Maris, 'Meentgenootschappen', 193–4.

111 See the map at Erichem in RAR, Oud Archief Buren, 0692, no. 743. Some inhabitants got permission to build on the commons; Idem, no. 747.

112 Ibid., no. 746.

113 Kos, 'De goede luden', 182.

the plethora of opportunities to be found outside the Betuwe, particularly to the west in nearby Holland which began to flourish economically in the late Middle Ages. Holland became a magnet for those impoverished rural dwellers of the Betuwe who had been divorced from the productive process. Indeed, Holland displayed some unusual demographic trends in that although it was affected in the short term by the Black Death, population quickly began to rise again during the fourteenth and fifteenth centuries – quite anomalous to what was happening in many parts of Western Europe during the period.[114] Rural population figures only started to level off towards 1600 in Holland, first in the South and later in the North.[115] This levelling-off of the rural population in Holland was likely caused by two processes which evolved over the sixteenth century: an increase in the age of marriage (lowering the birth rate in turn) and widespread migration to the cities and towns linked to the plethora of opportunity there and expropriation of peasant property by wealthy urbanites.[116] Similar to the Holland peasants, impoverished wage labourers of the Betuwe also flocked towards the towns and cities of Holland. Sixteenth- and seventeenth-century urbanisation in the core economically developed region of Holland owed as much to rural crisis as it did to vigour and buoyancy of the urban economies.[117] It is in this rural-urban migration that we can understand why the cities and towns of Holland kept growing in population during the seventeenth century after Holland's rural demographic boom had subsided.[118]

The cycle of deprivation and contraction may have continued in the Betuwe beyond the seventeenth century were it not for the chance introduction of potatoes after 1700, which gave the chance for agricultural labourers to secure a livelihood through highly intensive cultivation,[119] despite the fact that economic polarisation continued unabated.[120] Pressure was also eased later by the emergence of fruit production,[121] and (in the Neder-Betuwe) by opportunities

---

114 Van Bavel, 'Population and land'; Van Bavel and Van Zanden, 'The jump start of the Holland economy'.

115 Van Zanden, *Rise and decline of Holland's economy*, 35–40.

116 De Moor and Van Zanden, 'Girlpower'; Van Bavel, 'Rural development'.

117 De Boer, *Graaf en grafiek*, 211–45; De Vries and Van der Woude, *First modern economy*, 19.

118 Lourens and Lucassen, *Inwonertallen van Nederlandse steden*, 100–23; Prak and Van Zanden, 'Demographic change', 245.

119 GELA, Rechterlijk Archief Over-Betuwe, no. 481. Also Roessingh, 'Het begin van het aardappelteelt'; Bieleman, 'De Gelderse landbouw', 38–9, 48–50, 59–60.

120 Bieleman, 'De Gelderse landbouw', 57.

121 Sangers, *De ontwikkeling van de Nederlandse tuinbouw*, 111. See the high access to orchards in Buurmalsen and Tricht in SWB, Archief van de Dorpen Buurmalsen en Tricht (1581) 1594–1811 (1826), no. 225.

to work with tobacco crops,[122] often in sharecropping terms offered by former large tenant farmers who by the eighteenth century had bought their farms outright.[123] Nonetheless, eighteenth-century travellers to the region were still decidedly unimpressed: one unnamed 'English Gentleman' noted as late as 1786 that the roads of the Betuwe were muddy, miserable and impassable, with sparse populations who bore great signs of misery and poverty.[124] Another Englishman just a few years later described the route through the region as 'the worst that he had ever seen' and an abject vision of widespread poverty.[125]

Property and Power

The poor resilience of settlements in the Betuwe after the rupture of the fourteenth century was connected to the new paths taken in modes of economic exploitation around the same time. The question remains, however, why did these economic changes take place? Exogenous crisis such as plague and flooding hit Holland in the fourteenth century, and yet this did not stimulate the same kind of response seen in the Betuwe.[126] It is argued in this section that much was built upon the very particular underlying and interrelated constellations of property and power.

Vulnerability in the Betuwe villages was connected to the emergence of capital-intensive pastoral farming. This situation was only possible in the first place, however, through the ease with which tenant farmers could accumulate and consolidate their holdings – often to the detriment of their weaker neighbours. Although each parcel of land went up for lease every 6 to 10 years, often it would stay in the same families' hands for generations upon generations, if they were able to out-compete any rival bids from neighbours of inferior resources. The stability of some of these farms was reinforced by strong relationships between landlords and tenant farmers, who were offered favourable credit conditions and lower rents during periods of crisis such as exceptionally poor harvests.[127] The farmhouse and complex of 'Rijsen Ooijen' near Meteren is one example of considerable continuity in both ownership and occupation despite being farmed through a short-term lease.[128]

---

122 Roessingh, *Inlandse tabak.*

123 Brusse, *Overleven door ondernemen.*

124 Anon., *An entertaining tour*, 170–74.

125 Owen, *Travels*, i, letter 22.

126 See a positive interpretation of the response to crisis in Holland in Van Bavel and Van Zanden, 'The jump-start of the Holland economy'.

127 As seen in other parts of the Low Countries in Van der Woude, 'Large estates and small holdings', 194–5; Baars, *Geschiedenis van de landbouw*, 122–4, 200–204.

128 Van Olst, 'Rijsen Ooijen', 30.

The process described above is best highlighted through some individual examples, a good one being the fortunes of the 'Haag Spijk' farmhouse near Buurmalsen. It was almost certainly located in the same position of the modern-day farmhouse of 'Den Haag'. The Haag Spijk was not mentioned in the early cartularies belonging to Mariënweerd, though it was listed in the abbey's property register of 1347. By the mid-fourteenth century, the Haag Spijk was already clearly an important farmhouse for the abbey. It was listed as a '*hofstat op. die spijk*' (the term *hofstat* or *hofstede* tended to be reserved for more important farms) and consisted of around 30 hectares.[129] It was likely a compact unit at this time because the whole 30 hectares were recorded under one entry. Other lands belonging to Mariënweerd also came to 30 hectares or more in certain areas, but these were not under one entry but usually split between three or more fields. The farmhouse lay peripheral to the actual village of Buurmalsen (away from the central green though near the peripherally located aristocratic residences of 'Arkelshoef' and 'Reygersvoort')[130] though it was situated within what can now be identified as an open-field complex, made distinct by the irregular patchwork of plots and the characteristic 's'-shape of the boundaries caused by the poor turning circle of the heavy plough used.[131] The fact it was situated on older-cultivated ground (although away from the main village) and that it appeared to be a consolidated farm unit from an early date suggests that the Haag Spijk may originally have been an early '*uithof*' or grange belonging to Mariënweerd. Mariënweerd's first granges such as Ganshoevel and De Woerd were formed through gifts of land by the Van Cuijk family and lay within the 'Mariënweerdse Veld'.[132] Granges further away like the Haag Spijk, however, were built-up and extended by gifts and purchase from local smallholders and medium-sized proprietors, a chronology in line with Norbertine and Cistercian institutions elsewhere in Europe.[133]

As Mariënweerd moved from direct exploitation to indirect leasing of its estates from the mid-fourteenth century onwards, the compact farm of *Haag Spijk* was broken up into separate pieces and leased out to farmers. By 1456, it had been divided into three smaller units of 3.5 hectares each and one 12.5-hectare unit.[134] The lands were leased to two local farmers, Wouter Lamertssoen and William Pits. Wouter Lamertssoen had already started trying to accumulate lease land in the fifteenth century: indeed, he was one of the first land consolidators in the area. He held a total of almost 70 hectares from the

129 De Fremery (ed.), *Cartularium*, no. 363.

130 Belonje, 'Het huis Reygersfoort'.

131 Harten, 'Rivierkleilandschap'; 'Invloed van de mens op. het landschap'.

132 Muller and Bouman (eds), *OSU*, i, no. 18; De Fremery (ed.), *Cartularium*, nos 49, 51.

133 See the historiographical essay; Alfonso, 'Cistercians and feudalism'.

134 GELA, AMtB 2, 1170, no. 68, fos 5v–6r.

abbey in various places around Buurmalsen,[135] and feasibly he could even have had more than that, since there is nothing to say that he did not lease land from another institution or aristocrat, or perhaps even own land himself.

The Haag Spijk was still sub-divided into smaller plots in 1490; each averaged around 4 hectares, though by this time three-quarters of the plots were now consolidated into the hands of tenant farmer, Jan Wouterssoen, probably related to the aforementioned Wouter.[136] By the sixteenth century, the lease books show that the Haag Spijk had been rearranged into a complete farm unit once again. In 1550 the farm was now leased under a complete entity to individual farmers and was not sub-divided into different parcels.[137] It was during the sixteenth century that either a new farmhouse appeared at the Haag Spijk, or at the very least, an older inferior one was replaced or renovated into a larger and grander version. By the mid-century, it was described as a large farmhouse with a front and back house, a cellar, and glass windows. The costs of renovating the Haag Spijk in 1548 came to 477 *carolus* guilders, which were spent on materials such as wood, iron, stone, chalk, reeds, as well as the wage labour.[138] The high amount represents a long renovation process, probably equivalent to 6 years of wages payable to a carpenter at the time. The farmhouse was also surrounded by other buildings such as sheds, haystacks, sheep pens, as well as an orchard and a copse. The farmhouse was also situated on a '*terp*' (raised mound) as a mode of protection from flooding and to assert the status of the site.[139]

The Haag Spijk is just one example but is illustrative of a general process. The same sort of developments have been reconstructed from the manuscript sources for the isolated tenant farms of Treeft, Ganshoevel, De Woerd, and Dijstelcamp, to name but a few.[140] Many of the farms seemed to follow the same pattern of being important directly exploited granges or *uithoven* in the twelfth and thirteenth centuries, being dismantled through leasing in the fourteenth and fifteenth centuries, and then re-emerging on the same locations in the sixteenth century as tenant farms. This may have been a general trend for the whole Central Dutch River Area: for example, the 'Hoff te Heteren' in the Over-Betuwe grew into a large compact tenant farm in the fifteenth and sixteenth centuries (after being

135 GELA, AMtB 2, 1170, no. 68, fos 5v–6v.

136 GELA, AMtB 2, 1170, no. 69, fo. 3.

137 GELA, AMtB 2, 1170, no. 73, fo. 177, no. 74, fos 133–4.

138 GELA, AMtB 2, 1170, no. 171.

139 Bosschaert and Driessen, 'Terpen'.

140 For the *Treeft* see GELA, AMtB 2, 1170, no. 68, fo. 6r, no. 69; De Fremery (ed.), *Cartularium*, no. 363; GELA, AMtB 1, 0283, no. 9. For the *Ganshoevel* see De Fremery (ed.), *Cartularium*, nos 49, 51, 347; GELA, AMtB 2, 1170, no. 68, fo. 2, 6r, no. 73, no. 38; GELA, Oud Archief Tiel, 0001, nos 852–7. For *De Woerd* see De Fremery (ed.), *Cartularium*, no. 349; GELA, AMtB 2, 1170, no. 68, fos 1r–8r, no. 38. For the *Dijstelcamp* see GELA, AMtB 2, 1170, no. 68, fo. 3v, no. 73.

donated to the dean of St. Pieter at Utrecht)[141] but was an administrative centre earlier in the Middle Ages for the monastery of Renkum.[142] The distribution of possible granges and tenant farms connected to Mariënweerd is shown in Figure 5.4. These elements of continuity and discontinuity in farms have already been discussed for other parts of Europe such as the sharecropping *poderi* which often emerged on the previous relics of manorial *curtes* and granges.[143]

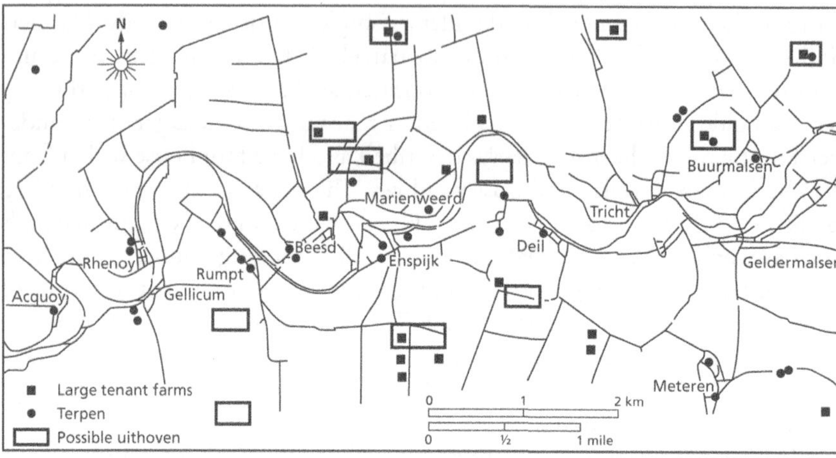

Figure 5.4 Distribution of Mariënweerd *uithoven* (1350) and locations of large tenant farms (1550) in the Betuwe

This capacity for accumulation and consolidation of lease land provided the basic contextual conditions for the emergence of capital-intensive pastoral farms. As a result of consolidation of lease land into the hands of the few, many rural dwellers ended up without access to even one morsel of land. Accumulation came at the expense of smaller farmers, many of whom lost the means of production and became proletarianised.[144] The average size of lease holdings doubled from 7 hectares in 1442 to 14 hectares in 1580, while the actual number of tenants decreased from 172 in 1442 to 93 in 1580.[145] As Figures 5.5 and 5.6 show, in 1456 there were no tenant farmers with more than 40 hectares but 100 years later in 1550 farms over 40 hectares took up around

141 Tersteeg and Scheepsma (eds), *Cartularium Renkum*, 31–2.

142 Van de Westeringh, 'Boerderij 't Hoff', 45.

143 Comba, 'Le origini medievali'; 'La dispersione dell'habitat'.

144 The landless labourers discussed in Van Bavel, 'Transition in the Low Countries'; 'Rural wage labour'.

145 Van Bavel, *Mariënweerd*, 396.

42 per cent of land belonging to the abbey of Mariënweerd. While in 1456 over 80 per cent of the land was distributed in farms of 3 to 20 hectares and worked by the peasant household, in 1550 this figure had dropped to just a third of the land. Lease land was distributed at a Gini index of 0.74 in 1456 (0.83 if you add the Mariënweerd self-exploited lands to the total) but in 1550 it was more unequal at 0.85. The proportion of land farmed in large units was also even higher than the lease books suggest, given that nobles and religious institutions such as Zennewijnen (68 hectares) or Mariënweerd (fluctuating around the 360-hectare mark) continued to exploit farms or demesne directly.[146] Across the whole of the Betuwe in its entirety, by the end of the sixteenth century there were around a hundred farms of more than 40 hectares.[147]

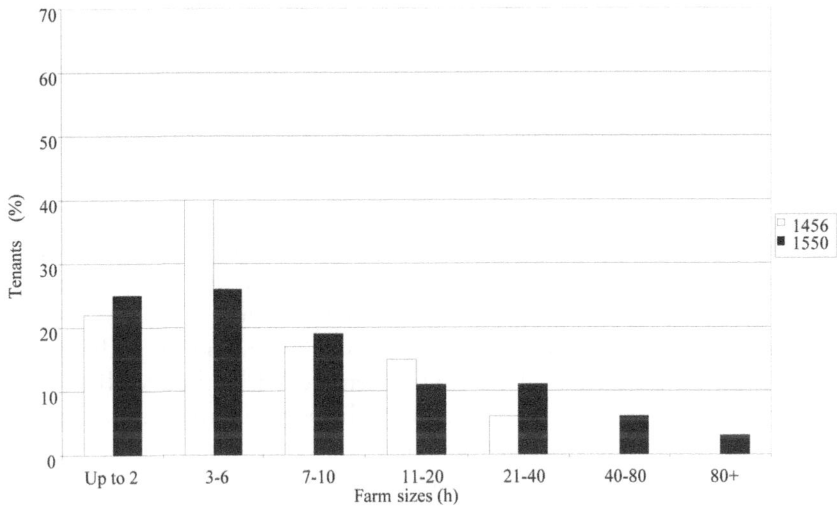

Figure 5.5 Size of tenant farms leased from Mariënweerd, 1456/1550 (divided by tenants)

Sources: GELA, AMtB 2, 1170, nos 68, 73.

[146] Van Bavel, *Transitie en continuitëit*, 575; GELA, Abdij Mariënweerd te Beesd 2, 1170, no. 67, no. 116, fos 35–36.

[147] Van Bavel, *Mariënweerd*, 396.

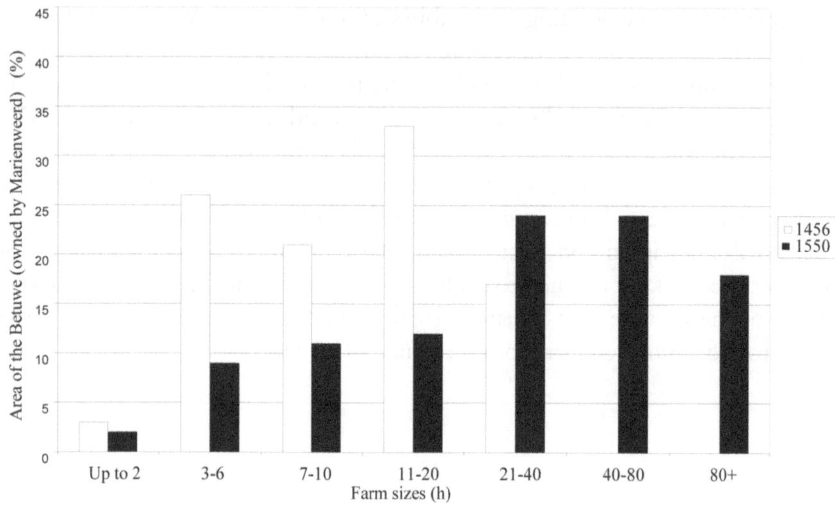

Figure 5.6 Size of tenant farms leased from Mariënweerd, 1456/1550 (divided by area)

Sources: GELA, AMtB 2, 1170, nos 68, 73.

Capital-intensive pastoral farming may have emerged on the back of the consolidation and polarised distribution of lease land at the user level, but then how do we explain the basic proliferation of the short-term lease? For this the answer lies in the social distribution of landownership seen in the Betuwe between the Middle Ages and the early modern period. By the late Middle Ages in many areas of Western Europe, land was being transferred between parties more freely leading to social and economic stratification in the countryside, as some peasants and tenants began to accumulate land to the detriment of their neighbours (for example see Chapter 4). After the decline of the manorial system in the Betuwe, however, this did not happen – land ownership barely changed at all. In fact, it remained proportionally in the hands of the same social interest groups over a number of centuries. A fluid and flexible market in land did not emerge at all. In the twelfth and thirteenth centuries, ecclesiastical institutions such as the abbey of Mariënweerd obtained vast amounts of land, first through concession by noble families and later by purchase, yet after 1300 very little change occurred in the structure of landownership. Land was actually very immobile, and a sale was made only every 45 to 55 years on average, which is a much lower turnover of land than for leasehold, where land went up for auction every 6 to 10 years.

Over a long period of 250 years and during a time of great social and economic upheaval in Western Europe, land in the Betuwe continued to be distributed unequally in the hands of certain elite social groups, these being the large ecclesiastical institutions (like Mariënweerd), local aristocratic families, and then to a much lesser extent, territorial lords and the urban bourgeoisie or institutions. Peasants and farmers in the Betuwe owned only between a fifth and quarter of the land in the period 1300 to 1550.

Table 5.2 Social distribution of landownership in the Western Betuwe, 1300–1600 (%)

	c. 1300	**c. 1400**	**c. 1500**	**c. 1600**
Aristocratic / noble	48	45	35	34
Ecclesiastical institutions	11	15	18	18
Lay / charitable institutions	4	7	13	15
Urban	6	8	9	11
Rural peasants / farmers	27	24	24	22
Total	**96**	**99**	**99**	**100**

Note: In 1300, 2 per cent of land was common and 2 per cent unknown. In 1400 and 1500, 1 per cent of land was common. Adapted from: Van Bavel, *Transitie en continuitëit*, 427.

The stability in this imbalanced property distribution between the late Middle Ages and the early modern period maintained inequality on a landownership level but also inadvertently stimulated a polarised distribution of land at the user level by providing ripe conditions for the emergence of short-term leasing. Already the rapid decline of manorialism had paved the way for the establishment of clear inalienable property rights.[148] The continued dominance of large landownership by former manorial lords and ecclesiastical institutions after the collapse of formalised manorialism in the late Middle Ages increased the likelihood of a system of short-term leasing to emerge as it stopped the peasantry getting its hands on a higher share of land. If peasants had been able to secure a larger share of land through the decline of manorialism in the Betuwe, short-term leasehold would never have become so influential as small peasants were more likely to cling onto their land and work it themselves.[149] Furthermore, peasants with restricted capital were much less likely to make financial investments in their farms, slowing the general commercialisation of agriculture.[150]

148 Van Bavel, 'Organisation and rise of land and lease markets'; 'Emergence and growth of short-term leasing'.

149 As noted recently, secure small peasant property structures limited leasehold's economic impact; Wilkin, 'Role of the secular canons'.

150 Van Bavel, 'Land, lease and agriculture', 29–30.

The final question of course is that if the proliferation of the short-term lease (which was so vital to late-medieval and early modern settlement change) was dependent on the stability of large landownership over many centuries, how did the large landowners (aristocrats, former manorial lords, and ecclesiastical institutions) achieve this? The answer is that these particular social groups were barely challenged for their position over the long term. Into the late Middle Ages and early modern period, towns had minimal influence over the countryside in the Betuwe, demonstrating how urbanisation and commercialisation in the pre-industrial period were never one and the same thing and urban growth cannot be a clear proxy for economic development.[151] Despite replacing Dorestad as a developing urban centre in the tenth century, Tiel had very little influence over the surrounding countryside in the late Middle Ages, partly due to the fact that its early merchant guild associations did not expand out of their eleventh-century roots[152] (the merchant guild of Tiel was mentioned by a cleric in 1020, one of the earliest references in Europe).[153] Furthermore, urban landownership in the Betuwe continued to play an insignificant role well into the sixteenth century and beyond, in complete contrast to other areas such as Flanders and Holland.[154] Even where it was more significant, it was never typical land associated with absentee burghers but actually citizens of small towns such as Culemborg farming their own plots just outside the town.[155] The eastern parts of the Central Dutch River Area such as the Neder-Betuwe and the Over-Betuwe, which were closer to the towns of Nijmegen and Arnhem, had slightly higher levels of burgher landownership but still the majority of this was ecclesiastical and composed of monasteries, vicarages, and hospitals.[156]

Territorial lords such as the Bishop of Utrecht, the Count of Holland, and the Duke of Guelders equally exerted minimal influence in the Betuwe. Admittedly the Duke of Guelders did hold the feudal over-lordship over half the feudal property in the Betuwe and owned eight per cent of the total land

---

151 Van Bavel, *Manors and markets*, 384.

152 For the end of Dorestad see Van Es, 'Dorestad centred'; Hodges, 'Dark Ages economics revisited'; Coupland, 'Trading places'. For the rise and decline of Tiel see Sarfatij, 'Tiel in succession to Dorestad'; Oudhof, 'De handelsfunctie van Tiel'. For the early guilds of Tiel see Akkerman, 'Het koopmansgilde'; De Munck, Lourens and Lucassen, 'Establishment and distribution of craft guilds', 34–5.

153 Mettensis, *De diversitate temporum et Fragmentum de Deoderico primo episcopo Mettensi*, 81.

154 However, urban institutions (especially from Zaltbommel) did gain more land in the Betuwe in the late sixteenth and seventeenth centuries; see GELA, Staten van het Kwartier van Nijmegen en hun Gedeputeerden, 0003, nos 368–72; GELA, Huis Enspijk, 0390, no. 39. Also Leupen, 'Zaltbommel'.

155 Van Bavel, *Transitie en continuitëit*, 509–11.

156 Van Schaïk, 'Nijmegen, Arnhem en de Betuwe', 104.

within the Tielerwaard.[157] A large portion of land came into the hands of the Duke in 1265 when he exchanged with Rodolf Cock his *curtes* at Opijnen and Neerijnen for an area stretching between Leerdam and Beesd – clearly a territorial strategy aimed at neutralising the threat of the Count of Holland.[158] However, most of this land was granted in fiefdom to various men of high social status, which became ever more frequent in the late Middle Ages when the Duke was beset by financial problems (as evidenced by increased tax pressure on subjects of the Duchy).[159] The Huis te Rumpt, Crayestein te Tricht and the Huis te Meteren are three examples of high-status properties bestowed to noble men as part of a fiefdom and traceable in the Gelre and Buren feudal books.[160] In that sense, the feudal land belonging to the Duke of Guelders did not give him great influence over the Betuwe, and in fact, by creating fiefs with the land he achieved the opposite. Rather than creating a group of loyal subjects in the countryside, the granting away of land to local nobles and aristocrats only served to strengthen the manorial lords as a social group vis-à-vis the territorial lords. It gave room for the crystallisation of independent lordships such as Arkel, Buren and Culemborg.[161] Furthermore, some areas of the Betuwe such as the Land van Buren began to claim immunity from the payment of taxes to the Duke.[162] An example of the tension between the territorial lords and the local nobles is seen in a fraught episode in 1457 between the Duke of Guelders and Arnt Pieck (who had previously held the fortified '*Hoge Huis*' of Beesd in fiefdom from the Duke).[163] The precise reason for the dispute is unclear but it seems to have been related to Arnt's recent installation as administrative overseer of the Ambt Beesd and Rhenoy.[164]

The large aristocratic or ecclesiastical landowners, furthermore, did not encounter any pressure from below from the local peasants and farmers. Indeed, as already noted, local rural people had such a small proportion of landownership in the Betuwe that they had no foundations or tools to disturb the imbalance of power weighted in favour of the large institutions and nobles. Van Bavel has shown that rural revolts were not that common in the Central Dutch River Area, especially in comparison to other parts of the Low Countries

157 Van Bavel, *Transitie en continuïteit*, 218–9.

158 GELA, Hertogelijk Archief, no. 25, fo. 13r.

159 Van Schaïk, 'Socio-economic inequality in town and countryside', 143.

160 Belonje, 'Crayesteyn'; Baelaerts van Blokland, 'Het in 1553 gebouwde huis te Rumpt'; Beresteyn, 'Het huis te Meteren'.

161 Palmboom, 'De stichting', 248.

162 Van Schaïk, 'Taxation, public finances', 268.

163 Schouten, 'Het Hoge Huis', 21.

164 GELA, Hertogelijk Archief, no. 860; GELA, Graven en Hertogen van Gelre, Graven van Zutphen, 0001, no. 645.

which had greater traditions of personal freedom and a conspicuous absence of manorialism.[165]

Conclusion

From the late Merovingian period, villages came to develop along the edges of the Linge River in the Betuwe. These proliferated in the Carolingian period and became bigger and more populous between the eleventh and thirteenth centuries, crystallised by the open-field system, manorialism and demesne agriculture, and fortifications. The Betuwe, like most areas of Western Europe, experienced a crisis period in the fourteenth century, however, characterised by repeat plagues (particularly in 1316 but also the Black Death) and exacerbated by flooding problems. From a medieval population nadir in the late fourteenth century, however, the villages in the Betuwe did not recover well. In fact the population of the early seventeenth century was even lower than that seen not so long after the terrible impact of the Black Death. Some of the villages have shown archaeological signs of late-medieval contraction and collapse.

Poor recovery of societies after the fourteenth century crises was not inevitable. In nearby Holland, it has been shown that the particular socio-political configurations inherited from the reclamation context gave this region high resilience against exogenous hazards. The Betuwe performed poorly because of its move towards particular modes of economic exploitation of resources: the emergence of the short-term lease, the move to capital-intensive pastoral farming, the poorly developed proto-industries and non-agricultural sector, and the expropriation of the commons. These developments pushed rural people out of the region in search of new opportunities, and furthermore, induced rural households to limit their numbers of children. Again this economic direction was not inevitable: it was formed against the background of particular constellations in property and power. These deep foundations included high inequality of property distribution at the user level, persistent and stable inequality in the social distribution of landownership, and a lack of dynamism and change in the social distribution of power.

Fitting the Findings into the Theoretical Framework

In this final section, the information taken from the case study in the late-medieval and early modern Betuwe is placed into the theoretical framework outlined in Chapter 2.

165 Van Bavel, 'Rural revolts'.

Property, Social Distribution of Property, and Power

Unfortunately it was not possible to account for all the property and how it was distributed at the user level between 1300 and 1600. Van Bavel has written two books (one of 500 and another of 600 pages) on property structure in the Betuwe region, and even he was not able to reconstruct property in its entirety (only at the owner level did he manage this). The Gini indexes as an indicator of property distribution in the Betuwe have been taken solely from distribution of lease land belonging to the abbey of Mariënweerd. In many administrative districts this accounted for between a third and a half of total land. Obviously there are some limitations to this method, the main one being that the source does not account for the landless – thus the Gini indexes are lower than they probably should be. However, given that the Gini indexes were 0.74 in 1456 (0.83 if you add Mariënweerd self-exploited land) and 0.85 in 1550, this problem is limited somewhat by the fact that the figures are already assessed as 'polarised'. Adding landless to the dataset would simply make the property distribution assessment 'more polarised'. Having Gini indexes for more than one date also allowed a good quantitative indicator for dynamism in the property structure. Indeed, between 1456 and 1550 the Gini index jumped from 0.74 to 0.85, a total of 0.11, which was above the 0.1 needed to acquire 'dynamic' status. Furthermore, it has been shown that the lease market was entirely fluid and lease land was put up for auction every 6 to 10 years.

Thanks to van Bavel, we have excellent data on social distribution of landownership in the Betuwe – data to rival any rural region in Western Europe in the late Middle Ages or early modern period. At no point between 1300 and 1600 did the rural-dwelling peasantry or farmers ever own more than 27 per cent of the land – thus firmly displaying the criteria needed to be assessed as 'polarised'. In the same period, large ecclesiastical institutions and aristocratic landlords owned between 52 and 60 per cent of the land. Another clear feature of this polarised social distribution of landownership was its persistence over the long term. The same social interest groups remained owners of the land from the fourteenth to the sixteenth century, regardless of demographic or economic changes. Between 1300 and 1600, the peasantry's share of the land went from 27 per cent to 22 per cent, hardly changing at all over a period of 300 years.

The distribution of power was less clear-cut. Prior to 1300 one surely could say that this was a really coercive and repressive region with the dominance of large manors and the preponderance of serfs. However, manorialism and serfdom had all but disappeared by 1300, thus giving the rural communities some freedoms. Repressive jurisdictions had gone and there is no evidence for harsh or onerous taxation after 1300. Yet at the same time, this has to be balanced out with other trends such as the loss of rights, privileges and access to the commons – protested by rural dwellers but seemingly ignored. Thus, power has been assessed as 'intermediate' in terms of distribution. It was clear, however, that the balance of power stayed very stable over many centuries after 1300. Many regions of Western Europe saw increased powers and freedoms given to the peasants after the Black Death or even peasant revolts. Other regions experienced greater political and economic connection between town and countryside. Power in the Betuwe, however, stayed almost in a vacuum over the long term – and even the territorial lord (Duke of Guelders) could not or did not gain a strong grip over jurisdictions in the region.

Table 5.3 The breakdown of the Betuwe (1300–1600) into quantifiable configurations

	Egalitarian-Polarised	**Dynamic-Persistent**
Property	0	1
Social distribution of property	0	0
Power	0.5	0
Total scores	**0.17**	**0.33**

Type of society: polarised-persistent.

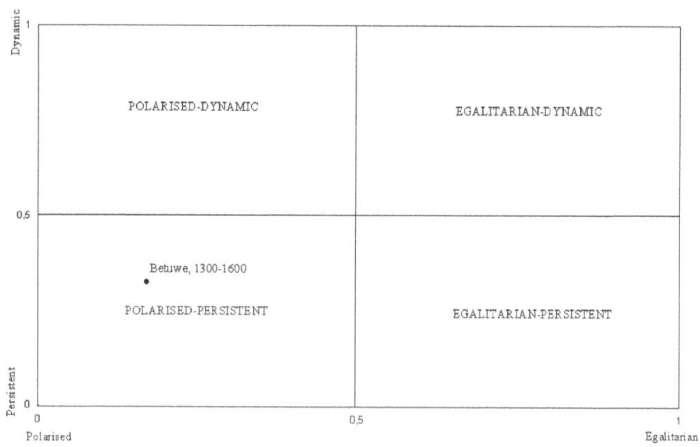

Figure 5.7 What type of society was the Betuwe, 1300–1600?

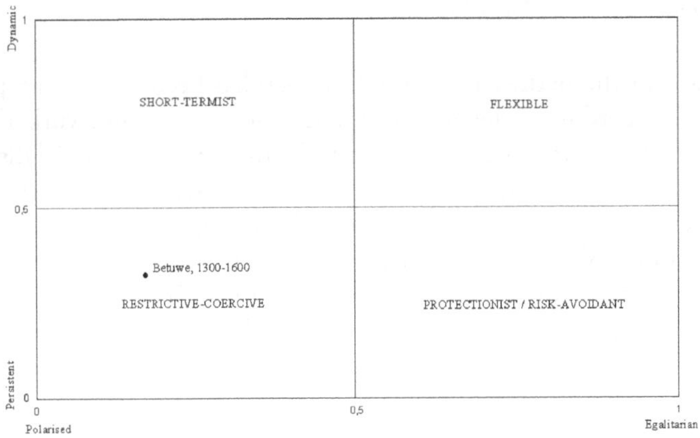

Figure 5.8 Predicted strategies for resource management in the Betuwe, 1300–1600

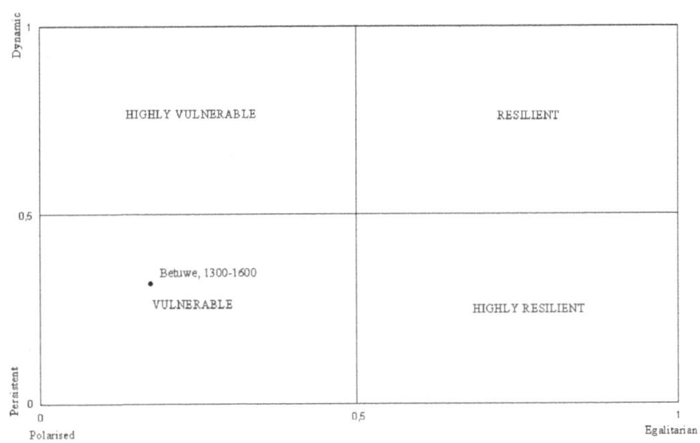

Figure 5.9 Predicted levels of settlement resilience or vulnerability in the Betuwe, 1300–1600

Assessing the Theoretical Model

The society of the Betuwe from 1300 to 1600 has been assessed as 'polarised-persistent'. According to the principles of the theoretical framework, this would mean that these arrangements of property (at the user level), social distribution of property, and power, led logically to 'restrictive-coercive' strategies for resource exploitation, and in turn 'vulnerable' settlements.

The 'vulnerable' status of settlements in the Betuwe suggested by the principles of the theoretical framework is confirmed by the evidence. In order to achieve 'vulnerable' status, a society needed to clearly exhibit two of the indicators or markers for settlement vulnerability defined in Chapter 1. The long demographic stagnation over a number of centuries after the crises of the 1300s is certainly testament to this. From a medieval demographic nadir after the Black Death, the villages held even fewer people some 250 years later in the early sixteenth century – despite the proliferation of new farms in isolated areas. Limited evidence also exists for the structural collapse of some of the settlements: even as early as the late thirteenth century some rural centres were being abandoned. One thing that cannot be argued for, however, is a retraction in the cultivated area. In fact, the reverse happened as more investment was put into draining the lower marshes and farmers started exploiting these areas more systematically through grazing. Thus, two of the indicators for settlement vulnerability were present. The links between property and power and the modes of economic exploitation are less clear, however. Although the particular arrangement of property and power should have brought about 'restrictive-coercive' strategies (in theory), it is difficult to classify the actual strategies seen in the Betuwe between 1300 and 1600 in this way. In fact the proliferation of short-term leases, capital-intensive pastoral farming, and the reclamation of new areas previously unsuited to agriculture, all in the pursuit of commercial profit for a limited pool of interest groups would conform more to the 'short-termist' extractive strategies for resource management. Thus, in this case study the connection between certain arrangements of power and property and settlement vulnerability is confirmed, but offers less security on the predicted 'causal link'. Some of these inconsistencies will be discussed further in the conclusion in Chapter 8.

Chapter 6

A North Sea Coastal Area Under Pressure of Land Consolidation. Transition from a Farmers' Republic to an Unequal Polder Society in the Oldambt of Groningen, 1700–1900

From the late Middle Ages onwards, many regions of Western Europe experienced heightened levels of inequality in the distribution of land caused by the consolidation of property in the hands of various interest groups. There was no one set path to land accumulation: there were many routes. In some cases (particularly in areas that had once known strong formalised manorialism) inequality in the distribution of land was connected to the long-term maintenance of inequitable structures inherited from the Middle Ages. Large landlords retained control over the land, farming it out at competitive prices, thus leading in the 'Brennerian' sense to innovation and agricultural specialisation.[1] Already wealthy noble and aristocratic families carefully enlarged landed estates through tactical marriage.[2] Elsewhere land accumulation was achieved by urban encroachment into the countryside, whereby wealthy urban burghers or institutions expropriated land from rural-dwelling peasants, or instead invested capital in new land reclamation schemes.[3] Another route was land accumulation evident within the layers of rural society itself; new distinctions were made between ordinary smallholding peasants and those peasants that were able to 'better themselves' by slowly consolidating property – effectively becoming '*les coqs du village*'.[4] Often this kind of interpretation is linked less with forced

1 Brenner, 'Agrarian class structure', 16–9; 'Agrarian roots of European capitalism', 102–3.

2 McFarlane, *Nobility of later medieval England*, 79–80, 152–3; Habakkuk, 'Rise and fall of English landed families, 192.

3 Richards, *The unending frontier*; Ciriacono, *Acque e agricoltura*. 208–42.

4 Duby, *L'économie rurale*, ii, 524, 591; Hilton, *The English peasantry*, 40–41. On the opening up of new stratifications within village communities see Bourin, 'Peasant elites and village communities'; Hilton, 'Les communautés villageoises'. Even more so by the early modern period; Wrightson, 'Aspects of social differentiation'.

expropriation, but instead with voluntary and active participation in fluid land markets.[5]

Given these developments, what happened to those unfortunate rural groups (often impoverished) who lost their land to wealthier or more powerful interest groups (often absentee)? In this chapter the impact of land consolidation on pre-industrial rural communities is assessed. As noted in Chapter 1, a great amount of literature has noted the connection between land accumulation and strong population decline or stagnation in the countryside.[6] Given the importance of the topic (for societies both past and present), this chapter explores the link between land consolidation and rural population movements a little more closely by recourse to empirical case study analysis. The reason for this is that while land consolidation has been frequently found in the literature to have been linked to downward demographic trends (caused mainly by outward rural-urban migration), this outcome was not always inevitable – something not explicitly appreciated widely in the scholarly literature. Actually there were cases in certain regions of pre-industrial Western Europe where an inequitable distribution of land did not lead to population contraction – quite the opposite. In Andalusia, great estates granted to nobles in the thirteenth century remained in aristocratic hands up to the first half of the nineteenth century.[7] In the eighteenth and nineteenth century, however, inequality in the distribution of land increased further as former church and municipal lands were consolidated into extended *latifundia* (sometimes thousands of hectares at a time), and began to be leased as large farms (cereal not olives) to substantial tenants.[8] However, this did not lead to population contraction or outward migration: instead agricultural labourers continued to crowd themselves into growing agro-towns all the way up to the mid-twentieth century.[9]

In that sense, while land consolidation may in many cases have been the motor which set in motion outward migration towards cities, depopulation could have been avoided or limited within certain pre-industrial rural societies. In other words, this chapter considers the capacity of a rural economy to resiliently maintain and retain its labouring (and often landless) population – a test performed by looking more closely at a historical case in the far north-east of the Low Countries where peasant expropriation, land consolidation

5 Whittle, *Development of agrarian capitalism*, 314–5; Coote and Parker, 'Agrarian class structure', 85; Glennie, 'In search of agrarian capitalism', 14–20; Campbell, 'Population pressure'.

6 For an overview see Curtis, 'The impact of land accumulation'.

7 Montes Romero-Camacho, *Propiedad y explotación*.

8 Artola et al., *El latifundio*.

9 Gilmore, 'Patronage and class conflict'; 'Social organization of space'. For comparable chronologies in parts of southern Italy see Curtis, 'Is there an 'agro-town' model for Southern Italy?'.

and a transition to a rural economy dominated by large farms occurred at the same time as settlement expansion. The Oldambt region of Groningen (the furthest north-easterly point of present-day Netherlands) was transformed from an independent society of free peasant farmers with a shallow hierarchy in the sixteenth and seventeenth centuries into a society characterised by a sharp division between a group of prosperous 'gentleman' farmers and a mass labouring poor by roughly the late eighteenth century. While in the previous chapter this process led to the contraction of villages in the early modern Betuwe, heightened inequality in the distribution of land did not produce the same demographic effects in the Oldambt. The rise of a group of large 'gentleman' farmers in the Oldambt occurred simultaneously with rapid settlement expansion and demographic growth. Indeed, the Oldambt had a population of roughly 10,000 at the beginning of the eighteenth century, but this total by the end of the nineteenth century had increased threefold to over 40,000.

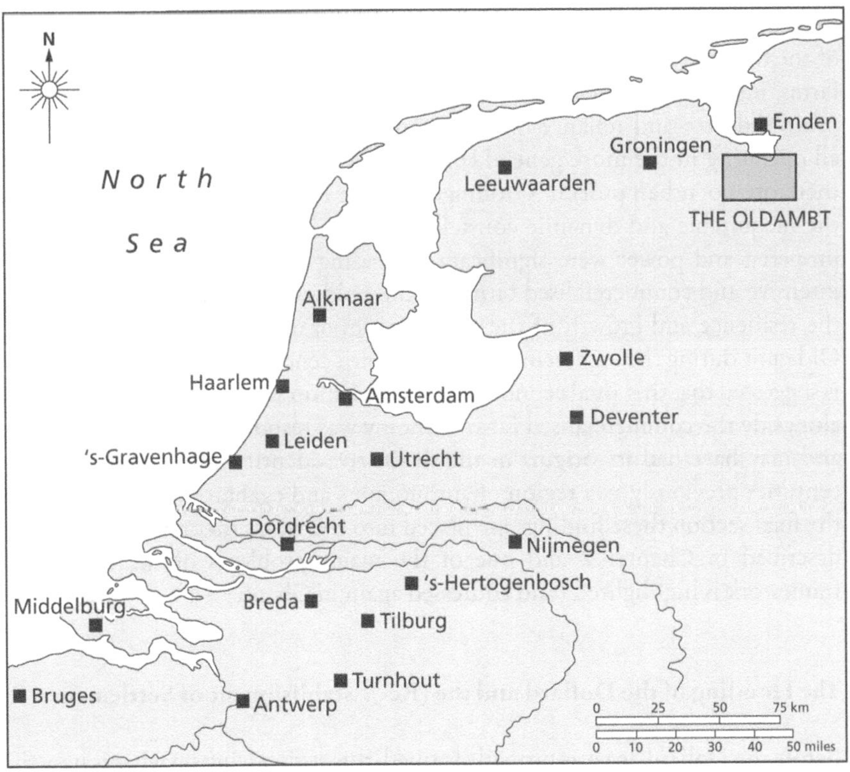

Figure 6.1 Location of the Oldambt in the Northern Low Countries, c.1700

In the first section, the long-term context for the development of settlement in the Oldambt is laid out with an emphasis on the disastrous flooding of the late fifteenth and early sixteenth centuries, the shifting of villages, and the initial reclamation of the marshes which brings us up to the beginning of the eighteenth century. In the second section, the exceptional demographic growth and settlement expansion is shown for the period 1730–1900 (after the crises of the mid-seventeenth century through plague and flooding). Rural settlement in the Oldambt during these centuries was not just resilient but actually responded favourably to the same pressures (i.e. intense land consolidation) which drove many other pre-industrial societies to stagnation and contraction. In the third section, it is shown that this was connected to very particular modes of exploitation. It is clear that in the Oldambt there emerged a group of very successful tenant farmers (exploiting a long-term hereditary lease known as *beklemrecht*), who invested significant amounts of capital in modernised and commercialised grain farms on newly reclaimed fertile polders. However, this development did not destroy the rural communities. Newly proletarianised rural inhabitants instead developed an alternative economy distinct from that of the farmers. The facets of this 'dual economy' were wage labour on the large farms, intensive production of vegetables on micro-plots, the development of proto-industry and reliance on an initially well-functioning welfare system – all operating in the more general context of a stagnating urban economy (and therefore no 'urban pull) of Groningen. In the fourth section, it is shown that the inequitable and dynamic constellations in property, social distribution of property, and power were significant in leading to the emergence of capital-intensive and commercialised farms on the polders – yet this does not explain the resilience and growth of the communities of agricultural labourers in the Oldambt during the eighteenth and nineteenth centuries. In the fifth section, it is suggested that this 'dual economy' of the agricultural labourers which emerged alongside the commercialised farm economy was responsible for the resilience, and may have had its origins in the distinctive identity already forged many centuries previously as a region of autonomous and egalitarian free farmers. In the final section these findings are placed into the wider theoretical framework described in Chapter 2 and one of the major problems of the theoretical framework is highlighted (and addressed again in Chapter 8).

The Flooding of the Dollard and the (Re-)Establishment of Settlement

Before the Dollard Sea was properly formed, this region lying on what is now the borderland between Northeast Netherlands and Northeast Germany was where the Eems river mouth flowed into the Wadden Sea. The region prior to, and throughout the Middle Ages, was essentially characterised predominantly by peat soils, with salt marshes at the peat-edges and along the banks of the river.[10] Higher sandy ridges were formed further back from the coast. From the earliest dates of permanent settlement in this region, inhabitants knew a precarious existence – as did many parts along the Northern coastal marshes. In the early Middle Ages, settlements were given some protection from the water by being placed on raised mounds known as *terpen* (or *wierden* in Groningen).[11] A number of raised farmsteads are traceable in the landscape between Woldendorp and Nieuwolda on the edge of the Dollard area.[12] On the other side of the Dollard (over the German border), isolated early-medieval settlements were raised on riverside levees and may have been points of origin for peat-land reclamation.[13]

Settlement could only expand over the peat areas of the Dollard, however, when the methods of water management and drainage became more sophisticated. From the high Middle Ages onwards, this came in the form of dike construction, the proliferation of small windmills, and through the practice of mixing peat with sand.[14] Some of this early peat colonisation and dike building was financed and organised by large ecclesiastical institutions: there were a number of monasteries belonging to various orders that were founded in the twelfth and thirteenth centuries in this area of the Dollard. This included Cistercian monasteries at Midwolda (1259) and Menterwolde at Nieuwolda (1247), the Johanitter institution of Goldhoorn at Finsterwolde (1319), and two Premonstratensian monasteries at Palmar (far out in the Dollard marshes) and Heigerlee near Winschoten.[15] These monasteries were interested in maintaining effective drainage systems in order to cultivate their large farms and granges known as *voorwerken*, often worked by lay brothers. Regional magnates holding foreign leases and dignities may have stimulated other early reclamation.[16] Some high-ranking nobles certainly had interests in the region in the eleventh and twelfth centuries – a manor at Hatzum-Alte Boomborg has been identified, as well as a proliferation of estates.[17] The maintenance of the dikes and sluices was coordinated through a system of local waterboards known as *zijlvesten*,[18] and frequently such cooperation was facilitated by key figures from the monasteries such as abbots acting as chairpersons and negotiators.[19]

---

10 Vos and Knol, 'De ontstaansgeschiedenis van het Dollardlandschap'.

11 Bierma et al. (eds), *Terpen en wierden.*

12 Tuinstra et al., *Middeleeuwse bewoningssporen.*

13 Schleicher, 'Zur Entstehung der Sog'.

14 Engelen, 'Oude dijken'; Groenendijk, 'Middeleeuwse bedijking'. On the mixing of sand; Molema, 'Van de Mierden, Egeste en Broke', 313.

15 All described in Tromp, *Groninger kloosters,* 34–8, 57–9, 74–5.

16 Knottnerus, 'Reclamations and submerged lands', 257.

17 Strahl, 'Reiderland', 357; Jongbloed, 'Wanburtich: Heinrichs II', 46.

18 Ligtendag, *De Wolden en het water.*

19 Knottnerus, 'Reclamations', 258.

These early attempts at diking and colonisation allowed for the emergence of some precariously sited settlements all around the Dollard area from the eleventh and twelfth centuries.[20] New districts were formed in the Dollard area in the thirteenth century: the Reiderland to the north and the Oldambt to the south mentioned for the first time in 1271.[21] A number of parish churches began to appear also between 1150 and 1300, though waterlogged conditions necessitated that they over time be moved towards the higher ridges.[22] The problem with the colonisation of the peat lands, however, became more apparent in the course of the late Middle Ages. Between 1250 and 1450, it is suggested that the soil surface was reduced from 2m to 0.3m above sea level. Present-day practices with the *Nieuwe Statenzijl* leads us to suppose that all land below 0.4m above sea level was flooded for long periods during the winter. Reclamation of the peat bogs and swamps caused erosion of the top layer of soil, leading to exposure to oxygen (oxidisation) and general soil subsidence.[23] Matters were made worse when excess water ran down from the peat highlands in the Veenkoloniën to the south.[24] The situation was then further exacerbated by the particular socio-political configuration of the region. Foreign overlords, for one reason or another, failed to maintain a jurisdictional grip over much of the Dollard, and local noble families such as the Addingas were pushed out into neighbouring Westerwolde to the south. Peasant colonists and their local leaders were left to their own devices, in turn stimulating by the late Middle Ages a situation of consistent tribal conflict and power struggle. In this battle for supremacy, sluices at Reide were set alight in 1413,[25] and a number of documents record situations where local peasants were unable to repair dikes, while absentee owners were simply unwilling.[26] One sixteenth-century document suggests that a locally powerful nobleman had explicitly refused to act unless waves went 'as high as a lance over his property'.[27] Constant warring disrupted the process of dike repair, and water had begun to seep through as far Winschoten by 1445.[28] Thus, Dollard settlements were under constant threat of being submerged under water.

Despite this vulnerability, culminating in localised flooding and seasonal drainage problems, the Dollard region did not experience its devastating flood until the sixteenth century – in contrast to what previous scholarship has

20 Groenendijk and Schwarz, 'Mittelalterliche Besiedlung der Moore'.

21 Van Lengen, 'Tota Frisia'.

22 Molema, 'Verdwenen kerken'.

23 Casparie and Molema, 'Het middeleeuwse veenontginningslandschap'; Knol, 'Het verleden van kwelders'.

24 Groenendijk and Bärenfänger, *Gelaagd landschap*, 38–9.

25 Rinzema, 'Een burger vertelt', 71.

26 Stratingh and Venema, *De Dollard*, 316–21.

27 Knottnerus, 'Verdwenen dorpen', 3.

28 Möhlmann (red.), *Ostfriesisches Urkundenbuch*, no. 359.

suggested. One particular myth suggested that the Dollard was entirely flooded through a storm surge on St. Stephen's Eve 1277 – yet Otto Knottnerus has shown this to be a complete myth.[29] Other scholarly works pinpointed the Saint Lucia Flood of 1287,[30] or the Saint Marcellus Flood of 1362, as key dates for the collapse of the dikes and formation of the Dollard Sea.[31] Again Knottnerus has disputed these accounts on lack of evidence, and has shown that many of the late-medieval chronicles on which sixteenth-century documents and mapping was based, entirely over-exaggerated the devastation. In particular, a fable is noted where the drowned monastery of Oosterreide is meant to have held 180 resident sisters, but in reality a tiny group of nuns simply moved away to Trimunt (near Marum) in 1528.[32] Furthermore, it is clear that many of the Reiderland and Oldambt settlements were still in existence even in the second half of the fifteenth century, since a key protective dike was constructed as late as 1454 from the banks of the Eems across the high peat-lands by Palmar to Finsterwolde, under pressure from the city of Groningen.[33]

Nonetheless it is clear that signs of what was to come in 1509, were already being seen in incipient stages throughout the fifteenth century. Tidal foreshores and barrier islands began to be washed away – creating more exposure.[34] The old village of Scheemda was apparently deserted before the terrible storms of 1508/9, its former position shown by the remains of an isolated church not far from Nieuwolda known as 'Ol Kerkhof' with a grave containing 50 skeletons.[35] Settlements such as Meeden and Midwolda were also shifted from their original sites.[36] The remains of monasteries also provide evidence for incremental displacement in the Dollard region.[37] Menterwolde (*Campis Silvae*) monastery was relocated from its position east of Nieuwolda to Termunten in the late fourteenth- or early fifteenth century.[38] Palmar monastery was evacuated in

29 Knottnerus, 'Dollardgeschiedenis(sen)'.

30 Gottschalk (ed.), *Stormvloeden*, I, 49, 269–71, 485; II, 40–1.

31 Behre, 'Die Veränderungen der niedersächsischen Küstenlinien'; Homeier, 'Einbruch und weitere Entwicklung des Dollart'.

32 Knottnerus, 'Verdwenen dorpen', 5; citing also Tromp, *Groninger kloosters*, 91–3.

33 Groninger Archieven, Losse stukken register Feith, meest charters, 1246–1864, 2241, no. 48.

34 Oost, *Dynamics and sedimentary development of the Dutch Wadden Sea*, 213–4.

35 Uytterschaut, 'The human skeletons'; Groenendijk and Molema, 'Het 'Ol Kerkhof' van Scheemda', 9; Molema, 'Het 'Ol Kerkhof' te Scheemda (Gr.)'; 'De opgravingen op het kerkhof'; Prummel, 'Draught horses'.

36 Molema, 'Kerken in de voormalige Dollardboezem'; 'Een steenhuis te Midwolde'; 'Meeden in de Middeleeuwen'; Bärenfänger & Groenendijk, 'Versunkene Siedlungen am Dollart'.

37 Halbertsma, 'Sporen van verdronken dorpen'; 'Het vergeten klooster te Dallingeweer'.

38 Georgius and De Smet (eds), *Honderd jaar Landbouwvereniging*, 34–7.

1446, with its property including significant *voorwerken* divided up between the monasteries of Wittewierum and Dockum.[39] Thus, even before the terrible storms at the beginning of the sixteenth century, people were beginning to slowly move themselves away from the coast, and settle further inland in a new series of villages (seen today) sitting upon safer sandy ridges separating the Dollard regions from the peat area of the Veenkoloniën. Residents were seemingly well aware of the impending doom that they would soon have to face.[40] However, the break-through of the key 1454 dike caused by violent storm surges in 1508/9 was the final death-knell to much peat-land settlement and cultivation in the Dollard region – by 1509 the Dollard Sea had been born. Otto Knottnerus has usefully listed all the known and potential settlement sites that were either drowned or displaced as a result (suggesting a total figure of 26–27 abandoned 'villages with churches').[41] Many of the settlements mentioned in a register of territories under the bishopric of Munster in the late fifteenth century, disappeared from record thereafter.[42]

After the floods and settlement relocation, the sixteenth century represented the initial human 'fightback' against the sea. The water which had swept over the former farmlands had turned these areas into swampy marshes. Displaced villagers, therefore, began to set about reclaiming these marshes – turning wastes into cultivable fields. Colonising farmers were armed with the '*recht van opstrek*', an old jurisdiction possibly originating with the *Fries-Hollandse* colonisation of the marshes of the lower Netherlands.[43] As well as receiving the equivalent amount of land in their new locations in compensation for the lands lost in the floods, the displaced peasants also had ownership over all uncultivated salt marshes backing onto their property. This was accompanied by written evidence, and people were fined if claiming for more than they previously had. Any unclaimed land reverted to urban institutions of Groningen.[44] This situation then contrasted with that found in fourteenth-century Friesland where the Count of Hainaut simply ordered that drowned lands could go to anyone with the wherewithal to start building dikes,[45] or the island of Nordstrand in the seventeenth century where all inhabitants lost their property rights after the floods.[46] In fact, early allotment of the first polders was based on differing

39 Knottnerus, 'Verdwenen dorpen', 8; Stratingh and Venema, *De Dollard*, 327–8.
40 Duijvendak, 'Storm watching', 153.
41 Knottnerus, 'Alle verdronken Dollarddorpen'.
42 Find a copy of this register in Stratingh and Venema, *De Dollard*, 313–5.
43 Ketelaar, *Oude zakelijke rechten*, 250–61; Keuning, *De Groninger Veenkoloniën*, 37–8.
44 Stratingh and Venema, *De Dollard*, 330–31.
45 Wauters (ed.), *Table chronologique des chartes et diplômes*, ix, 26–7.
46 Müller and Fischer, *Das Wasserwesen*, 27.

hereditary rights belonging to each colonist.[47] From each farmhouse (placed in a parallel row along a street), the *recht van opstrek* allowed the colonisers to go as far as they wanted into the marshes until a natural barrier was met or until it met up with another property. These boundaries were frequently negotiated.[48] Some of the narrow reclaimed strips extended for many kilometres, a pattern still seen in the parish of Slochteren.[49] The linear strip reclamation may have taken its cue from the monasteries, which were already colonising land in this way. The Grijzevrouwen priory of Midwolda was positioned out on the '*Oud-Nieuwland*' in front of the village and had land consolidated in an elongated formation.[50] The same went for the Menterwolde abbey at Nieuwolda, which had a strip of consolidated land that went straight through the older polders and joined up with the settlement at Midwolda.[51]

Settlement Resilience (and Growth) in a Period of Extreme Land Consolidation

Thus settlement and cultivation expanded between the sixteenth and early seventeenth centuries in the Oldambt, stimulated by peasant reclamations into the marshes. This growth was reversed only around the middle of the seventeenth century as a result of the cumulative effect of a number of crises which included some severe repeat flooding, continuous malaria epidemics[52] and, most significantly, the outbreak of terrible cattle pestilences. The lands and goods of the unfortunate began to fall into the hands of those not brought to ultimate ruination. As peasants lost their herds of animals, this had a knock-on effect as small farmers turned slowly away from the mixed pattern of arable and pastoral farming towards cultivation alone.[53] The area of arable began to increase from the second half of the seventeenth century, while the numbers of cattle declined.[54] By 1771, the cattle population of the Oldambt had been

[47] For parallels to this process of sixteenth-century farmer-led colonisation in the coastal marshes see Brandt, 'Die mittelalterliche Siedlungentwicklung'; Ey, 'Late medieval and early-modern reclamation', 214–5.

[48] GA, Losse stukken register Feith, meest charters, 1246–1864, 2241, no. 433.

[49] De Cock, 'Ontginningsgeschiedenis'.

[50] Tromp, *Groninger kloosters*, 37–8.

[51] Ibid., 34–5.

[52] Knottnerus, 'Malaria'.

[53] De Vries, *Dutch rural economy*, 171. More and more land was turned over to arable in the eighteenth century; Van Schaik, 'Omvang en kwaliteit van het cultuurareaal', table 1; Harten, 'Ontwikkeling van de landbouw'; Van der Poel, 'De landbouw na 1800', 512; *Heren en boeren*, 49–57.

[54] Knottnerus, 'Land kanaän', 59.

halved from what it had been in 1697, while arable extended across almost 60 per cent of the total area – two to three times the level seen in 1662.[55] The late seventeenth-century crises were exacerbated by severe flooding in the early eighteenth century, the worst of which was the Christmas Floods of 1717 which reduced Oldambt populations further.[56] Further pestilence continued in the early eighteenth century.[57]

The early eighteenth century probably represented a population nadir for the Oldambt. However from roughly the 1730s onwards, a demographic revival once again began. It started slowly, as from 1735 to 1760, the population of the Oldambt increased by around 15 per cent.[58] The greatest demographic explosion came in the first half of the nineteenth century, however, as the number of inhabitants almost doubled between 1795 and 1859. The last decades of the nineteenth century also showed demographic growth with the expansion of the regional capital, Winschoten, into a small town. The Oldambt population in 1899 had increased by a ratio of 2.78 from what it was in 1795, and furthermore, there appears to have been a relentless upward demographic push all the way from 1730 to 1900. Demographic growth in the Oldambt exceeded the general rate for the whole province of Groningen. It has also been shown by Evert Hofstee that by the late nineteenth century, the Oldambt had one of the highest rates of fertility in the whole of the Netherlands for a rural region.[59] Indeed recent work has also empirically shown the unrestricted nature of marriage practices in the province of Groningen during the nineteenth century. Groningers married early in their twenties and almost ten years earlier than counterparts to the south in Drenthe, an area dominated by small farmers.[60]

Table 6.1 Population figures for the Oldambt, 1795–1899

	1795	**1830**	**1859**	**1869**	**1879**	**1899**
Population	14,898	20,302	28,051	31,132	35,059	41,383
Population ratio	100	136	188	209	235	278
Pop. (Gr. prov.)	114,555	157,504	207,688	225,336	253,256	299,602
Pop. ratio (Gr. prov.)	100	138	181	197	221	262

Sources: CBS, 'Volkstellingen 1795–1971'.

55 GA, Gewestelijke Besturen, no. 574.

56 Ufkes, 'De Kerstvloed', 117–20.

57 Matthey, 'Op. fiscaal kompas', 261.

58 Knottnerus, 'Land kanaän', 44.

59 Hofstee, 'De ontwikkeling van de huwelijksvruchtbaarheid'.

60 Karel and Paping, 'Rural succession myth'; 'Searching for a place to live', 19–20.

The prolonged and intense demographic growth in the Oldambt is curious given that it occurred at the same time as the great structural changes in the economy of the region – in particular the beginnings of land consolidation and accumulation, the emergence of a dominant group of elite large tenant farmers, and the transition of many former peasant farmers towards the status of (almost) an agricultural proletariat. Given the negative demographic consequences associated with this process highlighted in Chapter 1, why was it in the Oldambt that the rural communities not only were resilient in the face of widespread expropriation of their main means of livelihood but were able to grow and proliferate? Despite land loss and impoverishment, very few of the emigrants to the Americas from the Northern Netherlands came from the Oldambt – in fact, migration tended to be short distances between villages in search of work.[61] While land consolidation and agricultural modernisation led to high levels of labourer emigration from Zeeland and Northern Groningen, Oldambt labourers did not decide to leave.[62] Settlement decline in the Oldambt was only a twentieth-century phenomenon, exacerbated after the Second World War when the region lost many distinctive characteristics.[63]

Linking Settlement Resilience (and Growth) with Resource Exploitation

After the crises of the late seventeenth and early eighteenth centuries, the way in which the economy was arranged in the Oldambt also underwent some significant structural changes. One of the key breaks from the past was the crystallisation and proliferation of the long-term hereditary leases known as *beklemrecht*, which took off from the mid-eighteenth century in particular. The rules concerning this lease contract are contained in a '*beklembrief*' addressing eight hectares of land in Nieuwolda in 1739. It noted that the land under *beklemming* should follow a hereditary line with the tenant, could be used to the tenant's own pleasure, with a fixed yearly rent that could not be lowered or raised, and a one-off purchase fee (which may explain why landlords chose *beklemrecht*). The tenant's rights to the land were so strong that by the end of the eighteenth century it would be a fallacy to even describe Oldambt farmers as 'tenants'. Indeed, when the province was forced to sell off its former monastery lands between 1764 and 1773, a significant portion went to rural nobles and elite urban landowners in the Ommelanden, yet in the Oldambt about a quarter of the purchasers were existing tenants in *beklemming*, who essentially became

61 Paping, 'Family strategies concerning migration', 159.

62 Wintle, 'Push-factors in emigration', 525–6; Swierenga, 'Exodus Netherlands', 522.

63 Knottnerus, 'Tragiek van het platteland'; 'Het land dat wij gekend hebben ... '; Westerman, *Graanrepubliek*.

owners.[64] By the nineteenth century many lands in the Oldambt leased by urban institutions to farmers in *beklemming* were sold to the stewards outright.[65]

The *beklemrecht* lease gave full inalienable rights of the land to the tenant farmer (in contrast to more insecure tenancies in neighbouring Friesland),[66] whereby it could not be split into smaller pieces without consent of both parties. The system developed in the first instance in the sixteenth century, replacing what had been a dominant method of short-term lease prevalent in other parts of the Low Countries. However, secure rights to the land for the tenant farmer were only established fully in the eighteenth century, which has parallels with elsewhere in the Northern Low Countries such as the Over-Betuwe in the Central Dutch River Area.[67] *Beklemrecht* found a foothold and perpetuated itself in Groningen for two reasons. The first was the right that the tenant had to build a house on the leased land. The owner had to reimburse the costs, often quite high since farms were large and built of stone. If the tenant broke the agreement, then he paid back all the costs to the owner; both parties therefore had an interest in preserving the contract and the integrity of the landholdings, which were truly tied to the house. The second was connected to the *Reductie van Groningen* in 1594 where all monastic property was secularised and passed into the hands of Groningen city or province. Most of this land was leased out on fixed perpetual terms, contributing to a culture of long-term leasing.[68]

Thus from the mid-eighteenth century onwards, farmers began to enjoy simultaneously high prices for their agricultural produce and rents which were fixed and could not be raised by the real owners of the land. Prices for grain in the province of Groningen were at their highest during the years around 1800, and were two or occasionally three times as high as they were in 1700.[69] A farming elite emerged by investing their increasing surpluses in their own agricultural enterprises, intensifying and bringing more land under cultivation, consolidating more land, investing in better drainage systems, and constructing grandiose farmhouses and farm buildings. Larger farmers were also aided in their consolidation of agriculture by ease of access to credit facilities, which they had obtained by their increasingly extensive social networks and political influence at village level.[70] As the farmers of the Oldambt saw profits soar, and agriculture become intensified and commercialised, more and more land was

---

64 Feenstra, *Bloeitijd en het verval van de Ommelander adel*, 31–3, 360; Paping, 'Groningse provinciale rekeningen', 116.

65 GA, Losse stukken Register Feith, meest charters, 1246–1864, 2241, no. 1034; GA, Gemeentebestuur van Groningen (1), 1816–1916, 1399, no. 4276.

66 Knibbe, *Lokkich Fryslan*, chp 4.

67 Brusse, *Overleven door ondernemen*.

68 Priester, *Economische ontwikkeling van de landbouw*, 110.

69 Tijms, *Groninger graanprijzen*.

70 Knottnerus, 'Yeoman and farmers', 26.

put under the plough, while the growing of fodder crops meant that less pasture was needed for the animals providing manure. The concern over intensifying the arable cultivation on the newer polders from the eighteenth century onwards is reflected in an ordinance from the city in 1742, which forbade the grazing of sheep and cows on the new Groninger and Egypter dikes behind the Kroonpolder.[71] By 1910, only around 4 per cent of land on the newer polders was devoted to pasture, which stands out when compared with a tax register from 1662 which shows the Oldambt to have only around 30 per cent of the land under grain cultivation.[72] The newer polders had more arable land than in the older polders, peat edges and sandy soils, and were probably the most fertile soils in the whole of the Low Countries. Numerous corn mills from the eighteenth century began to appear in areas of the Oldambt outside the older villages, for example on the Kroonpolder and Oostwolderhamrik, to cater for the increased demand for milled grain.[73] Such increased scale of production further played into the hands of large elite farmers as new technological innovations such as horse-driven churns and winnowing mills could only be worked by large farms.[74]

This situation was a significant difference from what was described in the previous chapter for the early modern Betuwe. While both regions underwent (at different times) a move towards more capital-intensive, modernised, and commercialised methods of farming, the Oldambt farmers specialised in cultivation, not pastoral products. During the eighteenth century, farmers were putting more emphasis on arable cultivation and more and more land was being reclaimed from the marshes. Thus those without land found opportunities to work on these farms on new lands, and even led to the development of new 'labourer villages' clustered on the edges of the Dollard. Work was not just restricted to tilling the fields, but agriculture on the polders necessitated large amounts of labour for digging the dikes and ditches and maintaining the sluices.[75] Fortunately for the labourers, maintenance works were concentrated in the winter when farm work availability was lower.[76] Figures for the Groningen province show that up to 1850, large farmers were employing more 'live-in' servants and workers on their farms in order to cope with the greater workloads, but also a higher number of fixed contract workers and seasonal or day labourers.[77] Work was seemingly plentiful and reports from the late eighteenth century

---

71 GA, Plakkaten en ordonnanties GAG, 1595–1795, no. 527.

72 Priester, 'Economische ontwikkeling van de landbouw ', 102. For 1662 see GA, Ommelander Archief, no. 1058.

73 Knottnerus, 'Korenmolens in Oost-Groningen'; Paping, 'Industriële windmolens'.

74 Priester, *Economische ontwikkeling van de landbouw*, 99–103; Van der Poel, *Honderd jaar landbouwmechanisatie*, 37–44.

75 Knottnerus, 'Het Oldambt'.

76 A point made in Van Dam, 'Digging for a dike', 222–4.

77 Collenteur and Paping, 'De arbeidsmarkt voor inwonend boerenpersoneel', 101.

suggest labourers were known to consistently eat hearty breakfasts of bread, ham, and glasses of beer.[78] The success of the large farms was built upon the efficient market and consistent supply of wage labour. Furthermore, excellent wages attracted seasonal workers from further afield, in particular from the neighbouring Reiderland, but also Westfalen and East Frisia.

Nevertheless, the further we go into the nineteenth century, the less applicable such a positive interpretation becomes. For example, in the Oldambt the notion of a 'fixed contract' worker employed for a year was a bit of misnomer. Although employed on a fixed contract, the availability of work was so polarised between the busy harvest and summer periods and the quiet winter periods that many barely did a week of work in the whole of the winter.[79] Indeed, the levels of winter unemployment on the farms were actually higher in the Oldambt in comparison with the Ommelanden, and the levels of truly fixed contract labourers were lower.[80] The labourer contracts and relationships to the farmers were slightly different in the Oldambt to the rest of the clay-lands, and it was not unusual for labourers who had a long and fixed relationship with a particular farmer to also work on the side for other farmers. Nonetheless, the demand for work was so high on the large farms during the early nineteenth century that many farmers also employed seasonal labourers taken on from the Veenkolonien, Eemsland, Reiderland and other parts of the Westfalen.[81] The continued employment of outsiders became a contested issue in the nineteenth century, as shown by a letter sent in 1846 by 31 labourers from Drieborg to the king himself, requesting something be done about foreign workers 'taking bread from their mouths'.[82] While the agricultural labourer in 1770 benefited from a high availability of work, good wages, and lower prices for foodstuffs, the world the agricultural labourer knew in 1850 was very different. In 1813 around 3 per cent of the Oldambt men over 16 were said to have no work, but by 1859 this had grown to 6 per cent.[83] As the Oldambt became more heavily populated into the nineteenth century, the large farmers benefited from an over-supply in labour, and real wages accordingly dropped.[84] The wages of the nineteenth century did not increase much at all from what they were in the middle of the eighteenth century, but of course prices went up, so much so that by the mid-nineteenth century, labouring families could not even afford to buy bread

78 Van den Bosch, 'Natuur- en geneeskundige verhandeling', 606.

79 Paping, *Voor een handvol stuivers*, 102–4.

80 Paping, 'Vaste en losse arbeiders', 153–5; Hofstee, *Het Oldambt*, 217–8.

81 Lucassen, *Naar de kusten van de Noordzee*, 274; Knottnerus, 'Wanderarbeiter'.

82 Priester and De Raad, *De iezeren kette van d'armoude*, 28, 138.

83 GA, Gewestelijke Besturen in Groningen, 1798–1814 (1815), 3, nos 1898–9, 1901; *Uitkomsten der Vierde Tienjarige Volkstelling*, i.

84 Paping, *Voor een handvol stuivers*, 344.

from their local bakery.[85] By the turn of the century terrible economic conditions for many Oldambt people had been translated into political strife.[86] The labourer strikes of 1929 produced numerous tragic stories and violent clashes, the military police's shooting dead of an impoverished vegetable peddler (a mere onlooker on the riots) being one of a number of typical examples.[87] So given this general downturn in economic conditions during the nineteenth century, why did the settlements continue to swell with people?

The answer may lie in what can be termed the development of a 'dual economy'. Those pushed to the margins through land consolidation and accumulation were able to create their 'own' economy based around a number of flexible and diverse strategies – in contrast to what was seen in the sixteenth-century Betuwe. Many of the Oldambt labourers also worked their own plots of land, managing subsistence through a combination of dependent labour and independent cultivation of potatoes.[88] Indeed, the precarious reliance on this crop by a high proportion of labourers meant that Groningen was almost the hardest hit province in the Netherlands during the potato disease of the mid-nineteenth century, which even led to revolt in the city of Groningen.[89] These small plots were generally what was sold or leased by the larger farmers from their own lands, often whole pieces of fenland onto which the labourers built themselves simple huts and small houses.[90] Farmers realised that their own farms required the stable provision of labour at close hand. The owner of the old aristocratic house '*Ennemaborg*' in Midwolda leased plots of one hectare to labourers from Meerland.[91] Some of the labourers were later caught stealing peat from larger holdings.[92]

---

85 Paping, 'Nijverheid op. het Groninger platteland', 99, 113; De Jager, 'De Oldambster landbouwer', 70–73.

86 Hoekman, 'Van spontaan verzet naar socialisme', 31; *Socialisme en arbeidersbeweging* ; Buning, 'Sociale beroering'; Hibma, Hoekstra and Uil (eds), *'We hadden geen keus'*; *Verslagen betreffende den oeconomischen toestand der landarbeiders*, i, 113–55; Frieswijk, *Om een beter leven*; Voerman (ed.), *Tussen Moskou en Finsterwolde.*

87 Karel, 'Oost-Groningen', 4. On the labour strikes of 1929 see Knottnerus, 'Boeren en landarbeiders'; Meulenkamp, *'Wie willen boas blieven'*.

88 The importance of the potato to Groningen discussed in Paping and Tassenaar, 'Consequences of the potato disease ', esp. 152, 154. Also Terlouw, 'Aardappelziekte'; Bergman, 'Potato blight'.

89 In contrast to a mistaken view suggesting the crisis was less in Groningen due to a larger share of freeholders in Van Zanden, *'Den zedelijk materiëlen toestand der arbeidende bevolking ten platten lande'*, 8. For revolts see Gout, 'Het broodoproer'.

90 Georgius and De Smet (eds), *Honderd jaar Landbouwvereniging*, i, 15; Commissie Fotoboek Nieuw-Scheemda/'t Waar, *Tussen 't Zieldaip en 't Grootmoar*, 24.

91 GA, NV Ennemaborg te Midwolda, 1660–1964, 402, no. 63.

92 GA, NV Ennemaborg te Midwolda, 1660–1964, 402, no. 355.

'Labour pool villages' operated through a 'dual economy', whereby the inhabitants would act as agricultural labourers from 6 a.m. to 1 or 2 p.m. in a shortened day, and travel back to their own plots to work on them in the afternoon. As well as having shorter work days, Oldambt labourers held a higher proportion of land themselves than labourers in other parts of Groningen. According to the data taken from the 1832 cadaster, labourers on the newer polders had on average 0.58 hectares for their own use, which is close to Priester's calculation of 0.6 hectares for 1909/10.[93] Compared with Priester's figures for the whole of Groningen, the average landholding of 0.58 hectares for the Oldambt labourers was the highest in the province, (though this amount of land was nowhere near enough to support a family on its own).

Many agricultural labourers supported themselves in the tougher winter periods by securing work as peat diggers in the Veenkoloniën to the south. Some also offered their services as transporters of goods and people along the waterways of the region. Labourers secured some work improving the footpaths by putting down and compacting gravel.[94] After 1860 labourers began to find it less easy to secure work, as the farmers made labour cuts in response to the lowering of prices for agricultural products – a process stimulated by the flooding of the market of cheap grain from the Americas. Less labour was required as a consequence of the development of more sophisticated labour-saving machinery and chemical fertilisers.[95] When the agricultural conditions worsened in the second half of the nineteenth century, demographic pressure slowed somewhat compared with the period 1795–1850. However the polder villages continued to swell through extra houses and this can be seen as the result of the final cultural break between farmer and labourer. The days of the in-living labourer on the large farm were well and truly over, as all labourers began to live independently in their own houses – often in the polder villages. This can be seen almost as the physical manifestation of the emergence of the 'dual economy': one economy for the farmers and another for the labourers. The decline of the in-living servants and maids only exacerbated this trend, and it has been convincingly argued that labourer family strategy by 1850 tended towards keeping the children at home for longer, not moving them out into the service of others.[96]

The very poorest households of the Oldambt were aided in their struggle to survive by the widespread provision of poor relief. During the eighteenth century this support was provided by parish institutions of the reformed church, although the number of Oldambt people who received relief was decidedly

93 Own data collected from the GA, Kadaster 1832; Priester, *Economische ontwikkeling van de landbouw*, 160. For 1910 also see *Uitkomsten der telling in zake grondgebruik en veestapel 1910*, 2–11.

94 Teenstra (ed.), *Landhuiskundige almanak*, 131.

95 Knottnerus, 'Oldambt: het puukje'.

96 Paping, 'Family strategies'; 'Gezinnen en cohorten'.

limited. The limited gifts had less to do with the workings of poor relief itself, and was more a function of the higher living standards experienced by farmers and labourers alike. As mentioned already, work was still plentiful then, wages were high, and more importantly real wages were high. Poor relief in the eighteenth century did help the really destitute however, and cash payment and food parcels were reserved for widows or families who supported 'burdens' to the household.[97] Through the course of the nineteenth century the nature of this support changed quite a bit according to data from Richard Paping, as more Oldambt inhabitants received welfare, though each gift was a lower amount. This was testament to the widening disparities in the region between rich and poor, and the increasing numbers of agricultural labourers. Nevertheless, constant distributions of food through parish relief in the likes of Beerta, Finsterwolde, Nieuwschans, Winschoten, Nieuwolda, and Termunten, meant that many households were saved from absolute poverty and starvation in the very worst years.[98]

Furthermore, the Oldambt cannot simply be seen as an example of a diametric opposition between a large group of poor agricultural labourers and a small group of wealthy farmers. In fact, the Oldambt had long known forms of industrial, craft and artisanal employment. In the early seventeenth century there were at least four bakers and three brewers in the village of Noordbroek, for example, occupations allowed to proliferate because the monopolies on economic activity imposed by the city of Groningen on the Ommelanden did not apply for the Oldambt.[99] By the nineteenth century craft or artisan work was more numerous, and in the same village of Noordbroek there were at least seven bakers in 1866 and eighteen in 1900.[100] Quite simply more people required more bread, and taxes on the milling of grain drove up these prices – this was deeply resented when the potatoes failed and real poverty set in.

The increasing number of industrial and artisanal opportunities in the Oldambt from the second half of the eighteenth century through to the beginning of the twentieth century supported the population and settlement expansion between the rough period of 1730 to 1900. The occupational registers from 1807 suggest that around a fifth of the population were employed in a more permanent industrial or craft capacity, while the conscription registers of 1813 indicate the proportion was more like a quarter. Whether the Oldambt had more industrial opportunities than the rest of the Groningen clay-lands at

97 For example in Midwolda numerous cash and food payments were made in the late eighteenth century to widows, while one Hindrick Jurriens in the same parish received a large yearly payment for keeping his mother in his house; GA, Archief Nederlands Hervormde Gemeente Midwolda, no. 5.

98 Paping, *Voor een handvol stuivers*, 289–90.

99 Abels, *Doopsgezinde families*, 150–53.

100 Last, *Noordbroek*, 181; Antonides, *Noord- en Zuidbroek*, 254–6.

this point is not clear; certainly in 1807 the proportion of industrial occupations was higher outside of the Oldambt in the 1807 registers, but when comparing the 1813 Oldambt registers with the civil registers for the rest of the clay-area from 1811, the Oldambt figures were higher.[101] What we can say at the very least is that industrial, personal service and administrative occupations had an important role to play in the Groningen clay-areas in general.

Table 6.2 Occupational distribution of the Oldambt population by parish, 1807 (%)

	Farmer	Labourer	Craft	Administrative	Other
Beerta	21	42	16	2	20
Finsterwolde	20	43	14	2	21
Midwolda	22	44	16	2	16
Nieuweschans	11	14	35	7	33
Nieuwolda	21	39	15	2	23
Scheemda	18	42	15	3	23
Termunten	19	40	15	4	22
Winschoten	9	28	19	3	41
Oldambt	17	38	17	3	25
Other parts of the Groningen clay-lands	24	29	22	4	22

Source: GA, Gewestelijke Besturen in Groningen, 1798–1814 (1815), 3, nos 855–6.

A problem which always comes up when taking occupational data from censuses is how the assessors came up with the classification system.[102] We have limited instructions on the procedures by which the categories were formed.[103] One basic uncertainty is the distinction made between farmers and labourers. We can only assume that farmers were those people who never had to perform labour tasks on other people's farms, while labourers often did so (despite perhaps working small lands of their own). In the 1807 register the biggest uncertainties, however, are the administrative and 'other' categories. From what is known

[101] The Oldambt figures were compared with figures from other parts of the Groningen clay areas recorded in Paping, *Voor een handvol stuivers*, 322–3.

[102] For a discussion of these sources from 1807, 1811, and 1813 see Van Zanden, *Economische ontwikkeling van de Nederlandse landbouw*, 63–7; 'De volkstelling'; 'De Registres Civiques'.

[103] Instructions to the assessors are provided in GA, Gewestelijke Besturen in Groningen, 1798–1814 (1815), 3, no. 1662.

Table 6.3 Occupational distribution of the Oldambt population by parish, 1813 (%)

	Farmers	**Labourers**	**Farm servants**	**Industry**	**Service**	**No work**
Beerta	16	20	39	21	4	1
Finsterwolde	12	28	33	14	10	3
Midwolda	13	24	30	26	6	2
Nieuweschans	11	4	15	33	30	7
Nieuwolda	15	20	36	20	8	2
Scheemda	8	23	29	28	8	5
Termunten	11	29	23	26	10	1
Winschoten	3	21	2	34	33	7
Oldambt	11	22	27	25	12	3
Other parts of the Gr. Clay-lands	27	28	5	21	16	3

Source: GA, Gewestelijke Besturen in Groningen, 1798–1814 (1815), 3, nos 1642–4, 1898–9, 1901.

about the categories taken from a much later occupational register in 1889, administrative positions were reserved for higher status inhabitants with certain amounts of local political power or clerics.[104] Given the absence of a 'service' category, the 'other' classification probably refers to those inhabitants offering an economic service or in personal household service – made more likely by the fact that the regional capital Winschoten had a higher proportion of this type of occupation. In the 1813 registers the distinction between industry and service-based occupations is a little clearer, although a new category under the heading 'farm servants' is included. Probably this was a more agricultural service, and may have referred to fixed labourers (even if fixed labour was more in name and not economic reality, especially in the winter) while the labourer column referred to temporary, unattached labourers.

From the tables, it is clear that by the early nineteenth century, farming was almost an elite activity, and perhaps even more so in the Oldambt than elsewhere in the clay regions, since in 1813 only a tenth of the people were classified as farmers in the Oldambt, compared to over a quarter elsewhere. A large majority of people in the Oldambt would never be farmers and had to forge an existence by other means. Given the interpretation of the categories used in the registers in the paragraph above, the tables tell two slightly different stories. In the 1807 registers it is suggested that 38 per cent of the population of the Oldambt were

[104] *Uitkomsten der beroepstelling in het Koninkrijk der Nederlanden.*

destined for agricultural labouring, while 45 per cent of the population pursued industrial, craft, administrative or service-provision occupations. In the 1813 registers the figures are reversed, as almost half the population is involved in agricultural work, while 40 per cent are engaged in industrial or service trades. The second set of figures is more reliable just for the fact that the greatest uncertainty surrounds the interpretation of the 'other' category in the 1807 registers.[105] Furthermore, the proportion involved in industrial or service-based occupations (40 per cent) matches up more closely with what was going on elsewhere in the province.

Thus, it is clear that even by the early nineteenth century the Oldambt (as with elsewhere in Groningen) was able to absorb a lot of labour not just in tasks linked to the cultivation of the great farms. It was this industrial, service, and craft aspect to the economy which also supported the great population expansion in the Oldambt, and the industrial-service character of the economy was only strengthened by the later stages of the nineteenth century, especially with the growth of Winschoten into a regional trading centre with more urban functions. The province-wide statistics calculated in 1862 suggest this, whereby the total number of those considered 'farmers' or 'agricultural labourers' came to just over half of the Oldambt population. Even accounting for the permanently unemployed, those unable to work, and those with religious or administrative functions, the proportion of people engaged in industrial, craft or service occupations was high at this stage.

The settlement of Winschoten in particular in the second half of the nineteenth century began to grow quickly, and the industrial or commercial character of the small town is shown in the 1862 figures, as only one fifth of the inhabitants were considered a farmer or agricultural labourer. In fact the intensification and expansion of grain cultivation on the fertile polders of the Oldambt also created new industrial opportunities. The left-over stalks from the arable fields were used in new cardboard factories. The first cardboard factory in the Netherlands actually appeared in Hoogezand in 1869 (*Hooites en Beukema*), and by the beginning of the twentieth century there were around 20 in the vicinity of the Oldambt; 9 in the village of Oude Pekela, but also in Scheemda, Winschoten, Sappemeer, and Nieuweschans.[106] The factory in Scheemda known as '*De Toekomst*', employed over 60 local labourers in 1909.[107] Some labourers

---

[105] The reliability of the figures had also been brought into question in Paping, *Voor een handvol stuivers*, 322.

[106] Friedrich, *125 jaar de fabriek*; Van Hoorn, '*Reiderland*'. Also in the Veenkoloniën; Broekhuis, *Voorheen de vooruitgang*.

[107] GA, Coöperatieve strokartonfabriek 'De Toekomst', 1899–1971, 388, nos 160, 166. See also the wage books of the '*Reiderland*' cardboard factory in GA, Coöperatieve strokartonfabriek 'Reiderland', 1913–1988, 2045, no. 122. Furthermore see the numerous

Table 6.4 Oldambt agricultural sector, 1862 (%)

	Population	Agricultural labourers	Farmers	Agricultural sector	Other sectors
Finsterwolde	2089	45	21	66	34
Beerta	3519	30	24	54	46
Meeden	1412	46	21	67	33
Midwolda	3448	53	17	70	30
Muntendam	2412	14	25	39	61
Nieuweschans	1075	13	11	24	76
Nieuwolda	1627	33	33	66	34
Noordbroek	2145	40	25	65	35
Scheemda	4183	39	19	58	42
Termunten	2690	29	21	50	50
Winschoten	5085	11	9	20	80
Zuidbroek	1905	20	22	42	58
Total	**31590**	**31**	**20**	**51**	**49**

Source: 'Landbouwstatistiek'.

also crossed the border into the Westfalen to work in factories.[108] Women found more limited opportunities in the Oldambt by the second half of the nineteenth century but some sought work as seamstresses or in factories.[109] Other important factories were those producing starch, making use of surplus potatoes, with particularly significant ones located in Foxhol (*Eureka*), Muntendam, Zuidbroek (*Motké*), and Oude Pekela (*Oranja*) which burnt down in 1898.[110]

A final point to make on the emergence of the 'dual economy' and the resilience and growth of rural settlements in the Oldambt during the nineteenth century is that this took place within a context of de-urbanisation and a stagnant urban economy of Groningen. Already mentioned is the lack of Oldambt participation in the emigration to the Americas in the second half of the nineteenth century, but it must be emphasised also that the city of Groningen failed to be an attractive option during this period. Groningen failed to absorb labour from the countryside.[111] During the first half of the nineteenth century this is perhaps to be expected given that agriculture was still going through an

labourers employed in other factories; for example GA, W.A. Scholten NV, ca 1840–ca 1965', 1100, nos. 56, 106, 110, 171, 176, 190, 199, 203, 206, 208.

108 GA, W.A. Scholten NV, ca 1840– ca 1965', 1100, nos. 215–6.

109 Hibma et al. (eds), *'We hadden geen keus'*, 12–5; *Verslagen betreffende den oeconomischen toestand der landarbeiders*, i, 105, 153.

110 Voerman, *Verstedelijking en migratie*, 49.

111 The same process has for example been plotted for Zeeland in Brusse, *Gevallen stad.*

intensifying and expansion process in the clay-areas, and work was still being created in the countryside (even if it was seasonal). An important observation must be, however, that the Netherlands in general during the nineteenth century was going through a retarded or slower urbanising process in comparison with other areas of Europe.[112] Indeed it has long been remarked that the Netherlands retained a certain agricultural character during the nineteenth century, strangely at odds with its early commercialisation of the sixteenth and seventeenth centuries.[113] The Netherlands was slow to latch onto urbanisation of the Industrial Revolution from the late eighteenth century. It is in this final context that we can understand the lack of drive for Oldambtster agricultural labourers to seek their fortune in the city of Groningen in the 1800s.

Property and Power

The growth of rural settlement in the Oldambt from 1730 onwards occurred simultaneously with two processes: the emergence of capital-intensive arable-orientated commercial farms and the development of a flexible 'dual economy' by those who had lost their means of production. These processes were built upon the very particular underlying constellations of property, social distribution of property, and power – all very much interrelated.

The move towards this new form of highly commercialised arable farming on the fertile polders of the Oldambt was only possible in the very first instance through the accumulation and consolidation of land (at the user level) into the hands of a group of large farmers. However, the distribution of property in the Oldambt was not always so polarised. In fact the earliest colonists of the 'older polders' after the flooding of the Dollard in 1508 were small peasant farmers. Peter Hoppenbrouwers suggested that in three-quarters of the parishes in the Oldambt in 1660, over 50 per cent of the land was used by farmers with fewer than 6 hectares.[114] Such figures are likely an over-exaggeration however, given the methodological problems surrounding this approach. Hoppenbrouwers explicitly acknowledges that many farmers used land in a number of different parishes; he suggests this problem can only be overcome by creating a regional database of land users, and yet continues to pursue his investigation into farm sizes using the 1660 copy of the *verponding* (fiscal registration of land) on a

112 De Vries, 'Dutch economic growth'; Brusse and Mijnhardt, *Towards a new template.*

113 On early Dutch urbanisation see De Vries, *European urbanization*, 65. On the slow loss of position in comparison with other countries in the nineteenth century with regard to a per capita income see Maddison, *Dynamic forces*, 7; Smits, Horlings and Van Zanden, 'Sprekende cijfers!'.

114 Hoppenbrouwers, 'Grondgebruik', 80.

strictly parish by parish basis.[115] Such an approach was always going to give a false impression of the number of smallholders. Actually only around 12 per cent of the land in the Oldambt was used by farmers with fewer than 6 hectares. Nonetheless, despite reservations over Hoppenbrouwers' methodology, he was correct in his assertion that the seventeenth-century Oldambt was dominated by a property structure of small farmers and tenants. In 1630, 1660 and 1721, the Gini index for property distribution was 0.54, 0.56, and 0.54 respectively, reflecting a quite egalitarian distribution of land with a shallow hierarchy.

The graphs below show that between 1630 and 1721, polarisation of landed resources was not exaggerated. The number of very large farms did increase from two in 1660 to six in 1721, but they still only represented 6 per cent of the total land. Furthermore, there was no proliferation of tiny holdings associated with agricultural labourers. In fact, the number of very small landholders (possibly impoverished) decreased between 1630 and 1721, and represented an even smaller proportion of the total land – less than 1 per cent in 1721. There were some changes however. More farmers by 1721 had moved up into the threshold of medium-sized enterprises. The proportion of small farmers who held anything from 3 to 10 hectares had declined by 1721, and the highest proportion of land in the Oldambt now was worked on farms of 21 to 40 hectares (40 per cent of the land), and this figure went up to around 60 per cent if we extend the band from 11 to 40 hectares. Thus, larger farms were being formed from the late seventeenth century, though there were no signs of obvious polarisation yet or great divides between rich and poor.

While some limited consolidation of farms had occurred by 1721, the consolidation of property in the Oldambt by the time of the 1832 cadastral survey was on a whole new level. The Gini index by this point was 0.83, a far more skewed distribution of landholding than in 1630 when the Gini index was 0.54. While in 1721 there were still only six farmers with more than 80 hectares, comprising just 1 per cent of the total Oldambt area, in 1832 almost a third of the Oldambt was in the hands of 31 exceptionally large farmers. Furthermore, another third of the Oldambt was in the hands of large farmers holding between 41 and 80 hectares, which meant that two-thirds of the Oldambt was controlled by a local farming elite. Emerging medium-sized farmers seen in 1721 now played an insubstantial role in the region. A big division had opened up between those 2 per cent of the population who farmed a third of the land, and the 62 per cent of the population who farmed fewer than 2 hectares each. In fact, many of these lowly sorts did not even reach 2 hectares, often cultivating tiny morsels consisting of a house plot and garden, where vegetables were grown. The trends generally corroborate what Richard Paping has shown for other areas of the

115 Ibid., 76.

Groningen clay-lands.[116] It was a polarisation in fortunes, only exacerbated as the nineteenth century went on.

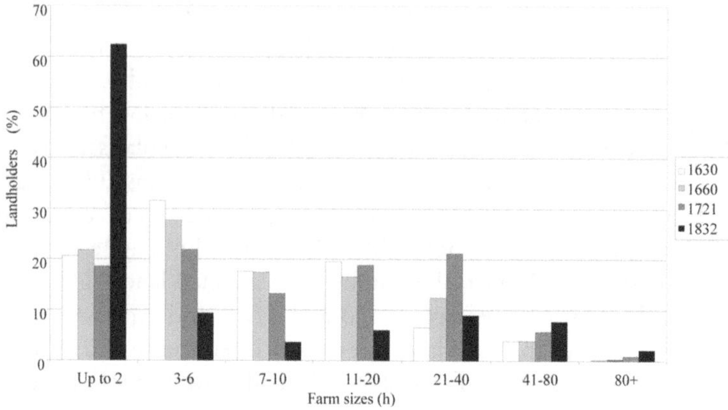

Figure 6.2 Farm sizes in the Oldambt, 1630–1832 (divided by total landholders)

Sources: GA, Archief Staten van Stad en Lande, nos 2133, 2139–41, 2143; GA, Kadaster, 1832.

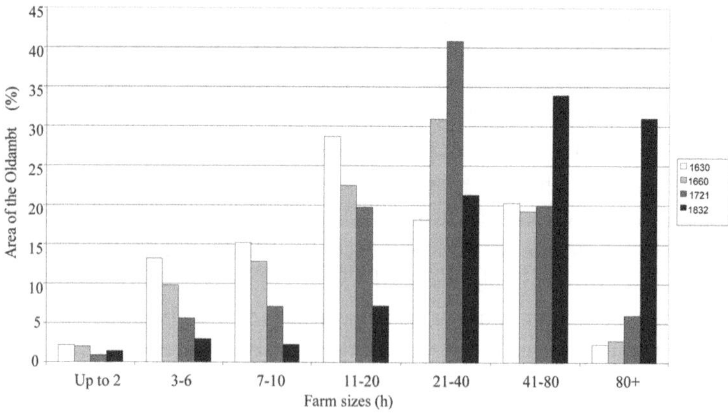

Figure 6.3 Farm sizes in the Oldambt, 1630–1832 (divided by total area)

Sources: GA, Archief Staten van Stad en Lande, nos 2133, 2139–41, 2143; GA, Kadaster, 1832.

116 Paping, *Voor een handvol stuivers*, 71–4.

The seeds were sown in the eighteenth century, but it was in the nineteenth century that the classic dichotomy between the successful, wealthy farmers and the poor, disadvantaged agricultural labourers became clearer, the former residing in large farmhouses of almost aristocratic grandeur in design and the latter confined to small sombre hovels, often sinking into the mud on the peaty edges of the Dollard. A large pool of literature has been devoted to the emergence of the *herenboeren* in Groningen, and the Oldambt provided some of the most typical examples of the 'gentleman farmer'. Numerous travellers to the Oldambt in the late eighteenth and nineteenth centuries commented with surprise on the size and splendour of the farms.[117] From the late eighteenth century, the farms began to change in design, as both living-quarters and barns were incorporated under one roof, and the sheds were lengthened in order to store more produce.[118] The literature has focused not just on the heightened importance of arable cultivation or the commercial orientation of the enterprises, but also the development of a new enlightened culture of farmer, at odds with the more pious farming culture of the eighteenth century.[119] These large farmers were interested in science and philosophy, were influenced by agricultural ideas from the university, had hoards of books and paintings, and were anxious to turn economic success into political influence.[120] The most successful farmers went on not only to dominate village politics but also got involved in provincial affairs.[121]

Some of the large farmers had their farmhouses within the 'original' linear villages on the sandy ridges and consolidated their land lengthways into the polders in long narrow strips – often barely wider than the farmhouse. However, the large farms on the newer polders (reclaimed from at least the late seventeenth century onwards) such as the Kroon- and Stadspolder were consolidated differently to the farms in the villages. Here land was accumulated around the farmhouse in coherent blocks, as seen in Figure 6.4.

117 NADH, Archief Familie van Hogendorp, no. 186; Van Lennep, *Nederland in den goeden ouden tijd*, 91–5; Marshall, *Travels*, i, 190; Fischer, *Lotgevallen op. eene reize*, 18; De Roo van Alderwerelt, 'Een reis', 22.

118 Havik, 'De Oldambster boerderij', 291.

119 Knottnerus, 'Land kanaän', 35–9; 'Het Oldambt'.

120 Schuurman, *Materiële cultuur en levensstijl*; Botke, *Boer en heer*; "k had nooit in mijn stoutste dromen eenigzins gedacht'; 'Provinciaal, maar niet zonder smaak'; "Van de boer hangt alles of"; Boer, 'Een Oldambster herenboer'; Doornbos, 'Groningers en hun boeken'; Goudschaal, *Herinneringen uit mijn bijna zeventigjaren leeftijd*, 14.

121 Formsma, *Beklemrecht en landbouw*, 98–108. Also a feature in Friesland; Blauw, *Van Friese grond*, 251–3.

Figure 6.4 Isolated farms on the Kroonpolder and Stadspolder, 1832

At the same time, in contrast to the grand isolated farmhouses stuck out on the polders, a network of small villages and hamlets grew up on the edges of the Dollard, often on peat soils where plots were leased out by large farmers, in order to secure a constant base of settled labour.[122] These were true 'labour pools', new places like Drieborg, Hongerige Wolf, Kromme Elleboog, and Ganzedijk. Labourer housing expanded even further in the late nineteenth century, sometimes purposely built by urban government institutions so labourers could work city-owned farms.[123] Another variation (see Figure 6.5) was the example of Nieuw Beerta, where important farmhouses were lined up along a main street, and a separate cluster of labourer houses was attached at the end.[124] The spatial separation of labourer and farmer on the polders did not apply to the older linear villages such as Midwolda, Finsterwolde, or Beerta, however. Here, labourers

[122] Schuurman, 'Tussen 'beschaving' en 'verwildering'', 117.

[123] For example in Beerta and Finsterwolde; GA, Gemeentebestuur van Groningen (3), 1916–1965, 1841, no. 1324.

[124] Hofstee, *Het Oldambt*, 222.

Figure 6.5 Farmhouses on the main street and labourer houses on the side-road, 1832 (Nieuw Beerta)

and large farmers lived intermixed, although some of the labourer houses were congregated on the side-roads.[125]

As well as increasing inequality in the distribution of property caused by the accumulation of land at the user level, the establishment of the commercialised arable farms was also facilitated by increasing inequalities in the social distribution of land. Indeed, the increased amount of absentee landownership in the region from wealthy urbanites and urban institutions laid the favourable institutional conditions for the long-term hereditary leases (*beklemrecht*) to emerge. By creating a database from the fiscal registers of 1721, it is calculated that urban social groups owned around 44 per cent of the land in the region.[126] Just a third of the land was owned by non-noble locals (i.e. peasants or farmers), and the proportion of landowners who farmed the soil they owned was even lower at 29 per cent because some land was owned by rural-dwelling *rentier* widows. Seventy-one per cent of land in the Oldambt was used by a third party.

---

125 On the spatial relationship between labourer housing and farmhouses see De Boer, 'Dorpen'.

126 The *verpondingen* do not give all the explicit occupational or social categories of landowners: this information had to be extracted from cross-referencing a number of works; GA, 'Lijst van gezagsdragers'; Abels, *Doopsgezinde families*; Boelema-Diddens (ed.), *Boerderijen* ; Stichting Boerderijenboek Wold-Oldambt (ed.), *Boerderijen*; Feenstra, *Spinnen in het web*.

Table 6.5 Social distribution of landownership in the Oldambt, 1721 (%)

	Oldambt, 1721	**Groningen clay-areas, 1755**
Aristocratic / noble	3	12
Ecclesiastical institutions	13	17
Lay / charitable institutions	1	1
Urban	44	22
Rural peasants / farmers	33	25
Total	**93**	77

Note: 'Groningen clay-areas' comprised Hunsingo, Fivelingo and the N-W Kwartier (areas of the Groningen Ommelanden) from the '*grastallen*' of 1755 found in Paping, *Voor een handvol stuivers*, 184. In 1721, 7 per cent of land was in the hands of 'provincial' or 'Ommelanden' administration. For the Groningen clay-areas in 1755, 23 per cent was in the same hands.
Source: GA, Staten van Stad en Lande, 1, no. 2143.

The problem with the *verpondingen* however, is that we cannot make a systematic comparison of the social distribution of landownership in 1721, with the situations in 1660 or 1630. We can compare size of farms at the user level, but not social composition of ownership. The reason for this is that the 1721 *verpondingkohier* is the only version which explicitly separates owners and users.[127] Thus, all we can say at present is that there was a high level of urban landownership in the Oldambt in 1721. Whether that was already the case in, say, 1650, we cannot be sure. However, through indirect evidence it is suggested here that the city of Groningen and its burghers likely expanded their landownership in the Oldambt from the late seventeenth century onwards.

The expansion in urban landowning was highly likely given the increased urban finance put into the reclamation of new polders. These new polders were not created in the same way as the 'older ones' (peasant colonists benefiting from the '*recht van opstrek*' over the wastelands), and looked different. Instead, city institutions and burghers provided large amounts of capital investment to employ large pools of labour for the reclamation tasks, in the process digging new dikes and incorporating new drainage mills.[128] The Drieborg Kroonpolder was reclaimed from the sea in 1696 and then the Stadspolder in 1740, which just from its name can highlight the role that the city played in the colonisation process.[129] A map from 1699 shows the extent of the newly won land around Midwolda, Oostwold and Oostwolder Hamrik, and a map from 1690

127 Paping, 'Groningse verpondingsregisters', 331.
128 Schroor, *Wotter*, 58.
129 GA, Kaartenverzameling, no. 1307.

shows land reclaimed around Beerta, Nieuwe Beerta and Ulsda.[130] If urban landownership in the Oldambt was high in 1721, then further reclamation projects only increased that percentage as we can see from charters which show large portions of land in the seventeenth and eighteenth centuries from these new polders being sold to officials of the city.[131] Despite financial difficulties in the nineteenth century, the city of Groningen owned over 400 hectares on the Oldambt polders in 1832, some of which constituted marshes.[132] The city also had rights to the water behind the polders.

Later in the eighteenth century the Oostwolder Polder was reclaimed, followed by the Finsterwolder Polder in 1819, although the Groningen institutions had slightly less ownership in these two areas, for example, just 116 hectares on the last named polder. A visual illustration of the differences between the city's land ownership and reclamation on the Finsterwolder Polder and the Stadspolder is shown in a map centred on the hamlet of Hongerige Wolf.[133] On the 27 July 1819, the city decided to sell the property rights over its *beklemmingen* on the Finsterwolder Polder for 90,000 guilders, indicative of its general financial troubles.[134] Nonetheless the city did have great influence over the further reclamation of the Reiderwolderpolder in 1869, the marshes to the north of the Stadspolder in 1874, and finally the Carel Coenraadpolder in 1924 where Groningen self-exploited three farms comprising 162 hectares until 1985.[135] In the eastern parts of the Reiderwolderpolder around 202 hectares belonged to the city. The Johannes Kerkhovenpolder was reclaimed in 1874 through large investments by a banker from Amsterdam, whose family had a long association with tea plantations in the Dutch Indies.[136]

The reclamation of the Finsterwolder and Oostwolder Polders was undertaken through a combined effort of absentee landowners (rather than urban or provincial administrative institutions), though many still had links to the city of Groningen (governors or notable office holders of the city, wealthy clerics, but also some rich local *rentiers* as well). These wealthy individuals bought the rights to huge swathes of mud and salt marsh which backed onto their newly acquired lands, and many charters recording the transfer of land mention 'considerable' access to the wastelands.[137] For example, the cadaster of 1832 showed that

130 GA, Kaartenverzameling, no. 990–1.

131 GA, Losse stukken Register Feith, meest charters, 1246–1864, 2241, nos 353, 371, 456, 467, 499, 535, 668, 766, 776, 854, 880, 903, 909, 936–7, 944, 957, 1017, 1019–20,1029.

132 GA, Kadaster, 1832.

133 GA, Kaartenverzameling, no. 1311.

134 GA, Gemeentebestuur van Groningen (1), 1816–1916, 1399, no. 3584.

135 Schroor, *Stadsstaat Groningen*, 179.

136 Vis, *Johannes Kerkhovenpolder*; Feith (ed.), *Archief der maatschappij tot exploitatie van den Johannes Kerkhovenpolder*.

137 GA, Losse stukken Register Feith, meest charters, 1246–1864, 2241, no. 880.

Johan Hora Siccama van Slochteren owned hundreds of hectares of land in the Finsterwolder Polder, Oostwolder Polder and around Nieuwolda.[138] Although the cadaster suggested he actually lived in nearby Slochteren (and was mayor there in 1811), it is clear he was part of the Siccama family which throughout the eighteenth century had occupied important administrative offices in Groningen. Indeed, his namesake and father had served as a councillor in Groningen as well as chairing the *Nationale Vergadering* in The Hague. Siccama van Slochteren was in 1817 a member of the '*Societé Royale d'Ariculture et de Botanique*' in Ghent, and had written in 1826 a complete doctoral thesis at the Rijksuniversiteit Groningen.[139] He was also a member of the Second Chamber (*de Tweede Kamer*). This important governor had purchased the rights to masses of uncultivated land behind his holding. As well as his 54-hectare farmlands on the polder, he also had the rights to 72 hectares of salt marsh and 458 hectares of wet mud. It was men of high status like Siccama van Slochteren that were the driving force behind the reclamation of new polders.

The question of course remains: why were urban groups able to invest so heavily in the Oldambt from around the late seventeenth century onwards? This is where property distribution and social distribution of property become closely connected to power. In fact, initially power alignments in the Oldambt were such that it was difficult for urban interest groups to encroach into this rural region. This can be explained on two different levels: the wider political context and urban-network balance and the equilibrium of social interest groups at the local level of Oldambt society. These two constellations formed a 'protective shield' against urban predations and encroachment before the late seventeenth century.

The isolated geographical position of Groningen and the lack of other large urban centres in close proximity theoretically gave the city a clear position to subdue its rural hinterlands from the Middle Ages onwards. Certainly in the early sixteenth century, Groningen was still able to compete with important coastal trading centres to the east like Hamburg, although this economic strength dissipated through the course of the century as the economic centre of gravity shifted west to Holland. More than this though, Groningen initially struggled to bring much of its countryside to heel – and the Oldambt in the first half of the seventeenth century proved particularly troublesome. Although Groningen was at the head of its regional urban network by default (no other urban centres around), its hopes of building a city-state were actually limited by its position in relation to two key interest groups. The first was the so-called 'Ommelanden',

138 Although he died in Brussels in 1829 before the cadaster was finalised; Formsma, Luitjens-Dijkveld Stol and Pathuis, *Ommelander borgen*, 369.

139 GA, Families Siccama, Hora Siccama, Hora Siccama van Harkstede en Rengers Hora Siccama, 1597–1970, 535, nos 65, 496.

a part of the province which obtained sovereign rights separate to the city and restricted urban political powers. The second was the States General based in The Hague, which looked to resolve disputes such as that which emerged between Groningen and the Oldambt in the interests of maintaining the constitution of the free Republic of the United Netherlands.

Although the city of Groningen increasingly wanted to subject the Oldambt to its jurisdictional and seigneurial powers in the seventeenth century in order to economically exploit the region, the dominance of Groningen was countered by the two powerful external allies. Thus during initial points of contention, the States General stepped in on behalf of the Oldambt, disarming the Groningen militia, imposing taxes on the city, and removing their privileges, such as the right to levy troops.[140] Similarly the Ommelanden acted on behalf of the Oldambt. For example, in one case the city of Groningen tried to arrest and banish three *volmachten* (representatives of the local interest in the Oldambt) on the grounds they had revolted against the lawful sovereign power. The Ommelanden administration challenged this, however, suggesting the city had no right to banish people when the city authority did not extend to the furthest borders of the province. The persecuted men from the Oldambt were protected by Ommelanden intervention.[141]

Furthermore, the rural society of the Oldambt was initially up to the mid-seventeenth century well placed to fend off any perceived urban attacks on their autonomy, and defended themselves well in the face of the imposition of urban jurisdictions. One of the reasons was the presence and consolidation of a social balance in the region, with an absence of dominant and elite interest groups looking to further their own ends. The Oldambt was governed by a collective of village representatives, dike supervisors, church ministers, and most significantly, all landowning peasant farmers known as '*eigenerfden*', who participated in annual meetings and held free and unencumbered title to their property.[142] Representatives of the collective interest (*volmachten*) were voted in on two-year terms.[143] The flat hierarchy and egalitarian distribution of property gave a broad base of participation in local political structures, and furthermore, a broad consensus on what was in the interests of the region.[144] This strong consensus was further strengthened by the absence of a local nobility or gentry (only three per cent of the total land in 1721), who played a more significant role in other parts of

140 't Hart, 'Rulers and repertoires', 199.

141 Van Aitzema, *Saken van staet en oorlogh in*, ii, 18th book.

142 Formsma, 'Staatsinstellingen'; Prak, *Dutch Republic*, 172.

143 't Hart, 'Rulers and repertoires', 199.

144 An argument also made for rich farmers defending themselves against 'external pressures' in nearby Friesland; see Frieswijk (ed.), *Fryslân, staat en macht*; Nijdam, *Lichaam, eer en recht*.

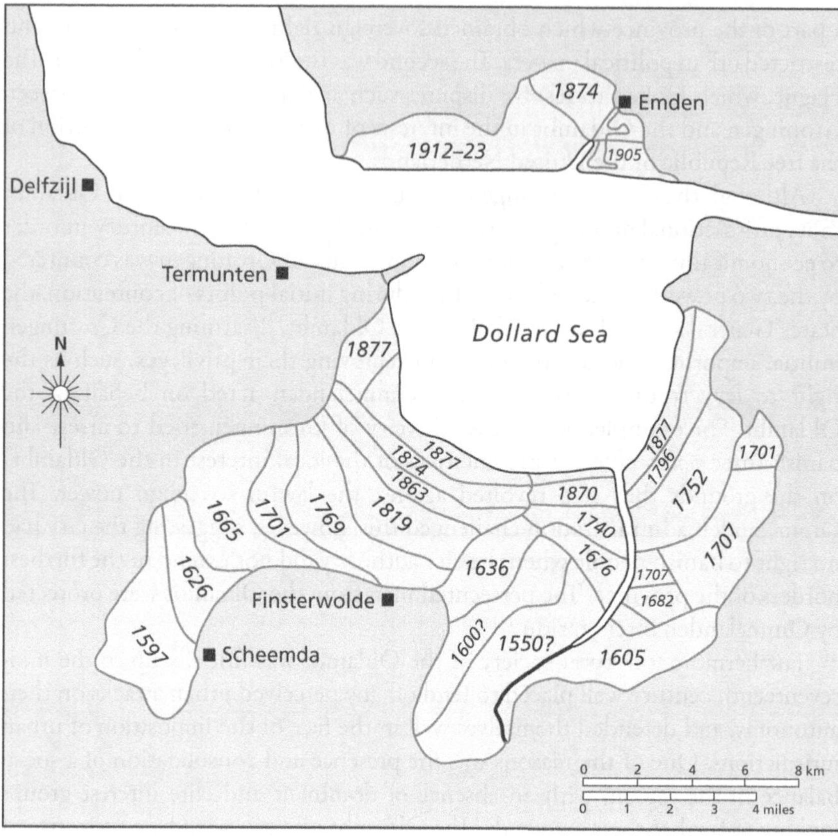

Figure 6.6 Development of the polders in the Dollard, c.1550–1923

Groningen province.[145] As shown elsewhere in Western Europe, secure property rights and rural autonomy were important factors in maintaining distance from urban jurisdictions.[146] Aside from any political ambitions that Groningen had over the Oldambt, the city was also hindered by many of the Oldambt peasant farmers who still invoked their rights over the wastelands (*recht van opstrek*).[147] This made urban accumulation of rural lands, and in particular, the purchase of lands suitable for peat extraction, much more difficult.

Thus, the Oldambt was able to stave off potential urban predation from the city of Groningen all the way up to the later stages of the seventeenth century. Consistently throughout the transition to the early modern period, Groningen

145 Hoppenbrouwers, 'Grondgebruik'.

146 Blickle, *Studien zur geschichtlichen Bedeutung des deutschen Bauernstandes*, 208.

147 Ketelaar, *Oude zakelijke rechten*, 250–61; Keuning, *De Groninger Veenkoloniën*, 37–8.

tried to invoke jurisdictional rule over the Oldambt through the implementation of a number of 'quasi-seigneurial' rights based on an earlier perceived territorial dominion of the city inherited from the Middle Ages.[148] This jurisdictional pressure failed, however, and their declaration of sovereignty in 1619 was firmly rejected.[149] To counter the demands from Groningen, peasant farmers of the Oldambt looked to ancient precedents of autonomy to assert their claims for freedom from urban control.[150] Thus up to the sixteenth century, Oldambt producers rarely used the Groningen market for trade, instead looking east towards Emden and other towns of north-west Germany. For example, the Grijzemonniken monastery shipped 25,000 kilos of barley to the Westfalen in exchange for wheat in 1493, while timber came in the other direction from Emden to Groningen via the Oldambt.[151] Groningen invoked a monopoly (*stapelrecht*) over other parts of the countryside such as the Ommelanden (rural areas closer to the city), which stipulated that farmers of the surrounding hinterland had to bring their produce to the city of Groningen first, before being distributed.[152] It also blocked certain economic activities in the countryside such as brewing.[153] The Oldambt was able to avoid these onerous obligations, however.[154] After 1600, Oldambt producers looked instead to benefit from the development of major markets in the western part of the Republic.[155]

Indeed, much of the Oldambt's history between the late Middle Ages and the seventeenth century was characterised by their own tradition of independence and autonomy, and in the literature have been referred to as a true 'farmers' republic'.[156] Any attempt by the city of Groningen to bring the region to heel was met with stubborn resistance. Groningen's attempts to improve their transport connections with the Westfalen by building canals through the Oldambt were

148 On this early territorial formation see Noomen, 'Koningsgoed'.

149 Unsuccessful in the Oldambt but Groningen secured seigneurial jurisdiction over nearby Westerwolde in 1618; Adriaenssen and 't Hart, 'Farming communities at risk', 18.

150 Dijkstra, 'Oldambten tegen de stad', 56–8. Invoking historical precedents from Hapsburg rule; De Blécourt, *Oldambt en de Ommelanden*, 361; Knottnerus, 'De kleistreken', 8–9. In particular invoking old land rights from 1471 described in Feith, 'Geschiedkundig berigt'.

151 Friedländer (ed.), *Ostfriesisches Urkundenbuch*, ii, no. 112; GA, Stadsarchief tot 1594, no. 732, fos 289–312.

152 Van den Broek, *Groningen, een stad apart*, 63–5; Feenstra, 'Van stapelrecht en vrije markteconomie'.

153 Unger, *Beer*, 202.

154 Van den Broek, 'Graven bij Stootshorn', 100.

155 Meihuizen, 'Sociaal-economische geschiedenis van het Groningerland', 298–9.

156 Knottnerus, 'Oldambt: het puukje'. On the coastal tradition of independence in general see Idem, 'Moral economy behind the dikes'; Slicher van Bath, *Boerenvrijheid*; Wiemann, 'Die Bauern'.

met with great protest in the sixteenth century.[157] Much of the seventeenth century was marked by bitter battle and revolt of the Oldambt people, against increasing urban influence and sanctions.[158] Farmers complained bitterly about urban investment into dikes which drained the nearby fenlands to the south, building up water pressure on over-burdened system, and ended leaving farmers at Zuidbroek with flooded lands.[159]

However, this situation did not last. Around the late seventeenth century, the wider political balance began to shift against the interests of the Oldambt inhabitants – they lost their 'protective shield' as the city of Groningen had more room to subdue its rural territories. The States General began to side with the city, forcing Oldambt farmers to pay for dikes and sluices which urbanites had constructed against a torrent of discontent. Groningen even used Republican troops against the Oldambt in 1643 and 1648, only to be blocked at the last minute by the rural nobility of the Ommelanden (*jonkers*).[160] Eventually in a States General ruling in 1648, what let the Oldambt down was their lack of documents to prove their independence from urban jurisdiction – of course the original manuscripts were kept in the city.[161] Thus, eventually the city of Groningen was supported by the States General in its legal battle with the Oldambt – ruling against Oldambt autonomy, its representation in the diet, and an installation of a separate judicial system. Essentially Groningen benefited from the States General's bias towards cities, based upon security concerns and the fact their wealth was indispensable for the maintenance of the Republic.[162] The Oldambt also lost its support from the Ommelanden; the rural nobles eventually became discontented with sharing its participation in the diet with a group of Oldambt farmers.[163] In that sense, urban domination of the Oldambt was facilitated by a changing position of Groningen not within an urban network as such, but within wider political structures.

Groningen managed to gain a foothold in the Oldambt from the late seventeenth century onwards, not by direct application of jurisdictions or powers, but by increasing its economic and political stranglehold over other parts of the province, achieved in three ways. First, in some parts of the province, the city began to easily acquire property outside its walls. This was in part aided by the *Reductie van Groningen* in 1594, where a large proportion of confiscated monastic property ended up in city hands, particularly in the fens.[164] By 1755,

157 Schroor and Knottnerus, 'De opstand', 136–7.
158 Dijkstra, 'Oldambten tegen de stad'.
159 't Hart, 'Rulers and repertoires', 202.
160 GA, Archief van de Staten van Stad en Lande, 0001, no. 475.
161 't Hart, 'Rulers and repertoires', 207.
162 On this issue see 't Hart, *Making of a bourgeois state*; 'Intercity rivalries'.
163 Blécourt, *Oldambt en de Ommelanden*, 119.
164 Hurenkamp, 'Groningen van stadstaat tot stad van het noorden', 45.

22 per cent of the Ommelanden was in the hands of urban elites and institutions such as '*gasthuizen*', increasing when urbanites of the Ommelanden acquired properties from the provincial administration from 1764 to 1773.[165] Second was the implementation of market staples in the Ommelanden. Third, the city developed an efficient taxation system on property. Investment in the expansion of the Veenkoloniën allowed them to exploit this avenue, particularly from the 1600s.[166] Its profits from the peateries came to be substantial under this intensification of activity.[167] In 1619, the city received all the jurisdictional rights of exploitation in Westerwolde.[168] As well as the benefits of peat extraction, the tax on newly reclaimed land represented 4 per cent of the city's income in 1600.[169] In 1608, the city bought over 100 hectares of peat-land from peasant farmers in the parish of Zuidbroek, and between 1614 and 1628 bought peat lands in Foxhol, Kropswolde, Kolham and Slochteren, so they owned the rights to a wide expanse of fenland stretching across the border between Drenthe and Groningen.[170] New boundaries were drawn between city-owned peat and the peat-lands of local farmers.[171] In sum, Groningen institutions and its administrators were in a good position to finally subject the Oldambt to its influence in the late seventeenth century, mainly down to the huge power that it had built up over the centuries by exploiting other parts of the province.

Incorporating the 'Dual Economy'

It is clear that the eighteenth and nineteenth centuries were periods of dynamic change for the Oldambt. The particular alignment (and change) in power and property structures allowed for the emergence of new modes of resource exploitation characterised by large commercialised tenant farms profiting from arable cultivation on fertile polders, and worked mainly by wage labourers. It has been suggested that the reason why the Oldambt settlements responded positively to these developments (in contrast to what one might expect from the principles of the theoretical framework outlined in Chapter 2) is that the Oldambt inhabitants (mainly comprised of agricultural labourers) were able to

---

165 Paping, *Voor een handvol stuivers*, 181–5.

166 Schroor, 'Een vlucht voorwaarts'. For urban influence on the development of this region see Voerman, *Verstedelijking en migratie*.

167 Gerding, *Vier eeuwen turfwinning*, 360.

168 Keuning, *De regio Groningen*, 49.

169 Schroor, *Stadsstaat Groningen*, 46. Also see Matthey, 'Op. fiscaal kompas', 231.

170 GA, Losse stukken register Feith, meest charters, 1246–1864, 2241, no. 307; De Blécourt, *Het stadsmeierrecht*, i, v; GA, Archief Veenkantoor, no. 384. Also Hurenkamp, 'Groningen van stadsstaat tot stad van het noorden', 45.

171 GA, Losse stukken register Feith, meest charters, 1246–1864, 2241, nos 582, 1151.

develop an alternative economy which functioned alongside and separate to the 'farmers' economy'. A question remains, however, why were they able to do that? Why did the Oldambt inhabitants manage this, when the Betuwe labourers described in the previous chapter failed?

Probably one of the major differences was in the development of both societies over the long term. In the Betuwe, the sixteenth-century polarisation between farmers and labourers was simply a new form of inequality: the Betuwe had always been inequitable in its distribution of power and property. The capacity for the labourers of the Oldambt to create their own economy, however, lay in the fact that the inequalities of the eighteenth and nineteenth centuries were a sharp break from the past. The point is that despite the heightened and sharpened inequalities seen in the Oldambt in this period and in particular the widespread impoverishment of proletarianised labourers in the nineteenth century, this society of labourers had already forged and crystallised a very distinct identity for themselves on the basis of high levels of freedom, autonomy, and equality experienced before 1700. In that sense the 'farmers' republic' may have disappeared but the social cohesion did not. Communal tradition and agrarian capitalism could (uneasily) co-exist, and pronounced social distinctions between farmers and labourers could still be compatible with an egalitarian ethos.[172] It was on this foundation that the labourers managed to eke out a precarious state of living in the far north-east of the Netherlands and on this foundation that they developed their very own 'dual economy' distinct from the commercialised economies of the large polder farms. Through this dual economy, we can understand the curious simultaneous development of land consolidation, inequality, and settlement growth from 1730 well into the twentieth century.

Fitting the Findings into the Theoretical Framework

In this final section, the information taken from the case study in the Oldambt between 1700 and 1900 is placed into the theoretical framework outlined in Chapter 2.

Property, Social Distribution of Property, and Power

If we take property distribution at the beginning of the eighteenth century, the tax registers from 1721 showed that land was divided very equally in the Oldambt, and that smallholders still held sway. However, it is clear that for the most of the period in question, land was distributed far more inequitably.

172 Knottnerus, 'Moral economy'.

The Gini index of 0.83 for the year 1832 was well over the 'polarised' threshold of 0.75 outlined in Chapter 2. The earlier Gini indexes do allow us to have an excellent idea of the levels of dynamism in property structure seen in the Oldambt, however. In 1630, 1660 and 1721, the Gini indexes were 0.54, 0.56, and 0.54 respectively – all well below the threshold of 0.65 which is the marker for 'egalitarian' status. The change in the Gini between 1721 and 1832 was well above the 0.1 figure stated in Chapter 2 (a change of 0.29), and thus can clearly be categorised as 'dynamic'.

The tax register from 1721 also allowed an excellent reconstruction of the social distribution of landownership in the Oldambt. Urban landowners had by this time already encroached significantly into the region: 44 per cent of the land belonged to wealthy urban citizens or urban institutions, while another 8 per cent belonged to provincial and Ommelanden institutions. In fact less than one-third of the land was in the hands of local farmers by 1721, which was far below the marker of 45 per cent – indicating a 'polarised' status. Reconstructing change in this situation is far more difficult to assess quantitatively because the cadastral surveys of the nineteenth century did not distinguish effectively between 'actual owners' and the long-term hereditary leaseholders who farmed the land. This was testament to the high security of the *beklemrecht* lease which really obscured the owner/user boundary and where farmers basically became 'owners' in everything but name. Some indirect qualitative evidence does suggest that the social distribution of land ownership continued to change – initially becoming more polarised in the hands of urban institutions in the eighteenth century thanks to land reclamation, but then later more coming into the hands of the large tenant farmers who ended up becoming effective owners of the land in the nineteenth century. However, given that the quantitative data is lacking, a cautionary figure of 0.5 is awarded here.

The distribution of power before 1700 would certainly be classified as highly egalitarian in the Oldambt due to the wide political participation of local stakeholders and the strong stance of independence and freedom presented in the face of urban encroachments. The period between 1700 and 1900 was different, however. While it would be difficult to classify it as 'polarised', it was also neither 'egalitarian' and thus receives an 'intermediate' status. Agricultural labourers of the Oldambt did not experience any kind of direct extra-economic coercion or suffer oppressive jurisdictions or limitations on their mobility, however, the political fracas and labour strikes at the end of the nineteenth century and into the twentieth century were revealing of their weak position in respect of the powerful farmers, many of whom dominated provincial offices in Groningen. The distribution of power (over the long term) can be seen as quite dynamic, however. Before the end of the seventeenth century, the equilibrium of social interest groups at the local level and the equilibrium of political interest groups at the regional level (the States General and the Ommelanden) proved to be checks on the power of the city of Groningen and stifled their control over the Oldambt. Eventually, however, the States General began to align themselves with the city, and the Oldambt lost their support from the rural nobles of the Ommelanden. Power distributions began to change – particularly with large farmers securing more power for themselves in provincial positions in Groningen, and farmers and labourers began to align themselves with differing political ideologies.

Table 6.6 The breakdown of the Oldambt (1700–1900) into quantifiable configurations

	Egalitarian-Polarised	Dynamic-Persistent
Property	0	1
Social distribution of property	0	0.5
Power	0.5	1
Total scores	**0.17**	**0.83**

Type of society: polarised-dynamic.

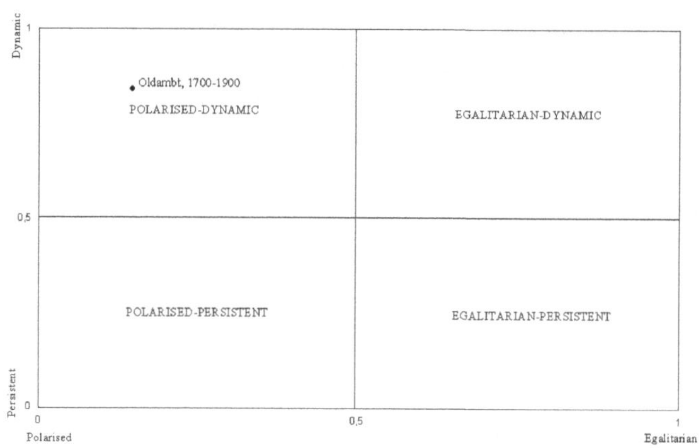

Figure 6.7 What type of society was the Oldambt, 1700–1900?

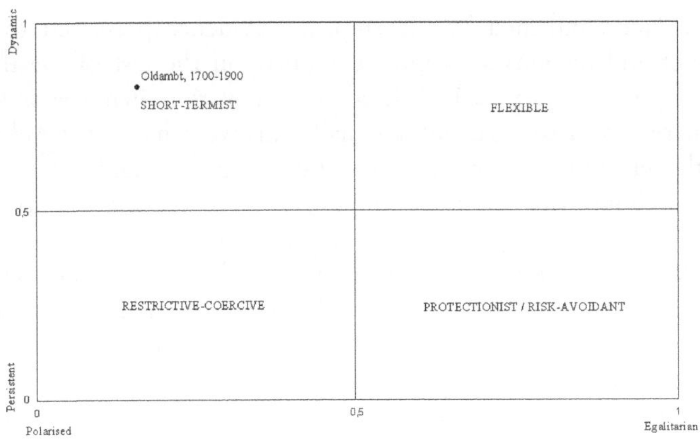

Figure 6.8 Predicted strategies for resource management in the Oldambt, 1700–1900

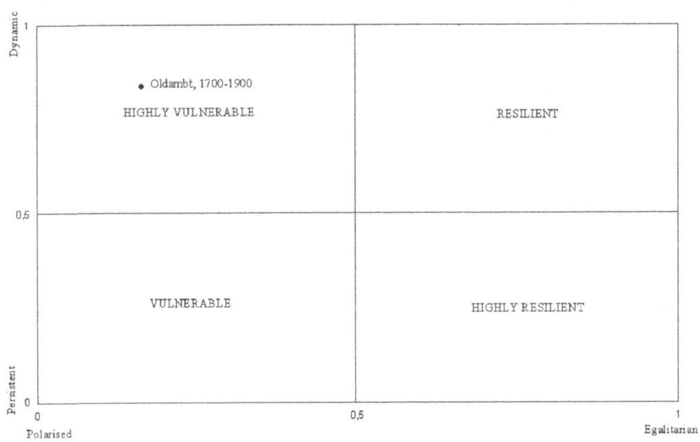

Figure 6.9 Predicted levels of settlement resilience or vulnerability in the Oldambt, 1700–1900

Assessing the Theoretical Model

The society of the Oldambt from 1700 to 1900 has been assessed as 'polarised-dynamic'. According to the principles of the theoretical framework, this would mean that these arrangements of property (at the user level), social distribution of property, and power, led logically to 'short-termist' strategies for resource exploitation, and in turn 'highly vulnerable' settlements.

This is not confirmed by the empirical evidence presented throughout the chapter and remains a significant anomaly in the test of the theoretical framework. Despite the polarised-dynamic constellations in power and property reconstructed from the Oldambt, actually this went hand in hand with not only settlement resilience but intense settlement growth and expansion. From 1730 and well into the twentieth century there was an almost continuous and (at times) intense population growth. Existing villages became bigger (some like Winschoten developed into small towns), and completely new settlements began to emerge in the new polder areas. Rather than land loss, more and more land was brought into cultivation – probably the most fertile land in the whole of the Low Countries at that time. Farmhouses began to be expanded and built out of more expensive stone; possibly the only 'downturn' was the quality of housing of the very poorest members of society, as labourer cottages tended to be very squalid with the walls even made out of mud.

Why did the principles of the theoretical model not apply here? It seems the reason is that the framework only operates by approaching settlement vulnerability through the lens of 'one society' and therefore one predominant mode of exploitation. Dividing pre-industrial societies into four basic 'types' is a useful process and brings more advantages than disadvantages, but one problem brought out by the Oldambt is that it cannot account for those societies which have 'societies within societies'. In that sense the settlement growth seen in the Oldambt between 1730 and 1900 was possible even with very distorted alignments of property and power and short-termist, rent-seeking modes of exploitation employed by elite farmers because the agricultural labourers formed their 'own society' and by that token their own modes of exploitation and coping strategies. Much of this was inherited from their distinct past: indeed the society of the Oldambt was quite different before the study period of 1700–1900. If we put the Oldambt of roughly 1500–1700 through the same process, we would get entirely different results, as seen in Table 6.7.

Table 6.7 The breakdown of the Oldambt (1500–1700) into quantifiable configurations

	Egalitarian-Polarised	Dynamic-Persistent
Property	1	0
Social distribution of property	0.5	0.5
Power	1	1
Total scores	**0.83**	**0.5**

Type of society: egalitarian-intermediate.

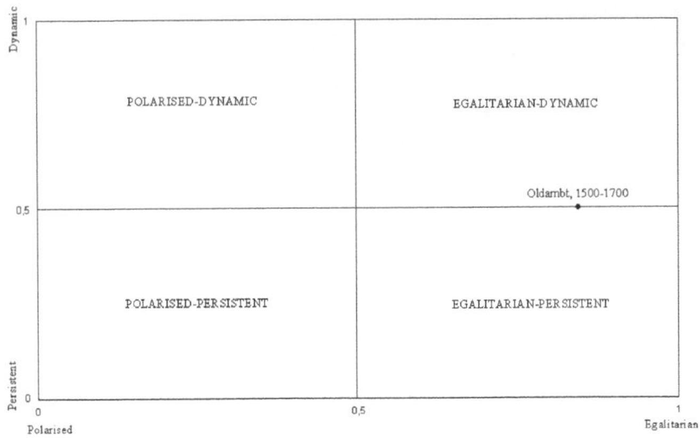

Figure 6.10 What type of society was the Oldambt, 1500–1700?

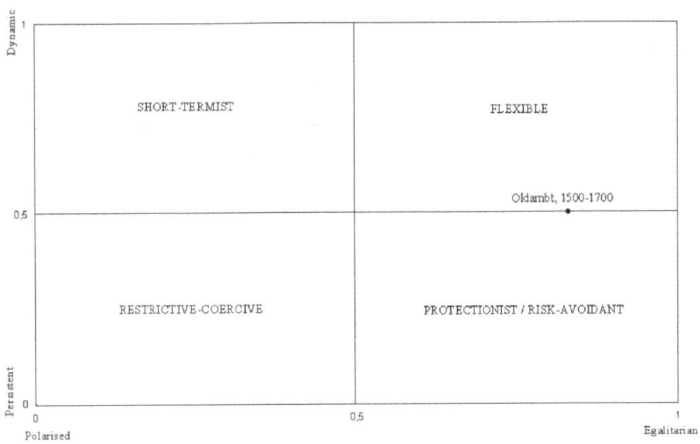

Figure 6.11 Predicted strategies for resource management in the Oldambt, 1500–1700

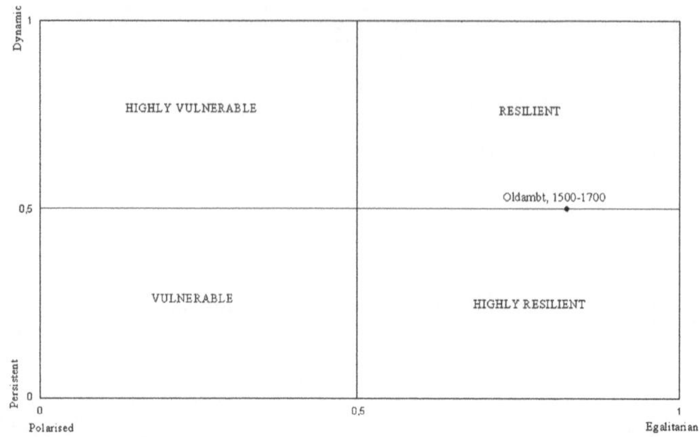

Figure 6.12 Predicted levels of settlement resilience or vulnerability in the Oldambt, 1500–1700

The sharp rupture in property and power structures around the early eighteenth century can account for the unusual results seen in this case study, although this can be seen as a positive aspect of the testing process. It shows that the theoretical framework needs further modification in order to account not only for differences between societies, but internal stratifications of societies within societies.

Chapter 7

Exploring Long-Term Inequality and Agro-Towns in the Kingdom of Naples, 1600–1900: A Comparative Study in Apulia

> What do people do here? I once asked at a little town between Rome and Naples; and the man with whom I talked, shrugging his shoulders, answered curtly, 'c'è miseria', there's nothing but poverty ... I have seen poverty enough, and squalid conditions of life, but the most ugly and repulsive collection of houses I ever came upon was the town of Squillace.[1]

George Gissing's 'rambles' through Southern Italy at the turn of the twentieth century led him to remark extensively on the topography. In particular, he frequently mentioned the miserable living conditions of the people he encountered who tended to live huddled together in large impoverished towns. His account is made all the more interesting by the fact that (a) Southern Italy is today more economically disadvantaged than Northern Italy with some of the poorest social and economic infrastructures in Western Europe,[2] and (b) this habitation pattern within large towns has been retained in large parts of modern Southern Italy. While alternative settlement patterns do exist in Southern Italy including small villages and isolated farms, it is undeniable that the distribution of large concentrated towns is prolific.[3] It is also a settlement structure often seen in other areas of the Mediterranean such as in central and southern parts of the Iberian Peninsula, regions of mainland Greece, and in parts of Northern Africa. These large agglomerated settlements are often referred to as 'agro-towns', pointing to their essentially agricultural function.

The prevalence and persistence of agro-towns across Southern Italy (and indeed across large parts of the Mediterranean) is curious, but as yet is not well explained in the literature. This is unfortunate because understanding the roots behind the agro-town structure may shed some light on economic underdevelopment in Southern Italy and Spain, especially given that an

---

1 Gissing, *By the Ionian Sea*, 65.

2 Ginsborg, *Italy and its discontents*.

3 See Figure 7.1 for a rough geographical distribution of agro-towns in Southern Italy.

explicit link has often been made between these towns and poverty. The Italian government in fact recognised the problems linked to persistent habitation within agro-towns in the south, and in the mid-twentieth century actually expropriated land from large estates to give to poor labouring families to entice them into living away from the towns.[4] The purpose of this chapter is two-fold: to assess the supposed 'impoverishment' and inherent 'vulnerability' of these towns, and to understand the reasons behind their development and proliferation.

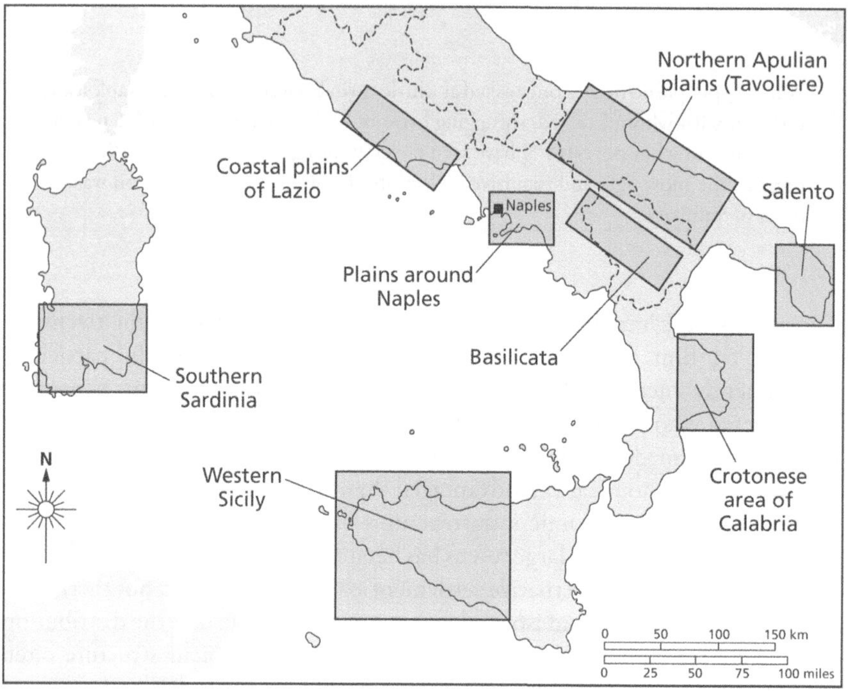

Figure 7.1 Rough locations of main agro-town areas of Southern Italy

Note: Even the concentrated towns vary in structure. In Western Sicily and the Northern Apulian plains there is a proliferation of very large agro-towns, while in areas such as Southern Basilicata (Lucania) or Principato Ultra there is a pattern of concentrated settlement amongst mainly deserted countryside – but settlements are smaller.

[4] These attempts at land reform largely failed due to the inadequate quality and size of the land given out and the lack of infrastructure in place for settlement; Blok, 'Land reform'; Bonanno, 'Theories of the state'. Farms were abandoned soon after occupation; Marciani, *L'esperienza di Riforma Agraria*, 120.

Very initial work on agro-towns saw their formation as a logical grouping together of vulnerable people in what was an essentially harsh environment. Early twentieth-century geographers highlighted poor access to water as a reason for settlement concentration.[5] Connected to this point, some geographers put precedence on the incidence and threat of malaria, particularly out on the plains.[6] After all, at the end of the nineteenth century, malaria killed around nine times more people in Southern Italy than in Northern and Central Italy combined.[7] Other scholars, even famous ones such as Max Weber and Fernand Braudel, alluded to the fact that many parts of Southern Italy were subject to widespread lawlessness and perpetual insecurity, and that living in the countryside was not a 'rational' decision.[8] These arguments were not convincing at all. Many of the same conditions are found all over the world even today, in places not necessarily characterised by agro-towns. Environmental determinism was not a satisfactory explanation and causal conditions were not dealt with systematically.

A new group of scholars based largely (though not exclusively) around the disciplines of ethnology and anthropology later added some sophistication to these environmentally deterministic interpretations. Nonetheless, these scholars still generally framed the proliferation of agro-towns across much of the Mediterranean in a negative light, emphasising the role played by specific social and economic conditions such as high levels of inequality and widespread poverty.[9] In particular, scholars tended to link Southern Italian agro-towns with grain cultivation exploited through a series of large estates known as *latifundia* with minimal capital investment.[10] Latifundist estates tended to be hundreds and sometimes over a thousand hectares in area, cultivated almost entirely by agricultural labourers, often on short-term contracts and even on a day-by-day basis with no security.[11] As a result, the towns had entirely unpredictable and constantly fluctuating populations, exhibiting both rapid growth and rapid decline in a short space of time, which was linked to the insecure and temporary nature of agricultural work.[12]

---

5 Semple, *Geography of a Mediterranean region*, 539–40; Ahlmann, 'Etudes de géographie humaine', 113–5; Maranelli, *Considerazioni geografiche*, 26–8.

6 Kish, 'The marine of Calabria', 496; Compagna, *La questione meridionale*, 78; Ahlmann, 'The geographical study of settlements'; Le Lannou, 'Le rôle géographique de la malaria'; Unger, 'Rural settlement in Campania', 508.

7 Snowden, 'Fields of death', 27.

8 Weber, *The city*, 82; Braudel, *The Mediterranean*, ii, 734, 865.

9 Boissevain, 'Poverty and politics in a Sicilian agro-town'.

10 Blok, 'South Italian agro-towns'; Tentori, 'Social classes and family'; Mack Smith, 'Latifundia in modern Sicilian history'; Rossi-Doria, 'Land tenure system'.

11 Labrot, 'La città meridionale', 221.

12 Djurfeldt, 'Classes as clients of the state', 174–5

Other 'negative' interpretations of agro-towns in parts of the Mediterranean were linked to scholarly interest in the so-called 'Mediterranean mind-set' or embedded cultural values. These kinds of towns were logical given a widespread culturally ingrained distaste for the countryside, whereby inhabitants exalted virtues of 'urban' life.[13] Connected with this was the apparent 'regionalism' of many areas of the south, where inhabitants had high levels of local patriotism and identification with their town of origin.[14] Such towns were home to internal discontent expressed in hostile entrenched class-based conflict between landowners and labourers.[15] The inhabitants of these agro-towns apparently displayed animosity to other towns in the vicinity, indicative of a closed character.[16] Culture and politics came together most closely in the work of Robert Putnam, whose famous and somewhat controversial thesis posited that Southern Italy was a place where people had no concept of 'citizenship' or civic tradition.[17] The lack of trust apparently offered fertile conditions for the proliferation of mafia organisation,[18] led to the poor performance of southern credit cooperation,[19] and led in a more general sense to dysfunction of financial institutions.[20] Of course, these kinds of views on Southern Italy were informed by wider literature linking culture to economic performance.[21] Furthermore, Putnam's thesis at the time seemed convincing, given that other works had suggested agro-towns in Southern Italy lacked urban functions and municipal institutions,[22] and furthermore had no tradition of jurisdictional control over

---

13 Blok and Driessen, 'Mediterranean agro-towns'; Schneider and Schneider, *Culture and political economy*, 66, 151; Silverman, *Three bells of civilization*; Davis, *People of the Mediterranean*; Kenny and Kertzer (eds), *Urban life in Mediterranean Europe*; Driessen, 'Male sociability and rituals of masculinity', 125.

14 As seen in Gilmore, *People of the plain*.

15 Gilmore, 'Class, culture, and community size', 100; Mintz, 'The folk-urban continuum'; Caro Baroja, 'City and the country', 38; Kaplan, *Anarchists of Andalusia*; Mintz, *Anarchists of Casas Viejas*. On class stratification see Corbin, 'Social class and patron-clientage'; Tolosana, *Belmonte de los Caballeros*.

16 Chapman, *Milocca*, 150; Behar, *Santa María del Monte*; Freeman, 'Corporate village organization'; Herzfeld, *Poetics of manhood*; Loizos, *The Greek gift*, 94–5.

17 Putnam, *Making democracy work*. See also the earlier controversial 'amoral familism' of Banfield, *Moral basis of a backward society*.

18 Gambetta, *La mafia siciliana*.

19 A'Hearn, 'Could Southern Italians cooperate?', 91.

20 Guiso, Sapienza and Zingales, 'Role of social capital in financial development'.

21 Landes, *Wealth and poverty of nations*, 516; Fukuyama, *Trust*; Gambetta, 'Can we trust trust?'.

22 Silverman, 'Agricultural organization'.

their rural hinterlands in the way that Northern and Central Italian city-states controlled their own surrounding countryside.[23]

In that sense, the explanation of the agro-town in the Mediterranean came to be framed in an entirely negative story of inequality. Some might even say these ideas were placed within a narrative of southern 'backwardness'; a place of extreme social and economic polarities, a place without a civic consciousness, of closed societies, and a place which never appeared to take the 'step forward' towards modernisation.[24] Southern Italy was portrayed as a place mired in antiquated feudal relations with little room for dynamic change: some historians emphasised the reinforcement of feudal powers in the transition to the early modern period.[25] Agro-towns were linked in a general sense then (without real causal links established) to inequality, widespread '*miseria*', societal vulnerability, and persistent institutional and economic structures.[26] Apparently they varied little in their economic function and one study even goes as far as to say 'one agrotown resembled most others economically'.[27] The development of the agro-town was something negative and to be avoided, not encouraged.

The problem with this negative explanatory framework for the agro-town in Southern Italy was that it was rarely historically rigorous.[28] Thus, from the literature cited above we cannot easily discern whether agro-towns are a recent phenomenon, only emerged within the past few centuries, or have medieval or even ancient antecedents. The long-term processes leading to the emergence of the agro-towns were not properly considered, with little explicit focus on chronology. Even some of the best sociological work identifying many different 'types' of society in the *Mezzogiorno* (Southern Italy) failed to go back much before 1860.[29] In some cases historical sources were not used at all.[30]

Fortunately, some of the best historical scholarship on Southern Italy in the past 30 years (driven forward by impressive work from the *Istituto di Studi sulle Società del Mediterraneo* based in Naples) has gone some way to addressing flaws in the previous methodology. In fact, in contrast to agro-towns being framed in an entirely negative story of southern stagnation, vulnerability, and backwardness, historians have focused on different regions of Southern Italy and shown agro-towns as embedded within a more 'positive' narrative. Biagio

23 Vivanti, 'Città e campagne', 267–70; Berengo, 'Città e "contado"', 107; Galasso, 'Gli insediamenti e il territorio', 58; Di Ciommo, 'Piccole e medie città meridionali', 357.

24 Levine, 'Modernity, backwardness, and capitalism'.

25 Romano, 'La storia economica'.

26 Friedmann, 'The world of "la miseria"'.

27 Gabaccia, *From Sicily to Elizabeth Street*, 13–4.

28 A criticism made in Abse, 'Recent works', 1021.

29 Arlacchi, *Mafia, peasants, and great estates*. Criticism of Arlacchi (of the original book in Italian) made in Bevilacqua, 'Calabria fra antropologia e storia', 667.

30 Broegger, *Montevarese*.

Salvemini in his study on an area of Central Apulia skilfully went back as far as the sixteenth century to show the view of agro-towns as being 'backward', immobile, economically irrational, dysfunctional, and with market weaknesses, totally without foundation.[31] Salvemini instead highlighted how agro-towns fitted into an adaptive agricultural and economic system, subject to the pressure of international markets and changing balances between arable and pastoral lands.[32] Rather than a simplistic association between agro-towns and *latifundia*, scholars such as Angelo Massafra, Saverio Russo and Annastella Carino have shown a greater complexity of tenurial structure including the proliferation of micro-plots in the early modern period.[33]

Similarly, Eleni Sakellariou has shown that real urban centres emerged in Apulia as early as the fifteenth and sixteenth centuries; these were outward-looking places with high numbers of their inhabitants involved in non-agricultural activity and economically integrated into regional markets.[34] Apulian merchants and artisans actively participated in commercial exchange in a combination of regional and long-distance trading opportunities.[35] This was in contrast to a previous view likening Apulia almost to a 'colony' of the Venetian State, a significant client for agricultural produce.[36] Sakellariou's interpretation finds wider consensus with other scholars working on Apulia from the early modern period.[37] Rather than emphasising the overarching grip of central political power from Naples or the economic might of northern city-states,[38] these studies lend themselves more to economic development stimulated through local or regional interest groups.[39] Some of these towns even came to have some limited jurisdictional control over subordinate settlements

---

31 Salvemini, 'Prima della Puglia', 114.

32 Salvemini, *L'innovazione precaria*; 'Arrogance of the market', 60–62.

33 Carrino, 'Messagne: una agrotown?', 20–2; Massafra and Russo, 'Microfondi e borghi rurali'.

34 Sakellariou, 'Cities of Puglia'; 'I centri minori'; *Southern Italy in the late Middle Ages*.

35 Salvemini and Visceglia, 'Bari e l'Adriatico', 172–3.

36 Leone, 'Caratteri dell'economia mercantile pugliese'; 'Il versante adriatico del Regno', 231. A view perpetuated by the fact that Northern city-states were reliant on trade with the South in the Middle Ages; Abulafia, *The two Italies*; 'Southern Italy and the Florentine economy'.

37 Ciuffreda, 'Massari e mercanti di piazza', 175–9; Galasso, 'La provincializzazione del Regno'; Massafra, 'Equilibri territoriali'.

38 Musi, *Mezzogiorno spagnolo*, 81; Cernigliaro, *Sovranità e feudo nel Regno di Napoli*.

39 In the form of local feudal lords; Visceglia, *Territorio, feudo e potere locale*, 215. Also in the form of the provincial landed bourgeoisie; Russo, *Storia di famiglia*; Macry, 'Le elites urbane', 808–11; Antonacci, *Terra e potere*, 156–7.

in their rural hinterlands, not just in Apulia but also in Campania.[40] Scholars have even disputed the perceived wisdom that Southern Italian agro-towns had no municipal or urban functions, for example in parts of Salerno, and also in the towns of Reggio Calabria and Avellino.[41] One such function of these towns was increasingly to hold periodic markets and fairs.[42]

The formation of agro-towns in Sicily was initially linked by Henri Bresc to a reliance on a complete grain monoculture dictated by the exploitation of southern markets by northern commercial elites.[43] However, exceptional work from Stephan Epstein was able to challenge Bresc's view by showing how Sicilian towns from the late Middle Ages onwards exhibited highly diversified economies and produced a vast array of items for regional trade.[44] In fact Sicily benefited from a lack of urban monopolies or protectionism, institutional configurations which conversely held back regions such as Tuscany in the transition to the early modern period.[45] The development of the south is no longer approached simply through a north–south paradigm.[46] Like Apulia, concentrated towns in Sicily also developed in a context of regional networks of trade.[47] Where previous 'negative' interpretations of the development of agro-towns had highlighted their almost exclusively agricultural and closed character, more recent historical work on Southern Italy is instead putting forward their diversified and integrated features.[48] Agro-towns apparently were products of more complex ecological systems, connected with wider territories and other networks of towns.[49] This same complexity in the *Mezzogiorno* has been extended to research at the household level too: while early work suggested that Northern and Central Italy were typified by larger complex households while the small nuclear household was characteristic of Southern Italy,[50] later work has shown an entire diversity in

---

40 Spagnoletti, *L'incostanza delle umane cose*; 'Il patriziato barese', 115; Massaro, 'La città e i casali'; Marin, 'Les bourgs ruraux'; Musi, 'La città assente'.

41 Musi, 'Piccole e medie città', 156–7; Placanica, *La Calabria*, i; Barra, *Storia di Avellino*.

42 Grohmann, *La fiere del Regno di Napoli*, 68–72.

43 Bresc, *Un monde méditerranéen*.

44 Epstein, *An island for itself*; 'Cities, regions'; 'The textile industry'.

45 Epstein, 'Cities, regions', 46.

46 On this point; Bevilacqua, *Breve storia dell'Italia meridionale*; Davis, 'Casting off the 'Southern Problem'.

47 Benigno, 'Assetti territoriali e ruralizzazione nella Sicilia'.

48 Bevilacqua and Gorgoni, 'Mercati'; Bevilacqua, 'Clima, mercato e paesaggio agrario'; Petrusewicz, 'Agromania'; *Latifundium*, 1–21; Lupo, *Il Giardino degli aranci*; Antonacci, 'Le città rurali'.

49 Delille, *Famiglia e proprietà*; 'La famiglia contadina'.

50 Banfield, *Moral basis of a backward society*; Silverman, 'Agricultural organization'; Davis, *Land and family in Pisticci*, 42. Also for the wider Mediterranean; Peristiany (ed.),

household structure, proving a death-knell to big theories about the Southern Italian family.[51]

Previous historical literature had suggested that an economic divergence between Northern and Southern Italy had already been drawn in the Middle Ages.[52] However, the economic position of the Kingdom of Naples is also beginning to be revised in a much more general sense, particularly through the influence of important and skilled research by Paolo Malanima. Malanima has used comparative data such as wage series to argue that before the end of the nineteenth century a gap between Northern and Southern Italy barely existed.[53] Similar lines of argument have been made with GDP.[54] The notion of pre-industrial backwardness in the south has drastically been revised, also with support from Stefano Fenoaltea and Giovanni Federico.[55] Even the scale of nineteenth- and twentieth-century *latifundia* has now been reconsidered, where new literature is highlighting a greater variety of modes of exploitation.[56] Old views of conservative landlords more concerned with ostentation than agricultural improvements have been challenged.[57] Furthermore, it has even been suggested that in 1860, numbers engaged in 'industrial' occupations were higher in the south than the north.[58] That is not to say the pre-twentieth-century *Mezzogiorno* has now been painted as some sort of utopia, however: scholars have also recognised that at the time of Unification, Southern Italy displayed in many areas very low levels of literacy and life-expectancy.[59]

Thus, it is clear that scholarly literature on the economics and society of Southern Italy has become far more nuanced and sophisticated in recent years. A particular feature of these new interpretations is a greater appreciation of diversity and dynamism in economic activity in the south supported by a wide

---

Mediterranean family structures.

51 The historiography provided by Viazzo, 'What's so special about the Mediterranean?'. See the diversity in Southern Italian household structure in Douglass, 'South Italian family', 340; Da Molin, 'Family forms'; Delille, *Famiglia e proprietà*; Colclough, 'Continuity and change'; Barbagli, 'Marriage and the family', 119; Benigno, 'Southern Italian family'

52 Galasso, *Il Mezzogiorno*; Cafagna, 'Intorno alle origini del dualismo economico'.

53 Malanima, 'An age of decline'.

54 Daniele and Malanima, 'Il prodotto delle regioni'; Felice, 'Regional value added'.

55 Fenoaltea, 'La crescita industriale'; *L'economia italiana dall'Unità alla Grande Guerra*, 217; Federico, 'Ma l'agricoltura meridionale era davvero arretrata?'; 'L'agricoltura italiana: successo o fallimento?'.

56 Galassi and Cohen, 'Economics of tenancy', 585.

57 Lupo, 'I proprietari terrieri nel Mezzogiorno'. Despite the persistence of negative views of latifundist agriculture in Toniolo, *L'economia dell'Italia fascista*; Zamagni, *Dalla periferia al centro*.

58 De Rosa, *La provincia subordinata*, 3–19.

59 Felice, 'I divari regionali in Italia'.

variety of institutional structures. However, this still poses some problems for understanding why the agro-town was a general phenomenon across a large part of Southern Italy (and the Mediterranean at large). We know now that Southern Italy was not as backward, isolated and conservative as once thought and exhibited a level of market integration, non-agricultural activity and tenurial complexity. But the point is so did many places in pre-industrial Europe – it did not mean that all these places were characterised by an overwhelming tendency for habitation within very large towns (with very unpredictable rates of fluctuating growth and decline), however. In a comparative sense, their proliferation is still curious. This aim of this chapter is to shed some light on their development. Some of their features will be teased out of a comparative case study of two towns within Apulia: Ascoli Satriano and Locorotondo between 1600 and 1900.

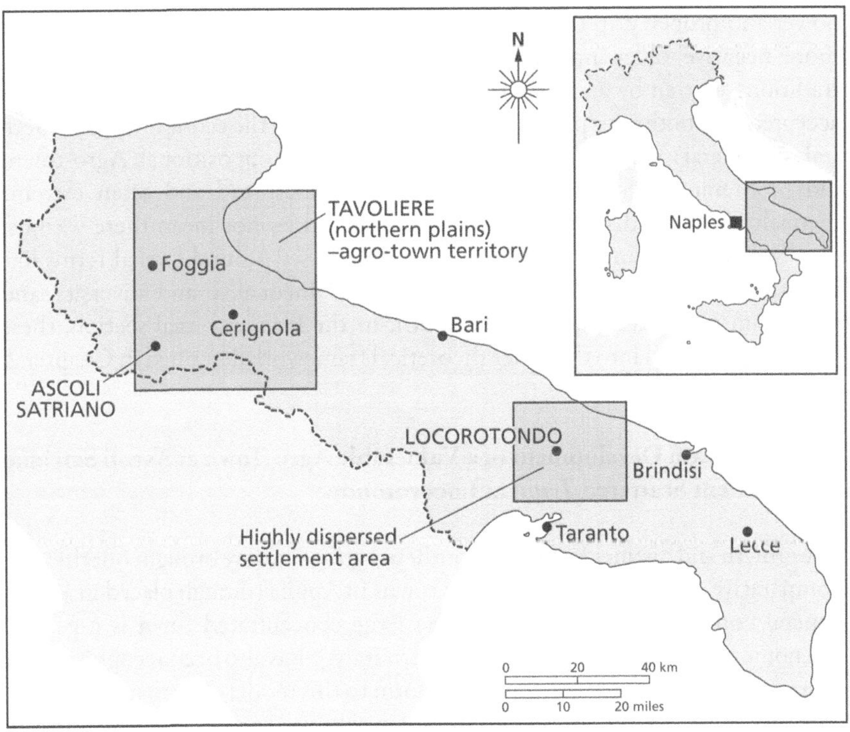

Figure 7.2 Map of Apulia and locations of towns

In the first section, it will be shown that agro-towns in Southern Italy frequently did have some distinctly 'negative' characteristics which led to heightened societal vulnerability of their inhabitants. In the second section, the question of why agro-towns developed is addressed. Here it is shown that in Apulia, agro-towns did not necessarily develop through latifundist agriculture and conservative structures but were actually part of dynamic and flexible modes of exploitation for managing economy, agriculture, and resources. *Latifundia* did not develop until much later in the nineteenth century (after the essential large concentrated town structure had taken shape). In that sense, this part of the chapter lends support to the more recent work (of the historical, economic and archaeological tradition mainly written in Italian) revising a previous image of Southern Italy as conservative and backward. However, in the third section, the reasons for the emergence of these distinct modes of exploitation are considered. It is suggested that these dynamic and diverse modes of exploitation were built upon very polarised and entrenched inequitable distributions of power and property. In that sense, this part of the chapter lends support to the more 'negative' older interpretations (of the anthropologist and ethnographic tradition) written by an international scholarship. Thus in the conclusion it is accepted that both interpretations of agro-towns (and the economy of Southern Italy in general) are correct and need not be mutually oppositional. Agro-towns did proliferate in Southern Italy because of widespread and often extreme inequalities in the distribution of land but that does not mean there was just one 'Southern Italian path' towards inequality based around loaded terms like 'stagnation', 'conservatism', or 'backwardness'.[60] Inequality and diversity and dynamism go hand-in-hand in the south. In the fifth and final section, these findings are placed into the wider theoretical framework described in Chapter 2.

The Long-Term Development of a Vulnerable Agro-Town at Ascoli Satriano and Resilient Scattered *Trulli* at Locorotondo

The growth and distinct features of southern agro-towns are brought out through comparative case study analysis of two towns in Apulia (though placed in a more general context). Indeed, although the large concentrated town is a general phenomenon across large parts of Southern Italy, it has also been recognised that there are certain areas which do not conform to this model of settlement. In fact, there are some areas of Southern Italy which exhibited a more dispersed pattern of settlement – smaller villages and hamlets or scattered houses and farmsteads. The Murgia in Central Apulia, most of the Abruzzi and Molise, parts of Eastern

[60] A criticism of the vague notion of 'backwardness' is made in Davis, *Naples and Napoleon*, 7; 'Remapping Italy's path'. Also Morris, 'Challenging Meridionalismo'.

Sicily, and the Cosentino area of Central Calabria certainly did not conform to the agro-town model.[61] The same is true of other parts of the Mediterranean such as Portugal: large towns may dominate in the Alentejo regions to the south (south of Lisbon and particularly dominant around inland Evora), but further to the north small scattered hamlets dominate.[62] To highlight some of the agro-town's characteristic features, the demographic development of the agro-town of Ascoli Satriano is contrasted with the town of Locorotondo – not an agro-town but actually characterised by the dispersed distribution of farms and conical stone houses known as *trulli*. Did agro-towns exhibit more signs of settlement vulnerability?

Ascoli Satriano is located on the edge of a large plain in Northern Apulia known as the Tavoliere, but within a shallow valley (*La Valle del Carapelle*) formed by three hills. Archaeological evidence suggests that earliest human habitation at Ascoli was around the ninth century BCE.[63] Similar dated earthworks have been found all over these plains.[64] In the Roman period, Ascoli ('*Ausculum*' as it was known then[65]) was a small cluster of habitations connected to a wider network of scattered villas operated by slave labour and focused on grain cultivation.[66] When the Western Roman Empire began to collapse in the fourth and fifth centuries, many of these farms were abandoned.[67] On the surface this fits with the influential thesis of Jean-Marie Martin, who framed early medieval settlement on the Apulian plains as a case of total depopulation with a retraction of cultivation and a re-growth of woodlands.[68] Nonetheless, there were some signs of continuity between the Roman and early medieval periods at Ascoli (and on the plains in general).[69] An archaeological project at the villa of Faragola, 2 km outside the current location of Ascoli, has shown how the settlement readapted from an elite aristocratic residence into a small peasant village and point of production.[70]

61 Dickinson, 'Dispersed settlement'; *The population problem*, 24; Arlacchi, *Mafia, peasants, and great estates*, chp. 1; Galt, *Far from the church bells*; Rochefort, *Le travail en Sicile*, 100–101; Palumbo, *Madre madrina*; Piselli, *Parentela ed emigrazione*.

62 Compare Cutileiro, *Portuguese rural society*, 7, 42; Juan O'Neill, *Social inequality*, 31–3.

63 Goffredo and Ficco, 'Tra Ausculum e Herdonia', 29.

64 Delano Smith, 'Ancient landscapes', 96.

65 Campopiano (ed.), *Liber Guidonis*, lxxvii

66 Accorsi et al., 'Ricerche archeoambientali'; Volpe, *La Daunia*, 56–60; Sanpaolo, 'Appunti preliminari'.

67 Volpe, 'Herdonia romana, tardoantica e medievale'.

68 Martin, *La Pouillé*, 148–50; Martin and Noyé, 'Il popolamento del Tavoliere'; Volpe, 'Villaggi e insediamento sparso'; 'Paesaggi e insediamenti rurali'; Martin and Noyé, 'Guerre, fortifications et habitats', 227–9.

69 Christie, *The Lombards*, 90; Favia, 'Temi, approcci, metodologici'.

70 Volpe et al., 'L'abitato altomedievale '; Volpe, 'A late Roman villa', 44–5.

The medieval reconstruction of settlement in many parts of Apulia is difficult due to paucity of sources, and Ascoli is no different in that respect.[71] Essentially, Ascoli's development from the high Middle Ages into the early modern period seemed to be characterised by total instability: a cycle of decline followed by re-emergence, perhaps unsurprising given the political struggles associated with this frontier region. Ascoli was subjected to the rule of the Vandals and Goths, Lombard princes, Byzantine and Norman lords from the fifth to the twelfth centuries, not to mention Saracen invasions in the late tenth century. Norman soldiers burnt Ascoli to the ground in 1082,[72] though it had been rebuilt in a different location by 1111 'without its previous beauty'.[73] The settlement was fortified with walls by 1180.[74]

Late-medieval Ascoli is particularly difficult to reconstruct. Certainly we know that it began to descend as a feudal fee through aristocratic families who received lands and jurisdictions there in return for services rendered to sovereigns.[75] We also know that absentee landowners already had managed to secure land in the territory by the thirteenth century,[76] as had happened all over this area of Apulia.[77] Settlement evidence is vague, however. One significant event was an earthquake on 5 December 1456, which totally destroyed Ascoli, and the surviving inhabitants had to relocate to a new spot where the current town is positioned.[78] The 1456 earthquake reaped havoc in Southern Italy, with the number of victims estimated in Molise, Campania, Abruzzo, Basilicata, and Apulia estimated between 30,000 and 100,000.[79] After relocation, Ascoli grew from 420 households in 1532 to 870 households by 1648 (a population of 4,350), enough to warrant 'small town' status, though we cannot be sure of the location of these houses. Twenty-one years later however, Ascoli was absolutely devastated and reduced to less than half of its former size, badly hit by outbreaks

---

71 Worsened by a fire in 1667 destroying the important ecclesiastical documents; Todisco Grande, 'Memoria dell'antichità', 133.

72 Protospata, 'Chronicon', 18.

73 Todisco Grande, 'Memoria dell'antichità', 131.

74 Lupriore, *Ascoli di Capitanata*, 79.

75 Checchia de Ambrosio (ed.), *Ricordi storici di Capitanata*, 54; Perthes Gotha (ed.), *Almanach de Gotha*, 314; De Lellis, *Discorsi delle famiglie nobili*, 157; Siena Chianese, *La nobiltà napoletana*, 101; Magdaleno, *Títulos y privilegios de Nápoles*, i, 320; Romano, *Gli apprezzi e le platee dell'Archivio Caracciolo di Torella*, 58, 125, 126, 249, 266; Della Marra, *Famiglie estinte fuorestiere*, 163; Marinaccio, 'Una famiglia feudale', 133.

76 Gilsdorf, 'Foundation of a French monastery', 250.

77 Houben, *Die Abtei Venosa*, 203–9.

78 Todisco Grande, 'Memoria dell'antichità', 131.

79 Helly, 'Case studies', 139.

of pestilence with a great loss of human and animal life.[80] Nonetheless, a sketch made of Ascoli in 1703, shows the general form of a concentrated town, even though the population in 1709 was half of what it had been before the plague epidemic with narrowly more houses than in 1532.

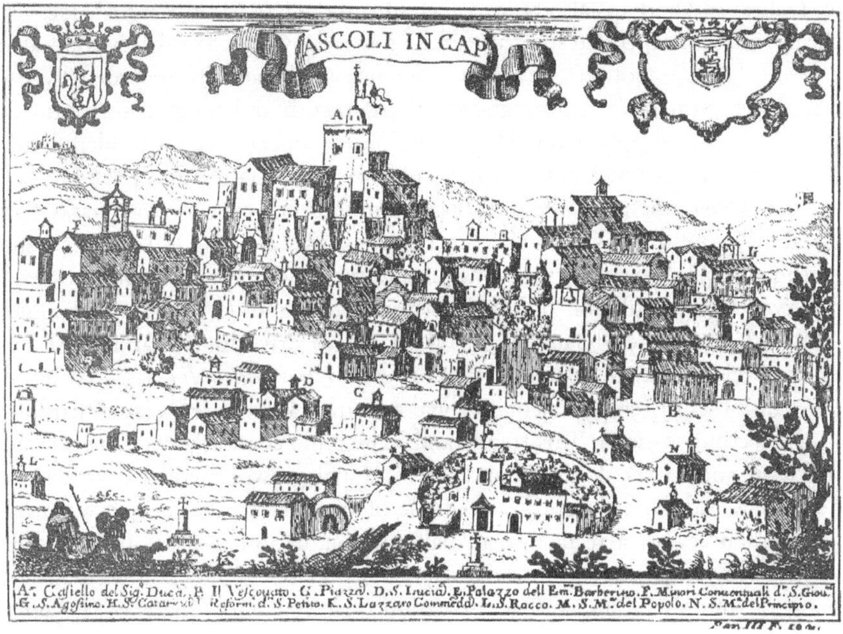

Figure 7.3 Ascoli Satriano in 1703

Source: Pacichelli, *Il Regno di Napoli.*

By the time of the Catasto Onciario (a fiscal assessment of property in the Kingdom of Naples) in 1753, Ascoli had surpassed the houses recorded a century before.[81] Nearly every house was recorded within the town centre or in a *contrada* (neighbourhood) near the walls. The transmission of property through women via marriage contracts (dowries) had led to the establishment of many

[80] The proportion of survivors was suggested as just one-sixth of the former population in a chronicle though this may have been exaggerated; see Todisco Grande, 'Memoria dell'antichità', 131. For the overall Kingdom of Naples figures see Marino, *Pastoral economics*, 65–6.

[81] The higher number of houses in 1753 than in 1648 despite lower population figures is because there were more absentee owners of real estate with more than one house by 1753.

'new' nuclear households (77 per cent of all households in 1753);[82] however, houses were positioned very close together as daughters inherited houses within the same *contrada* as their parents.[83] The dividing line between 'neo-locality' and 'extension of households' is somewhat blurred here then. The only houses far from the walls were large farms (*masserie*) belonging to elite landowners.[84] Many of these *masserie* were located in exactly the same spots as former Roman *fattorie* and villas, and perhaps also failed villages from the late Middle Ages.[85] Despite the obvious concentrated structure of the town, the Catasto probably concealed a level of settlement in the countryside not systematically recorded by the assessors.[86] Nonetheless, throughout the eighteenth and nineteenth centuries, Ascoli Satriano simply became bigger and more concentrated – hindered only during brief phases such as the typhus epidemics of 1764–67 and 1815–17.[87]

The development of Ascoli up to the nineteenth century was marked by instability – rapid growth and decline caused by warfare, plague, pestilence, and earthquakes. The instability after 1850 was at a much more pronounced level, however. The population doubled between 1861 and 1951 from just under 6,000 inhabitants to just under 12,000. In just 90 years this was an intense and rapid development stimulated by the conversion to a *latifundia*-based economy with an influx of temporary or seasonal agricultural labourers (explained later in the second section). This fragile and vulnerable economy could never last, however, and under domestic and international pressures collapsed after the Second World War. As quick as the rise of Ascoli was, the decline was even more intense with a retraction in half the population in just 50 years. The actual living situation within the town of Ascoli after 1850 was quite poor for many of the inhabitants and is a situation mirrored across many of the agro-towns in Northern Apulia during this time with impoverishment of a mass rank of wage workers. This is the kind of image portrayed by Frank Snowden when he described the late nineteenth- and early twentieth-century 'Company Towns' – places like Cerignola or Andria where poor people were crowded into

---

82 Ventura (ed.), *Onciario 1753*. This figure is actually not as high as some of the other 'agro-town' areas of Apulia where levels of 90 per cent were sometimes recorded; see Da Molin, 'Family forms', 506–7.

83 Colclough, 'Invisible patrimonies'.

84 Di Cicco, *Il Tavoliere*, 199–209.

85 Licinio, *Masserie medievali*, 13–25. It has been suggested elsewhere in Apulia that *masserie* were on the same sites as former Roman villas; Ambrosi, 'Schemi propositivi per lo studio dell'architettura della masseria pugliese'; Mongiello, *Le masserie di Puglia*. The fortified *masseria* of Torre Alemania near Ascoli had a small clustered habitation as early as the thirteenth century; Licinio, *Castelli medievali*, 145.

86 Colclough, 'Famiglie catastali', 53.

87 On concerted demographic growth in the Kingdom of Naples; Massafra, 'Economia e società nel periodo Spagnola', 79.

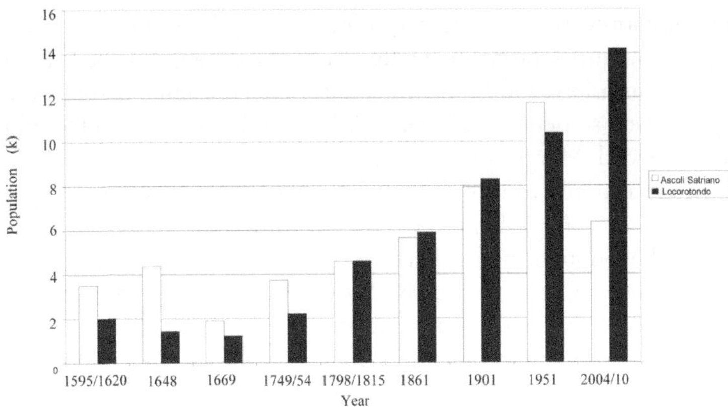

Figure 7.4 Population trends in comparison: Ascoli Satriano and Locorotondo, 1595–2010

Sources: Giustiniani (ed.), *Dizionario geografico*, ii, 8–9, 282; Colclough, 'Family and the spatial distribution of kin'; Ventura (ed.), *Onciario 1753*; ISTAT, *Catasto agrario 1929. Compartimento delle Puglie. Provincia di Bari,* no. 71; *Secondo censimento generale dell'agricoltura*; ASB, 1749 Catasto Onciario di Locorotondo; Mele, *Una famiglia in ascesa,* 138–41.

rented hovels in terrible living conditions, often with no windows and located underground.[88] These kinds of conditions gave rise to endemic and epidemic diseases, as described also by Snowden for Barletta in 1910.[89] In a report from 1889, it was noted 'misery had become more terrible'. One peasant was recorded as having died from starvation leaving three children behind, while the very next day another agricultural worker had fallen into the public highway exhausted by lack of food.[90] The troubling aspect of the report was its note that such cases were so common, it was becoming almost impossible to provide support to the destitute – the town of Andria was described as entirely 'over-populated'. In the countryside surrounding the towns under the pressure of bringing more land under the plough, woodland disappeared, and soil became all but ruined.[91]

Locorotondo showed a different course of development over the long term, however. The settlement is located further south to Ascoli, on a raised rocky inland plateau in Central Apulia known as the Murgia. Locorotondo also knew

88 Snowden, *Violence and great estates*, 41–61.

89 Snowden, 'Cholera in Barletta'.

90 ASB, Fondo Intendenza-Prefettura (agricoltura, industria e commercio), no. 7, fo. 41.

91 Russo, *Grano, pascolo e bosco*.

human habitation from around the ninth century BCE, but the first settled farming communities probably emerged much later around the fifth century CE. Saracen invasions and Lombard counter-attacks caused destruction of the principle coastal settlements of Brindisi, Bari, and Taranto, and forced people into the wooded Murgia to seek refuge.[92] As with Ascoli, there is limited documentary material to reconstruct the medieval settlement development of Locorotondo. Around 1086, the Count of Conversano founded the abbey of S. Stefano of Monopoli, giving them, amongst other feudal property, the fee of Casale San Giorgio, later to become Locorotondo. The Knights of Jerusalem fortified the settlement in the fourteenth century, and from the fifteenth century, Locorotondo descended through the hands of various aristocratic families.[93]

The demographic development of Locorotondo was less dramatic and unstable than Ascoli's trajectory, as seen from Figure 7.4. In 1648, it was less than half the size of Ascoli, yet Locorotondo was also less severely hit by bouts of pestilence in the mid-seventeenth century which had been so disruptive in Ascoli.[94] Locorotondo was less afflicted by cattle plagues as its more rocky and wooded environment did not support this sort of specialised pastoral economy. The epidemic evened out population differences between the two places, and Locorotondo re-grew during the eighteenth century, though not into a concentrated town like Ascoli. Certainly there was a town centre tucked away behind the walls, home to the church, taverns, and artisan shops. However, this co-existed with a level of dispersed settlement. Clusters of *trulli* (conical stone houses) known as '*jazzeleri*' were mentioned by notaries, and were clearly out in the countryside.[95] By the census of 1811, 37 per cent of inhabitants were living outside the walls and in new areas (*nuovi borghi*).[96] The scattered pattern of settlement has continued to the modern day, a contrast to the stereotypical vision of the concentrated town in the Mediterranean. In 1971 over half the population lived outside the walls, as shown in Figure 7.5. Locorotondo did not experience the sharp ups and downs seen in Ascoli after 1850 (since *latifundia* did not become dominant here at all) and while Ascoli suffered a complete retraction after the Second World War, Locorotondo continued to blossom with steady demographic growth up to the modern day. The terrible living conditions described for the late nineteenth-century agro-towns were not immediately recognisable here.

92 Di Michele, *Locorotondo.*

93 Montanaro and Tursi, *Guida di Locorotondo*, 15.

94 Massella, 'Economia e società nel periodo Spagnolo', 36.

95 Galt, *Far from the church bells*, 76–7.

96 Ibid., 151.

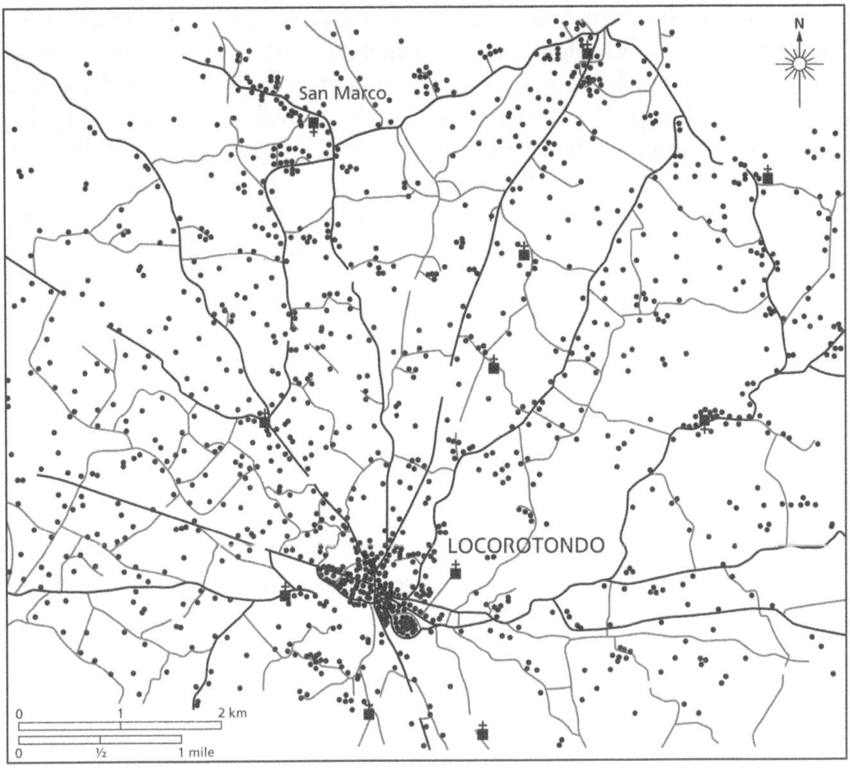

Figure 7.5 Distribution of dispersed *trulli* in Locorotondo, end of the twentieth century

Linking Settlement Resilience and Vulnerability with Resource Exploitation

As noted in the above section, Ascoli Satriano (like many agro-towns) was an altogether more vulnerable settlement than that of Locorotondo, characterised by rapid and frequent swings of upward and downward population trends. In this section, the context behind the emergence and proliferation of agro-towns such as Ascoli is considered. Why did Ascoli develop into this large concentrated town after the terrible cattle pestilences of the mid- to late seventeenth century, while Locorotondo some 100 km to the south developed a highly dispersed pattern? Traditional explanations of *latifundia* do not hold, because it is clear from the settlement chronology presented above that the concentrated town structure of Ascoli (as with many settlements on the plains of the Tavoliere) developed far earlier than the *latifundia*, which only became dominant after roughly 1850. Actually what is shown in this section is that concentrated agro-towns on the Northern Apulian plains were established and perpetuated in a context of a carefully ecologically managed mixed system of arable and pastoral farming with high levels of capital investment in large flocks and herds of animals. Ascoli in particular was crystallised into a real commercial and trading centre based around urban functions.[97] While agro-towns were locked into this system managed centrally through the government in Naples, the more dispersed settlements of Locorotondo (and more generally on the Murgia) had autonomy over their own adaptable strategies – achieving control over their own land thanks in combination to greater independence from Naples and internal weaknesses of their elite feudal landlords. Locorotondo became orientated towards international markets through the coastal ports of Apulia rather than the overarching coercive arm of Naples.

Ascoli, the Plains of the Tavoliere, and the Royal Customhouse of Naples

The emergence of the large concentrated towns such as Cerignola, Troia, Foggia, Lucera, Candela, Andria, and Ascoli Satriano on the northern plains of Apulia (the Tavoliere), emerged in a context of strict economic and agricultural management from the Royal Customhouse of Naples. The system was based around a rigorous supervision of transhumant sheep farming between the Apulian plains and the mountains of the Abruzzo.[98] Transhumance between the two regions had Roman origins, though the system retracted in the early Middle Ages with the collapse of the long-distance trading networks.[99] When the Normans arrived in Apulia, transhumant sheep farming probably picked up again (from around the eleventh century onwards), although the Royal Customhouse only formalised the institutions necessary for its management in 1447.[100] Some evidence points to local cloth production in parts of late-medieval Northern Apulia.[101]

The rationale behind the Royal Customhouse of Naples was to create a balance between arable and pastoral land on the Tavoliere.[102] Alongside the Castilian *Mesta*, it was Europe's largest managed pastoral economy. Privately owned arable land was grazed during fallow periods, while royal pastures were never cultivated. It that sense, it was an early exercise in environmental sustainability and a way of avoiding ecological degradation. It also lent itself to

97 Colclough, 'Variation and change', 9–11.

98 For a superb explanation of how it worked see Marino, *Pastoral economics*.

99 Barker, 'Archaeology of the Italian shepherd', 13; Corbier, 'La transhumance', 161. Some argue even earlier; Lomas, *Rome and the western Greeks*, 122–3.

100 The founding charter from Alfonso of Aragon who conquered the Kingdom of Naples in 1447 has been printed in Grana, *Istituzioni delle leggi della Regia Dogana*, 72–9.

101 De Gennaro, 'Le lane di Puglia'.

102 Di Stefano, *Della ragion pastorale*.

flexible manipulation in the economic interests of the Neapolitan political and commercial elite. Wool and wheat were cash products which were to be sold in Naples, and fortunately for Ascoli, it was located on a key overland transport link through the Basilicata to Naples.[103] Naples was one of the most populous cities in Western Europe before the plagues of 1656;[104] the ratio therefore between arable and pasture fluctuated with the trends of demand and prices for agricultural goods. Grain fed the kingdom while taxes on sheep provided its riches.[105] Apulia accounted for over a fifth of total grain imported into Naples between the mid-1500s and the mid-1600s, and in 1486 around 655,200 kg of grain was shipped from Manfredonia in Northern Apulia to Naples.[106] Tax exemptions and privileges granted by Naples on certain Apulian centres eased the export of grain.[107] Of course, the ratios between arable and pasture were not entirely dictated by demand. For example, the pestilences of 1656 in Northern Apulia led to an entirely contracted labour force, thereby halting any trend towards large-scale arable cultivation.[108] Elite landowners quickly shifted investment strategy towards sheep farming with smaller labour intensive demands – an extreme case being the estates of the Prince of Melfi.[109] However, when population began to increase on the plains again, pressure was once again put on producers to bring more land into grain cultivation.[110]

The incipient town structure on the Northern Apulian plains had its roots in the rigorous management of the Tavoliere by Naples from its regional base in Foggia. The building of farms and houses out in the countryside became entirely restricted. In that respect the Tavoliere became depicted as a barren wilderness, comparable to the Steppes of Central Asia. It was the second biggest province in the Kingdom of Naples in terms of area, and frequently the least populous in the early modern period.[111] Land became divided into *locazioni*, each comprised of a number of isolated farms known as *masserie*. Livestock farms were more complex than grain farms, took up more space, and included a wider range of buildings such as dog kennels, animal stables, sheep pens, cheese processing

103 Massafra, *Campagna e territorio nel Mezzogiorno*, 199.

104 Sakellariou, *Southern Italy in the late Middle Ages*, 446.

105 Calabria, *The cost of empire*, 33–6.

106 Coniglio, *Il viceregno di Napoli*, 37; Salvati (ed.), *Copia quarteni Bernardi de Anghono mag. Actorum penes mag. portulanum Apulie de tractis extraxtis (1486–87)*, 18–23.

107 Fenicia, 'Tendencias comerciales', 14.

108 See the descriptions in Ardoini, *Descrizione del Stato di Melfi*. Also Marino, 'I meccanismi della crisi'.

109 Zotta, 'Momenti e problemi'. Prior to the pestilence, investment was restricted to grain farming; Lepre, *Feudi e masserie*, 85–123.

110 Cerrito, 'Ambiente, insediamento e regime agrario', 113–5.

111 La Cava, 'La demografia di un comune Pugliese'.

sites, and threshing floors.[112] In particular the complex belonging to the abbey of S. Leonardo di Siponto at their Feudo di Torre Alemanna had all these things as well as taverns, olive presses, and bakeries inside an almost fortified design.[113] *Locazioni* were also subdivided between smaller huts (*capanne*), which belonged to shepherds, and often included a church nearby. In sum, the potential for local inhabitants to construct their own habitations where they wanted on the plains was limited. The point is reinforced by the fact that on the Tavoliere lie the remnants of former villages, abandoned between the fourteenth and sixteenth centuries. Up to around the fifteenth century, this sort of settlement structure was possible on the plains of the Tavoliere, but was quickly destroyed when the Royal Customhouse management of agriculture was institutionally formalised.[114]

Yet while institutional restrictions on habitation in the countryside of Northern Apulia in the early modern period may be part of the story, it cannot explain why the development of capital intensive and labour extensive forms of commercialised pastoral farming occurred at the same time as the intense growth of these concentrated towns after the pestilences of the mid-seventeenth century. How can we account for the large inward migration into Ascoli in the eighteenth century, and where was the attraction? Indeed, 32 per cent of households in the Catasto of 1753 were living in Ascoli as immigrants, indicative of high mobility. Unfortunately while we know the place of origin for all of these people (people came from all over Apulia and Basilicata to live and work in Ascoli),[115] the Catasto did not record occupations for immigrants. They were not all poor labourers looking for work, though. Some were referred to as 'magnificent', indicative of elite status, while others were doctors, clerics, and widows.[116]

It seems the town of Ascoli expanded its population as a result of its well-developed trading and commercial sector: essentially, it was an urban sector. Obviously this kind of situation contrasts entirely with some of the views crystallised by Putnam, who emphasised Southern Italy's agricultural character, its sense of a closed community, and its lack of civic amenities. Ascoli blossomed in the eighteenth century (despite its extreme inequality in the distribution of land, explained in the next section) as traders and artisans were able to provision large estates and transhumant pastoralists with produce.[117] Neville Colclough

112 La Sorsa, 'La pastorizia pugliese'; Bissanti, 'Il Tavoliere'.

113 Laurenti, 'Visita dell'abbatia'.

114 Licinio, *Uomini e terre nella Puglia medievale*; *Masserie medievali*; Delano Smith, 'Villages désertés dans les Pouilles'; Klapisch-Zuber, 'Villaggi abbandonati', 345–9.

115 The diverse place of origin for Ascoli immigrants is also noted in Russo, 'Uomini e colture', 81.

116 The diverse status of eighteenth- and nineteenth-century immigrants in Northern Apulia is discussed in Russo, *Storie di famiglie*; 'La cerealicoltura del Tavoliere'.

117 Colclough, 'Variation and change', 4.

actually showed through a hearth tax of 1728 that only about 35 per cent of the population worked on large estates, and these were not always grain. Actually, more of this kind of work was taken on by temporary seasonal workers from the Southern Apulia and the Central Uplands who did not own property in Ascoli and rented rooms from wealthy aristocrats in the town, taking up notarised six-month contracts to work the estates.[118] Agricultural labourers made up a minority of the population. In fact, Ascoli had a high number of inhabitants working outside agriculture, either in professional or clerical roles, or in mercantile or industrial roles as craftsmen or apprentices. Colclough's figures from 1728 suggested that almost half the people in Ascoli worked in the 'urban sector',[119] and this is supported by my data from 1753 which recorded 40 per cent of the inhabitants in urban occupations.[120] Some of those in the 'urban sector' supported their trades with work on micro-plots of vines attached to the town walls.[121] Elsewhere on the agro-town plains such as at Orsara di Puglia, high levels of non-agricultural labour have been found.[122] These figures can be contrasted with Locorotondo where only 14 per cent of households were involved in non-agricultural occupations in the mid-eighteenth century or Santo Marco dei Cavoti in Northern Basilicata (an area characterised by small villages and dispersed farms) where only 10 per cent of the heads of households were classed as 'artisans'.[123]

Thus, the large concentrated town structure of Ascoli was crystallised in place a long time before monoculture and latifundist estates started to dominate on the Tavoliere. In 1806 the Royal Customhouse of Naples and its management of the Apulian plains collapsed in line with a Europe-wide ideological move away from communal property forms at the end of the eighteenth century.[124] The same solution was devised for the Sila Forest in Calabria.[125] Neo-Malthusian and neo-liberal ideological reforms necessitated a dismantlement of a system deemed antithetical to new visions of modernity.[126] This had been preceded by the writings of a number of 'enlightened thinkers' such as Antonio Genovesi, Gaetano Filangieri, and Giuseppe Galanati discontented with the persistence

118 As in Cerignola; Russo, 'I lavoratori delle masserie', 29–31.

119 Colclough, 'Variation and change', 5.

120 Ventura (ed.), *Onciario 1753.*

121 Ventura, 'L'Onciario di Ascoli Satriano', 63.

122 Anzivino, 'Fuochi, famiglie e donne nel catasto onciario'.

123 Palumbo, 'Casa di mugliera', 7.

124 Deméelas and Vivier (eds), *Les propriétés collectives*; Congost and Miguel Lana (eds), *Cerrados, debates abiertos.*

125 Corona, *Demani ed individualismo agrario*, 23–62.

126 Colapietra, 'Gli economisti settecenteschi dinanzi al problema del Tavoliere'; Di Cicco, 'Il problema della Dogana delle Pecore'; *Censuazione ed affrancazione del Tavoliere di Puglia.*

of old feudal structures across the Kingdom of Naples.[127] One such Neapolitan reformer, Ferdinando Galiani, went as far as to describe the collective transhumance system in Apulia as 'barbarous' and having parallel nowhere across 'civilised Europe'.[128] It was certainly true that the commons of the south were far closely tied up in feudal relationships than the commons found further north in the peninsula.[129] However, the collapse of the Royal Customhouse did nothing to change inequitable property distribution on the Tavoliere. In fact it exacerbated inequality, since 'communal land' was simply divided up and sold to the highest bidders at public auction.[130] In that way land was consolidated into the hands of already wealthy interest groups in Northern Apulia: former feudal lords and barons, urban entrepreneurs, and property speculators.[131] The same skewed process happened in Sicily when newly wealthy rent collectors expropriated communal parcels allocated to peasants as compensation.[132] Thus, finally the labour intensive and environmentally exhaustive system of *latifundia* dominated the region towards the late 1800s – a far cry from what had gone before.[133] Old sheep-orientated *masserie* were readapted for this purpose.[134] As production shifted, flocks of immigrant workers came to fill the suburbs (vineyards and meadows were converted into habitations) – yet this labourer migration merely added to a pattern of towns already fixed in place in another economic and ecological context.[135] Of course this was the context behind the great population boom between 1850 and 1950 in Ascoli and the perpetuation of some terrible living conditions, and the pretext for the eventual population contraction after the Second World War once the system of *latifundia* collapsed and unemployment soared. The local economy to this day is highly government-subsidy driven.[136]

---

127 See Venturi (ed.), *Illuministi Italiani*, 28, 618–9; Galanti, *Nuova descrizione storia e geografica della Sicilie*, i, 273–4, ii, 7, iii, 261–9; *Breve descrizione di Napoli*, iii, 309.

128 Marino, *Pastoral economics*, 245.

129 Bulgarelli Lukacs, 'La gestione delle risorse collettive'.

130 Massafra, 'Equilibri territoriali', 40–44; Russo, *Grano, pascolo e bosco*, 54; D'Atri, 'Censuazione del Tavoliere '. Despite initial promises of dividing up land into small farms; Davis, *Naples and Napoleon*, 178.

131 Lupo and Mangiameli, 'La modernizzazione difficile', 227; Martucci, 'La riforma del Tavoliere'.

132 Riall, 'Ill-contrived, badly executed [and] ... of no avail?', 136–9.

133 De Felice, *L'agricoltura di Terra di Bari*; Cormio, 'Le campagne pugliesi nella fase di transizione'; Massella, 'La Puglia contemporanea'.

134 Russo and Mercurio, 'L'organizzazione spaziale della grande azienda'.

135 Colclough, 'Variation and change', 9.

136 Colclough, 'How elections are fought in Ascoli', 186.

Peasant Power and Adaptive Strategies in Locorotondo

In contrast to the centrally managed system of large commercialised pastoral and arable farms owned by large absentee landowners in Ascoli, the conditions in Locorotondo in the eighteenth century were ripe for the proliferation of viticulture. Peasants began to build their rural *trulli* away from the walls of the town of Locorotondo and instead next to their newly acquired vineyard plots. This kind of peasant adaptive strategy was aided by their greater autonomy to make their own economic decisions. Neapolitan coercion did not extend so strongly this far into the Murgia of Apulia, especially with the government less able to secure a steady stream of taxes with the absence of large-scale sheep farming. Despite being characterised by a large band of small peasant farmers in the eighteenth and nineteenth centuries, Locorotondo was highly commercialised.[137] In particular, it was plugged into newly emerging international wine markets, and much trade was conducted through the ports of Bari and Monopoli.[138] These ports showed steady commercial expansion from 1750 onwards.[139] Wine from Locorotondo was sent on Sicilian and Venetian ships abroad.[140] The port of Taranto also became important for the Murgia.[141] Nearby Martina Franca with its workforce dedicated towards specialised livestock rearing and leather production was a ready eighteenth-century market, especially since its own wine production did not take off until the 1800s.[142] The institutional monopolies imposed by Naples and seen on the Tavoliere did not apply for Locorotondo and surrounding regions, and Locorotondese peasants used their grip on property and production to benefit from the misfortunes which hit wine producers in Southern France or Catalonia, as vineyards in the late 1800s were ruined by phylloxera.[143] In 1883 it was noted that Locorotondo's domestic and international wine trade gave rise to prosperity within the town.[144]

As argued by Anthony Galt, this peasant-owner system of viticulture can be explained by the dissemination of emphyteutic leases from the mid-eighteenth century onwards.[145] These contracts specified to the tenant that they must improve the property and this was common to the Mediterranean.[146] Initially

137 Galt, *Far from the church bells*, 225.

138 Visceglia, 'Il commercio dei porti pugliesi'. Taxes on wine traded through Monopoli are found as early as the 1400s; Muciaccia (ed.), *Il Libro Rosso*, 242.

139 Chorley, *Oil, silk and enlightenment*, 38.

140 Galt, 'Emphyteusis', 80.

141 Visceglia, 'Commercio e mercato in Terra d'Otranto', 153–4; *Territorio, feudo*, 156.

142 Boso, *Martina Franca*, 33–7; Montanaro, 'Quotizzazione delle masserie'.

143 Simpson, 'Cooperation and conflicts'.

144 Mele, *Annuario storico-statistico-commerciale di Bari*, 230.

145 Galt, 'Emphyteusis '.

146 For example see Marfany, *Land, proto-industry and population in Catalonia*, chp. 2.

ecclesiastical institutions but later lay feudal aristocrats decided to offer their land out on long-term heritable leases with the stipulation that the receiving peasant tenants had to improve the land by preparing the soil for viticulture.[147] The landlords' plan was that after the initial labour intensive and back-breaking work undertaken by the tenants, they would take the land back into hand – after 20 to 30 years. However, due to the weaknesses of the elite landowning class (explained in the next section), this never happened. Landlords lost their grip and security on the land, and eventually it was actually owned by the peasants themselves. In that sense, the proliferation of the lease allowed a larger proportion of Locorotondese inhabitants to gain access to their own land, with many of the farmers actually deciding it was in their interests to build their stone *trulli* out in the fields next to their vineyards.[148] In fact the inheritance practice in Locorotondo shifted in the eighteenth and nineteenth centuries in line with these changes: real estate in the town transferred to the daughter upon marriage was replaced by a system whereby sons received a rural *trullo* out in the countryside while daughters received cash payments.[149]

Power and Property

Rather than an assumed connection between *latifundia* and agro-town formation, the case seen in Northern Apulia shows that these concentrated towns actually formed in quite a dynamic context of capital intensive and commercialised pastoral agriculture, alongside a well-developed urban and trade sector. *Latifundia* were only applied over the top of an existing settlement structure. In that sense, the more recent literature emphasising diversity and dynamism in the economy and society of the Kingdom of Naples is supported. However, the obvious follow-up question to ask is why did such diverse economic arrangements emerge? Indeed, why was there such a divergence in economic paths between Ascoli Satriano and Locorotondo, separated by less than 100 km? It is shown in this section that while the modes of exploitation in the Kingdom of Naples could be dynamic and diverse, these (in the agro-town areas especially) were built upon a foundation of highly inequitable and persistent configurations of property, social distribution of property, and power.

The re-emergence of the concentrated town structure (after the disastrous pestilences of the late seventeenth century) and the development and

---

147 On ecclesiastical institutions laying the seeds of emphyteusis in the Terra di Bari; Poli, 'Appunti per una tipologia dei contratti agrari'. For similar chronology in Salento (Southern Apulia); Villari, *Mezzogiorno e contadini*, 73.

148 Massafra, 'Murgia dei Trulli'.

149 Galt, 'Marital property'.

crystallisation of the Royal Customhouse-managed system of commercial pastoral agriculture at Ascoli was founded on a context of extreme inequality, as shown by fiscal registers from the mid-eighteenth century. The Catasto Onciario was a register of taxable property combined with a census of households for the Kingdom of Naples, mandated by the Bourbon King Charles VII of Naples (Charles III of Spain) in order to make the tax system more efficient and equitable.[150] The declarations of property varied from settlement to settlement – the first ones were conducted in 1741 yet some were still being completed some 20 years later.[151] Resentment and resistance in the rural hinterlands of the Kingdom meant the recording process was uneven at best.[152] One of the helpful features of the Catasto was that it included all households, regardless of whether they had land or not, thus making it a good source for reconstructing inequality.[153] Some caution needs to be taken nonetheless in the sense that the new tax was still based on simple estimates rather than sophisticated measuring or consistent evaluations.[154] By making databases of the Catasto entries, it was confirmed that the agro-town of Ascoli was far more inequitable than the dispersed settlement of Locorotondo. Ascoli received an astonishing 0.97 on the Gini index for distribution of land (including all types of land: arable, pastoral, vineyards, and olives) compared to 0.77 in Locorotondo.[155] The scale of inequality in Ascoli can be further highlighted by comparing Gini indexes elsewhere in Italy in the early modern period. For example, in Piedmont in Northern Italy, the small town of Ivrea had a Gini index which oscillated between 0.6 and 0.7 all the way from the late fifteenth to the late seventeenth century.[156] Even when compared to the famously inequitable distribution of property in the fifteenth-century Florentine *contado* (a Gini index of 0.8 – see Chapter 3), Ascoli exhibited far greater levels of polarisation. Gini indexes between 0.65 and 0.75 were quite common for small towns and rural areas across pre-industrial Western Europe from the fourteenth up to the eighteenth century.[157]

Thus inequality in Ascoli proved sharp. A small handful (1 per cent) of Ascoli households and institutions owned 58 per cent of the land. Furthermore, 93 per

---

150 The background to this new fiscal system can be found in Cuoco, 'La funzione del catasto onciario', 143–5.

151 Galt, 'Social class', 422.

152 Villani, 'Il catasto onciario', 107–8.

153 The uses of the *catasto* for research into settlement, economy and demography are explained in Assante, 'Il catasto onciario come fonte di storia demografica'; Da Molin, *La famiglia nel passato*, 27–37; Carbone, 'Tra storia e demografia'.

154 Davis, *Naples and Napoleon*, 37.

155 My database of Ventura (ed.), *Onciario 1753*.

156 Alfani, 'Wealth inequalities and population dynamics in early modern Northern Italy', appendix.

157 Van Zanden, 'Tracing the beginning of the Kuznets Curve', 645–7.

cent of the land was in the hands of feudal lords such as the Duke of Ascoli, lesser aristocratic families, or absentee ecclesiastical institutions, leaving just 7 per cent in the hands of local peasants, labourers and tradesmen. In Locorotondo, 55 per cent of the land was in the hands of local agriculturalists and tradesmen. Three-quarters of the population had no access to land at all in Ascoli compared to just under a fifth in Locorotondo. In fact, most of the Ascoli residents did not even own houses (just a quarter of the households did), often renting a room from ecclesiastical institutions or wealthy aristocrats who monopolised real estate in the town.

Table 7.1 Access to land in Locorotondo (1749) and Ascoli Satriano (1753) (%)

	Households and institutions with land in Ascoli	**Households and institutions with land in Locorotondo**
Arable	15	74
Vineyards	17	74
Pasture	4	25
Total land	**26**	**82**

Sources: Ventura (ed.), *Onciario 1753*; ASB, 1749 Catasto Onciario di Locorotondo.

Table 7.2 Social distribution of land in Locorotondo (1749) and Ascoli Satriano (1753)

	Ascoli Satriano		**Locorotondo**	
	Hectares	**%**	**Hectares**	**%**
Aristocrats	13118	37	296	15
Urban	0	0	0	0
Ecclesiastical institutions	20016	56	599	31
Farmers and tradesmen	2491	7	1070	55
Total	35625	100	4855	101

Sources: Ventura (ed.), *Onciario 1753*; ASB, 1749 Catasto Onciario di Locorotondo.

Locorotondo's Gini index was much lower than Ascoli's, although at 0.77 it was still quite high (especially given 0.75 is the marker laid down in Chapter 2 for 'polarised' distribution of land status). However, a note must be made on this. Locorotondo may have had a Gini of 0.77 in 1749, but this figure was stretched somewhat by the large amount of forest in the hands of the Duke of

Martina Franca (without the forest it was 0.7). Furthermore, by the twentieth century this general figure was as low as 0.56.[158] Essentially, the more equitable distribution of property in Locorotondo laid the platform for the dissemination of emphyteutic leases, and once disseminated, the proliferation of this lease reduced inequality by giving more people access to land. Vineyards as the backbone of small peasant property in Locorotondo were distributed much more equally than land taken in its entirety in 1749 – a Gini index of 0.56 in comparison to 0.77 mentioned above.

Further historical data taken from other parts of Southern Italy also support this link between agro-towns and inequitable distribution of property. For example, the large concentrated town of Calopezzati in Calabria knew a Gini index of 0.87 for distribution of land in the eighteenth century.[159] Further calculations by the author of transcribed *catasti* for a cluster of small towns close to Naples in the Campania (Crispano, Frattapiccolo and Pomigliano d'Atella) also showed a highly skewed distribution of land in the eighteenth century, all recording Gini indexes close to 0.9.[160] Eighty-six per cent of the households or institutions listed in the Catasto for Crispano worked fewer than two hectares, and well over half of those recorded neither owned nor had any access to land through lease. These figures can be contrasted with the author's database of Gini indexes taken from the Cosentino region of Calabria, which was a part of Southern Italy identified by Pino Arlacchi as not conforming to the agro-town model. Here people lived in very small villages and hamlets.[161] As Table 7.3 shows, the distribution of land here was much more equitable, with Gini indexes even below 0.5 in places. Some of the Cosentino achieved the same level of equality as the famously egalitarian mountain villages studied by Robert Netting in the Swiss Alps in the twentieth century.[162] The link between agro-town proliferation and inequitable distribution of property also continued into the twentieth century in Southern Italy, as seen from Table 7.4, even after the government land reform projects.

---

158 Calella, *Colonizzazione e ruralizzazione*, 112.

159 Assante, *Calopezzati*, 41.

160 Libertini (ed.), *Documenti per la storia di Crispano*; *Documenti per la storia di Frattaminore*.

161 Arlacchi, *Mafia, peasants, and great estates*, chp. 1; Rossi-Doria, 'La Calabria agricola', 1176.

162 Netting and McGuire, 'Leveling peasants?', 273–4.

Table 7.3 Gini indexes for villages in the Cosentino area of Calabria, mid-eighteenth century

Village	Gini index
Cavellerizzo	0.52
Serra di Leo	0.48
S. Ippolito	0.68
Francolisi	0.69
Marri	0.47
S. Benedetto	0.73
S. Lauro	0.51
Casole	0.69
Lappano	0.59
Cerzeto	0.48

Source: ASC, III. Catasti, notai e archivi non statali, Catasti, Catasto Onciario, (various nos).

Thus, inequality at Ascoli (and on the plains of Northern Apulia in general) proved to be a favourable context for the establishment and crystallisation of Neapolitan state control over the regional economy of the Tavoliere. From the sixteenth century onwards, Naples favoured the large landowners and those with the larger flocks, and they were often given the best grazing lands.[163] The best grazing lands were very close to Ascoli, especially the *locazioni* of Orta and Ordona, because they had previously gone under the plough.[164] The skewed property distribution came to be locked in over the long term and made more inequitable from the sixteenth century onwards with smallholders put at a constant disadvantage.[165] The State in fact on occasion supported the expropriation of small cultivators – reintegrating the land as part of larger pastoral complexes.[166] This was in contrast to the Royal Customhouse's belief that they were 'pacifying' the countryside and promoting harmony through balanced justice and good government.[167]

In particular, the commercialised pastoral economy which emerged in Ascoli came to be entirely polarised in the hands of powerful interest groups in the eighteenth century, many of whom employed armed retainers to protect their

[163] See the abuses of power and concessions to favourites listed in De Dominicis, *Lo stato politico, ed economico della Dogana della Mena della Pecore di Puglia*, iii, 37–9.

[164] Guadiani, *Notizie per il buon governo della Regia Dogana*, 100.

[165] Nardella, 'Terre di portata'; 'Produzione mercantile e intervento dello Stato'.

[166] Altobella and Muscio, 'Aspetti del contrasto agro-pastorale dei territori della Dogana delle pecore', 40–43.

[167] Marino, 'Economic idylls', 232–3.

flocks and land.[168] In Ascoli, the Catasto Onciario recorded nearly 30,000 animals, a significant amount in comparison to the 2,000 found in Locorotondo, and almost 95 per cent of these were goats or sheep. The pastures had the most inequitable distribution of all the land – only 3 per cent of the population had access to grazing in the eighteenth century, while the average size of a pastoral landholding belonging to an individual or institution was over 200 hectares.[169] Only 15 per cent of the population had access to an animal, and it was only this high because some of the impoverished labourers had a donkey to carry goods from the fields. Eighty-five per cent of all animals were consolidated in the hands of the top ten landowners in Ascoli. Some of these landowners had extremely large herds, such as the Marquis of Basilicata, Don Alessandro Rinuccini, who by himself owned a third of all animals listed in the Catasto, including 10,000 sheep amongst others. These animals were grazed out on *masserie* belonging to the Locazione del Feudo, west of Ascoli and centred on the present-day hamlet of Palazzo d'Ascoli. Until the late seventeenth century, these enterprises were run by the Crown, which specialised in horse-breeding for the army; royal debts, however, had led many of the *masserie* to be transferred into the hands of the Marquis.[170] These large pastoral enterprises were frequently in the hands of absentee institutions since 80 per cent of the pastures belonged to non-residents, often ecclesiastical institutions. The Jesuits controlled many of these commercial estates until they were dissolved by royal decree in 1767.[171]

In contrast the emergence of viticulture and emphyteutic leasing in Locorotondo was supported by a much more equitable distribution of property and power. In Galt's book on Locorotondo, he emphasised the importance of widespread access to land and the diffusion of emphyteutic leases as the main reasons why settlement structure developed differently from the agro-town pattern seen elsewhere in Southern Italy.[172] This argument was highly convincing. What he failed to show, however, were the mechanisms behind these developments in Locorotondo. His argument was that landlords had trouble finding labour to work large estates in the eighteenth century, putting them off grain cultivation, and instead they resorted to emphyteutic leasing of vineyards to local peasants.[173] On the surface the argument made sense, particularly given

168 Villari, *Mezzogiorno e contadini*, 14–58; Marino, *Pastoral economics*, 255–9; Russo, *Tra Abruzzo e Puglia*.

169 Ventura (ed.), *Onciario 1753*.

170 Giustiniani (ed.), *Dizionario-geografico*, ii, 6.

171 See a study of two Jesuit estates to the south-west of Ascoli in Vitolo, *Introduzione-documenti Cavesi*. Alienation of ecclesiastical estates was common throughout parts of Southern Italy in the late 1700s; Placanica, 'Note sull'alienazione dei beni ecclesiastici'.

172 Galt, *Far from the church bells*. Also Richioni, 'Aspetti della trasformazione fondiaria'.

173 In particular Galt attributes significance to the wave of transatlantic emigration in the nineteenth century as noted in Presutti (ed.), *Puglie. Relazione del Delegato Tecnico*, i, 147.

that emphyteutic leasing had been used in Sicily in the sixteenth century with the explicit intention of bringing people to under-populated areas.[174] His rationale on further inspection, however, was not logical. Although the population of Locorotondo was behind Ascoli's by some way in the mid-eighteenth century, demographic boom between 1750 and 1850 meant that by 1861, Locorotondo actually had more inhabitants than Ascoli (see Figure 7.4). Furthermore, the territory of Locorotondo was one-eighth of the size of Ascoli. Given this information, it is really doubtful that Locorotondo landlords would have found it difficult to find workers for hypothetical estates, considering large estates were formed elsewhere in places with lower population densities.

Instead, the more equitable property structure seen in Locorotondo had its roots in the first instance in its colonisation and reclamation context. In Locorotondo, local peasants were by the sixteenth century colonising the woodlands and wastes with their own private enclosures. At the time when the town of Locorotondo bought its hinterlands from the Royal Court in 1566 (establishing its territorial borders),[175] the settlement was located in the middle of a large common territory which ran from Monopoli on the coast to Ostuni in the south-east.[176] The communities of nearby Martina Franca, Fasano, Cisterino, as well as Locorotondo, benefited from the common rights of grazing and collection of wood.[177] Sixteenth-century fulling mills existed in various places along the River Cervaro, very close to this territory, indicative of silvo-pastoral farming.[178] Around the mid-sixteenth century, however, inhabitants began to encroach into the commons, something which the Royal Court struggled to prevent. It was noted in the document from 1566 that much of the land was now enclosed and had vineyards belonging to farmers from Locorotondo and Martina Franca.[179] The document also mentioned two *jazzèleri*, Trito and S. Marco, showing how the seeds of dispersed settlement had already been laid. It was also noted that it was now legal to plant vineyards and gardens under private ownership, which effectively meant that by the eighteenth century, all common land ceased to exist in Locorotondo.[180] As iterated in Chapter 2 already, the commons must not be seen as an institution leading inevitably to higher levels of equality within pre-industrial societies, but sometimes even were the

---

174 Benigno, *Una casa, una terra*; Davies, 'Village-building in Sicily'; Richioni, 'Della proprietà fondiaria privata nel Mezzogiorno'; Mack Smith, *Medieval Sicily*, 195–8.

175 Sampietro, *Fasano*, 254–63.

176 Galt, *Far from the church bells*, 69.

177 On the early rights see Cascella, 'I magistri forestarii'; Travaglini, *I limiti della foresta oritana*.

178 Sakellariou, 'The cities of Puglia', 107.

179 Chirulli (ed.), *Istoria cronologica della Franca Martina*, 217–41.

180 See the reports on the condition of the commons in ASB, Atti Demaniali (1809), no. 69.

Table 7.4 Gini indexes for various places in the Mediterranean, twentieth century

	Place	**Region**	**Year**	**GI**	**Sources**
Agro-towns	(Genuardo)	Sicily, Italy	Pre-1966	0.88	Blok
	Trapani	Sicily, Italy	1947	0.76	INEA
	Pisticci	Basilicata, Italy	1972	0.81	Davis
	Crotone	Calabria, Italy	1972	0.89	ISTAT
	Alcala	Andalucia, Spain	1970	0.87	Davis
	Vila Velha	Beira Baixa, Portugal	1970	0.75	Davis
	Huelva (prov.)	Andalucia, Spain	1982	0.86	Sanchez
	Cádiz (prov.)	Andalucia, Spain	1982	0.83	Sanchez
Small villages / dispersed settlements	Conversano	Apulia, Italy	1972	0.57	Galt
	Locorotondo	Apulia, Italy	1972	0.56	Galt
	Alberobello	Apulia, Italy	1972	0.63	Galt
	Cisternino	Apulia, Italy	1972	0.52	Galt
	Fontelas	Alto Douro, Portugal	1978	0.56	O'Neill
	Cosentino area	Calabria, Italy	1929	0.63	CA 1929
	Zumpano	Calabria, Italy	1972	0.59	Davis
	Belmonte	Asturias, Spain	1970	0.70	Galt 'Social'

Notes: Parentheses indicate a pseudonym since the place's real identity is unknown. For Fontelas, a calculation has been made using a database of O'Neill's transcribed landholding survey. The 'Cosentino area' includes the same individual settlements as in Table 7.3 for the eighteenth century.

Sources: Galt, *Far from the church bells*, 28–9; 'Social stratification', 410; Blok, *Mafia of a Sicilian village*, 251; INEA, *La distribuzione della proprietà fondiaria*; ISTAT, *Secondo censimento generale dell'agricoltura*, 25 ottobre 1970; *Catasto agrario 1929. Compartimento delle Calabrie. Provincia di Cosenza*, fo. 79; Davis, *People of the Mediterranean*, table 6; Rafael Peña Sánchez and Rodríguez García, 'La concentración de la tierra'; Juan O'Neill, *Social inequality*, 72–3.

'vehicles' through which inequality was perpetuated and crystallised. This early encroachment by local farmers allowed them to build up a firm property base by the eighteenth century, which gave them stronger foundations in opposition to feudal lords. Indeed, the fact that a wider section of the population in Locorotondo received access to land through emphyteutic concessions from the 1700s onwards was down to the fact that the elite landowners in Locorotondo were a lot weaker than to be found in other parts of Southern Italy such as Ascoli. In Locorotondo, there was a greater power struggle between social groups than seen in typical agro-town areas.

The fee of Locorotondo had belonged to the Duke of Martina, Francesco Caracciolo I, since 1645, bought from another noble family of the town of Monopoli.[181] The Duke was the largest landowner in Locorotondo in 1749 with 355 hectares to his name (7 per cent of the territory). Proportionally, the Duke of Ascoli, Don Sebastiano Marulli did not hold much more – around 9 per cent of the total. However, the territory of Ascoli Satriano was a lot larger than that of Locorotondo (the 9 per cent corresponded to 3,290 hectares); it thus comprised an estate around 10 times the size of that of the Duke of Martina Franca. Furthermore, the quality and fertility of the Locorotondo land was significantly lower than the lush plains around Ascoli. The Caracciolo family did have estates outside Locorotondo in the nearby regions, but at the same time the Marulli family of Ascoli similarly had *masserie* in other parts – particularly to the south.[182] The landed weaknesses of the large landowners in Locorotondo in comparison to the agro-town regions of Apulia is shown by the fact that the top 10 Locorotondese landowners only comprised 14 per cent of the total land, paling in comparison to the 58 per cent in the hands of the top 10 Ascoli landowners. The Duke of Martina Franca (lord of Locorotondo) had all the things one would associate with feudal estates: a castle, a tavern, a butchery, craft shops, furnaces, a mill – even underground snow-storage facilities.[183] The Duke of Ascoli, however, had all these things but in greater quantity.

The weak position of the Locorotondo landlords translated itself into jurisdictional problems, especially for the feudal lord, the Duke of Martina Franca.[184] The relationship between the local municipal authorities (*università*) and the aristocratic elite was symptomatic of the general weakening of large landlords' power. Before 1550, the municipal government tended to support the prevailing aristocratic and baronial groups. However, as the woodlands began to be cleared and more investment was put into agriculture, the municipal authorities instead began to align themselves away from the barons and more towards serving the interests of the local community which was expanding in size and influence.[185] As the Duke of Martina Franca began to see his jurisdictional powers over Locorotondo waning in the eighteenth century, his only recourse was increasingly to ancient rights found in old documents in an attempt to stem the general trend towards heightened municipal autonomy.[186] In 1754, conflict had led the Duke to make demands on the municipal authorities, arguing that

[181] Capograssi, 'Due secoli di successioni feudali registrati', 192; Carrino, *La città aristocratica*, 253–61.

[182] Papagna, *Sogni e bisogni di una famiglia aristocratica*, 67. The distribution of these lands is mapped in Idem, 'Dimensione territoriali'.

[183] Guarella, 'Niviere e vendita della neve'.

[184] Cofano, *Storia antifeudale della Franca Martina*.

[185] Di Michele, 'Fermenti di rivolta anti baronale', 113.

[186] In particular a pact from 1605; Guarella, 'L'università di Locorotondo', 28.

they owed him three annual sums.[187] First, a sum of 48 ducats for ovens, mills and herbage, as agreed in 1502 and 1509 with previous barons Alberico and Alessandro Carafe. Second, a sum of 200 ducats as a tribute for autonomy afforded to the municipal authorities by the barons. Third, a sum of 50 ducats as a direct charge to the municipal authorities covering a fine for the marriage of daughters in the territory, and also as compensation for underpayment by the *università* for half the land bought from former barons, the Loffredo family. The weak position of the feudal lords was highlighted by the fact the *università* refused outright to pay these sums, and in fact, turned the claims around by suggesting they themselves had been overcharged over the years. Eventually the Duke lost his tithe of a twentieth,[188] and while the feudal lords renewed their complaints in 1785, by this time they were well beaten.[189] During the course of the eighteenth century, the municipal authorities stopped paying rent to the Duke, the *decime* and twentieth had disappeared, and total ducal income in 1794 was down from its 1667 level.[190] Demographic expansion and rising prices further reduced the relative value of feudal revenues.[191]

In sum, the more equitable distribution of land and the divergence from agro-town settlement pattern in Locorotondo had its seeds sown in its particular colonisation context and the more equitable power balance between interest groups. These jurisdictional and landed weaknesses of the elite landlords led them down the route of emphyteutic leasing in the eighteenth century. What is more, the weaknesses of the landlords also led the emphyteutic leases to become almost heritable, where landlords lost their grip on property to peasants and emphyteutical income was eroded by inflation over the long term.[192] The same process has been traced for parts of eighteenth-century Southern France and Catalonia.[193] The importance of this process can be highlighted by comparison with events in Northern Apulia dominated by large towns. Improvement contracts were also actually attempted here in the 1800s. From Cerignola to Bitonto in the nineteenth century, attempts were made to plant vineyards by enticing labour through improvement contracts, especially by the great landowners such as the Pavoncelli family. In the first phase of Pavoncelli planting, 1,022 tenants were created, each with small plots of 1 to 5 hectares.[194] In this situation, however, once the terms of the lease had ended after 27 to 29 years

---

187 Fumarola, 'Appunti della storia di Locorotondo'.

188 A common feature in this part of Apulia in the seventeenth and eighteenth centuries; Massella, 'Decime e demani'.

189 Baccari, *Memorie storiche di Locorotondo*, 90–91.

190 Papagna, *Sogni e bisogni di una famiglia aristocratica*, 91.

191 Aymard, 'La transizione dal feudalismo al capitalismo'.

192 Galt, *Far from the church bells*, 238.

193 Congost, 'Property rights and historical analysis'.

194 Pavoncelli, *Un azienda vinaria*, 16.

with improvements made, the land reverted back into the hands of landlords who retained a strong grip on property and agricultural production.[195] A similar story was seen in the agro-towns of the Crotonese in Calabria.[196]

Conclusion: Institutional Diversity and Inequality in the Kingdom of Naples

In this chapter it is shown that Ascoli Satriano (like many agro-towns in Northern Apulia) was a settlement which experienced rapid growth and rapid decline in very short periods. Ascoli in particular has had a disrupted and unstable history of re-emergence after decline or crisis. In contrast, the development of the dispersed settlement of Locorotondo was far less unstable and unpredictable. It was less afflicted by crises seen in the seventeenth century, and over the long term seems to have been characterised by steady population growth (which continues to this day, in stark contrast to many stagnating former agro-towns). In this chapter it is argued that the settlement divergence between Ascoli and Locorotondo was linked to their different modes of exploitation. The towns on the plains of the Tavoliere were crystallised through a commercialised pastoral economy managed by elite absentee stakeholders in Naples. Once established, these towns grew in size (particularly after 1850) when the Royal Customhouse-managed pastoral economy was replaced by the ecologically insensitive system of arable monoculture and *latifundia*. Locorotondo did not go down this route, instead being shaped by the proliferation of viticulture and the dissemination of emphyteutic leases, which allowed for the development of peasant adaptive strategies – one of which was actually an increased trend towards settlement away from the town centre and out in the fields. Despite the dynamic and diverse modes of exploitation, however, these economic paths were founded on the back of quite deep and persistent constellations in power and property. The commercialised pastoral economy which emerged on the northern plains of Apulia was facilitated by an inequitable distribution of property and an imbalance in the social distribution of landownership. On the distribution of power we know less concrete information. In contrast viticulture and emphyteusis in Locorotondo were facilitated by a much more equitable distribution of property (originating from the very particular colonisation context seen in the fifteenth and sixteenth centuries), a more equitable social distribution of landownership, and a weakened elite group unable to dominate its peasantry by the eighteenth century.

195 Snowden, *Violence and great estates*, 35–40.
196 Sereni, *Il capitalismo nella campagne*, 171–2.

In that way, this chapter has lent support to two different pools of literature on the pre-industrial Italian South. The diversity and dynamism of the modes of exploitation seen in Apulia support the more recent view that the Mezzogiorno exhibited much more change and transition than previously appreciated. Indeed, it is clear that agro-towns were not simply a function of *latifundia* or linked in any way to some loose notion of conservative agricultural and economic systems, the long perpetuation of feudal structures, or the lack of 'urban functions' and 'civic consciousness' previously argued for Southern Italy. Yet at the same time, it is argued in this chapter that a recurrent feature associated with agro-towns is the inequitable distribution of power and property – perhaps going back quite far into the past. It is this phenomenon which likely lies at the core of explaining the general proliferation of the agro-town model in the Mediterranean.

Of course, the views put forward in this chapter have been teased out of a comparative case study restricted to some limited areas of Apulia. It is clear that the institutional management of the agricultural systems on the Tavoliere through the coercive arm of Naples in a mutually beneficial consensus with large landowners cannot explain the perpetuation of inequality and agro-towns across all of Southern Italy, let alone the whole of the Mediterranean world. This chapter is simply a first step – recognising the co-existence of inequality and dynamism, continuity and change. In parts of Sicily or Calabria, for example, the roots of inequitable land distribution likely informed very different (perhaps dynamic) institutional configurations, completely different from those seen in Northern Apulia. It is argued in this chapter then that there is a 'Southern Italian agro-town model': a general framework connected to the perpetuation of inequitable distributions of land in many areas of the *Mezzogiorno* over the long term. However, there was no 'Southern Italian model for inequitable property distribution' – the social context in which inequality was embedded was frequently diverse. In that sense, the old story of the south being a place of persistent inequality forged through conservatism and backwardness may soon come to be replaced by a new appreciation of how widespread inequality existed simultaneously with (and facilitating) very dynamic and diverse institutional structures.

Fitting the Findings into the Theoretical Framework

In this final section, the information taken from the case study in Apulia between 1600 and 1900 is placed in the theoretical framework outlined in Chapter 2.

Property, Social Distribution of Property, and Power

In Ascoli Satriano, it is clear that there existed an extreme level of inequality in the distribution of property by the eighteenth century. The Catasto Onciario is a good source for reconstructing inequality because it is a document which records all resident households and institutions regardless of whether they hold land or not (and also absentee landholders). In that sense the Gini index taken from this source is as accurate as one is going to get. In Ascoli the Gini was around 0.97 – hardly surprising when one considers that only 3 per cent of the population had access to grazing, the average size of pastoral estates was 200 hectares, and 85 per cent of the animals in the territory were in the hands of the top 10 landowners. In Locorotondo the distribution of land was not entirely equitable in 1749 but also not polarised as seen in the agro-town areas. When one accounts for the large amount of feudal forest in the territory, the Gini index goes down from 0.77 to 0.7 – an intermediate status. Furthermore, after the proliferation of the emphyteutic lease in the eighteenth and nineteenth centuries, property became more equally distributed over time with a Gini index of just 0.56 in 1929. Figures from the Catasto Provvisorio of 1811, but also from general literature on nineteenth-century landholding on the Tavoliere, suggest inequality at Ascoli persisted well into the twentieth century. Unfortunately the Catasto Onciario is our earliest systematic record of land distribution so it is uncertain how far back in the past such inequality went – but there is nothing obvious to suggest that it was more equitable in the seventeenth century, and there is much qualitative evidence available which attests to the influence of large landholders. The distribution of land in Locorotondo during the period of focus was more dynamic. The Gini index went from 0.77 (0.7 without feudal forest) to 0.56 between 1749 and 1929, and we have much documentary evidence for the proliferation of emphyteutic leases during this time.

The social distribution of landownership also contrasted between the two towns and territories. In Ascoli a tiny 7 per cent of the land was owned by local non-noble inhabitants such as farmers, tradesmen, peasants and labourers. Land was consolidated instead in the hands of aristocratic lords and territorial lords (including the Duke of Ascoli) and ecclesiastical institutions – frequently absentee. Locorotondo was much different: 55 per cent of land was in the hands of local peasants or tradesmen in 1749 (securing 'egalitarian' status), and local aristocrats only owned around 15 per cent of the territory (much of this being forest also). Quantitative data on change over time of landownership is less plentiful, but inferences can still be made. In Ascoli this social distribution did not change at all in the nineteenth century, despite the parcelling out and auctioning off of the Royal Customhouse land in 1806. It simply went into the hands of the already dominant elite groups such as grain-speculators from Naples or former feudal lords. In Locorotondo some change was inevitable given the proliferation of the emphyteutic lease and the loss of security which landlords experienced over their land given their weak position. Peasants continued to gain at the expense of 'elites', though arguably peasants already had a decent grip on property even in the sixteenth century as a result of the early colonisation of the communal woodlands, and thus this must be deemed 'intermediate'.

Power was also highly imbalanced in Ascoli. There is no evidence of internal polarisation in the distribution of power, indeed, despite their domination of landownership, elite aristocratic lords and ecclesiastical institutions did not have any real tools of repression such as coercive jurisdictions or extra-economic powers (at least none of any significance by the eighteenth century). Any power these landlords had was precisely in their domination in the means of production, and the fact they could pick and choose from an over-supply in the workforce. The power imbalance in Ascoli and on the Tavoliere came from the fact that the whole economic and agricultural system was managed to the commercial interests of the State itself – many hundreds of kilometres away in Naples. Towns like Ascoli became pawns supporting the much larger urban economy of the Kingdom of Naples. Locorotondo was more equitable in its distribution of power – the Murgia being freer from the overarching grip of Naples played its part. Furthermore, the feudal rights of aristocratic lords and barons became entirely eroded by the eighteenth century, linked to the rise of a formalised commune (*università*) which switched allegiance from the elites to the community itself. The fact that we can trace this erosion between the seventeenth and eighteenth centuries, and the changing alignment of the *università* of Locorotondo towards its inhabitants, means this constellation is also assessed as dynamic. In Ascoli, the distribution of power was more persistent – particularly viewed from the relationship between Naples and its outlying rural kingdom. Big changes in economic structure took place in the nineteenth century, partly pushed through on a wave of new political ideologies based around neo-liberal 'enlightened' philosophy. Yet this did nothing to change the balance in power between the Tavoliere and the Neapolitan State, and the fact that the whole agricultural system could be rapidly taken apart by the state ruling elites is indicative of this complete imbalance of power and lack of control that Ascoli inhabitants had over their own economic decisions over the long term.

Table 7.5 The breakdown of Ascoli Satriano (1600–1900) into quantifiable configurations

	Egalitarian-Polarised	Dynamic-Persistent
Property	0	0
Social distribution of property	0	0
Power	0	0
Total scores	**0**	**0**

Type of society: polarised-persistent.

Table 7.6 The breakdown of Locorotondo (1600–1900) into quantifiable configurations

	Egalitarian-Polarised	Dynamic-Persistent
Property	1	1
Social distribution of property	1	0.5
Power	1	1
Total scores	**1**	**0.83**

Type of society: egalitarian-dynamic.

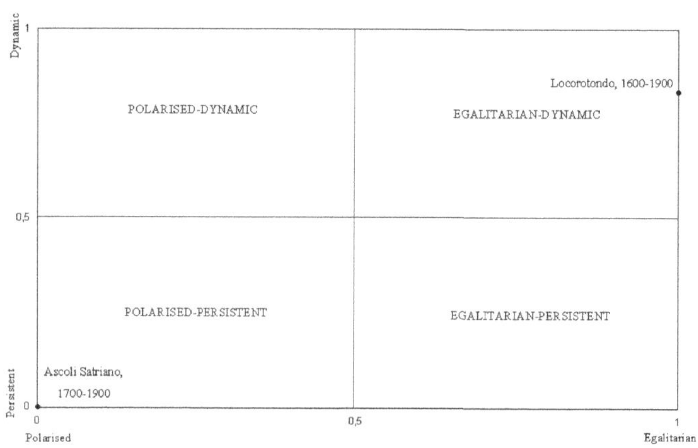

Figure 7.6 What type of society was Ascoli Satriano and Locorotondo, 1600–1900?

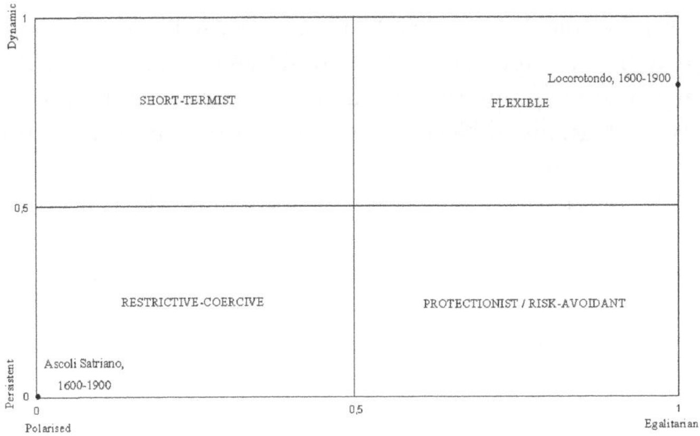

Figure 7.7 Predicted strategies for resource management in Ascoli Satriano and Locorotondo, 1600–1900

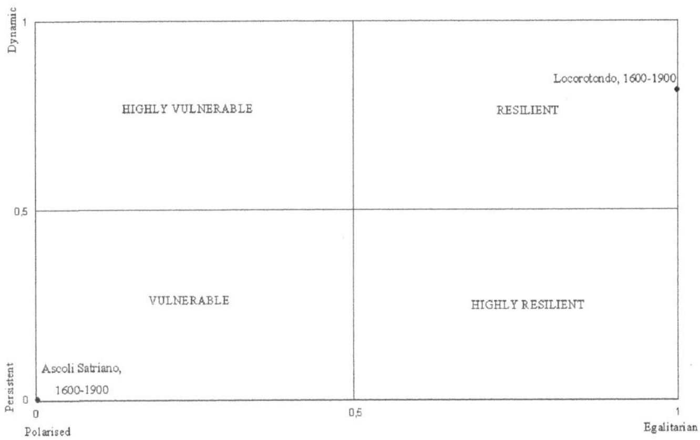

Figure 7.8 Predicted levels of settlement resilience or vulnerability in Ascoli Satriano and Locorotondo, 1600–1900

Assessing the Theoretical Model

The society of Ascoli Satriano from 1600 to 1900 has been assessed as 'polarised-persistent'. According to the principles of the theoretical framework, this would mean that these arrangements of property (at the user level), social distribution of property, and power, led logically to 'restrictive-coercive' strategies for resource exploitation, and in turn 'vulnerable' settlements. In contrast the society of Locorotondo from 1600 to 1900 has been assessed as 'egalitarian-dynamic'. According to the principles of the theoretical framework, this would mean that these arrangements of property (at the user level), social distribution of property, and power, led logically to 'flexible' strategies for resource exploitation, and in turn 'resilient' settlements.

Certainly the classifications of settlement vulnerability are confirmed by the results. Ascoli Satriano displayed an entirely unstable and unpredictable demographic pattern between 1600 and 1900 (and also earlier than 1600 and later than 1900). Terrible crises such as plague and pestilence hit this town hard in the seventeenth century, reducing its population by around half. In some periods the population would go through intense and rapid growth, such as between 1860 and 1950, though this was inevitably followed up by even quicker decline and retraction. Furthermore, the conditions of settlement were sometimes terrible. In the eighteenth century many people lived in small one-room hovels (sometimes underground) rented from an elite real estate owner, and conditions only worsened once *latifundia* took hold in the late nineteenth century and the flood of temporary labourers arrived. In fact, in many respects Ascoli often suffered in this period from 'over-population'. The only indicator not pointing to 'vulnerability' was the fate of cultivated land. Through the Royal Customhouse management of the pastoral economy, an ecologically sensitive balance between arable and pastoral land was maintained over the long term. However, it must be noted that with the development of proliferation of *latifundia* after 1850, soil was quickly worked into ruination. Locorotondo showed more signs of resilience. It was only minimally affected in terms of population figures by the mid-seventeenth-century pestilences. Furthermore, between 1669 and the present day (a period of around 340 years), it has seemingly known persistent and consistent demographic expansion – not the unstable decline and re-emergence seen in Ascoli but a more gentle upward trend. Over time the value of building materials generally increased with the proliferation of elaborate stone *trulli*, which required expert local craftsmanship. The same can be said of the improvement of local infrastructures such as roads and stone walls between *trulli*, and the development of sophisticated irrigation systems through aqueducts in order to bring water to the dispersed houses. Despite being a region with infertile soil for arable farming, the land was well-prepared by peasants using back-breaking labour through improvement contracts in order to facilitate the planting of vines. Thus the soils were well preserved and little land went out of cultivation.

The link between settlement resilience and the 'egalitarian-dynamic' society of Locorotondo in the form of 'flexible' strategies for resource exploitation is also confirmed almost perfectly. Indeed, the expansion of market-orientated viticulture, emphyteutic leasing, and the establishment of settlement away from the town centre was a real peasant adaptive strategy. The link between settlement vulnerability and the 'polarised-persistent' society of Ascoli is less clear-cut. Probably the establishment of the Royal Customhouse-managed system of commercial pastoral farming was 'restrictive-coercive'. The desires and economic autonomy of the inhabitants of the Tavoliere were checked and limited by the economic and political goals of urban elites in Naples. It was not an economic system set up for the producers on the Northern Apulian plains themselves but for absentee stakeholders. The system of *latifundia* which came after 1850, however, was surely more 'short-termist' in nature, given the ultimate degradation of the soil and exploitation of the local wage labour workforce with little in the way of capital investment in economic or agricultural institutions or local infrastructure. Elite landlords saw no logic in that. The main point of potential confusion, however, lies in the notion of it being a 'polarised-persistent' society as dictated by its distribution of power and property. Indeed, how does that square with the fact that throughout the chapter it has been emphasised how dynamic and diverse the modes of exploitation in Southern Italy could be? The point is, however, that this is all relative. The point emphasised in the chapter is that Southern Italian economic exploitation was not all conservative, backward and limited only to *latifundia* – there was a diversity not always appreciated for the pre-industrial *Mezzogiorno*. However, this does not detract from the fact that power and property distributions in Ascoli were very stable and persistent over the long term – and furthermore, the system of ecologically sensitive pastoral farming was also locked in over many centuries, maintained by small adaptations to exogenous conditions such as prices, wages, labour supply and urban demand.

Chapter 8
Conclusion

Comparing the Case Studies through the Theoretical Framework

Here the case studies are laid out side-by-side to assess in a relative sense their 'type of society', their 'strategy for resource exploitation', and their overall 'settlement resilience or vulnerability'.

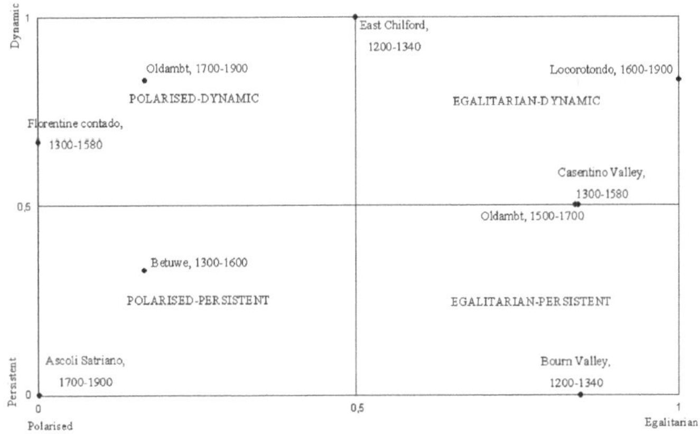

Figure 8.1 What types of societies were the case studies?

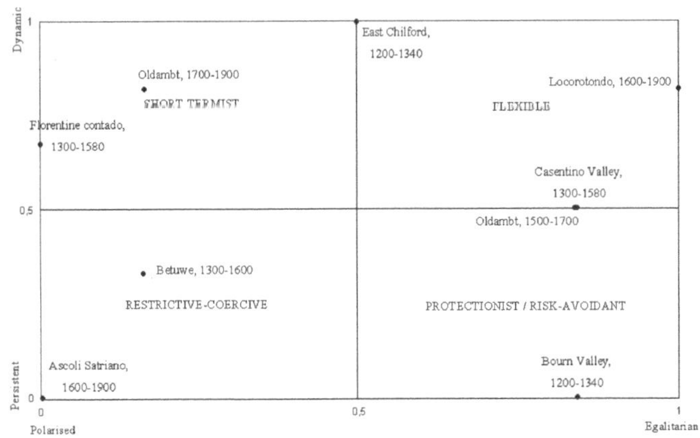

Figure 8.2 Predicted strategies for resource management in the case studies

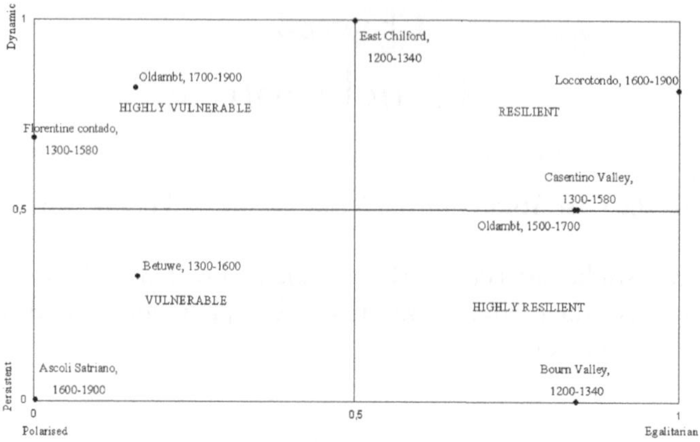

Figure 8.3 Predicted levels of settlement resilience or vulnerability in the case studies

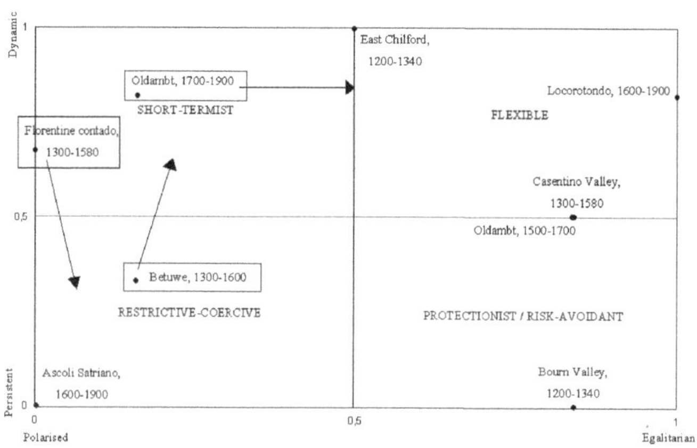

Figure 8.4 Number of 'matches' between predicted and actual strategies for resource management

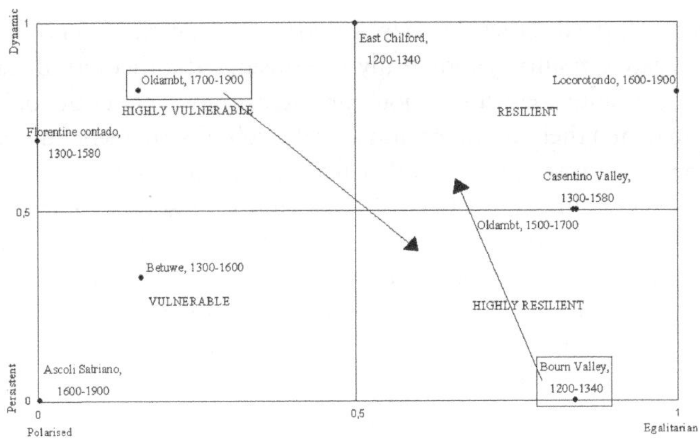

Figure 8.5 Number of 'matches' between predicted and actual levels of settlement resilience or vulnerability in the case studies

Assessing the Framework: Strengths and Limitations

Out of the nine different pre-industrial societies identified, two were deemed 'polarised-dynamic', two were 'polarised-persistent', one was 'egalitarian-dynamic', one was 'egalitarian-persistent', and then two were 'egalitarian-intermediate' while one was 'intermediate-egalitarian'. In this section, we assess to what extent the framework is a convincing one for predicting both the strategy and institutions for resource exploitation that a society may adopt and in turn a good one for predicting the resilience or vulnerability of settlements within that society against crises. The limitations are discussed first, followed by the strengths and opportunities it offers.

Clearly not all the results from the case studies matched up with what might have been 'expected' according to the basic principles of the theoretical framework. Out of the nine predicted institutions or strategies for resource exploitation marked in Figure 8.2, six were confirmed by what happened in practice, as seen in Figure 8.4. Out of the nine predicted levels of settlement resilience or vulnerability marked in Figure 8.3, seven were confirmed by what happened in practice, as seen in Figure 8.5. The Betuwe (1300–1600) was assessed as exhibiting 'restrictive-coercive' strategies for resource exploitation but in reality they were more 'short-termist', while the strategies in the Florentine *contado* (1300–1580) had the opposite problem: assessed as 'short-termist', in reality they were more 'restrictive-coercive'. The theoretical framework is not an absolute set of universal and infallible rules, however; there are going to be occasions when societies do not easily fit into neat classifications. No theoretical framework can ever cater for every single nuance and complexity in historical development. Indeed, a theoretical framework or model that cannot be falsified through negative results cannot really be considered a theoretical framework at all. These results were not serious problems, however: both societies still correctly matched their predicted and actual levels of settlement vulnerability.

Another issue was those cases that fell on the boundaries of two different 'types of society'. In some cases this was easy to resolve. For example, the Casentino Valley (1300–1580) fell on the boundary between 'egalitarian-dynamic' and 'egalitarian-persistent', which led to being on the boundary between 'protective' and 'flexible' resource-exploitation strategies and in turn on the boundary between 'resilient' and 'highly resilient' settlements. This was not a problem, however. It was clear that the society used a combination of 'protectionist' and 'flexible' strategies in order to secure a certain level of resilience – the precise or 'exact' level is not so important. The theoretical framework acts as an indicator of general trends, not a precise statistical measurement device. More troublesome were those cases that fell on the boundary between 'resilient' settlements and 'highly vulnerable' settlements such as East Chilford (1200–1340) – how do we interpret this? Essentially these kinds of societies had some resource-exploitation strategies leading to vulnerability, but had some modes of exploitation and institutions in place which offered resilience. Thus in the case of East Chilford, an 'in-between' compromise is sought – between 'highly vulnerable' and 'resilient' it becomes simply 'vulnerable' (i.e. displaying two indicators for settlement vulnerability outlined in Chapter 1). Similarly for any society on the boundary between 'vulnerable' and 'highly resilient' settlements, it becomes assessed as simply 'resilient'. Figure 8.6 clarifies this.

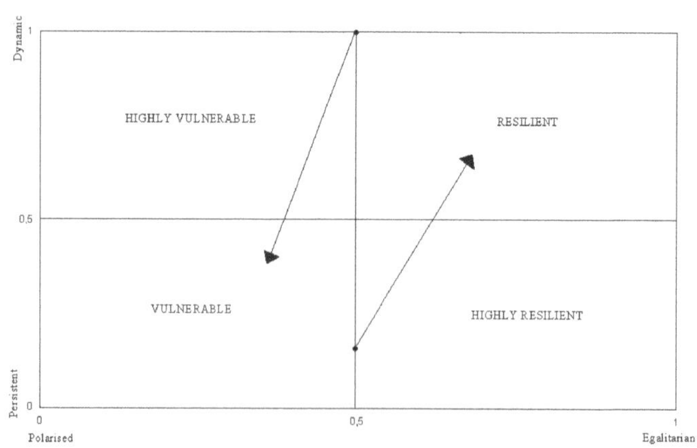

Figure 8.6 Societies on the 'boundary'

The most serious 'anomaly' from what was predicted according to the theoretical framework, however, surrounded the Oldambt (1700–1900). This matched neither the 'strategies for resource exploitation' nor the 'levels of settlement resilience or vulnerability', and the mismatches were not simply by 'degree' (i.e. highly vulnerable instead of vulnerable), but were completely counter to what would be expected (i.e. highly vulnerable instead of resilient or highly resilient). As already noted in Chapter 6, this was down to the fact that while the 'polarised-dynamic' society did lead to 'short-termist' resource-exploitation strategies in the form of large commercialised monoculture arable polder farms, the mass ranks of the poor (those former free farmers who had over time become proletarianised) formed their own economy (a dual economy), very distinct from the wealthy and dominant elites. In that sense, the biggest limitation of the theoretical framework not yet resolved is the fact it cannot at the moment distinguish between 'societies within societies'. Internal stratifications in pre-industrial societies could lead to two or more different types of institutional frameworks for exploiting resources within one geographical area.

Notwithstanding that anomaly and broader issue, however, the strengths of the framework seem to far outweigh the limitations. Indeed, most of the misalignments in predicted and actual results are by 'degree' or 'extent' rather than entirely incorrect. For example, the Bourn Valley (1200–1340) was assessed as 'highly resilient' by the principles of the framework though in reality it could be judged as just 'resilient'. This is of course dependent on the markers and indicators for settlement resilience/vulnerability chosen, and other scholars may argue for different parameters. Certainly other indicators do exist, and it simply was not realistic to be able to measure them all. However, the basic point is that the framework predicted a certain level of resilience (i.e. not vulnerability) and this was confirmed by the results, regardless of precise degree. Indeed, if we take the final figure presented above in its entirety, all five of the societies on the 'resilient side' (the right-hand side) were resilient to certain degrees, while three out of the four societies on the 'vulnerable side' (the left-hand side) were vulnerable to certain degrees. Although not absolutely precise, the general confirmation of expected resilient settlements in the 'resilient side' and expected vulnerable settlements in the 'vulnerable side' suggests this theoretical framework operates at the very least 'on the right track' and that there is something to be said for this approach.

Academic Statement and Societal Relevance of the Framework

The confirmation of expected results according to the framework allows us to make some more general statements. First of all, by using a method which distinguishes between different 'types of societies' in order to see if this led to any differences in resilience or vulnerability, it seems that we are able to say (at least to some degree) that the arrangement of society itself is important for achieving resilience against crises, and that the impact of even exogenous events can be limited or negated by the way society is configured. A more explicit statement is the test of an important hypothesis. In Chapter 1, it was noted that the recent 'disaster studies' literature has been tentatively putting forward an idea (in some quarters) that more 'equitable' societies were more resilient against terrible hazards and disasters, although this has not been systematically tested and has only been suggested through description in contemporary contexts. This explicitly historical and systematically comparative test has confirmed that a link may exist between 'equality' in the distribution of property and power and the extent to which a society is able to create coping strategies in order to protect or shield itself from crises (or adapt to crisis) in the pre-industrial context. Indeed, it is significant that all of the most 'equitable' or 'egalitarian' societies studied turned out to be more resilient with their human habitations than the more 'inequitable' or 'polarised' societies. *This book then asserts a general statement that equality in the distribution of property and power was a vital component in pre-industrial societies' capacity to deal or recover from crises.* The level of dynamism or persistence in these constellations merely dictated the precise direction or method of achieving resilience – be it through 'protective' or 'adaptive' institutions. By the same token, dynamism or vulnerability in these constellations also dictated the precise direction or method of experiencing vulnerability – be that 'coercive' or 'short-termist' in nature.

More specifically, what is being suggested here is that where property and power were distributed unequally, people lost their capacity to control their own destiny or benefit from the fruits of their own labour – and ultimately did not exert themselves or did not make efforts to put in place institutions and resource management strategies needed for long-term environmental and societal sustainability. In more equitable and freer societies, protective or adaptable institutions such as the commons, the open fields, or water management systems operated more effectively – less hindered by problems of participation and incentive. Producers could choose what and when they wanted to produce, and change, adapt and combine avenues of production if necessary. They could also decide whether they wanted to consume produce for themselves, save and store it for hazardous events possibly on the horizon, or trade it at the market. In that way in equitable and freer societies, rural producers could also use the market as one component of a survival strategy including a whole 'package' of other strategies – thus neither 'coerced' into trading as Robert Brenner suggested nor in the aspiration consumption way of the 'Industrious Revolution' as argued by

Jan de Vries.[1] Furthermore, if rural people were not satisfied with their own lot in these more equitable and freer societies, they had the opportunity and the capacity to freely migrate in search of better prospects for themselves. On the other side of the coin, in those societies with highly inequitable distributions of property and power and with very weakly configured sets of property rights, ordinary rural producers and tenants received and retained smaller shares of the total surplus, which in turn gave people less opportunity and incentive to make any effort to increase agricultural productivity. Essentially the ways in which power and property were configured dictated to what extent 'favourable' or 'unfavourable' institutions were likely to emerge in a given pre-industrial society, and naturally, the presence or absence of these different kinds of institutions and ways of managing resources had an important role to play in defining a society's capacity to deal with crises. Those societies founded upon more equitable distributions of power and property gave a wider proportion of people a greater stake in local institutions and accordingly an optimum level of participation within them, and furthermore, gave people the freedom and room to choose their own fate – not necessarily reliant on one coping strategy but with the capacity to combine many different ones in search of optimum resilience. Equitable and freer societies did not produce one 'special' method for achieving societal resilience against crises, but instead offered the social context for its inhabitants to flexibly choose which ones suited particular circumstances.

This statement is a clear and provocative one, and requires further systematic testing on different parts of the pre-industrial world. Do the central tenets hold up for parts of early-medieval Iraq, seventeenth-century Barbados or the Cape Colonies, or the nineteenth-century British Punjab, or does being tested on select regions of pre-industrial Western Europe intrinsically inhibit the framework? By bringing in, for example, the colonial context, new levels of extremes in power and property would have to be catered for in light of slavery and plantation economies. Is it possible that this kind of theoretical framework could also be applied to contemporary 'underdeveloped' and 'developing' societies? Of course the pre-industrial world and the modern-day underdeveloped world are not absolutely comparable, and caution must always be taken when making comparisons. Nonetheless it is undeniable that despite the passing of the Industrial Revolution and the emergence of global capitalism, much of the world today can still be effectively classed as 'pre-industrial' in some respects. A significant proportion of the world still lives in the countryside, a significant proportion still works the land, a significant proportion is terribly poor, and it is sometimes easy to forget that post-industrial modernised society is not the 'norm' and applies to very restricted parts of the globe. What this theoretical

[1] See Brenner, 'Agrarian roots'; De Vries, 'The Industrial Revolution and the Industrious Revolution'; 'Peasant demand patterns'.

framework may offer is a general philosophy moving away from contemporary thinking that still suggests many of the world's problems can be solved by (a seemingly relentless) pursuit of economic growth. There is still a perception that protection in the face of crises and sustainable societies in underdeveloped countries can be achieved through technological innovation, the provision of medicines, or through big-business capital investments and philanthropy. The World Bank not so long ago suggested the market and the emergence of clear 'modern' property rights in private hands were the best institutional conditions for coping with terrible hazards such as famine.[2] These views were echoed by one of the (eventually unsuccessful) candidates for the Republican Party in the 2012 US Presidential Election Campaign, Ron Paul, who noted that 'the key to sound environmental policy is respect for private property rights'.[3]

Yet what is clear from this book is that there may currently be an over-reliance and too much faith put in the protective functions of the market, the state, or technological innovations. In fact none of these concepts and their institutions has any intrinsic or inherent value on their own. In some cases the market or the state may protect inhabitants of a society, but in other cases it may produce the opposite effect – the different types of social context in which they operate determine their qualities.[4] Just as the state was unable to respond effectively to disasters in pre-industrial periods,[5] states today can be equally ineffective. A system of collective property rights or 'the commons' may be employed in some cases to halt environmental degradation, but at the same time its effectiveness can be limited by its employment in entirely unfavourable social contexts.[6] Thus, even if the thesis that 'more equitable pre-industrial societies were more resilient' does not end up being applicable to modern underdeveloped societies, at the very least it is put forward that we must start explicitly incorporating social context into our resilience and vulnerability modelling rather than an application of overarching broad ideologies or political convictions.

---

2 World Bank, 'Agriculture for development'.

3 Quote taken from Van Bavel and Thoen, 'Rural history and the environment', 28.

4 Nee and Ingram, 'Embeddedness and beyond'.

5 Sharp, 'Royal paternalism'.

6 Ostrom, *Governing the commons.*

Bibliography

Archives

Archivio di Stato di Arezzo

Diplomatico, pergamene e carte varie, no. 91.
Fondo di Murello, no. 1269.
S. Fiora, no. 704.

Archivio di Stato di Bari

1749 Catasto Onciario di Locorotondo.
Atti Demaniali (1809), no. 69.
Fondo Intendenza-Prefettura (agricoltura, industria e commercio), no. 7.

Archivio di Stato di Cosenza

III. Catasti, notai e archivi non statali, Catasti, Catasto Onciario.

Archivio di Stato di Firenze (Florence)

Arte della Lana, no. 15.
Camaldoli, nos 117–18, 123, 125, 136, 183, 191, 589–90, 935.
Carte Strozziane, i, no. 24.
Catasto, nos 116–17, 179–81, 246, 250, 307, 330, 886.
Corporazioni religiose soppresse dal Governo Francese, no. 39.
Decima Granducale, no. 6852.
Diplomatico, Olivetani d'Arezzo, 8 August 1346.
Misc. Medicea, no. 459.
Notarile Antecosimiano, nos 92–4, 9495–7.
Pratica Segreta, nos 157, 174, 178.
Provvisioni Registri, nos 4, 109, 175–6.
Reale Arcispedale di Santa Maria Nuova, nos 474–5.
Statuti delle comunità autonome e soggette, nos 79, 696.

Archivio Storico dell'Eremo e Monastero di Camaldoli

Atti Capitolari, no. 156.

Biblioteca Comunale di Poppi

'Relazione della peste in Poppi nel 1630 e memorie della più distinte famiglie della stessa città scritta da Bernardo di Giuliano Lapini nel XVII secolo', no. 160.

Biblioteca Nazionale di Firenze (Florence)

EB, 15, no. 2.
Magliabechi, ii, nos 120, 359.

British Library (London)

Add. Ch., no. 44797.
Add. MS., nos 5823, 5861.
Cott. MS. Claud C., no. 9.
Cott. MS. Tib. C., no. 9.
MS Lansdowne Manuscripts, no. 375.

Cambridgeshire County Record Office (Shire Hall, Cambridge)

588/T124.
P10/27/1.
PB X/18.

Cambridge University Library

Add. MS. 6081.
QC, 3 & 4.
QC, 6, nos 5–6.
QC, 8, no. 4
QC, 11.
QC, 15, no. 67.
QC, 52, nos 9, 22, 101.
QC, 59, no. 36.

Essex Record Office (Chelmsford)

D/D Q 1, no. 1.

Gelders Archief (Arnhem)

Abdij Mariënweerd te Beesd 1, 0283, no. 9.
Abdij Mariënweerd te Beesd 2, 1170, nos 38, 67–9, 73–4, 106, 112, 116, 171.
Archief van de Familie van der Capellen, 0467, no. 278.
Archief van de Familie van Randwijck, 6090, no. 1324.
Familie Pieck, 0480, no. 46.
Graven en Hertogen van Gelre, Graven van Zutphen, 0001, no. 645.
Hertogelijk Archief, nos 25, 860.
Huis Enspijk, 0390, no. 39.
Nassause Domeinen, no. 148.
ORA Deil, no. 1089.
Oud Archief Tiel, 0001, nos 852–7.
Rechterlijk Archief Over-Betuwe, no. 481.
Staten van het Kwartier van Nijmegen en hun Gedeputeerden, 0003, nos 368–72.
Waardenburg, no. 584.

Groninger Archieven

Archief Nederlands Hervormde Gemeente Midwolda, no. 5.
Archief Staten van Stad en Lande, nos 475, 2133, 2139–41, 2143.
Archief Veenkantoor, no. 384.
Coöperatieve strokartonfabriek 'De Toekomst', 1899–1971, 388, nos 160, 166.
Coöperatieve strokartonfabriek 'Reiderland', 1913–1988, 2045, no. 122.
Families Siccama, Hora Siccama, Hora Siccama van Harkstede en Rengers Hora Siccama, 1597–1970, 535, nos 65, 496.
Gemeentebestuur van Groningen (1), 1816–1916, 1399, nos 3584, 4276.
Gemeentebestuur van Groningen (3), 1916–1965, 1841, no. 1324.
Gewestelijke Besturen, no. 574.
Gewestelijke Besturen in Groningen, 1798–1814 (1815), 3, nos 855–6, 1642–4, 1662, 1898–9, 1901.
Kaartenverzameling, nos 990–91, 1307, 1311.
Kadaster 1832.
Losse stukken register Feith, meest charters, 1246–1864, 2241, nos 48, 307, 353, 371, 433, 456, 467, 499, 535, 582, 668, 766, 776, 854, 880, 903, 909, 936–7, 944, 957, 1017, 1019–20, 1029, 1034, 1151.
NV Ennemaborg te Midwolda, 1660–1964, 402, nos 63, 355.
Ommelander Archief, no. 1058.
Plakkaten en ordonnanties GAG, 1595–1795, no. 527.
Stadsarchief tot 1594, no. 732.
W.A. Scholten NV, ca 1840–ca 1965, 1100, nos 56, 106, 110, 171, 176, 190, 199, 203, 206, 208, 215–6.

King's College Archives (Cambridge)

BAR/4, nos 6–11, 13–40, 42–103, 105–16, 122–32, 134–6, 138.

Merton College (Cambridge)

Muniments, nos 5394–6.

Pembroke College Archives (Cambridge)

Barham, AA, nos 2–3.

Nationaal Archief Den Haag (The Hague)

Archief Familie van Hogendorp, no. 186.

Regionaal Archief Rivierenland (Tiel)

Archief Dijkstoel Beesd, 1552–1838, Verpondingen over Beesd 1690, no. 26.
Oud Archief Buren, 0692, nos 743, 746–7.

St. Catherine's College (Cambridge)

6/175, nos 15–16.

Streekarchivariaat West-Betuwe (Geldermalsen)

Archief van de Dorpen Buurmalsen en Tricht (1581) 1594–1811 (1826), no. 225.

The National Archives (Kew)

C133/94/5, no. 3; C134/22/10; C135/28/17, no. 8; C135/54/9; C135/131/8, no. 19; C135/137/3; C135/222, no. 15; C137/34/2; C139/37/4; C142/63/33; C142/170/12; C143/75/12; C143/118/4
CP25(1)/26/43, no. 31; CP25(1)/26/44, no. 20; CP25(1)/26/49, no. 17; CP25(1)/27/57, no. 7; CP25(1)/28/67, no. 21; CP25(2)/51/270, no. 2; CP25(2)/93/835; CP40/236
E150/74/4; E150/106/2; E179/81/130; E179/242/8.

Utrechts Archief

Stichting Armen de Poth te Amersfoort, 1342–1999, 0100, no. 582.

Primary Printed

Aa, A. van der, *Aardrijkskundig woordenboek der Nederlanden*, iii (Gorinchem 1851).

Aitzema, L. van, *Saken van Staet en oorlogh in, ende omtrent de Vereenigde Nederlanden. Beginnende met het Jaer 1633, ende eyndigende met het Jaer 1644*, ii, 18th book (The Hague 1669).

Anon (ed.), *An entertaining tour, containing a variety of incidents and adventures, in a journey through part of Flanders, Germany and Holland, historical, political and entertaining (...) with an account of the various paintings, pictures, coins, inns, mode of travelling, and a history of the various places* (London 1791).

———, *Monumenta Historica ad provincias parmensem et Placentia pertinentia* (Parma 1860).

———, *Uitkomsten der Vierde Tienjarige Volkstelling in het Koninkrijk der Nederlanden op. de een en dertigste December 1859*, i (The Hague 1863).

———, 'Landbouwstatistiek van de provincie Groningen over het jaar 1862', in *Bijdragen tot de kennis van den tegenwoordigen staat der provincie Groningen*, v (Groningen 1870).

———, *Uitkomsten der beroepstelling in het Koninkrijk der Nederlanden op. den een en dertigsten December 1889* (The Hague 1894).

———, *Verslagen betreffende den oeconomischen toestand der landarbeiders in Nederland*, i (Groningen 1908).

———, *Uitkomsten der telling in zake grondgebruik en veestapel 1910* (The Hague 1912).

Ardoini, P., *Descrizione del Stato di Melfi (1674)*, (ed.) E. Navazio (Lavello 1980).

Baccari, G., *Memorie storiche di Locorotondo* (Fasano 1869).

Bailey, M. (ed.), *The English manor, c. 1200–1500: selected sources translated and annotated* (Manchester 2002).

Berger, E. and Delaborde, H-F. (eds), *Recueil des actes de Philippe Auguste*, i (Paris 1916).

Bianchi, S. and Granuzzo, R. (eds), *Statuti di Verona nel 1327* (Rome 1992).

Birch, W. (ed.), *Cartularium Saxonicum: a collection of charters relating to Anglo-Saxon history AD 948–975*, iii (London 1964).

Bland, A., Brown, P. and Tawney, R. (eds), *English economic history, select documents* (London 1915).

Bliss, W. (ed.), *Calendar of papal registers relating to Great Britain and Ireland*, ii (London 1895).

Bosch, I. van den, 'Natuur- en geneeskundige verhandeling van de oorzaken, voorbehoeding en geneezing, uit de natuurlijke gesteldheid van het vaderland voortvloeijende', in *Verhandelingen, uitgegeeven door de Hollandsche Maatschappij der Weetenschappen te Haarlem* (Haarlem 1778).
Brooke, C. and Postan, M. (eds), *Carte nativorum: a Peterborough Abbey cartulary of the fourteenth century* (Northampton 1960).
Bruhl, C-R. and C. Violante (eds), *Honorantie Civitatis Papiae* (Tübingen 1983).
Caley, J. and Illingworth, W. (eds), *Rotuli Hundredorum*, ii (London 1818).
Campanini, A. (ed.), *I rubricari degli statuti comunali di Reggio Emilia (secc. XIII–XVI)* (Reggio Emilia 1997).
Campopiano, M. (ed.), *Liber Guidonis compositus de variis historiis. Studio ed edizione critica dei testi inediti* (Florence 2008).
Cerlini, A. (ed.), *Consuetudini e statuti reggiani del sec. XIII* (Milan 1933).
Cerutti, F. (ed.), *Hoofdstukken uit de Nederlandse rechtsgeschiedenis* (Nijmegen 1972).
Checchia de Ambrosio, G. (ed.), *Ricordi storici di Capitanata* (San Severo 1987).
Clark, J. and Maitland, F. (eds), *Liber Memorandum Ecclesie de Bernewelle* (Cambridge 1907).
Cunningham, W., *Common rights at Cottenham and Stretham in Cambridgeshire* (London 1910).
De Dominicis, F., *Lo stato politico, ed economico della Dogana della Mena della Pecore di Puglia*, iii (Naples 1781).
De Lellis, C., *Discorsi delle famiglie nobili del Regno di Napoli* (Naples 1654).
Della Marra, F., *Famiglie estinte fuorestiere o non comprese ne' Seggi di Napoli imparentate colla casa della Marra* (Naples 1641).
Di Stefano, S., *Della ragion pastorale* (Naples 1731).
Doorninck, P. van and Veen, J. van (eds), *Acten betreffende Gelre en Zutphen, 1107–1415* (Haarlem 1908).
Evelyn-White, C. (ed.), *Cambridgeshire and the Isle of Ely: lay subsidy for the year 1327: names of the taxpayers in every parish* (Cambridge 1911).
Feith, R. 'Geschiedkundig berigt van de vorenstaande oud-Oldambster en Reiderlandsche landregten van 1471 en 1327', *Pro Excolendo Jure Patrio* 6 (1846) 745–67.
———, (ed.), *Archief der maatschappij tot exploitatie van den Johannes Kerkhovenpolder* (Groningen 1902).
Fenwick, C. (ed.), *The poll taxes of 1377, 1379 and 1381*, iii (Oxford 2005).
Fischer, A., *Lotgevallen op. eene reize van Riga, over Holland, door Spanjen en een gedeelte van Italien* (Amsterdam 1802).
Fremery, J. de (ed.), *Cartularium der abdij Mariënweerd* (The Hague 1890).
Friedländer, E. (ed.), *Ostfriesisches Urkundenbuch*, ii (Emden 1881).
Galanti, G., *Nuova descrizione storia e geografica della Sicilie*, 3 vols (Naples 1786).
———, *Breve descrizione di Napoli e del suo contorno*, iii (Naples 1792).

Gemeente Winschoten, *Verslag van de commissie, benoemd door het departement Winschoten der Maatschappij tot Nut van 't Algemeen, betrekkelijk de arbeiders-quaestie* (Winschoten 1872).
Gilsdorf, S., 'Foundation of a French monastery in Abruzzo: Santa Maria della Vittoria (1277)', in K. Jansen, J. Drell and F. Andrews (eds), *Medieval Italy: texts in translation* (Philadelphia 2009) 249–53.
Gissing, G., *By the Ionian Sea: notes of a ramble in Southern Italy* (Teddington 2007 [1901]).
Giustiniani, L. (ed.), *Dizionario geografico ragionato del Regno di Napoli di Lorenzo Giustiniani*, ii (Naples 1797).
Goldsmith, O., *The deserted village* (Boston 1866 [1770]).
Gottschalk, M. (ed.), *Stormvloeden en rivieroverstrommingen in Nederland, 500–1700*, 3 vols (Assen 1971–7).
Grana, S., *Istituzioni delle leggi della Regia Dogana di Foggia* (Naples 1770).
Graswinckel, D. (ed.), *Het oud-archief der gemeente Arnhem* (Arnhem 1935).
Guadiani, A., *Notizie per il buon governo della Regia Dogana della mena della pecore di Puglia*, ed. P. Di Cicco (Foggia 1981 [1715]).
Guasti, C. (ed.), *I capitoli del comune di Firenze. Inventario e regesto*, i (Florence 1866).
Herlihy, D. and Klapisch-Zuber, C. (eds), *Census and property survey of Florentine domains and the city of Verona in the fifteenth century* (Cambridge MA 1981).
Illingworth, W. (ed.), *Placitorum in domo capitulari Westmonasteriensi asservatorum abbreviatio* (London 1811).
Imberciadori, I. (ed.), 'Il primo statuto della dogana dei paschi maremmani (1419)', in *Per la storia della società rurale. Amiata e Maremma tra il IX e il XX secolo* (Parma 1971) 107–40.
INEA, *La distribuzione della proprietà fondiaria in Italia* (Rome 1947).
ISTAT, *Catasto agrario (1929–VIII. Compartimento delle Puglie. Provincia di Bari* (Rome 1933).
———, *Catasto agrario 1929. Compartimento delle Calabrie. Provincia di Cosenza* (Rome 1936).
———, *Secondo censimento generale dell'agricoltura, 25 ottobre 1970* (Rome 1972).
———, *Secondo censimento generale dell'agricoltura*; *Dodicesimo censimento generale della popolazione* (Rome 1983).
Kastner, D., *Das Schoffenbuch der Stadt Zülpich und die Urkunden des Stadtarchivs* (Cologne 1996).
Kort, J. (ed.), 'Reportorium op. de Cuykse lenen in Holland, het Sticht en Gelre, 1129–1649', *OV* 44 (1989) 252–66.
Kuys, J. (ed.), *De Tielse kroniek. Een geschiedenis van de Lage Landen van de volksverhuizingen tot het midden van de vijftiende eeuw, met een vervolg over de jaren 1552–1566* (Amsterdam 1983).

Laurenti, G., 'Visita dell'abbatia o precettoria di S. Leonardo di Puglia e dell'abbatia di S. Maria di Banzi', in A. Massafra and A. Ventura (eds), *Il patrimonio dell'Abbazia di S. Leonardo di Siponto: illustrazione e trascrizione del manoscritto di una visita pastorale di fine secolo XVII conservato nella Biblioteca provinciale di Foggia* (Foggia 1978) 43–89.

Lennep, J. van, *Nederland in den goeden ouden tijd zijnde het dagboek van hunne reis te voet, per trekschuit en per diligence van Jacob van Lennep en zijn vriend Dirk van Hogendorp door de Noord-Nederlandsche provintien in den jare 1823*, ed. M. Elisabeth Kluit (Utrecht 1942).

Libertini, G. (ed.), *Documenti per la storia di Crispano* (Naples 2003).

———, (ed.), *Documenti per la storia di Frattaminore (Frattapiccola, Pomigliano d'Atella e Pardinola)* (Naples 2005).

Longeville, N. (ed.), *Newington Longeville charters* (Oxford 1921).

Manaresi, C. (ed.), *I placiti del 'Regnum Italiae'*, i (Rome 1955).

Marshall, J., *Travels through Holland, Flanders, Germany, Denmark, Sweden, Lapland, Russia, the Ukraine and Poland in the years 1768, 1769, and 1770*, i (London 1772).

Meihuizen, L. (ed.), *De rekening betreffende het graafschap Gelre, 1294/1295* (Arnhem 1953).

Meister, A. (ed.), 'Niederdeutsche Chroniken aus dem XV. Jahrhundert', *Annalen des Historischen Vereins für den Niederrhein* 70 (1901) 43–64.

Mele, D., *Annuario storico-statistico-commerciale di Bari e Provincia* (Bari 1883).

Mettensis, A., *De diversitate temporum et Fragmentum de Deoderico primo episcopo Mettensi*, ed. H. van Rij (Amsterdam 1980).

Mittarelli, G. and Costadoni, A. (eds), *Annales Camaldulenses ordinis S. Benedicti*, ix (Venice 1773).

Möhlmann, G. (red.), *Ostfriesisches Urkundenbuch. Dritter Band: Ergänzende Regesten und Urkunden zu Band I und II* (Aurich 1975).

Moor, C. *Knights of Edward I*, iii (London 1930).

Muciaccia, F. (ed.), *Il Libro Rosso della città di Monopoli* (Bari 1906).

Muller, S. and Bouman, A. (eds), *Oorkondenboek van het Sticht Utrecht*, i (Utrecht 1920).

Otway-Ruthven, J., 'Translation of the text of Cambridgeshire Domesday', in L. Salzman (ed.), *VCH*, i (London 1938) 358–99.

Owen, D. (ed.), *The making of King's Lynn. A documentary survey* (London 1984).

Owen, J., *Travels into different parts of Europe in the years 1791 and 1792, with familiar remarks on places, men, and manners*, i (London 1796).

Pacichelli, G., *Il Regno di Napoli in prospettiva ...* (Naples, 1703).

Palmer, W. and Saunders, H. (eds), *Documents relating to Cambridgeshire villages* (Cambridge 1928).

Pampaloni, G. (ed.), *Firenze al tempo di Dante: documenti sull'urbanistica fiorentina* (Rome 1973).

Pasqui, U. (ed.), *Documenti per la storia della città di Arezzo*, 3 vols (Florence 1899–1937).
Pavoncelli, G., *Un azienda vinaria in Capitanata* (Cerignola 1897).
Perthes Gotha, J. (ed.), *Almanach de Gotha, Annuaire généalogique, diplomatique et statistique, cent-quatorzième année* (unknown 1877).
Pignoni, Z., *Bando, e prohibizione di non poter pescare nel fiume de l'Oia in Casentino nel Vicariato di Poppi. E non poter pescare dal principio d'Arno fino al ponte di Stia sopra Arno* (Florence 1619).
Presutti, E. (ed.), *Puglie. Relazione del Delegato Tecnico. In Inchiesta Parlamentare sulle Condizioni dei Contadini nelle Provincie Meridionali e nella Sicilia*, i (Rome 1909).
PRO (TNA) (ed.), *Calendar of Charter Rolls AD 1226–1257*, i (London 1908).
———, *Calendar of Charter Rolls AD 1257–1300*, ii (London 1902).
———, *Calendar of Charter Rolls AD 1300–1326*, iii (London 1908).
———, *Calendar of Close Rolls AD 1341–1343*, vi (London 1902).
———, *Calendar of Inquisitions Miscellaneous, Chancery*, vi (London 1916).
———, *Calendar of Patent Rolls AD 1266–1272*, vi (London 1913).
———, *Calendar of Patent Rolls AD 1307–1313*, i (London 1894).
———, *Calendar of the Patent Rolls, 1281–1292, Edward I*, ii (London 1893).
———, *Calendar of the Patent Rolls, 1313–1317, Edward II*, iii (London 1898).
———, *Curia Regis rolls*, vii (London 1935).
———, *IPM AD 1336–1347*, viii (London 1913).
———, *IPM AD 1352–1361*, x (London 1921).
———, *IPM AD 1377–1384*, xv (London 1970).
———, 'Nomina Villarum: Comitatus Cantebrigie', in *Inquisitions and assessments relating to feudal aids with other analogous documents preserved in the Public Record Office: 1284–1431*, i (London 1899) 152–7.
———, *The assizes held at Cambridge A.D. 1260: being a condensed translation of assize roll 82 in the Public Record Office* (Linton 1930).
Protospata, L., 'Chronicon', in A. Silba (ed.), *Frammenti di storia nella città dei tre colli: Ascoli Satriano in tre antiche documenti* (Ascoli Satriano 2007) 3–38.
Ronchini, A. (ed.), *Statuta communis Parmae* (Parma 1855–56).
Roo van Alderwerelt, D. de, 'Een reis door Friesland, Drente, en Groningen in het jaar 1845', *De Vrije Fries* 48 (1968) 5–29.
Sacchetti, F., *Il libro del rime*, ed. F. Ageno (Florence 1990).
Salter, H. (ed.), *A cartulary of the Hospital of St. John the Baptist*, i (Oxford 1914).
Salvati, C. (ed.), *Copia quarteni Bernardi de Anghono mag. Actorum penes mag. portulanum Apulie de tractis extraxtis (1486–87)* (Naples 1968).
Santini, P. (ed.), *Documenti dell'Antica Costituzione del Comune di Firenze* (Florence 1895).
Schiaparelli, L., Baldesseroni, F. and Lasinio, E. (eds), *Regesto di Camaldoli*, 4 vols (Rome, 1907–22).

Singleton, C. (ed.), *Canti carnascialeschi del Rinascimento* (Bari 1936).
Sloet, J., Veen, J. van, and Martens van Sevenhoven, A. (eds), *Register op. de leenaktenboeken van het vorstendom Gelre en het graafschap Zutphen. Het Kwartier van Nijmegen* (Arnhem 1924).
Tersteeg, J. and Scheepsma, W. (eds), *Cartularium van de brieven van het O.L. Vrouweklooster te Renkum (1383–1609)* (Arnhem 1992).
Todisco Grande, L., 'Memoria dell'antichità del sito del governo di Ascoli Satriano', in A. Silba (ed.), *Frammenti di storia nella città dei tre colli: Ascoli Satriano in tre antiche documenti* (Ascoli Satriano 2007) 125–70.
Torelli, P. (ed.), *Regesto mantovano. Le carte degli archivi Gonzaga e di Stato in Mantova e dei monasteri Mantovani soppressi (Archivio di Stato in Milano)*, i (Rome 1914).
Vanderzee, G. (ed.), *Nonarum Inquisitiones in Curia Scaccarii* (London 1807).
Ventura, A. (ed.), *Onciario della città di Ascoli 1753* (Foggia 2006).
Venturi, F. (ed.), *Illuministi Italiani, v: riformatori napoletani* (Milan 1962).
Villani, G., *Cronica*, vols 1–4, ed. I. Moutier (Florence 1826).
Wauters, A. (ed.), *Table chronologique des chartes et diplômes imprimés concernant l'histoire de la Belgique*, ix (Brussels 1896).
Weiler, P. (ed.), *Urkundenbuch des Stiftes Xanten, (vor590)–1359*, i (Bonn 1935).
Westermann, J. (ed.), *De rekeningen van de landsheerlijke riviertollen in Gelderland, 1394/1395* (Arnhem 1939).
World Bank, *Agriculture for development. World Development Report 2008* (Washington 2007).

Internet

CBS, 'Volkstellingen 1795–1971', <http://www.volkstellingen.nl/nl/>.
Colclough, N., 'Family and the spatial distribution of kin in eighteenth century Ascoli', <http://lucy.ukc.ac.uk/jb6/archives/ascpaper/ascfr.html>.
Doesburg, J. van, Hesselink, A. and Smit, M., 'Het Rivierengebied in de middeleeuwen en vroegmoderne tijd', <http://archeologieinnederland.nl/sites/default/files/21%20Doesburg%20ME%20rivierengebied%20%2Blinks.pdf>, (2007).
Fumarola, F., 'Appunti della storia di Locorotondo: la Valle d'Itria e le origini di Locorotondo', <http://digilander.libero.it/locomind/storia/fumarola%201.html>.
GA, 'Lijst van gezagsdragers vermeld in het Regeringsboek afkomstig uit het Gemeente-archief Groningen, 1594 – ca. 1811', <http://files.archieven.nl/5/f/1700/1700_16.pdf>

Knottnerus, O., 'De korenmolens in Oost-Groningen vóór 1855: met een overzicht van de molens in de gemeente Menterwolde', <http://ottoknot.home.xs4all.nl/werk/>.

———, 'Boeren en landarbeiders in het Oldambt: de landarbeidersstaking van 1929 en haar voorgeschiedenis', <http://ottoknot.home.xs4all.nl/werk/>.

Migration Policy Centre, 'Syrian refugees: a snapshot of the crisis – in the Middle East and Europe', <http://syrianrefugees.eu/>.

Unpublished

Adriaenssen, L. and 't Hart, M., 'Farming communities at risk. War and economic structures in the Netherlands; some evidence from the Meierij and Westerwolde, c. 1550–1700' (unpub. paper, University of Amsterdam 2005).

Ali, I., 'The Punjab canal colonies, 1885–1940' (unpub. PhD, Australian National University 1980).

Bin Wong, R., 'China before capitalism' (unpub. paper, Utrecht Social and Econ. History Ser. 2013).

Bolton, M., 'Recovery for whom? Social conflict after the San Francisco earthquake and fire, 1906–1915' (unpub. PhD, University of California [Davis] 1997).

Curtis, D., 'A comparative study of the impact of social structure and tenure on nucleated and dispersed settlement in eight Cambridgeshire parishes, 1275–1340' (unpub. MPhil, University of Cambridge 2009).

Curtis, D., Van Onacker, E. and De Keyzer, M., 'Parasite or stimulant? Explaining divergent relationships between pre-industrial rural societies and cities: the growth of late-medieval and early-modern Antwerp and Florence compared' (unpub. Paper, University of Antwerp Seminar Ser. 2013).

Dilli, S., 'The roots of persistent global gaps in democracy: making the family count', (unpub. Paper, Utrecht University Seminar Ser. 2013) 1–40.

Karel, E., 'Oost-Groningen: een eeuwige periferie?' (unpub. conference paper, Sociaal-Historisch Centrum Limburg te Maastricht 2012) 1–20.

Karel, E. and Paping, R., 'Searching for a place to live. Succession and child career strategies of peasant and farmer households in rural Drenthe and Groningen in the first half of the nineteenth century' (unpub. Posthumus Conference Paper, University of Antwerp 2011) 1–35.

Oudhof, J., 'De handelsfunctie van Tiel in de periode late negende eeuw tot en met het begin van de elfde eeuw. Een historisch-archeologische verkenning aan de hand van vier stadskernopgravingen in de binnenstad van Tiel' (unpub. PhD, University of Amsterdam 1996).

Postgate, M., 'The open fields of Cambridgeshire' (unpublished PhD thesis, University of Cambridge 1964).

Sapoznik, A., 'Productivity of peasant agriculture at Oakington, Cambridgeshire, c.1290–1400' (unpub. PhD, University of Cambridge, 2010).
Slota, L., 'The land market on the St. Albans manors of Park and Codicote 1237–1399' (unpub. PhD, University of Michigan, 1984).
Ufkes, T., 'De Kerstvloed van 1717. Oorzaken en gevolgen van een natuurramp' (unpub. PhD, University of Groningen 1984).

Secondary Literature

Abatantuono, M. and Righetti, L., *I conti Alberti (secoli XI–XIV). Strategie di una signoria territoriale. La montagna tra Bologna e Prato* (Rastigano 2000).
Abel, W., *Agrarkrisen und Agrarkonjunktur* (Berlin 1935).
———, *Agricultural fluctuations in Europe from the thirteenth to the twentieth centuries* (New York 1978).
———, *Die Wüstungen des ausgehenden Mittelalters. Ein Beitrag zur Siedlung- und Agrargeschichte Deutschlands* (Jena 1943).
Abels, S., *Doopsgezinde families in het Oldambt 1520–1811* (Eextrerzandvoort 2002).
Abreu, L., 'Beggars, vagrants and romanies: repression and persecution in Portuguese society (14th–18th centuries)', *Hygiea Internationalis* 6 (2007) 41–66.
Abse, T., 'Recent works on nineteenth- and twentieth-century Italian history', *Hist. J.* 27 (1984) 1019–36.
Abulafia, D., *The two Italies* (Cambridge 1977).
———, 'Southern Italy and the Florentine economy, 1265–1370', *EcHR* 34 (1981) 377–88.
Accorsi, C., Bandini Mazzanti, M., Marchesini, M. and Marvelli, S., 'Ricerche archeoambientali nella Daunia antica. Dati pollinici sull'insediamento di Arpi e sulla villa romana di Ascoli Satriano', in L. Quilici and S.Q. Gigli (eds), *Agricoltura e commerci nell'Italia antica* (Rome 1995) 108–13.
Acheson, J., 'The politics of managing the Maine lobster industry: 1860 to the present', *Human Ecology* 25 (1997) 3–27.
Achilles, W., *Vermögensverhältnisse Braunschweigischer Bauernhöfe im 17. und 18. Jahrhundert* (Stuttgart 1965).
Ackerberg, D. and Botticini, M., 'The choice of agrarian contracts in early Renaissance Tuscany: risk sharing, moral hazard or capital market imperfections?', *ExEH* 37 (2000) 241–57.
Adriaenssen, L., *Staatsvormend geweld. Overleven aan de frontlinies in de Meierij van Den Bosch, 1572–1629* (Tilburg 2007).
Agnew, H., *The Czechs and the lands of the Bohemian Crown* (Stanford 2004).

Aguirre, B., 'Better disaster statistics: the Lisbon earthquake', *JIH* 43 (2012) 27–42.
Agrawal, A. and Chhatre, A., 'Explaining success on the commons: community forest governance in the Indian Himalaya', *World Development* 34 (2006) 149–66.
Agrawal, A. and Ostrom, E., 'Collective action, property rights and decentralization in resource use in India and Nepal', *Politics & Soc.* 29 (2001) 485–514.
A'Hearn, B., 'Could Southern Italians cooperate? Banche Popolari in the Mezzogiorno', *JEH* 60 (2000) 67–93.
Ahlmann, H., 'Etudes de géographie humaine sur l'Italie subtropicale. Calabre, Basilicate et Apulie', *Geografiska Annaler* 8 (1926) 74–124.
———, 'The geographical study of settlements: examples from Italy, Germany, Denmark, and Norway', *Geog. Rev.* 18 (1928) 93–128.
Ahmad, S., *Class and power in a Punjabi village* (New York 1977).
Ahuja, R., 'State formation and "famine policy" in early colonial South India', *Indian Econ. & Social History Rev.* 39 (2002) 351–80.
Akkerman, J., 'Het koopmansgilde omstreeks het jaar 1000', *Tijdschrift voor Rechtsgeschiedenis* 30 (1962) 409–74.
Alavi, H., 'The politics of dependence: a village in West Punjab', *South Asian Rev.* 4 (1970–1) 111–25.
Alberts, W., 'Gelderland van 1543–1566', in P. Meij and W.J. Alberts (eds), *Geschiedenis van Gelderland, 1492–1795* (Zutphen 1975) 79–96.
Albini, G., *Guerra, fame, peste: crisi di mortalità e sistema sanitario nella Lombardia tardomedioevale* (Bologna 1982).
Alchon, S., *A pest in the land: New World epidemics in a global perspective* (Albuquerque 2003).
Alfani, G., 'Population and environment in Northern Italy during the sixteenth century', *Population* 62 (2007) 559–95.
———, 'Wealth inequalities and population dynamics in early modern Northern Italy', *JIH* 40 (2010) 513–49.
———, *Calamities and the economy in Renaissance Italy: the Grand Tour of the Horsemen of the Apocalypse*, trans. C. Calvert (Basingstoke 2013).
Alfonso Antón, I., 'Conflict in the behetrías', in C. Pérez-Alfaro and C. Estepa Díez (eds), *Land, power and society in medieval Castile: a study of behetría lordship* (Turnhout 2010) 275–316.
Alfonso, I., 'Cistercians and feudalism', *P&P* 133.1 (1991) 3–30.
Ali, I., 'Malign growth? Agricultural colonization and the roots of backwardness in the Punjab', *P&P* 114 (1987) 110–33.
Allemeyer, M., *'Kein land ohne Deich ... !'. Lebenswelten einer Küstengesellschaft in der Frühen Neuzeit* (Göttingen 2006).
Allen, R., *Enclosure and the yeoman* (Oxford 1992).

Alos, L., 'When there was no male heir: the transfer of wealth through women in Catalonia (the pubilla)', *C&C* 20 (2005) 27–52.

Altobella, C. and Muscio, A., 'Aspetti del contrasto agro-pastorale dei territori della Dogana delle pecore di Puglia: usurpazioni, reintegre e trasformazioni', in *Agricoltura e pastorizia in Capitanata: la storia e le ragioni di un conflitto (secc. xv–xix)* (Bari 1997) 1–62.

Ambrosi, A., 'Schemi propositivi per lo studio dell'architettura della masseria pugliese', in *Contribuiti allo studio del paesaggio urbano e rurale della masseria in Puglia; quaderni della scuola di perfezionamento in pianifacazione urbana e territorale* (Bari 1983) 7–20.

Anantha Ram, K., Tsunekawab, A., Sahac, D. and Miyazaki, T., 'Subdivision and fragmentation of land holdings and their implication in desertification in the Thar Desert, India', *J. Arid Environments* 41 (1999) 463–77.

André, C. and Platteau, J-P., 'Land relations under unbearable stress: Rwanda caught in the Malthusian trap', *J. Econ. Behaviour & Organization* 34 (1998) 1–47.

Andreae Fockema, S., *Studien over Waterschapsgeschiedenis: De Grote of Zuidhollandse Waard* (Leiden 1950).

Andreolli, A., 'Formule di pertinenza e paesaggio. Il castagneto nella Lucchesia altomedievale', *Rivista di Archeologia, Storia, Economia, Costume* 3 (1977) 7–18.

Andreolli, A. and Montanari, M., *L'azienda curtense in Italia. Proprietà della terra e lavoro contadino nei secoli VIII–XI* (Bologna 1983).

Andrews, D., 'Castelli e incastellamento nell'Italia centrale' in R. Comba (ed.) *Castelli storia e archeologia* (Cuneo 1981) 123–36.

Angelis, L. de, 'Intorno all'attività di Deo di Buono, fabbro casentinese', *AM* 3 (1976) 429–46.

Antonacci, N., *Terra e potere in una città rurale del Mezzogiorno. Le elites di Andria nell'Ottocento* (Bari 1996).

———, 'Le città rurali dell'Italia meridionale nel XIX e XX secolo. Rassegna critica e prospettive di ricerca', *Società e Storia* 71 (1996) 19–31.

Antoniadis-Bibicou, H., 'Villages désertés en Grèce – un bilan provisoire', in R. Romano and P. Corbin (eds), *Villages désertés et histoire economique. XI–XVIII siècles* (Paris 1965) 343–417.

Antonides, H., *Noord- en Zuidbroek in vroegere jaren* (Noordbroek 1973).

Antonson, H., 'The extent of farm desertion in central Sweden during the late medieval agrarian crisis: landscape as a source', *JHG* 35 (2009) 619–41.

Anzivino, A., 'Fuochi, famiglie e donne nel catasto onciario di Orsara di Puglia', *Carte di Puglia* 12 (2004) 30–40.

Aparisi, F. and Royo, V. (eds), *Beyond lords and peasants: rural elites and economic differentiation in pre-modern Europe* (Valencia 2013).

Appleby, A., 'Grain prices and subsistence crises in England and France, 1690–1740', *JEH* 39 (1979) 871–87.
Arlacchi, P., *Mafia, peasants, and great estates: society in traditional Calabria* (Cambridge 1983).
Arnold, D., *The problem of nature: environment, culture and European expansion* (Oxford 1996).
Artola, M., Bernal, A., and Contreras, J., *El latifundio. Propiedad y explotación, ss. XVIII–XX* (Madrid 1978).
Asaji, K., 'The Baron's War and the Hundred jurors in Cambridgeshire', *JMH* 21 (1995) 153–65.
Ashtor, E., *A social and economic history of the Near East in the Middle Ages* (London 1976).
Assante, F., *Calopezzati: proprietà fondiaria e classi rurali in un Comune della Calabria (1740–1886)* (Naples 1964).
———, 'Il catasto onciario come fonte di storia demografica', in *Le fonti della demografia storica in Italia* (Rome 1973) 273–83.
Astarita, T., *The continuity of feudal power: the Caracciolo di Brienza in Spanish Naples* (Cambridge 1992).
Astill, G., 'The long and the short: rural settlement in medieval England', in R. Goddard, J. Langdon and M. Müller (eds), *Survival and discord in medieval society. Essays in honour of Christopher Dyer* (Turnhout 2010) 11–28.
Astin, T., Eckhardt, H. and Hay, S., 'Resitivity imaging survey of the Roman Barrows at Bartlow, Cambridgeshire', *Arch. Protection* 14 (2007) 24–37.
d'Atri, S., 'Censuazione del Tavoliere e proprietà fondiaria a Cerignola', in *Il paesaggio agrario di Cerignola fra Settecento e Ottocento* (Cerignola 1999) 33–46.
Augusto Padua, J., 'European colonialism and tropical forest destruction in Brazil', in J. McNeill, J. Augusto Padua and M. Rangarajan (eds), *Environmental history: as if nature existed* (Oxford 2010) 130–50.
Ault, W., *Open-field farming in medieval England. A study of village by-laws* (London 1972).
Austermann, M., 'Archäologische Forschungen zu den mittelalterlichen Siedlungen in der Wetterau. Ergebnisse der Arbeit von 1993–1997', *Siedlungforschung* 17 (1999) 47–64.
Averill, S., 'The Shed People and the opening of the Yangzi highlands', *Modern China* 9 (1983) 84–126.
Aymard, M., 'Mesures et interprétations de la croissance. Rendements et productivité agricole dans l'Italie moderne', *Annales: ESC* 28 (1973) 475–98.
———, 'La transizione dal feudalismo al capitalismo', in R. Romero and C. Vivanti (eds), *Storia d'Italia, Annali,* i (Turin 1978) 1155–69.
———, 'L'Europe moderne: féodalité ou féodalités?', *Annales: ESC* 36 (1981) 426–35.

———, 'From feudalism to capitalism in Italy: the case that doesn't fit', *Rev.* 6 (1982) 131–208.

Baars, C., *De geschiedenis van de landbouw in de Beijerlanden* (Wageningen 1973).

———, 'Oorspronkelijke verkaveling en grootte van de bezittingen in enige polders in Noord-Holland', *Landbouwkundig Tijdschrift* 92 (1981) 193–201.

Bacchi, T., 'Conquista del territorio e modificazione dei modelli impeditive. Le aziende fondiarie nel Ferrarese (secoli XI–XII)', in B. Andreolli, V. Fumagalli and M. Montanari (eds), *Le campagne italiane prima e dopo il Mille. Una società in trasformazione* (Bologna 1985) 133–61.

Backmund, N., 'Verkoop en afbraak van Heigerlee en Nyeklooster-op.-den-Dam in 1597', *Sacris Erudiri. Jaarboek voor Godsdienstwetenschappen* 7 (1955) 381–5.

Baelaerts van Blokland, W., 'Het in 1553 gebouwde huis te Rumpt', *BMGelre* 35 (1932) 105–16.

Bahn, P. and Flenley, J., *Easter Island. Earth Island* (London 1992).

Bailey, M., 'The concept of the margin in the medieval economy', *EcHR* 42 (1989) 1–17.

———, *A marginal economy? East Anglian Breckland in the later Middle Ages* (Cambridge 1989).

———, 'Sand into gold: the evolution of the foldcourse system in west Suffolk, 1200–1600', *AgHR* 38 (1990) 40–57.

———, 'Per impetum maris: natural disaster and economic decline in Eastern England, 1275–1350', in B. Campbell (ed.), *Before the Black Death. Essays in the crisis of the early fourteenth century* (Manchester 1991) 184–208.

———, 'The Prior and Convent of Ely and their management of the manor of Lakenheath in the fourteenth century', in M. Franklin and C. Harper-Bill (eds), *Medieval ecclesiastical studies in honour of Dorothy M. Owen* (Woodbridge 1995) 1–20.

———, 'Peasant welfare in England, 1290–1348', *EcHR* 51 (1998) 223–51.

———, 'Beyond the Midland field system: the determinants of common rights over the arable in medieval England', *AgHR* 58 (2010) 153–71.

Bailey, M. and Hatcher, J., *Modelling the Middle Ages: the history and theory of England's economic development* (Oxford 2001).

Baker, A., 'Evidence in the "Nonarum Inquisitiones" of contracting arable lands in England during the early fourteenth century', *EcHR* 19 (1966) 518–32.

Balard, M., 'Le commerce du blé en mer Noire (XIIIe–XVe siècles)', in *Aspetti della vita economica medievale: studi nell'archivio Datini di Prato* (Florence 1985) 64–80.

Baldari, E. and Farina, S., 'Il Casentino. Una vallata montana dalleo sfruttamento feudale all'annessione al contado urbano', in E. Guidoni (ed.), *Città, contado e feudi nell'urbanistica medievale* (Rome 1974) 64–99.

Balducci, O., 'La dimora silvo-pastorale appenninica', in G. Barbieri and L. Gambi (eds), *La casa rurale in Italia* (Florence 1970) 299–308.

Balestracci, D., 'Lavoro e povertà in Toscana alla fine del medioevo', *SS* 23 (1982) 565–82.

———, 'La politica delle acque urbane nell'Italia comunale', *Mélanges de l'Ecole Française de Rome. Moyen Age* 104 (1992) 431–79.

Banfield, E., *The moral basis of a backward society* (New York 1958).

Bankoff, G., 'Rendering the world unsafe: 'vulnerability' as Western discourse', *Disasters* 25 (2001) 19–35.

———, 'Constructing vulnerability: the historical, natural and social generation of flooding in metropolitan Manila', *Disasters* 27 (2003) 224–38.

———, *Cultures of disaster: society and natural hazard in Philippines* (London 2003).

———, 'Time is of the essence: disasters, vulnerability, and history', *International J. Mass Emergencies & Disasters* 22 (2004) 23–42.

———, 'Dangers to going it alone: social capital and the origins of community resilience in the Philippines', *C&C* 22 (2007) 327–55.

Bankoff, G., Frerks, G. and Hilhorst, D. (eds), *Mapping vulnerability: disasters, development and people* (London 2004).

Banks, S., 'Nineteenth century scandal or twentieth century model? A new look at open and close parishes', *EcHR* 41 (1988) 51–73.

Baquero Moreno, H., *Marginalidade e conflitos sociais em Portugal nos séculos XIV e XV* (Lisbon 1985).

Barbagli, M., 'Marriage and the family in Italy in the early nineteenth century', in J. Davis and P. Ginsborg (eds), *Society and politics in the age of the Risorgimento: essays in honour of Mack Smith* (Cambridge 1991) 92–127.

Barbieri, G., *Memoria illustrativa della carta della utilizzazione del suolo della Toscana* (Rome 1966).

Bärenfänger, R. and Groenendijk, H., 'Versunkene Siedlungen am Dollart', *Archäologie in Niedersachsen* 2 (1999) 116–9.

Barg, M., 'The social structure of manorial freeholders: an analysis of the Hundred Rolls of 1279', *AgHR* 39 (1991) 108–15.

Bargiacchi, R., 'I conti Guidi e l'incastellamento del Casentino: il caso di Poppi', *AM* 35 (2008) 255–73.

———, 'I castelli dei conti Guidi in Casentino: storia di un contesto archeologico', in F. Canaccini (ed.), *La lunga storia di un stirpe comitale: i conti Guidi tra Romagna e Toscana* (Florence 2009) 211–44.

Barker, G., 'The archaeology of the Italian shepherd', *Proc. Phil. Soc.* 25 (1989) 1–19.

Barlucchi, A., 'La lavorazione del ferro nell'economia casentinese alla fine del medioevo (tra Campaldino e la battaglia di Anghiari)', *Annali Aretini* 14 (2006) 169–200.

Barnett, J. and Adger, N., 'Climate change, human security, and violent conflict', *Pol. Geography* 26 (2007) 639–55.

Barra, F., *Storia di Avellino* (Avellino 1992).

Bartlett, R., *The making of Europe: conquest, colonisation and cultural change, 950–1350* (London 1993).

———, *England under the Norman and Angevin Kings 1075–1225* (Oxford 2000).

Bavel, B. van, *Goederenverwerving en goederenbeheer van de abdij Mariënweerd, 1129–1592* (Hilversum 1993).

———, 'Stichtingsplaats, ontginning en goederenverwerving. De economische ontwikkeling van Norbertijner abdijen in de Nederlanden', *Ideaal en Werkelijkheid: Verslagen van de Contactdag van de Werkgroep Norbertijnse Geschiedenis in de Nederlanden* 3 (1993) 44–53.

———, 'Pachtboek, pachtcontract, legger, pachtrekening-courant en rekening: typologie en interpretatie van de laat-middeleeuwse bronnensoorten met betrekking tot de verpachting van grondbezit', in J. Smit, D. den Boer and J. Marsilje (eds), *Vander rekeninghe. Bijdragen aan het symposium* (The Hague 1998) 99–110.

———, 'A valuation of arable productivity in the central part of the Dutch river area, c.1360–1570', in B. van Bavel and E. Thoen (eds), *Land productivity and agro-systems in the North Sea area (Middle Ages – 20th century). Elements for comparison* (Turnhout 1999) 297–310.

———, *Transitie en continuitëit: de bezitsverhoudingen en de plattelands-economie in het westelijke gedeelte van het Gelderse rivierengebied, ca. 1300 – ca. 1570* (Hilversum 1999).

———, 'Land, lease and agriculture: the transition of the rural economy in the Dutch river area from the fourteenth to the sixteenth century', *P&P* 172 (2001), 3–43.

———, 'Landbouw, bosbouw en visserij', in J. Stinner and K-H, Tekath (eds), *Gelre, Geldern, Gelderland. Geschiedenis en cultuur van het hertogdom Gelre* (Geldern 2001) 261–7.

———, 'People and land: rural population developments and property structures in the Low Countries, c. 1300 – c. 1600', *C&C* 17 (2002) 9–37.

———, 'Proto-industrie tussen de Gelderse rivieren? Een eerste verkenning naar de niet-agrarische, marktgerichte activiteiten op. het platteland van het Gelderse rivierengebied, 1300–1600', *BMGelre* 93 (2002) 55–78.

———, 'Eendenkooien in het Hollandse en Gelderse rivierengebied. Aanleg en vroegste exploitatie', *Historisch-Geografisch Tijdschrift* 20 (2002) 16–20.

———, 'The land market in the North Sea area from a comparative perspective, 13th–18th centuries', in S. Cavaciocchi (ed.), *Il mercato della terra secc. XIII–XVIII* (Prato 2003) 119–46.

———, 'Early proto-industrialization in the Low Countries? The importance and nature of non-agricultural activities on the countryside in Flanders and Holland', *RBPH* 81 (2003) 1109–65.

———, 'Rural wage labour in the sixteenth-century Low Countries: an assessment of the importance and nature of wage labour in the countryside of Holland, Guelders, and Flanders', *C&C* 21 (2006) 37–72.

———, 'The transition in the Low Countries. Wage labour as an indicator of the rise of capitalism in the countryside, 14th–17th centuries', *P&P* 195 (2007) 286–303.

———, 'The organisation and rise of land and lease markets in northwestern Europe and Italy, c.1000–1800', *C&C* 23 (2008) 13–53.

———, 'The emergence and growth of short-term leasing in the Netherlands and other parts of Northwestern Europe (eleventh–seventeenth centuries). A chronology and a tentative investigation into its causes', in B. van Bavel and P. Schofield (eds), *The development of leasehold in northwestern Europe c. 1200–1600* (Turnhout 2008) 179–213.

———, 'Rural development and landownership in Holland, c. 1400–1650', in O. Gelderblom (ed.), *The political economy of the Dutch Republic* (Farnham 2009) 197–222.

———, *Manors and markets: economy and society in the Low Countries, 500–1600* (Oxford 2010).

———, 'Beyond the Midland field system. The determinants of common rights over arable land in medieval England', *AgHR* 58 (2010) 153–71.

———, 'The medieval origins of capitalism in the Netherlands', *BMGN* 125 (2010) 45–80.

———, 'Rural revolts and structural change in the Low Countries, thirteenth–early fourteenth centuries', in R. Goddard, J. Langdon and M. Müller (eds), *Survival and discord in medieval society. Essays in honour of Christopher Dyer* (Turnhout 2010) 249–67.

———, 'Mariënweerd en de heren van Culemborg. Machtsverhoudingen, goederenbezit en ontginningen in het gebied tussen Lek en Linge', in A. Blommers (ed.), *Rond de Kulenburg. Ridders en ontginningen tussen Lek en Linge 1100–1318* (Culemborg 2010) 43–58.

———, 'Markets for land, labor, and capital in northern Italy and the Low Countries, twelfth to seventeenth centuries', *JIH* 41 (2011) 13–53.

Bavel, B. van and Hoyle, R., 'Introduction: social relations, property and power in the North Sea Area, 500–2000', in *Rural economy and society in North-western Europe, 500–2000* (Turnhout 2010) 1–23.

Bavel, B. van and Thoen, E., 'Rural history and the environment. A survey of the relationship between property rights, social structures and sustainability of land use', in *Rural societies and environments at risk. Ecology, property rights and social organisation in fragile areas (Middle Ages-twentieth century)* (Turnhout 2013) 15–42.

Bavel, B. van and Zanden, J.L. van, 'The jump-start of the Holland economy during the late-medieval crisis, *c.*1350–*c.*1500', *EcHR* 57 (2004) 503–32.

Bazzana, A., Guichard, P. and Poisson, J-M., *Habitats fortifiés et organisation de l'espace* (Lyon 1983).

Béaur, G., *La marché foncier à la veille de la Révolution: les mouvements de propriété beaucerons dans les régions de Maintenon et de Janville de 1761 à 1790* (Paris 1984).

———, *La terre et les hommes : France et Angleterre, XVIIe–XVIIIe siècle* (Paris 1998).

Becker, M., *Florence in transition. Studies in the rise of the territorial state*, ii (Baltimore 1968).

Behar, R., *Santa María del Monte: the presence of the past in a Spanish village* (Princeton 1986).

Behre, K., 'Die Veränderungen der niedersächsischen Küstenlinien in den letzten 3000 Jahren und deren Ursachen', *Probleme der Küstenforschung im südlichen Nordseegebiet* 26 (1999) 9–34.

Beier, A., 'A new serfdom: labor laws, vagrancy statutes, and labor discipline in England, 1350–1800', in A. Beier and P. Ocobock (eds), *Cast out: vagrancy and homelessness in global and historical perspective* (Athens OH 2008) 35–63.

Beinart, W. and Hughes, L., *Environment and empire* (Oxford 2007).

Bekar, C. and Reed, C., 'Open fields, risk, and land divisibility', *ExEH* 40 (2003) 308–25.

Belfanti, C., 'Dalla città alla campagna: industrie tessili a Mantova tra carestie ed epidemie (1550–1630)', *Critica Storica* 25 (1988) 443–53.

———, *Mestieri e forestieri. Immigrazione ed economia urbana a Mantova fra Sei e Settecento* (Milan 1994).

———, 'Town and country in central and northern Italy, 1400–1800', in S. Epstein (ed.), *Town and country in Europe, 1300–1800* (Cambridge 2001) 292–315.

Bell, C., 'Alternative theories of sharecropping: some tests using evidence from northeast India', *J. Development Stud.* 13 (1977) 317–46.

Bellwood, P., *The first farmers: the origins of agricultural societies* (Oxford 2005).

Belonje, J., 'Crayesteyn onder Tricht', *BMGelre* 47 (1944) 41–72.

———, 'Het huis Reygersfoort bij Tricht', *BMGelre* 49 (1949) 267–310.

Beltjes, P., 'Het kerkhof van Paveie', *BMGelre* 51 (1951) 149–52.

Beltjes, P. and Blommers, A., 'Eer Culemborg was … Iets over de ontginningsgeschiedenis van het gebied tussen Lek en Linge, waar in de middeleeuwen de heerlijkheid Culemborg is gevormd', in A. Blommers (ed.),

Rond de Kulenburg. Ridders en ontginningen tussen Lek en Linge 1100–1318 (Culemborg 2010) 83–132.

Benadusi, G., 'Ceti dirigenti locali e bande granducali nella provincia Toscana: Poppi tra Sedicesimo and Diciassettesimo secolo', in C. Lamioni (ed.), *Istituzioni e società in Toscana nell'età moderna* (Rome 1994) 231–44.

———, *A provincial elite in early modern Tuscany: family and power in the creation of the state* (Baltimore 1996).

———, 'Rethinking the state: family strategies in early modern Tuscany', *Social History* 20 (1996) 157–78.

Benders, J., 'Item instituimus ibidem singulis annis nundinas. Fairs in the principality of Guelders, 1294–1543', in S. Cavaciocchi (ed.), *Fiere e mercati nella integrazione delle economie Europee secc. XIII–XVIII* (Prato 2000) 645–67.

Benedictow, O., 'New perspectives in medieval demography: the medieval demographic system', in M. Bailey and S. Rigby (eds), *Town and countryside in the age of the Black Death: essays in honour of John Hatcher* (Turnhout 2012) 3–42.

Beni, C., *Guida del Casentino* (Florence 1983).

Benigno, F., *Una casa, una terra: ricerche su Paceco, paese nuovo nella Sicilia del Sei e Ottocento* (Catania 1985).

———, 'The Southern Italian family in the early modern period: a discussion of co-residential patterns', *C&C* 4 (1989) 165–94.

———, 'Assetti territoriali e ruralizzazione nella Sicilia del Seicento: note per una discussione', in *La popolazione delle campagne italiane in età moderna* (Bologna 1993) 55–70.

Bennett, J., 'Spouses, siblings and surnames: Reconstructing families from medieval village court rolls', *J. British Stud.* 23 (1983) 26–46.

———, *Women in the medieval English countryside: gender and household in Brigstock before the Plague* (Oxford 1987).

Berendsen, H., *Landschappelijk Nederland: de fysisch-geografische regio's* (Assen 2005).

Berengo, M., 'Città e 'contado' in Italia dal XV al XVIII secolo', *Storia dell Città* 36 (1986) 107–11.

Beresford, M., *The lost villages of England* (London 1954).

Beresford, M. and Hurst, J., *Deserted medieval villages* (London 1971).

Beresteyn, E., 'Het huis te Meteren en zij bezitters (1267–1907)', *BMGelre* 11 (1908) 335–72.

Bergman, M., 'The potato blight in the Netherlands and its social consequences, 1845–47', *IRSH* 12 (1967) 390–431.

Berkner, L., 'The stem family and the development cycle of the peasant household: an eighteenth-century Austrian example', *AHR* 77 (1972) 398–418.

Berry, M., 'Public peace and private attachment: the goals and conduct of power in early modern Japan', *J. Japanese Stud.* 12 (1986) 237–71.

Bertelli, S., *Il potere oligarchico nello stato-città medievale* (Florence 1978).

Bevilacqua, P., 'Calabria fra antropologia e storia', *SS* 22 (1981) 665–70.

———, 'Clima, mercato e paesaggio agrario nel Mezzogiorno', in *Storia dell'agricoltura italiana in età contemporanea: spazi e paesaggi*, i (Venice 1989) 643–67.

———, *Breve storia dell'Italia meridionale* (Rome 1997).

Bevilacqua, P. and Gorgoni, M., 'Mercati', *Meridiana* 1 (1987) 11–8.

Biasutti, R., *Casa rurale nella Toscana* (Bologna 1938).

Bicchierai, M., *Il castello di Raggiolo e i conti Guidi. Signoria e società di antico regime: Raggiolo in Casentino* (Raggiolo-Montepulciano 1994).

———, 'La signoria dei conti Guidi in Valdarno. Osservazioni ed ipotesi', in G. Pinto and P. Pirillo (eds), *Lontana dalle città. Il Valdarno di Sopra nei secoli XII–XIII* (Rome 2005) 83–116.

———, *Una comunità rurale toscana di antico regime: Raggiolo in Casentino* (Florence 2006).

———, 'La lunga durata dei beni comuni in una comunità Toscana: il caso di Raggiolo in Casentino', in R. Zagnini (ed.), *Comunità e beni comuni dal medioevo ad oggi* (Pistoia 2007) 45–60.

Biddick, K., 'Missing links: taxable wealth, markets, and stratification among medieval English peasants', *JIH* 18 (1987) 277–98.

Bieleman, J., 'De Gelderse landbouw voor 1850', in *Anderhalve eeuw Gelderse landbouw. De geschiedenis van de Geldersche maatschappij van landbouw en het Gelderse platteland* (Groningen 1995) 34–64.

Bierbrauer, P., 'Die Ausbildung bäuerlicher Landschaften im Raum der Eidgenossenschaft', *Parliaments, Estates & Representation* 11 (1991) 91–102.

Bierma, M., Clason, A., Kramer, E. and Langen, G. de (eds), *Terpen en wierden in het Fries-Groningse kustgebied* (Groningen 1988).

Bin Wong, R., *China transformed: historical change and the limits of the European experience* (Ithaca 1997).

Birrell, J., 'Common rights in the medieval forest: disputes and conflicts in the thirteenth century', *P&P* 117 (1987) 22–49.

———, 'Peasant deer poachers in the medieval forest', in R. Britnell and J. Hatcher (eds), *Progress and problems in medieval England* (Cambridge 1996) 68–88.

Bissanti, A., 'Il Tavoliere di Puglia', in C. Colamonico (ed.), *La casa rurale nella Puglia* (Florence 1970) 70–91.

Blaikie, P., Wisner, B., Cannon, T. and Davis, I. (eds), *At risk. Natural hazards, people's vulnerability, and disasters* (London 1997).

Blake, W., 'Norfolk manorial lords in 1316', *Norfolk Archaeology* 30 (1952) 234–86.

Blanshei, S., 'Population, wealth, and patronage in medieval and Renaissance Perugia', *JIH* 9 (1979) 597–619.

Blanton, R., 'Review', *Amer. Antiquity* 55 (1990) 421–3.

Blarel, B., Hazell, P., Place, F. and Quiggin, J., 'The economics of farm fragmentation: evidence from Ghana and Rwanda', *World Bank Econ. Rev.* 6 (1992) 233–54.

Blauw, M., *Van Friese grond. Agrarische eigendoms- en gebruiksverhoudingen en de ontwikkelingen in de Friese landbouw in de negentiende eeuw* (Leeuwarden 1995).

Blécourt, A. de, *Het stadsmeierrecht in de Groninger Veenkoloniën*, i (Groningen 1907).

———, *Oldambt en de Ommelanden: rechtshistorische opstellen met bijlagen* (Assen 1935).

Blickle, P., 'Wem gehörte der Wald? Konflikte zwischen Bauern und Obrigkeiten um Nutzungs- und Eigentumsansprüche', *Zeitschrift für Württembergischen Landesgeschichte* 45 (1986) 167–78.

———, *Studien zur geschichtlichen Bedeutung des deutschen Bauernstandes* (Stuttgart 1989).

Blockmans, W., 'The social and economic effect of the plague in the Low Countries', *RBPH* 58 (1980) 833–63.

———, 'Stadt, Region und Staat: ein Dreiecksverhältnis: der Kasus der Niederlande im 15. Jahrhundert', in F. Seibt and W. Eberhard (eds), *Europa 1500* (Stuttgart 1987) 211–26.

Blok, A., 'Land reform in a west Sicilian Latifondo village: the persistence of a feudal structure', *Anthropological Quart.* 39 (1966) 1–16.

———, 'South Italian agro-towns', *CSSH* 11 (1969) 121–35.

———, *The mafia of a Sicilian village, 1860 to 1960: a study of violent peasant entrepreneurs* (Oxford 1974).

Blok, A. and Driessen, H., 'Mediterranean agro-towns as a form of cultural dominance; with special reference to Sicily and Andalusia', *Ethnologia Europaea* 14 (1984) 111–24.

Blok, D., 'De enken', *Driemaandelijkse Bladen* 10 (1958) 1–5.

———, 'De eigen inbreng van de plaatsnaamkunde in de nederzettinggeschiedenis', *Naamkunde* 5 (1973) 223–41.

———, *De Franken in Nederland* (Bussum 1974).

Blondé, B. and Damme, I. van, 'Retail growth and consumer changes in a declining urban economy: Antwerp (1650–1750)', *EcHR* 63 (2010) 638–63.

Blum, J., *The end of the social order in rural Europe* (Princeton 1978).

Boadu, F., 'The efficiency of share contracts in Ghana's cocoa industry', *J. Development Stud.* 29 (1992) 108–20.

Boddington, A., 'Models of burial, settlement and worship: the final phase reviewed', in E. Southworth (ed.), *Anglo Saxon cemeteries: a reappraisal* (London 1990) 177–99.

Boelema-Diddens, T. (ed.), *Boerderijen en hun inwoners in Noord- en Zuidbroek* (Zuidbroek 1990).

Boer, D. de, *Graaf en grafiek. Sociale en economische ontwikkelingen in het middeleeuwse 'Noordholland' tussen 1345 en 1415* (Leiden 1978).

Boer, J. de, 'Dorpen in Groningen', *Noorderbreedte* 12 (1988) 145–51.

Boer, L., 'Een Oldambster herenboer op. het Haagse pluche. J.F. Zijlker (1805–1868) en het Oldambt', *Veenkoloniale Volksalmanak* 11 (1999) 9–22.

Bois, G., *Crise du féodalisme. Economie rurale et démographie en Normandie orientale du début du 14e siècle au milieu du 16e siècle* (Paris 1974).

Boissevain, J., 'Poverty and politics in a Sicilian agro-town: a preliminary report', *Int. Arch. Ethnography* 50 (1966) 198–236.

Bolòs, J., 'Changes and survival: the territory of Lleida (Catalonia) after the twelfth-century conquest', *JMH* 27 (2001) 313–39.

Bonanno, A., 'Theories of the state: the case of land reform in Italy, 1944–1961', *Sociological Quart.* 29 (1988) 131–47.

Boomgaard, P., 'Oriental nature, its friends, and its enemies: conservation of nature in late-colonial Indonesia, 1889–1949', *Environment & History* 5 (1999) 257–92.

Borsch, S., 'Environment and population: the collapse of large irrigation systems reconsidered', *CSSH* 46 (2004) 451–68.

Borst, A., 'Das Erdbeben von 1348. Ein historischer Beitrag zur Katastrophenforschung', *Historisch Zeitschrift* 233 (1981) 529–68.

Boschi, E., Guidoboni, E., Ferrari, G., Valensise, G. and Gasperini, P., *Catalogo dei forti terremoti in Italia dal 461 a.C. al 1990* (Bologna 1997).

Boserup, E., *The conditions of agricultural growth: the economics of agrarian change under population pressure* (London 1965).

Boso, P., *Martina Franca nel 1755* (Taranto 1969).

Bosschaert, A. and Driessen, P., 'Terpen in de Neder-Betuwe en de Tielerwaard', *Historisch-Geografisch Tijdschrift* 7 (1989) 10–17.

Botke, I., ''Van de boer hangt alles of'. De Groninger landbouwer in eigen en andermans ogen, 1800–1900', in P. Boekholt, A. Huussen jr., P. Kooij, F. Postma and H. Wedman (eds), *Rondom de reductie. Vierhonderd jaar provincie Groningen 1594–1994* (Groningen 1994) 287–308.

———, 'Provinciaal, maar niet zonder smaak. Schilders, ververs, glazenmakers en de Groninger boerenwoning in de eerste helft van de negentiende eeuw. Een verkenning', *Veenkoloniale Volksalmanak* 8 (1996) 9–37.

———, ''k had nooit in mijn stoutste dromen eenigzins gedacht'. De wording van een nieuwe plattelandselite', in I. Botke and H. Maring (eds), *De Groninger boer. De wording van een nieuwe plattelandselite 1775–1875* (Leeuwarden 1999) 5–60.

———, *Boer en heer. 'De Groninger boer' 1760–1960* (Groningen 2002).

Botman, A. and Kenemans, M., 'Sporen en structuren', in A. Verhoeven and O. Brinkkemper (eds), *Twaalf eeuwen bewoning langs de Linge bij De Stenen Kamer in Kerk-Avezaath* (Amersfoort 2001) 59–130.

Botticini, M., 'A tale of benevolent governments: private credit markets, public finance, and the role of Jewish lenders in medieval and Renaissance Italy', *JEH* 60 (2000) 164–89.

Boucheron, P., 'Water and power in Milan, c. 1200–1500', *Urban History* 28 (2001) 180–93.

Bourin, M., *Villages médiévaux en Bas-Languedoc : genèse d'une sociabilité: Xe–XIVe siècle. 1, Du château au village : Xe–XIIe* (L'Harmattan 1987).

———, 'Peasant elites and village communities in the south of France, 1200–1350', *P&P* 195 (2007) 101–14.

Boustan, L., Kahn, M. and Rhode, P., 'Moving to higher ground: migration responses to natural disasters in the early twentieth century', *Amer. Econ. Rev.* 102 (2012) 238–44.

Boutruche, R., *La crise d'une société. Seigneurs et paysans du Bordelais pendant la Guerre de Cent Ans* (Paris 1947).

Bowden, P., 'Agricultural prices, farm profits, and rents', in H. Finberg and J. Thirsk (eds), *The Agrarian History of England and Wales: 1500–1640*, iv (Cambridge 1966) 593–695.

Bowerstock, G., 'Review', *J. Field Archaeology* 18 (1991) 119–21.

Boyer, J-P., '1245–1380: l'éphémère paix du prince', in M. Aurell, J-P Boyer and N. Coulet (eds), *La Provence au Moyen* Âge (Aix-en-Provence 2005) 254–78.

Braams, B., *Weyden en zeyden in het broek: middeleeuwse ontginning en exploitatie van de kommen in het Land van Heusden en Altena* (Wageningen 1995).

Bradbury, R., *The Benin Kingdom and the Edo-speaking peoples of south-western Nigeria* (London 1957).

Bradford, J., *Ancient landscapes* (London 1957).

Brakensiek, S., 'Farms and land – a commodity? Land markets, family strategies and manorial control in Germany (18th–19th centuries)', in B. van Bavel and P. Hoppenbrouwers (eds), *Landholding and land transfer in the North Sea are (late Middle Ages – 19th century)* (Turnhout 2004) 218–34.

Bramall, C. and Jones, M., 'The fate of the Chinese peasantry since 1978', in D. Bryceson, C. Kay and J. Mooij (eds), *Disappearing peasantries? Rural labour in Africa, Asia, and Latin America* (London 2000) 262–78.

Brandler, J., 'Viewpoint: sustainability: Malthus revisited?', *Canadian J. Economics* 40 (2007) 1–38.

Brandt, K., 'Die mittelalterliche Siedlungentwicklung in der Marsch von Butjadingen (Landkreis Wesermarsch). Ergebnisse archäologischer Untersuchungen', *Siedlungforschung* 2 (1984) 123–46.

Braudel, P., *The Mediterranean and the Mediterranean World in the age of Phillip II*, trans. S. Reynolds, ii (New York 1972).

Breen, T., *Tobacco culture: the mentality of the great tidewater planters on the eve of revolution* (Princeton 1985).

Brennan, E., James, A. and Morill, W., 'Inheritance, demographic structure, and marriage: a cross-cultural perspective', *JFH* 7 (1982) 289–98.

Brenner, R., 'Agrarian class structure and economic development in pre-industrial England', *P&P* 70 (1976) 30–75.

———, 'The agrarian roots of European capitalism', *P&P* 97 (1982) 16–113.

———, 'Economic backwardness in eastern Europe in light of developments in the West', in D. Chirot (ed.), *The origins of backwardness in eastern Europe* (Berkeley 1989) 15–52.

Bresc, H., *Un monde méditerranéen:* économie *et société en Sicilie, 1300–1450*, 2 vols (Rome 1986).

Bridenbaugh, C. and Bridenbaugh, R., *No peace beyond the line: the English in the Caribbean, 1624–1690* (New York 1972).

Briffa, K., Jones, P., Schweingruber, F. and Osborn, T., 'Influence of volcanic eruptions on Northern Hemisphere summer temperatures over the past 600 years', *Nature* 393 (1998) 450–55.

Briggs, C., 'Creditors and debtors and their relationships at Oakington, Cottenham and Dry Drayton (Cambridgeshire), 1291–1350', in P. Schofield and N. Mayhew (eds), *Credit and debt in medieval England c.1180–c.1350* (Oxford 2002) 136–43.

———, 'Seigniorial control of villagers' litigation beyond the manor in later medieval England', *Hist. Research* 81 (2008) 399–422.

———, 'Credit and the freehold land market in England, c.1200–c.1350: possibilities and problems for research', in P. Schofield and T. Lambrecht (eds), *Credit and the rural economy in Europe, c. 1100–1850* (Turnhout 2009) 109–27.

———, *Credit and village society in fourteenth-century England* (Oxford 2009).

———, 'Monitoring demesne managers through the manor court before and after the Black Death', in R. Goddard, J. Langdon and M. Müller (eds), *Survival and discord in medieval society. Essays in honour of Christopher Dyer* (Turnhout 2010) 179–95.

Britnell, R., 'The proliferation of markets in England, 1200–1349', *EcHR* 34 (1981) 209–21.

———, *Growth and decline in Colchester, 1300–1525* (Cambridge 1986).

———, 'Feudal reaction after the Black Death in County Durham', *P&P* 128 (1990) 28–47.

———, 'The towns of England and Northern Italy in the early fourteenth century', *EcHR* 64 (1991) 21–35.

———, *The commercialisation of English society, 1000–1500* (Cambridge 1993).

———, 'Specialization of work in England, 1100–1300', *EcHR* 54 (2001) 1–16.

———, *The Winchester pipe rolls and medieval English society* (Woodbridge 2003).

Britton, E., *The community of the vill: a study in the history of the family and village life in fourteenth century England* (Toronto 1977).

Brocklebank, C., 'The Bartlow Hills', *J. British Archaeological Assoc.* 19 (1913) 249–54.

Broegger, J., *Montevarese: a study of peasant society and culture in southern Italy* (Oslo 1971).

Broek, J. van den, *Groningen, een stad apart. Over het verleden van een eigenzinnige stad (1000–1600)* (Assen 2007).

———, 'Graven bij Stootshorn. De verbinding tussen Groningen en het Oldambt gedurende de oorlogsjaren 1580–1594', in G. Collenteur, M. Duijvendak, R. Paping and H. de Vries (eds), *Stad en regio* (Assen 2010) 99–113.

Broekhuis, T., *Voorheen de vooruitgang. Voormalige aardappelmeel- en strokartonfabrieken in de Veenkoloniën* (Amsterdam 1986).

Brown, A. and Foard, G., 'The Saxon landscape: a regional perspective', in *The archaeology of landscape* (Manchester 1998) 67–94.

Brown, J., *In the shadow of Florence: provincial society in Renaissance Pescia* (New York 1982).

———, 'The 'economic decline' of Tuscany: the role of the rural economy', in C. Smyth and G. Garfagnini (eds), *Florence and Milan: comparisons and relations* (Florence 1989) 101–15.

Brown, P., 'Arable land as commons: land reallocation in early modern Japan', *Social Science History* 30 (2006) 431–61.

Browne, D., Cra'ster, M., Denston, C., and Smith, M., 'Archaeological notes', *PCAS* 64 (1973) 28–9.

Bruce-Chwatt, L. and Zulueta, J. de, *The rise and fall of malaria in Europe: a historico-epidemiological study* (Oxford 1980).

Brucker, G., *Renaissance Florence* (Berkeley and Los Angeles 1969).

———, 'Bureaucracy and social welfare in the Renaissance: a Florentine case study', *J. Modern History* 55 (1983) 1–21.

———, 'Florentine voices from the "Catasto", 1427–1480', *I Tatti Studies: Essays in the Renaissance* 5 (1993) 11–32.

———, *Florence, the Golden Age, 1138–1737* (Berkeley and Los Angeles 1998).

Brusse, P., *Overleven door ondernemen. De geschiedenis van de Over-Betuwe 1650–1850* (Wageningen 1999).

———, *Gevallen stad. Stedelijke netwerken en het platteland. Zeeland 1750–1850* (Wageningen 2011).

Brusse, P. and Mijnhardt, W., *Towards a new template for Dutch history. De-urbanization and the balance between city and countryside* (Utrecht 2011).

Buisman, J. and Engelen, A. van, *Duizen jaar weer, wind en water in de lage landen*, 2 vols (Franeker 1996–2000).

Buitelaar, A., *De Stichtse ministerialiteit en de ontginningen in de Utrechtse Vechtstreek* (Hilversum 1993).

Bulgarelli Lukacs, 'La gestione delle risorse collettive nel Regno di Napoli in età moderna: un percorso comparativo', in G. Alfani and R. Rao (eds), *La gestione delle risorse collettive nell'Italia settentrionale (secoli XII-XVIII)* (Milan 2011) 227–45.

Bullard, R., *Dumping in Dixie: race, class, and environmental quality* (Boulder 1990).

Bult, E., 'Moated sites in their economical and social context in Delfland', *Château Gaillard. Etudes de Castellogie Médiévale* (1987) 127–42.

Bult, E. and Hallewas, D., 'Archaeological evidence for the early-medieval settlement around the Meuse and Rhine deltas up to ca. AD 1000', in J. Besteman, J. Bos and H. Heidinga (eds), *Medieval archaeology in the Netherlands. Studies presented to H.H. van Regeteren Altena* (Assen 1990) 71–90.

Bunce, M., *Rural settlement in an urban world* (London 1982).

Buning, L., 'Sociale beroering in Oostelijk Groningen', *Groningse Volksalmanak* (1979) 125–53.

Büntgen, U. and Hellman, L., 'The Little Ice Age in scientific perspective: cold spells and caveats', *JIT* 44 (2013) 353–68.

Cacciamani, G., *L'antica foresta di Camaldoli. Storia e codice forestale* (Arezzo 1965).

———, 'L'antica farmacia di Camaldoli', *Camaldoli Cittadella di Dio* 16 (1968) 103–9.

Caduff, C., 'Publici latrones', *Ricerche Storiche* (1988) 497–522.

Cafagna, L., 'Intorno alle origini del dualismo economico in Italia', in A. Caracciolo (ed.), *Problemi storici dell'industrializzazione e dello sviluppo* (Urbino 1965) 103–50.

Caferro, W., 'City and countryside in Siena in the second half of the fourteenth century', *JEH* 54 (1994) 85–103.

Caiati, V., 'The peasant household under Tuscan mezzadria: a socioeconomic analysis of some Sienese mezzadri households, 1591–1640'. *JFH* 9 (1984) 111–26.

Calabria, A., *The cost of empire: the finances of the Kingdom of Naples in the time of Spanish rule* (Cambridge 1991).

Calamari, G., 'La lega dei comuni di Valdinievole e la loro pace Firenze (1328–1329)', *Bullettino Storico Pistoiese* 28 (1966) 144–59.

Calella, S., *Colonizzazione e ruralizzazione. Un modello: il territorio di Locorotondo, Martina Franca, Aquaro e Dragonetti* (Cardone 1972).

Campbell, B., 'Arable productivity in medieval England: some evidence from Norfolk', *JEH* 43 (1983) 379–404.

———, 'Population pressure, inheritance and the land market in a fourteenth-century peasant community', in R. Smith (ed.), *Land, kinship and life-cycle* (Cambridge 1984) 87–134.

———, 'The complexity of manorial structure in medieval Norfolk: a case study', *Norfolk Archaeology* 39 (1986) 225–61.

———, 'Land, labour, livestock, and productivity trends in English seigniorial agriculture, 1208–1450', in B. Campbell and M. Overton (eds), *Land, labour, and livestock: historical studies in European agricultural productivity* (Manchester 1991) 59–74.

———, 'Ecology versus economics in late thirteenth and early fourteenth century English agriculture', in D. Sweeney (ed.), *Agriculture in the Middle Ages: technology, practice, and representation* (Philadelphia 1995) 76–108.

———, 'Economic rent and the intensification of English agriculture, 1086–1350', in G. Astill and J. Langdon (eds), *Medieval farming and technology: the impact of agricultural change in Northwest Europe* (Leiden 1997) 225–50.

———, *English seigniorial agriculture, 1250–1450* (Cambridge 2002).

———, 'The agrarian problem in the early 14th century', *P&P* 188 (2005) 3–70.

———, 'Nature as historical protagonist: environment and society in pre-industrial England', *EcHR* 63 (2010) 281–314.

Campbell, B. and Bartley, K., *England on the eve of the Black Death: an atlas of lay lordship, land, and wealth, 1300–49* (Manchester 2006).

Campbell, B., Galloway, J., Keene, D. and Murphy, M., *A medieval capital and its grain supply: agrarian production and distribution in the London region, c.1300* (London 1993).

Campopiano, M., 'Land tax 'alā l-misāha and muqānama. Legal theory and the balance of social forces in early medieval Iraq (6th–8th centuries C.E.), *J. Econ. & Social History of the Orient* 54 (2011) 239–69.

———, 'State, land tax and agriculture in Iraq from the Arab Conquest to the crisis of the Abbasid Caliphate (seventh-tenth centuries)', *Studia Islamica* 1 (2012) 5–50.

———, 'Land clearance and water management in the Po Valley in the central and late Middle Ages (ninth-fifteenth centuries): the role of rural communities', *JMH* 39.4 (2013) 377–93.

Camuffo, D. and Enzi, S., 'Reconstructing the climate of Northern Italy from archive sources', in R. Bradley and P. Jones (eds), *Climate since A.D. 1500* (London 1992) 143–54.

Capograssi, M., 'Due secoli di successioni feudali registrati nei cedolari di Terra di Bari', *Rivista Araldica* (1956) 161–210.

Carbone, A., 'Tra storia e demografia: Cassano delle Murge e il catasto onciario del 1752', *Archivio Storico Pugliese* 52 (1999) 135–63.

Caro Baroja, J., 'The city and the country: reflections on some ancient commonplaces', in J. Pitt-Rivers (ed.), *Mediterranean countrymen: essays in the social anthropology of the Mediterranean* (Paris 1963) 27–40.

Carrino, A., 'Messagne: una agrotown?', in *Parentela, mestiere, potere: gruppi sociali in un borgo meridionale di antico regime (Messagne: secoli XVII–XVIII)* (Bari 1995) 17–36.

———, *La città aristocratica. Linguaggi e pratiche della politica a Monopoli fra Cinque e Seicento* (Bari 2000).

Casari, M., 'Emergence of endogenous legal institutions: property rights and community governance in the Italian Alps', *JEH* 67 (2007) 191–225.

Cascella, B., 'I magistri forestarii e la gestione delle foreste', in R. Licinio (ed.), *Castelli, foreste, masserie: potere centrale e funzionari periferici nella Puglia del secolo XIII* (Bari 1991) 47–94.

Casini, T., 'The minor rural aristocracy and great lords in thirteenth-century Tuscany: three cases from the entourage of the Guidi counts', *JMH* 37 (2011) 180–96.

Casparie, W. and Molema, J., 'Het middeleeuwse veenontginningslandschap bij Scheemda', *Palaeohistoria* 22 (1990) 271–89.

Castagnetti, A., 'Primi aspetti di politica annonaria nell'Italia comunale: la bonifica della 'palus comunis Verone (1194–99)', *Studi Medievali* 13 (1974) 363–48.

———, *Le comunità rurali dalla soggezione signorile alla giurisdizione del comune cittadino* (Verona 1983).

Cerman, M., 'Social structure and land markets in late medieval central and east-central Europe', *C&C* 23 (2008) 55–100.

Cernigliaro, A., *Sovranità e feudo nel Regno di Napoli (1505–1557)*, 2 vols (Naples 1983).

Cerrito, E., 'Ambiente, insediamento e regime agrario nella pianura dauna agli inizi del secolo XIX', *Rivista di Storia dell'Agricoltura* 2 (1981) 111–34.

Chao, K., *Man and land in Chinese history* (Stanford 1986).

Chapman, C., *Milocca: a Sicilian village* (Cambridge 1971).

Charge, B., 'Cropmark survey reports 1982–1983', *J. Haverhill & District Arch. Group* 3 (1984) 141–7.

———, 'A field survey of Castle Camps, Cambs.', *J. Haverhill & District Arch. Group* 6 (1997) 132–273.

Cherubini, G., 'Aspetti della proprietà fondiaria nell'aretino durante il XIII secolo', *ASI* 121 (1963) 3–40.

———, 'La signoria degli Ubertini sui comuni rurali casentinesi di Chitgnano, Rosina e Taena all'inizio del Quattrocento', *ASI* 126 (1968) 151–69.

———, 'La carestia del 1346–47 nell'inventario dei beni di un monastero del contado aretino', *Rivista di Storia dell'Agricoltura* 10 (1970) 178–93.

———, *Una comunità dell'Appennino dal XIII al XV secolo: Montecoronaro dalla signoria dell'abbazia del Trivio al Dominio di Firenze* (Florence 1972).

———, 'La società dell'Appennino settentrionale (sec. 13–15)', *Modena* 6 (1972) 23–36.

———, 'Un problema aperto: le crisi della proprietà ecclesiastica fra Quattro e Cinquecento', *Rivista Storica Italiana* 85 (1973) 235–92.

———, 'La società dell'Appennino settentrionale (secoli XIII–XV)', in *Signori, contadini, borghesi: ricerche sulla società italiana del basso medioevo* (Florence 1974) 121–42.

———, 'La 'bannalità' del mulino in una signoria casentinese (1350)', in *Signori, contadini, borghesi: ricerche sulla società italiana del basso medioevo* (Florence 1974) 219–28.

———, 'La proprietà fondiaria nei secoli XV–XVI nella storiografia italiana', *Società e Storia* 1 (1978) 9–33.

———, 'Appunti sul brigantaggio in Italia alla fine del medioevo', in *Studi di storia medievale e moderna per Enesto Sestan: medioevo*, i (Florence 1980) 103–33.

———, 'La 'civiltà' del castagno in Italia alla fine del medioevo', *AM* 8 (1981) 247–80.

———, 'Risorse, paesaggio et utilizzazione agricola del territorio della Toscana sud-occidentale nei secc. XIV–XV', in *Civiltà ed economia agricola in Toscana dei secoli XIII–XV: problemi della vita delle campagne nel tardo medioevo* (Pistoia 1981) 91–115.

———, 'Paesaggio agrario, insediamenti e attività silvo-pastorali sulla montagna tosco-romagnola alla fine del medioevo', in S. Anselmi (ed.), *La montagna fra Toscana e Marche* (Milan 1984) 58–92.

———, 'Il montanaro della novellistica', in R. Zagnoni (ed.), *Homo Appenninicus. Donne e uomini delle montagne* (Pistoia 2007) 7–15.

Cherubini, G. and Francovich, R., 'Forme e vicende degli insediamenti nella campagna Toscana dei secoli XIII–XV', *Quaderni Storici* 24 (1973) 877–905.

Cherubini, G., Indrizzi, G., Lachi, A., Biagini, P., Mandriani, C., Conti, L., Caldelli, A., Tacchetti, G., Gelli, V. and Lorenzini, P., 'La proprietà fondiaria in alcune zone del territorio senese all'inizio del Trecento', *Rivista di Storia dell'Agricoltura* 14 (1974) 2–176.

Chew, S., *World ecological degradation: accumulation, urbanization, and deforestation, 3000 B.C. – A.D. 2000* (Walnut Creek CA 2001).

Chirulli, D. (ed.), *Istoria cronologica della Franca Martina cogli avvenimenti piu notabili del Regno di Napoli* (Martina Franca 1982).
Chittolini, G., 'Un problema aperto: la crisi della proprietà ecclesiastica fra Quattrocento e Cinquecento', *Rivista Storica Italiana* 85 (1973) 353–93.
———, 'Alle origini delle "grandi aziende" della bassa lombarda: l'agricoltura dell'irriguo fra XV e XVI secolo', *Quaderni Storici* 39 (1978) 828–44.
———, 'I capitoli di dedizione delle comunità lombarde a Francesco Sforza: motivi di contrasto fra città e contado', in *Felix olim Lombardia: studi di storia padana in onore di G. Martini* (Milan 1978) 673–93.
———, 'Governo ducale e poteri locali', in *Gli Sforza a Milano e in Lombardia e i loro rapporti con gli stati italiani ed europei (1450–1535)* (Milan 1982) 27–42.
———, 'Legislazione statutaria e autonomie nella pianura bergamasca', in M. Cortesi (ed.), *Statuti rurali e statuti di valle. La provincia di Bergamo nei secoli XIII–XVIII* (Bergamo 1984) 93–114.
———, 'Cities, city-states, and regional states in North-Central Italy', *Theory & Soc.* 18 (1989) 689–706.
Chittolini, G. and Fasano Guarini, E., 'Citta soggette e contadi nel dominio fiorentino tra Quattro e Cinquecento: il caso pisano', in M. Mirri (ed.), *Ricerche di storia moderna*, i (Pisa 1976) 1–94.
Chorley, P., *Oil, silk and enlightenment: economic problems in eighteenth-century Naples* (Naples 1965).
Christie, N., *The Lombards. The ancient Longobards* (Oxford 1997).
Ciampelli, P., *Badia Prataglia antica e moderna* (Bagno di Romagna 1910).
Cipolla, C., 'Une crise ignorée: comment s'est perdue la propriété ecclésiastique dans l'italie du nord entre le XIe et le XVIe siècle', *Annales: ESC* 2 (1947) 317–27.
———, *Before the Industrial Revolution: European society and economy, 1000–1700* (New York 1976).
Ciriacono, S., 'Venise et ses villes. Structuration et déstructuration d'un marché regionale (XVIe–XVIIIe siècle)', *Revue Historique* 276 (1986) 288–9.
———, 'L'economia regionale veneta in epoca moderna. Note a margine del caso bergamasco', in *Venezia e la Terraferma. Economia e società* (Bergamo 1989) 43–76.
———, *Acque e agricoltura. Venezia, l'Olanda e la bonfica europea in Età Moderna* (Milan 1994).
Ciuffreda, A., 'Massari e mercanti di piazza. Storie di famiglia e percorsi individuali nelle medie città pugliesi tra sei e settecento', *Mélanges de l'Ecole Française de Rome* 112 (2000) 173–91.
Clapham, J., 'A thirteenth-century market town: Linton, Cambs', *Cambridge Hist. J.* 4 (1933) 194–202.

Clark, E., 'Social welfare and mutual aid in the medieval countryside', *J. British Stud.* 33 (1994) 405–6.
Clark, G., 'Labour productivity in English agriculture, 1300–1860', in B. Campbell and M. Overton (eds), *Land, labour, and livestock: historical studies in European agricultural productivity* (Manchester 1991) 211–35.
———, 'Commons sense: common property rights, efficiency, and institutional change', *JEH* 58 (1998) 73–102.
———, *A farewell to alms: a brief economic history of the world* (Princeton 2007).
Clark, P., *European cities and towns: 400–2000* (Oxford 2009).
Clark, S., *State and status: the rise of the state and aristocratic power in Western Europe* (Quebec 1995).
Cock, J. de, 'Ontginningsgeschiedenis van de gemeente Slochteren', *Groningse Volksalmanak* 67 (1967) 162–85.
Cofano, A., *Storia antifeudale della Franca Martina* (Fasano 1977).
Cohn, S., 'Criminality and the state in Renaissance Florence, 1344–1466'. *J. Social History* 14 (1980) 211–33.
———, 'Insurrezioni contadine e demografia: il mito della povertà nell montagne toscane (1348–1460)', *SS* 36 (1995) 1023–49.
———, *Women in the streets: essays on sex and power in Renaissance Italy* (Baltimore 1996).
———, 'Inventing Braudel's mountains: the Florentine Alps after the Black Death', in S. Cohn and S. Epstein (eds), *Portraits of medieval and Renaissance living. Essays in honour of David Herlihy* (Ann Arbor 1996) 383–416.
———, *Creating the Florentine State: peasants and rebellion, 1348–1434* (Cambridge 1999).
———, 'Demography and the politics of fiscality', in W. Connell and A. Zorzi (eds), *Florentine Tuscany: structures and practices of power* (Cambridge 2000) 183–206.
———, 'Highlands and lowlands in late medieval Tuscany', in D. Broun and M. MacGregor (eds), *Mìorun Mòr nan Gall, 'The great ill-will of the lowlander'? Lowland perceptions of the highlands, medieval and modern* (Glasgow 2007) 110–27.
———, 'After the Black Death: labour legislation and attitudes towards labour in late-medieval Western Europe', *EcHR* 60 (2007) 457–85.
Colapietra, R., 'Gli economisti settecenteschi dinanzi al problema del Tavoliere', *Rassegna di Politica e di Storia* 58 (1959) 24–32.
Colclough, N., 'Continuity and change in marriage patterns and group formation in a south Italian town', *L'Uomo* 7 (1994) 17–37.
———, 'How elections are fought in Ascoli: kinship, politics, history and culture', *J. Modern Italian Stud.* 5 (2000) 186–206.

———, 'Invisible patrimonies – Capitoli matrimoniali in ancien régime Ascoli', in H. Grandis and P. Heady (eds), *Distinct inheritances: property, family and community in a changing Europe* (Munster 2003) 145–58.

———, 'Famiglie catastali – la dinamica delle relazioni di parentela e dell'organizzazione familiare nella Ascoli dell'ancien régime', in A. Ventura (ed.), *Onciaro della città di Ascoli 1753* (Foggia 2006) 46–56.

———, 'Variation and change in land use and settlement patterns in South Italy: Ascoli Satriano 1700–1990. The making of a southern agro-town', *History & Anthropology* 21 (2010) 1–17.

Collantes, F., 'The decline of agrarian societies in the European countryside: a case study of Spain in the twentieth century', *Agr. History* 81 (2007) 76–97.

Collantes, F. and Pinilla, V., 'Extreme depopulation in the Spanish rural mountain areas: a case study of Aragon in the nineteenth and twentieth centuries', *Rural History* 15 (2004) 149–66.

Collenteur, G. and Paping, R., 'De arbeidsmarkt voor inwonend boerenpersoneel in het Groningse kleigebied 1830–1920', *NEHA-Jaarboek voor Economische, Bedrijfs- en Techniekgeschiedenis* 60 (1997) 96–135.

Coltelli, D., 'La civiltà del castagno in Lunigiana', *Cronaca e Storia di Val di Magra* 6 (1977) 157–79.

Comba, R., 'La dispersione dell'habitat nell'Italia centro-settentrionale tra XII e XV secolo. Vent'anni di ricerche', *SS* 25 (1984) 765–83.

———, 'Le origini medievali dell'assetto insediativo moderno nelle campagne italiane', in *Storia d'Italia: annali*, viii (Turin 1985) 393–404.

Comino, G., 'Sfruttamento e ridistribuzione di risorse collettive: il caso della confraria del S. Spirito nel Monregalese dei secoli XIII–XVIII', *Quaderni Storici* 81 (1992) 687–702.

Commissie Fotoboek Nieuw-Scheemda/'t Waar, *Tussen 't Zieldaip en 't Grootmoar: view eeuwen leven en werken in Nieuw-Scheemda en 't Waar* (Nieuw Scheemda 1985).

Compagna, F., *La questione meridionale* (Milan 1963).

Condorelli, S., *Un tirrimoti ranni. Lectures du tremblement de terre de Sicile de 1693* (Catania 2012).

Congost, R., 'Property rights and historical analysis: what rights? What history?', *P&P* 181 (2003) 73–106.

Congost, R. and Miguel Lana, J. (eds), *Cerrados, debates abiertos. Análisis histórico y propiedad de la tierra en Europa (siglos XVI–XIX)* (Pamplona 2007).

Congost, R. and Santos, R., 'Working out the frame: from formal institutions to the social contexts of property', in R. Congost and R. Santos (eds), *Contexts of property: the social embeddedness of property rights to land in Europe in historical perspective* (Turnhout 2010) 15–38.

Coniglio, G., *Il viceregno di Napoli nel secolo XVII. Notizie sulla commerciale e finanziaria secondo nuove ricerche negli archivi italiani e spagnoli* (Rome 1955).

Conti, E., *La formazione della struttura agraria moderna. I catasti agrari della Repubblica fiorentina e il catasto particellare toscano (secoli XIV–XIX)*, iii (Rome 1966).

———, 'Le proprietà fondiarie del vescovado di Firenze nel Dugento', in R. Nelli (ed.), *Signoria ecclesiastica e proprietà cittadina: Monte di Croce tra XIII e XIV secolo* (Pontassieve 1985) xi–xliii.

Cooper, C. and Block, R., *Disaster: Hurricane Katrina and the failure of homeland security* (New York 2006).

Coote, P. and Parker, D., 'Agrarian class structure and the development of capitalism: France and England compared', in T. Aston and C. Philpin (eds), *The Brenner Debate: agrarian class structure and economic development in pre-industrial Europe* (Cambridge 1985) 79–90.

Corbier, M., 'La transhumance entre le Samnium et l'Apulie: continuités entre l'époque républicaine et l'époque impériale', in G. d'Henry (ed.), *La romanisation du Samnium aux IIe et le siècles av. J.-C.* (Naples 1991) 149–67.

Corbin, J., 'Social class and patron-clientage in Andalusia: some problems of comparing ethnographies', *Anthropological Quart.* 52 (1979) 99–114.

Cormio, A., 'Le campagne pugliesi nella fase di transizione (1880–1914', in *La modernizzazione difficile. Città e campagne nel Mezzogiorno dall'età giolittiana al fascismo* (Bari 1983) 147–216.

Corona, G., *Demani ed individualismo agrario nel Regno di Napoli (1780–1806)* (Naples 1995).

Cortese, M., 'L'incastellamento nel territorio di Arezzo (secoli X–XII)', in R. Francovich and M. Ginatempo (eds) *Castelli. Storia e archeologia del potere nella Toscana medievale* (Florence 2002) 67–109.

Coss, P., *The origins of the English gentry* (Cambridge 2003).

Coulet, N., 'Encore les villages disparus. Dépeuplement et repeuplement autour d'Aix-en-Provence, XIVe–XVIe siècles', *Annales: ESC* 28 (1973) 1463–83.

Coupland, S., 'Trading places: Quentovic and Dorestad reassessed', *Early Med. Europe* 11 (2002) 209–32.

Crais, C., *White supremacy and black resistance in pre-industrial South Africa: the making of the colonial order in the Eastern Cape, 1700–1865* (Cambridge 1992).

Crosby, A., *The Columbian exchange: biological and cultural consequences of 1492* (Westport 1972).

———, 'Virgin soil epidemics as a factor in the Aboriginal depopulation in America', *William & Mary Quart.* 33 (1976) 289–99.

———, *Ecological imperialism: the biological expansion of Europe, 900–1900* (Cambridge 1986).

———, 'Infectious disease and the demography of the Atlantic peoples', *J. World Hist* 2 (1991) 119–33.

Cruyningen, P. van, 'Profits and risks in drainage projects in Staats-Vlaanderen, c. 1590–1665', *Jaarboek voor Ecologische Geschiedenis* (2005/6) 123–42.

———, 'State, property rights and sustainability of drained areas along the North Sea coast, sixteenth-eighteenth centuries', in B. van Bavel and E. Thoen (eds), *Rural societies and environments at risk. Ecology, property rights and social organisation in fragile areas (Middle Ages-twentieth century)* (Turnhout 2013) 181–207.

Culbert, T., 'The collapse of classic Maya civilization', in N. Yoffee and G. Cowgill (eds), *The collapse of ancient states and civilizations* (Tuscon 1988) 69–101.

Cuny, F., *Disasters and development* (New York 1983).

Cuoco, P., 'La funzione del catasto onciario attraverso la sua disciplina giuridica', in M. Mafrici (ed.), *Il Mezzogiorno settecentesco attraverso i catasti onciari. Aspetti e problemi della catastazione borbonica*, i (Naples 1983) 148–58.

Curtis, D., 'Florence and its hinterlands in the late Middle Ages: contrasting fortunes in the Tuscan countryside, 1300–1500', *JMH* 38 (2012) 472–99.

———, 'Tine De Moor's 'Silent Revolution'. Reconsidering her framework for explaining the emergence of institutions for the collective management of resources', *International J. Commons* 7 (2013) 209–29.

———, 'Is there an "agro-town" model for Southern Italy? Exploring the diverse roots and development of the agro-town structure through a comparative case study in Apulia', *C&C* 28.3 (2013) 377–419.

———, 'The emergence of concentrated settlements in medieval Western Europe: explanatory frameworks in the historiography', *Canadian J. History* 48.2 (2013) 223–51.

———, 'The impact of land accumulation and consolidation on population trends in the pre-industrial period: two contrasting cases in the Low Countries', *Hist. Research* 87 (2014).

Curtis, D. and Campopiano, M., 'Medieval land reclamation and the creation of new societies. Comparing Holland and the Po Valley, 800–1500', *JHG* 44 (2014), 93–103.

Cutileiro, J., *A Portuguese rural society* (Oxford 1971).

Dahlman, C., *The open field system and beyond* (Cambridge 1980).

———, 'The tragedy of the commons that wasn't: on technical solutions to the institutions game', *Population & Environment: J. Interdisciplinary Stud.* 12 (1991) 285–96.

Dal Lago, E., *Agrarian elites: American slaveholders and southern Italian landowners, 1815–1861* (Baton Rouge 2005).

Dam, P. van, 'Sinking peat bogs: environmental change in Holland, 1350–1550', *Env. History* 6 (2001) 32–45.

———, 'Digging for a dike. Holland's labor market ca. 1510' in P. Hoppenbrouwers and J.L. van Zanden (eds), *Peasants into farmers? The*

transformation of rural economy and society in the Low Countries (Middle Ages – 19th century) in light of the Brenner Debate (Turnhout 2001) 220–56.
———, 'Water en land', *BMGN* 124 (2009) 459–66.
Dameron, G., *Episcopal power and Florentine society, 1000–1320* (Cambridge MA 1991).
Da Molin, G., 'Family forms and domestic service in southern Italy from the seventeenth to the nineteenth century', *JFH* 15 (1990) 504–27.
———, *La famiglia nel passato. Strutture familiari nel Regno di Napoli in età moderna*, ii (Bari 1995).
Daniele, V. and Malanima, P., 'Il prodotto delle regioni e il divario Nord-Sud in Italia, 1861–2004', *Rivista di Politica Economica* 97 (2007) 267–315.
Dansma, D. and Kok, J., 'Ingedroogde harten? Partnerkeuze en sociale reproductie van de Noord-Hollandse boerenstand in de negentiende en vroeg-twintigste eeuw', in J. Kok and M. van Leeuwen (eds), *Genegenheid en gelegenheid. Twee eeuwen partnerkeuze en huwelijk* (Amsterdam 2005) 285–308.
Dash, N., Peacock, W. and Morrow, B., 'And the poor get poorer: a neglected black community', in W. Peacock, B. Morrow and H. Gladwin (eds), *Hurricane Andrew: ethnicity, gender and the sociology of disaster* (London 1997) 206–25.
Dasmann, R., 'Environmental changes before and after the Gold Rush', in J. Rawls, J. Orsi and M. Smith-Baranzini (eds), *A golden state: mining and economic development in gold rush California* (Los Angeles 1999) 105–22.
Davidsohn, R., *Forschungen zur* älteren *Geschichte von Florenz*, i (Berlin 1896).
———, *Storia di Firenze*, i (Florence 1956).
Davies, M. and Kissock, J., 'The feet of fines, the land market, and the English agricultural crisis of 1315 to 1322', *JHG* 30 (2004) 215–30.
Davies, T., 'Village-building in Sicily: an aristocratic remedy for the crisis of the 1590s', in P. Clark (ed.), *The European crisis of the 1590s. Essays in comparative history* (London 1985) 191–208.
Davis, J., *Land and family in Pisticci* (London 1973).
———, *The people of the Mediterranean: an essay in comparative social anthropology* (London 1977).
———, 'Remapping Italy's path to the twentieth century', *J. Modern History* 66 (1994) 291–320.
———, 'Casting off the 'Southern Problem': or the peculiarities of the South reconsidered', in J. Schneider (ed.), *Italy's Southern Question. Orientalism in one country* (Oxford 1998) 205–24.
———, *Naples and Napoleon: Southern Italy and the European revolutions, 1780–1860* (Oxford 2006).
Davison, A., 'The evolution of settlement in three parishes in south-east Norfolk', *East Anglian Archaeology* 49 (1990) 1–93.

Dean, W., *With broadax and firebrand: the destruction of the Brazilian Atlantic forest* (Berkeley 1995).

De Felice, F., *L'agricoltura di Terra di Bari dal 1880 al 1914* (Milan 1971).

De Gennaro, G., 'Le lane di Puglia nel basso medioevo', in M. Spallanzani (ed.), *La lana come materia prima. I fenomeni della sua produzione e circolazione nei secoli XIII–XVII* (Florence 1974) 149–67.

De Jonge, E., 'De hopteelt in Gelderland (15e–19e eeuw). Het telen, oogsten, eesten en verhandelen van een ingrediënt', *BMGelre* 102 (2012) 78.

Dejongh, G. and Thoen, E., 'Arable productivity in Flanders and the former territory of Belgium in a long-term perspective (from the Middle Ages to the end of the Ancien Régime)', in B. van Bavel and E. Thoen (eds), *Land productivity and agro-systems in the North Sea area (Middle Ages – 20th century). Elements for comparison* (Turnhout 1999) 30–64.

Dekker, A., 'Buurmalsen, een merkwaardig dorp', *HKWB* 9 (1979) 4–9.

Dekker, C., *Het Kromme Rijngebied in de middeleeuwen: een institutioneel-geografische studie* (Utrecht 1983).

De Keyzer, M., 'The common denominator: regulation of the community of users of common waste within the Campine Area during the 16th century', in F. Aparisi and V. Royo (eds), *Beyond lords and peasants: rural elites and economic differentiation in pre-modern Europe* (Valencia 2013) 217–38.

———, 'The impact of different distributions of power on access rights to the common wastelands: the Campine, Brecklands, and Geest compared', *J. Institutional Economics* 9 (2013) 517–42.

Delano Smith, C., 'Ancient landscapes of the Tavoliere, Apulia', *Trans. Inst. British Geographers* 41 (1967) 203–8.

———, 'Villages désertés dans les Pouilles: le Tavolière', in *I paesaggi rurali europei* (Perugia 1975) 125–40.

Delille, G., *Famiglia e proprietà nel Regno di Napoli, XV–XIX secolo* (Turin 1988).

———, 'La famiglia Contadina nell'Italia moderno', in P. Bevilacqua (ed.), *Storia dell'agricoltura Italiana in età contemporanea: uomini e classi*, ii (Venice 1990) 507–34.

Della Bordella, P., *L'arte della lana in Casentino. Storia dei lanifici* (Cortona 1996).

Delort, R., *Le commerce des fourrures en Occident* à *la fin du moyen age (vers 1300–vers 1450)*, i (Rome 1978).

Deméelas, M-D. and Vivier, N. (eds), *Les propriétés collectives face aux attaques libérales (1750–1914). Europe occidentale et Amérique latine* (Rennes 2003).

De Moor, T., 'The Silent Revolution: a new perspective on the emergence of commons, guilds, and other forms of corporate collective action in Western Europe', *IRSH* 53 (2008) 179–212.

———, 'Avoiding tragedies: a Flemish common and its commoners under the pressure of social and economic change during the eighteenth century', *EcHR* 62 (2009) 1–22.

De Moor, T., Shaw-Taylor, L. and Warde, P. (eds), *The management of common land in north west Europe, c. 1500–1850* (Turnhout 2002).
De Moor, T. and Zanden, J.L. van, 'Girl power: the European Marriage Pattern and labour markets in the North Sea region in the late medieval and early modern period', *EcHR* 63 (2010) 1–33.
De Munck, B., Lourens, P. and Lucassen, J., 'The establishment and distribution of craft guilds in the Low Countries, 1000–1800', in M. Prak, C. Lis, J. Lucassen and H. Soly (eds), *Craft guilds in the early modern Low Countries: work, power, and representation* (Farnham 2006) 32–73.
Dennison, T., 'Contract enforcement in Russian serf society', *EcHR* EV (2013) 1–18.
Dennison, T. and Ogilvie, S., 'Serfdom and social capital in Bohemia and Russia', *EcHR* 60 (2007) 513–44.
De Rosa, L., *La provincia subordinata. Saggio sulla questione meridionale* (Rome 2004).
Despy, G., 'Villes et campagnes aux IX et Xe siècles. L'exemple du pays mosan', *Revue du Nord* 50 (1968) 145–68.
Devailly, G., *Le Berry du Xe siècle au milieu du XIIIe:* étude *politique, religieuse, sociale et* économique (Paris 1973).
Devroey, J-P., 'Mansi absi: indices de crise ou de croissance de l'économie rurale du haut Moyen Age?', *Le Moyen Age* 82 (1976) 97–118.
De Wachter, A., 'De opname van de Kempen in het hertogdom Brabant (elfde tot dertiende–veertiende eeuw). Een politiek-geografische probleemstelling', *Tijdschrift van de Belgische Vereniging voor Aardrijkskundige Studies* 68 (1999) 111–40.
Dewindt, E., *Land and people in Holywell-cum-Needingworth: structures of tenure and patterns of social organisation in an east Midlands village, 1252–1457* (Toronto 1971).
DeWitte, S. and Slavin, P., 'Between famine and death: England on the eve of the Black Death – evidence from paleoepidemiology and manorial accounts', *JIT* 44 (2013) 37–60.
Diamond, J., *Guns, germs, and steel: the fates of human societies* (New York 1997).
———, *Collapse: how societies choose to fail or succeed* (New York 2005).
Di Cicco, P., *Il Tavoliere di Puglia nella prima metà del XIX secolo* (Foggia 1966).
———, 'Il problema della Dogana delle Pecore nella seconda metà del XVIII secolo', *La Capitanata* 4 (1966) 63–72.
———, *Censuazione ed affrancazione del Tavoliere di Puglia (1789–1865)* (Rome 1964).
Dickinson, R., *The population problem of Southern Italy: an essay in social geography* (Syracuse 1955).
———, 'Dispersed settlement in southern Italy', *Erdkunde* 10 (1956) 282–97.

Di Ciommo, E., 'Piccole e medie città meridionali tra antico regime e periodo napoleonico', in *Villes et territoire pendant la période napoléonienne (France et Italie)* (Rome 1987) 355–42.

Dijkman, J., *Shaping medieval markets: the organisation of commodity markets in Holland, c. 1200–1450* (Leiden 2011).

Dijkstra, C., 'De Oldambten tegen de stad – een vruchteloze strijd', *Groningse Volksalmanak* (1974/5) 39–58.

Dijkstra, M., *Rondom de mondelingen van Rijn en Maas* (Leiden 2011).

Dikötter, F., *Mao's Great Famine. The history of China's most devastating catastrophe, 1958–62* (London 2010).

Di Michele, V., *Locorotondo: rinvenimenti archeologici in Contrada Grofoleo: origini di un centro abitato della Valle d'Itria* (Martina Franca 1986).

———, 'Fermenti di rivolta anti baronale nella Locorotondo della prima metà del Settecento', *Locorotondo* 4 (1988) 110–20.

Dirks, R., *The black saturnalia: conflict and its ritual expression on British West Indian slave plantations* (Gainesville 1987).

Djurfeldt, G., 'Classes as clients of the state: landlords and labourers in Andalusia', *CSSH* 35 (1993) 159–82.

Dobson, M., 'Marsh fever: the geography of malaria in England', *JHG* 6 (1980) 357–89.

Dodds, B., 'Estimating arable output using Durham Priory tithe receipts, 1341–1450', *EcHR* 57 (2004) 245–85.

Doesburg, J. van, 'Medieval castles in the Dutch central river area: towers of power?', *Concilium Medii Aevi* 14 (2011) 63–78.

Doesburg, J. van and Schut, P., *Die hofstat tot Zoelen, daer dat hues op. plach te staen – Een waarderend booronderzoek op. de motte Aldenhaag (gemeente Buren, Gelderland)* (Amersfoort 2007).

Donahue, B., *The great meadow: farmers and the land in colonial Concord* (New Haven 2004).

Doornbos, W., 'De Groningers en hun boeken', *Gruoninga. Jaarboek voor Genealogie, Naam- en Wapenkunde* 41–2 (1996–7) 160–70.

Dorsey, M., 'Globalizing justice: against environmental racism in the age of globalization', in N. Arias and I. Yánez (eds), *Resistance: a path towards sustainability* (Quito 2000) 37–50.

Douglass, W., 'The South Italian family: a critique', *JFH* 5 (1980) 338–59.

Dribe, M. and Lundh, C., 'Gender aspects of inheritance strategies and land transmission in rural Scania, Sweden, 1720–1840', *The History of the Family* 10 (2005) 293–308.

Dribe, M., Olsson, M. and Svensson, P., 'If the landlord so wanted ... Family, farm production, and land transfers in the manorial system', *EcHR* 65 (2012) 746–69.

Driessen, H., 'Male sociability and rituals of masculinity in rural Andalusia', *Anthropological Quart.* 56 (1983) 125–33.

Du Boulay, F., 'Who were farming the English demesnes at the end of the Middle Ages?', *EcHR* 17 (1964–5) 443–55.

Duby, G., *L'économie rurale et la vie des campagnes dans l'Occident médiéval*, 2 vols (Paris 1962).

———, *Early growth of the European economy* (London 1974).

Dugsdale, W., *The history of imbanking and draining* (London 1772).

Duijvendak, M., 'Storm watching: de invloed van de Cosmas en Damianus stromvloed 500 jaar later', in K. Essink (red.), *Stormvloed 1509 – geschiedenis van de Dollard* (Groningen 2013) 149–55.

Dun, O. and Gemenne, F., 'Defining environmental migration', *Forced Migration Rev.* 31 (2008) 10–11.

Dunbabin, J., 'The revolt of the field: the agricultural labourers' movement in the 1870s', *P&P* 26 (1983) 68–97.

Dunsford, H. and Harris, S., 'Colonization of the wasteland in County Durham, 1100–1400', *EcHR* 56 (2003) 34–56.

Dyer, C., *Lords and peasants in a changing society: the estates of the Bishopric of Worcester, 680–1540* (Cambridge 1980).

———, 'Deserted medieval villages in the West Midlands', *EcHR* 35 (1982) 19–34.

———, 'Changes in the link between families and land in the West Midlands in the fourteenth and fifteenth centuries', in R. Smith (ed.), *Land, kinship and life-cycle* (Cambridge 1984) 305–11.

———, 'The retreat from marginal land: the growth and decline of medieval rural settlements', in M. Aston, D. Austin, and C. Dyer (eds), *The rural settlements of medieval England: studies dedicated to Maurice Beresford and John Hurst* (Oxford 1989) 45–57.

———, 'The consumer and the market in the late Middle Ages', *EcHR* 42 (1989) 305–27.

———, *Standards of living in the later Middle Ages: social change in England, c. 1200–1520* (Cambridge 1989).

———, 'Occupation of the land: the West Midlands', in J. Thirsk and E. Miller (eds), *The Agrarian History of England and Wales, 1348–1500*, iii (Cambridge 1991) 77–91.

———, *Making a living in the Middle Ages. The people of Britain 850–1520* (London 2002).

———, 'Villages and non-villages in the medieval Cotswolds', *Trans. Bristol & Gloucestershire Arch. Soc.* 120 (2002) 11–35.

———, *An age of transition? Economy and society in England in the later Middle Ages* (Oxford 2005).

———, 'Conflict in the landscape: the enclosure movement in England, 1220–1349', *LH* 28 (2006) 21–33.

———, 'The ineffectiveness of lordship in England, 1200–1400', *P&P* 195 (2007) 69–86.

———, 'Were late medieval English villages "self-contained"?', in *The self-contained village? The social history of rural communities 1250–1900* (Hatfield 2007) 6–27.

———, 'Villages in crisis: social dislocation and desertion, 1370–1520', in C. Dyer and R. Jones (eds), *Deserted villages revisited* (Hatfield 2010) 28–45.

Dyer, C. and Jones, R. (eds), *Deserted villages revisited* (Hatfield 2010).

Eckhardt, H., 'Roman barrows and their landscape context: a GIS case study at Bartlow', *Cambridgeshire Britannia* 30 (2009) 65–98.

Eckhardt, H., Clarke, S., Hay, S., Macaulay, S., Ryan, P., Thornley, D. and Timby, J., 'The Bartlow Hills in context', *PCAS* 98 (2009) 47–64.

Edelman, C., 'Oudheidkundige resultaten van de bodemkartering', *Boor en Spade* 4 (1951) 307–26.

Edelman, C. and Edelman-Vlam, A., *Over de perceelsnamen van het Nederlandse rivierkleigebied* (Amsterdam 1949).

Edmonds, R., *Patterns of China's lost harmony. A survey of the country's environmental degradation and protection* (London 1994).

Ehbrecht, W., 'Gemeinschaft, Land und Bund im Friesland des 12. bis 14. Jahrhunderts', in H. van Lengen (ed.), *Die Friesische Freiheit des Mittelalters: Leben und Legende* (Aurich 2003) 154–60.

Elvin, M., 'On water control and management during the Ming and Ch'ing periods: a review article', *Ch'ing-shih Wen-t'I* 3 (1975) 82–103.

———, 'Three thousand years of unsustainable growth: China's environment from archaic times to the present', *East Asian History* 6 (1993) 7–46.

———, 'The environmental legacy of Imperial China', *The China Quart.* 156 (1998) 733–56.

Elvin, M. and Ninghu, S., 'Engineering the sea: hydraulic systems and pre-modern technological lock-in in the Hangzhen Bay area, circa 1000–1800', in I. Suntato and Y. Yoshinori (eds), *Nature and humankind in the age of environmental crisis* (Kyoto 1995) 79–137.

Elrington, C. (ed.), *VCH*, v (London 1968).

Emery, F., 'Moated settlements in England', *Geography* 47 (1962) 378–88.

Emigh, R., 'Loans and livestock: comparing landlords' and tenants' declarations from the Catasto of 1427', *J. Europ. Econ. History* 25 (1996) 705–23.

———, 'The mystery of the missing middle-tenants: the 'negative' case of fixed-term leasing and agricultural investment in fifteenth-century Tuscany', *Theory & Soc.* 27 (1998) 351–75.

———, 'Forms of property rights or class capacities? The example of Tuscan sharecropping', *Archives Européennes de Sociologie* 41 (2000) 22–52.

———, *The undevelopment of capitalism: sectors and markets in fifteenth-century Tuscany* (Philadelphia 2009).

Endfield, G. and O'Hara, S., 'Degradation, drought, and dissent: an environmental history of colonial Michoacán, West Central Mexico', *Annals of the Assoc. Amer. Geographers* 89 (1999) 402–19.

Engelen, G., 'Oude dijken in de westelijke Dollardboezem', *Tijdschrift Koninklijk Nederlands Aardrijkskundig Genootschap* 82 (1965) 72–82.

Ensminger, J., *Making a market: the institutional transformation of an African society* (Cambridge 1996).

Epstein, S., 'The textile industry and the foreign cloth trade in late medieval Sicily (1300–1500): a colonial relationship?', *JMH* 15 (1989) 141–83.

———, 'Cities, regions and the late medieval crisis: Sicily and Tuscany compared', *P&P* 130 (1991) 3–50.

———, *An island for itself: economic development and social change in late medieval Sicily* (Cambridge 1992).

———, 'Town and country: economy and institutions in late medieval Italy', *EcHR* 46 (1993) 453–77.

———, 'Regional fairs, institutional innovation, and economic growth in late-medieval Europe', *EcHR* 47 (1994) 459–82.

———, 'Tuscans and their farms', *Rivista di Storia Economica* 11 (1994) 111–23.

———, 'Moral hazard and risk sharing in late medieval Tuscany', *Rivista di Storia Economica* 11 (1994) 131–7.

———, 'The peasantries of Italy', in T. Scott (ed.), *The peasantries of Europe from the fourteenth to the eighteenth century* (London 1998) 75–109.

———, *Freedom and growth: the rise of states and markets in Europe, 1300–1750* (London 2000).

———, 'Market structures', in W. Connell and A. Zorzi (eds), *Florentine Tuscany: structures and practices of power* (Cambridge 2000) 90–121.

Es, W. van, 'Dorestad centred', in J. Besteman, J. Bos and H. Heidinga (eds), *Medieval archaeology in the Netherlands. Studies presented to H.H. van Regeteren Altena* (Assen 1990) 151–82.

———, 'Volksverhuizing en continuiteit', in W. van Es and W. Hessing (eds), *Romeinen, Friezen en Franken in het hart van Nederland; van Traiectum tot Dorestad 50 v. C. – 900 n. C.* (Utrecht 1994) 64–81.

———, 'Friezen, Franken en Vikingen', in W. van Es and W. Hessing (eds), *Romeinen, Friezen en Franken in het hart van Nederland; van Traiectum tot Dorestad 50 v. C. – 900 n. C.* (Utrecht 1994) 82–119.

Es, W. van, Doesburg, J. van and Koningsbruggen, I. van, *Van Dorestad naar Wijk bij Duurstede. Het ontstaan van een stad ca. 600–1500 na Chr.* (Abcoude 1998).

Escaleras, M., Anbarci, N. and Register, C., 'Public sector corruption and major earthquakes: a potentially deadly interaction', *Public Choice* 132 (2007) 209–30.

Ey, J., 'Late medieval and early-modern reclamation of marsh lands: the role of the state and of village communities. A case-study of the north-western Weser-marshes under the Counts of Oldenburg', in H-J., Nitz (ed.), *The medieval and early-modern rural landscape of Europe under the impact of the commercial economy* (Göttingen 1987) 211–7.

Fabbri, C., *Statuti e riforme del comune di Terranuova, 1487–1685* (Florence 1989).

Faini, E., 'Da Bagno a Ripoli a Firenze (e ritorno)', in P. Pirillo (ed.), *Alle porte di Firenze: il territorio di Bagno a Ripoli in età medievale* (Rome 2008) 41–56.

Faith, R., 'Seigneurial control of women's marriage', *P&P* 99 (1983) 133–48.

———, *The English peasantry and the growth of lordship* (London 1997).

Fantoni, G., *L'acqua a Milano. Uso e gestione nel basso medioevo (1385–1535)* (Bologna 1990).

Farmer, D., 'Prices and wages, 1350–1500', in E. Miller (ed.), *The Agrarian History of England and Wales: 1348–1500*, iii (Cambridge 1991) 431–525.

Farolfi, B., *Strutture agrarie e crisi cittadina nel primo Cinquecento bolognese* (Bologna 1977).

Fauve-Chamoux, A., 'Family reproduction and stem-family system: from Pyrenean valleys to Norwegian farms', *The History of the Family* 11 (2006) 171–84.

Favia, P., 'Temi, approcci, metodologici, modalità e problematiche della ricerca archeologica in un paesaggio di pianura di età medievale: il caso del Tavoliere di Puglia', in N. Mancassola and F. Saggioro (eds), *Medioevo, paesaggi e metodi* (Mantua 2006) 179–98.

Federico, G., 'L'agricoltura italiana: successo o fallimento?', in P. Ciocca and G. Toniolo (eds), *Storia economica d'Italia 3.1. Industrie, mercati e istituzioni* (Rome 2003) 71–98.

———, 'Ma l'agricoltura meridionale era davvero arretrata?', *Rivista di Politica Economica* 97 (2007) 1–24.

Feenstra, H., *De bloeitijd en het verval van de Ommelander adel (1600–1800)* (Groningen 1981).

———, 'Van stapelrecht en vrije markteconomie. Stad en Ommelanden in de 16de eeuw', in P. Brood (ed.), *Van beeldenstorm tot Reductie van Groningen* (Groningen 1994) 143–82.

———, *Spinnen in het web. Groningse regenten in relatie tot het omringende platteland tijdens de Republiek* (Assen 2007).

Felice, E., 'I divari regionali in Italia sulla base degli indicatori sociali (1871–2001)', *Rivista di Politica Economica* 97 (2007) 359–405.

———, 'Regional value added in Italy, 1891–2001, and the foundation of a long-term picture', *EcHR* 64 (2011) 929–50.

Feller, L., *Les abruzzes médiévales – territoire, économie et société en Italie centrale du IX au XII siècle* (Rome 1998).

———, 'Quelques problèmes liés à l'étude du marché de la terre durant le Moyen Age', in S. Cavaciocchi (ed.), *Il mercato della terra secc. XIII–XVIII* (Prato 2003) 21–45.

Fenicia, G., 'Tendencias comerciales en el Reino de Nápoles durante la primera mitad del siglo XVI (1503–1556)', *Estudis* 19 (1993) 7–38.

Fenoaltea, S., 'Risk, transaction costs, and the organization of medieval agriculture', *ExEH* 13 (1976) 129–51.

———, 'Transaction costs, Whig history, and the common fields', *Politics & Soc.* 16 (1988) 171–240.

———, 'La crescita industriale delle regioni d'Italia dall'Unità alla Grande Guerra: una prima stima per gli anni censuari', *Quaderni dell'Ufficio Ricerche Storiche* 1 (2001) 9–77.

———, *L'economia italiana dall'Unità alla Grande Guerra* (Rome 2006).

Finkler, K., 'From sharecroppers to entrepreneurs: peasant household production strategies under the Ejido system of Mexico', *Econ. Development & Cultural Change* 27 (1978) 103–20.

Fiumi, E., 'La demografia fiorentina nelle pagine di Giovanni Villani', *ASI* 108 (1950) 78–158.

———, *Storia economica e sociale di San Gimignano* (Florence 1961).

———, 'La popolazione del territorio volterrano-sangimignanese ed il problema demografico dell'età comunale', in *Studi in onore di A. Fanfani*, i (Milan 1962) 248–90.

Flinn, M., *The European demographic system, 1500–1820* (Baltimore 1981).

Foard, G., 'Systematic fieldwalking and the investigation of Saxon settlement in Northamptonshire', *World Archaeology* 9 (1978) 357–74.

Folkerts, A., 'Op. zoek naar Romeinen en Batavieren in de Betuwe', *HKWB* 20 (1992) 35–8.

Formsma, W., 'Staatsinstellingen', in W. Formsma, M. Buist and W. Koops (eds), *Historie van Groningen. Stad en land* (Groningen 1976) 277–92.

———, *Beklemrecht en landbouw. Een agronomisch-historische studie over beklemrecht in Groningen, in vergelijking met ontwikkelingen elders* (Groningen 1980).

Formsma, W. Luitjens-Dijkveld Stol, R. and Pathuis, A., *De Ommelander borgen en steenhuizen* (Assen 1987).

Forquet, G., 'Das Erdbeben in Basel 1356. Für eine Kulturgeschichte der Katastrophen', *Basler Zeitschrift für Geschichte und Altertumskunde* 103 (2003) 31–49.

Fossier, R., 'L'économie cistercienne dans les plaines du nord-ouest d'Europe', in *Flaran 3, L'économie cistercienne-Géographie-Mutations* (Auch 1983) 53–75.

Fothergill, A., 'Gender, risk, and disaster', *Int. J. Mass Emergencies & Disasters* 14 (1996) 33–56.

Fothergill, A. and Peek, L., 'Poverty and disasters in the United States: a review of recent sociological findings', *Natural Hazards* 32 (2004) 89–110.

Fox, C., *The archaeology of the Cambridge region* (London 1923).

Fox, H., 'Some ecological dimensions of medieval field systems', in K. Biddick (ed.), *Archaeological approaches to medieval Europe* (Kalamazoo 1984) 119–58.

———, 'Exploitation of the landless by lords and tenants in early medieval England', in Z. Razi and R. Smith (eds), *Medieval society and the manor court* (Oxford 1996) 518–69.

———, 'The Wolds before c. 1500', in J. Thirsk (ed.), *Rural England* (Oxford 2000) 50–61.

———, *The evolution of the fishing village: landscape and society along the South Devon coast, 1086–1550* (Leicester 2001).

Francovich, R., 'The beginnings of hilltop villages in early medieval Tuscany', in J. Davis and M. McCormick (eds) *The long morning of medieval Europe: new directions in early medieval studies* (Aldershot 2008) 55–82.

Francovich, R., Augenti, A., Farinelli, R. and Elena Cortese, M., 'Verso un atlante dei castelli della Toscana: primi risultati', in S. Gelichi (ed.), *I congresso nazionale di archeologia medievale* (Florence 1997) 97–101.

Francovich, R., Boldrini, E. and Di Luca, D., 'Archeologia delle terre nuove in Toscana: il caso di San Giovanni Valdarno', in R. Comba and A. Settia (eds), *I borghi nuovi, secoli XII–XIV* (Cuneo 1993) 155–94.

Francovich, R. and Hodges, R., *Villa to village* (London 2003).

Frankema, E., *Has Latin America always been unequal? A comparative study of asset and income inequality in the long twentieth century* (Leiden 2009).

Franklin, P., 'Gloucestershire's medieval taxpayers', *Local Population Stud.* 54 (1995) 22–5.

Frêche, G., *Toulouse et la région Midi-Pyrénées au siècle des lumières (vers 1670–vers 1789)* (Paris 1974).

Freeman, S., 'Corporate village organization in the Sierra Ministra: an Iberian structural type' *Man* 3 (1968) 477–87.

Freedman, P., *The origins of peasant servitude in medieval Catalonia* (Cambridge 2004).

French, H. and Hoyle, R., 'English individualism refuted: and reasserted: the land market of Earls Colne (Essex), 1550–1750', *EcHR* 56 (2003) 595–622.

Friedmann, F., 'The world of "la miseria"', *Partisan Rev.* 20 (1953) 218–31.

Friedrich, W., *125 jaar de fabriek. Karton in Nieuweschans* (Nieuweschans 1995).

Frieswijk, J., *Om een beter leven. Strijd en organisatie van land- en veenarbeiders in het noorden van Nederland (1850–1914)* (Leeuwarden 1989).

———, (ed.), *Fryslân, staat en macht, 1450–1650* (Hilversum 1999).
Fukuyama, F., *Trust: the social virtues and the creation of prosperity* (New York 1995).
Fumagalli, V., *Terra e società nell'Italia padana. I secoli IX e X* (Turin 1976).
———, 'L'evoluzione dell'economia agraria e dei patti colonici dall'alto al basso Medioevo. Osservazioni su alcune zone dell'Italia settentrionale', in B. Andreolli, V. Fumagalli and M. Montanari (eds), *Le campagne italiane prima e dopo il Mille. Una società in trasformazione* (Bologna 1985) 13–42.
———, 'Il paesaggio si trasforma. Colonizzazione e bonifica durante il Medioevo. L'esempio emiliano', in B. Andreolli, V. Fumagalli and M. Montanari (eds), *Le campagne italiane prima e dopo il Mille. Una società in trasformazione* (Bologna 1985) 95–132.
Gabaccia, D., *From Sicily to Elizabeth Street: housing and social change among Italian immigrants, 1880–1930* (New York 1984).
Galassi, F. 'Tuscans and their farms: the economics of share tenancy in fifteenth-century Florence', *Rivista di Storia Economica* 9 (1992) 77–94.
Galassi, F. and Cohen, J., 'The economics of tenancy in early twentieth-century southern Italy', *EcHR* 47 (1994) 585–600.
Galasso, G., *Il Mezzogiorno nella storia d'Italia* (Florence 1977).
———, 'Gli insediamenti e il territorio', in *L'altra Europa. Per un'antropologia storica del Mezzogiorno d'Italia* (Milan 1982) 21–70.
———, 'La provincializzazione del Regno e l'egemonia napoletana nel secolo XVI: il caso pugliese', in D. Fonseca (ed.), *La Puglia tra Barocco e Rococò* (Milan 1982) 373–87.
Galloway, J., 'London's grain supply: changes in production, distribution and consumption during the fourteenth century', *Franco-British Stud.* 20 (1995) 23–34.
———, 'Town and country in England, 1300–1570', in S. Epstein (ed.), *Town and country in Europe, 1300–1800* (New York 2001) 106–31.
———, 'Storm flooding, coastal defence and land use around the Thames estuary and tidal river c. 1250–1450', *JMH* 35 (2009) 171–88.
Galloway, J. and Potts, J., 'Marine flooding in the Thames estuary and tidal river, c. 1250–1450: impact and response', *Area* 39 (2007) 370–79.
Galt, A., 'Social stratification on Pantelleria, Italy', *Ethnology* 19 (1980) 405–25.
———, 'Social class in a mid-eighteenth century Apulian town: indications from the Catasto Onciario', *Ethnohistory* 33 (1986) 419–47.
———, *Far from the church bells: settlement and society in an Apulian town* (Cambridge 1991).
———, 'Marital property in an Apulian town during the eighteenth and early nineteenth centuries', in D. Kertzer and R. Saller (eds), *The family in Italy* (New Haven 1991) 304–20.

———, 'Emphyteusis and indigenous agricultural development: the case of Locorotondo, Italy', in R. Herr (ed.), *Themes in the rural history of the Western world* (Iowa 1993) 67–98.

Gambetta, D., *La mafia siciliana. Un'industria della protezione private* (Turin 1992).

———, 'Can we trust trust?', in *Trust: making and breaking cooperative relations* (Oxford 2000) 213–37.

Ganapati, N., Cheng, S. and Ganapati, S., 'Resilient rural communities: housing recovery patterns following Hurricane Katrina', in E. Kapucu, C. Hawkins and F. Rivera (eds), *Disaster resiliency: interdisciplinary perspectives* (London 2012) 99–120.

Gardiner, M., 'Planned medieval land division in Withyham, East Sussex', *Sussex Arch. Collections* 123 (1985) 109–14.

Gavitt, P., *Charity and children in Renaissance Florence: the Ospedale degli Innocenti 1410–1536* (Ann Arbor 1990).

Gelderblom, O., 'The decline of fairs and merchant guilds in the Low Countries, 1250–1650', *Jaarboek voor Middeleeuwse Geschiedenis* 7 (2004) 199–238.

Genicot, L., *L'économie rurale Namuroise au Bas Moyen Age*, 3 vols (Louvain 1974–82).

———, 'Crisis: from the Middle Ages to modern times', in M. Postan (ed.), *Cambridge economic history of Europe*, i (Cambridge 1966) 703–21.

Georgius, R. and Smet, L. de, (eds), *Honderd jaar Landbouwvereniging 'Nieuwolda-Nieuw-Scheemda' (1860–1960)*, i (Nieuwolda 1960).

Gerding, M., *Vier eeuwen turfwinning. De vervening in Groningen, Friesland, Drenthe en Overijssel tussen 1500 en 1950* (Wageningen 1995).

Germain, R., 'Les migrations comme facteur d'équilibre démographique (Bourbonnais XIVe–XVe siècles)', in *Population et démographie au Moyen Age* (Paris 1995) 251–66.

Gestrich, A., 'Religion in der Hungerkrise von 1816–1817', in M. Jakubowski-Tiessen and H. Lehmann (eds), *Um Himmels Willen. Religion in Katastrophenzeiten* (Göttingen 2003), 275–93.

Gilmore, D., 'Class, culture, and community size in Spain: the relevance of models', *Anthropological Quart.* 49 (1976) 89–106.

———, 'The class consciousness of the Andalusian rural proletarians in historical perspective', *Ethnohistory* 24 (1977) 149–61.

———, 'Patronage and class conflict in Southern Spain', *Man* 12 (1977) 446–58.

———, 'The social organization of space: class, cognition, and residence in a Spanish town', *Amer. Ethnologist* 4 (1988) 437–51.

———, *The people of the plain. Class and community in lower Andalusia* (New York 1980).

Ginatempo, M. and Sandri, L., *L'Italia delle città. Il popolamento urbano tra Medioevo e Rinascimento (secoli XIII–XVI)* (Florence 1990).

Ginsborg, P., *Italy and its discontents: family, civil society, state 1980–2001* (London 2003).

Gissel, S., Jutikkala, E., Osterberg, E., Sandnes, J. and Teitsson, B., *Desertion and land colonization in the Nordic Countries c.1300–1600* (Stockholm 1981).

Glaeser, E., *Triumph of the city: how our greatest invention makes us richer, smarter, greener, healthier, and happier* (New York 2011).

Gleave, M., 'Hill settlements and their abandonment in tropical Africa', *Trans. Inst. British Geographers* 40 (1966) 9–49.

Glennie, P., 'In search of agrarian capitalism: manorial land markets and the acquisition of land in the Lea Valley, c.1450–c.1650', *C&C* 3 (1988) 11–40.

Gobbi Sica, G., *The Florentine villa: architecture, history, society* (Abingdon 2007).

Goddard, R., 'Small boroughs and the manorial economy: enterprise zones or urban failures?', *P&P* 210 (2011) 3–31.

Goelst Meijer, A. van, 'Het verdwenen kasteel Bulckestein', *HKWB* 2 (1974) 2–10.

Goffredo, R. and Ficco, V., 'Tra Ausculum e Herdonia: i paesaggi di età daunia e romana della Valle del Carapelle', in G. Volpe and M. Turchiano (eds), *Faragola 1. Un insediamento rurale nella Valle del Carapelle. Ricerche e studi* (Bari 2010) 25–56.

Goldthwaite, R., 'I prezzi del grano a Firenze dal XIV al XVI secolo', *Quaderni Storici* 10 (1975) 5–36.

———, *The building of Renaissance Florence* (Baltimore 1980).

Goss, S., 'Handing down the farm: values, strategies, and outcomes in inheritance practices among rural German Americans', *JFH* 21 (1996) 192–217.

Goubert, P., *Beauvais et le Beauvaisis de 1600 à 1730. Contribution à l'histoire sociale de la France du XVIIe siècle* (Paris 1960).

Goudschaal, U., *Herinneringen uit mijn bijna zeventigjaren leeftijd* (Groningen 1877).

Goudswaard, B., 'Archeologie en Betuweroute', *BMGelre* 88 (1997) 173–92.

Gout, D., 'Het broodoproer in Groningen in 1847', *Groningse Volksalmanak* (1976/7) 63–84.

Grant, O., *Migration and inequality in Germany 1870–1913* (Oxford 2005).

Grantham, G., 'Divisions of labour, agricultural productivity and occupational specialisation in a pre-industrial France', *EcHR* 46 (1993) 478–502.

———, 'Espaces privilégiés: productivité agricole et zones d'approvisionnement dans l'Europe pré-industrielle', *Annales: Histoire, Sciences Sociales* 52 (1997) 697–725.

Gray, H., *English field systems* (Cambridge MA 1915).

Greif, A., 'Institutions and impersonal exchange: from communal to individual responsibility', *J. Institutional & Theoretical Economics* 158 (2002) 168–204.

———, *Institutions and the path to the modern economy: lessons from medieval trade* (Cambridge 2006).

Grigg, D., *The dynamics of agricultural change: the historical experience* (London 1982).

Grillo, P., 'Comuni urbani e poteri locali nel governo del territorio in Lombardia (XII–inizi XIV secolo)', in L. Chiappa Mauri (ed.), *Contado e città in dialogo. Comuni urbani e comunità rurali nella Lombardia medievale* (Milan 2003) 41–82.

Gritt, A., 'Making good land from bad: the drainage of West Lancashire, c. 1650–1850', *Rural History* 19 (2008) 1–27.

Groenendijk, H., 'Middeleeuwse bedijking aan de rand van de Dollard bij Zuidbroek', *Paleo-aktueel* 2 (1991) 47–51.

Groenendijk, H. and Molema, J., 'Het 'Ol Kerkhof' van Scheemda: een kerk onder klei', *Noorderbreedte* 13 (1989) 8–10.

Groenendijk, H. and Schwarz, W., 'Mittelalterliche Besiedlung der Moore im Einflussbereich des Dollarts', *Archäologische Mitteilungen aus Nordwestdeutschland* 14 (1991) 39–68.

Groenendijk, H. and Bärenfänger, R., *Gelaagd landschap; veenkolonisten en kleiboeren in het Dollardgebied* (Bedum 2008).

Grohmann, A., *La fiere del Regno di Napoli in età aragonese* (Naples 1969).

Grossi, P., *Le abbazie benedettine nell'alto medioevo italiano* (Florence 1957).

Grove, R., Grove, *Green Imperialism: colonial expansion, tropical island edens, and the origins of environmentalism, 1600–1860* (Cambridge 1995).

———, *Ecology, climate, and empire: colonialism and global environmental history, 1400–1940* (Cambridge 1997).

Gruter, E., *La naissance d'un grand vignoble: les seigneuries de Pizay et Tanay en Beaujolais au XVIe et au XVIIe siècles* (Lyon 1977).

Guarducci, P. and Ottanelli, V., *I servitori domestici della casa borghese toscana nel basso medioevo* (Florence 1982).

Guarella, G., 'Niviere e vendita della neve nelle carte del passato', *Riflessioni Umanesimo della Pietra* 11 (1988) 117–24.

———, 'L'università di Locorotondo: i Borassa e le capitolazioni del 1605', *Locorotondo* 4 (1988) 20–40.

Gubbels, M., 'Boeren, bezit en bodemproblemen. Verklaringsmodellen voor de transitie van de Hollandse economie in de late middeleeuwen', *Holland* 42 (2010) 65–84.

Guerra, F., 'El efecto demográfico de las epidemias trás el descubrimiento de América', *Rivista de Indias* 46 (1986) 41–58.

Guidoboni, E., 'Human factors, extreme events and floods in the lower Po Plain (Northern Italy) in the 16th century', *Environment & History* 4 (1998) 279–308.

Guinnane, T. and Miller, R., 'Bonds without bondsmen: tenant-right in nineteenth-century Ireland', *JEH* 56 (1996) 113–42.

Guiso, L., Sapienza, P. and Zingales, L., 'The role of social capital in financial development', *Amer. Econ. Rev.* 94 (2004) 526–56.
Gullino, G., 'Quando il mercante costruì la villa: le proprietà dei Veneziani nella Terraferma', in G. Cozzi and P. Prodi (eds), *Storia di Venezia. Dal Rinascimento al Barocco*, vi (Rome 1994) 875–924.
Gutton, J., *La société et les pauvres en Europe, XVIe–XVIIIe siècles* (Paris 1974).
Haan, H. de, *In the shadow of the tree. Kinship, property and inheritance among farm families* (Amsterdam 1994).
Haarnagel, W., 'De prähistorischen Siedlungsformen in Küstengebiet der Nordsee', in *Beiträge zur Genese der Siedlungs- und Agrarlandschaft in Europa* (Wiesbaden 1968) 67–84.
Habakkuk, H., 'The rise and fall of English landed families, 1600–1800', *Trans. Royal Hist. Soc.* 29 (1979) 187–207.
Haber, S. and Menaldo, V., 'Do natural resources fuel authoritarianism? A reappraisal of the resource curse', *Amer. Pol. Science Rev.* 105.1 (2010) 1–26.
Hadwin, J., 'The medieval lay subsidies and economic history', *EcHR* 36 (1983) 200–17.
Hagen, W., 'Seventeenth-century crisis in Brandenburg: the Thirty Years' War, the destabilization of serfdom, and the rise of absolutism', *AHR* 94 (1989) 302–35.
———, 'Village life in east-Elbian Germany and Poland, 1400–1800: subjection, self-defence, survival', in T. Scott (ed.), *The peasantries of Europe from the fourteenth to the eighteenth centuries* (London 1998) 145–89.
———, *Ordinary Prussians. Brandenburg Junkers and villagers, 1500–1840* (New York 2002).
Hahn, P-M., 'Kriegserfahrungen von Kindern und Jugendlichen im Zeitalter des Dreißigjärigen Krieges', in D. Dahlmann (ed.), *Kinder und Jugendliche in Krieg und Revolution. Vom Dreißigjärigen Krieg bis zu den Kindersoldaten Afrikas* (Paderborn 2000) 1–15.
Halbertsma, H., 'Sporen van verdronken dorpen en verlaten Cisterciënzer kloosters, Dollardgebieden (Groningen)', *Berichten van de Rijksdienst voor het Oudheidkundig Bodemonderzoek* 3 (1952) 18–20.
Hallam, H., *Rural England, 1066–1348* (London 1981).
———, 'Population movements in England, 1086–1350', in *The agrarian history of England and Wales*, ii (Cambridge 1988) 508–94.
Haller, T., *Understanding institutions and their links to resource management from the perspective of new institutionalism* (Bern 2007).
Hamerow, H., 'Settlement mobility and the 'Middle Saxon shift': rural settlements and settlement patterns in Anglo-Saxon England', *Anglo-Saxon England* 20 (1991) 1–17.
———, *Early medieval settlements: the archaeology of rural communities in North-West Europe 400–900* (Oxford 2004).

Hanawalt, B., *Crime and conflict in English communities, 1300–1348* (Cambridge MA 1979).

Hanus, J., 'Real inequality in the early modern Low Countries: the city of 's-Hertogenbosch, 1500–1660', *EcHR* 66 (2013) 733–56.

Hardin, G., 'The tragedy of the commons', *Science* 162 (1968) 1243–8.

Harley, J., 'Population trends and agricultural developments from the Warwickshire Hundred Rolls of 1279', *EcHR* 11 (1958) 8–18.

———, 'The settlement geography of early medieval Warwickshire', *Trans. & Papers of the Inst. British Geographers* 34 (1964) 115–30.

Harris, D., *Plants, animals, and man in the Outer Leeward Islands, West Indies* (Los Angeles 1965).

Harris, S., 'Wastes, the margins and the abandonment of land: the Bishop of Durham's estate, 1350–1480', in C. Liddy and R. Britnell (eds), *North-east England in the later Middle Ages* (Woodbridge 2005) 196–219.

Harris, W., 'War and settlement change: the Gohan Heights and the Jordan Rift, 1967–77', *Trans. Inst. British Geographers* 3 (1978) 309–30.

Harrison, D., 'Bridges and economic development, 1300–1800', *EcHR* 45 (1992) 240–61.

Harriss, G., *King, parliament and public finance in medieval England to 1369* (Oxford 1975).

Hart, M. 't, *The making of a bourgeois state: war, politics, and finance during the Dutch Revolt* (Manchester 1993).

———, 'Intercity rivalries and the making of the Dutch state', in C. Tilly and W. Blockmans (eds), *Cities and the rise of states in Europe, A.D. 1000 to 1800* (Boulder 1994) 196–217.

———, 'Een boerenopstand op. Walcheren. De strijd om het waterschap 1655–1671', *Tijdschrift voor Sociale Geschiedenis* 20 (1994) 265–81.

———, 'Rulers and repertoires: the revolt of a farmers' republic in the early modern Netherlands', in M. Hanagan, L. Page Morch and W. te Brake (eds), *Challenging authority: the historical study of contentious politics* (Minneapolis 1998) 197–212.

Harten, J., 'De ontwikkeling van de landbouw in Groningen gedurende de achttiende en de negentiende eeuw', *Tijdschrift Koninklijk Nederlands Aardrijkskundig Genootschap* 83 (1966) 346–57.

———, 'Oude nederzettingsvormen in de Bommelerwaard', in H. Berendsen (ed.), *Het landschap van de Bommelerwaard* (Amsterdam 1986) 67–90.

———, 'Dorpen in het rivierengebied: speurtocht naar planning', *Nederlandse Geografische Studies* 68 (1988) 155–76.

———, 'De invloed van de mens op. het landschap', in H. de Bruin (ed.), *Het Gelders rivierengebied uit zijn isolement. Een halve eeuw plattelandsvernieuwing* (Zutphen 1988) 16–38.

———, 'Rivierkleilandschap', in S. Barends, J. Renes, T. Stol, J. van Triest, R. de Vries and F. van Woudenberg (eds), *Het Nederlandse landschap. Een historisch geografische benadering* (Utrecht 2005) 92–103.

Harten, J. and Schuyf, J., 'Possible planned medieval villages in the Netherlands', in B. Roberts and R. Glasscock (eds), *Villages, fields and frontiers: studies in European rural settlement in the medieval and early modern periods* (Oxford 1983) 43–59.

Hartman, C. and Squires, G. (eds), *There is no such thing as a natural disaster. Race, class and Hurricane Katrina* (New York 2006).

Harvey, B., 'The population trend in England between 1300 and 1348', *Trans. Royal Hist. Soc.* 16 (1966) 23–42.

———, 'The leasing of the abbot of Westminster's demesnes in the later Middle Ages', *EcHR* 22 (1969) 17–27.

Harvey, I., *Jack Cade's rebellion of 1450* (Oxford 1991).

Harvey, M., 'Regular field and tenurial arrangements in Holderness, Yorkshire', *JHG* 6 (1980) 3–16.

Harvey, P., *A medieval Oxfordshire village, Cuxham, 1240 to 1400* (London 1965).

Harvey, S., 'The knight and the knight's fee', *P&P* 49 (1970) 3–43.

Hatcher, J., *Plague, population, and the English economy 1348–1530* (London 1977).

———, 'English serfdom and villeinage: towards a reassessment', *P&P* 90 (1981) 3–39.

Hauptmeyer, C-H., 'Bäuerlicher Widerstand in den Grafschaften Schaumburg-Lippe, im Fürstentum Calenberg und im Hochstift Hildesheim. Zur Frage der qualitativen Veränderung bäuerlicher Opposition am Ende des 18. Jahrhunderts', in W. Schulze (ed.), *Aufstände, Revolten, Prozesse. Beiträge zu bäuerlichen Widerstandsbewegungen im frühneuzeitlichen Europa* (Stuttgart 1983) 217–32.

Hauser, W., 'Osaka Castle', in J. Mass and W. Hauser (eds), *The Bakufu in Japanese history* (Stanford CA 1985) 153–72.

Haverhill and District Archaeological Group, 'A field survey of sites at Yen Hall, West Wickham, Cambs.', *J. Haverhill & District Arch. Group* 6 (1995) 6–55.

Havik, P., 'De Oldambster boerderij', in O. Knottnerus, P. Brood, W. Deeters and H. van Lengen (eds), *Rund um Eems und Dollart. Historische Erkundungen im Grenzgebiet der Nordostniederlande und Nordwestdeutschlands* (Groningen 1992) 290–303.

Hayhoe, J., 'Litigation and the policing of communal farming in northern Burgundy, 1750–1790', *AgHR* 50 (2002) 51–68.

Hazelhoff, B., 'Wagenborgen aan en van de kust', *Bulletin van de Historische Kring 'De Marne'* 4 (1977) 33–50.

———, 'Het vergeten klooster te Dallingeweer', *Bulletin van de Historische Kring 'De Marne'* 6 (1979) 81–6.

Healey, M., *The ruins of New Argentina: Peronism and the remaking of San Juan after the 1944 earthquake* (Durham NC 2011).

Heidinga, H., 'From Kootwijk to Rhenen: in search of the elite in the Central Netherlands in the early Middle Ages', in J. Besteman, J. Bos and H. Heidinga (eds), *Medieval archaeology in the Netherlands. Studies presented to H.H. van Regeteren Altena* (Assen 1990) 9–40.

Heimpel, H., 'Die Federschnur: Wasserrecht und Fischrecht in der Reformation Kaiser Sigismunds', *Deutsches Archiv für Erforschung des Mittelalters* 19 (1963) 474–88.

Heiningen, H. van, *Dijken en dijkdoorbraken in het Nederlandse rivierengebied* (The Hague 1978).

Held, W., *Zwischen Marktplatz und Anger: Stadt-Land-Beziehungen im 16. Jahrhundert in Thüringen* (Weimar 1988).

Helly, H., 'Case studies', in F. Ferrigni, B. Helly, A. Mauro, L. Mendes Victor, O. Pierotti, A. Rideaud and P. Teves Costa (eds), *Ancient buildings and earthquakes. The local seismic culture approach: principles, methods, potentialities* (Bari 2005).

Heming, L., Waley, P. and Rees, P., 'Reservoir resettlement in China: past experience and the Three Gorges Dam', *The Geog. Journal* 167 (2001) 195–212.

Henderikx, P., *De beneden-delta van Rijn en Maas: landschap en bewoning van de Romeinse tijd tot ca. 1000* (Hilversum 1987).

———, 'De ringwalburgen in het mondingsgebied van de Schelde in historisch perspectief', in R. van Heeringen, P. Henderikx and A. Mars (eds), *Vroeg-middeleeuwse ringwalburgen in Zeeland* (Amersfoort 1995) 71–112.

Henderson, J., *Piety and charity in late medieval Florence* (Oxford 1994).

Herlihy, D., 'Church property on the European continent 701–1200', *Speculum* 36 (1961) 81–105.

———, 'Population, plague and social change in rural Pistoia, 1201–1430', *EcHR* 18 (1965) 225–44.

———, *Medieval and Renaissance Pistoia: the social history of an Italian town, 1200–1430* (New Haven 1967).

———, 'Santa Maria Impruneta: a rural commune in the late Middle Ages', in N. Rubinstein (ed.), *Florentine studies: politics and society in Renaissance Florence* (London 1968) 242–76.

———, *The Black Death and the transformation of the West* (Cambridge 1999).

Herlihy, D. and Klapisch-Zuber, C., *Les toscans et leurs familles: une* étude *du 'catasto' florentin de 1427* (Paris 1978).

———, *Tuscans and their families: a study of the Florentine Catasto of 1427* (New Haven 1985).

Herzfeld, M., *The poetics of manhood: contest and identity in a Cretan mountain village* (Princeton 1985).

Heston, A. and Kumar, D., 'The persistence of land fragmentation in peasant agriculture: an analysis of south Asian cases', *ExEH* 20 (1983) 199–220.

Hibma, A., Hoekstra, W. and Uil, T. (eds), *'We hadden geen keus'. Interviews met landarbeidsters uit het Oldambt 1920–1940* (Groningen 1987).

Higounet, C., *Nouvelle approche sur les bastides du Sud-Ouest aquitain* (Paris 1967).

———, *Les Villeneuves de Piémont et les bastides de Gascogne (XIIe –XIVe siècles)* (Paris 1970).

———, *Paysages et villages neufs d'Aquitane* (Bordeaux 1975).

———, 'Congregare populationem: politiques de peuplement dans l'Europe méridionale (Xe–XIVe siècles)', *Annales de Démographie Historique* (1979) 135–44.

———, 'Les origines et la fondation de la bastide de Vianne (1284)', *Revue de l'Agenais* (1984) 5–24.

———, 'Hospitaliers et Templiers: peuplement et exploitation rurale dans le sud-ouest de la France au Moyen Âge', *Cahiers de Flaran* 6 (1984) 61–78.

Higounet-Nadal, A., *Perpignan aux XIV et XV siècles. Etude de démographique historique* (Bordeaux 1978).

Hildebrandt, H., 'Systems of agriculture in Central Europe up to the tenth and eleventh centuries', in D. Hooke (ed.), *Anglo-Saxon settlements* (Oxford 1998) 81–101.

Hilton, R., *The economic development of some Leicestershire estates in the fourteenth and fifteenth centuries* (Oxford 1947).

———, 'Freedom and villeinage in England', *P&P* 31 (1965) 3–19.

———, 'Villages désertés et histoire économique: recherches françaises et anglaises', *Études Rurales* 32 (1968) 104–9.

———, *Bondsmen made free. Medieval peasant movements and the English rising of 1381* (London 1973).

———, *The English peasantry in the later Middle Ages* (Oxford 1975).

———, 'A crisis of feudalism?', *P&P* 80 (1978) 3–19.

———, 'Les communautés villageoises en Angleterre au Moyen Age', in *Les communautés villageoises en Europe occidentale* (Auch 1984) 118–28.

———, 'Small town society in England before the Black Death', *P&P* 105 (1984) 53–78.

———, 'Medieval market towns', *P&P* 109 (1985) 3–23.

Hinton, D., 'Demography: from Domesday and beyond', *JMH* EV (2013) 1–33.

Ho, P-t., *Studies on the population of China, 1368–1953* (Cambridge MA 1959).

Hobsbawm, E. and Rude, G., *Captain Swing* (London 1969).

Hochstadt, S., *Mobility and modernity. Migration in Germany, 1820–1989* (Michigan 1999).

Hodges, R., 'Dark Ages economics revisited. W.A. van Es and the end of the mercantile model in early medieval Europe', in H. Sarfatij, W. Verwers and P. Woltering (eds), *In discussion with the past. Archaeological studies presented to W.A. van Es* (Zwolle 1999) 227–32.

Hoed, J. den, 'Beschouwingen rond de Culemborgse stadsrechtbrief van 1318', *Spiegel der Historie* 3 (1968) 346–53.

Hoek, C., 'Moated sites in the County of Holland', *Moated Sites Research Group Report* 2 (1975) 18–20.

Hoekman, P., *Socialisme en arbeidersbeweging in het Oldambt 1881–1894* (Groningen 1985).

———, 'Van spontaan verzet naar socialisme', in P. Hoekman, J. Houkes and O. Knottnerus (eds), *Een eeuw socialisme en arbeidersbeweging in Groningen 1885–1985* (Groningen 1986) 29–40.

Hoffman, P., 'The economic theory of sharecropping in early modern France', *JEH* 44 (1984) 303–19.

———, *Growth in a traditional society: the French countryside 1450–1815* (Princeton 1996).

Hoffmann, R., 'Medieval origins of the common fields', in W. Parker and E. Jones (eds), *European peasants and their markets* (Princeton 1975) 23–71.

———, 'Fishing for sport in medieval Europe: new evidence', *Speculum* 60 (1985) 877–902.

———, 'Economic development and aquatic ecosystems in medieval Europe', *AHR* 101 (1996) 631–69.

Hofstee, E., *Het Oldambt. Een sociografie. Deel 1: vormende krachten* (Groningen 1937).

———, 'De ontwikkeling van de huwelijksvruchtbaarheid in het Oldambt in de periode 1880–1950', in *De wereld der mensen. Sociaal-wetenschappelijke opstellen aangeboden aan prof.dr. J.J. Fahrenfort* (Groningen 1955) 295–353.

Holderness, B., 'Open and close parishes in England in the eighteenth and nineteenth centuries', *AgHR* 20 (1972) 126–39.

Holmes, G., *The estates of the higher nobility in fourteenth-century England* (Cambridge 1957).

Hombergh, F. van den, 'Brugman en de broodnijd: problemen rond de Culemborgse paardenmarkt', *De Drie Steden* 8 (1987) 3–9.

Homeier, H., 'Einbruch und weitere Entwicklung des Dollart bis um 1600', *Forschungsstelle für Insel- und Küstenschutz der Niedersächsischen Wasserwirtschaftsverwaltung, Jahresbericht* 28 (1976) 39–81.

Homer-Dixon, T., 'On the threshold: environmental changes as causes of acute conflict', *Int. Security* 16 (1991) 76–116.

———, *The upside of down: catastrophe, creativity, and the renewal of civilization* (Washington 2007).

Hoorn, W. van, *'Reiderland', het verhaal van een Coöperatieve strokartonfabriek* (Winschoten 1968).

Hopcroft, R. and Emigh, R., 'Divergent paths of agrarian change. Eastern England and Tuscany compared', *J. Europ. Econ. History* 29 (2000) 9–51.

Hoppenbrouwers, P., 'Grondgebruik en agrarische bedrijfsstructuur in het Oldambt na de vroegste inpolderingen (ca. 1630 – ca. 1720)', in J. Elerie and P. Hoppenbrouwers (eds), *Het Oldambt, deel 2. Nieuw visies op. geschiedenis en actuele problemen* (Groningen 1991) 73–95.

———, 'Op. zoek naar de "kerels". De dorpsgemeente in de dagen van graaf Floris V', in D. de Boer, E. Cordfunke and H. Sarfatij (eds), *Wi Florens ... De Hollandse graaf Floris V in de samenleving van de dertiende eeuw* (Utrecht 1996) 224–42.

———, 'Agricultural production and technology in the Netherlands, c. 1000–1500', in G. Astill and J. Langdon (eds), *Medieval farming and technology: the impact of agricultural change in northwest Europe, c.1500–1850* (Turnhout 2002) 99–101.

———, 'The use and management of commons in the Netherlands. An overview', in T. De Moor, L. Shaw-Taylor and P. Warde (eds), *The management of common land in north west Europe, c.1500–1850* (Turnhout 2002) 88–112.

Hoppenbrouwers, P. and J.L. van Zanden, 'Restyling the transition from feudalism to capitalism. Some critical reflections on the Brenner Thesis', in P. Hoppenbrouwers and J.L. van Zanden (eds), *Peasants into farmers? The transformation of rural economy and society in the Low Countries (Middle Ages – 19th century) in light of the Brenner Debate* (Turnhout 2001) 19–40.

Hoshino, H., 'Per la storia dell'arte della lana in Firenze nel Trecento e nel Quattrocento: un riesame', *Istituto Giapponese di Cultura. Annuario* 10 (1972–3) 33–80.

Houben, H., *Die Abtei Venosa und das Mönchtum im normannisch-staufischen Süditalien* (Tübingen 1995).

Howard, P., 'The history of ecological marginalization in Chiapas', *Env. History* 3 (1998) 357–77.

Hoyle, R., 'Disafforestation and drainage: the Crown as entrepreneur?', in *The estates of the English crown 1558–1640* (Cambridge 1992) 353–88.

Hoyt, R., 'Farm of the manor and community of the vill in Domesday Book', *Speculum* 30 (1955) 147–69.

Huang, P., *The peasant family and rural development in the Yangzi Delta, 1350–1988* (Stanford 1990).

Huang, T-L., Orazem, P. and Wohlgemuth, D., 'Rural population growth, 1950–1990: the roles of human capital, industry structure, and government policy', *Amer. J. Agr. Econ.* 84 (2002) 615–27.

Humm, A., *Villages et hameaux disparus de basse Alsace. Contribution* à *l'histoire de l'habitat rural, XIIe–XVIIIe siècles* (Strasbourg 1971).

Humphries, J., 'Enclosures, common rights, and women: the proletarianization of families in the late eighteenth and early nineteenth centuries', *JEH* 50 (1990) 17–42.

Hunt, E., *The medieval super-companies: a study of the Peruzzi Company of Florence* (Cambridge 1994).

Hurenkamp, H., 'Groningen van stadstaat tot stad van het noorden', in G. Collenteur, M. Duijvendak, R. Paping and H. de Vries (eds), *Stad en regio* (Assen 2010) 42–56.

Ingen, K. van, 'Enige wetenswaardigheden over het huis Soelen', *Tabula Batavorum* 15 (1997) 6–13.

Innes, F., 'The pre-sugar era of European settlement in Barbados', *J. Caribbean History* 1 (1970) 1–22.

Innes, M., *State and society in the early Middle Ages: the middle Rhine Valley, 400–1000* (Cambridge 2001).

Iriate-Goñi, I., 'Common lands in Spain, 1800–1995: persistence, change and adaptation', *Rural History* 13 (2002) 19–37.

Iriarte-Goñi, I. and Miguel Lana, J., 'The 'concurrence' and 'hierarchization' of rights to property: the case of public lands in Spain', in G. Beaur, P. Schofield, J-M. Chevet and M.T. Pérez Picazo (eds), *Property rights, land markets and economic growth in the European countryside (thirteenth-twentieth centuries)* (Turnhout 2013) 123–38.

Irsigler, F., 'Divites und Pauperes in der Vita Meinwerci. Untersuchungen zur wirtschaftlichen und sozialen Differenzierung der Bevölkerung Westfalens im Hochmittelalter', *Vierteljahrschrift für Sozial- und Wirtschaftsgeschichte* 57 (1970) 449–99.

Jabarin, A. and Epplin, F., 'Impact of land fragmentation on the cost of production of wheat in the rain-fed region of northern Jordan', *Agr. Economics* 11 (1994), 191–6.

Jackson, J., *Migration and urbanisation in the Ruhr Valley, 1820–1914* (Atlantic Highlands 1997).

Jacobi, P., 'Environmental problems in Sao Paolo: the challenge for co-responsibility and innovative crisis management', *J. Contingencies & Crisis Management* 5 (1997) 131–9.

Jager, G. de, 'De Oldambster landbouwer en zijn bedrijf voor 60 jaar en thans', *Groningen, Cultureel Maandblad* 10 (1927) 70–3.

Jager, H., 'Die Ausdehnung der Wälder in Mitteleuropa über offenes Siedlungsland', in *Géographie et histoire agraires* (Nancy 1959) 300–312.

Jakubowski-Tiessen, M., 'Gotteszorn und Meereswüten. Deutungen von Strumfluten vom 16. Bis 19. Jahrhundert', in D. Groh, M. Kempe and F. Mauelshagen (eds), *Naturkatastrophen. Beiträge zu ihrer Deutung, Wahrnehmung und Darstellung in Text und Bild von der Antike bis ins 20. Jahrhundert* (Tübingen 2003) 101–18.

Janssen, H., 'The castles of the Bishop of Utrecht and their function in the political and administrative development of the bishopric', *Château Gaillard. Etudes de Castellologie Médiévale* 7 (1977) 135–57.

———, 'The archaeology of the medieval castle in the Netherlands. Results and prospects for future research', in J. Besteman, J. Bos and H. Heidinga (eds), *Medieval archaeology in the Netherlands. Studies presented to H.H. van Regeteren Altena* (Assen 1990) 219–64.

———, 'Tussen woning en versterking. Het kasteel in de middeleeuwen', in H. Janssen, J. Kylstra-Wielinga and B. Olde Meierink (eds), *1000 jaar kastelen in Nederland: functie en vorm door de eeuwen heen* (Utrecht, 1996), 32–45.

Jacquart, J., *La crise rurale en Ile-de-France, 1550–1670* (Paris 1974).

Jing, J., 'Rural resettlement: past lessons for the Three Gorges project', *The China J.* 38 (1997) 65–92.

———, 'Villages dammed, villages repossessed: a memorial movement in northwest China', *Amer. Ethnologist* 26 (1999) 324–43.

John, T., 'Population change in medieval Warwickshire: Domesday Book to the Hundred Rolls of 1279–80', *Local Population Stud.* 59 (1997) 41–53.

Jones, A. and Kupper, J-L., 'Villes, bourgs et franchises en Wallonie de 1250 à 1477', in H. Hasquin (ed.), *La Wallonie. Le pays et les hommes*, i (Brussels 1982) 131–59.

Jones, E., 'Review', *EcHR* 42 (1989) 634.

———, 'Agricultural origins of industry', *P&P* 40 (1968) 58–71.

Jones, P., 'Florentine families and Florentine diaries in the fourteenth century', *Papers of the British School at Rome* 24 (1954) 183–205.

———, 'A Tuscan monastic lordship in the later Middle Ages: Camaldoli', *J. Ecclesiastical History* 5 (1954) 168–83.

———, 'An Italian estate, 900–1200', *EcHR* 7 (1954) 18–32.

———, 'From manor to mezzadria: a Tuscan case study in the medieval origins of agrarian society', in N. Rubinstein (ed.), *Florentine studies: politics and society in Renaissance Florence* (London 1968) 193–241.

———, *Economia e società nell'Italia medievale* (Turin 1980).

———, *The Italian city-state: from signoria to commune* (Oxford 1997).

Jones, R., 'Contrasting patterns of village and hamlet desertion in England', in C. Dyer and R. Jones (eds), *Deserted villages revisited* (Hatfield 2010) 8–27.

Jones, R. and Lewis, C., 'The Midlands: medieval settlements and landscapes', in N. Christie and P. Stamper (eds), *Medieval rural settlement: Britain and Ireland, AD 800–1600* (Oxford 2012) 186–205.

Jongbloed, H., 'Wanburtich: Heinrichs II. Beteiligung an der Wahl von Kamba (1024)', *Deutsches Archiv für die Erforschung des Mittelalters* 62 (2006) 1–63.

Jordan, W., *The Great Famine. Northern Europe in the early fourteenth century* (Princeton 1996).

Juan O'Neill, B., *Social inequality in a Portuguese hamlet: land, late marriage, and bastardy, 1870–1978* (Cambridge 1987).
Kahn, M., 'The death toll from natural disasters: the role of income, geography, and institutions', *Review of Economics & Statistics* 87 (2005) 271–84.
Kalela-Brundin, M., *Climate information from tree rings* (Umeå 1999).
Kälin, U., *Die Urner Magistraten-Familien. Herrschaft,* ökonomische *Lage und Lebensstil einer ländlichen Oberschicht, 1700–1850* (Zurich 1991).
Kanzaka, J., 'Villein rents in thirteenth-century England', *EcHR* 55 (2002) 593–618.
Kaplan, S., *Provisioning Paris: merchants and millers in the grain trade in the eighteenth century* (Ithaca 1984).
Kaplan, T., *Anarchists of Andalusia, 1868–1903* (Princeton 1973).
Karel, E. and Paping, R., 'The rural succession myth. Occupational careers and household formation of peasants' and farmers' offspring around 1800', *TSEG* 4 (2011) 44–75.
Karl O'Brien, P., 'Final considerations: aristocracies and economic progress under the Ancien Régime', in P. Janssens and B. Yun-Casalilla (eds), *European aristocracies and colonial elites: patrimonial management strategies and economic development, 15th–18th centuries* (Aldershot 2005) 247–64.
Katajala, K., 'Against tithes and taxes, for king and province. Peasant unrest and medieval Scandinavian political culture', in *Northern revolts. Medieval and early modern unrest in the Nordic countries* (Helsinki 2004) 32–52.
Keene, D., 'Medieval London and its region', *London J.* 14 (1989) 99–111.
———, 'The property market in English towns, AD 1100–1600', in J-C Maire Vigueur (ed.), *D'une ville à l'autre: structures matérielles et organisation de l'espace dans les villes européennes (XIIIe–XVIe siècle)* (Rome 1989) 201–26.
Kelly, M. and Ó Gráda, C., 'The waning of the Little Ice Age: climate change in early modern Europe', *JIH* 44 (2013) 301–25.
Kelter, E., 'Das deutsche Wirtschaftsleben des 14. und 15. Jahrhundert im Schatten der Pestepidemien', *Jahrbuch für Nationalökonomie und Statistik* 165 (1953) 161–208.
Kempe, M., 'Noah's flood: the Genesis story and natural disasters in early modern times', *Environment & History* 4 (1998) 279–308.
Kenny, M. and Kertzer, D. (eds), *Urban life in Mediterranean Europe* (Chicago 1983).
Kershaw, I., 'The Great Famine and agrarian crisis in England, 1315–1322', *P&P* 59 (1973) 3–50.
Ketelaar, F., *Oude zakelijke rechten vroeger, nu en in de toekomst* (Zwolle 1978).
Keuning, H., *De Groninger Veenkoloniën: een sociaal-geografische studie* (Amsterdam 1933).
———, *De regio Groningen* (Groningen 1974).

Kim, N., 'How much more exposed are the poor to natural disasters? Global and regional measurement', *Disasters* 36 (2012) 195–211.

Kimber, C., *Martinique revisited: the changing plant geographies of a West Indian island* (College Station 1988).

Kish, G., 'The marine of Calabria', *Geog. Rev.* 43 (1953) 495–505.

Kiss, A., 'Floods and weather in 1342 and 1343 in the Carpathian Basin', *J. Env. Geography* 2 (2009) 37–47.

Kitsikopoulos, H., 'Technological change in medieval England: a critique of the Neo-Malthusian argument', *Proc. Amer. Phil. Soc.* 144 (2000) 397–449.

———, 'Standards of living and capital formation in pre-plague England: a peasant budget model', *EcHR* 53 (2000) 237–61.

Klapisch-Zuber, C., 'Villaggi abbandonati ed emigrazioni interne', in R. Romano and C. Vivanti (eds), *Storia d'Italia: i documenti*, v (Turin 1973) 311–69.

———, 'Mezzadria e insediamenti rurali alla fine del medio evo', in *Civiltà ed economia agricola in Toscana dei secoli XIII–XV: problemi della vita delle campagne nel tardo medioevo* (Pistoia 1981) 149–64.

———, 'Blood parents and milk parents: wet nursing in Florence, 1300–1550', in *Women, family and ritual in Renaissance Italy* (Chicago 1985) 132–64.

Klapisch-Zuber, C. and Day, J., 'Villages désertés en Italie: esquisse', in R. Romano and P. Corbin (eds), *Villages désertés et histoire économique. XI–XVIII siècles* (Paris 1965) 419–59.

Knibbe, M., *Lokkich Fryslan. Een studie naar de ontwikkeling van de productiviteit van de Friese landbouw, 1505–1830* (Wageningen 2006).

Knol, E., 'Het verleden van kwelders, wierden en dijken; werk voor natuurwetenschappers', in G. Borger, P. Breuker and H. de Jong (reds), *Van Groningen tot Zeeland. Geschiedenis van het cultuurhistorisch onderzoek naar het kustlandschap* (Hilversum 2010) 11–27.

Knottnerus, O., 'Land kanaän aan de Noordzee: een vergeten hoofdstuk', in J. Elerie and P. Hoppenbrouwers (eds), *Het Oldambt, deel 2. Nieuw visies op. geschiedenis en actuele problemen* (Groningen 1991) 25–72.

———, 'Moral economy behind the dikes. Class relations along the Frisian and German North Sea coast during the early modern age', *Tijdschrift voor Sociale Geschiedenis* 18 (1992) 333–52.

———, 'Wanderarbeiter auf der andere Seite der Grenze', in P. Schoneville (red.), *Wanderarbeit jenseits der Grenze* (Assen 1993) 12–21.

———, 'De kleistreken: van historisch kernlandschap naar randgebied', in H. Elerie, W. Foorthuis and K. Siderius (eds), *Grenzeloos. De identiteit van het landschap in de Eems Dollard regio* (Groningen 1993) 8–13.

———, 'Oldambt: het puukje van de geheele provincie', *Jaarverslag Stichting Historisch Boerderij Onderzoek* (1996) 35–55.

———, 'Het Oldambt in de achttiende eeuw – een inleiding', in H. Perton (ed.), *Het loeit in het Oldambt. Kroniek van de boerenopstand van 1748* (Scheemda 1998) 9–37.

———, 'Malaria in den Nordseemarschen. Gedanken über Mensch und Umwelt', in K. Lorenzen-Schmidt and M. Jakubowski-Tiessen (eds), *Dünger und Dynamit. Beiträge zur Umweltgeschichte Schleswig-Holsteins* (Neumünster 1999) 25–39.

———, 'De tragiek van het platteland: herinneringen aan het Oldambt', *Gronings Historisch Jaarboek* (2000) 124–43.

———, 'Het land dat wij gekend hebben ... De onstuitbare transformatie van het polderland', in M. Bemelman (ed.), *Alles wordt anders. De transformatie van Nederlands Noorden* (Alphen aan de Rijn 2001) 11–22.

———, 'Yeoman and farmers in the Wadden Sea coastal marshes, c. 1500–1900', in B. van Bavel and P. Hoppenbrouwers (eds), *Landholding and land transfer in the North Sea area (late Middle Ages–19th century)* (Turnhout 2004) 149–86.

———, 'Verdwenen dorpen', *Groninger Kerken* 28 (2011) 3–8.

———, 'Dollardgeschiedenis(sen) – mythe en realiteit', in K. Essink (red.), *Stormvloed 1509 – geschiedenis van de Dollard* (Groningen 2013) 95–116.

———, 'Reclamations and submerged lands in the Ems River estuary (900–1500)', in E. Thoen, G. Borger, A. de Kraker, T. Soens, D. Tys, L. Vervaet and H. Weerts (eds), *Landscapes or seascapes? The history of the coastal environment in the North Sea area reconsidered* (Turnhout 2013) 241–66.

Koch, A. and Maris, A., 'Meentgenootschappen in Land van Buren', *BMGelre* 99 (1949) 163–204.

Kochanowicz, J., 'The Polish economy and the evolution of dependency', in D. Chirot (ed.), *The origins of backwardness in eastern Europe* (Berkeley 1989) 92–131.

Komlos, J. and Landes, R., 'Anachronistic economics: grain storage in medieval England', *EcHR* 44 (1991) 36–45.

Körner, M., 'Trotz, Hochmuot und Rebellion macht guotte Viceÿ zergon. Ein Konflikt um die rechte Ordnung zwischen Stadt und Landschaft Basel im ausgehenden 16. Jahrhundert', in B. Bietenart (ed.), *Ansichten von der rechten Ordnung. Bilder* über *Normen und Normenverletzungen in der Geschichte. Festschrift Beatrix Mesmer* (Bern 1991) 115–26.

Kortekaas, G., 'Archeologie in 2007 en 2008', *Hervonden Stad* 13 (2008) 6–59.

Koo, H-W., 'Deer hunting and preserving the commons in Dutch colonial Taiwan', *JIH* 42 (2011) 185–203.

Kos, A., 'De geode luden van Gooiland. Oorsprong en wording van de Gooise marke', *Jaarboek voor Middeleeuwse Geschiedenis* 7 (2004) 142–98.

Kosminsky, E., 'The Hundred Rolls of 1279–80 as a source for English agrarian history', *EcHR* 3 (1931–2) 16–44.

———, 'Services and money rents in the thirteenth century', *EcHR* 5 (1935) 24–45.

———, *Studies in the agrarian history of England in the 13th Century* (Oxford 1956).

Kotel'nikova, L., 'La produzione dei panni di lana nella campagna Toscana nei secoli XIII–XIV', in M. Spallanzani (ed.), *Produzione, commercio et consumo dei panni di lana* (Florence 1976) 221–30.

———, 'Tendenze progressive e regressive nello sviluppo socio-economico della Toscana nei secoli xiii–xv (campagna e città nella loro interdipendenza)', in A. Guarducci (ed.), *Sviluppo e sottosviluppo in Europa e fuori d'Europa dal secolo XIII alla rivoluzione industriale* (Florence 1983) 103–51.

———, 'Artigiani-affittuari nelle città e nelle campagne toscane del XV–XVI Secolo', in *Aspetti della vita economica medievale* (Florence 1985) 747–58.

———, 'Rendita in natura e rendita in denaro nell'Italia medievale', in R. Romano (ed.), *Storia d'Italia*, vi (Turin 1983) 93–112.

Kowaleski, M., *Local markets and regional trade in medieval Exeter* (Cambridge 1995).

Kraker, A. de, 'Reconstruction of storm frequency in the North Sea Area of the preindustrial period, 1400–1625', *History of Meteorology* 2 (2005) 51–69.

———, 'Flood events in the Southwestern Netherlands and coastal Belgium, 1400–1953', *Hydrological Sciences J.* 51 (2006) 913–29.

———, 'Storminess in the Low Countries, 1390–1725', *Environment & History* 19 (2013) 149–71.

Kreutz, B., *Before the Normans: Southern Italy in the ninth and tenth centuries* (Philadelphia 1991).

Kriedte, P., *Peasants, landlords and merchant capitalists: Europe and the world economy, 1500–1800* (Oxford 1983).

Kruger, F., 'Taking advantage of rural assets as a coping strategy for the urban poor: the case of rural urban interrelations in Botswana', *Environment & Urbanization* 10 (1998) 119–34.

Krugman, P., 'Increasing returns and economic geography', *J. Pol. Economy* 99 (1991) 483–99.

Kueh, Y., *Agricultural instability in China, 1931–1991: weather, technology, and institutions* (Oxford 1995).

Kuehn, T., 'Understanding gender inequality in Renaissance Florence: personhood and gifts of maternal inheritance by women', *J. Women's History* 8 (1996) 58–80.

Kulisheck, J., 'Pueblo population movements, abandonment and settlement change in sixteenth and seventeenth century New Mexico', *Kiva* 69 (2003) 30–54.

Kupperman, K., 'Apathy and death in early Jamestown', *J. Amer. History* 66 (1979) 24–40.

———, 'The puzzle of the American climate in the early Colonial Period', *AHR* 87 (1982) 1262–89.

Kurze, W., 'Campus Malduli. Die Frühgeschichte Camaldolis', *Quellen und Forschungen aus Italienischen Archiven und Bibliotheken* 44 (1964) 1–34.

Kuys, J., 'Dagelijkse heerlijkheden in de Bommeler- en Tielerwaard tot omstreeks het midden van de zeventiende eeuw', *BMGelre* 70 (1978/9) 1–35.

———, *De ambtman in het kwartier van Nijmegen (ca. 1250–1543)* (Nijmegen 1987).

Laborda Pemán, M. and De Moor, T., 'A tale of two commons. Some preliminary hypotheses on the long-term development of the commons in Western and Eastern Europe, 11th–19th centuries'. *Int. J. Commons* 7 (2013) 7–33.

Labrot, G., 'La città meridionale', in G. Galasso and R. Romeo (eds), *Storia del Mezzogiorno*, viii (Rome 1984) 215–92.

La Cava, A., 'La demografia di un comune Pugliese nell'età moderna', *Archivio Storico per le Province Napoletane* 25 (1939) 25–66.

Lachman, J., 'Golden promises, abandoned dreams: a brief history and portfolio of photographs of Bodie, California', *California History* 73 (1994) 308–21.

Laiou, A., 'The agrarian economy, thirteenth–fifteenth centuries', in *The economic history of Byzantium* (Washington 2007) 311–77.

Lalanne, J-M., 'Le domaine des Prémontrés de Belval aux XIIe et XIIIe siècles', *Annales de l'Est* 36 (1984) 287–305.

Lalik, T., 'Märkte des 12. Jahrhunderts in Polen', *Kwartalnik Historii Kultury Materialnej* 10 (1962) 364–7.

Lambrecht, T., 'Reciprocal exchange, credit and cash: agricultural labour markets and local economies in the southern Low Countries during the eighteenth century', *C&C* 18 (2003) 237–61.

Landes, D., *The wealth and poverty of nations* (New York 1998).

Lane, P., 'Agricultural labourers and rural violence, 1850–1914', *Studia Hibernica* 27 (1993) 77–87.

Langdon, J., 'Inland water transport in medieval England', *JHG* 19 (1993) 1–11.

Lange, R., 'Bilder eines Deichbruchs. Katastrophendarstellung zwischen Ereignisbericht und moralischem Exempel', *Zeitschrift für Geschichte* 2 (2003) 67–74.

Lapidus, I., 'Arab settlement and economic development of Iraq and Iran in the Age of Umayyad and early Abbasid Caliphs', in A. Udovitch (ed.), *The Islamic Middle East, 700–1900. Studies in economic and social history* (Princeton 1981) 183–7.

Larner, J., 'Chivalric culture in the age of Dante', *Renaissance Stud.* 2 (1988) 117–30.

———, 'Crossing the Romagnol Appennines in the Renaissance', in T. Dean and C. Wickham (eds), *City and countryside in late medieval and Renaissance Italy: essays presented to Phillip Jones* (London 1990) 147–70.

La Sorsa, S., 'La pastorizia pugliese e le sue costumanze', *Archivio 'Vittorio Scioloja' per le Consuetudine Giuridiche Agrarie e le Tradizioni Popolari Italiane* 8 (1941) 8–11.

Last, G., *Noordbroek: een dorp in de Franse Tijd* (Noordbroek 1964).

Lavelly, W. and Bin Wong, R., 'Revising the Malthusian narrative: the comparative study of population dynamics in Late Imperial China', *J. Asian Stud.* 57 (1998) 714–48.

Lawless, R., 'The lost Berber villages of eastern Morocco and western Algeria', *Man* 7 (1972) 114–21.

Lawton, R., 'Rural depopulation in England and Wales', in D. Mills (eds), *English rural communities: the impact of a specialized economy* (London 1973) 195–219.

Lee, J., 'Tracing regional and local changes in population and wealth during the later Middle Ages using taxation records: Cambridgeshire, 1334–1563', *Local Population Stud.* 69 (2002) 32–50.

———, 'Feeding the colleges: Cambridge's food and fuel supplies, 1450–1560', *EcHR* 56 (2003) 243–62.

Leijonhufvud, L., *Grain tithes and manorial yields in early modern Sweden: trends and patterns of production and productivity c.1540–1680* (Uppsala 2001).

Le Lannou, M., 'Le rôle géographique de la malaria', *Annales de Géographie* 45 (1938) 121–6.

Lengen, H. van, 'Tota Frisia: sieben Seelande und mehr. Die territoriale Gliederung des freien Frieslands im Mittelalter: ein Überblick mit einer Karte', in *Die Friesische Freiheit des Mittelalters: Leben und Legende* (Aurich 2003) 67–70.

Leone, A., 'Caratteri dell'economia mercantile pugliese (1467–1488)', *Annali dell'Istituto Italiano per gli Studi Storici* 6 (1979–80) 105–9.

———, 'Il versante adriatico del Regno nell'ultimo quarto del sec. XV: Trani, 1484–1488', *Archivio Storico per le Province Napoletane* 99 (1981) 221–31.

Le Patourel, J., *Moated sites of Yorkshire* (London 1973).

———, 'Documentary evidence', in F. Aberg (ed.), *Medieval moated sites: research report* (London 1978) 21–8.

Le Patourel, J. and Roberts, B., 'The significance of moated sites', in F. Aberg (ed.), *Medieval moated sites: research report* (London 1978) 46–51.

Lepre, A., *Feudi e masserie, problemi della società meridionale nel '600 e nel '700* (Naples 1973).

Le Roy Ladurie, E., 'Climat et récoltes aux XVIIe et XVIII siècles', *Annales: Histoire, Sciences Sociales* 15 (1960) 434–65.

———, *Les paysans de Languedoc*, 2 vols (Paris 1966).

———, 'L'histoire immobile', *Annales: ESC* 29 (1974) 673–92.
Le Roy Ladurie, E. and Pesez, J-M., 'Les villages désertés en France', *Annales: ESC* 20 (1965) 257–90.
Lethbridge, T., 'A cemetery at Shudy Camps, Cambridgeshire. Report of the excavation of a cemetery of the Christian Anglo-Saxon period in 1933', *CAS Quarto Publications* 5 (1936) 1–30.
Leupen, P., 'Zaltbommel en zijn waarden: een verkenning van de relatie tussen een kleine stad en het platteland in het begin der zestiende eeuw', *BMGelre* 69 (1976/7) 80–101.
Leeuwen, M. van, 'Rwanda's Imidugudu programme and earlier experiences with villagisation and resettlement in East Africa', *J. Modern African Stud.* 39 (2001) 623–44.
Levine, B., 'Modernity, backwardness, and capitalism in the Two Souths', in E. Dal Lago and R. Halpern (eds), *The American South and the Italian Mezzogiorno: essays in comparative history* (Basingstoke 2002) 231–7.
Lewis, C., Mitchell-Fox, P. and Dyer, C., *Village, hamlet and field. Changing medieval settlements in central England* (London 1997).
Li, C-y., 'Beneficiary pays: forging reciprocal connections between private profit and public good in hydraulic reform in the Lower Yangzi Delta, 1520s–1640s', *T'oung Pao* 98 (2012) 385–438.
Licinio, R., *Uomini e terre nella Puglia medievale. Dagli svevi agli Aragonesi* (Bari 1983).
———, *Castelli medievali: Puglia e Basilicata, dai Normanni a Federico II e Carlo I D'Angiò* (Bari 1994).
———, *Masserie medievali. Masserie massari e carestie da Federico II alla Dogana delle Pecore* (Bari 1998).
Ligtendag, W., *De Wolden en het water. De landschaps- en waterstaatsontwikkeling in het lage land ten oosten van de stad Groningen vanaf de volle middeleeuwen tot ca. 1870* (Groningen 1995).
Lillie, A., *Florentine villas in the fifteenth century: an architectural and social history* (New York 2005).
Linden, H. van der, *De cope: bijdrage tot de rechtsgeschiedenis van de openlegging der Hollands-Utrechtse laagvlakte* (Assen 1956).
———, 'Het platteland in het Noordwesten met de nadruk op. de occupatie circa 1000–1300', *Algemene Geschiedenis der Nederlanden* 2 (1982) 48–82.
Liu, T., 'Dike construction in Ching-chou', *Papers on China* 23 (1970) 1–28.
Livingstone, A., *Out of love for my kin: aristocratic family life in the lands of the Loire, 1000–1200* (Ithaca 2010).
Lloyd, T., *The English wool trade in the Middle Ages* (Cambridge 1977).
Löffler, U., *Lissabons Fall – Europas Schrecken. Die Deutung des Erdbebens von Lissabon im deutschsprachigen Protestantismus des 18. Jahrhunderts* (Berlin 1999).

Loizos, P., *The Greek gift: politics in a Cypriot village* (Oxford 1975).
Lomas, K., *Rome and the western Greeks 350 BC – AD 200. Conquest and acculturation in southern Italy* (London 1993).
Lomas, R., 'The Priory of Durham and its demesnes in the fourteenth and fifteenth centuries', *EcHR* 31 (1978) 185–94.
———, *North-East England in the Middle Ages* (Edinburgh 1992).
Lopez, R., 'The trade of medieval Europe: the South', in M. Postan and E. Miller (eds), *The Cambridge Economic History: trade and industry in the Middle Ages*, ii (Cambridge 1987) 306–401.
Lorenzen-Schmidt, K-L., 'Gutsherrschaft über reiche Bauern. Übersicht über bäuerliche Widerständigkeit in den Marschgütern an der Westküste Schleswig-Holsteins und Jütlands', in J. Peters (ed.), *Gutsherrschaft als Soziales Modell: vergleichende Betrachtungen zur Funktionsweise frühneuzeitlicher Agrargesellschaften* (München 1995) 261–78.
Loud, G., 'Continuity and change in Norman Italy: the Campania during the eleventh and twelfth centuries', *JMH* 22 (1996) 313–43.
Lourens, P. and Lucassen, J., *Inwonertallen van Nederlandse steden ca. 1300–1800* (Amsterdam 1997).
Lübken, U., 'Chasing a ghost? Environmental change and migration in history', *Global Environment* 9 (2012) 5–24.
Lübken, U. and Mauch, C., 'Uncertain environments: natural hazards, risks, and insurance in historical perspective', *Environment & History* 17 (2011) 1–12.
Lucassen, J., *Naar de kusten van de Noordzee: trekarbeid in Europees perspektief, 1600–1900* (Gouda 1984).
Lucassen, L. and Lucassen, J., 'The world we lost. European migrations 1500–1830', in D. Knauf and B. Moreno (eds), *Leaving home. Migration yesterday and today* (Bremen 2009) 11–24.
Lucassen, L. and Willems, W., 'Why people want to live in the city: looking back', in *Living in the city. Urban institutions in the Low Countries, 1200–2010* (London 2012) 216–26.
Lundahl, M., *The political economy of disaster: destitution, plunder and disaster in Haiti* (New York 2013).
Lupo, S., 'I proprietari terrieri nel Mezzogiorno', in P. Bevilacqua (ed.), *Storia dell'agricoltura Italiana in età contemporanea: uomini e classi*, ii (Venice 1990) 105–50.
———, *Il Giardino degli aranci. Il mondo degli agrumi nella storia del Mezzogiorno* (Venice 1990).
Lupo, S. and Mangiameli, R., 'La modernizzazione difficile: blocchi corporativi e conflitto di classe in una società "arretrata"', in *La modernizzazione difficile. Città e campagne nel Mezzogiorno dall'età giolittiana al fascismo* (Bari 1983) 219–29.
Lupriore, L., *Ascoli di Capitanata tra medioevo ed età moderna* (Foggia 2008).

Luzzati, M., 'Firenze e le origini della banca moderna', *SS* 28 (1987) 423–34.
———, 'I contadini e la guerra di Pisa (1494–1509): nuovi dati sulla base dei registri battesimali', in R. Pozzi and A. Prosperi (eds), *Studi in onore di Armando Saitta dei suoi allievi pisani* (Pisa 1989) 11–22.
Lyon, B., 'Medieval real estate developments and freedom', *AHR* 63 (1957) 47–61.
Mack Smith, D., *The latifundia in modern Sicilian history* (Oxford 1965).
———, 'The latifundia in modern Sicilian history', *Proc. British Academy* 51 (1965) 87–93.
———, *Medieval Sicily, 800–1713* (London 1968).
Macry, P., 'Le elites urbane: stratificazione e mobilità sociale, le forme del potere locale e la cultura dei ceti emergenti', in A. Massafra (ed.), *Il Mezzogiorno preunitario. Economia, società e istituzioni* (Bari 1988) 799–820.
Maddicott, J., 'The English peasantry and the demands of the crown 1294–1341', in T. Aston (ed.), *Landlords, peasants and politics* (Cambridge 1987) 285–359.
Maddison, A., *Dynamic forces in capitalist development* (Oxford 1991).
Magdaleno, R., *Títulos y privilegios de Nápoles siglos XVI–XVIII*, i (Valladollid 1980).
Maitland, F., 'The history of a Cambridgeshire manor', *EHR* 9 (1894) 417–39.
Maitland, F. and Pollock, F. (eds), *The history of English law before the time of Edward I*, 2 vols (Cambridge [red.] 1968).
Malanima, P., *La decadenza di un'economia cittadina: l'industria di Firenze nei secoli XVI–XVIII* (Bologna 1982).
———, 'Urbanisation and the Italian economy during the last Millennium', *Europ. Rev. Econ. History* 9 (2005) 97–122.
———, 'An age of decline. Product and income in eighteenth–nineteenth century Italy', *Rivista di Storia Economica* 22 (2006) 91–134.
Mallett, M., 'Pisa and Florence in the fifteenth century: aspects of the period of the first Florentine domination', in N. Rubinstein (ed.), *Florentine studies: politics and society in Renaissance Florence* (London 1968) 403–31.
Maranelli, C., *Considerazioni geografiche sulla questione meridionale* (Bari 1946).
Marciani, C., *L'esperienza di Riforma Agraria in Italia* (Rome 1966).
Marcos Martín, A., 'Before the liberal *desamortizaciones*: the sale of *baldíos* in sixteenth-century Castille', in G. Beaur, P. Schofield, J-M. Chevet and M.T. Pérez Picazo (eds), *Property rights, land markets and economic growth in the European countryside (thirteenth-twentieth centuries)* (Turnhout 2013) 105–22.
Marfany, J., 'Is it still helpful to talk about proto-industrialization? Some suggestions from a Catalan case study', *EcHR* 63 (2010) 942–73.
———, *Land, proto-industry and population in Catalonia, c. 1680–1829: an alternative transition to capitalism?* (Farnham 2012).

Mariani, L., 'Clima ed agricoltura in Europa e nel bacino del Mediterraneo dalla fine dell'ultima glaciazione', *Rivista di Storia dell'Agricoltura* 46 (2006) 3–42.

Maria Pult Quaglia, A., 'Aspetti della proprietà fiorentina e medicea nella zona del Padule. Il Padule di Fucecchio', in A. Prosperi (ed.), *La lunga storia di un ambiente naturale* (Rome 1995) 107–22.

———, 'Early modern Tuscany: "regional" borders and internal boundaries', in S. Ellis and R. Esser (eds), *Frontiers, regions and identities in Europe* (Pisa 2009) 129–42.

Marignani, R., 'I mulini ad acqua della zona casentinese fino alla metà del secolo XII', *Argomenti Storici* 6–7 (1981) 22–50.

Marin, B., 'Les bourgs ruraux sous juridiction de la ville: les casali', in C. Vallat, B. Marin and G. Biondi (eds), *Naples. Démythifier la ville* (Paris 1998) 98–104.

Marinaccio, M., 'Una famiglia feudale ed il suo patrimonio nella seconda metà del 1700: i Marulli di Ascoli', in *La daunia felix* (Foggia 2000) 133–8.

Marino, J., 'I meccanismi della crisi nella dogana di Foggia nel XVII secolo', in A. Massafra (ed.), *Problemi di storia delle campagne meridionali nell'età moderna e contemporanea* (Bari 1981) 309–20.

———, 'Economic idylls and pastoral realities: the 'trickster economy' in the Kingdom of Naples', *CSSH* 24 (1982) 211–34.

———, *Pastoral economics in the Kingdom of Naples* (Baltimore 1988).

Martin, E. and Satchell, M., 'Wheare most inclosures be – East Anglian fields: History, morphology and management', *East Anglian Archaeology* 124 (2008) 1–270.

Martin, J., 'The parliamentary enclosure movement and rural society in Warwickshire', *AgHR* 15 (1967) 19–39.

Martin, J-M., 'Note sur l'habitat fortifié médiéval en Pouillé', in A. Bazzana, P. Guichard and J-M, Poisson (eds), *Habitats fortifiés et organisation de l'éspace en Méditerranée medieval* (Paris 1983) 105–8.

———, *La Pouillé du VIe au XIIe siècle* (Rome 1993).

Martin, J-M., and Noyé, G., 'Guerre, fortifications et habitats en Italie méridionale du Ve au IXe siècle', in A. Bazzana (ed.), *Castrum 3. Guerre, fortification et habitat dans le monde méditerranéen au Moyen Age* (Madrid 1988) 225–36.

———, 'Il popolamento del Tavoliere e dei suoi dintorni (provincia di Foggia, Italia)', in *La Capitanata nella storia del Mezzogiorno medievale* (Bari 1991) 47–63.

Martin Viso, I., 'Riflessioni sull'incastellamento nella penisola iberica: la Castiglia dell'Ebro e la Transierra di Madrid', *AM* 28 (2001) 83–110.

Martucci, L., 'La riforma del Tavoliere e l'eversione della feudalità', *Quaderni Storici* 19 (1972) 253–83.

Marx, K., *Capital: a critical analysis of capitalist production*, i, ed. F. Engels (New York 1967)

———, *Capital*, trans. B. Fowkes, i (Harmondsworth 1976).

Massafra, A., 'Economia e società nel periodo Spagnola', in G. Musca (ed.), *Storia della Puglia*, ii (Bari 1979) 27–44.

———, 'Murgia dei Trulli: trasformazione del paesaggio agrario dai primi dell'Ottocento ai giorni nostri', *Umanesimo della Pietra* 1 (1983) 9–16.

———, 'Equilibri territoriali, assetti produttivi e mercato in Capitanata nella prima metà dell'Ottocento', in *Produzione, mercato e classi sociali nella Capitanata moderna e contemporanea* (Foggia 1984) 5–56.

———, *Campagna e territorio nel Mezzogiorno fra Settecento e Ottocento* (Bari 1984).

Massafra, A. and Russo, S., 'Microfondi e borghi rurali nel Mezzogiorno', in P. Bevilacqua (ed.), *Storia dell'agricoltura italiana: spazi e paesaggi*, i (Padua 1989) 181–228.

Massaro, C., 'La città e i casali', in B. Vetere (ed.), *Storia di Lecce. Dai Bizantini agli Aragonesi* (Rome 1993) 345–92.

Masschaele, J., *Peasants, merchants and markets: inland trade in medieval England, 1150–1350* (New York 1997).

Massella, L., 'Decime e demani: l'eversione della feudalità in terra d'Otranto', *Quaderni Storici* 19 (1972) 284–301.

———, 'Economia e società nel periodo Spagnolo', in G. Musca (ed.), *Storia della Puglia*, ii (Bari 1979) 27–44.

———, 'La Puglia contemporanea', in *Storia del Mezzogiorno. Regioni e province nell'Unità d'Italia*, xv (Rome 1986) 607–708.

Mate, M., 'The farming out of manors: a new look at the evidence from Canterbury Cathedral Priory', *JMH* 9 (1983) 331–44.

———, 'Agrarian economy after the Black Death: the manors of Canterbury Cathedral Priory, 1348–91', *EcHR* 37 (1984) 341–54.

Matthey, I., 'Op. fiscaal kompas; een bijdrage tot de economische geschiedenis van het gewest Groningen in de 17e en 18e eeuw, met toespitsing op. de dorpen in de huidige gemeente Stedum', in *Westeremden; het verleden van een Gronings terpdorp* (Groningen 1975) 195–360.

Max Edelson, S., 'Clearing swamps, harvesting forests: trees and the making of a plantation landscape in the colonial South Carolina lowcountry', *Agr. History* 81 (2007) 381–406.

Mayhew, L., 'Ascription in modern societies', in E. Laumann, P. Siegel and R. Hodge (eds), *The logic of social hierarchies* (Chicago 1971) 308–23.

Mazzi, M., 'Ai margini del lavoro: i mestieri per "campare la vita"', *SS* 27 (1986) 359–69.

Mazzi, M. and Raveggi, S., *Gli uomini e le cose nelle campagne fiorentine del Quattrocento* (Florence 1983).

McAdams, R., *Land behind Baghdad. A history of settlement on the Diyala plain* (Chicago 1965).

———, 'Intensified large-scale irrigation as an aspect of Imperial policy: strategies of statecraft on the late Sasanian plain', in J. Marcus and C. Stanis (eds), *Agricultural strategies* (Los Angeles 2006) 17–37.

McAdams, R. and Nissen, H., *The Uruk countryside. The natural setting of urban societies* (Chicago 1972).

McArdle, F., *Altopascio: a study in Tuscan rural society, 1587–1784* (Cambridge 1978).

McCants, A., 'Inequality among the poor of eighteenth-century Amsterdam', *ExEH* 44 (2007) 1–21.

McCay, B. and Jentoft, S., 'From the bottom up. Participatory issues in fisheries management: issues in institutional design', *Soc. & Natural Resources* 9 (1996) 237–50.

McCloskey, D., 'English open fields as behaviour toward risk', *Research in Econ. History* 1 (1976) 124–70.

———, 'The prudent peasant: new findings on open fields', *JEH* 51 (1991) 343–55.

McCloskey, De., *Bourgeois dignity: why economics can't explain the modern world* (Chicago 2010).

McCloskey, D. and Nash, J., 'Corn at interest: the extent and cost of grain storage in medieval England', *Amer. Econ. Rev.* 74 (1984) 174–87.

McFarlane, K., *The nobility of later medieval England* (Oxford 1973).

McKean, M., 'The Japanese experience with scarcity: management of traditional common lands', in K. Bailes (ed.), *Environmental history: critical issues in comparative perspective* (Lanham 1985) 334–59.

———, 'Success on the commons: a comparative examination of institutions for common property resource management', *J. Theoretical Politics* 4 (1992) 247–82.

McKintosh, M., *Autonomy and community: the royal manor of Havering, 1200–1500* (Cambridge 1986).

McNeill, J., 'Observations on the nature and culture of environmental history', *History & Theory* 2 (2003) 5–43.

McNeill, W., *Plagues and peoples* (Garden City 1976).

Meaney, A., *Gazetteer of early Anglo-Saxon burial sites* (London 1964).

Meek, C., *Lucca, 1369–*1400: *politics and society in and early Renaissance city-state* (Oxford 1978).

Meibeyer, W., 'Der Rundling – eine koloniale Siedlungsform des hohen Mittelalters', *Niedersächsisches Jahrbuch für Landesgeschichte* 44 (1972) 27–49.

Meihuizen, L., 'Sociaal-economische geschiedenis van het Groningerland', in W. Formsma, M. Buist and W. Koops (eds), *Historie van Groningen. Stad en land* (Groningen 1976) 293–330.

Meijering, J., 'Oldambt, streek van de verplaatste dorpen', *Noorderbreedte* 3 (1987) 88–92.

Mele, A., *Una famiglia in ascesa nel Regno di Napoli. I Marulli duchi di Ascoli tra Sei e Settecento* (Foggia 2000).

Melis, F., *Aspetti della vita economica medievali (Studi nell'Archivio Datini di Prato)*, i (Siena 1962).

———, 'Momenti dell'economia del Casentino nei secoli XIV e XV', in B. Dini (ed.), *Industria e commercio nella Toscana medievale* (Florence 1989) 192–7.

———, 'Lazzaro Bracci (la funzione di Arezzo nell'economia dei secoli XIV–XV', in B. Dini (ed.), *Industria e commercio nella Toscana medievale* (Florence 1989) 175–91.

Menant, F., *Campagnes lombardes du Moyen Age. L'économie et la société rurales dans la région du Bergame, de Crémone et de Brescia du Xe au XIIIe siècle* (Rome 1993).

———, 'Les chartes de franchises de l'Italie communale: un tour d'horizon et quelques études de cas', in M. Bourin and P. Martin (eds), *Pour anthropologie du prélèvement seigneurial dans les campagnes médiévales (XIe–XIVe). Réalités et représentations paysannes* (Paris 2004).

Menant, F. and Jessenne, J.P. (eds), *Les élites rurales dans l'Europe médiévale et moderne* (Toulouse 2007).

Meriwether, M., *The kin who count: family and society in Ottoman Aleppo, 1770–1840* (Austin 1999).

Merlo, E., *Le corporazioni. Conflitti e soppressioni a Milano nei Sei e Settecento* (Milan 1996).

Meulenkamp, J., *'Wie willen boas blieven'. De Oostgroninger landarbeidersstaking van 1929* (Groningen 1983).

Miguel Lana, J., 'From equilibrium to equity. The survival of the commons in the Ebro Basin: Navarra from the 15th to the 20th centuries', *Int. J. Commons* 2 (2008) 162–91.

Miller, E., *The Abbey and Bishopric of Ely: social history of an ecclesiastical estate* (Cambridge 1951).

———, 'The English economy in the thirteenth century: implications of recent research', *P&P* 28 (1964) 21–40.

Miller, E. and Hatcher, J., *Medieval England: rural society and economic change, 1086–1348* (London 1978).

Mintz, J., *The anarchists of Casas Viejas* (London 1983).

Mintz, S., 'The folk-urban continuum and the rural proletarian community', *Amer. J. Sociology* 59 (1953) 136–43.

Mitterauer, M., 'Die Wirtschaftspolitik der österreichischen Landesfürsten im Spätmittalter und ihre Auswirkungen auf den Arbeitsmarkt', in H. Kellenbenz (ed.), *Wirtschaftspolitik und Arbeitsmarkt* (Vienna 1974) 15–46.

Moberg, V., *A history of the Swedish people*, i (New York 1973).

Modderman, P., 'Het oudheidkundig onderzoek van de oude woongronden in de Over- en Neder-Betuwe', *Oudheidkundig Mededelingen uit het Rijksmuseum van Oudheden te Leiden* 30 (1949) 25–61.

Mol, J., 'Aduard 1192–1594. Een korte geschiedenis van het klooster', in *Een klooster, drie dorpen. Geschiedenis van Aduard, Den Ham en Den Horn* (Bedum 1992) 19–36.

Molducci, C., 'L'incastellamento dei conti Guidi nel Valdarno superiore fra X e XII secolo', in G. Vannini (ed.), *Rocca Ricciarda, dai Guidi ai Ricasoli. Storia e archeologia di un castrum medievale nel Pratomagno aretino* (Florence 2009) 53–69.

Molema, J., 'Het "Ol Kerkhof" te Scheemda (Gr.); tussentijds verslag van een opgraving', *Paleo-Aktueel* 1 (1989) 107–11.

———, 'De opgravingen op. het kerkhof van het verdronken dorp Scheemda', *Paleohistoria* 32 (1990) 247–70.

———, 'Kerken in de voormalige Dollardboezem (Gr.)', *Paleo-Aktueel* 2 (1991) 123–6.

———, 'Van de Mierden, Egeste en Broke: de middeleeuwse nederzettingsgeschiedenis van het zuidwestelijk Wold-Oldambt in kort bestek', *Palaeohistoria* 33/4 (1991–2) 311–21.

———, 'Een steenhuis te Midwolde (Oldambt, Gr.)', *Paleo-Aktueel* 6 (1995) 129–32.

———, 'Meeden in de middeleeuwen', in *Boerderijen 'Wold-Oldambt'*, ii (1997) 221–7.

Molho, A., *Florentine public finances in the Early Renaissance, 1400–1433* (Cambridge MA 1971).

———, *Marriage alliance in late medieval Florence* (Cambridge 1994).

Mongiello, L., *Le masserie di Puglia* (Bari 1984).

Montanari, M., *L'alimentazione contadina nell'Alto Medioevo* (Naples 1979).

Montanari, M. and Baruzzi, M., 'Silva runcare. Storie di cose, di parole e di immagini', in B. Andreoli and M. Montanari (eds), *Il bosco nel medioevo* (Bologna 1988) 125–36.

Montanaro, A., 'Quotizzazione delle masserie – ascesa e declino della viticoltura a Martina Franca', *Umanesimo della Pietra* 1 (1983) 35–42.

Montanaro, P. and Tursi, P., *Guida di Locorotondo* (Bari 1991).

Montes Romero-Camacho, I., *Propiedad y explotación de la tierra en la Sevilla de la baja Edad Media* (Seville 1988).

Mooers, C., *The making of bourgeois Europe: absolutism, revolution, and the rise of capitalism in England, France, and Germany* (London 1991).

Moore, J., "'Quot homines'? The population of Domesday Book', *Anglo-Norman Stud.* 19 (1997) 307–34.

Moreno Fraginals, M., *The sugarmill. The socioeconomic complex of sugar in Cuba, 1760–1860* (New York 1976).

Morera, R., 'Environmental change and globalization in seventeenth-century France: Dutch traders and draining of French wetlands (Arles, Petit Poitou)', *IRSH* 55 (2010) 79–101.

Moriceau, J-M., *Les fermiers de l'Ile-de-France. L'ascension d'un patronat agricole (XVe–XVIIIe siècle)* (Paris 1994).

Morita, A., 清代水利史研究，森田明[著 (A study of water management in the Qing dynasty) (Tokyo 1974).

Morony, M., 'Landholding in seventh-century Iraq: late Sasanian and early Islamic patterns', in A. Udovitch (ed.), *The Islamic Middle East, 700–1900. Studies in economic and social history* (Princeton 1981) 135–76.

———, 'Landholding and social change: lower al'-Iraq in the early Islamic period', in T. Khalidi (ed.), *Land tenure and social transformation in the Middle East* (Beirut 1984) 209–22.

Morris, J., 'Challenging Meridionalismo: constructing a new history for Southern Italy', in J. Morris and R. Lumley (eds), *A new history of the Italian South: the Mezzogiorno revisited* (Exeter 1997) 1–19.

Mostert, M., 'De goederen van de abdij Berne in het Land van Heusden tot 1236', *Holland* 14 (1982) 133–9.

Muendel, J., 'The 'French mill' in Tuscany', *JMH* 10 (1984) 83–115.

Muir, R., *The Yorkshire countryside: a landscape history* (Edinburgh 1997).

Mulcahy, M., *Hurricanes and society in the British Greater Caribbean, 1624–1783* (Baltimore 2006).

Mulder, J., 'Het veranderende landschap tussen Lek en Linge (900–1300)', in A. Blommers (ed.), *Rond de Kulenburg. Ridders en ontginningen tussen Lek en Linge 1100–1318* (Culemborg 2010) 59–82.

Müller, F. and Fischer, O., *Das Wasserwesen an der Schleswig-Holsteinischen Nordseeküste*, ii (Berlin 1936).

Mundy, M., 'The family, inheritance, and Islam: a re-examination of the sociology of Farā'id Law', in A. Al-Azmeh (ed.), *Islamic law: social and historical contexts* (London 1988) 49–65.

Munro, J., 'Changing fortunes of fairs in medieval and early modern Europe: the textile trades, warfare, and transaction costs', *Vierteljahrschrift für Sozial- und Wirtschaftsgeschichte*, 88.1 (2001), 1–47.

Musi, A., 'La città assente: Salerno nella provincializzazione del Mezzogiorno spagnolo', *Rassegna Storica Salernitana* 5 (1988) 63–88.

———, *Mezzogiorno spagnolo. La via napoletana allo stato moderno* (Naples 1991).

———, 'Piccole e medie città nella storia moderna del Mezzogiorno continentale', *Rassegna Storica Salernitana* 10 (1994) 145–64.

Myers, N. and Tucker, R., 'Deforestation in Central America: Spanish legacy and North American consumers', *Env. Rev.* 11 (1987) 55–71.

Nadeau, R., *Ghost towns and mining camps of California* (Los Angeles 1965).

Najafi, B. and Bakhshoodeh, M., 'The effects of land fragmentation on the efficiency of Iranian farmers: a case study', *J. Agr. Science & Technology* 1 (1992) 15–22.

Najemy, J., *A history of Florence, 1200–1575* (Oxford 2006).

Nanni, P., 'Lorenzo agricolture. Sulla proprietà fondiaria dei Medici nella seconda metà del Quattrocento'. *Rivista Storia dell'Agricoltura* 2 (1992) 1–148.

Nardella, M., 'Terre di portata e terre salde di Regia corte: le aree di cerealicoltura estensiva nei territori soggetti alla giurisdizione della Dogana', in *Decimo convegno sulla preistoria, protostoria e storia della Daunia* (San Severo 1989) 187–92.

———, 'Produzione mercantile e intervento dello Stato nella seconda metà del Cinquecento: le terre a cerealicoltura estensiva della Dogana delle pecore di Foggia', in *Undicesimo convegno sulla preistoria, protostoria e storia della Daunia* (San Severo 1990) 279–90.

Nash, A., 'Customary measure and open field strip size in Sussex', *Sussex Arch. Collections* 121 (1983) 109–17.

Neave, S., 'Rural settlement contraction in the East Riding of Yorkshire between the mid-seventeenth and mid-eighteenth centuries', *AgHR* 41 (1993) 124–36.

Nee, V. and Ingram, P., 'Embeddedness and beyond: institutions, exchange and social structure', in M. Brinton and V. Nee (eds), *The new institutionalism in sociology* (New York 1998) 19–45.

Nenci, M., 'Ricerche sull'immigrazione dal contado alla città di Firenze nella seconda metà del XIII secolo', *Studi e Ricerche* 1 (1981) 139–77.

Netting, R. and McGuire, R., 'Leveling peasants? The maintenance of equality in a Swiss Alpine community', *Amer. Ethnologist* 9 (1982) 269–90.

Nève, P., 'De overdracht van onroerend goed in de middeleeuwen', *Ars Notariatus* 32 (1985) 23–37.

Neveux, H., *Les révoltes paysannes en Europe: XIVe–XVIIe siècle* (Paris 1997).

Nguyen, T., Cheng, E. and Findlay, C., 'Land fragmentation and farm productivity in China in the 1990s', *China Econ. Rev.* 7 (1996) 169–80.

Nicolas, J., *La rébellion française: mouvements populaires et conscience sociale, 1661–1789* (Paris 2002).

Nicholas, D., 'Town and countryside: social and economic tensions in fourteenth-century Flanders', *CSSH* 10 (1968) 458–85.

Niermeyer, F., 'Het klooster Berne en de ontginning van de oostelijke Meierij omstreeks 1200', in N. Addens, S. Fockema Andreae and J. Kuperus (eds), *Ceres en Clio, zeven variaties op. het thema landbouwgeschiedenis* (Wageningen 1964) 113–28.

Nijdam, H., *Lichaam, eer en recht in middeleeuws Friesland*, 2 vols (Hilversum 2008).

Nitz, H-J., *Die ländliche Siedlungsformen des Odenwaldes: Untersuchungen* über *ihre Typologie und Genese die Prinzipien der räumlichen Organisation des mittelalterlichen Siedlungsbildes* (Heidelberg 1962).

———, 'The Church as colonist: The Benedictine Abbey of Lorsch and planned Waldhufen colonization in the Oldenwald', *J. Hist. Geography* 9 (1983) 105–23.

———, 'Planmäßige Siedlungsformen zwischen dem österreichischen Waldviertel und dem Passauer Abteiland', *Ostbairische Grenzmarken* 27 (1985) 47–62.

Noomen, P., 'Koningsgoed in Groningen. Het domaniale verleden van de stad', in *Groningen 1040* (Bedum 1990) 97–144.

———, 'Middeleeuwse bezitsverhoudingen in Noordoost Fivelingo', in E. de Boer, L. Bos and O. Mulder-Steenbrink (eds), *Het Bierumer Boerderijenboek. Een bijdrage tot de geschiedenis van noordoost-Fivelingo* (Scheemda 1996) 59–82.

Norden, W., *Eine Bevölkerung in der Krise: Historisch-demographische Untersuchungen zur Biographie einer norddeutschen Küstenregion* (Hildesheim 1984).

North, D. and Thomas, R., *The rise of the Western World: a new economic history* (Cambridge 1973).

Oberholzner, F., 'From an act of God to an insurable risk: the change in the perception of hailstorms and thunderstorms since the early modern period', *Environment & History* 17 (2011) 133–52.

O'Brien, P., 'Path dependency, or why Britain became an industrialised and urbanized economy long before France', *EcHR* 49 (1996) 213–49.

Occhipinti, E., 'L'economia agraria in territorio milanese fra continuità e spinte innovative', in *Milano ed il suo territorio in età comunale* (Spoleto 1989) 245–63.

Oels, A., 'From "securitization" of climate change to "climitization" of the security field: comparing three theoretical perspectives', in J. Scheffran, M. Broszka, H. Brauch, P. Link and J. Schilling (eds) *Climate change, human security and violent conflict* (New York 2011) 185–206.

Ogilvie, S., 'Whatever is, is right? Economic institutions in pre-industrial Europe', *EcHR* 60 (2007) 649–84.

Ogilvie, S., Küpker, M. and Maegraith, J., 'Household debt in seventeenth-century Württemburg: evidence from personal inventories', *JEH* 72 (2012) 134–68.

O'Grada, C., 'The ripple that drowns? Twentieth-century famines in China and India as economic history', *EcHR* 61 (2008) 5–37.

Oldfield, P., 'Rural settlement and economic development in Southern Italy: Troia and its contado, c. 1020 – c. 1230', *JMH* 31 (2005) 327–45.

Oliver-Smith, A., 'Peru's five-hundred-year earthquake: vulnerability in historical context', in A. Oliver-Smith and S. Hoffman (eds), *The angry earth: disaster in anthropological perspective* (London 1999) 74–88.

Olst, E. van, 'Rijsen Ooijen, een historische boerderij in de Tielerwaard', *SHBO Stichting Historisch Boerderij-onderzoek, Jaarverslag* (1987) 28–53.

Oost, A., *Dynamics and sedimentary development of the Dutch Wadden Sea, with emphasis on the Frisian inlet. A study of the barrier islands, ebb-tidal deltas, inlets, amd drainage basins* (Utrecht 1995).

Oosthuizen, S., 'Saxon commons in South Cambridgeshire', *PCAS* 83 (1994) 93–100.

———, 'Medieval settlement relocation in west Cambridgeshire: three case studies', *LH* 19 (1997) 43–55.

———, 'Medieval settlement plans in west Cambridgeshire: a re-examination', *LH* 18 (1997) 43–55.

———, 'Prehistoric fields into medieval furlongs? Evidence from Caxton, South Cambridgeshire', *PCAS* 86 (1998) 145–52.

———, 'Ancient greens in 'Midland' landscapes: Barrington, South Cambridgeshire', *Med. Archaeology* 46 (2002) 110–15.

———, 'Medieval greens and moats in the central province: evidence from the Bourn Valley, Cambridgeshire', *LH* 24 (2002) 73–88.

———, 'The roots of the common fields: linking prehistoric and medieval field systems in west Cambridgeshire', *Landscapes* 4 (2003) 40–64.

———, 'New light on the origins of open field farming?', *Medieval Archaeology* 49 (2005) 165–93.

———, *Landscapes decoded: the origins and development of Cambridgeshire's medieval fields* (Hatfield 2006).

———, 'Sokemen and freemen: tenure, status and landscape conservatism in eleventh-century Cambridgeshire', in S. Keynes and A. Smith (eds), *Anglo-Saxons: studies present to Cyril Roy Hart* (Dublin 2006) 184–207.

———, 'The Anglo Saxon Kindom of Mercia and the origins and distribution of common fields', *AgHR* 55 (2007) 153–80.

———, 'Field-names in reconstructing late Anglo-Saxon agricultural land-use in the Bourn Valley, West Cambridgeshire', in A. Chadwick (ed.), *Recent approaches to the archaeology of land allotment* (Oxford 2008) 325–33.

———, 'The deserted medieval settlements of Cambridgeshire: a gazetteer', *Medieval Settlements Research Group Annual Report* 24 (2009) 14–9.

———, 'A note concerning the distribution of two- and three-field systems in south Cambridgeshire before about 1350', *Medieval Settlement Research Group Annual Report* 25 (2010) 21–31.

———, 'Medieval field systems and settlement nucleation: common or separate origins?', in N. Higham (ed.), *The landscapes of Anglo-Saxon England* (Woodbridge 2010) 108–31.

Opsommer, R., *'Omme dat leengoed es thoochste dinc van der weerelt': het leenrecht in Vlaanderen in de 14de en 15de eeuw* (Brussels 1995).

Oris, M., 'Cultures de l'espace et cultures économiques parmi les populations urbaines liégeoises au XIXe siècle', in Y. Landry, J. Dickinson, S. Pasleau and C. Desama (eds), *Les chemins de la migration en Belgique et au Québec du XVIIe au XXe siècle* (Louvain 1995) 165–72.

Orliac, C., 'The wooded vegetation of Easter Island between the early 14th and the mid-17th centuries AD', in C. Stevenson and W. Ayres (eds), *Easter Island archaeology: research on early Rapanui culture* (Los Osos CA 2000) 211–20.

Orrman, E., 'The conditions of the rural population (c. 1350–1520)', in K. Helle (ed.), *The Cambridge History of Scandinavia; prehistory to 1520*, i (Cambridge 2003) 581–611.

Osheim, D., 'Countrymen and the law in late-medieval Tuscany', *Speculum* 64 (1989) 317–37.

———, 'Rural Italy', in D. Abulafia (ed.), *Italy in the central Middle Ages* (Oxford 2004) 161–82.

Oudhof, J., 'Sporen en structuren', in J. Oudhof, J. Dijkstra and A. Verhoeven (eds), *'Huis Malburg' van spoor tot spoor. Een middeleeuwse nederzetting in Kerk-Avezaath* (Amersfoort 2000) 45–77.

Osborne, A., 'The local politics of land reclamation in the lower Yangzi highlands', *Late Imperial China* 15 (1994) 1–46.

Ostrom, E., *Governing the commons: the evolution of institutions for collective actions* (Cambridge 1990).

———, 'Design principles of robust property rights institutions: what have we learned?', in G. Ingram and Y. Hong (eds), *Property rights and land policies* (Cambridge MA 2009) 25–51.

Ostrom, O., Walker, J. and Gardner, R., 'Covenants with and without a sword: self-governance is possible', *Amer. Pol. Science Rev.* 86 (1992) 404–17.

Overton, M., *Agricultural revolution in England: the transformation of the agrarian economy 1500–1850* (Cambridge 1996).

Page, F., 'The customary poor-law of three Cambridgeshire manors', *Cambridge Hist. J.* 3 (1930) 125–33.

———, *The estates of Crowland Abbey: a study in manorial organisation* (Cambridge 1934).

Pallot, J., 'Rural depopulation and the restoration of the Russian village under Gorbachev', *Soviet Stud.* 42 (1990) 655–74.

Palmboom, E., *Het kapittel van Sint Jan te Utrecht. Een onderzoek naar verwerving, beheer en administratie van het oudste goederenbezit (elfde-veertiende eeuw)* (Amsterdam 1992).

———, 'De stichting van het kapittel van Culemborg', in E. Erkelens-Buttinger (ed.), *De kerk en de Nederlanden: archieven, instellingen, samenleving* (Hilversum 1997) 245–57.

Palumbo, B., *Madre madrina: rituale, parentela e identità in un paese del Sannio* (Milan 1991).

———, 'Casa di mugliera, casa di galera. Identità, residenza e parentela in un paese del Sannio', *La Ricerca Folklorica* 25 (1992) 7–24.

Pamuk, S., 'The Black Death and the origins of the "Great Divergence" across Europe, 1300–1600', *Europ. Rev. Econ. History* 11 (2007) 239–317.

Panero, F., *Terre in concessione e mobilità contadina. Le campagne fra Po, Sesia, e Dora Baltea (secoli XII e XIII)* (Bologna 1984).

Panjek, A., 'Not demesne but money: land and peasant economies in early modern western Slovenia', *AgHR* 59 (2011) 293–311.

Panjek, G., 'Beni comunali: note storiche e proposte di ricerca', in A. Tagliaferri (ed.), *Venezia e la Terraferma attraverso le relazioni dei Rettori* (Milan 1981) 371–82.

Papagna, E., *Sogni e bisogni di una famiglia aristocratica: i Caracciolo di Martina Franca in età moderna* (Milan 2002).

———, 'Dimensione territoriali e rappresentazione cartografica di una signoria feudale in età moderna', in G. Giarrizzo and E. Iachello (eds), *Le mappe nella storia. Proposte per una cartografia del Mezzogiorno e della Sicilia in età moderna* (Milan 2002) 33–43.

Paping, R., 'De Groningse verpondingsregisters', *Broncommentaren* 4 (1985) 310–39.

———, 'De nijverheid op. het Groninger platteland 1800–1860. Bedrijfsstructuur en loonontwikkeling', *Economisch en Sociaal-Historisch Jaarboek* 53 (1990) 80–116.

———, 'Industriële windmolens op. de Groninger klei 1770–1860', *Jaarboek voor Geschiedenis van Bedrijf en Techniek* 9 (1992) 69–94.

———, 'Vaste en losse arbeiders en de werkloosheid op. de Groninger klei 1760–1820', *NEHA-Jaarboek voor Economische, Bedrijfs- en Techniekgeschiedenis* 57 (1994) 122–58.

———, *Voor een handvol stuivers: de levensstandaard van boeren, arbeiders en middenstanders op. de Groninger klei, 1770–1860* (Groningen 1995).

———, 'Gezinnen en cohorten: arbeidsstrategieën in een marktgericht agrarische economie: de Groningse kleigebieden 1830–1920', in J. Kok, A. Knotter, R. Paping and E. Vanhaute (eds), *Levensloop en levenslot. Arbeidstrategieën van gezinnen in de negentiende en twintigste eeuw* (Groningen 1999) 17–88.

———, 'De Groningse provinciale rekeningen van de voormalige kloosterlanderijen', in R. van Synghel (ed.), *Broncommentaren. Bronnen betreffende de registratie van onroerend goed in de Middeleeuwen en Ancien Regime* (The Hague 2001) 108–36.

———, 'Family strategies concerning migration and occupations of children in a market-orientated agricultural economy', *The History of the Family* 9 (2004) 159–91.

———, 'Family strategies, wage labour, and the family life cycle in the Groningen countryside, c.1850–1910', in P. Kooij and R. Paping (eds), *Where the twain meet again. New results of the Dutch-Russian project on regional development 1750–1917* (Wageningen 2004) 147–67.

Paping, R. and Tassenaar, V., 'The consequences of the potato disease in the Netherlands, 1845–60: a regional approach', in C. O'Grada. R. Paping and E. Vanhaute (eds), *When the potato failed: causes and effects of the 'last' European subsistence crisis* (Turnhout 2007) 149–84.

Pappacio, G., 'I mulini e i porti sull'Arno a monte di Firenze', in *Lontano dalle città. Il Valdarno di sopra nei secoli XII–XIII* (Florence 2005) 191–210.

———, 'Mulini, pescaie e porti sull'Arno a monte di Firenze: la politica di acquisizione e gestione degli impianti idraulica del monastero di San Salvi tra XII e XV secolo', in F. Sznura (ed.), *Fiumi e laghi toscani fra passato e presente: pesca, memorie, regole* (Florence 2010) 157–76.

Parrinello, G., 'Post-disaster migrations and returns in Sicily: the 1908 Messina earthquake and the 1968 Belice Valley earthquake', *Global Environment* 9 (2012) 26–49.

Parry, M., *Climatic change, agriculture and settlement* (Folkestone 1978).

Parry, V., 'The Ottoman Empire, 1566–1617', in *The New Cambridge Modern History*, iii (Cambridge 1968) 347–76.

Parsa, M., *Social origins of the Iranian Revolution* (New Jersey 1989).

Parsons, C., 'A Romano-British site in Horseheath', *PCAS* 31 (1931), 99–104.

Pavese, M. and Gregori, G., 'An analysis of six centuries (XII through XVII century A.D.) of the climatic records from the upper Po Valley', in W. Schröder (ed.), *Historical events and people in geosciences* (Frankfurt am Main 1985) 185–220.

Pawloski, K., 'Villes et villages circulaire du Languedoc', *Annales du Midi* 9 (1987) 407–28.

Pearson, R., '"A menace to the neighbourhood": housing and African Americans in Portland, 1941–1945', *Oregon Hist. Quart.* 102 (2001) 158–79.

Pelling, M., *The vulnerability of cities: natural disasters and social resilience* (London 2003).
Penco, G., *Storia del monachesimo in Italia* (Rome 1961).
Perdue, P., 'Official goals and local interests: water control in the Dongting Lake region during the Ming and Qing periods', *J. Asian Stud.* 41 (1982) 747–65.
Pereira, A., 'The opportunity of a disaster. The economic impact of the 1755 Lisbon earthquake', *JEH* 69 (2009) 466–99.
Peristiany, J. (ed.), *Mediterranean family structures* (Cambridge 1976).
Peters, J. (ed.), *Gutsherrschaftsgesellschaften im europäischen Vergleich* (Berlin, 1997).
Petralia, G., 'Lo sviluppo dell'economia toscana medievale', in G. Petralia, E. Guarini and P. Pezzino (eds) *Storia della toscana: dalle origini al Settecento*, i (Rome 2004) 116–32.
Petrusewicz, M., 'Agromania: innovatori agricoli alla periferia dell'Ottocento', in P. Bevilacqua (ed.), *Storia dell'agricoltura italiana: mercati e istituzioni*, iii (Venice 1991) 295–343.
———, *Latifundium: moral economy and material life in a nineteenth-century periphery* (Ann Arbor 1996).
Pfister, C., 'Learning from nature-induced disasters: theoretical considerations and case studies from Western Europe', in C. Mauch and C. Pfister (eds), *Natural disasters, cultural responses: case studies toward a global environmental history* (Lanham 2009) 17–40.
Pfister, C., Schwarz-Zanetti, G. and Wegmann, M., 'Winter severity in Europe: the fourteenth century' *Climatic Change* 34 (1996) 91–108.
Phillips, D., 'The growth and decline of states in Mesoamerica', *J. Steward Anthropological Soc.* 10 (1979) 137–59.
Pichard, G., 'L'espace absorbé par l'économique? Endettement communautaire et pression sur l'environnement en Provence (1640–1730)', *Histoire et Sociétés Rurales* 16 (2001) 81–115.
Pietz, D., *Engineering the state: the Huai River and reconstruction in nationalist China, 1927–1937* (London 2002).
Piffanelli, L., 'Sustanze e beni nel contado fiorentino. Evoluzione del patrimonio fondiario di Bongianni Gianfigliazzi, Gonfaloniere di Giustizia, tra Cosimo e Lorenzo de' Medici'. *Eurostudium* 3 (2012) 3–39.
Pinto, G., *Il libro del Biadaiolo: carestie e annona a Firenze dalla metà del '200 al 1348* (Florence 1978).
———, 'Coltura e produzione dei cereali in Toscana nei secoli XIII–XV', in *Civiltà ed economia agricola in Toscana dei secoli XIII–XV: problemi della vita delle campagne nel tardo medioevo* (Pistoia 1981) 203–20.
———, 'Honour and profit: landed property and trade in medieval Siena', in T. Dean and C. Wickham (eds), *City and countryside in late medieval and Renaissance Italy: essays presented to Phillip Jones* (London 1990) 81–91.

———, 'Commercio del grano e politica annonaria nella Toscana del Quattrocento: la corrispondenza dell'ufficio fiorentino dell'Abbondanza negli anni 1411–1412', in *Città e spazi economici nell'Italia comunale* (Bologna 1996) 97–122.

Pirillo, P., 'Il popolamento tra signorie territoriali e dominio fiorentino', in *Costruzione di un contado. I fiorentini e il loro territorio nel Basso Medioevo* (Florence 2001) 39–53.

Piselli, F., *Parentela ed emigrazione. Mutamenti e continuità in una comunità calabrese* (Turin 1981).

Placanica, A., 'Note sull'alienazione dei beni ecclesiastici in Calabria nel tardo Settecento: a proposito del carteggio di un ispettore di Cassa Sacra del 1790', *SS* 6 (1965) 435–82.

———, *La Calabria nell'età moderna: uomini, strutture, economie*, i (Naples 1985).

Platt, C., *The monastic grange in medieval England: a reassessment* (London 1969).

Plesner, J., *L'émigration de la campagne* à *la ville libre de Florence au XIIIe siècle* (Copenhagen 1934).

Poel, J. van der, *Heren en boeren. Een studie over de Commissiën van Landbouw (1801–1851)* (Wageningen 1949).

———, 'De landbouw na 1800', in W. Formsma, M. Buist and W. Koops (eds), *Historie van Groningen. Stad en land* (Groningen 1976) 507–30.

———, *Honderd jaar landbouwmechanisatie in Nederland* (Wageningen 1983).

Poli, G., 'Appunti per una tipologia dei contratti agrari nella fascia costiera di Terra di Bari nel Cinquecento', in A. Massafra (ed.), *Problemi di storia delle campagne meridionali nell'età moderna e contemporanea* (Bari 1981) 321–34.

Polica, S., 'An attempted "reconversion" of wealth in fifteenth-century Lucca: the lands of Michele di Giovanni Guinigi', *J. Europ. Econ. History* 9 (1980) 655–707.

Poni, C., 'Per la storia del distretto industriale serico di Bologna (secoli XVI–XIX)', *Quaderni Storici* 25 (1990) 93–167.

Poos, L., 'The rural population of Essex in the later Middle Ages', *EcHR* 38 (1985) 515–30.

Poos, L. and Smith, R., 'Legal windows onto historical populations? Recent research on demography and the manor court in medieval England', *Law & History Rev.* 2 (1984) 128–52.

———, 'Shades still on the window: a reply to Zvi Razi', *Law & History Rev.* 4 (1985) 409–29.

Post, J., 'Manorial amercements and peasant poverty', *EcHR* 28 (1975) 304–11.

Postan, M., 'The manor in the Hundred Rolls', *EcHR* 3 (1950) 119–25.

———, 'Some agrarian evidence of declining population in the later Middle Ages', in *Essays on medieval agriculture and general problems of the medieval economy* (Cambridge 1973) 186–213.

Postan, M. and Hatcher, J., 'Population and class relations in feudal society', in T. Aston and C. Philpin (eds), *The Brenner Debate: agrarian class structure and economic development in pre-industrial Europe* (Cambridge 1985) 64–78.

Postan, M. and Titow, J., 'Heriots and prices on Winchester manors', in M. Postan (ed.), *Essays on medieval agriculture and general problems of the medieval economy* (Cambridge 1973) 186–213.

Postgate, M., 'Field systems of East Anglia', in A. Baker and R. Butlin (eds), *Studies of field systems in the British Isles* (Cambridge 1973) 281–324.

Poulsen, B., 'Schleswigsche Bauern und europäischer Markt. Ein Aufstand aus dem Jahre 1472', *Demokratische Geschichte* 4 (1989) 9–26.

Pouw, G., 'Onontgonnen geschiedenis. Vragen naar de middeleeuwse ontginningsgeschiedenis van Culemborg', *Culemborgse 'Voet'-noten* 10 (1993) 14–7.

Powell, W. (ed.), *VCH of Essex. Roman Essex*, iii (London 1963).

Powers, D., 'The Islamic inheritance system: a socio-historical approach', in C. Mallat and J. Connors (eds), *Islamic family law* (London 1990) 19–27.

Prak, M., *The Dutch Republic in the seventeenth century: the Golden Age* (Cambridge 2002).

Prak, M. and Van Zanden, J.L., 'Demographic change and migration flows in Holland between 1500 and 1800', in M. van der Linden and L. Lucassen (eds), *Working on labor. Essays in honor of Jan Lucassen* (Leiden 2012) 237–45.

Pretty, J., 'Sustainable agriculture in the Middle Ages on the English manor', *AgHR* 38 (1990) 1–19.

Priester, P., *De economische ontwikkeling van de landbouw in Groningen, 1800–1910. Een kwalitatieve en kwantitatieve analyse* (Wageningen 1991).

———, 'De economische ontwikkeling van de landbouw in het Oldambt in de negentiende eeuw', in J. Elerie and P. Hoppenbrouwers (eds), *Het Oldambt, deel 2. Nieuw visies op. geschiedenis en actuele problemen* (Groningen 1991) 95–104.

Priester, P. and Raad, H. de, *De iezeren kette van d'armoude. Aspecten van de sociale-economische geschiedenis van Beerta, 1800–1870* (Groningen 1983).

Provero, F., 'Le corvées nelle campagne dell'Italia settentrionale', in M. Bourin and P. Martinez Sopena (eds), *Pour une anthropologie du prélèvement seigneurial dans les campagnes médiévales (XIe–XIVe siècles). Réalités et représentations paysannes* (Paris 2004) 365–80.

Prummel, W., 'Draught horses and other animals at late-medieval Scheemda', *Paleohistoria* 32 (1990) 299–314.

Pullan, B., 'Support and redeem: charity and poor relief in Italian cities from the fourteenth to the seventeenth century', *C&C* 3 (1988) 177–208.

Putnam, R., *Making democracy work: civic traditions in modern Italy* (Princeton 1993).

Raban, S. (ed.), *A second Domesday? The Hundred Rolls of 1279–80* (Oxford 2004).

Rackham, O., 'The medieval landscape of Essex', in D. Buckley (ed.), *Archaeology in Essex to AD 1500* (London 1980) 103–7.

———, *The history of the countryside* (London 1986).

Rafael Peña Sánchez, A. and Rodríguez García, J., 'La concentración de la tierra en Andalucía en la década de los 80: una aproximación cuantitativa', *Estudios Regionales* 46 (1996) 211–39.

Raftis, J., *Tenure and mobility: studies in the social history of the mediaeval English village* (Toronto 1964).

———, 'East Midlands', in H. Hallam (ed.), *The Agrarian History of England and Wales: 1042–1350*, ii (Cambridge 1988) 325–41.

Ragin, C., *The comparative method: moving beyond qualitative and quantitative strategies* (London 1987).

Rahimi-Laridjani, F., *Die Entwicklung der Bewässerungslandwirtschaft im Iran bis in sasanidisch-frühislamische Zeit* (Wiesbaden 1988).

Rao, R., 'Risorse collettive e tensioni giurisdizionali nella pianura vercellese e novarese (XII–XIII secolo)', *Quaderni Storici* 120 (2005) 753–76.

Ravensdale, J., 'Population changes and the transfer of customary land on a Cambridgeshire manor in the fourteenth century', in R. Smith (ed.), *Land, kinship and life-cycle* (Cambridge 1984) 197–225.

Razi, Z., 'The Toronto School's reconstitution of medieval peasant society: A critical view', *P&P* 141 (1979) 141–57.

———, 'The use of manorial court rolls in demographic analysis: A reconsideration', *Law & History Rev.* 3 (1985) 191–200.

———, 'The struggles between the Abbots of Halesowen and their tenants in the thirteenth and fourteenth centuries', in T. Aston, P. Coss, C. Dyer and J. Thirsk (eds) *Social relations and ideas: essays in honour of R. H. Hilton* (Cambridge 1983) 151–67.

———, 'Family, land and the village community in late medieval England', in T. Aston (ed.), *Landlords, peasants and politics in medieval England* (Cambridge 1987) 360–93.

———, 'The demographic transparency of manorial court rolls', *Law & History Rev.* 5 (1987) 523–35.

———, *Life, marriage, and death in a medieval parish: economy, society, and demography in Halesowen, 1270–1400* (Cambridge 1990).

———, 'The myth of the immutable English family', *P&P* 140 (1993) 3–44.

Reaney, P., *The place-names of Cambridgeshire and the Isle of Ely* (London 1943).

Rees, W., 'Carrying capacity and sustainability: waking Malthus' ghost', in D. Bell and Y. Cheung (eds), *Encyclopedia of life support systems* (Oxford 2002) accessed online at <http://www.eolss.net>.

Reis, J., Pereira, A. and Martins, C., 'How unequal were the Latins? The 'strange' case of Portugal, 1550–1770', in *Wellbeing and inequality in the long run: measurement, history and ideas* (Madrid 2012) 1–25.

Renaud, J., 'Het kerkhof van Paveien', *Bulletin KNOB* 4 (1951) 118–22.

Renes, J., 'Culemborg-Redichem', *Gelders Oudheidkundig Contactbericht* 90 (1981) 5–8.

———, 'Culemborg en omgeving', *Geografisch Tijdschrift* 16 (1982) 476–8.

———, 'Historisch Culemborg in vogelvlucht', *Culemborgse 'Voet'-noten* 3 (1989) 1–3.

———, 'Grainlands. The landscape of open fields in a European perspective', *LH* 31 (2010) 37–70.

———, *Op. zoek naar de geschiedenis van het landschap. Handleiding voor onderzoek naar onze historische omgeving* (Hilversum 2010).

Renes, J. and Ven, G. van de, 'Siedlung und Landschaft im östlichen Rhein-Maas-Delta', *Siedlungsforschung* 7 (1989) 173–9.

Renswoude, J. van, *Archeologische onderzoek in de dorpskern van Kapel-Avezaath, gemeente Tiel: een uitzonderlijk rijk 13de-eeuws erf en een 14-de eeuwse gracht in het plangebied Muggenborch* (Amsterdam 2011).

Riall, L., 'Ill-contrived, badly executed [and] ... of no avail? Reform and its impact in the Sicilian latifondo (c.1770–1910)', in E. Dal Lago and R. Halpern (eds), *The American South and the Italian Mezzogiorno: essays in comparative history* (Basingstoke 2002) 132–54.

Ribbe, W., 'Die Anfänge von Berlin/Cölln als Forschungproblem', *Jahrbuch für die Geschichte Mittel- und Ostdeutschlands* 34 (1985) 1–9.

Ribot, J., 'Theorizing access: forest profits along Senegal's charcoal commodity chain', *Development & Change* 29 (1998) 307–41.

Richards, J., *The unending frontier: an environmental history of the early modern World* (Berkeley 2003).

Richardson, B., *Caribbean migrants: environment and human survival on St. Kitts and Nevis* (Knoxville 1983).

———, 'Slavery to freedom in the British Caribbean: ecological considerations', *Caribbean Geography* 1 (1984) 164–75.

———, *The Caribbean in the wider world, 1492–1992. A regional geography* (Cambridge 1992).

Richioni, V., 'Della proprietà fondiaria privata nel Mezzogiorno avanti le riforme francesi', in *Studi storici di economia dell'agricoltura meridionale* (Florence 1952) 39–42.

———, 'Aspetti della trasformazione fondiaria nella Murgia dei Trulli', *Atti del Congresso Geografico Italiano* 18 (1957) 330–45.

Richter, G., 'Kulturlandschaft und Wirtschaft', in H. Heckmann (ed.), *Mecklenburg-Vorpommern. Historische Landeskunde Mitteldeutschlands* (Würzburg 1989) 127–58.

Rigby, S., 'Urban society in the fourteenth century: the evidence of the lay subsidies', *Bulletin of the John Rylands Library of Manchester* 72 (1990) 169–84.

———, *English society in the later Middle Ages: class, status and gender* (New York 1995).

Rinaldi, R., 'Le origini dei Guidi nelle terre di Romagna (secoli IX–X)', in *Formazione e strutture dei ceti dominanti nel Medioevo: marchesi conti e visconti nel Regno italico (secc. IX–XII)*, ii (Rome 1996) 211–40.

Rinzema, A., 'Een burger vertelt: de kroniek van Johan van Lemego', in B. Ebels-Hoving, C. Santing and C. Tilmans (eds), *Genoechlicke ende lustige historiën: laatmiddeleeuwse geschiedschrijving in Nederland* (Hilversum 1987) 61–78.

Rippon, S., *The transformation of coastal wetlands. Exploitation and management of marshland landscapes in North West Europe during the Roman and medieval periods* (Oxford 2008).

Roberts, B., 'Moated sites in Midland England', *Trans. & Proc. Birmingham Arch. Soc.* 80 (1965) 26–37.

———, 'Moats and mottes', *Medieval Archaeology* 8 (1965) 219–22.

———, 'Moated sites', *Amateur Historian* 10 (1972) 34–8.

———, 'The historical geography of moated homesteads: the Forest of Arden, Warwickshire', *Trans. Birmingham & Warwickshire Arch. Soc.* 88 (1976–7) 61–70.

———, *Rural settlements in Britain* (Folkestone 1977).

Roberts, B. and Wrathmell, S., *An atlas of rural settlement in England* (Swindon 2000).

———, *Region and place: a study of English rural settlement* (London 2002).

Roblin, M., *Le terroir de Paris aux* époques *gallo-romaine et franque* (Paris 1971).

Rochefort, R., *Le travail en Sicile* (Paris 1961).

Roden, D., 'Field systems of the Chiltern Hills and their environs', in A. Baker and R. Butlin (eds), *Studies of field systems in the British Isles* (Cambridge 1973) 325–76.

Rodríguez, H. and Barnshaw, J., 'The social construction of disasters: from heat waves to worst-case scenarios', *Contemporary Sociology* 35 (2006) 218–23.

Rodwell, W., 'Relict landscapes in Essex', in H. Bowen and P. Fowler (eds), *Early land allotment in the British Isles* (London 1978) 89–98.

Roessingh, H., 'Het begin van de aardappelteelt en de aardappelconsumptie in Gelderland', *Gelders Oudheidkundig Contactbericht* 68 (1976) 1–9.

———, *Inlandse tabak. Expansie en contractie van een handelsgewas in de 17de en 18de eeuw in Nederland* (Wageningen 1976).

Rohr, C., 'Man and natural disaster in the late Middle Ages: the earthquake in Carinthia and Northern Italy on 25 January 1348 and its perception', *Environment & History* 9 (2003) 127–49.

Romá, A., 'El terremoto de Lisboa en el contexto del catastrofismo natural en la Espana de la primera mitad del siglo XVIII', *Cuardenos Dieciochistas* 6 (2005) 19–42.

Romano, M., *Gli apprezzi e le platee dell'Archivio Caracciolo di Torella come fonte per la ricostruzione del paesaggio e della 'Forma Urbi' medievale degli insediamenti del Vulture* (Potenza 2004).

Romano, R., 'L'Italia nella crisi del secolo XV', *Nuova Rivista Storica* 1 (1966) 580–95.

———, 'La storia economica dal secolo XIV al Settecento', in R. Romano and C. Vivanti (eds), *Storia d'Italia*, ii (Turin 1974) 1811–913.

Romano, R. and Corbin, P. (eds), *Villages désertés et histoire économique. XI–XVIII siècles* (Paris 1965).

Roncière, C. de la, 'Indirect taxes or "gabelles" at Florence in the fourteenth century: the evolution of tariffs and the problems of collection', in N. Rubinstein (ed.), *Florentine studies: politics and society in Renaissance Florence* (London 1968) 140–91.

———, *Un changeur florentin du trecento: Lippo di Fede del Sega (1285 env.–1363 env.)* (Paris 1973).

———, 'Pauvres et pauvreté à Florence au XIVe siècle', in M. Mollat (ed.), Études *sur l'histoire de la pauvreté* (Paris 1974) 661–745.

———, *Florence: centre* économique *régional au XIVe siècle*, iii (Aix-en-Provence 1976).

———, 'Le vignoble florentin et ses transformations au XIVe siècle', in *Le vin au Moyen Age: production et producteurs* (Grenoble 1978) 125–59.

———, 'Alimentation et ravitaillement à Florence au XIVe siècle', *AM* 8 (1981) 183–92.

———, 'Condition des salariés à Florence au XIVe siècle', in *Il tumulto dei Ciompi : un momento di storia fiorentina ed europea* (Florence 1981) 13–40.

———, *Prix et salaires* à *Florence au XIVe siècle (1280–1380)* (Rome 1982).

———, 'Fidélités, patronages, clientèles dans le contado florentin au XIVe siècle', *Ricerche Storiche* 15 (1985) 35–60.

———, 'A monastic clientele? The abbey of Settimo, its neighbours and its tenants (Tuscany, 1280–1340)', in T. Dean and C. Wickham (eds), *City and countryside in late medieval and Renaissance Italy: essays presented to Phillip Jones* (London 1990) 55–67.

———, 'Rentabilité, bien commun, écologie. La forêt communale de San Gimignano', in *Milieux naturels, espaces sociaux.* Études *offertes* à *Robert Delort* (Paris 1997) 131–9.

Ronsijn, W., 'Mediated and unmediated market dependence in the Flemish countryside in the nineteenth century: two paths of rural development', *C&C* 28 (2013) 89–120.

Rösener, W., 'L'économie cistercienne de l'Allemagne Occidentale (XIIe–XVe siècle)', in *Flaran 3, L'économie cistercienne-Géographie-Mutations* (Auch 1983) 135–56.

———, *Bauern im Mittelalter* (Munich 1985).

———, *Peasants in the Middle Ages* (Chicago 1992).

Rosenthal, P-A., *Les sentiers invisibles. Espace, familles, et migrations dans la France du 19e siècle* (Paris 1999).

Rossi-Doria, M., 'La Calabria agricola e il suo avvenire', *Il Ponte* 9–10 (1950) 1173–86.

———, 'The land tenure system and class in southern Italy', *AHR* 44 (1958) 46–53.

Rossini, A., *Le campagne Bresciane nel Cinquecento: territorio, fisco, società* (Milan 1994).

Roy Meterns, H. and Terry, G., 'Dying in paradise: malaria, mortality, and the perceptual environment in colonial South Carolina', *J. Southern History* 50 (1984) 533–50.

Royo, V., 'Manifestations of difference: conflicts of interest in rural Valencia during the late Middle Ages', in F. Aparisi and V. Royo (eds), *Beyond lords and peasants: rural elites and economic differentiation in pre-modern Europe* (Valencia 2013) 87–110. Rucquoi, A., 'Pouvoir royal et oligarchies urbaines d'Alfonso X à Fernando IV de Castille', in *Genesis medieval del estado moderno: Castilla y Navarra, 1250–1370* (Valladolid 1987) 173–92.

Russell, W., 'The pre-plague population of England', *J. British Stud.* 5 (1966) 1–21.

Russo, S., *Grano, pascolo e bosco in Capitanata tra Sette e Ottocento* (Bari 1990).

———, *Storie di famiglia. Mobilità della ricchezza in Capitanata tra Sette e Ottocento* (Bari 1995).

———, 'I lavoratori delle masserie: geografia della provenienze', in *Il paesaggio agrario di Cerignola fra Settecento e Ottocento* (Cerignola 1999) 21–32.

———, *Tra Abruzzo e Puglia. La transumanza dopo la Dogana* (Milan 2002).

———, 'La cerealicoltura del Tavoliere e la montagna appenninica (secoli XVIII–XIX)', in A. Calafati and E. Sori (eds), *Economie del tempo. Persistenze e cambiamenti negli Appennini in età moderna* (Milan 2004) 117–25.

———, 'Uomini e colture: questioni di carte', in R. De Lorenzo (ed.), *Storia e misura. Indicatori sociali ed economici nel Mezzogiorno d'Italia (secoli XVIII–XX)* (Milan 2007) 75–86.

Russo, S. and Mercurio, F., 'L'organizzazione spaziale della grande azienda', *Meridiana* 10 (1990) 94–124.

Rutte, R., *Stedenpolitiek en stadsplanning in de Lage Landen (12de–13de eeuw)* (Zutphen 2002).
Ryang, S., 'The Great Kanto earthquake and the massacre of Koreans in 1923: notes on Japan's modern national sovereignty', *Anthropological Quart.* 76 (2003) 731–48.
Rydström, J., *Sinners and citizens: bestiality and homosexuality in Sweden, 1880–1950* (Chicago 2003).
Sabean, D., *Propery, production, and family in Neckarhausen, 1700–1870* (Cambridge 1990).
Saggioro, F., 'Insediamenti, proprietà ed economie nei territori di pianura tra Adda e Adige (VII–IX secolo)', in G. Brogiolo, A. Chavarria and M. Valenti (eds), *Dopo la fine delle ville. Evoluzione nelle campagne tra VI e IX secolo* (Mantua 2005) 81–104.
Saint-Denis, A., 'Les débuts du temporel de Saint-Martin de Laon, 1124–1155', *Actes Officiels du Colloque du Centre d'Études et de Recherches Prémontrés* 14 (1988) 37–55.
Saito, O., 'Land, labour and market forces in Tokugawa Japan', *C&C* 24 (2009) 169–96.
Sakellariou, E., 'The cities of Puglia in the fifteenth and sixteenth centuries: their economy and society', in A. Cowan (ed.), *Mediterranean urban culture, 1400–1700* (Exeter 2000) 97–114.
———, 'I centri minori del Regno di Napoli nel tardo medioevo. Problemi e prospettive', *Incontri Mediterranei* 5 (2004) 194–207.
———, *Southern Italy in the late Middle Ages: demographic, institutional and economic change in the Kingdom of Naples, c.1440–c.1530* (Leiden 2012).
Salas, J., 'La evolución demográfica aragonesa en los siglos XVI y XVII', in J. Nadal (ed.), *La evolución demográfica bajo los Austrias* (Madrid 1991) 169–79.
Salvemini, B., 'Prima della Puglia. Terra di Bari e il sistema regionale in età moderna', in P. Villani and P. Macry (eds), *Storia d'Italia. Le regioni dall'Unità ad oggi. La Puglia* (Turin 1989) 1–218.
———, *L'innovazione precaria. Spazi, mercati e società nel Mezzogiorno fra Sette e Ottocento* (Rome 1995).
———, 'The arrogance of the market: the economy of the Kingdom between the Mediterranean and Europe', in G. Imbruglia (ed.), *Naples in the eighteenth century: the birth and death of a nation state* (Cambridge 2000) 44–69.
Salvemini, B. and Visceglia, M., 'Bari e l'Adriatico', in A. Massafra and F. Tateo (eds), *Storia di Bari nell'antico regime*, i (Bari 1991) 169–217.
Salzman, L. (ed.), *VCH*, vols 1–2 (London 1938–48).
———, 'Early taxation in Sussex', *Sussex Arch. Collection* 98 (1960) 29–43.
Sampietro, G., *Fasano: indagni storiche* (Fasano 1922).

Sangers, W., *De ontwikkeling van de Nederlandse tuinbouw (tot het jaar 1930)* (Zwolle 1952).

Sanpaolo, E., 'Appunti preliminari per la storia dell'insediamento nel territorio di Ascoli Satriano', in *Atti del 12 Convegno Nazionale sulla Preistoria, Protostoria e Storia della Daunia* (San Severo 1991) 117–30.

Santiago Caballero, C., 'Income inequality in central Spain, 1690–1800', *ExEH* 48 (2011) 83–96.

Sarfatij, H., 'Tiel in succession to Dorestad', in H. Sarfatij, W. Verwers and P. Woltering (eds), *In discussion with the past. Archaeological studies presented to W.A. van Es* (Zwolle 1999) 267–78.

Scales, L., 'The Cambridgeshire Ragman Rolls', *EHR* 113 (1998) 553–79.

Schaïk, R. van, 'Nijmegen, Arnhem en de Betuwe. De relatie stad-platteland rond 1500', *Numaga* 26 (1979) 97–113.

———, 'Socio-economic inequality in town and countryside. The Duchy of Guelders in the fifteenth and sixteenth centuries', in J. Renaud (ed.), *Rotterdam Papers. A contribution to medieval archaeology*, iv (Rotterdam 1982) 143–9.

———, 'Omvang en kwaliteit van het cultuurareaal in Groningerland tijdens de 16de en 17de eeuw', *Historisch-Geografisch Tijdschrift* 2 (1984) 9–19.

———, *Belasting, bevolking en bezit in Gelre en Zutphen, 1350–1550* (Hilversum 1987).

———, 'Taxation, public finances and the state-making process in the late Middle Ages: the case of the Duchy of Guelders', *JMH* 19 (1993) 251–71.

Schenk, G., 'Historical disaster research. State of research, concepts, methods and case studies', *Hist. Social Research* 32 (2007) 9–31.

Schleicher, S., 'Zur Entstehung der Sog. Ostfriesischen Registers in den frühen Werdener Urbaren', *Emder Jahrbuch* 77 (1997) 7–40.

Schmidt, H., 'Hochmittelalterliche Bauernaufstände im südlichen Nordseekustengebiet', in W. Rösener (ed.), *Grundherrschaft und bäuerliche Gesellschaft im Hochmittelalter* (Göttingen 1995) 416–25.

Schneider, J. and Schneider, P., *Culture and political economy in western Sicily* (New York 1976).

Schofield, P., 'Dearth, debt and the local land market in a thirteenth-century village community', *AgHR* 45 (1997) 1–17.

———, *Peasant and community in medieval England 1200–1500* (Basingstoke 2003).

———, 'The social economy of the medieval village in the early fourteenth century', *EcHR* 61 (2008) 38–63.

Schofield, P. and Lambrecht, T. (eds), *Credit and the rural economy in North-Western Europe, c. 1200-c.1850* (Turnhout 2009).

Scholliers, E., 'Vrije en onvrije arbeiders, voornamelijk te Antwerpen in de 16de eeuw', *Bijdragen voor de Geschiedenis der Nederlanden* 11 (1956) 283–322.

Schouten, H., 'Het Hoge Huis te Beesd en zijn bewoners', *HKWB* 28 (2000) 20–32.

Schroor, M., *Wotter. Waterstaat en waterschappen in de provincie Groningen, 1850–1995* (Groningen 1995).

———, *Stadsstaat Groningen: de Groninger stadsrechten en buitenbezittingen 1612–2000* (Groningen 1999).

———, 'Een vlucht voorwaarts. Bespiegelingen rond de economisch-geografische politiek van het stadsbestuur van Groningen in het begin van de 17de eeuw', *Historisch Jaarboek Groningen* (2003) 37–58.

Schroor, M. and Knottnerus, O., 'De opstand 1568–1596', in M. Duijvendak and H. Feenstra (eds), *Geschiedenis van Groningen*, ii (Zwolle 2008) 107–51.

Schubert, D., 'The Great Fire of Hamburg, 1842. From catastrophe to reform', in G. Bankoff, U. Lübken and J. Sand (eds), *Flammable cities: urban fires and the making of the modern world* (Madison 2012) 212–34.

Schütte, L., 'Markenrecht und Markengerichtsbarkeit in Nordwestdeutschland', in U. Meiners and W. Rösener (eds), *Allmenden und Marken vom Mittelalter bis zur Neuzeit* (Cloppenburg 2004) 31–45.

Schuyf, J., 'Beyond the castle: moated sites in the Netherlands', in T. Hoekstra, H. Janssen and I. Moerman (eds) *Liber castellorum: 40 variaties op. het thema kasteel* (Zutphen 1981) 144–53.

Schuurman, A., *Materiële cultuur en levensstijl. Een onderzoek naar de taal der dingen op. het Nederlandse platteland in de negentiende eeuw: de Zaanstreek, Oost-Groningen, Oost-Brabant* (Wageningen 1989).

———, 'Tussen "beschaving" en "verwildering": de ontwikkeling van de materiele cultuur van de boeren in oost-Groningen in de negentiende eeuw', in J. Elerie and P. Hoppenbrouwers (eds), *Het Oldambt, deel 2. Nieuw visies op. geschiedenis en actuele problemen* (Groningen 1991) 95–104.

Schwartz, G. and Nichols, J., (eds), *After collapse: the regeneration of complex societies* (Tuscon 2006).

Scott, T., *Freiburg and the Breisgau: town-country relations in the Age of Reformation and Peasants' War* (Oxford 1986).

———, *The city-state in Europe, 1000–1600: hinterland, territory, region* (Oxford 2012).

Searle, E., *Lordship and community: Battle Abbey and its Banlieu, 1066–1538* (Toronto 1974).

———, 'Seigneurial control of women's marriage: the antecedents and function of merchet in England', *P&P* 82 (1979) 3–43.

Segalen, M., *Fifteen generations of Bretons: kinship and society in lower Brittany 1720–1980* (Cambridge 1991).

Seghi, A., *Alla macchia. Carbonai, vetturini, tagliatori* (Stia 1983).

Sen, A., *Poverty and famines. An essay on entitlement and deprivation* (Oxford 1988).

Sen, A. and Drèze, J., *Hunger and public action* (Oxford 1989).
Semple, E., *The geography of a Mediterranean region. Its relation to ancient history* (London 1932).
Sengupta, N., 'Fragmented landholding, productivity, and resilience management', *Environment & Development Economics* 11 (2006) 507–32.
Sereni, E., *Il capitalismo nella campagne (1860–1900)* (Turin 1968).
Serrão, J.V. and Santos, R., 'Land policies and land markets: Portugal, late eighteenth and early nineteenth century', in G. Béaur and P. Schofield (eds), *Property rights, land markets, and economic growth in the European countryside in the European countryside (13th–19th centuries)* (Turnhout 2013) 317–42.
Sestan, E., 'I conti Guidi e il Casentino', in *Italia medievale* (Naples 1966) 356–78.
Settia, A., *Castelli e villaggi dell'Italia padana: popolamento, potere e sicurezza fra IX e XIII secolo* (Naples 1984).
Sharp, B., 'Royal paternalism and the moral economy in the reign of Edward II: the response to the Great Famine', *EcHR* 66 (2013) 628–47.
Shaw, W., 'They stole our land: debating the expropriation of white farms in Zimbabwe', *J. Modern African Stud.* 41 (2003) 75–89.
Shaw-Taylor, L., 'Labourers, cows, common rights and parliamentary enclosure: the evidence of contemporary comment c. 1760–1810', *P&P* 171 (2001) 95–126.
———, 'The rise of agrarian capitalism and the decline of family farming in England', *EcHR* 65 (2012) 26–60.
Sheppard, J., 'East Yorkshire's agricultural labour force in the mid-nineteenth century', *AgHR* 9 (1961) 43–54.
Sheridan, R., *Sugar and slavery: an economic history of the British West Indies, 1623–1775* (Baltimore 1973).
Shughart, W., 'Katrinanomics: the politics and economics of disaster relief', *Public Choice* 127 (2006) 31–53.
Siena Chianese, A., *La nobiltà napoletana oggi, incontri* (Naples 1995).
Silverman, S., 'Agricultural organization, social structure, and values in Italy: amoral familism reconsidered', *Amer. Anthropologist* 70 (1968) 1–20.
———, *The three bells of civilization: the life of an Italian hill town* (New York 1975).
Simmons, S., 'Land fragmentation in developing countries: the optimal choice and policy implications', *ExEH* 25 (1988) 254–62.
Simon, P., 'Les castra du Néracais et du Condomnois d'après les hommages de 1286', *Revue de l'Agenais* (1984) 25–34.
Simpson, J., 'Cooperation and conflicts: institutional innovation in France's wine markets, 1870–1911', *Business History Rev.* 79 (2005) 527–58.
Skovgaard, D., 'Oregon voices: memories of the 1948 Vanport Flood', *Oregon Hist. Quart.* 108 (2007) 88–106.

Slicher van Bath, B., *Boerenvrijheid* (Groningen 1948).

———, *De agrarische geschiedenis van West-Europa (500–1850)* (Utrecht 1960).

Small, C., 'Grain for the Countess: the hidden costs of cereal production in fourteenth-century Artois', *Proc. Annual Meeting of the Western Soc. for French History* 17 (1990) 56–63.

Smith, A., *An inquiry into the nature and causes of the wealth of nations* (Edinburgh 1863).

Smith, R., 'Kin and neighbors in a thirteenth-century Suffolk community', *JFH* 4 (1979) 219–56.

———, 'Families and their land in an area of partible inheritance: Redgrave, Suffolk 1260–1320', in *Land, kinship and life-cycle* (Cambridge 1984) 135–96.

———, 'Demographic developments in rural England, 1300–48: a survey', in B. Campbell (ed.), *Before the Black Death. Essays in the crisis of the early fourteenth century* (Manchester 1991) 25–78.

Smith, S., 'Volcanic hazard in a slave society: the 1812 eruption of Mount Soufrière in St. Vincent', *JHG* 37 (2011) 55–67.

Smits, J., Horlings, E. and Zanden, J.L. van, 'Sprekende cijfers! De historische nationale rekeningen van Nederland, 1807–1913', *NEHA-Jaarboek voor Economische, Bedrijfs- en Techniekgeschiedenis* 62 (1999) 51–110.

Smout, T., *A history of the Scottish people, 1560–1830* (London 1969).

Snell, K., 'Settlement, poor law and the rural historian: new approaches and opportunities', *Rural History* 3 (1992) 145–72.

Snowden, F., *Violence and great estates in the south of Italy: Apulia. 1900–1922* (Cambridge 1986).

———, 'Cholera in Barletta, 1910', *P&P* 132 (1991) 67–103.

———, 'Fields of death: malaria in Italy, 1861–1962', *Modern Italy* 4 (1999) 25–57.

Soens, T., 'Explaining deficiencies of water management in the late medieval Flemish coastal plain (13th–16th centuries)', *Jaarboek voor Ecologische Geschiedenis* (2005/6) 35–62.

———, 'Polders zonder poldermodel? Een onderzoek naar de rol van inspraak en overleg in de waterstaat van de laatmiddeleeuwse Vlaamse kustvlakte (1250–1600)', *TSEG* 4 (2006) 3–36.

———, 'The origins of leasehold in the former county of Flanders', in B. van Bavel and P. Schofield (eds), *The development of leasehold in Northwestern Europe, c. 1200–1600* (Turnhout 2008), 19–38.

———, *De spade in de dijk? Waterbeheer en rurale samenleving in de Vlaamse kustvlakte (1280–1580)* (Ghent 2009).

———, 'Floods and money: funding drainage and flood control in coastal Flanders from the thirteenth to the sixteenth centuries', *C&C* 26 (2011) 333–65.

———, 'The social distribution of land and flood risk along the North Sea coast: Flanders, Holland and Romney Marsh compared (c.1200–1750)', in B. van Bavel and E. Thoen (eds), *Rural societies and environments at risk. Ecology, property rights and social organisation in fragile areas (Middle Ages–twentieth century)* (Turnhout 2013) 147–80.

Soens, T., Van Onacker, E. and Dombrecht, K., 'Metropolis and hinterland? A comment on the role of rural economy and society in the urban heart of the medieval Low Countries', *BMGN* 127 (2012) 82–8.

Sogner, S., 'The legal status of servants in Norway from the seventeenth to the twentieth century', in A. Fauve-Chamoux (ed.), *Domestic service and the formation of European identity: understanding the globalization of domestic work, 16th–21st centuries* (Bern 2004) 175–87.

Sommé, M., 'Règlements, délits et organisation des ventes dans la forêt de Nieppe (début XIVe siècle – début XVIe siècle)', *Revue du Nord* 72 (1990) 511–31.

Spagnoletti, A., *L'incostanza delle umane cose'. Il patriziato di Terra di Bari fra egemonia e crisi* (Bari 1981).

———, 'Il patriziato barese nei secoli XVI e XVII. La costruzione di una difficile egemonia', in M. Visceglia (ed.), *Signori, patrizi, cavalieri nell'età moderna* (Rome 1992) 108–21.

Spufford, M., *Contrasting communities. English villagers in the sixteenth and seventeenth centuries* (Cambridge 1974).

Stabel, P., *De kleine stad in Vlaanderen. Bevolkingsdynamiek en economische functies van de kleine en secundaire centra in het Gentse kwartier (14de–16de eeuw)* (Brussels 1995).

———, *Dwarfs among giants. The Flemish urban network in the late Middle Ages* (Louvain 1997).

Stein, M., 'Rivierverleggingen van Maas en Waal in de omgeving van de Bommelerwaard, sinds de bedijking in de Middeleeuwen', in H. Berendsen (ed.), *Het landschap van de Bommelerwaard* (Utrecht 1986) 91–110.

Steinberg, T., *Acts of God. The unnatural history of natural disaster in America* (Oxford 2000).

Stephenson, M., 'Risk and capital formation: seigneurial investment in an age of adversity', in M. Bailey and S. Rigby (eds), *Town and countryside in the age of the Black Death: essays in honour of John Hatcher* (Turnhout 2012) 175–212.

Sterpos, D., 'Evoluzione delle comunicazioni transappenniniche attraverso tre passi del Mugello', in *Percorsi e Valichi dell'Appennino fra storia e leggenda. Futa, Osteria Bruciata, Giogo. Manifestazione espositiva itinerante* (Florence 1985) 7–22.

Steurs, W., 'Seigneuries et franchises dans le duché de Brabant au moyen âge. L'exemple de Dongelberg (1217)', in *Wavre 1222–1972: 750me anniversaire des libertés communales* (Wavre 1973) 57–93.

———, 'La région entre Dommel et Peel (Brabant septentrional). Peuplement rural, géographie politique et création de villes, 1200–1400 environ', *RBPH* 60 (1982) 791–808.

———, *Naissance d'une région. Aux origines de la mairie de Bois-le-Duc. Recherches sur Brabant septentrional aux 12 et 13 siècles* (Brussels 1993).

Stevenson, C. and Haoa, S., 'Diminishing agricultural productivity and the collapse of ranked society on Easter Island', in *Archaeology, agriculture and identity* (Oslo 1999) 4–12.

Stewart, M., *'What nature suffers to groe': life, labor, and landscape on the Georgia coast, 1680–1920* (Athens 1996).

Stichting Boerderijenboek Wold-Oldambt (ed.), *De boerderijen in het 'Wold-Oldambt'. Scheemda, Midwolda, Ekamp, Meerland, Heiligerlee, Westerlee, Meerden*, 2 vols (Scheemda 1997).

Stone, D., 'The productivity of hired and customary labour: evidence from Wisbech Barton in the fourteenth century', *EcHR* 50 (1997) 640–56.

———, *Decision-making in medieval agriculture* (Oxford 2005).

———, 'The consumption of field crops in late medieval England', in C. Woolgar, D. Serjeantson and T. Waldron (eds), *Food in medieval England: diet and nutrition* (Oxford 2006) 1–26.

Stone, R., 'Three Gorges Dam: into the unknown', *Science* 321 (2008) 628–32.

Stopani, R., *Medievali 'Case da Lavoratore' nella campagna fiorentina* (Florence 1978).

Stumpo, E., 'Problema di ricerca: per la storia della crisi della proprietà ecclesiastica fra Quattro e Cinquecento', *Critica Storica* 1 (1976) 62–80.

Strahl, E., 'Reiderland', *Reallexikon der Germanischen Altertumskunde* 24 (2003) 348–61.

Stratingh, G. and Venema, G., *De Dollard of geschied-, aardrijks- en natuurkundige beschrijving van dezen boezem der Eems* (Groningen 1855).

Strömberg, D., 'Natural disasters, economic development, and humanitarian aid', *J. Econ. Perspectives* 21 (2007) 199–222.

Strupp, C., 'Dealing with disaster: the San Francisco earthquake of 1906', *Inst. Europ. Stud. Paper Ser.* (2006) 1–44.

Sundberg, K., 'Nordic common lands and common rights. Some interpretations of Swedish cases and debates', in T. De Moor, L., Shaw-Taylor and P. Warde (eds), *The Management of Common Land in North West Europe, c. 1500–1850* (Turnhout 2002) 173–94.

Sunseri, T., 'Reinterpreting a colonial rebellion: forestry and social control in German East Africa, 1874–1915', *Env. History* 8 (2003) 430–51.

Swierenga, R., 'Exodus Netherlands, promised land America', *BMGN* 97 (1982) 517–37.

Tabacco, G., 'La data di fondazione di Camaldoli', *Rivista di Storia della Chiesa in Italia* 16 (1962) 451–5.

Taconis, G. and Verhelst, E., 'Archeologische verkenningen in Midden- en Neder-Betuwe', *Tabula Batavorum* 6 (1988) 26–34.
Tainter, J., *The collapse of complex societies* (Cambridge 1988).
———, 'Archaeology of overshoot and collapse', *Annual Rev. Anthropology* 35 (2006) 59–74.
Takahashi, T., 'I bambini e i genitori-'espositori' dello spedale di Santa Maria degli Innocenti di Firenze nel XV secolo', *Annuario dell'Istituto Giapponese di Cultura* 25 (1991) 35–57.
Tan, E., 'The bull is half the herd: property rights and enclosures in England, 1750–1850', *ExEH* 13 (2002) 470–89.
Tawney, R., *The agrarian problem in the sixteenth century* (London 1967).
Taylor, C., 'Medieval moats in Cambridgeshire', in P. Fowler (ed.), *Archaeology and the landscape* (Cambridge 1972) 237–49.
———, *Cambridgeshire landscape: Cambridgeshire and the Southern Fens* (Cambridge 1973).
———, 'Cambridgeshire earthworks surveys: motte and bailey castle and deserted village, Castle Camps', *PCAS* 64 (1973) 38–41.
———, 'Medieval market grants and village morphology', *LH* 4 (1982) 21–8.
———, *Village and farmstead: a history of rural settlement in England* (London 1983).
———, 'Dispersed settlement in nucleated areas', *LH* 17 (1995) 27–34.
———, 'Medieval ornamental landscapes', *Landscapes* 1 (2000) 38–55.
———, 'Nucleated settlement: a view from the frontier', *LH* 24 (2002) 53–71.
Teenstra, M. (ed.), *Landhuiskundige almanak ten dienste van de land- en buitenman* (Groningen 1859).
Tentori, T., 'Social classes and family in a southern Italian town: Matera', in J. Perstiniany (ed.), *Mediterranean family structures* (Cambridge 1976) 273–85.
Terlouw, F., 'De aardappelziekte in Nederland in 1845 en volgende jaren', *Economisch- en Sociaal-Historisch Jaarboek* 34 (1971) 263–308.
Terrier, D., *Les deux âges de la proto-industrie. Les tisserands du Cambrésis et du Saint-Quentinois, 1730–1880* (Paris 1996).
Thaxton, R., *Catastrophe and contention in rural China: Mao's Great Leap Forward, famine and the origins of the righteous resistance in Da Fo village* (New York 2008).
Theibault, J., *German villages in crisis. The rural life in Hesse-Kassel and the Thirty Years' War, 1580–1720* (New Jersey 1995).
Thirsk, J., 'The common fields', *P&P* 29 (1964) 3–25.
Thoen, E., 'Warfare and the countryside: social and economic aspects of the military destruction in Flanders during the late Middle Ages and the early modern period', *Acta Historiae Neerlandicae. The Low Countries History Yearbook* 13 (1980) 25–38.

———, *Landbouwekonomie en bevolking in Vlaanderen gedurende de late Middeleeuwen en het begin van de moderne tijden. Testregio: de kasselrijen van Oudenaarde en Aalst, eind 13de – eerste helft van de 16de eeuw* (Ghent 1988).

———, 'A commercial survival economy in evolution. The Flemish countryside and the transition to capitalism (Middle Ages – 19th century)', in P. Hoppenbrouwers and J.L. van Zanden (eds), *Peasants into farmers? The transformation of rural economy and society in the Low Countries (Middle Ages – 19th century) in light of the Brenner Debate* (Turnhout 2001) 102–57.

———, 'Social agrosystems as an economic concept to explain regional differences. An essay taking the former county of Flanders as an example (Middle Ages – 19th century)', in B. van Bavel and P. Hoppenbrouwers (eds), *Landholding and land transfer in the North Sea area (late Middle Ages–19th century)* (Turnhout 2004) 47–66.

Thomas, H., 'Subinfeudation and alienation of land, economic development, and the wealth of nobles on the Honor of Richmond', *Albion* 26 (1994) 397–417.

Thornton, R., *American Indian holocaust and survival: a population history since 1492* (Norman 1987).

Tielhof, M. van, 'Eendenkooien in Rijnland in de vroegmoderne tijd', *Tijdschrift voor Waterstaatsgeschiedenis* 13 (2004) 47–59.

———, 'Op. zoek naar het poldermodel in de waterstaatsgeschiedenis', *Tijdschrift voor Geschiedenis* 122 (2009) 149–61.

———, 'Texel, kerstavond 1593. De ramp die Tesselschade haar nam gaf', in M. Damen and L. Sicking (eds), *Bourgondië voorbij. De Nederlanden 1250–1650. Liber alumnorum Wim Blockmans* (Hilversum 2010) 311–24.

Tierney, K., 'From the margins to the mainstream? Disaster research at the crossroads', *Annual Rev. Sociology* 33 (2007) 503–25.

Tijms, W., *Groninger graanprijzen. De prijzen van agrarische producten tussen 1546 en 1990* (Wageningen 2000).

Tilburg, J. van, *Easter Island: archaeology, ecology and culture* (Washington 1994).

Tilly, C., 'Migration in modern European history', in W. McNeill and R. Adams (eds), *Human migration, patterns, and policies* (Bloomington 1978) 51–7.

———, *Coercion, capital, and European states, AD 990–1990* (Cambridge MA 1990).

———, *Durable inequality* (Berkeley 1998).

Tilly, L., 'Food entitlement, famine, and conflict', *JIH* 14 (1983) 333–349.

Tindley, A., 'The Iron Duke: land reclamation and public relations in Sutherland, 1868–95', *Hist. Research* 82 (2009) 303–19.

Titow, J., *English rural society, 1200–1350* (London 1969).

Tobriner, S., 'La casa baraccata: earthquake-resistant construction in 18th-century Calabria', *J. Soc. Architectural Historians* 42 (1983) 131–8.

Tocci, G., *Le terre traverse. Poteri e territori nei ducati di Parma e Piacenza tra Sei e Settecento* (Bologna 1985).

Tolosana, L., *Belmonte de los Caballeros: anthropology and history in an Aragonese community* (Princeton 1983).

Toniolo, G., *L'economia dell'Italia fascista* (Rome 1980).

Toubert, P., 'Les statuts communaux et l'histoire des campagnes lombardes au XIVe siècle', *Mélanges d'Archéologie et d'Histoire* 72 (1960) 397–508.

———, *Dalla terra ai castelli. Paesaggi, agricoltura e poteri nell'Italia medievale* (Turin 1997).

Travaglini, R., *I limiti della foresta oritana in documenti e carte dal 1432 al 1809* (Oria 1977).

Trexler, R., 'The foundlings of Florence', *History of Childhood Quart.* 1 (1973) 259–84.

———, 'Measures against water pollution in fifteenth-century Florence', *Viator* 5 (1974) 455–67.

Trigger, B., 'Review', *Man* 24 (1989) 374–5.

Tromp, C., *Groninger kloosters* (Assen 1989).

Tuinstra, S., Bosma, K. and Ufkes, A., *Middeleeuwse bewoningssporen op. de wierde van Woldendorp. Een archeologische opgraving aan de Burgemeester Garreltsweg te Woldendorp, gemeente Delfzijl (Gr.)* (Groningen 2006).

Tukker, A., 'Sanctionering en controle als sleutel tot overleving. Gemene gronden in Gelderland en Overijssel van de vijtiende tot de achttiende eeuw', *Leidschrift Historisch Tijdschrift* 25 (2010) 115–30.

Tys, D., 'Medieval moated sites in Coastal Flanders: the impact of social groups on the formation of the landscape in relation to the early estates of the Count of Flanders', in K. De Groote, D. Tys and M. Pieters (eds), *Exchanging medieval material culture. Studies on archaeology and history presented to Frans Verhaeghe* (Brussels 2010) 289–98.

Tys, D. and Pieters, M., 'Understanding a medieval fishing settlement along the southern Northern Sea: Walraversijde, c. 1200–1630', in L. Sicking and D. Abreu-Ferreira (eds), *Beyond the catch: fisheries of the North Atlantic, the North Sea and the Baltic, 900–1850* (Leiden 2009) 91–122.

Ulsig, E., *Danske adelsgodser i middelalderen* (Copenhagen 1968).

Unger, L., 'Rural settlement in Campania', *Geog. Rev.* 43 (1953) 506–24.

Unger, R., *Beer in the Middle Ages and the Renaissance* (Philadelphia 2004).

Utterstrom, G., 'Climate fluctuations and population problems in early modern history', *Scandinavian Econ. History Rev.* 3 (1955) 3–47.

Uyl, R. den, 'Dorpen in het rivierengebied', *Bulletin KNOB* 11 (1958) 97–114.

Uytterschaut, H., 'The human skeletons from the late-medieval graveyard of Scheemda', *Palaeohistoria* 32 (1990) 323–30.

Uytven, R. Van, 'Vorst, adel en steden: een driehoeksverhouding in Brabant van de XIIde tot de XVIde eeuw', *Bijdragen tot de Geschiedenis* 59 (1973) 93–122.

Valenti, M., *L'insediamento altomedievale delle campagne toscane* (Florence 2004).

Val Valdivieso, I. del, 'Urban growth and royal interventionism in late medieval Castile', *Urban History* 24 (1997) 129–40.

Vardi, L., 'Construing the harvest: gleaners, farmers, and officials in early modern France', *AHR* 98 (1993) 1427–47.

———, *The land and the loom: peasants and profit in Northern France, 1680–1800* (Durham 1993).

Vedovato, G., *Camaldoli e la sua congregazione dalle origini al 1184. Storia e documentazione* (Cesena 1994).

Veit, L., *Passau: Das Hochstift. Historischer Atlas von Bayern* (Munich 1978).

Venditelli, M., 'Diritti ed impianti di pesca degli enti ecclesiastici Romani tra X e XIII secolo', *Mélanges de l'École Francaise de Rome. Moyen Age* 104 (1992) 387–430.

Ventura, A., 'L'Onciario di Ascoli Satriano', in *Onciario della città di Ascoli 1753* (Foggia 2006) 57–76.

Verhaeghe, F., 'Moated sites in Flanders: features and significance', in T. Hoekstra, H. Janssen and I. Moerman (eds) *Liber castellorum: 40 variaties op. het thema kasteel* (Zutphen 1981) 98–121.

Verhelst, E., Boreel, G., Beurden, L. van, Groot, M. and Kerckhove, J. van, *De nederzetting Zandwijk, door een rivier geschieden van Tiel. Bewoningssporen uit de 10de en 11de eeuw na Chr. in het plangebied Tiel-Binnenheuvel* (Amsterdam 2006).

Verhulst, A., 'La diversité du régime domanial entre Loire et Rhin à l'époque carolingienne', in W. Janssen and D. Lohrmann (eds), *Villa, Curtis, Grangia: Landwirtschaft zwischen Loire und Rhein von der Romerzeit zum Hochmittelalter* (Munich 1983) 133–48.

———, 'Medieval socio-economic historiography in Western Europe: towards and integrated approach', *JMH* 23 (1997) 89–101.

———, *The Carolingian economy* (Cambridge 2002).

Verhulst, A. and Bock-Doehaerd, R. de, 'Het social-economische leven tot circa 1000', in D. Blok, W. Prevenier and D. Roorda (eds), *Algemene geschiedenis der Nederlanden* (Haarlem 1981) 183–215.

Vermeer, E., 'The mountain frontier in late Imperial China: economic and social developments in the Dabashan', *T'oung Pao* 77 (1991) 306–35.

Viazzo, P-P., 'What's so special about the Mediterranean? Thirty years of research on household and family in Italy', *C&C* 18 (2003) 111–37.

Villani, P., 'Il catasto onciario e il sistema tributario', in *Mezzogiorno tra riforme e rivoluzione* (Rome 1974) 105–53.

Villari, R., *Mezzogiorno e contadini nell'Età moderna* (Bari 1977).

Vis, D., *De Johannes Kerkhovenpolder: een episode uit de herovering van de Dollard* (Hoorn 1962).

Visceglia, M., 'Commercio e mercato in Terra d'Otranto nella seconda metà del XVIII secolo', *Quaderni Storici* 28 (1975) 151–98.

———, 'Il commercio dei porti pugliesi nel Settecento: ipotesi di ricerca', in P. Villani (ed.), *Economia e classi sociali nella Puglia moderna* (Naples 1976) 187–220.

———, 'Linee per uno studio unitario dei testamenti e dei contratti matrimoniali dell'aristocrazia feudale napoletana tra fine Quattrocento e Settecento', *Mélanges de l'Ecole Française de Rome* 95 (1983) 393–470.

———, *Territorio, feudo e potere locale. Terra d'Otranto tra medioevo ed età moderna* (Naples 1988).

———, *Il bisogno di eternità: comportamenti aristocratici in età moderna* (Naples 1988).

Vitolo, G., *Introduzione-documenti Cavesi per la storia di Rocchetta S. Antonio*, ed. P. Carlone (Altavilla Silentina 1987).

Vivanti, C., 'Città e campagne', in R. Romano (ed.), *Storia dell economica italiana. L'età moderna: verso la crisi*, ii (Turin 1991) 243–83.

Voerman, G. (ed.), *Tussen Moskou en Finsterwolde. Over de geschiedenis van het communisme in Oost-Groningen* (Scheemda 1993).

Voerman, J., *Verstedelijking en migratie in het Oost-Groningse veengebied 1800–1940* (Assen 2001).

Volpe, G., *La Daunia nell'età della romanizzazione. Paesaggio agrario, produzione, scambi* (Bari 1990).

———, 'Herdonia romana, tardoantica e medievale alla luce dei recenti scavi', *Ordona* 10 (2000) 533–6.

———, 'Paesaggi e insediamenti rurali dell'Apulia tardoantica e altomedievale', in G. Volpe and M. Turchiano (eds), *Paesaggi e insediamenti rurali in Italia meridionale fra Tardoantico e Altomedioevo* (Bari 2004) 299–314.

———, 'Villaggi e insediamento sparso in Italia meridionale fra tardoantico e altomedioevo: alcune note', in G. Brogiolo, A. Chavarria and M. Valenti (eds), *Dopo la fine delle ville: evoluzione delle campagne dal VI al IX secolo* (Mantua 2005) 221–49.

———, 'A late Roman villa at Faragola, Italy', *Minerva. International Rev. Ancient Art & Archaeology* 17 (2006) 44–5.

Volpe, G., De Venuto, G., Goffredo, R. and Turchiano, M., 'L'abitato altomedievale di Faragola (Ascoli Satriano)', in G. Volpe and P. Favia (eds), *V Congresso Nazionale di Archeologia Medievale* (Florence 2009) 284–90.

Vos, P. and Knol, E., 'De ontstaansgeschiedenis van het Dollardlandschap; natuurlijke en antropogene processen', in K. Essink (red.), *Stormvloed 1509 – geschiedenis van de Dollard* (Groningen 2013) 31–43.

Vries, J. de, *The Dutch rural economy in the Golden Age, 1500–1700* (New Haven 1974).

———, 'Peasant demand patterns and economic development: Friesland, 1550–1750', in W. Parker and E. Jones (eds), *European peasants and their markets: essays in agrarian economic history* (Princeton 1975) 179–96.

———, *European urbanization* (London 1984).

———, 'The Industrial Revolution and the Industrious Revolution', *JEH* 54 (1994) 249–70.

———, 'Dutch economic growth in comparative-historical perspective, 1500–2000', *De Economist* 148 (2000) 443–67.

Vries, J. de and Woude, A. van der, *The first modern economy: success, failure and perseverance of the Dutch economy, 1500–1815* (Cambridge 1997).

Wagstaff, J., 'War and settlement desertion in the Morea, 1685–1830', *Trans. Inst. British Geographers* 3 (1978) 295–308.

Waley, D., *The Italian city-republics* (New York 1988).

Wallerstein, I., *The modern world-system. Capitalist agriculture and the origins of the world-economy in the sixteenth century* (New York 1974).

Walter, J., 'The social economy of dearth in early modern England', in J. Walter and R. Schofield (eds), *Famine, disease and the social order in early modern society* (Cambridge 1989) 75–128.

Warner, P., *Greens, commons and clayland colonization: the origins and development of green-side settlement in east Suffolk* (Leicester 1987).

Watkins, A., 'Cattle grazing in the Forest of Arden in the later Middle Ages', *AgHR* 37 (1989) 12–25.

Watts, D., *The West Indies: patterns of development, culture, and environmental change since 1492* (Cambridge 1987).

Way, T., *A study of the impact of imparkment on the social landscape of Cambridgeshire from c. 1080 to 1760* (Oxford 1997).

Weber, M., *The city* (New York 1962).

———, *Economy and society*, eds G. Roth and C. Wittich, ii (Berkeley 1978).

Weijschedé, T., Exaltus, R., Koomen, A., and van Bemmel, B., *Gaafheid van bodem en reliëf gemeente Lingewaal en gemeente Geldermalsen. Kennisinstrument bij de relatie culturhistorie en ruimtelijke ontwikkelingen* (Wageningen 2006).

Weil, B., 'The rivers come: colonial flood control and knowledge systems in the Indus Basin, 1840s–1930s', *Environment & History* 12 (2006) 3–29.

Weiss, H. and Bradley, R., 'What drives societal collapse?', *Science* 291 (2001) 609–10.

Westeringh, W. van de, 'Boerderij 't Hoff te Heteren 1406–1945', *Tabula Batavorum* 15 (1997) 44–8.

Westerman, F., *De Graanrepubliek* (Amsterdam 1999).

Weststrate, J., 'The organisation of trade and transport on the Lower Rhine and Waal rivers around 1550', in H. Brand (ed.), *Trade, diplomacy and cultural exchange: continuity and change in the North Sea area and the Baltic c. 1350–1750* (Hilversum 2005) 95–113.

———, *In het kielzog van moderne markten. Handel en scheepvaart op. de Rijn, Waal en Ijssel, ca. 1360 – ca. 1560* (Hilversum 2008).

Wetherell, C., Plakans, A. and Wellman, B., 'Social networks, kinship, and community in Eastern Europe', *JIH* 24 (1994) 639–63.

Wheaton, R., 'Family and kinship in Western Europe: the problem of the joint family household', *JIH* 5 (1975) 601–28.

White, S., 'The real Little Ice Age', *JIT* 44 (2013) 327–52.

Whittle, J., 'Individualism and the family-land bond: a reassessment of land transfer patterns along the English peasantry, c.1270–1580', *P&P* 160 (1998) 25–63.

———, *The development of agrarian capitalism: land and labour in Norfolk, 1440–1580* (Oxford 2000).

Wickham, C., *Early medieval Italy: central power and local society, 400–1000* (London 1981).

———, *The mountains and the city: the Tuscan Apennines in the early Middle Ages* (Oxford 1988).

———, 'European forests in the early Middle Ages: landscape and land clearance', in *L'ambiente vegetale nell'alto medioevo*, xxxvii (Spoleto 1990) 479–548.

———, 'Land sales and land market in the eleventh century', in *Land and power: studies in Italian and European social history, 400–1200* (London 1994) 257–74.

———, *Community and clientele in twelfth-century Tuscany. The origins of the rural commune in the plain of Lucca* (Oxford 1998).

Wiemann, H., 'Die Bauern in der Ostfriesischen Landschaft im 16.–18. Jahrhundert', in G. Franz (ed.), *Bauernschaft und Bauernstand 1500–1970* (Limburg-Lahn 1975) 153–64.

Wijkman, A. and Timberlake, L., *Natural disasters: acts of God or acts of man?* (Washington DC 1984).

Wilkin, A., 'The role of the secular canons in the introduction of leaseholding in the thirteenth century. Case study: the Liege area', in B. van Bavel and P. Schofield (eds), *The development of leasehold in northwestern Europe c. 1200–1600* (Turnhout 2008) 57–80.

Will, P.-E. and Bin Wong, R., *Nourish the people: the state civilian granary stem in China, 1650–1850* (Ann Arbor 1991).

Willard, J., *Parliamentary taxes on personal property 1290 to 1334* (Cambridge MA 1934).

Willems, W., 'Romans and Batavians: regional developments at the Imperial frontier', in R. Brandt and J. Slofstra (eds), *Romans and natives in the Low Countries: spheres of interaction* (Oxford 1983) 105–28.

Williamson, T., 'The Roman countryside: settlement and agriculture in N. W. Essex', *Britannia* 15 (1984) 225–30.

———, *Shaping medieval landscapes: settlement, society, environment* (Macclesfield 2003).

Wilson, D., *Moated sites* (Princes Risborough 1985).

Wintle, M., 'Push-factors in emigration: the case of the Province of Zeeland in the nineteenth-century', *Population Stud.* 46 (1992) 523–37.

Wokeck, M., *Trade in strangers: the beginnings of mass migration to North America* (University Park 1999).

Woude, A. van der, 'Large estates and small holdings. Lords and peasants in the Netherlands during the late Middle Ages and early modern times', in P. Gunst and T. Hoffmann (eds), *Grand domaine et petites exploitations en Europe au Moyen Age et dans le temps modernes* (Budapest 1982) 193–207.

Wright, A. (ed.), *VCH*, vi (London 1978).

Wrightson, K., 'Aspects of social differentiation in rural England, c. 1580–1660', *J. Peasant Stud.* 5 (1977–8) 33–47.

Wrigley, E., 'Parasite or stimulus: the town in a pre-industrial economy', in P. Abrams and E. Wrigley (eds), *Towns in societies. Essays in economic history and historical sociology* (Cambridge 1978) 295–309.

———, 'Urban growth and agricultural change: England and the Continent in the early modern period', *JIH* 15 (1985) 683–728.

———, 'Men on the land and men in the countryside: employment in agriculture in early nineteenth century England', in L. Bonfield, R. Smith and K. Wrightson (eds), *The world we have gained: histories of population and social structure* (Oxford 1986) 295–336.

Wymer, J. (ed.), *Gazetteer of Mesolithic sites* (London 1977).

Yacoob, M. and Kelly, M., 'Secondary cities in West Africa: the challenge for environmental health and prevention', *Comparative Urban Stud. Occasional Paper Ser.* 21 (1999) 1–28.

Yates, M., 'The market in freehold land, 1300–1509: the evidence of feet of fines', *EcHR* EV (2012) 1–22.

Yoffee, N. and Cowgill, G., (eds), *The collapse of ancient states and civilizations* (Tuscon 2003).

Yun, B., 'Economic cycles and structural changes', in T. Brady Jr., H. Oberman and J. Tracy (eds), *Handbook of European history, 1400–1600* (Leiden 1994) 113–46.

Zadora-Rio, E., 'Parcs à gibier et garennes à Lapins: contribution à une étude archéologique des territoires de chasse dans le paysage médiéval', *Hommes et Terres du Nord* 2–3 (1986) 133–9.

Zagnoni, R., 'La coltivazione del castagno nella montagna fra Bologna e Pistoia nei secoli XI–XIII', in G. Pinto (ed.), *Villaggi, boschi e campi dell'Appennino dal Medioevo all'età contemporanea* (Pistoia 1997) 41–57.

———, 'Comunità e beni comuni nella montagna fra Bologna e Pistoia nel medioevo', in *Comunità e beni comuni dal medioevo ad oggi* (Pistoia 2007) 17–44.

Zamagni, V., *Dalla periferia al centro. La seconda rinascita economica dell'Italia (1861–1990)* (Bologna 1993).

Zanden, J.L. van, *De economische ontwikkeling van de Nederlandse landbouw in de negentiende eeuw, 1800–1914* (Utrecht 1985).

———, 'De volkstelling van 1807/8', in M. Duijghuisen (ed.), *Broncommentaren*, iii (The Hague 1987) 43–50.

———, 'De Registres Civiques 1811 (1812, 1813)', in M. Duijghuisen (ed.), *Broncommentaren*, iv (The Hague 1987) 53–8.

———, *'Den zedelijk materiëlen toestand der arbeidende bevolking ten platten lande'. Een reeks rapporten uit 1851* (Groningen 1991).

———, *The rise and decline of Holland's economy: merchant capitalism and the labour market* (Manchester 1993).

———, 'Tracing the beginning of the Kuznets Curve: Western Europe during the early modern period', *EcHR* 48 (1995) 643–64.

———, 'The paradox of the Marks. The exploitation of the commons in the eastern Netherlands, 1250–1850', *AgHR* 47 (1999) 125–45.

———, 'A third road to capitalism? Proto-industrialisation and the moderate nature of the late medieval crisis in Flanders and Holland, 1350–1550', in P. Hoppenbrouwers and J.L. van Zanden (eds), *Peasants into farmers? The transformation of rural economy and society in the Low Countries (Middle Ages – 19th century) in light of the Brenner Debate* (Turnhout 2001) 85–101.

———, 'Taking the measure of the early modern economy. Historical national accounts for Holland in 1510/14', *Europ. Rev. Econ. History* 6 (2002) 131–63.

Zanden, J.L. van, and Prak, M., 'State formation and citizenship: the Dutch Republic between medieval communes and modern nation states', in J.L. van Zanden, *The long road to the Industrial Revolution: the European economy in a global perspective, 1000–1800* (Leiden 2009) 205–32.

Zanetti, D., *Problemi alimentari di una economia preindustriale. Cereali a Pavia dal 1398 al 1700* (Turin 1964).

Zeitlhofer, H., 'Besitztransfer in frühneuzeitlichen ländlichen Gesellschaften: die südböhmische Pfarre Kapličky (Herrschaft Vyšši Brod), 1640–1840', in R. Cerman and H. Zeitlhofer (eds), *Soziale Strukturen im Böhmen. Ein regionaler Vergleich von Wirtschaft und Gesellschaft in Gutsherrschaften 16.–19. Jahrhundert* (Munich 2002) 240–61.

Zotta, S., 'Momenti e problemi di una crisi agraria in uno 'stato' feudale napoletano (1585–1615)', *Mélanges de l'École Française de Rome* 90 (1978) 717–96.

Zuijderduijn, J., *Medieval capital markets: markets for rents between state formation and private investment in Holland (1300–1550)* (Boston 2009).

———, 'Accessing a medieval capital market. The capacity of the market for renten in Edam and De Zeevang (1462–1563)', *Jaarboek voor Middeleeuwse Geschiedenis* 11 (2009) 138–64.

Zuijderduijn and De Moor, T., 'Spending, saving, or investing? Risk-management in sixteenth-century Dutch households', *EcHR* 66 (2013) 38–56.

———, 'Preferences of the poor: market participation and asset management of poor households in sixteenth-century Holland', *Europ. Rev. Econ. History* 17 (2013) 233–49.

Zuijderduijn, J., Zanden, J.L. van and De Moor, T., 'Microcredit in late medieval Waterland. Households and the efficiency of capital markets in Edam and De Zeevang (1462–1563)', in S. Cavaciocchi (ed.), *La famiglia nell'economia europea. Secc. XIII–XVIII* (Florence 2009) 651–68.

———, 'Small is beautiful. On the efficiency of credit markets in late medieval Holland', *Europ. Rev. Econ. History* 16 (2012) 3–22.

Zupko, R. and Laures, R., *Straws in the wind. Medieval urban environmental law: the case of Northern Italy* (Boulder 1996).

Zytkowicz, L., 'Trends of agrarian economy in Poland, Bohemia and Hungary from the middle of the fifteenth to the middle of the seventeenth century', in A. Mączak, H. Samsonowicz and P. Burke (eds), *East-Central Europe in transition. From the fourteenth to the seventeenth century* (Cambridge 1985) 59–83.

Index

Abruzzo 234, 279
Africa 42
Arezzo 73, 74, 75, 81, 87, 88, 97, 281, 300, 307, 344
Arno 72, 85, 87, 89, 281, 352
Arnt Pieck 175

Banzena 76
Bartlow 112, 115, 123, 314
Barton 112, 131, 132
Basilicata 242, 338
Beerta 197, 198, 199, 201, 206, 207, 208, 355
Beesd 156, 175, 275, 362
Beklemrecht 192, 205, 317
Beusichem 163, 165
Bibbiena 74, 76, 77, 86, 87, 97
Bishop of Utrecht 155, 157, 174, 331
Black Death 31, 127, 128, 158, 166, 298
Bourn Brook 127
Brabant 363, 366
Buren 165, 175, 276, 312, 334
Buurmalsen 153, 156, 168, 169

Camaldoli 72, 75, 80, 81, 83, 84, 87, 88, 89, 93, 95, 273, 281, 300, 367
Cambridge 112, 123, 127, 128, 278, 279, 281, 284, 287, 301, 304, 305, 308, 313, 315, 319, 320, 321, 330, 338, 340, 343, 344, 345, 350, 354, 356, 360, 363, 365, 368, 371
Campi 76
Carel Coenraadpolder 209
Castel Focognano 74
Castel San Niccolo 97
Castle Camps 112, 115, 126, 302
Catasto 75, 76, 77, 83, 86, 88, 93, 94, 237, 248, 279, 314
Cerignola 243, 244, 281, 287
Cetica 76, 95
Chilford 111, 112, 115, 124, 132, 133
Chitignano 97
Cistercian 168
Corezzo 73
Count of Holland 174
Credit 298
Culemborg 153, 154, 155, 162, 174, 291, 293, 355, 356

Deil 155
Demesnes 129
Dollard 188, 193, 205, 206, 212, 322, 367, 371
Domesday 116, 119, 127, 131, 280, 329, 331, 355
Dorestad 160, 174, 315
Drenthe 164, 215
Drieborg 194, 206, 208
Duke of Gelre 174

Earl of Oxford 112, 126, 136
Emphyteusis 245, 320
Enspijk 153, 155, 174, 275

Fairs 293
Famine 106, 331, 332
Faragola 233, 321, 372
Finsterwolde 195, 197, 198, 199, 201, 206, 372
Flanders 157, 163, 174, 280, 310, 368, 371, 376
Florence 25, 26, 71, 78, 81, 82, 85, 89, 91, 92, 94, 96, 97, 278, 279, 281, 282, 289, 293, 294, 299, 303, 307, 309, 316, 317, 320, 321, 322, 333, 335,

340, 344, 345, 352, 353, 357, 367, 372
Foggia 240, 241, 279, 280, 282, 306, 339, 341, 347, 371
Friesland 205, 281

Ganzedijk 206
Gello 73, 74, 76
Gini 91, 203
Granges 168
Gressa 74, 76
Groningen 188, 189, 190, 192, 193, 194, 195, 196, 197, 198, 199, 200, 201, 204, 205, 206, 207, 208, 209, 213, 214, 215, 275, 281, 282, 283, 284, 295, 296, 297, 299, 312, 316, 323, 324, 325, 328, 330, 332, 338, 342, 351, 352, 355, 362, 363, 367, 368, 370
Guidi 74, 81, 83, 87, 96, 97, 289, 294, 345, 364

Harlton 112, 128, 129
Holland 154, 157, 166, 174, 279, 280, 312, 328, 346, 376
Horseheath 112, 115, 123, 124, 125, 137, 352

Incastellamento 74
Inheritance 24, 298

Kingston 112, 122, 127, 129, 134
Knights 134, 280
Kroonpolder 193, 206, 208

Labourer 198, 206
Linge 153, 155, 156, 160, 165, 291, 293, 297, 346
Linton 123, 281, 304
Locazioni 242
Locorotondo 237, 238, 239, 248, 254, 255, 282, 312, 320, 345

Manors 25, 56, 131, 161, 291
Marciano 74, 75, 76, 77
Marienweerd 154, 155, 156, 161, 168, 170, 172, 173, 275, 278, 290, 291
Masserie 236, 242, 338
Meeden 201, 345
mezzadria 79, 82, 98, 331
Midwolda 189, 195, 197, 198, 199, 201, 206, 208, 275, 367
migration 77, 78, 82, 191, 201, 351, 369, 374
Moats 110, 358
Monopoli 302
Montecchio 74, 75
Muntendam 201
Murgia 357

Naples 235, 240, 250, 278, 279, 280, 287, 307, 308, 337, 341, 364
Netherlands 153, 157, 162, 164, 188, 192, 195, 200, 202, 291, 300, 315, 325, 326, 329, 331, 352, 363, 375
Nieuwolda 189, 191, 197, 198, 199, 201, 210, 320
Norbertine 155, 168

Oldambt 190, 193, 194, 195, 196, 197, 198, 199, 200, 201, 202, 203, 205, 206, 207, 208, 209, 210, 213, 214, 295, 299, 328, 333, 334, 344, 345, 355
Ommelanden 191, 194, 213, 215, 295
Oostwold 208
Oostwolder Polder 209, 210
Ortignano 76, 83

Partina 73, 74, 76, 87
Paveien 154, 155, 356
Pavoncelli 255, 281
Poderi 79
Poppi 71, 74, 75, 77, 85, 88, 89, 97, 281, 289, 293
Po Valley 95
Prataglia 88, 304
Pratovecchio 76, 77, 86, 88, 95, 97

Raggiolo 76, 83, 86, 87, 88, 95, 97, 294

Reiderwolderpolder 209
Romena 74, 76, 77
Rumpt 175, 288

Scheemda 195, 198, 199, 200, 201, 302, 306, 320, 348, 367, 372
Shudy Camps 112, 115, 123, 124, 136, 338
Sicily 295
Slochteren 189, 209, 215, 305
Stadspolder 206, 208, 209
Strumi 74

Tavoliere 233, 236, 240, 242, 244, 287, 294, 311, 316, 341, 360
Taxation 162, 175, 362
Termunten 197, 198, 199, 201
Terpen 157, 169, 294, 296
Tiel 163, 169, 174, 275
Tricht 152, 168, 175, 292
Trulli 251, 357

Ubertini 81, 86, 96, 97, 303

Vado 76, 86
van Cuijk 155, 168
Veenkolonien 188, 194, 196, 200, 215, 295, 296, 332
Vijfheerenlanden 156
Vineyards 88, 248

Wagenborgen 325
Western Roman Empire 153
Westerwolde 215
Westfalen 194
West Wickham 112, 115, 123, 131, 136, 325
Winschoten 190, 197, 198, 199, 200, 201, 279, 328
Woldendorp 370

Yen Hall 115, 325

Zaltbommel 163, 174
Zeeland 201
Zoelen 312
Zuidbroek 197, 201, 207, 215, 286, 296, 322